World Development Report 1995

D0206546

WORKERS *in an* INTEGRATING WORLD

PUBLISHED FOR THE WORLD BANK

OXFORD UNIVERSITY PRESS

Oxford University Press

OXFORD   NEW YORK   TORONTO   DELHI   BOMBAY   CALCUTTA
MADRAS   KARACHI   KUALA LUMPUR   SINGAPORE   HONG KONG
TOKYO   NAIROBI   DAR ES SALAAM   CAPE TOWN   MELBOURNE
AUCKLAND

and associated companies in

BERLIN   IBADAN

© 1995 The International Bank for Reconstruction and
Development / The World Bank
1818 H Street, N.W., Washington, D.C. 20433, U.S.A.

Published by Oxford University Press, Inc.
200 Madison Avenue, New York, N.Y. 10016

Oxford is a registered trademark of Oxford University Press.

Manufactured in the United States of America
First printing June 1995

The cover illustration is *Eight Builders* (1982) by Jacob Lawrence, repro-
duced courtesy of the artist and the Francine Seders Gallery. Original art-
work is part of the Seattle City Light Portable Works Collection administered by the Seattle Arts Commission. Photograph by Steve Young.

ISBN 0-19-521103-0 clothbound
ISBN 0-19-521102-2 paperback
ISSN 0163-5085

Text printed on recycled paper that conforms to the American
Standard for Permanence of Paper for Printed Library Material,
Z39.48-1984

Foreword

WORK—SAFE, PRODUCTIVE, AND environmentally sound—is the key to economic and social progress everywhere. In the advice it gives governments and in the policies it promotes, the World Bank has long recognized the critical value of work. This is more than an economic issue; it is at the heart of human development. As such, work is a more than worthy subject for this, the eighteenth annual *World Development Report.* It focuses on the incomes workers receive, the risks they face, and the conditions under which they work. Inevitably, work has almost as significant implications for those who do not work—children, the old, and those unable to work—as for those who do.

What makes the Report even more timely is the growing impact of two distinct global trends: reduced government intervention in markets, and the increased integration of trade, capital flows, and the exchange of information and technology. In such a climate of profound change, basic decisions about wages and working conditions are driven by global competitive pressures. The harsh reality of a global market is that policy failures are punished hard—through currency movements, shifts in market share, and, ultimately, through fluctuations in employment and wage levels.

Some see the new global marketplace as a source of opportunity, where industry and energy bring swift rewards; others regard the changes as a threat to security, and in parts of the industrial and the developing world the cause of protectionism is far from defeated.

This Report makes four key points:

First, building on earlier research—notably that of *World Development Report 1990*—it emphasizes the benefits to workers in all countries, and especially poor ones, of productivity-raising economic growth driven by sound investments in capital and in people's health and education.

Second, increased integration between countries, including through migration, can benefit workers in poor and rich countries at the same time. But governments have an important role in helping workers who are adversely affected by changes in trade patterns and capital flows. This can involve not just providing a social safety net, but also helping to equip workers for change.

Third, labor policies in many countries have been misguided in favoring those in good jobs at the expense of workers in the rural and informal sectors and the unemployed. Governments have a distinct role in setting the legal and regulatory frameworks within which trade unions and firms can operate and in ensuring that those frameworks encourage their positive contributions to development. Governments also need to define minimum standards and prevent exploitation and discrimination. Successful labor policies are those that work in harmony with the market and avoid providing special protections and privileges to particular labor groups at the expense of the poorest.

Fourth, workers eventually benefit from economic reform as states move from central planning to market systems and from protectionism to openness. The change, however, can be wrenching as employment and wages often decline temporarily and as workers have to move from old to new jobs. There remains a need for governments to provide strong support to workers and their families in such times of transition.

One goal of this Report is to spark a broad and informed debate on these often contentious issues. Another, more important, goal is to inspire policy changes that allow more of the right sort of jobs to be created. Work is, after all, the only foundation on which economies and people can build a success that lasts.

James D. Wolfensohn
President
The World Bank

June 1, 1995

This Report has been prepared by a team led by Michael Walton and comprising Arup Banerji, Alejandra Cox Edwards, Ishac Diwan, Hafez Ghanem, David Lindauer, Ana Revenga, and Michal Rutkowski. The team was assisted by Vinod Ahuja, Deon Filmer, Praveen Kumar, Claudio E. Montenegro, Sarbajit Sinha, and Zhi Wang. Edward Balls was the principal editor. The work was carried out under the general direction of Michael Bruno.

Many others in and outside the Bank provided helpful comments and contributions (see the Bibliographical Note). The International Economics Department contributed to the data appendix and was responsible for the World Development Indicators. The production staff of the Report included Amy Brooks, Kathryn Kline Dahl, Geoffrey Eaton, Stephanie Gerard, Audrey Heiligman, Cathe Kocak, Jeffrey N. Lecksell, Hugh Nees, Kathy Rosen, Beatrice Sito, Tracey A. Smith, and Michael Treadway. The design was by Brian Noyes of the Magazine Group. The support staff was headed by Rebecca Sugui and included Daniel Atchison, Elizabeth V. de Lima, and Michael Geller. Trinidad S. Angeles and later Maria D. Ameal served as administrative officer.

Preparation of the Report was greatly aided by background papers and by contributions from participants in the consultation meetings. The names of the participants in the consultation meetings are listed in the Bibliographical Note.

Contents

World Development Indicators   153

Boxes

Text figures

Text tables

Appendix tables

Definitions and Data Notes

Selected terms used in this Report

The labor force and its components. The *labor force* of a country consists of all those in its *working-age population* (those fifteen to sixty-four years of age) who are employed or seeking employment. It includes the *unemployed* (those seeking work but unable to find it) but excludes *discouraged workers* (those who have given up looking for work) as well as others who are neither working nor seeking work (family members caring for children, as well as students, retirees, disabled persons, and others). *Underemployment*, although variously defined in the literature, is used in this Report to mean employment at fewer hours during a given period than the worker desires. The *labor force participation rate* is the percentage of the working-age population that is in the labor force. The *work force* consists of all persons who are actually working, whether in the formal or the informal sector—that is, the labor force less the unemployed. The *formal sector* consists of those enterprises, public or private, that hire workers under contract and are subject to labor laws and regulations. For purposes of empirical analysis, the formal sector is defined to include all nonagricultural enterprises that hire workers as wage-earning employees.

Active labor market policies. Policies aimed at helping the unemployed return to work or improving the opportunities of those now working; they include job search assistance, training, and job creation initiatives and are distinguished from *passive* policies, which seek to support the standard of living of those not working by providing cash or other benefits.

Affirmative action. The granting of preferences in hiring to persons deemed to have suffered from job discrimination in the past.

Collective bargaining. Negotiations between a union (or other representatives of employees) and employers to establish wage levels and other conditions of employment.

Export processing zone. A defined geographic area in which manufacturers producing for export are ex-empted from paying duties on imported inputs and, often, from certain domestic regulation.

Freedom of association. The freedom of workers to form and join unions or other organizations whose purpose is to increase their collective bargaining power.

Human capital. The skills and capabilities embodied in an individual or a work force, in part acquired through improved health and nutrition, education, and training.

Incomes policy. Any attempt by a government to restrain increases in wages and salaries, usually for the purpose of holding down inflation or maintaining employment levels.

Pension schemes are of two basic types. *Pay-as-you-go schemes* are state-operated arrangements in which payments to retirees are made out of current revenues, thus constituting a transfer from those currently working. In *funded schemes,* in contrast, benefits are paid out of funds accumulated from past contributions and are therefore an intertemporal "transfer" from one generation of workers to itself.

Purchasing power parity (PPP) adjustment. The adjustment for research purposes of data on the money incomes of workers to reflect the actual power of a unit of local currency to buy goods and services in its country of issue, which may be more or less than what a unit of the same currency will buy of equivalent goods and services in foreign countries at current market exchange rates. PPP-adjusted incomes are useful for comparing the living standards of workers in different countries. In this Report, data stated "in international prices" are PPP-adjusted.

Country groups

For operational and analytical purposes the World Bank's main criterion for classifying economies is gross national product (GNP) per capita. Every economy is classified as either low-income, middle-income (subdivided into lower-middle and upper-middle), or high-income. Other analytical groups, based on regions, exports, and levels of external debt, are also used.

Because GNP per capita changes with time, the country composition of each income group may change from one edition to the next. Once the classification is fixed for any edition, all the historical data presented are based on the same country grouping. The income-based country groupings used in this year's Report are defined as follows.

Low-income economies are those with a GNP per capita of $695 or less in 1993.

Middle-income economies are those with a GNP per capita of more than $695 but less than $8,626 in 1993. A further division, at GNP per capita of $2,785 in 1993, is made between lower-middle-income and upper-middle-income economies.

High-income economies are those with a GNP per capita of $8,626 or more in 1993.

World comprises all economies, including economies with sparse data and those with less than 1 million population; these are not shown separately in the main tables but are presented in Table 1a in the technical notes to the World Development Indicators.

The income criteria used in the World Development Indicators may differ from those used in the text of the Report.

Classification by income does not necessarily reflect development status. (In the World Development Indicators, high-income economies classified as developing by the United Nations or regarded as developing by their authorities are identified by the symbol †.) The use of the term "countries" to refer to economies implies no judgment by the Bank about the legal or other status of a territory.

Countries included in regional groupings used in the Report are listed in Appendix table A-1.

Data notes

Billion is 1,000 million.

Trillion is 1,000 billion.

Tons are metric tons, equal to 1,000 kilograms, or 2,204.6 pounds.

Dollars are current U.S. dollars unless otherwise specified.

Growth rates are based on constant price data and, unless otherwise noted, have been computed with the use of the least-squares method. See the technical notes to the World Development Indicators for details of this method.

The symbol / in dates, as in "1990/91," means that the period of time may be less than two years but straddles two calendar years and refers to a crop year, a survey year, or a fiscal year.

The symbol .. in tables means not available.

The symbol — in tables means not applicable. (In the World Development Indicators, a blank is used to mean not applicable.)

The number 0 or 0.0 in tables and figures means zero or a quantity less than half the unit shown and not known more precisely.

The cutoff date for all data in the World Development Indicators is April 30, 1995.

Historical data in this Report may differ from those in previous editions because of continual updating as better data become available, because of a change to a new base year for constant price data, or because of changes in country composition in income and analytical groups.

Other economic and demographic terms are defined in the technical notes to the World Development Indicators.

Acronyms and initials

ASEAN	Association of South East Asian Nations (Brunei, Indonesia, Malaysia, the Philippines, Singapore, and Thailand)
CMEA	Council for Mutual Economic Assistance (the trading system of the former communist bloc)
FDI	Foreign direct investment
GATT	General Agreement on Tariffs and Trade
GDP	Gross domestic product
GNP	Gross national product
ILO	International Labour Office (or Organization)
NAFTA	North American Free Trade Agreement
NGO	Nongovernmental organization
NIE	Newly industrializing economy
PPP	Purchasing power parity (see "Selected terms used in this Report" above)
OECD	Organization for Economic Cooperation and Development (Australia, Austria, Belgium, Canada, Denmark, Finland, France, Germany, Greece, Iceland, Ireland, Italy, Japan, Luxembourg, Mexico, Netherlands, New Zealand, Norway, Portugal, Spain, Sweden, Switzerland, Turkey, United Kingdom, and United States)
UNICEF	United Nations Children's Fund
UNIDO	United Nations Industrial Development Organization

Overview

DUONG IS A VIETNAMESE PEASANT FARMER *who struggles to feed his family. He earns the equivalent of $10 a week for thirty-eight hours of work in the rice fields, but he works full-time only six months of the year—during the off-season he can earn very little. His wife and four children work with him in the fields, but the family can afford to send only the two youngest to school. Duong's eleven-year-old daughter stays at home to help with housework, while his thirteen-year-old son works as a street trader in town. By any standard Duong's family is living in poverty. Workers like Duong, laboring on family farms in low- and middle-income countries, account for about 40 percent of the world's labor force.*

• • •

Hoa is a young Vietnamese city dweller experiencing relative affluence for the first time. In Ho Chi Minh City she earns the equivalent of $30 a week working forty-eight hours in a garment factory—a joint venture with a French firm. She works hard for her living and spends many hours looking after her three children as well; her husband works as a janitor. But Hoa's family has several times the standard of living of Duong's and, by Vietnamese standards, is relatively well-off. There is every expectation that both she and her children will continue to have a vastly better standard of living than her parents had. Wage employees like Hoa, working in the formal sector in low- and middle-income countries, make up about 20 percent of the global labor force.

• • •

Françoise is an immigrant in France of Vietnamese origin who works long hours as a waitress to make ends meet. She takes home the equivalent of $220 a week, after taxes and including tips, for fifty hours' work. By French standards she is poor. Legally, Françoise is a casual worker and so has no job security, but she is much better off in France than she would have been in Viet Nam. Her wage is almost eight times that earned by Hoa in Ho Chi Minh City. Françoise and other services sector workers in high-income countries account for about 9 percent of the global labor force.

• • •

Jean-Paul is a fifty-year-old Frenchman whose employment prospects look bleak. For ten years he has worked in a garment factory in Toulouse, taking home the equivalent of $400 a week—twelve times the average wage in Viet Nam's garment industry. But next month he will lose his job when the factory closes. Unemployment benefits will partly shield him from the shock, but his chances of matching his old salary in a new job are slim. Frenchmen of Jean-Paul's age who lose their jobs are likely to stay unemployed for more than a year, and Jean-Paul is encouraging his son to work hard in school so he can go to college and study computer programming. Workers in industry in high-income countries, like Jean-Paul, make up just 4 percent of the world's labor force.

• • •

These four families—two living in Viet Nam, two in France—have vastly different standards of living and expectations for the future. Employment and wage prospects in Toulouse and Ho Chi Minh City are worlds apart, even when incomes are adjusted, as here, for differences in the cost of living. Françoise's poverty wage would clearly buy Hoa a vastly more affluent life-style. And much of the world's work force, like Duong, works outside the wage sector on family farms and in the informal sector, generally earning even lower labor incomes (Box 1). But the lives of urban workers in different parts of the world are increasingly intertwined. French consumers buy the product of Hoa's labor, and Jean-Paul believes it is Hoa's low wages that are taking his job, while immigrant workers like Françoise feel the brunt of Jean-Paul's anger. Meanwhile, Duong struggles to save so that his children can be educated and leave the countryside for the city, where foreign companies advertise new jobs at better wages.

These are revolutionary times in the global economy. The embrace of market-based development by many developing and former centrally planned economies, the opening of international markets, and great advances in the ease with which goods, capital, and ideas flow around the world are bringing new opportunities, as well as risks, to billions of people. In 1978 about a third of the world's work force lived in countries with centrally planned economies. At least another third lived in countries weakly linked to international interactions because of protective barriers to trade and investment. If recent trends continue, by the year 2000 fewer than 10 percent of workers may be living in such countries, largely disconnected from world markets.

But rapid change is never easy. In rich and poor countries alike there are fears of rising insecurity, as technological change, expanding international interactions, and the decline of traditional community structures seem to threaten jobs, wages, and support for the elderly. Nor have economic growth and rising integration solved the problem of world poverty and deprivation. Indeed, the numbers of the poor could rise still further as the world labor force grows from 2.5 billion today to a projected 3.7 billion in thirty years' time. The bulk of the more than a billion individuals living on a dollar or less a day depend, like Duong and his family,

Box 1 A world at work

For most households, poor and prosperous alike, income from work is the main determinant of their living conditions. Of the 2.5 billion people working in productive activities worldwide, over 1.4 billion live in poor countries, defined as those with annual income per capita below $695 in 1993. Another 660 million live in middle-income countries, and the remainder, some 380 million, live in high-income countries, with annual income per capita above $8,626 in 1993. There are vast differences in the patterns of employment across these three broad categories of countries. In poor countries 61 percent of the labor force works in agriculture, mainly tending family farms, while 22 percent work in the rural nonfarm and urban infor-

mal sectors, and 15 percent have wage contracts, mainly in urban industrial and service employment. In middle-income countries some 29 percent work on farms, 18 percent in rural and urban informal activities, and 46 percent in wage employment in industry and services. In rich countries the bulk of workers have jobs in the formal sector, with roughly 4 percent in agriculture, 27 percent in industry, and 60 percent in services. Some 120 million workers are unemployed worldwide. Workers in low-income countries dominate the world's agricultural work force but also, by their sheer numbers, account for nearly half of the world's industrial workers and about a third of its unemployed (see figure).

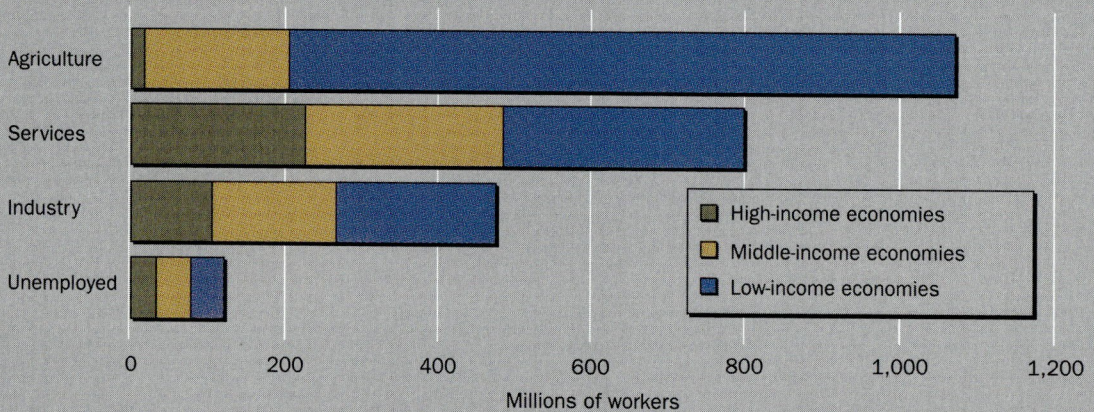

The world's labor force by sector and country income level. Data are projected for 1995 from a sample of countries in each income group. Source: World Bank staff estimates based on the following: EBRD 1994; ILO 1986 with ILO data updates; ILO, various years; and country sources.

on pitifully low returns to hard work. In many countries workers lack representation and work in unhealthy, dangerous, or demeaning conditions. Meanwhile 120 million or so are unemployed worldwide, and millions more have given up hope of finding work.

Yet fears that increased international trade and investment and less state intervention will hurt employment are mainly without basis. Workers have made great advances in many countries, especially those that have embraced these global trends, effectively engaging in international markets and avoiding excessive state intervention. Despite a doubling of the world's work force over the past three decades, the productivity of the world's median worker has doubled.

This Report concludes that problems of low incomes, poor working conditions, and insecurity affecting many of the world's workers *can* be effectively tackled in ways that

reduce poverty and regional inequality. But to do so will require sound domestic policy and a supportive international environment. This means that governments must:

■ pursue market-based growth paths that generate rapid growth in demand for labor, expansion in the skills of the work force, and rising productivity

■ take advantage of new opportunities at the international level, by opening up to trade and attracting capital—but manage the dislocations that international changes sometimes bring

■ construct a framework for labor policy that complements informal and rural labor markets, supports collective bargaining in the formal sector, provides safeguards for the vulnerable, and avoids biases that favor relatively well-off workers, and

- in those countries struggling with the transition to a more market-based and internationally integrated pattern of development, try to design the transition to make it as rapid as possible without excessive or permanent costs for labor.

Development strategy and workers

Manufacturing wages in a group of export-oriented East Asian economies rose 170 percent in real terms between 1970 and 1990, while manufacturing employment increased 400 percent. Wages of agricultural laborers in India rose 70 percent. But meanwhile industrial wages grew by only 12 percent in a group of Latin American countries and fell in many Sub-Saharan African countries.

• • •

Economic growth is good for workers. This has long been true for those living in what are now the world's rich countries, and it has been spectacularly true for the newly industrializing economies (NIEs) of East Asia over the past few decades. Growth has reduced poverty through rising employment, increased labor productivity, and higher real wages (Figure 1). Growth also tends to reduce poverty and inequality, including inequality between men and women. For today's low- and middle-income countries, the fear that growth will primarily benefit capital, create few jobs, and fail to raise wages is unfounded. Viet Nam's workers are now some of the poorest in the world. If their country follows the path of other East Asian successes, they could enjoy a doubling of their labor incomes in a decade or so.

Market-based development, which encourages firms and workers to invest in physical capital, new technologies, and skills, is the best way to deliver growth and rising living standards for workers. Countries that have attempted to help workers by biasing investment against agriculture and toward industry, protecting the jobs of a favored few industrial workers against international competition, dictating wage increases, or creating unneeded jobs in the public sector have failed over the long run—whether in Latin America, the former Soviet Union, or elsewhere. What any nation's work force needs most is stronger demand for its services, together with high levels of investment in schooling, training, roads, and machines. This has worked best where, as in East Asia, governments made good use of international markets, especially for expanding exports, and gave strong support to family farming. The public sectors in these economies supported the efficient functioning of markets by providing a stable macroeconomic environment

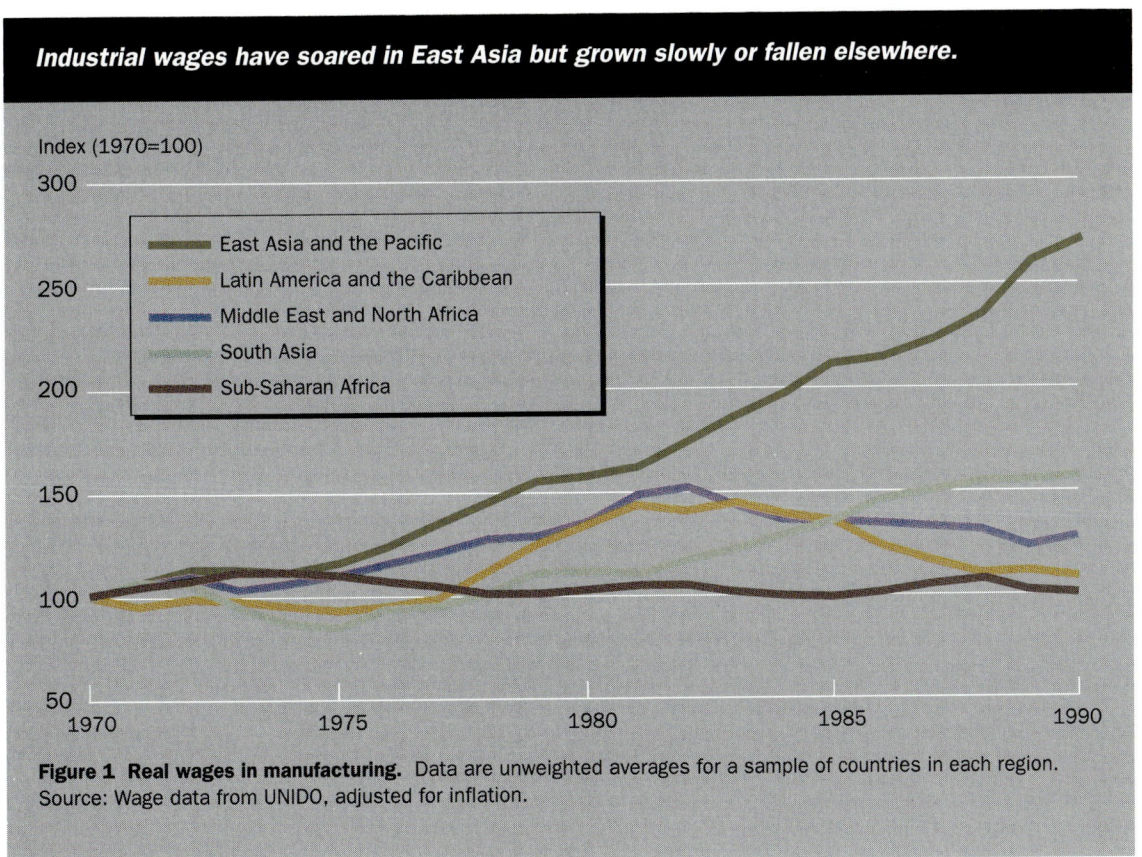

Industrial wages have soared in East Asia but grown slowly or fallen elsewhere.

Index (1970=100)

Legend:
- East Asia and the Pacific
- Latin America and the Caribbean
- Middle East and North Africa
- South Asia
- Sub-Saharan Africa

Figure 1 Real wages in manufacturing. Data are unweighted averages for a sample of countries in each region. Source: Wage data from UNIDO, adjusted for inflation.

for saving and investment and supporting the expansion of economic infrastructure and social services.

Investment in the skills, health, and nutrition of workers is key both to their welfare and to economic success. But some countries have performed badly despite investing in schooling. Investment—in physical or in human capital—does not guarantee growth (Figure 2). The former centrally planned economies of Europe and Central Asia represent an extreme case of high investment that led first to stagnating and eventually to collapsing labor incomes.

Market-based, labor-demanding growth also tends to reduce inequality—within countries and across regions—provided governments ensure broad-based investment in the capabilities of people and the complementary assets that determine their opportunities. It is true that the centrally planned economies achieved high degrees of equality and now generally face some rise in inequality. But the East Asian strategy—of supporting family farms, avoiding dual-

istic labor markets, and encouraging vigorous growth in formal employment through exporting—achieved rapid growth with declining poverty and lower inequality. By contrast, most Latin American countries have long had highly unequal income distributions, and most still do, with landholdings heavily concentrated in the hands of a few and growth paths biased against labor.

Inequalities between men and women, between ethnic groups, and between geographic regions are particularly tenacious. Women often work more but get paid less than men, because of a heavier burden of work in the home, less education, or weaker access to better paying jobs. Indian scheduled castes are confined to low-paying work. Poor regions, such as the state of Chiapas in Mexico, usually stay relatively poor even when the economy as a whole expands. Some of these groups do gain from development (in particular, wage differentials between men and women usually decline), but others miss out. Helping those left out is one of the toughest problems for policy, for poor and rich countries alike. From a hard-headed economic perspective, investing in such people may seem a poor risk, because many are old, socially ill adapted to work, or stuck in backward regions, but concern for their misery and for social cohesion demands that policy reach out to them. The longer people are left behind, the harder it becomes to break self-perpetuating intergenerational cycles of poverty.

Employment in an integrating world

The share of manufactures in developing country exports rose from 20 percent to 60 percent between 1960 and 1990. Low- and middle-income countries already account for almost 80 percent of the world's industrial work force.

• • •

International flows of goods, services, capital, and people bring new opportunities for most workers. Where exports have risen fast, so have real wages—by an average of 3 percent per year (Figure 3). Foreign direct investment, which now accounts for 30 percent of capital flows to low- and middle-income economies, is creating many new jobs: 60 percent of worldwide growth in the payrolls of multinational corporations occurred in these countries between 1985 and 1992. International migration, although so far less of a force for change than either trade or investment, has usually brought income gains to those who move, higher remittances to those who stay, and increased production of goods and services in the host countries.

Many workers, especially in the farms, factories, and services sectors of Asia, have seen great gains from international engagement. But for some it feels as though international integration has increased their vulnerability to volatile international conditions; others—especially those living in Sub-Saharan Africa—remain largely disconnected from international market opportunities. And within in-

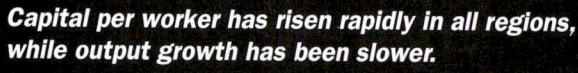

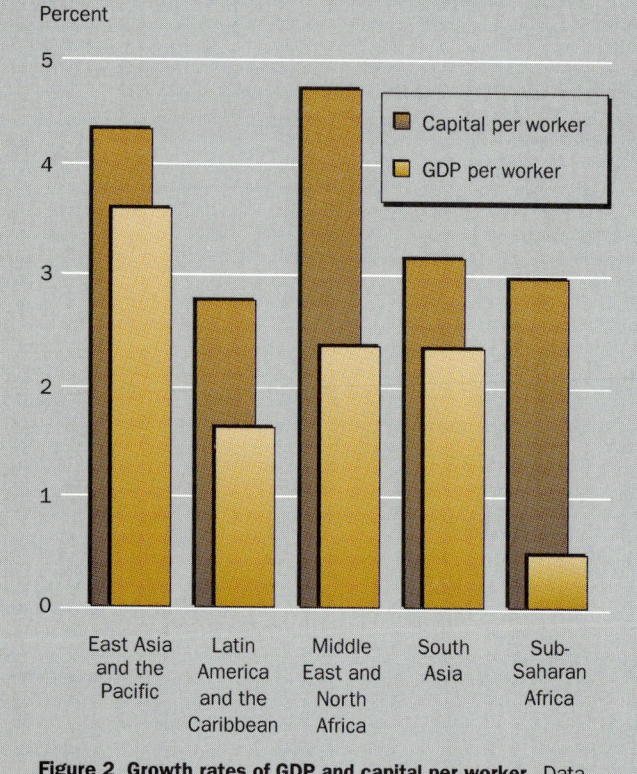

Capital per worker has risen rapidly in all regions, while output growth has been slower.

Percent

Capital per worker
GDP per worker

East Asia and the Pacific | Latin America and the Caribbean | Middle East and North Africa | South Asia | Sub-Saharan Africa

Figure 2 Growth rates of GDP and capital per worker. Data are annual averages for 1960-90. Source: ILO 1986 with ILO data updates; Nehru and Dhareshwar 1991; World Bank data.

dustrial countries there is a small but vocal minority who fear they will lose from the introduction of new technologies, the growth of international trade, and movements of capital and people across national boundaries.

Some workers will indeed be hurt if they are stuck in declining activities and lack the flexibility to change. However, international trade, immigration, and capital flows account for only a small part of the problem faced by laid-off workers in France, or by unskilled men in the United States who have seen their wages decline for decades, even as the wages of college graduates continue to rise. More important, restricting trade or capital is not an effective way of dealing with this problem—a better strategy for any country is to improve the skills of its people or ease their transition to new jobs, while staying engaged with the world economy. International migration, in contrast, is always controlled to some degree. To the extent this is done to reduce conflict while preserving the basic rights of migrants, it can actually help sustain moderate levels of international migration.

In any case, capital now crosses borders ever more rapidly despite the best efforts of some national governments to control it. But far from rendering national governments impotent, international capital movements intensify the impact of domestic policy on labor outcomes, richly rewarding policy when it is sound but punishing it hard when it is unsound. Faster and broader capital flows and greater openness in trade are making domestic policy more important for workers. Success breeds success, because good macroeconomic and structural policies are key to attracting or keeping capital and achieving the productivity necessary to create competitive jobs at rising wages. But when policies fail, portfolio investment and local savings leave the scene, and labor suffers the consequences.

Labor policy

Although 90 percent of developing countries have some form of social security system, at best it covers only workers in the formal sector, who make up just 15 percent of the labor force in low-income countries, 45 percent in middle-income countries.

• • •

Labor policies in low- and middle-income countries do not affect the majority of workers who, like Duong in Viet Nam, work in the rural or the urban informal sector. These are the poorest workers—often earning less than half what a formal sector employee earns—and therefore the most in need of protection. Moreover, labor regulations are often not enforced in many firms that are normally considered part of the modern sector (see Figure 11.2 in Chapter 11).

Does this mean that governments in low- and middle-income countries should not bother to intervene in the labor market, because their policies will not reach those who most need help and their regulations will not be enforced? The answer is no. Public action can complement

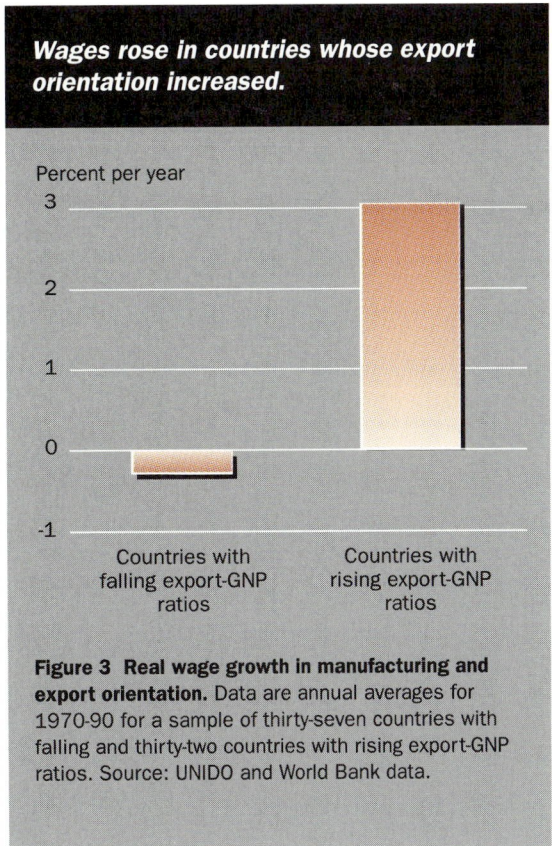

Wages rose in countries whose export orientation increased.

Percent per year

Figure 3 Real wage growth in manufacturing and export orientation. Data are annual averages for 1970-90 for a sample of thirty-seven countries with falling and thirty-two countries with rising export-GNP ratios. Source: UNIDO and World Bank data.

community arrangements and enhance the welfare of informal workers by improving the environment in which they operate. In the formal sector public action is sometimes needed to improve market outcomes, enhance equity, and protect vulnerable workers.

Informal and rural workers often must work under more hazardous and insecure conditions than their formal sector counterparts. Improved working conditions are best achieved not by legislation but by direct public action affecting the working environment and the health of workers, in areas such as provision of water and sanitation, roads and drainage in and near cities, and environmental health. The eradication of onchocerciasis (river blindness) in large parts of West Africa brought immense reductions in human suffering and large increases in labor supply. Informal income security arrangements can be complemented by public transfer programs: public works are usually the best transfer method for able-bodied men and women. In India's Maharashtra State, for many years rural workers were guaranteed work in public works schemes at the local wage rate.

For the formal sector, collective bargaining between firms and independent unions is an effective way to determine wages and working conditions. Yet governments have often repressed unions, as in the Republic of Korea until the 1980s, or politicized the bargaining process, as in Bangladesh today. Sometimes, as in Indonesia, they have responded to pressures for independent unions by directly raising standards, such as minimum wages, potentially at the cost of employment. Governments do need to establish the rules for labor-management negotiations, spelling out the rights of workers and firms, establishing dispute resolution mechanisms, and promulgating basic health and safety regulations, which unions can monitor. Where unions cover only a small proportion of the work force, as they do in most low- and middle-income countries, decentralized bargaining under conditions of competitive output markets produces the best results. This precept has long applied in Japan and Hong Kong and applies now in Chile and Korea.

Direct government intervention makes sense in dealing with child labor and in other cases where the market may produce adverse outcomes, such as discrimination against women. But legislation alone has been ineffective. It needs to be complemented by other policies such as low-cost education and better access for women to formal sector jobs. India has sound child labor laws, yet millions of children are working, often in hazardous conditions. Child labor is partly a reflection of poverty. But it is not necessary to wait for a reduction in the poverty rate to tackle the most life-threatening and demeaning aspects of child labor. In the town of Pagsanjan in the Philippines, civic action dramatically reduced child prostitution. In Brazil, India, and the Philippines, local action, with public support, is improving the health status of working children and giving them greater educational opportunities.

Governments also have to set policy for public employment. Many public sector workers work hard and productively. But in many low- and middle-income countries, notably in Sub-Saharan Africa and the Middle East, the quality of public service has suffered as its ethos has been destroyed by a combination of overstaffing, inadequate pay, and weak governance. Restoring levels of pay and reducing the number of public workers are often essential reforms, to be combined with improvements in the recruitment, promotion, and accountability of civil servants, teachers, nurses, and policymakers. The redefinition of the role of the state makes it all the more important that governments be effective in those areas where they do stay involved.

If support for the rights of workers to form unions and to bargain collectively and support for the reduction of child labor make sense in a national context, should these principles be linked to international trade agreements, with sanctions for their violation? Advocates of linkage make a distinction between "core" standards, which for many would be akin to basic rights and do not directly raise labor costs, and other standards, such as minimum wages, that are a direct function of the level of development. Such a division is sound, and there is a case for international concern over core standards. However, it is best to keep multilateral trade agreements confined to directly trade-related issues, to prevent protectionist interests from misusing such links to reduce the trade that workers in low- and middle-income countries need if their incomes are to rise. As the history of trade reform illustrates, even well-intentioned and rationally designed discretionary trade measures can be captured by protectionist interests.

Managing major changes

Of the world's 2.5 billion workers, 1.4 billion live in countries struggling with transitions from state interventionism, high degrees of trade protection, or central planning.

• • •

Many developing and transitional economies are struggling with one or both of two major changes in their development strategies: from protection to greater integration with international markets, and from massive state intervention to a market economy in which the state plays a smaller role in allocating resources. These changes can have a powerful labor market dimension. Their key characteristic is an acceleration in the destruction of unviable jobs and the creation of new ones. The process is often accompanied by macroeconomic decline and by a sharp drop in the demand for labor nationwide. In the short term, workers often feel the pain as real wages fall, unemployment rises, and employment shifts into informal activities. In Argentina, Bolivia, Chile, and Mexico, real wages fell by a third or more before recovering. In Bulgaria, the Czech Republic, Poland, Romania, and Russia, real wages fell between 18 and 40 percent in the first year of transition; in some countries, including Bulgaria and Poland, unemployment rose from negligible levels to 15 percent or more. But in Ghana and China wages rose during the adjustment process, and unemployment remained low.

Economic reform can create opportunities for some workers but have wrenching effects on others. Even the best-designed reforms produce gainers and losers in the short term. Moving the economy as quickly as possible to the new growth path is key to minimizing the pain and social costs of adjustment; macroeconomic stability and credibility of the overall reform package are therefore critical. Countries such as Chile and Estonia have done relatively well on these scores and have brought about—or are bringing about—recoveries in wages and employment. In contrast, Belarus and Venezuela have faltered and suffered declines or stagnation in wages and employment (Figure 4).

Is a strategy of gradual transition better for workers? Where initial conditions allow gradual job destruction without jeopardizing the reform that is needed to generate new jobs, gradualism makes sense. China exemplifies the truth of this proposition, but that country enjoyed a large margin for job expansion, first in agriculture and then in

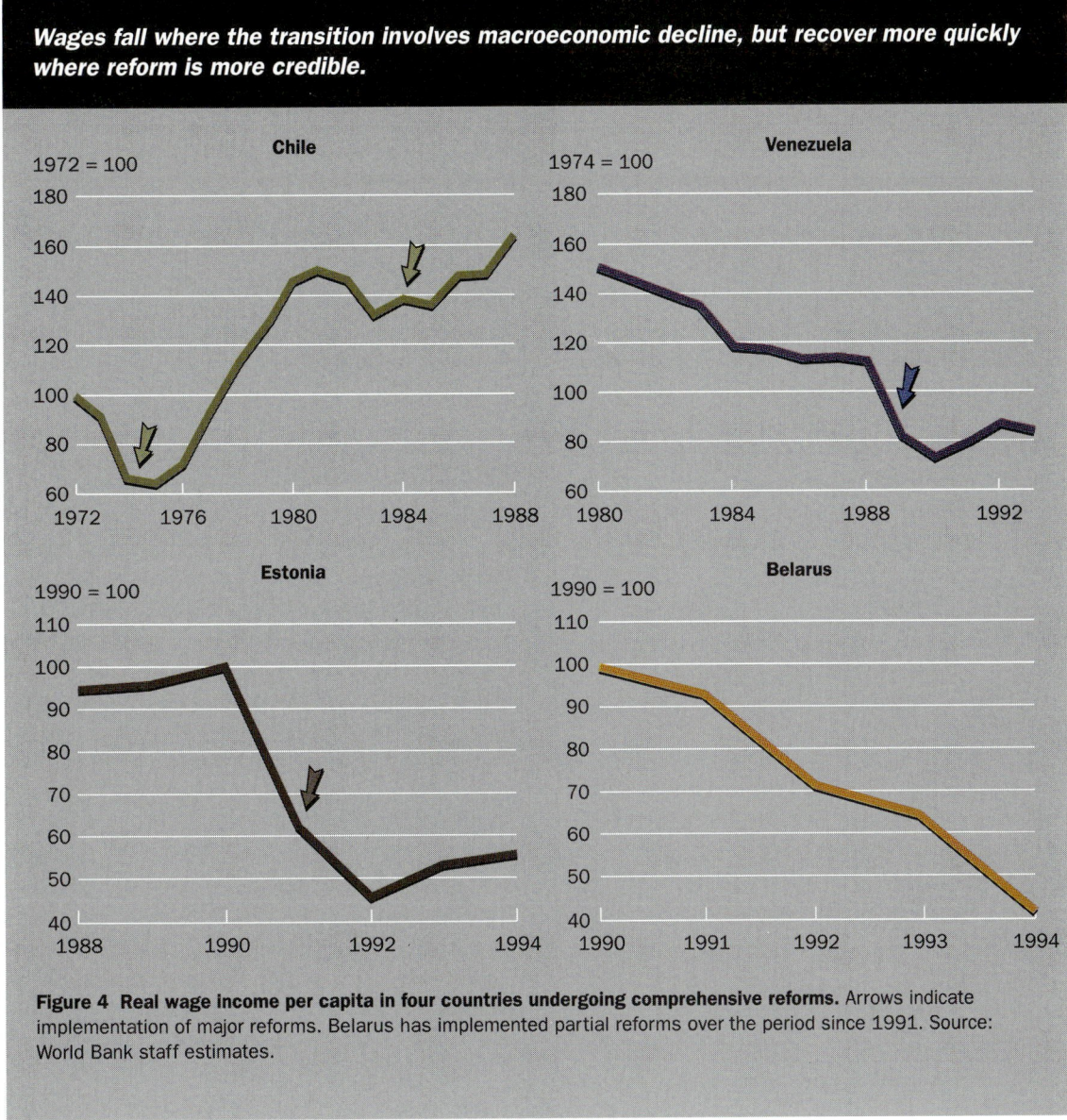

Wages fall where the transition involves macroeconomic decline, but recover more quickly where reform is more credible.

Figure 4 Real wage income per capita in four countries undergoing comprehensive reforms. Arrows indicate implementation of major reforms. Belarus has implemented partial reforms over the period since 1991. Source: World Bank staff estimates.

quasi-private industry, which could help finance the cost of the relatively inefficient state sector. In most other countries either macroeconomic imbalance or the costs of inefficient sectors make gradualism a nonstarter.

Microeconomic policies that affect the mobility and incomes of workers can play a major role both in influencing the overall pace of change and in safeguarding the welfare of workers over the transitional period. Good policy will generally involve action in three areas: enhancing mobility, reducing income insecurity, and equipping workers for change. These are highly complementary. Increased mobility will often involve measures to allow job destruction, including large layoffs from the public sector, to run its course. In many countries measures to separate entitlement

to social services from employment and to liberalize housing markets are required. But it is also important to consider the needs of those at risk of steep income declines. Income transfers can play an important role here. Retraining can help certain groups of workers but is unlikely to provide a panacea.

Divergence or inclusion?

About 99 percent of the 1 billion or so workers projected to join the world's labor force over the next thirty years will live in what are today's low- and middle-income countries. Some groups of relatively poor workers have experienced large gains in the past thirty years—especially in Asia. But there is no worldwide trend toward convergence between rich and poor workers. Indeed, there are risks that workers in poorer countries will fall further behind, as lower investment and educational attainment widen disparities. Some workers, especially in Sub-Saharan Africa, could become increasingly marginalized. And those left out of the general prosperity in countries that are enjoying growth could suffer permanent losses, setting in motion intergenerational cycles of neglect.

There is a substantial risk that inequality between rich and poor will grow over the coming decades, while poverty deepens. But it need not be so if countries choose the right international and domestic policies. Preserving open trading relations, preventing rich country fiscal deficits from crowding out investment elsewhere, and delivering high and stable growth in the high-income countries will maintain global demand and help head off any protectionist pressures in rich countries that might result from persistently high unemployment. Of even greater importance are domestic policies that promotes labor-demanding growth—and sound labor policy.

Governments and workers are adjusting to a changing world. The legacy of the past can make change difficult or frightening. Yet realization of a new world of work, in which all groups of workers are included in a dynamic of rising incomes, better working conditions, and enhanced job security, is fundamentally a question of sound choices—in the international and the domestic realm. The right choices involve using markets to create opportunities, taking care of those who are vulnerable or left out, and providing workers with the conditions to make their job choices freely, bargain over their conditions of work, and take advantage of better educational opportunities for their children. Duong, Hoa, Françoise, and Jean-Paul—and millions of workers like them—all have a powerful interest in good policy. They and their families have to live with the consequences.

CHAPTER 1

Introduction: A World at Work

THE GLOBAL LABOR FORCE HAS GROWN massively in recent decades. In 1995 there are an estimated 2.5 billion men and women of working age in the world's labor force, almost twice as many as in 1965. Estimates project a further worldwide increase of 1.2 billion by 2025. This expansion, moreover, has been geographically skewed. Since 1965 growth in the labor supply has varied substantially across regions: from 40 percent in the world's high-income economies to 93 percent in South Asia and 176 percent in the Middle East and North Africa. And 99 percent of the projected growth in the labor force from now to 2025 will occur in what are today's low- and middle-income economies (Table 1.1).

Burgeoning labor force growth heavily biased toward the poorer regions makes the task of raising the living standards of the world's poor seem daunting—even impossible. Yet the evidence of recent decades does not support prophecies of doom and gloom—of overpopulation, mass unemployment, and deepening poverty. Despite these unprecedented increases in labor supply, the world's median worker is better off today than thirty years ago.

But there can be no guarantee that the poorest workers will see their living standards rise. Not everyone has shared in the rising prosperity of recent decades—indeed, many countries and even whole regions have seen little increase in their incomes per capita. Inequality, both across regions and within countries, remains a significant feature of the global economy. By one estimate, in 1870 the average income per capita of the richest countries was eleven times that of the poorest; that ratio rose to thirty-eight in 1960 and to fifty-two in 1985.

Will this pattern of rising prosperity, unequally shared, persist? Two systemic shifts in the world's economies are profoundly affecting labor's outlook into the next millenium. One is the changing role of the state, mainly in response to past failures by governments to improve welfare through state action. This shift is seen most clearly in the demise of Soviet-style socialism, but government activism has come under scrutiny in almost every country in the world. The second change is that markets have become steadily more integrated, both within and between nations. This globalizing trend has been driven by breakthroughs in transportation, communications, and industrial technology

---

Low-income countries represent an increasing share of the world's labor force.

Table 1.1 The world's labor force by country income group and region

Income group or region	Millions of workers[a]			Percentage of total		
	1965	1995	2025	1965	1995	2025
World	1,329	2,476	3,656	100	100	100
Income group						
High-income	272	382	395	21	15	11
Middle-income	363	658	1,020	27	27	28
Low-income	694	1,436	2,241	52	58	61
Region						
Sub-Saharan Africa	102	214	537	8	9	15
East Asia and the Pacific	448	964	1,201	34	39	33
South Asia	228	440	779	17	18	21
Europe and Central Asia	180	239	281	14	10	8
Middle East and North Africa	29	80	204	2	3	6
Latin America and the Caribbean	73	166	270	5	6	7
High-income OECD	269	373	384	20	15	10

a. Ages fifteen to sixty-four.
Source: ILO 1986 with ILO data updates.

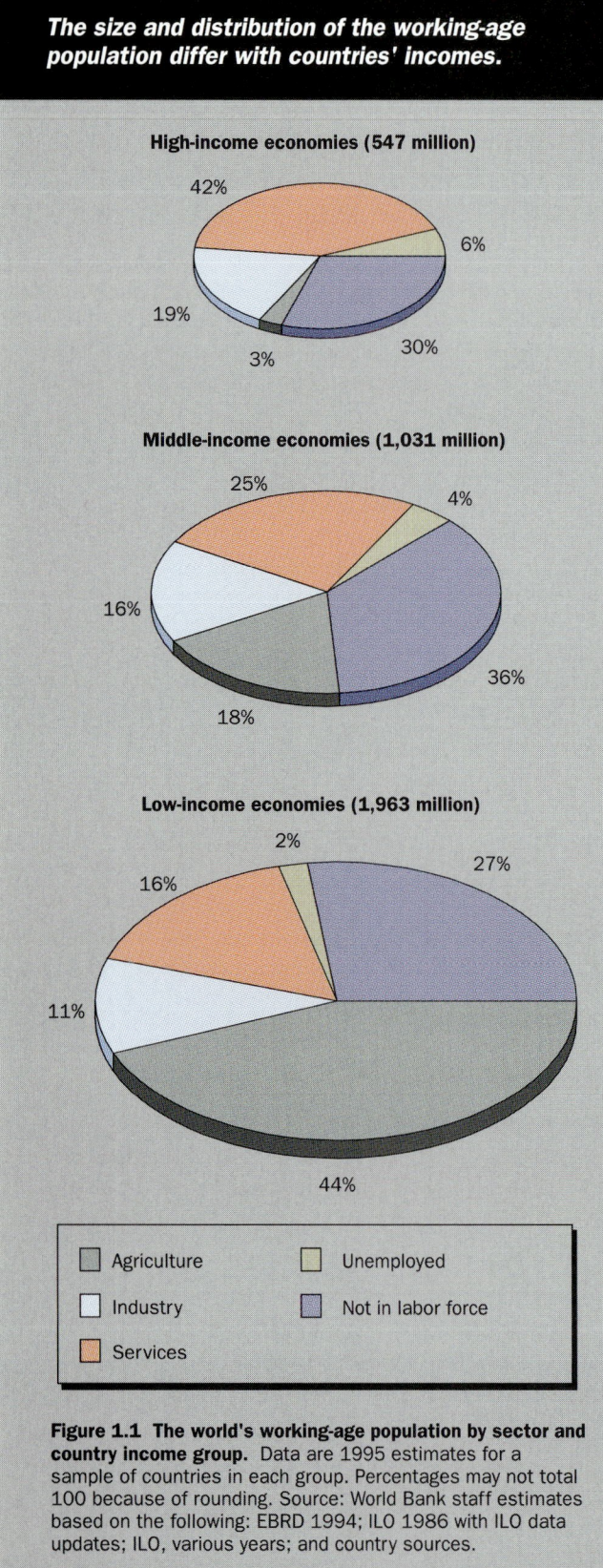

The size and distribution of the working-age population differ with countries' incomes.

High-income economies (547 million)

42%
6%
19%
3%
30%

Middle-income economies (1,031 million)

25%
4%
16%
36%
18%

Low-income economies (1,963 million)

2%
16%
27%
11%
44%

- ■ Agriculture
- □ Industry
- ■ Services
- ▨ Unemployed
- ▨ Not in labor force

Figure 1.1 The world's working-age population by sector and country income group. Data are 1995 estimates for a sample of countries in each group. Percentages may not total 100 because of rounding. Source: World Bank staff estimates based on the following: EBRD 1994; ILO 1986 with ILO data updates; ILO, various years; and country sources.

and above all by the opening of national markets to international trade. The countries that have achieved the greatest gains for their workers are those that decided early on to take advantage of international opportunities, and to rely increasingly on market forces rather than the state in allocating resources.

This Report evaluates what a more market-driven and economically integrated world means for workers. We focus on four questions: Which development strategies are best able to raise the incomes and working conditions of workers? Does growing integration offer an opportunity or pose a threat to workers, especially those in the world's poorest regions? What should be the role of domestic labor market policy in improving labor market outcomes: efficiency of markets, equity of incomes, job and income security, and workplace standards? How can countries making the transition from central planning, or from a closed market to one open to international transactions, take account of the needs of labor? This chapter frames the discussion by outlining the wide variation in, and the impact of policy on, employment and wages for workers around the world.

Wage and employment outcomes

The economic objectives of households are similar everywhere: families seek to meet their basic needs, improve their standards of living, manage the risks they face in an uncertain world, and expand opportunities for their children. But the opportunities to achieve these objectives through work vary substantially across regions at different stages of development. Well over half of the world's working-age population, some 2 billion people, live in low-income economies where annual income per capita was below $695 in 1993. Another 40 million elderly workers and a reported 50 million to 60 million children are at work. Because of widespread underreporting, child labor may actually involve tens of millions more.

About one-third of the working-age population in the low-income economies are not employed, some because they are attending school, raising children, or caring for their families, and others because they are unable to work or unable to find employment (Figure 1.1). But the majority are employed, and it is their low earnings at work, not unemployment, that are the main cause of their poverty. Of those at work, nearly six out of ten are engaged in agriculture. Of the remainder, almost 50 percent more are in the services sector than in industry (mining, manufacturing, construction, and utilities). Only about 15 percent of the labor force earn a living in the formal economy, defined as wage-paying nonagricultural private firms and the public sector.

The situation in the high-income economies is strikingly different. There, too, about one-third of the working-age population is outside the labor force or unemployed.

Nearly all the rest, however, about 350 million strong, work for wages. The services sector employs more than six out of every ten workers, more than double the number in industry. Agriculture employs 3 percent of the labor force. Some 30,000 children are estimated to be working. The situation in middle-income countries lies in between the low- and the high-income cases. Forty percent of all those of working age are not employed, about a third are in the formal economy (that is, working as regular, wage-earning employees in industry or services), about a fifth are in agriculture, and the remainder are in some type of informal employment. Over 7 million children in middle-income countries are reported as working.

Worldwide, unemployment—conventionally defined as those seeking work but unable to find any—is about 3 percent of the working-age population (about 5 percent of the labor force), although differences in national definitions and measurement difficulties make this estimate imprecise. Unemployment is often higher in high-income economies, but with rising incomes, increasing urbanization, and sweeping economic transitions, it has become more prevalent in a broad range of low- and middle-income economies.

Just as employment opportunities vary substantially across countries and regions, so do wages (Figure 1.2). Adjusted for differences in their currencies' purchasing power, the earnings of engineers in Frankfurt, Germany, are fifty-six times those of unskilled female textile workers in Nairobi, Kenya (Box 1.1). Part of this gap can be traced to the occupational pay structure within each domestic economy—the pay ratio of engineers to female textile workers is eight to one in Nairobi and three to one in Frankfurt. And part is due to international differences in returns to similar work—the pay ratio of German to Kenyan engineers is seven to one, and that of German to Kenyan female textile workers is eighteen to one. The 40 percent of the world's working-age population who work on family farms and in the informal sector typically earn far less than even unskilled urban workers—if the returns to their labor were

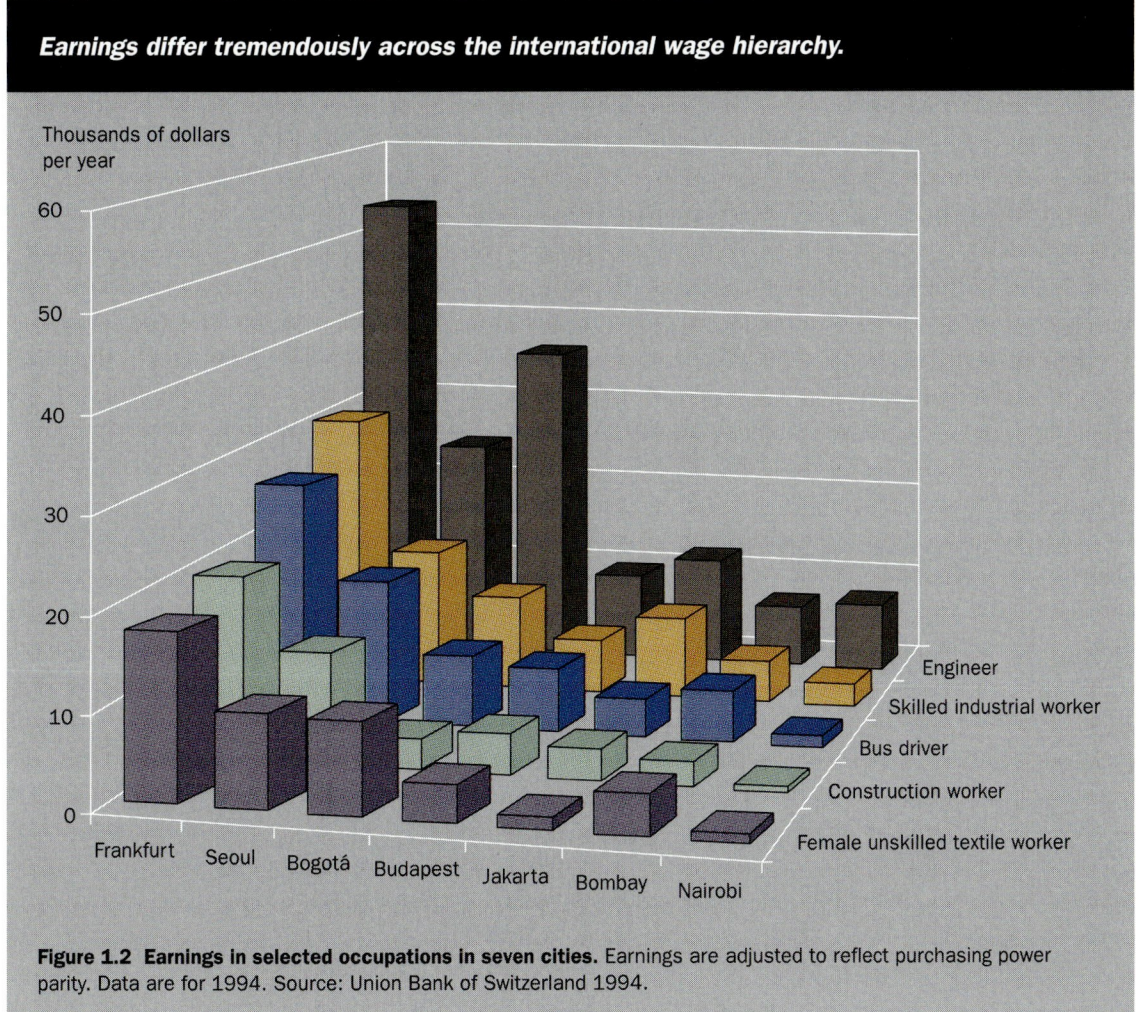

Earnings differ tremendously across the international wage hierarchy.

Figure 1.2 Earnings in selected occupations in seven cities. Earnings are adjusted to reflect purchasing power parity. Data are for 1994. Source: Union Bank of Switzerland 1994.

Box 1.1 How can we compare real wages across countries?

How much better off are workers in one country than their counterparts in another? This question often comes up in looking at cross-country data, but comparing the earnings of workers in different economies can be tricky because each is paid in domestic currency. The obvious solution is to convert wages into a common currency, usually the U.S. dollar. Until recently, the most common way of doing this was to use official exchange rates. However, dollar wages calculated in this manner do not adequately reflect workers' standards of living, because the prices of the goods they consume vary between countries. Prices of nontraded goods such as housing or personal services, in particular, differ widely, since they are determined by local demand and supply conditions.

To deal with such problems, wage comparisons in this Report use exchange rates adjusted for purchasing power parity (PPP), which equalize the price of the same bundle of goods and services across countries. For example, the Indian rupee PPP exchange rate measures the amount in rupees it would take in India to buy a selected basket of traded and nontraded goods that cost one dollar in the United States. This approach does not take into account differences in the bundles of goods that workers in different countries are likely to consume; even so, wages converted into dollars using PPP exchange rates provide a better estimate of the quantity of goods and services that workers in different countries can buy. (Whereas PPP exchange rates thus offer a better basis for welfare comparisons, official rates remain more appropriate for judging countries' international competitiveness.)

Using PPP rather than official exchange rates significantly affects the results reported in Figure 1.2. Poorer countries generally have larger adjustments, since their nontraded goods and services are cheaper. For example, in 1994 a bus driver in Seoul, Korea, earned $12,800 a year at the official exchange rate. A bus driver in Bombay, India, earned $1,700, also at the official rate. Is the Korean really more than seven times better off than the Indian? Converting to PPP dollars, we find that their earnings were $15,600 and $5,590, respectively. The Korean, in terms of purchasing power, was less than three times better off than his Indian counterpart, because the prices of nontraded goods were much lower in Bombay than in Seoul.

added to the picture, the spread in earnings, domestically as well as internationally, would be even greater.

Besides these cross-country differences in wage and employment outcomes, *within* countries there are significant differences between men and women. In most societies women work more hours for lower pay. Women are engaged disproportionately in the home, looking after children and maintaining the household—activities that fall outside the market. In many countries women receive less education, often are underrepresented in good jobs, and usually get paid less than men even for the same work. These differences may flow from cultural norms, but they lead to gender inequality and to inefficient use of a society's human resources.

Why some workers have done better than others

Why are there such large differences in employment and earnings, and hence in standards of living, across regions? Why does agriculture occupy so few working men and women in the high-income economies, but over half the labor force in the low-income countries? And why is there so much dispersion in earnings, both across occupations within an economy and among workers performing similar tasks but living in different countries?

Differences in labor market outcomes can mainly be traced back to the productivity of labor—the quantity and value of labor's contribution to output. When output per worker is high, a small fraction of the work force will be engaged in agriculture, because the economy's demand for food can be met by a small number of highly productive domestic farmers, or by the profitable exchange of goods made by highly productive industrial and service workers for food produced abroad. Across occupations, engineers earn more than textile workers because the market value of a year's work spent designing a machine that produces textiles is much greater than that of a year's supply of cloth produced by the worker operating it. Within occupations, pay differences across countries reflect the average level of *economy-wide* productivity. If a bus driver in Seoul earns three times as much as a bus driver in Bombay, it is not because the Korean is three times better at driving a bus. Instead, the higher level of labor productivity in the Korean economy overall, and hence the higher level of incomes there, mean that, on the one hand, the bus drivers must be paid enough to persuade them to drive a bus rather than do something else for a living, while on the other, consumers in Seoul are willing and able to pay more for a bus ride than consumers in Bombay.

In a market economy, differences in wages and employment are determined in the labor market, where households supplying their labor interact with employers who demand it. Where the market sets the price and quantity of labor, labor productivity must increase in order for wages to rise and employment opportunities to expand. This in turn requires expansion in productive capacity; that is, employers and households must mobilize savings to finance investments in physical capital, new technologies, and worker skills. With increased productivity, employers are both able and compelled to pay higher wages: able because of the increased amount of goods and services each worker produces in return; compelled because employers must compete for labor that is becoming increasingly productive across a whole range of activities.

In the low- and middle-income economies, cross-country differences in today's earnings largely reflect changes over the past two or three decades. Thirty-five years ago, for example, the earnings of bus drivers in Seoul, Bogotá, Jakarta, Bombay, and Nairobi were more similar than they are today. Some of these cities are located in economies that have experienced rapid changes in the demand for their output and in the productivity of their work forces, permitting significant growth in labor incomes (Figure 1.3).

The greatest successes have occurred in East Asia, where GDP per worker more than tripled from 1965 to 1993, and in South Asia, where average labor productivity doubled over the same period. Approximately two-thirds of the working-age populations of the low- and middle-income economies reside in regions where labor productivity has risen since 1980. But in Africa, Latin America, the Middle East, and the transitional economies of Europe and Central Asia—which together account for about 30 percent of the world's working-age population—output growth has declined over the past thirteen years, and in many of these countries growth in labor productivity has turned negative. In fact, the rate of decline has accelerated during the 1990s in all of these regions except Latin America. Explaining why some countries have prospered and others have not is key to understanding how the world can productively absorb its growing work force.

Three patterns

Rapid growth in output per worker in countries such as the Republic of Korea, Indonesia, and, most recently, China has brought rapid growth in the incomes of wage workers and the self-employed, together with a swift influx of rural labor into higher productivity employment in industry and services. All of these East Asian economies invested heavily in physical and human capital—with special emphasis on developing human resources throughout the population. Effective engagement in international markets has been key to expanding higher productivity employment, whether in primary products or in manufactures. This strategy included strong support for agriculture, especially for family farms, and mostly avoided sharp divides between modern sector and rural workers. A strong export orientation reduced economic rents, and labor policy did not favor privileged groups of workers. East Asia's record in labor relations

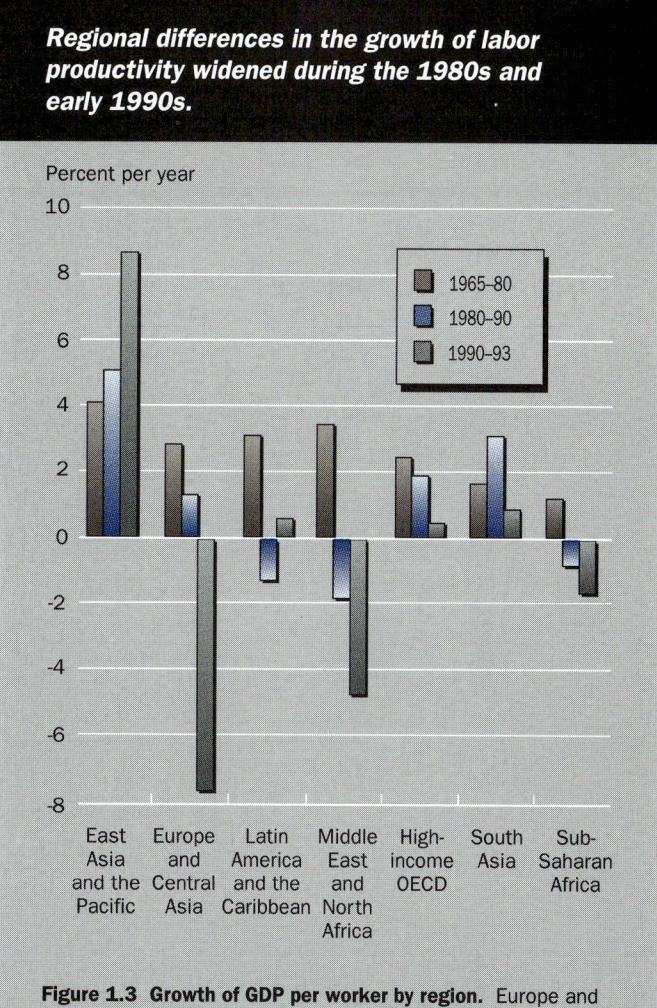

Regional differences in the growth of labor productivity widened during the 1980s and early 1990s.

Percent per year

Legend:
- 1965–80
- 1980–90
- 1990–93

Regions: East Asia and the Pacific; Europe and Central Asia; Latin America and the Caribbean; Middle East and North Africa; High-income OECD; South Asia; Sub-Saharan Africa

Figure 1.3 Growth of GDP per worker by region. Europe and Central Asia includes the middle-income economies of Europe. Source: EBRD 1994; Kornai 1992; World Bank data.

is less enviable: many countries imposed restrictions on unions, and some have endured labor-related violence. However, there is no evidence to suggest that such restrictions were necessary for East Asia's economic success.

In Sub-Saharan Africa, Latin America, the Middle East, and South Asia most countries pursued, to varying degrees, inward-oriented development paths that protected certain industries and were biased against agriculture. These strategies benefited a limited number of "insiders"—capital holders and workers employed in the protected sector. Attempts to maintain these workers' privileged positions often were based on institutional interventions—prohibitions on firing in Latin America or featherbedding of public employment in South Asia and Sub-Saharan Africa—rather than on raising labor demand or improving productivity. The consequences were slow growth in labor demand, especially in those industrial sectors that depended mainly on the domestic market, and a relatively large gap between workers in the formal sector and those working in the less privileged rural and informal sectors. A few countries, especially in South Asia, were able to achieve large gains for rural workers through effective support for family farms and adoption of new technologies. But even there labor's gains were substantially less than they would have been if industry had taken off.

The centrally planned economies, especially those of Europe and Central Asia, were for decades exemplars of an economic model antithetical to the market model of the high-income industrial countries. Regarding themselves as champions of labor, they delivered both rising wages and cradle-to-grave protection for their workers—and saw no need for free, independent trade unions. Like the East Asian economies they invested heavily in machines and skills, but unlike East Asia they weakened or destroyed family farming and pushed rather than attracted workers into industry—following a path dictated by a development strategy that was as disconnected from domestic economic reality as it was from international markets. Massive investments failed to offset severe resource misallocations and a lack of technological dynamism. Wage stagnation, shortages, a backward services sector, and some of the world's worst industrial pollution were all signs of the failure of central planning to improve workers' lives in a sustainable manner.

Two of these three divergent paths have reached their inevitable dead ends. Many workers are worse off than they were two or three decades ago. Today protectionist and centrally planned economies alike have been going through major changes toward greater reliance on international and domestic markets. These changes—in part forced by sharp macroeconomic shocks, in part driven by a radical turnaround in policy—have usually brought wrenching changes to workers in the transitional period before growth recovers.

The scope of this Report

This Report undertakes to explain how labor outcomes can be so extraordinarily different in different parts of the world, and how good policy choices can bring about desirable changes in the lives of workers. Part One reviews the long-run development experiences of different countries from the perspective of what they have meant for workers. It analyzes the relationship between the determinants of growth and policies influencing labor demand and human resource development. And it explores the relationship between inequality and the path of development. It concludes that high and broad-based investment in people and capital and reliance on markets can bring rapid and relatively equitable growth in labor incomes. The policy issue is not one of laissez-faire versus government intervention; rather it is how to take effective public action that supports the efficient functioning of markets, encourages productive investment, and responds to the particular needs of workers who are discriminated against or otherwise disadvantaged.

Part Two assesses the consequences of ongoing international developments for workers, with an emphasis on their likely future course. Economic integration is creating a global labor market where wage and employment decisions in one country are increasingly influenced by interactions with other countries. Trade, migration, and capital flows all have the potential to improve the welfare of workers, especially in poorer countries, with trade by far the most important channel. But this potential will be realized only if domestic policy is sound. In a world of mobile capital, success is well rewarded but failure punished hard. With increasingly open trade, workers in countries that do not keep up with improvements in their competitors' productivity will reap smaller gains.

Part Three turns to the role of government policy in labor markets and assesses what types of policies make sense in an increasingly open and often more democratic world. For a market-based strategy to succeed, governments must establish labor policies to deal with basic worker rights, discrimination and inequality, income security, and the government's own role as an employer. Such policy must take market realities into account. Rather than dictate outcomes, public action and legislation should complement both informal sector solutions and the outcomes of negotiated solutions between workers and employers in the formal sector. Government policy should enable workers and employers to negotiate with each other and should avoid helping a few insiders at the expense of the vast number of poor outsiders.

Part Four explores the consequences for workers of major shifts from protectionism and central planning. Initial conditions and macroeconomic policies matter for the path of wage and employment outcomes. Inevitably there are winners and losers, but the sooner economies begin to grow, the fewer are those workers who suffer permanent losses. Labor market policies can facilitate restructuring by encouraging wage flexibility and labor mobility, by designing transfers targeted to the casualties of transformation, and by adopting certain measures designed to help workers find employment.

With effective policy, there is great potential for the world's expanding labor force to enjoy significant gains in coming decades. But this optimistic outcome is not guaranteed. If poor countries do not pursue market-based policies, or if the trend toward greater global integration is halted by protectionism, the future could instead witness slow growth and increasing global inequality. The Report's concluding chapter reviews the implications of the earlier chapters' analysis for workers in the twenty-first century.

PART ONE

Which Development Strategies Are Good for Workers?

MARKET-BASED ECONOMIES have delivered faster growth than either centrally planned or protectionist economies. But how does growth affect workers? And what is the role of governments in supporting rising incomes for workers and their families? In this part of the Report we examine the relationship between long-term development and the fortunes of workers. We survey the consequences of economic growth for workers in Chapter 2, and the nature of interactions between households and labor markets in Chapter 3. We then, in Chapters 4 and 5, look at how policy choices can affect the growth of labor demand and the provision of skills. Finally, in Chapter 6, we ask how market outcomes affect inequalities in how the rewards of growth are distributed.

CHAPTER 2

Economic Growth and the Returns to Work

ECONOMIC GROWTH IS GOOD FOR WORK-
ers. Low- and middle-income countries cannot sustain the growth they need without
making the best use of their working-age
populations. Sustained growth with rising
labor demand has been achieved by countries that have relied on markets—domestic and international—to guide the
process of development, whereas inward-looking and centrally planned strategies have generally failed to bring sustainable gains to all workers. But the choice for governments today is not simply between free markets and state
intervention. The task is to determine which kinds of public intervention best support the efficient functioning of
markets, most encourage productive investment in plant,
technology, and people, and can assist disadvantaged workers. This is the new challenge of development.

This chapter investigates why some countries grow faster
than others, focusing on three countries that have had very
different experiences over the past three decades. It examines the determinants of growth and the importance of investment in physical capital and in people. And it considers
whether rapid population growth tends to depress growth
rates of GDP per capita and impoverish populations.

How do development strategies affect labor outcomes?

Ghana, Malaysia, and Poland are typical of their regions—
Sub-Saharan Africa, East Asia, and Eastern Europe. The
working-age populations of all three economies have grown

significantly over the past three decades. But their governments started out with different development strategies.
The result has been wide differences in economic growth
rates and labor outcomes (Figure 2.1).

Ghana was poorly integrated with global markets and
relied on government intervention in allocating resources,
for example through extensive use of state-run produce
marketing boards and stringent controls on foreign exchange. Malaysia also adopted various forms of intervention, including protected public enterprises and a broad
program of redistribution. But Malaysia's overall strategy
relied heavily on market processes; capital markets were
open, and the economy faced outward. In Poland resources
were allocated not by the market but by central planners.
Output targets were chosen and inputs allocated without
consideration of the real opportunity cost of resources; participation in international markets was limited mainly to
centrally negotiated trade with other planned economies.

Beginning in the 1960s Ghana experienced two decades
of economic decline, followed by a major reform program
and a modest recovery, which began in the late 1980s and
continues today. Between 1960 and 1990, GNP per capita
fell by 1.5 percent a year on average, and poverty deepened.
Meanwhile Ghana's working-age population doubled from
about 3.5 million to 7.8 million. Unemployment continued
to account for only a small percentage of the labor force: the
working-age population in 1989 was distributed roughly as
it had been thirty years earlier (Table 2.1). Self-employment
in urban and rural areas continued to absorb more than half

Growth and rising incomes bring more wage employment.

Table 2.1 Working-age population by employment status in Ghana, Malaysia, and Poland
(percentage of total)

Employment status	Ghana		Malaysia		Poland	
	1960	1989	1957	1989	1955	1990
Wage worker	14	14	35	42	41	52
Self-employed	58	59	27	20	32	23
Unemployed	4	2	1	3	0	5
Out of the labor force	24	24	37	35	27	20

Source: ILO, various years; Ghana Living Standards Measurement Study Survey data for 1988–89; Malaysia Labor Force Survey
data for 1989; *Statistical Yearbook of Poland* 1993.

of the working-age population. Another quarter were outside the labor force—raising children, attending school, or unable to work. Only 14 percent of the working-age population was occupied in wage labor, more than half of them in public employment. Private wage employment as a share of the labor force actually declined.

Malaysia's economy took off over this same period, and the number of households living in absolute poverty fell dramatically. Malaysia achieved growth in GNP per capita of 4 percent a year, despite a surge in the working-age population from 4.2 million to 10.4 million—a larger and faster increase than Ghana experienced. As in Ghana, labor force participation rates changed little over time, and unemployment accounted for only a small percentage of the labor force. What changed was wage employment, which rose, and self-employment, which fell, as jobs in industry and services increased dramatically (Table 2.1). In 1957 one in two employees worked on plantations; by 1989 only

one in ten workers did. Wage employment tripled between 1957 and 1989, while the share of the work force employed in agriculture fell from 58 percent to 26 percent.

Poland's economy also grew quickly during 1950–79, with net material product (GDP excluding most public and personal services) expanding by 4.1 percent a year and capital investment by 9.7 percent a year. The population grew slowly, at about 1.2 percent a year, and there was no unemployment—the state guaranteed workers jobs. The government moved thousands of workers from farms to the cities and pushed tens of thousands of women into the labor force. But growth proved unsustainable—it was based primarily on increasing the amount of capital and numbers of workers rather than on raising the productivity of capital and labor. Productivity slowed in the late 1960s, but heavy foreign borrowing postponed the crisis until eventually Poland's economy stopped growing altogether. By 1992, GDP was 9 percent lower than it had been in 1980. Over-

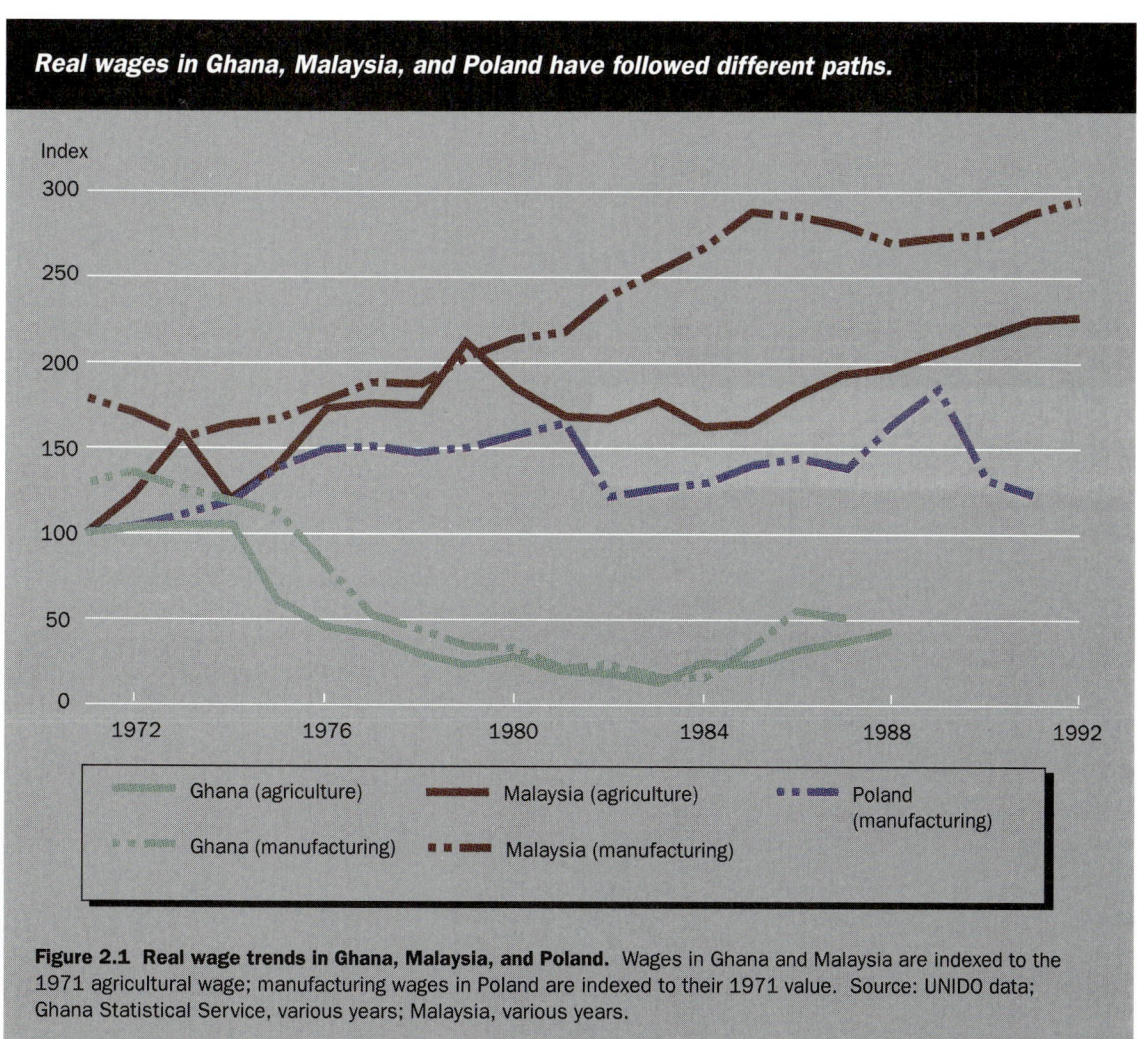

Real wages in Ghana, Malaysia, and Poland have followed different paths.

Figure 2.1 Real wage trends in Ghana, Malaysia, and Poland. Wages in Ghana and Malaysia are indexed to the 1971 agricultural wage; manufacturing wages in Poland are indexed to their 1971 value. Source: UNIDO data; Ghana Statistical Service, various years; Malaysia, various years.

all, between 1955 and 1990 the working-age population expanded from 17 million to 25 million. The share of the working population engaged in wage employment had increased, but so had the number of unemployed and the number living below the poverty line.

Wage increases mirrored aggregate economic performance in all three countries. Average real wages in manufacturing in Ghana remained roughly constant in the 1960s, but as growth turned negative, the purchasing power of wages in manufacturing collapsed: by 1984 real wages had plunged to 13 percent of their level a decade earlier; agricultural wages also collapsed (Figure 2.1). Had household incomes fallen as much as real wages, most families would have starved. Instead Ghanaians adjusted to falling wages in various ways. Farm families able to consume their own production had some protection against economic stagnation and rapid inflation. Urban workers held several jobs or migrated back to rural areas; some families relied on transfers from other households. Only recently have manufacturing wages started to rise again with economic recovery.

Malaysian workers, in contrast, have reaped the benefits of economic growth: all the major sectors experienced sustained increases in real wages, while more workers found jobs in higher paying, high-productivity activities. Both plantation wages and real earnings in manufacturing have doubled since the early 1970s. Most entrants to the labor force joined the modern industrial and service economy, where the average wages of workers in manufacturing were twice those of general plantation workers. Even those who did not work for wages experienced significant gains in their earnings from work. Self-employed workers such as street vendors, hairdressers, and truck drivers saw growth in their earnings that equaled or even exceeded the increase in manufacturing wages (Table 2.2).

Real wages in Poland also followed changes in GDP. Real wage growth remained high in the 1970s, even higher than in Malaysia. But in the 1980s Poland's wages fell, then stagnated, and unemployment rose in the 1990s. Poland was unable to sustain the past gains in the welfare of its workers. Real earnings in manufacturing dropped by a quarter between 1981 and 1991 (Figure 2.1).

Malaysian workers thus have benefited from economic growth, while Poles and Ghanaians have suffered from a lack of it. These countries are not unique. Evidence on long-run wage trends in low- and middle-income countries is not abundant, but in those countries for which data are available long-term growth is associated with rising real wages in agriculture and manufacturing (Figure 2.2). This is not surprising: GDP measures the value added by all factors of production—land, labor, and capital—and wages measure value added by labor. If GDP per worker is growing, then value added per worker must be growing—and under most circumstances so must wages.

Economic growth also changes the employment status of workers. In poor countries most labor is engaged in relatively low-productivity self-employment in agriculture or services. But as countries grow richer, more workers move into higher productivity, higher wage employment in industry and services (Figure 2.3). This transformation results from growth, but it also paves the way for further growth and increases in living standards. The formalization of employment relations is associated with increased opportunities for specialization and training, risk pooling, and greater income security.

What causes economic growth?

The benefits enjoyed by labor in fast-growing economies are not the result of job creation in the public sector or wage increases mandated by government. Expanding employment opportunities and rising wages are the consequences of growth and economy-wide increases in output per worker. A market-based development strategy achieves these outcomes through investment decisions by firms, households, and government. The search for more profitable activities encourages businesses—whether family farms, informal sector enterprises, or large corporations—to invest in equipment, new technology, and the training of workers. Households, seeking higher earnings from the hours they spend at work, will invest in their own human capital through improved health and nutrition and through schooling and training. Governments contribute directly by investing in public goods such as rural roads. But a market-

In Malaysia, growth has benefited workers in all sectors.

Table 2.2 Earnings in selected occupations in Malaysia

Occupation	Earnings in 1989 (manufacturing = 100)	Annual average growth rate of earnings, 1973–89 (percent)
Wage workers		
General plantation workers	50	3.0
Manufacturing workers	100	3.5
Self-employed workers		
Street vendors	111	4.4
Hairdressers	95	4.6
Launderers	42	−1.6
Tea preparers	64	2.5
Truck drivers	120	4.7
Shop owners	138	5.6

Source: Malaysia Labor Force Survey data for 1973, 1989.

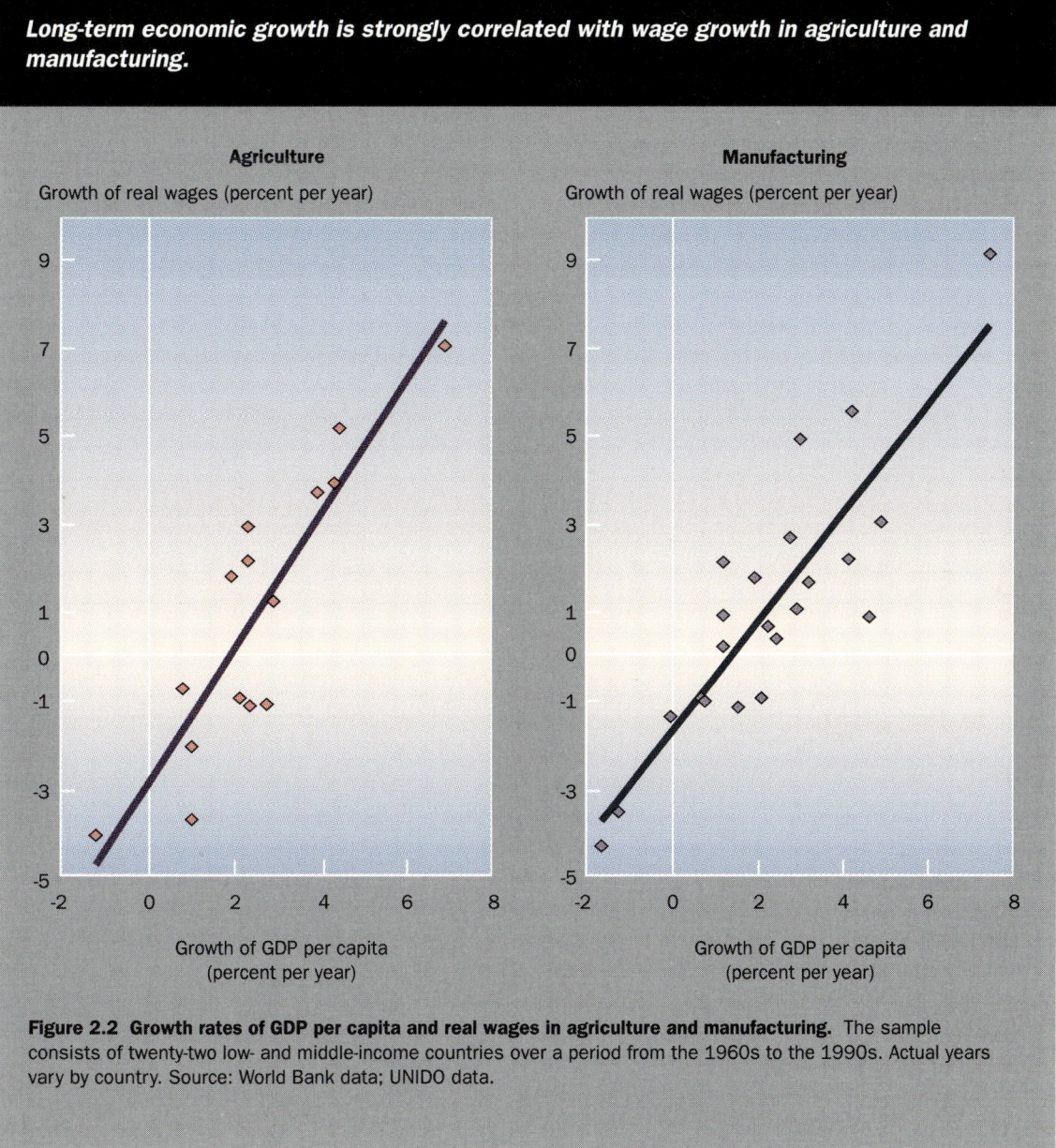

Long-term economic growth is strongly correlated with wage growth in agriculture and manufacturing.

Figure 2.2 Growth rates of GDP per capita and real wages in agriculture and manufacturing. The sample consists of twenty-two low- and middle-income countries over a period from the 1960s to the 1990s. Actual years vary by country. Source: World Bank data; UNIDO data.

based development strategy means that governments, above all, must enable businesses and households to invest in themselves, for example by protecting property rights and providing access to education.

The evidence linking economic growth to investment is overwhelming. For individuals, more schooling is strongly associated with increases in labor productivity and greater earning power (Chapter 5). At an aggregate level, the countries that have sustained high levels of economic growth are those that have experienced rapid increases in their stocks of physical and human capital. Between 1965 and 1990, the high-performing developing economies of East Asia sig-

nificantly increased their investment-GDP ratios, from an average of 22 percent in 1965 to an average of 35 percent in 1990. Human capital also increased rapidly: between 1965 and 1990 the gross primary school enrollment rate increased from 92 percent to 102 percent, and the gross secondary school enrollment rate went from 27 percent to 37 percent (gross enrollment rates include pupils who are not of the customary school age, and thus can exceed 100 percent of the relevant population). No other region matched this overall pattern of investment or the resulting payoffs in GDP growth, expanding wage employment, and increased earnings.

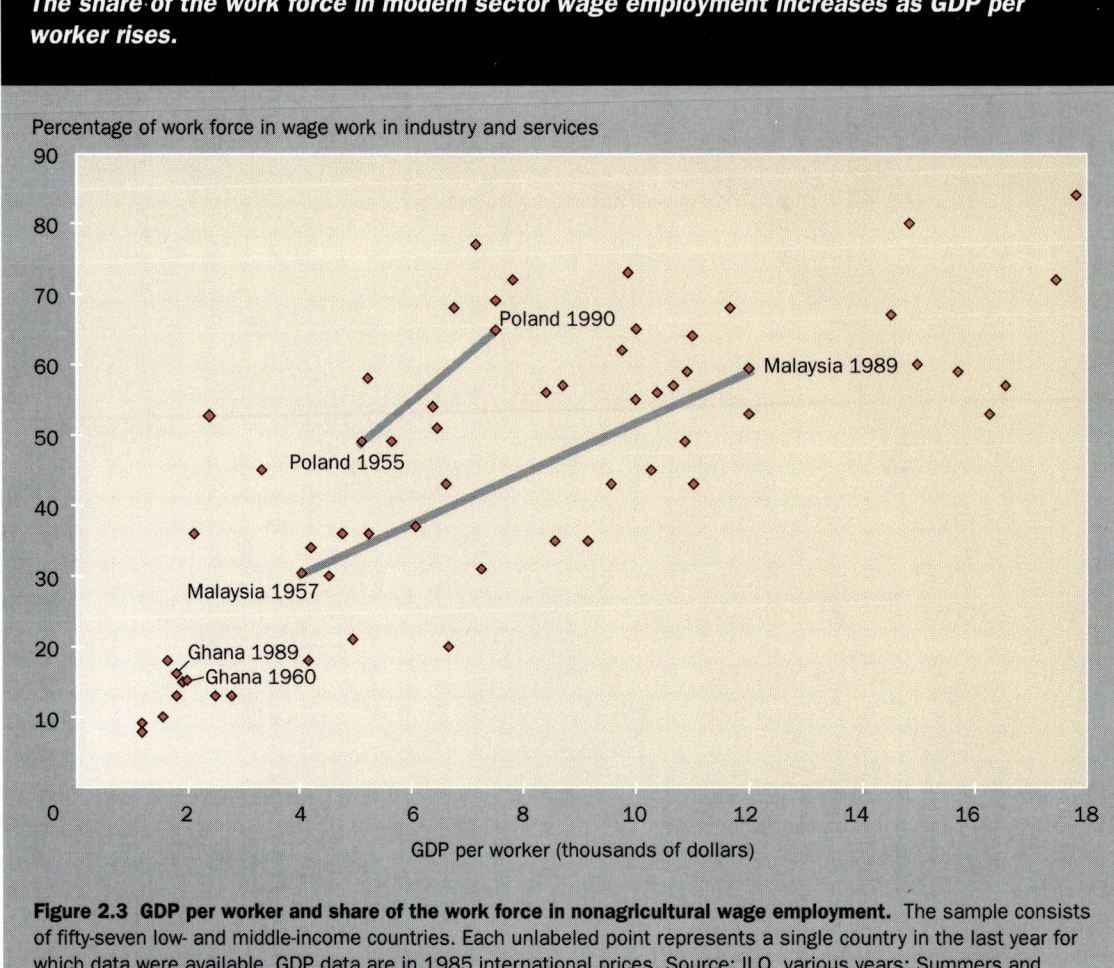

The share of the work force in modern sector wage employment increases as GDP per worker rises.

Percentage of work force in wage work in industry and services

Figure 2.3 **GDP per worker and share of the work force in nonagricultural wage employment.** The sample consists of fifty-seven low- and middle-income countries. Each unlabeled point represents a single country in the last year for which data were available. GDP data are in 1985 international prices. Source: ILO, various years; Summers and Heston 1991.

The relationship between investment and economic growth is captured by cross-country data comparing long-run (1960–85) growth rates in GDP per worker with recent estimates of the accumulation of physical capital and of years of schooling of workers (Figure 2.4). A sample of over sixty low- and middle-income countries, covering all regions except the transitional economies of Europe and Central Asia (for which comparable measures of investment are not yet available), exhibits a positive relationship between investment and growth in output per worker.

Fast-growing economies invest more, but investment alone does not necessarily deliver faster growth—the link between investment and productivity growth is far from automatic. Many economies expanded their stocks of physical and human capital per worker yet experienced low or even negative productivity growth rates. Some countries

that regularly invested more than 20 percent of GDP—including China in the 1970s, the former Soviet Union, Sri Lanka, and Tanzania—did not grow quickly. Changes in workers' average years of schooling are also weakly linked to faster growth. Many African countries expanded their educational systems, raising the average years of schooling of their labor force, but have seen little corresponding growth.

This far-from-automatic relationship between investment and productivity growth has two further implications. First, growth depends not only on how quickly inputs are accumulated, but also on the quality of those inputs, the technology embodied in them, and how efficiently they are employed. Fast-growing economies did not simply invest more but combined physical capital and educated workers in ways that increased output per worker.

Investment in physical and human capital is necessary but does not guarantee productivity growth.

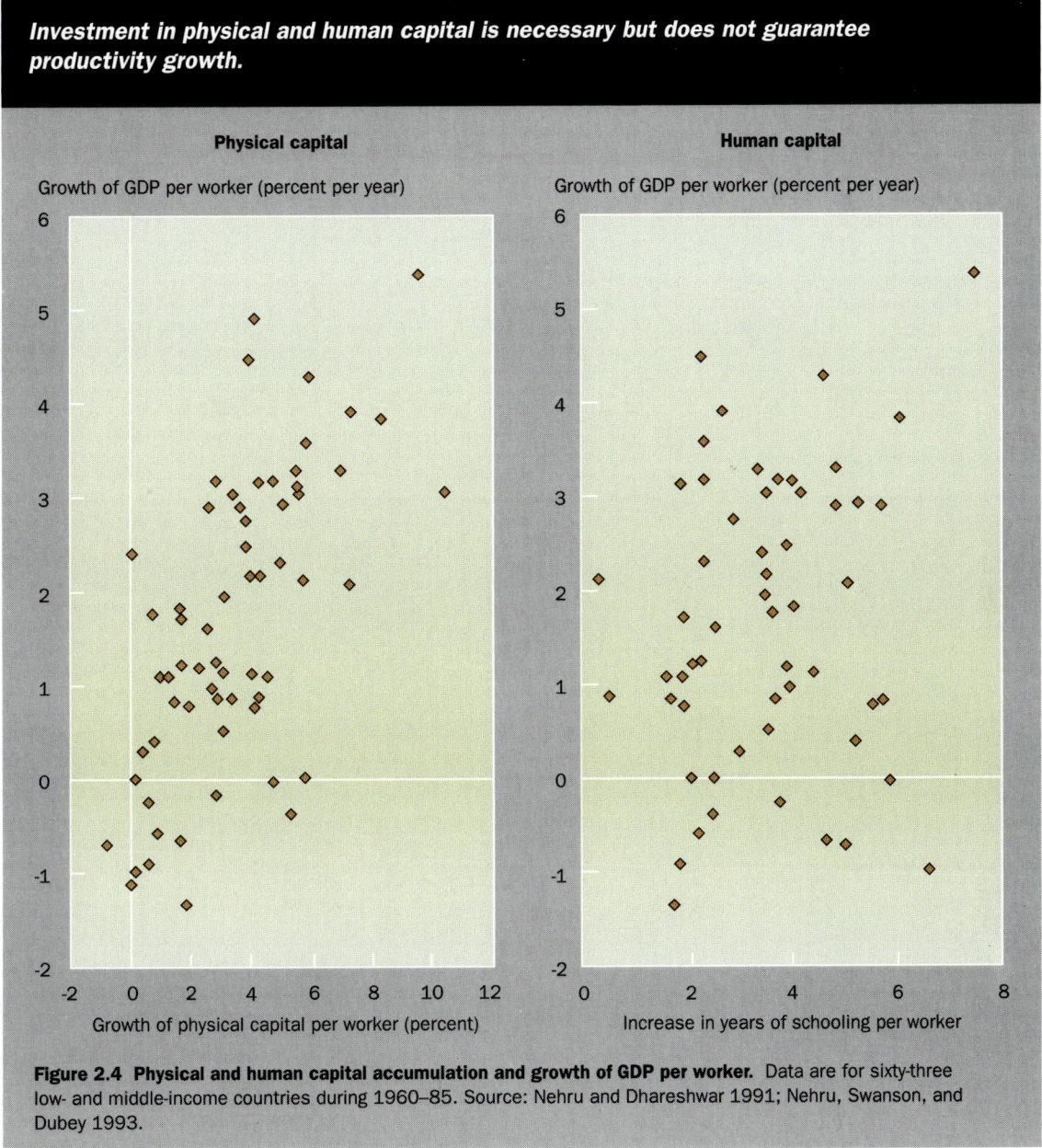

Figure 2.4 Physical and human capital accumulation and growth of GDP per worker. Data are for sixty-three low- and middle-income countries during 1960–85. Source: Nehru and Dhareshwar 1991; Nehru, Swanson, and Dubey 1993.

This finding points to the critical role of government policy in creating an environment that encourages *productive* investment.

Second, the relationship between investment in human capital and productivity growth is much weaker than that between investment in physical capital and productivity growth, as Figure 2.4 shows. But this is not to suggest that human capital is less important to growth. Detailed econometric studies find investment rates and initial endowments of education to be robust predictors of subsequent growth. Other things equal, the more educated a nation's workers, the greater their potential to catch up with prevail-

ing technologies and so achieve more rapid output growth. Rather, what weakens the relationship is that workers appear willing to invest in human capital even in the kinds of distorted, low-growth environments that tend to scare off private investment in physical capital. One reason is that capital is more mobile and can more easily seek out better opportunities in other regions or countries. Another is that households may continue to invest in education because they have longer run investment horizons or because public subsidies, by lowering private costs, continue to make education a worthwhile private investment. Households may also invest in schooling even when it does not translate into

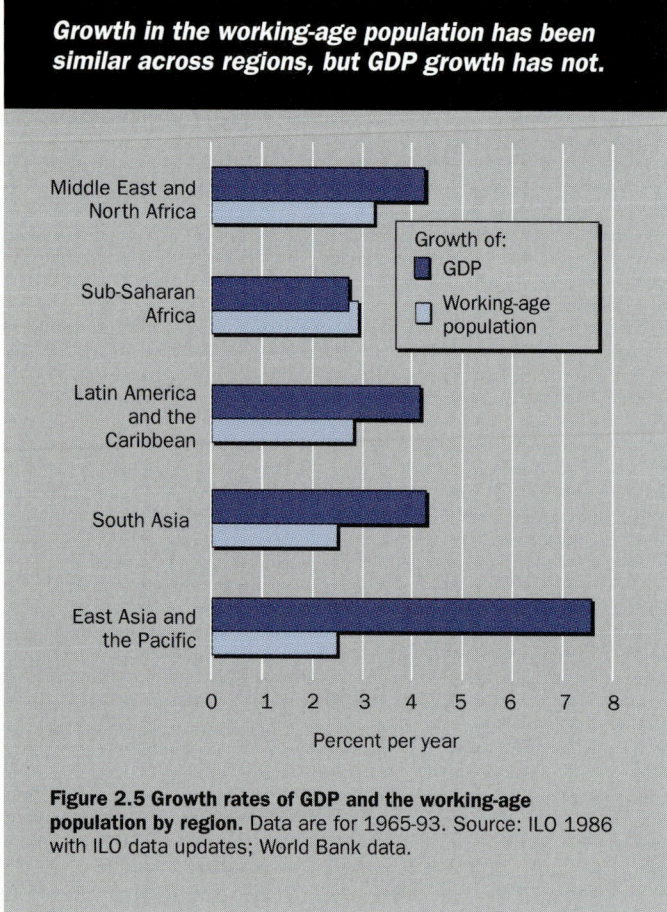

Growth in the working-age population has been similar across regions, but GDP growth has not.

Middle East and North Africa

Sub-Saharan Africa

Latin America and the Caribbean

South Asia

East Asia and the Pacific

Growth of:
- ■ GDP
- □ Working-age population

Percent per year

Figure 2.5 Growth rates of GDP and the working-age population by region. Data are for 1965-93. Source: ILO 1986 with ILO data updates; World Bank data.

higher levels of labor productivity because they value other benefits that education provides.

Economic growth and labor supply

Does rapid population growth depress growth and living standards? The argument that developing economies can have too many workers sounds persuasive. Economic growth requires rising productivity (output per worker), so more workers should, other things equal, mean lower productivity. But other things are not equal. More workers mean more output. And growth in output depends on the quantity and productivity of all inputs, including physical capital, human capital, and technology as well as the number of workers. Population growth need not have an adverse effect on investment, nor need it depress the productivity of inputs.

Poor labor outcomes may have little to do with the rate of growth of labor supply. Indeed, in recent decades, differences in the growth of potential labor supply in low- and middle-income economies do not explain differences in labor market conditions. During 1965–93, growth rates of the working-age population were remarkably similar across

regions, differing by only a few tenths of a percentage point. (The lone exception is the Europe and Central Asia region, which had already achieved low fertility rates by the 1960s.) But differences in GDP growth rates were huge, as Figure 2.5 shows. In East Asia output growth exceeded expansion of the working-age population by an average of about 5 percentage points a year; in Latin America the difference was less than 1.5 percentage points; and in Sub-Saharan Africa growth in the working-age population exceeded GDP growth. Where economic growth rates have been high, average output per worker has grown rapidly, doubling every fifteen years in East Asia compared with every fifty years in Latin America, and actually declining in Sub-Saharan Africa.

Economic growth and labor supply are interdependent, but the causality appears to run the other way than often claimed, with economic growth encouraging first faster, then slower labor supply growth. The Republic of Korea's working-age population was growing at a rapid 2.8 percent per year in the 1960s and 1970s, yet economic growth, by expanding employment opportunities, actually encouraged an *increase* in labor supply as participation rates of women went up. With growing incomes, and backed by family planning efforts, Korean households began to choose to have fewer children. As fertility declined, families invested more in each child they had, increasing the average number of years they spent in school. A growing economy also enabled government and households to devote more resources per pupil, improving the quality of Korea's education system. Investment in human capital helped to sustain Korea's rapid growth rates and closed the virtuous circle between economic growth and labor supply. Today Korea, like many other East Asian nations, has nearly completed its demographic transition from high to low fertility rates and faces the global marketplace with a slow-growing, highly skilled, and increasingly well-compensated work force.

The dilemma remains, however, about what to do about future labor supply in areas where economic growth is stagnant and populations continue to grow rapidly, as in much of Africa and the Middle East. There are no easy answers. It takes about twenty years for lowered fertility rates to appreciably slow the growth of the labor supply. And in the short run, lowering fertility can increase labor supply if women who would have been rearing children instead join the labor force. If the goal is to raise labor incomes, resources will have a higher return if used to encourage increases in labor demand—such measures will improve labor outcomes far sooner than will direct attempts to reduce future labor supply. While slowing population growth is thus no substitute for efforts to increase labor demand, there is reason to emphasize social policies that contribute to a decline in fertility—education of girls, improvements in women's status, and investments in reproductive health and family planning. These interventions can be justified in terms of their contribution to individual and family health and welfare.

• • •

Economic growth delivers higher wages and encourages workers to move to higher paid, high-productivity jobs in the formal sector, as Malaysia's experience demonstrates. Investment in physical capital and in people is key to economic growth and higher productivity—without investment, wages stagnate and living standards fall, as they did in Ghana before its reforms. But simply increasing the stock of physical capital and years of schooling will not automatically translate into sustained growth, as Poland discovered. A market-based development strategy that encourages enterprises and households to invest for the future in a productive and profitable manner can sustain rising labor demand. Such a strategy will enable low- and middle-income countries to expand employment opportunties and raise the wages of their often rapidly growing labor forces.

CHAPTER 3

Households, Growth, and Employment

OST PEOPLE, WHATEVER THEIR race, nationality, or the stage of development of their country, spend most of their lives working for a living. Economic growth and rising income per capita have a dramatic effect on the type of work households do, the incomes they receive, the way they manage their time, the sectors in which they work, and whether to migrate. Rising labor productivity and higher real wages affect decisions about who in the household should work, who should receive education and how much, and how households deal with risk and income security. For employers, higher productivity affects labor demand, the organization of production, and the nature of employment contracts. The interaction of households' supply of labor and employers' demand for it yields the employment outcomes we observe.

This chapter maps out the changes in household labor decisions and the organization of employment relationships that development brings. It then looks at what determines unemployment in rich and poor countries.

Household decisions and labor supply

Households everywhere have limited resources with which to meet their objectives. For most, especially in low- and middle-income countries, labor time is their primary resource.

Labor force participation

Households must decide how to allocate their collective labor time between home-based and market activity. Household income and the wages each member commands will influence their decisions. Low wages will not always mean long hours of work. In Ghana and Malaysia, evidence from household surveys suggests that workers from families in the bottom 40 percent of the income distribution worked 15 to 20 percent fewer hours on average than did individuals from the top 20 percent. This finding is probably due to a lack of opportunities, especially in rural areas. But at some point rising labor productivity and higher real wages raise household incomes enough so that individuals can choose to work fewer hours. One of the benefits of the sustained economic growth of today's high-income industrial countries has been an almost 40 percent decline in hours worked per person per year, from an average of 2,690 in 1900 to 1,630 in 1986.

Households must also decide who will work and in what activities. As work is conventionally measured, men work more than women. In a wide range of countries almost all men between twenty-five and fifty-four are directly engaged in income-generating activities, whether in the home, on the family farm or enterprise, or in the labor market (Figure 3.1). Differences between countries are confined to the young and the old. For example, a much larger fraction of male teenagers and elderly men work in Uganda than in Brazil, in part because of different income levels and hence different schooling and retirement patterns.

Among those who participate in market activities, wage employment is most common among the young; the incidence of self-employment and entrepreneurship increases with age; and unemployment is highest among young workers (who are more likely to change jobs). This suggests that, for a number of individuals, wage employment is a way to start out, earn some income and learn skills, save,

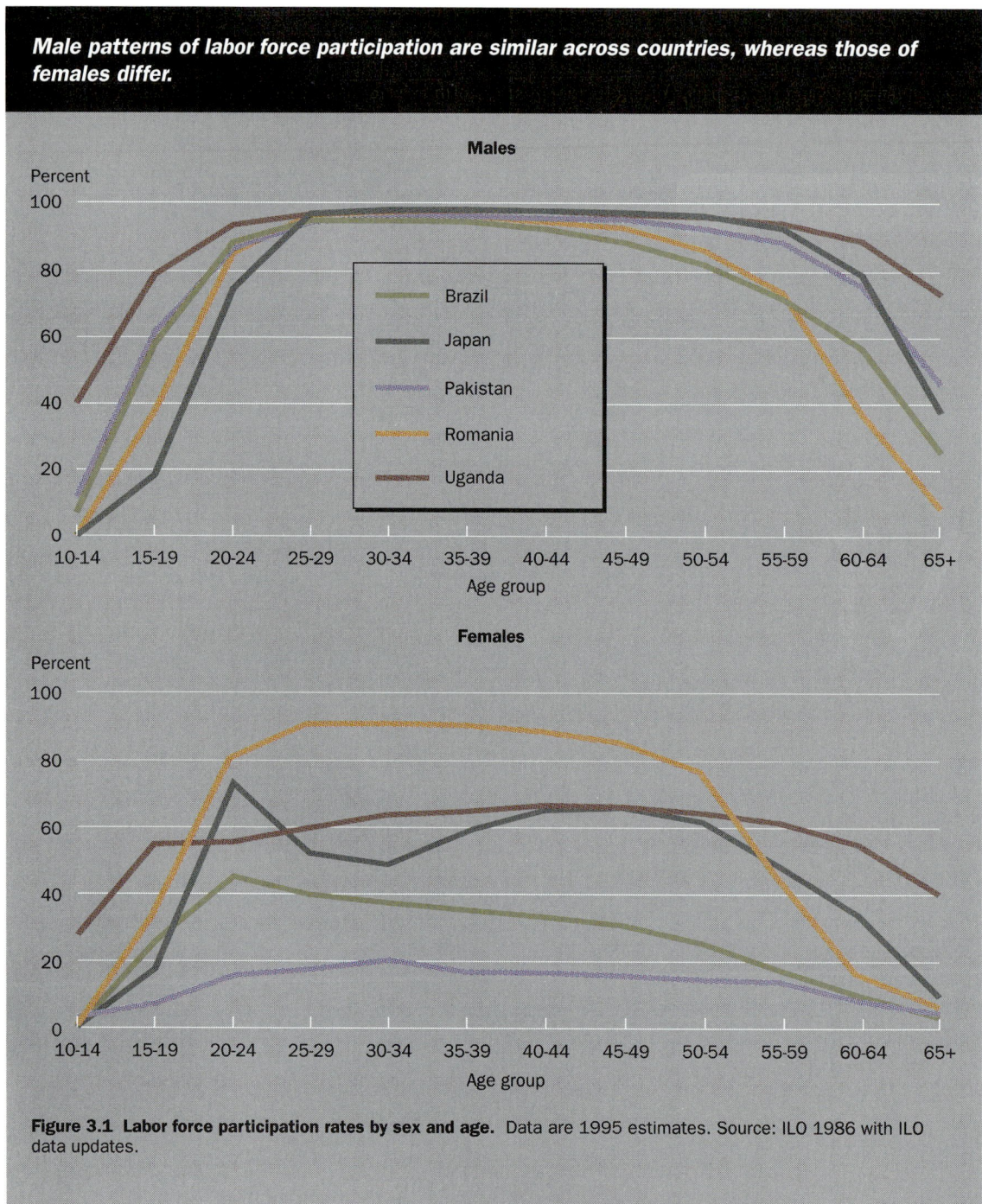

Male patterns of labor force participation are similar across countries, whereas those of females differ.

Males

Percent

Legend:
- Brazil
- Japan
- Pakistan
- Romania
- Uganda

Age group: 10-14, 15-19, 20-24, 25-29, 30-34, 35-39, 40-44, 45-49, 50-54, 55-59, 60-64, 65+

Females

Percent

Age group: 10-14, 15-19, 20-24, 25-29, 30-34, 35-39, 40-44, 45-49, 50-54, 55-59, 60-64, 65+

Figure 3.1 Labor force participation rates by sex and age. Data are 1995 estimates. Source: ILO 1986 with ILO data updates.

and ultimately set up an independent business. Figure 3.2 provides a snapshot of the working-age population in one country, Malaysia, showing how time allocation varies by age and sex.

But the conventional definition of "work" mischaracterizes relative effort, because time allocated to household activities other than agriculture is rarely counted. In almost all societies most households assign to women the bulk of childrearing and home management. Microeconomic studies often find women working longer hours than men—especially when they are also working in the market economy.

The labor force participation of women often changes in significant ways as development proceeds. Female participation rates tend to be higher when an economy is organized around family-based production in agriculture. With economic growth and increased urbanization, participation often declines, as women stay at home while men go out to work. At still higher levels of income per capita, female participation increases again as labor market options for women increase. Patterns of labor force participation also reflect cultural and ideological differences. A combination of economic and noneconomic factors is required to explain why Japan, Romania, and Uganda have higher female participation rates than Brazil and Pakistan (Figure 3.1).

Migration

Households also must decide where to work. Migration—be it permanent or temporary, domestic or international—is largely a labor market decision: household members move to where the jobs are. Where incomes are low, working for wages often requires members of rural households to move away, either temporarily or permanently. Migration also reflects a desire to diversify income sources—households may send one person to work in the city while others stay on the family farm or in the local wage economy. Temporary migration is generally associated with seasonal jobs and may involve crossing international borders: examples include Indonesian farm laborers traveling to Malaysia, Mexican workers to the United States, and Mozambicans to South Africa.

Economic development tends over time to increase urban employment opportunities and encourage workers to resettle to the cities. This process, however, can be distorted by policies biased against agriculture and toward urban areas in the creation of jobs, the supply of public services, or both (Chapter 4). Whatever the case, migration behavior needs to be understood as a household response to opportunities elsewhere, which means that attempts to control migration can be futile or costly to enforce.

Fertility and schooling

How many children a couple has largely reflects preferences about family size. Children of poor rural households are an

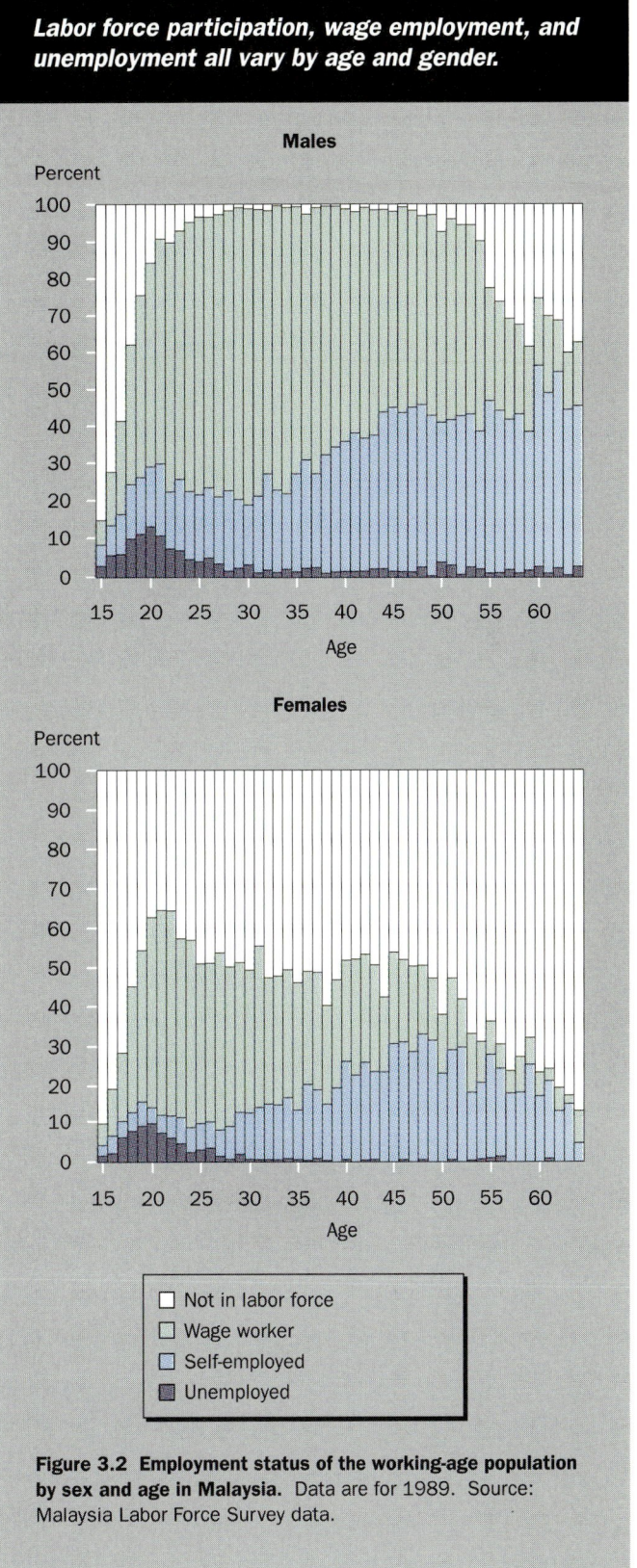

Labor force participation, wage employment, and unemployment all vary by age and gender.

Figure 3.2 Employment status of the working-age population by sex and age in Malaysia. Data are for 1989. Source: Malaysia Labor Force Survey data.

important source of farm labor and of security in old age. With development, most families desire fewer children, as employment opportunities and the market value of a woman's time increase and women opt to have fewer children. At the same time, rising incomes decrease the economic value of children as family workers and as a substitute for either public or more formal private systems of income security, including old age support.

As wealthier parents choose to have fewer children, they also invest more heavily in them, especially in the form of more education. In most countries girls get less education than boys—substantially so in South Asia and the Middle East—but in some regions, notably in Latin America, girls actually get more education. Less schooling for girls reflects fewer economic opportunities for women, as well as direct cultural influences. A feature of East Asian development was a rapid expansion of the education of girls as well as boys, bringing benefits to the next generation. More-educated mothers generally devote more household resources to the nutrition and upbringing of their children and give higher priority to their education. The cumulative effect of these household decisions is a slower growing and increasingly skilled work force—after a lag of some fifteen to twenty years.

Dealing with risk

A pervasive concern of households is how to manage the risks they face, whether of crop failure, unemployment, ill health, or incapacity in old age. Part of a household's strategy for allocating its labor time involves dealing with the risks of temporary or permanent falls in income. Even poor working households find ways of dealing with economic uncertainty and succeed in having much less variation in consumption than in income. This is achieved by a variety of mechanisms—the reallocation of labor time, fertility and marriage decisions, financial savings, transfers within the family or from the community, or borrowing. Fertility decisions, for example, are partly a function of the perceived risk that some children will die before reaching adulthood, jeopardizing parents' primary source of old age support.

The extent to which the allocation of labor responds to a strategy of risk management varies with the alternatives available. In Botswana and elsewhere it has been found that households decide how to allocate their members' time working at home and in other towns (or abroad) on the basis of reducing risks. With economic development, households tend to allocate more time to market-based activities. Labor market–related risks, particularly that of unemployment, become relatively more important.

Employment relationships

Half the world's workers are self-employed or work in family enterprises. But as economies grow, more workers work for wages, and employment relationships become increasingly formal, varied, and complex. Many forces typically come into play in eliciting and monitoring effort, sharing risks, and ensuring fairness. Arrangements that work well at one stage of development may not function later as the economy evolves.

The predominant form of labor organization in traditional economies is the family enterprise, typically a farm. Its main advantage is that the household reaps all the gains from its activity, so that all members have a direct interest in working productively; the disadvantages are small size and limited resources. Economies of scale are not important when most of production is agricultural; even where new techniques involving mechanization initially confer advantages on farms of larger size, rental markets usually develop that allow small farms to make use of them. Larger farms usually do have better access to credit, but this is generally outweighed by the advantages family farms have in eliciting effort. Family farms and other small-scale enterprises remain efficient forms of labor organization for much production in poorer societies.

Even where family farms and household enterprises predominate, other types of employment relationships coexist. The simplest form of labor contract is for purely casual work, for example by fruit pickers, taxi drivers, and temporary workers. In this part of the labor market productivity is easily measured, and piece rates are acceptable to workers and employers as a fair system of rewards. Demand for this labor is a function of the value of a worker's contribution to output, while supply depends on how much individuals value their time (or what they can earn elsewhere). As employment opportunities expand, this type of labor service becomes more specialized, and often a prearranged payment for services is required to secure labor supply at the appropriate time. Labor contractors emerge as important actors in this context, as they did in the fruit industry boom of the 1980s in the north of Chile. These entrepreneurs have been essential to a labor-intensive industry located in a sparsely populated area. They contract with farmers, act as employment agencies, and contribute to the flow of information across labor markets of neighboring regions.

Implicit contracts

Studies of rural labor markets in developing countries find that subtle social and economic forces often influence wages. In poor villages wages may be set at a level that ensures that workers have enough to eat to work effectively. More commonly, wages will be set for a given task for a season, and considerations of what is fair may apply. Studies in India find that daily wage rates in particular rural areas are strikingly uniform for workers of the same sex, despite differences in individual productivity. Wages do vary for different tasks, which are season-specific, but they do not directly reflect productivity. Instead more-productive workers tend to get more employment, while less productive ones have less employment in slack seasons. Such contracts contain incentives to reward effort and often have an element of risk sharing. Sharecropping contracts are popular for the same reasons, but they are more likely to be used where monitoring costs are high or where the relationship between effort and productivity is tenuous.

Formal contracts

With rising income per capita and industrialization, informal arrangements and small-scale production become less useful. Most manufacturing and many service activities exhibit greater economies of scale, in either production, marketing, or finance, than agriculture. In addition, workers are hired not just to accomplish a strictly contained task but to become part of a coordinated effort. They must be trained and given responsibilities, challenges, and incentives. Considerations of eliciting effort, concerns over risk, and social norms continue to interact with technology to produce the outcomes observed in the labor market, but this is increasingly resolved through formal contracts between employers and employees.

Formal labor contracts typically provide a framework for joint investments by employers and workers. Firms value a trusted and well-trained work force that knows the specific characteristics of its production process. They therefore devote resources to recruiting and training a work force tailored to their needs and offer incentives to those who remain loyal. Workers in turn value the security of a regular wage. Some firms offer "efficiency wages"—wages set deliberately above the market wage—to raise the cost of job loss to the worker and in return obtain, keep, and motivate good workers. The specifics of formal labor contracts must conform with a larger system of statutory workers' rights that typically governs labor relations in modern economies, covering minimum standards, union membership, and job security. We return to these issues in Part Three of the Report.

Unemployment

For almost half his fifty-two years Maciek was employed at the Star Truck Factory in Starachowice, Poland. Under new management the factory is being restructured, and he was among a thousand workers who lost their jobs. At his age and with his limited skills, Maciek will have great difficulty in finding a new job.

• • •

N'golo, a landless peasant living near Korhogo in northern Côte d'Ivoire, works fifteen hours a week on average. He would like to work more hours to improve his family's standard of living and pay for his children's education. But except in harvest season there is not enough work.

• • •

Zeba graduated three years ago from Dhaka University in Bangladesh. Nearly all of her male classmates have found work, but despite searching hard for a job in Dhaka, Chittagong, and her home town of Khulna, Zeba has had no offers. Employers prefer to hire men, believing they will be more committed to their careers.

• • •

Households supply labor, employers demand it, and this interaction along with self-employment and household production yields the employment and wage outcomes we observe. But many who want work cannot find it. Unemployment takes many forms, as illustrated by the contrasting stories of Maciek, N'golo, and Zeba. All involve human cost. The causes of unemployment are complex and often unrelated to the level of development. The difference between French and Japanese unemployment rates (11.6 and 2.5 percent, respectively, in 1993) clearly is not the result of differing incomes. But development does have an important impact on how unemployment manifests itself and is reported in official statistics (Box 3.1).

In low-income countries, informal and formal employment together usually absorb the entire labor force, especially in rural areas. Many of these workers are not fully employed. Some may work only part of the time, putting in long hours in peak agricultural seasons but otherwise mostly idle. But the nature of production in agricultural economies is such that open unemployment—defined as those without employment who are seeking work—is relatively rare. Individuals from poor households cannot afford to be without a job, and the sharing of low-productivity work in agriculture is widespread. But while open unemployment is low, underutilization of labor is pervasive. In Ghana rural laborers work on average only twenty-eight hours a week, whereas in Viet Nam nearly 10 percent of the labor force works less than fifteen hours per week, even though many of them would choose to work more. In Bangladesh the Bureau of Statistics estimated that nearly 43 percent of the country's labor force was underutilized in 1989.

In almost all countries there is underutilization of human resources—people who want to work cannot find as much work as they would like. In poorer, rural areas this mainly takes the form of seasonal underemployment. In urban areas one manifestation is that of the discouraged worker, who has given up searching for work. (In South Africa total unemployment of blacks is close to 40 percent, almost three-quarters of whom have given up even looking for a job.)

Over the course of development, and reflecting the structural transformation of the economy, the concentration of unemployment shifts from underemployment to some form of more open unemployment. This transition is

Box 3.1 What is unemployment?

Who are the unemployed? They include rural workers in Côte d'Ivoire and landless laborers in India who can find no work in the slack season; Polish steelworkers and Dutch longshoremen who have lost their jobs to sectoral shifts in the demand for their skills; members of the underclass in the United States and a generation of young workers in South Africa who have been unable to secure jobs or have been denied access to them; Egyptian university graduates and former civil servants in Nicaragua whose expectations for good jobs have failed to materialize and who are being supported by their extended families until suitable openings arise.

How many are unemployed? Most reported unemployment rates refer to the standard recommended by the International Labour Office (ILO): persons above a specified age who during the reference period (for example, the past week) are without work, currently available for work, and seeking work. By this definition the unemployed usually account for a relatively small percentage of the working-age population, although during acute episodes of adjustment—the United States in the 1930s, Chile in the early 1980s, Bulgaria in the 1990s—recorded unemployment can involve 15 to 25 percent of the labor force.

More comprehensive measures of labor underutilization come closer to capturing the true extent of idle labor time. Such measures include discouraged workers—those who are not working and would like to, but have given up looking because of a lack of opportunities. Another group not counted as unemployed consists of those who work less than full-time, not because they choose to but because more work is unavailable. This group includes those who remain formally fully employed but who no longer report to work (China's "off-post" employees) or who have been placed on indefinite unpaid leave (a common practice in Ukraine). Because the "availability" of work is partly subjective, precise estimates of the size of these groups are especially difficult. Nevertheless, when estimates of discouraged and underemployed workers are added to those counted as unemployed, the measured underutilization of labor rises significantly (see table).

Unemployment and underemployment in selected countries
(percentage of the labor force)

Country	Year	Unemployed	Discouraged workers	Underemployed[a]
Ghana	1988–89	1.6	1.5	24.1
Viet Nam	1992–93	1.3	3.5	10.0
Ukraine	1994	0.4	..	14.5
South Africa[b]	1993	11.9	25.5	5.5
Spain	1985	17.3	2.6	4.5
United States	1991	6.8	0.9	..

.. Not available.

Note: Countries are listed in ascending order of per capita income. Except for Ukraine, discouraged workers are counted in the labor force.

a. Those working fifteen hours or fewer per week.

b. Africans only.

Source: For Ghana and Viet Nam, Living Standards Measurement Study Survey data; for South Africa, Project for Statistics on Living Standards and Development data; for Spain, *La Encuesta de Condiciones de Vida y Trabajo*, 1985; for United States, Ehrenberg and Smith 1994; for Ukraine, *Labor Market Dynamics in Ukrainian Industry in 1992–94: Results from the Ukraine Labor Force Survey ILO-CEET*, Budapest 1994, and *Statisticheski Bulletin: Rynole Truda v stranakh SNE*, Moscow 1994.

partly due to rising incomes and urbanization. As countries grow and household incomes rise, individuals can begin to afford periods without work while waiting for a job. Also, more-modern economies organize work in ways that do not lend themselves as easily to work sharing or adjustment of hours as agricultural arrangements do. However, even among countries at the same level of income there are huge differences in open unemployment. Algeria, Brazil, and Poland have very similar incomes per capita, but in the early 1990s their rates of open unemployment, respectively, were 21.0, 3.9, and 16.0 percent (Figure 3.3). To under-

stand this variation it is important to recognize the various economic forces that generate unemployment.

Open unemployment can be driven by labor supply or labor demand: it can reflect a worker's decision to reject the jobs on offer and wait for a better one; it can be a sign of mistaken expectations; or it can result from policy failures or rigidities that reduce labor demand relative to supply. Unemployment is often subdivided by type or cause. Frictional unemployment results from the normal operation of markets, is typically of short duration, and is part of the process of workers looking for the right jobs, and employers for the right workers. Cyclical unemployment results from fluctuations in aggregate demand, and although sometimes widespread and severe it is usually temporary. Such unemployment can result in an increase in long-term unemployment if the unemployed find it difficult to reenter the work force once growth resumes. Structural unemployment is associated with economic stagnation, malfunctioning labor markets, or policy failures. It typically is of longer duration. Its elimination requires not only a recovery of aggregate demand, but also tackling problems of skill or geographic

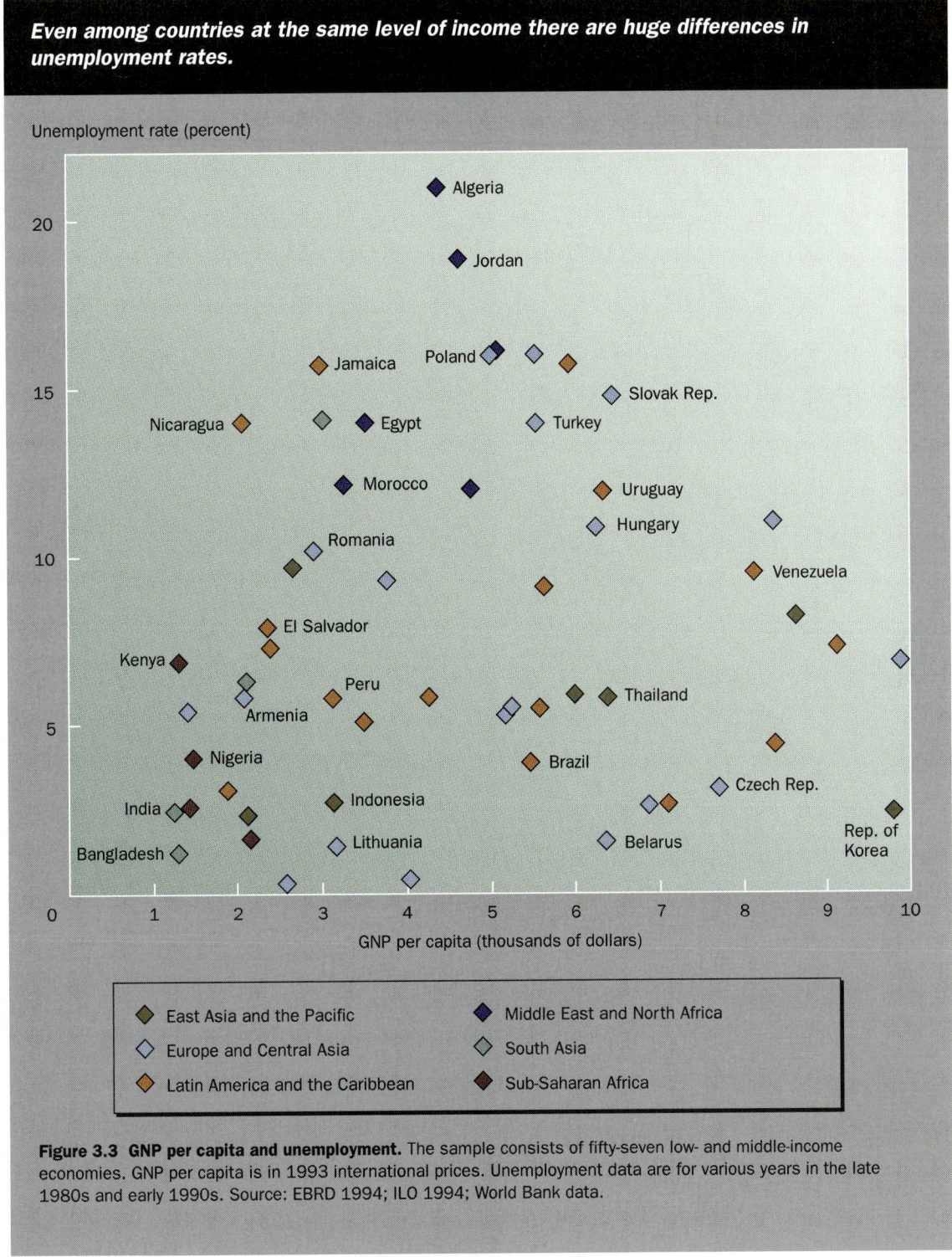

Even among countries at the same level of income there are huge differences in unemployment rates.

Figure 3.3 GNP per capita and unemployment. The sample consists of fifty-seven low- and middle-income economies. GNP per capita is in 1993 international prices. Unemployment data are for various years in the late 1980s and early 1990s. Source: EBRD 1994; ILO 1994; World Bank data.

mismatch between jobs and workers, eliminating rigid wage and employment practices, and upgrading the skills of workers.

Recent trends in unemployment are especially troubling. Despite a steady recovery in the world economy, open unemployment has grown in many countries. In Europe the persistence of high unemployment rates during the 1980s is believed to have been caused by a combination of weak growth in labor demand, real wage rigidities in the face of declining demand for unskilled workers, a welfare system that gives its beneficiaries disincentives to accept jobs, and restrictions in some service sectors that have held back employment growth.

Unemployment is particularly severe in many of the former centrally planned economies, where many enterprises, exposed for the first time to the discipline of markets, have been forced to cut back production or to shut down altogether. In Bulgaria, Hungary, and the Slovak Republic, officially recorded unemployment was negligible as recently as 1989. But by 1993 all three confronted open unemployment rates of between 12 and 16 percent. However, not all economies facing transition have had the same experience. In Belarus, the Czech Republic, and Russia open unemployment remains in single digits, although many workers in Belarus and Russia are effectively laid off or working part-time.

During the 1980s growth in modern sector employment stagnated in many poor countries in response to reductions in aggregate demand and public enterprise restructuring. In urban centers open unemployment grew as new entrants to the labor force and displaced workers failed to find work. Once viewed as a luxury, available only to better-off young people waiting for a modern sector job, unemployment now affects all social classes.

• • •

Economic development brings new and rapidly changing opportunities to participants in the labor market. Progress depends on the willingness and capacity of households to save and build up their productive assets, the willingness of entrepreneurs to organize productive factors so that gains from specialization can be achieved, and the willingness of governments to enhance rather than discourage these endeavors. Economic growth makes labor services increasingly expensive, inducing households to choose alternative ways of managing their time, and employers to discover better ways of organizing production. But these interactions are not perfect, and often many workers find that their labor is underutilized and their incomes are low.

CHAPTER 4

Policy and Patterns of Labor Demand

Economic development means dramatic changes in the structure of employment and enormous increases in productivity. The pattern of work in traditional industries changes as the rising cost of labor, together with technological advances, encourages new methods. Meanwhile job opportunities expand in services and industry, as employment in agriculture declines and workers move to urban areas and from the informal to the formal sector. Workers have prospered more when the process of productivity upgrading and labor transfer has been based on market realities. Attempts by governments to force the pace of change by protecting industry and formal employment have proved unsustainable and often counterproductive, slowing economic growth, depressing labor demand, and encouraging informalization.

This chapter seeks to explain why productivity growth changes the pattern of employment. It then asks how policy choices can help or hinder a process of labor-demanding growth and structural transformation.

The transformation from low- to high-productivity activities

Productivity growth and rising real wages change the way economies work. As skills and capital become more abundant, countries find it economical to use their labor to produce more skill- and capital-intensive manufactures and services and fewer labor-intensive agricultural goods. On average, agriculture's share of employment falls from 90 percent of the total in poor countries to roughly 5 percent in rich ones, as Figure 4.1 shows. Industry's share, which includes manufacturing, construction, and mining, rises from 4 percent to about 35 percent, and that of services from 6 percent to 60 percent. This shift is associated with the rise in formal employment discussed in Chapters 2 and 3. But different resource endowments can produce wide variations from this basic pattern. Those countries with a lot of agricultural land, such as the United States and New Zealand, remain highly efficient agricultural producers as they develop. Those well endowed with minerals, such as Indonesia and Venezuela, tend to allocate less labor to manufacturing and more to services.

Rising real wages also encourage producers within a given sector to adopt labor-saving production techniques as workers move from low- to high-productivity activities, as differences in the organization of milk production in Mexico, Ecuador, and Texas illustrate. Poor family farms in rural Mexico, each working with its own meager capital and without hiring specialized services, earn little more than a subsistence income producing only three to four liters per day per cow. In the Ecuadoran highlands small commercial dairy farms hire laborers at $100 per month, use a range of market services such as artificial insemination, and obtain thirteen liters per day from each cow. Texas ranches rely even more heavily on market transactions for such inputs as supplemental nutrients and veterinary services; their ranch hands get $1,200 per month, but their cows produce twenty or more liters per day.

As economies expand, new employment opportunities compete with existing ones. With demand rising elsewhere, workers move out of low-productivity, low-wage activities. Figure 4.2 outlines labor productivity trends within and between sectors in Malaysia and the Republic of Korea over the past three decades. Malaysia's impressive productivity performance partly reflects an expansion of employment in the high-productivity services and industrial sectors, but also the fact that agriculture substantially boosted its productivity while keeping the number of workers nearly constant. Korea's record was even more dramatic, although agricultural productivity began to improve only after the sector started to shed workers in the mid-1970s. In Korea and Malaysia, a breakdown of the sources of national labor productivity growth finds that about 60 percent of the total comes from rising labor productivity within sectors, and most of the rest from shifts between sectors.

Growth in labor productivity, whether within or between sectors, is not just a story of job creation; typically, some jobs must be eliminated as well. For example, employment in Korean industry grew from just over 1 million jobs in 1966 to more than 6 million in 1990, and during

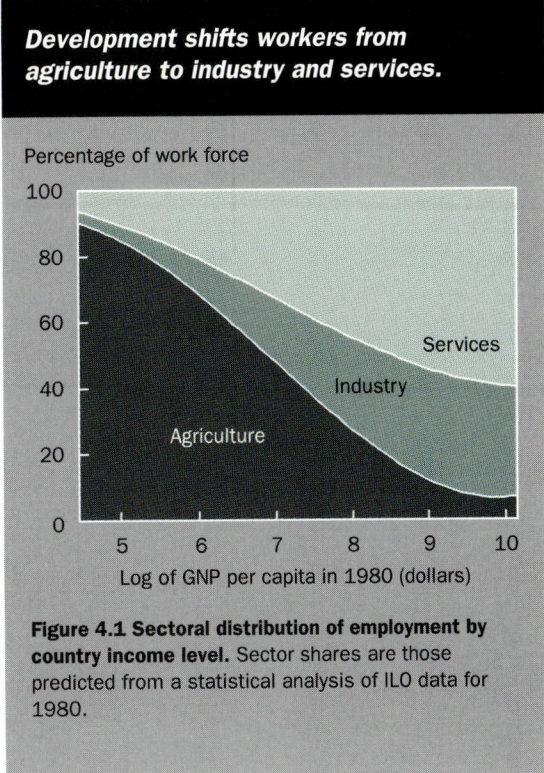

Development shifts workers from agriculture to industry and services.

Percentage of work force

Services

Industry

Agriculture

Log of GNP per capita in 1980 (dollars)

Figure 4.1 Sectoral distribution of employment by country income level. Sector shares are those predicted from a statistical analysis of ILO data for 1980.

this period manufacturing's share in total employment increased from 10 percent to 30 percent. But this economic success was unevenly distributed across industries and often resulted in the destruction of jobs. For example, employment in the plywood industry expanded from 23,000 jobs to 32,000 jobs between 1970 and 1979 but then fell after 1980. Real wages grew rapidly during this period, inducing a productivity-enhancing transformation in the industry.

Policy mistakes that lower labor demand

Too often the transformation of employment fails to reflect market-driven changes but instead results from government attempts to speed the shift from low- to high-productivity activities and sectors. There are three routes by which governments have tried to force change: policies that introduce a pro-industry, anti-agriculture bias; policies that are biased against labor demand within agriculture; and regulations designed to make formal sector employment more attractive to workers. All three suppress growth in labor demand and sooner or later hurt overall growth.

Pro-industry bias

Policies in a wide range of countries that emphasized import-substituting industrialization eventually proved bad for industrial employment, agricultural growth, and overall economic performance (Table 4.1). India, for example, enjoyed steady growth in wages, but experienced slow employment growth in manufacturing. Countries such as

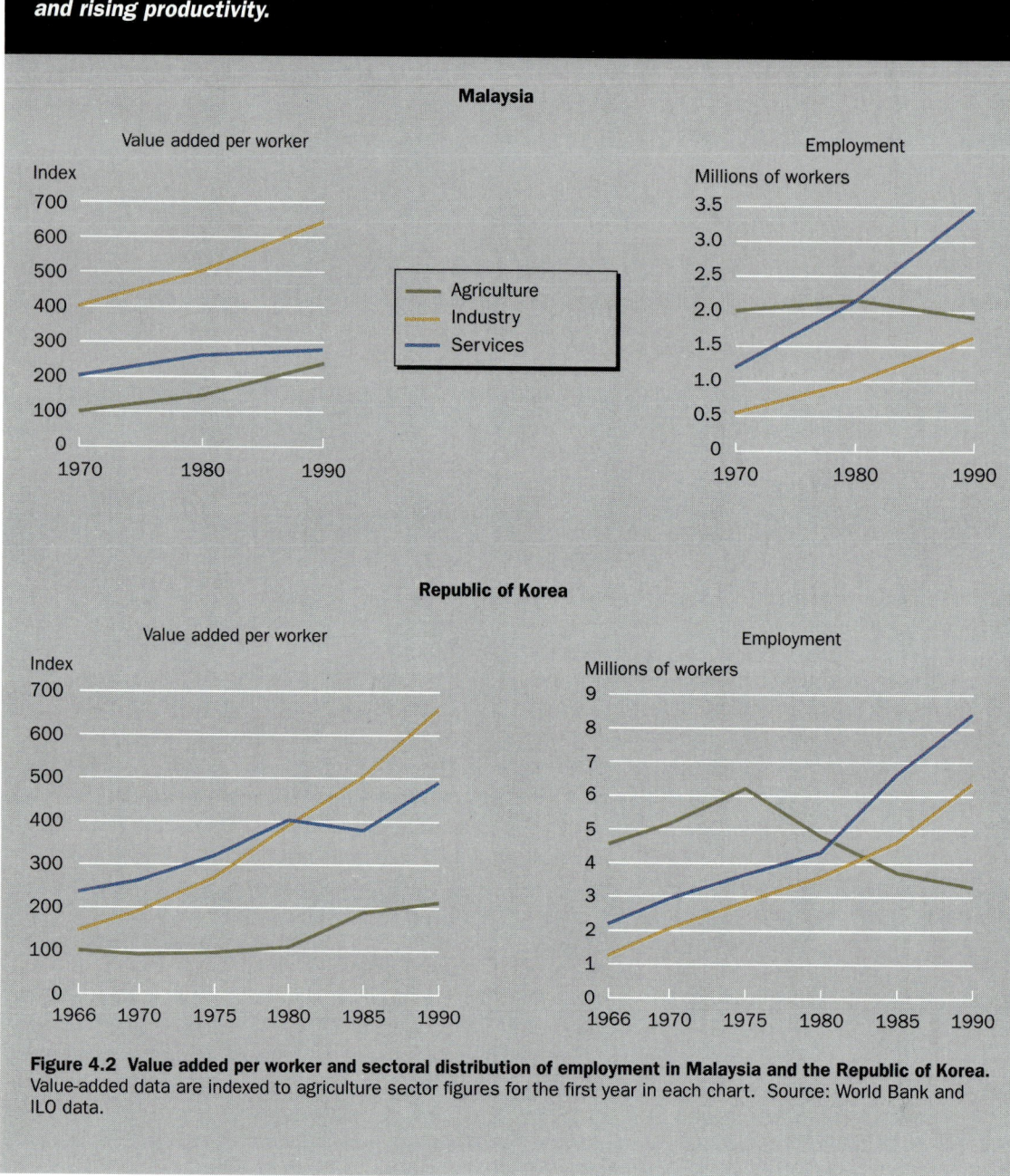

Workers in Malaysia and Korea have increasingly found employment in sectors with high and rising productivity.

Figure 4.2 Value added per worker and sectoral distribution of employment in Malaysia and the Republic of Korea. Value-added data are indexed to agriculture sector figures for the first year in each chart. Source: World Bank and ILO data.

Argentina and Peru, or Ghana and Zambia, suffered from both declining wages and slow (and in Argentina's case, negative) employment growth. Protection of industry failed to produce dynamic growth in industrial payrolls. It also introduced biases against labor within industry: studies show that in low- and middle-income countries export industries are usually more labor-intensive than import-substituting ones, but typically the former are disproportionately taxed rather than subsidized. Often capital is implicitly subsidized by lower protection for imported capital goods, and by overvalued currencies, further biasing industrialization against labor. In contrast, the successful East Asian economies emphasized exporting and had relatively moderate biases in favor of industry. They have seen wage employment growth far exceeding population growth, and significant growth in manufacturing wages.

Pampering of industry has proved good for a few industries but bad for growth in industrial employment. It has also been bad for agriculture. Given that agriculture is the major labor-intensive sector, this constitutes a bias against labor demand—and against the poorest groups of workers. The true tax on agriculture has often been huge. A study of eighteen countries found a total (explicit and implicit) tax on agriculture of 30 percent for the 1960–84 period—equivalent to a transfer to other sectors of 46 percent of agricultural value added per year. This transfer varied from around 50 percent for extreme taxers of agriculture such as Ghana and Zambia to 10 to 20 percent for relatively mild taxers such as Malaysia. Korea and Portugal actually subsidized agriculture. In most cases the primary source of taxation—some three-quarters of the total on average—was not explicit taxes but the indirect effects of industrial protection and the overvalued currencies that this brought. The study found that low taxation of agriculture meant faster agricultural growth and faster overall growth. Since this speeded the overall development process, lower taxes on agriculture paradoxically speeded the transformation from agricultural to industrial and services employment.

The pattern of technological change also matters. Where technological advance in a major labor-intensive sector is slow, that sector can become a laggard in the country's overall advance. This can be due to a failure to develop and adopt new techniques, as happened in agriculture during the industrial revolutions in the United Kingdom and the United States. There technical advances were concentrated in industry and communications, and this was one factor behind the stagnation of unskilled wages even as overall growth was taking off in these countries. But the green revolution has profoundly changed the situation in agriculture in the past three decades. Where farmers have been able to adopt the new technologies—notably in much of Asia—rural technical change has been rapid, bringing rapid overall rural income growth and powerful gains to rural workers through direct effects on farm incomes and agricultural wages. One study of rural India found that yield increases due to technical change reduced the incidence of poverty from 56 percent to 30 percent of the rural population between the mid-1970s and 1990, through both higher farm incomes and a 70 percent rise in agricultural wages. Many studies have found a substantial indirect effect in the expansion of the rural nonfarm sector, pulled up by rising demand for services, consumer goods, and inputs as farm incomes rise. However, for technological change to occur, the policy environment has to be supportive. Severe biases against agriculture, not unresponsive farmers, are the major reason for slow agricultural productivity growth in Sub-Saharan Africa.

Antilabor biases within agriculture

Between 1950 and the late 1970s, agriculture policies in both market-oriented and centrally planned economies

Table 4.1 Changes in manufacturing earnings and employment in highly protected and export-oriented economies
(percentage per year, 1970–90)

Country	Real earnings per worker	Wage employment
Highly protected economies		
Argentina	−0.9	−2.5
Ghana	−5.5	2.2
India	2.2	2.0
Peru	−3.3	2.6
Zambia	−0.9	2.0
Export-oriented economies		
Korea, Rep. of	8.2	6.6
Malaysia	2.2	8.2
Thailand	3.0	5.1

Source: Banerji, Campos, and Sabot, background paper.

were inspired by the view that peasants would be unlikely to respond to market incentives, that large farms were more efficient, and that the sector's best hope lay in capital-intensive modernization. This has been proved wrong. A few economies, mostly in East Asia, not only avoided excessive taxation of the agricultural sector but also provided strong infrastructural and service support for small-scale agriculture. This was facilitated by prior distributive land reforms (in Korea and Taiwan, China), by a history of small-farm production (in Indonesia and Thailand), or by a swift transition to small-farm production (in China after 1978). These economies enjoyed rapid rural growth and a significant shift to nonfarm employment within rural areas.

In many economies, however, a large proportion of land is held in excessively large and capital-intensive farms, which employ very little labor but enjoy preferential access to credit and other subsidies. In Latin America halfhearted land reforms that sought or threatened to give land rights to tenants only sharpened landowners' bias toward adopting labor-saving production practices. Colombia is a particularly striking example of the perverse incentive effects of such policies. Land that could be used efficiently for planting crops is instead used for ranching because of policy biases that favor large farms (Box 4.1). In many countries of the former CMEA bloc, land is still held in large-scale collective farms or their successors.

Privatization, land reform, or both are required in many countries. Viet Nam and Albania have already moved in

Box 4.1 Explaining weak labor demand in agriculture: the case of Colombia

Colombia is an example of a country that has taxed agriculture yet achieved a respectable rate of agricultural growth through an array of subsidies. But Colombia also vividly illustrates how policy biases within the sector can reduce labor demand. Poverty rates remain much higher in rural areas than in the cities, even as poverty has diminished in the country as a whole.

It is estimated that Colombia's implicit tax rate on agriculture reached 30 percent during 1960–84, yet agricultural growth averaged 3.5 percent per year between 1950 and 1987. The country's growth path was extremely capital- and land-intensive. Capital grew by 2.8 percent per year, and land area devoted to agriculture and livestock by 1.4 percent, but employment by only 0.6 percent. Preferential tax treatment, credit subsidies, and the virtual abolition of tenancy favored an excessively labor-saving pattern of agricultural growth. Beginning in 1936 and culminating with the *Ley de Aparcería* of 1975, a series of measures have had the effect—intentionally or otherwise—of reducing the incentive for large landowners to lease out land to tenants. The employment of sharecroppers and *colonos* was formally outlawed in 1968. Farmers reduced their dependency on labor through mechanization, usually with subsidized credit, or by converting to livestock ranching. A steep fall in rural employment—by 3.9 percent per year—occurred between 1970 and 1975.

Poor farmers resorted to squatting: during the 1970s there was a wave of illegal farm occupation, but this avenue for land acquisition was closed in 1988. The only option left for the poor was to occupy marginal and often ecologically unstable land at the frontier of the rain forest or in steep hills. In many areas mountain slopes are being denuded of vegetative and soil cover, and the resultant loss of moisture retention has an adverse affect on stream flow. Although lack of access to land and farm employment is by no means the only cause of rural violence in Colombia, it undoubtedly aggravates the situation. Those provinces most plagued by violence were found to have had a higher than average rate of decline in the land area operated by tenants and *colonos* between 1960 and 1988.

Colombia passed a different kind of land reform law in 1994, which proposes to increase the role of the market in transferring land to the rural poor. Eligible applicants will receive a subsidy of 70 percent toward purchase of a plot of land sufficient to support a farm family, and credit will be provided to cover the remaining 30 percent. It is intended that the subsidized farmers will group together in cooperatives to negotiate purchases of land from owners of large holdings. The new law also gives title to established squatters located on frontier lands and includes land improvement measures for indigenous communities. The law does not reform the restrictions on land tenancy, but it is a step in the right direction.

---

this direction, and a land reform program is getting under way in South Africa. Land reform is best executed within a market framework, with willing buyers and sellers, rather than through expropriation. To make reform work, the poor can be assisted with grants for farm purchase and development. Technical and marketing support and investment in rural infrastructure will also need to be redirected from larger farmers to smallholders.

Labor regulation, labor dualism, and the informal sector

The change in resource allocation that makes possible the productivity-enhancing transformation of an economy requires a labor market that is open to economic forces. Policies that favor the formation of small groups of workers in high-productivity activities lead to dualism (segmentation of the labor force into privileged and underprivileged groups) and tend to close the formal sector off from broader influences from the labor market, at the cost of job growth. These outcomes often occur when an output market that is sheltered from competition by trade protection or public ownership combines with government labor regulations designed—often with good intentions—to protect

or support the conditions of workers in the formal sector. This can create a small group of relatively privileged workers with an interest in perpetuating their favored status.

In many Latin American, South Asian, and Middle Eastern countries, labor laws establish onerous job security regulations, rendering hiring decisions practically irreversible; and the system of worker representation and dispute resolution is subject to often unpredictable government decisionmaking, adding uncertainty to firms' estimates of future labor costs. A proper bankruptcy law does not yet exist in India, rendering plant closings a matter of government discretion and complicating the political economy of adjustment in the industrial sector. Similarly, weak links between social security contributions and benefits have effectively transformed contributions into a tax, encouraging tax avoidance through changes in employment status. A study of the Brazilian social security system found evidence of workers staying in the informal sector as long as possible, switching eventually to formal employment only to meet the vesting requirements of the pension system.

The urban informal sector ranges from around 75 percent of the urban labor force in Burkina Faso and Sierra

Leone to around a quarter in Argentina. Informality tends to be higher in Sub-Saharan Africa and Latin America, and within each region informality and labor productivity are negatively related (Figure 4.3). But policy also matters. Onerous taxes and regulations can increase the size of the informal sector. A comparative study of El Salvador, Mexico, and Peru found the level of informality to be least in Mexico, where formal sector workers had less of an advantage over informal workers in terms of wages and legislated job security.

What should governments do about or for informal labor? Three types of policy initiative make sense. First, removing antilabor biases, whether against employment in agriculture or in formal sector establishments, reduces the pressure on the informal sector from agricultural workers who are leaving the land but cannot find formal jobs. Second, the tax and regulatory burden on formal activity needs to be put at moderate (and enforceable) levels. Third, there is some scope for direct public action, especially in the pattern of urban infrastructure provision and the avoidance of channeling subsidized credit to favored firms. Small firms see lack of credit as a constraint, but the experience of the East Asian countries shows that small firms can develop despite real rates of interest on the order of 40 percent, as long as they have access to credit and to markets.

As discussed in Chapter 3, in all economies there is a continuum of employment opportunities, from self-employment within the household to formal employment in registered enterprises. If labor policy overlooks the role of wages and working conditions as incentives and as market signals, it will end up closing the formal labor market to the influence of market forces and discouraging the formalization of labor contracts. Part Three discusses standards and income security provisions that are affordable and will be treated by workers as a benefit of employment, not by employers as a tax.

• • •

Economic growth and higher real wages mean that labor productivity will rise within sectors and that workers will move to higher productivity sectors such as industry and services. But governments will invariably fail if they try

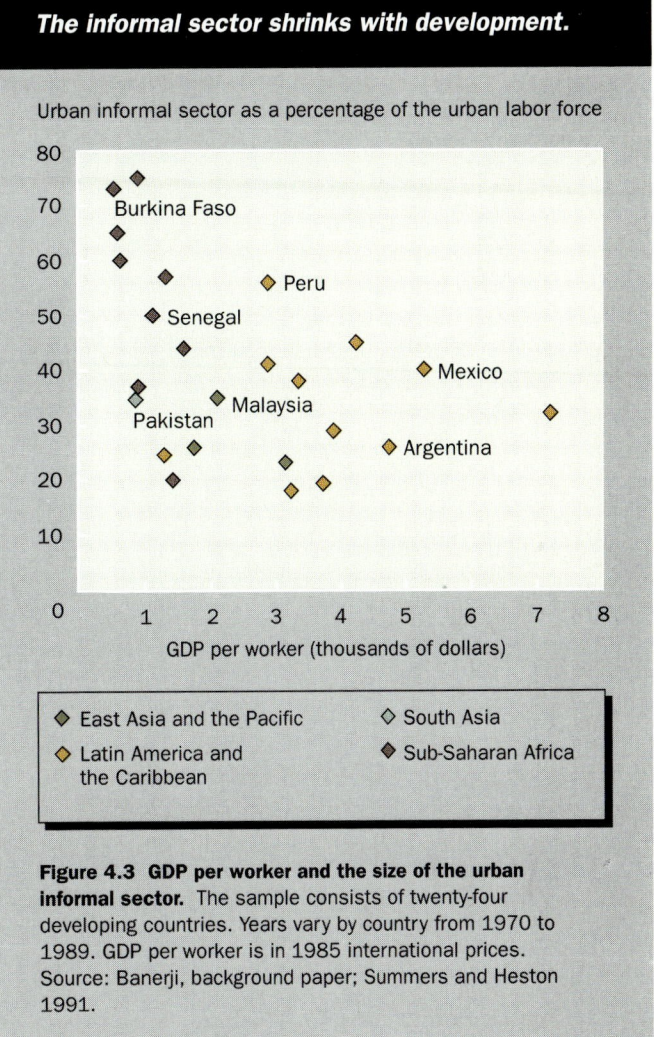

The informal sector shrinks with development.

Urban informal sector as a percentage of the urban labor force

(chart showing GDP per worker (thousands of dollars) on x-axis from 0 to 8, and urban informal sector percentage on y-axis from 0 to 80. Labeled points: Burkina Faso, Peru, Senegal, Mexico, Pakistan, Malaysia, Argentina.)

GDP per worker (thousands of dollars)

◆ East Asia and the Pacific   ◇ South Asia
◆ Latin America and the Caribbean   ◆ Sub-Saharan Africa

Figure 4.3 GDP per worker and the size of the urban informal sector. The sample consists of twenty-four developing countries. Years vary by country from 1970 to 1989. GDP per worker is in 1985 international prices. Source: Banerji, background paper; Summers and Heston 1991.

to speed this process by introducing biases toward high-productivity activities. Biases that favor industry over agriculture, capital over labor, and formal over informal work paradoxically tend to slow, not speed, the shift toward a more productive and more formalized economy.

CHAPTER 5

Skills for Development

INCREASING THE SKILLS AND CAPABILITIES OF workers is key to economic success in an increasingly integrated and competitive global economy. Investing in people can boost the living standards of households by expanding opportunities, raising productivity, attracting capital investment, and increasing earning power. Better health, nutrition, and education also have value in their own right, enabling people to lead more fulfilling lives. The importance of investing in human capital, especially education, for economic growth and household welfare is recognized worldwide; this realization has contributed to unprecedented global increases in schooling in recent decades. Yet these investments alone do not always lead to more rapid growth; in the wrong environment investments in people may only yield misspent or idle resources.

This chapter examines why human capital is important, why many countries have not been able to reap its benefits, and what role governments can play in supporting household investments in human capital.

What is human capital?

The livelihoods of farmers, industrial laborers, and service workers depend increasingly on their acquiring such basic skills as literacy and numeracy, as well as more specialized skills and the ability to manage complex tasks and organize the work of others. The human resources investments required to learn these skills—investments in health and nutrition, and in education and training—begin at an early age and extend over a lifetime. Such investments create the human capital necessary for raising the productivity of labor and the economic well-being of workers and their families.

Lowering protein-energy malnutrition, and increasing consumption of micronutrients such as iron and iodine, can increase labor productivity by improving mental and physical capacity. Analyses of farm households in southern India and on the island of Mindanao in the Philippines found that increased weight-for-height (a measure of long-term nutritional status) and height alone (a proxy for childhood nutrition) are both closely associated with greater adult output per worker. The quantitative impact on future productivity of better nutrition early in life appears in these cases to be at least as large as that often reported for primary schooling.

Education is essential for raising individual productivity. General education gives children skills that they can later transfer from job to job and the basic intellectual tools necessary for further learning. It augments the ability to perform standard tasks, to process and use information, and to adapt to new technologies and production practices. Evidence on the adoption of high-yielding varieties of food grains in China and India illustrates the point. After accounting for farm size and other production factors, studies found that better educated farmers in China's Hunan Province were more likely to adopt the more productive hybrids. In India, areas where relatively few farmers had primary schooling at the onset of the green revolution experienced less growth than areas with the same technological opportunities but better educated farmers.

Training for work exhibits a similar relationship with productivity. Enterprise-based training in Taiwan, China, has been associated with a significant rise in output per worker, with the largest gains realized in firms that invested simultaneously in training and technology. As in the case of the green revolution, human capital bears an especially high return when the opportunity to take advantage of new ideas is present.

Investments in people are often highly complementary. Adequate nutrition and health increase the ability of children to learn. Analysis of four Guatemalan villages indicates that protein-enriched food supplements delivered in childhood significantly improved scores on educational achievement tests administered some ten years later. Improving a country's general education increases the probability that workers will receive training after their formal education. In Peru male workers were 25 percent more likely to receive training from their employers if they had some rather than no secondary schooling; if they had completed secondary school, they were 52 percent more likely to receive training.

Increasing the human capital of workers boosts their earning power, because market-oriented economies reward the skilled worker who is able to deliver more output, or an output that is more highly valued in the marketplace. Rewards for education and skills, relative to those for unskilled labor, are now rising in some former centrally planned economies, where administrative rules rather than the market long determined wages. In Slovenia workers with education and prior work experience have seen their wages increase, as newly released market forces have begun to expand the wage structure in line with differences in the value of worker productivity.

Human capital: necessary but not sufficient

More education usually means more-productive individuals. So it is not surprising that, since 1960, world enrollments at all levels of education combined have increased fivefold. Today more than five of every ten secondary school graduates live in low- and middle-income countries; thirty years ago only three in ten did. In 1960 roughly one-third of all adults in developing countries were literate; in 1990 more than half were. This trend spans all regions, although the variance in outcomes remains large. Worldwide, women are increasingly better educated, although the distribution of schooling between men and women remains highly unequal in most regions.

So why has economic growth remained elusive in many parts of the world, despite rising levels of schooling and other forms of human capital? There are two reasons. First, human capital can be poorly used. Greater investment in human capital can neither compensate for nor overcome an environment inimical to economic growth. Second, human capital investments can be of the wrong type or of poor quality. Expenditures on human resources often fail to provide the quantity, quality, or type of human capital that it might have if the funds had been better spent. There are numerous examples—of food supplements having little effect on recipients' nutritional status; of increased school attendance yielding little change on standardized test scores; and of graduates of public training institutes finding no market for their new skills.

Underutilization of the education and skills of workers is mostly a problem of lack of labor demand due to inappropriate development strategies. This is evident in many regions, including Southeast Asia. The work forces of Viet Nam and the Philippines have historically had higher rates of adult literacy and educational attainment than other countries in the region. Yet both of these economies have grown relatively slowly, as Figure 5.1 shows, largely because both countries adopted development strategies—central planning in Viet Nam, import substitution in the Philippines—that proved incapable of taking full advantage of their stock of human capital. Some of the successful performers in Southeast Asia, in contrast, initially had relatively low levels of human capital but pursued strategies that expanded education and the demand for labor simultaneously.

The Philippines and Viet Nam did realize a return on their human resources investments. Many educated Filipinos took their skills abroad, and their remittances became the Philippine economy's largest source of foreign exchange earnings. In Viet Nam today, past investments in human capital are contributing to improved economic performance now that the country has adopted a more market-based approach to development. But what the Philippines and Viet Nam demonstrate is that the expansion of human capabilities delivers its full potential only when there is a corresponding increase in market-driven demand for labor skills.

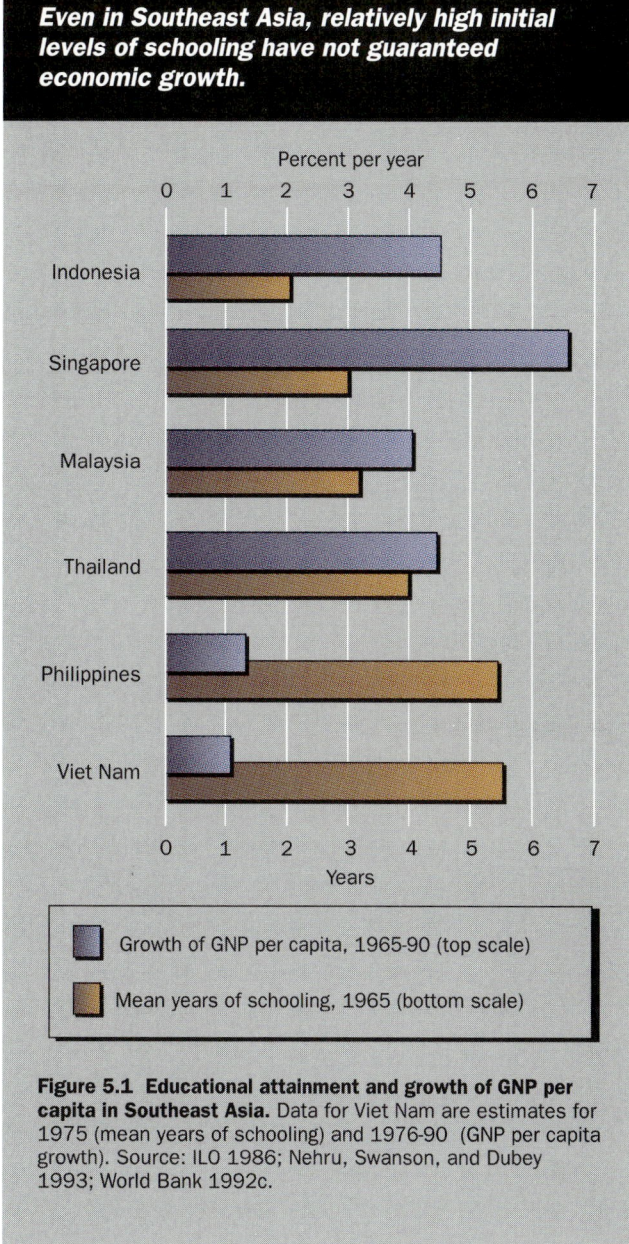

Even in Southeast Asia, relatively high initial levels of schooling have not guaranteed economic growth.

Growth of GNP per capita, 1965-90 (top scale)

Mean years of schooling, 1965 (bottom scale)

Figure 5.1 Educational attainment and growth of GNP per capita in Southeast Asia. Data for Viet Nam are estimates for 1975 (mean years of schooling) and 1976-90 (GNP per capita growth). Source: ILO 1986; Nehru, Swanson, and Dubey 1993; World Bank 1992c.

Government human resources policy also is part of the reason why investments in people do not always pay dividends. There are many examples; here we focus on education. Excessive spending on education bureaucracies and school infrastructure, rather than on teaching staff and supplies, depresses the quantity and quality of schooling. So do poorly trained teachers and failure to set high standards for students. Finally, human capital tends to be relatively unproductive where the skills acquired in school do not match market opportunities, or where higher education is promoted at the expense of primary and secondary schooling.

In all of these cases, improvements in education policy are needed to ensure that expenditures on schooling yield productive investments in human capital.

Supporting investment in people

Households willingly invest in their members' good health and education, because the benefits, which include the economic benefit of higher lifetime earnings, usually far exceed the costs (Box 5.1). Yet often households underinvest in human capital. When they do, governments have an essential role in supporting these investments in people.

Households are often poorly informed about the returns to human capital, especially in the areas of health and nutrition. Government-sponsored health and nutrition education can encourage them to undertake these high-return investments. Governments also intervene when families are willing to invest in human resources but cannot, because lenders are unwilling to extend credit against expected future earnings. Finally, the value to society of human capital investment can exceed its value to individual families: a more educated society is better able to adopt new technologies, and shared schooling experiences contribute to nation building. To capture these social benefits, governments can change the incentives households face, by targeting subsidies at the poor or, as in the case of primary education, providing the service for free.

Special efforts are often needed to offset the tendency for girls to receive less education than boys. Beyond the benefits it offers women in the labor market, education is linked to lower fertility, lower maternal mortality, and better health, nutrition, and education of children. These may not be fully realized without strong public intervention. The goals of combating discrimination, reducing poverty, and promoting equity therefore justify government action to promote the accumulation of human capital, especially among the poor.

Training as an investment

Productive learning does not end with school. Most individuals continue to build their skills throughout their working lives, through training on the job and in formal training centers. Training is an investment from the perspective of both workers and employers. Workers often willingly incur fees for training courses, or accept lower wages than they would receive if not engaged in on-the-job training, in return for expected higher wages in the future. Firms have an incentive to invest in their employees' training because they frequently need workers with certain skills. Neither side is completely sure that it will be able to appropriate fully the returns to its investment: workers may quit and transfer the gains to another employer, or may lose their jobs and find the skills they have acquired are not transferable. Employers and employees have found ways to work around this problem so that both sides can still gain: employers provide job security to reduce turnover; workers may agree to training contracts whereby they repay the employer if they leave before the employer's investment has been recouped; and workers and their employers can share the productivity gains associated with training.

Because training is often a good investment, most training takes place with little government involvement. The amount of training firms undertake varies, sometimes greatly, between countries and sectors, and even across firms within the same sector, depending on their size and type of ownership. In 1991, 24 percent of Mexican workers reported receiving some form of training to improve their skills on the job; the corresponding figure in Japan was 37 percent. Firms in high-technology industries in Indonesia are more likely to train their workers than those in low-technology sectors. Export-oriented enterprises in the chemical sector in Taiwan, China, are three times more likely to invest in training than those producing for the domestic sector, and six times more likely than the average Taiwanese textile firm. Export orientation, the pace of technological change, the education of the work force, and economic cycles and growth prospects all appear to determine a firm's willingness to train its workers.

If training is in the interest of both workers and employers, and in market economies takes place in response to underlying economic circumstances, should governments get involved? Governments should intervene in the market for training if there are particular market failures or imperfections, or to pursue goals other than economic efficiency. As with general education, individuals many underinvest in training because of lack of information or credit market failures, or because spillover effects drive a wedge between private and social returns. However, at least in the case of within-firm training, many of these problems may be secondary to constraints that inhibit firms from investing in skills.

When the level of skills in the labor market is low, firms may invest too little in training despite prospective returns that would justify the investment, for fear that their workers, once trained, will find other employment. How great a problem this is remains unknown. Where returns to training have been high, as in the Republic of Korea, firms still invested in training despite employee turnover that, throughout the 1970s and well into the 1980s, often amounted to 5 or 6 percent of the manufacturing work force leaving their employers *every month*.

Lack of training may also result from labor market regulations—including high minimum wages and rules governing job ladders within firms—that prevent firms from paying lower wages to trainees or restrict the placement of trained workers. In Mexico, federal labor legislation placing strict seniority-based rules on promotion reduces the incentive to train workers. The ideal solution would be to remove these policy constraints; failing that, alternatives in-

Box 5.1 By how much does education raise wages?

In every country, workers with more education tend to earn more than workers with less. Detailed statistical analyses of the countries shown in the figure confirm a positive association between wages and schooling for both men and women. The association was found both in economies that were growing quickly (Indonesia and Thailand) and in those with falling income per capita (Côte d'Ivoire, Peru, and Slovenia).

The wage premium associated with education varies considerably and appears related to the relative scarcity of educated workers—higher rewards where educated workers are in high demand (Thailand) or low supply (Côte d'Ivoire), lower re-

wards where educated workers are relatively abundant (Slovenia and the United States). The wage premium also depends on the level of education—among the low- and middle-income countries in the figure, the wage ratio between secondary and primary school graduates exceeds that between primary graduates and those with no schooling in all but one case. Wage premiums to education are sometimes higher for women than for men (in Indonesia, Peru, and Thailand, for example). This does not mean that women earn more than men, but only that the economic return to their schooling can be higher.

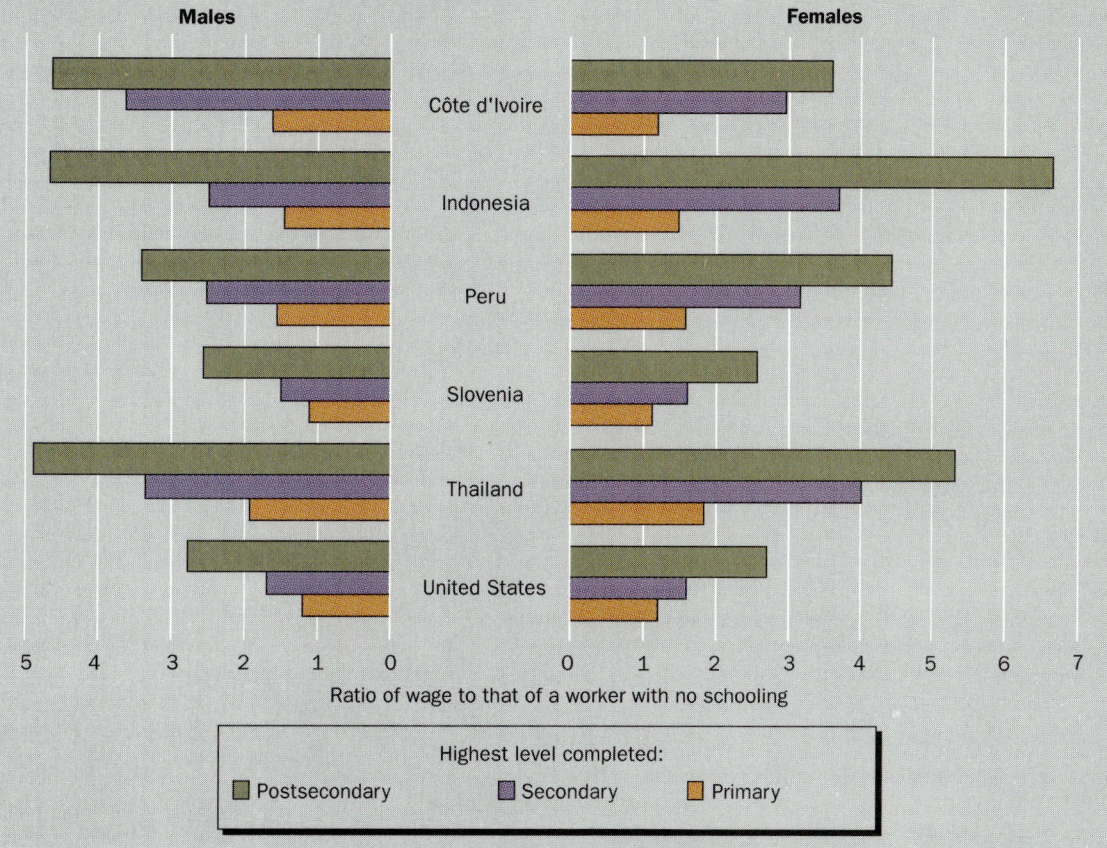

Wage premiums to education for male and female workers. Ratios are derived from statistical estimates that control for such variables as age. Data are for 1986 except Thailand (1988–89) and Slovenia and United States (1991). Source: Appleton, Collier, and Horsnell 1990; Behrman and Deolalikar 1994; Orazem and Vodopivec 1994; Schultz 1993; Khandker 1991.

clude compensatory measures to subsidize employer training costs.

Lack of information about what skills are in demand and the presence of scale economies in training are other grounds for government involvement. These constraints might be thought particularly relevant within the informal

sector, but on-the-job training is common there, especially in the form of traditional apprenticeship schemes. A recent survey of workers in Ghanaian small-scale manufacturing found that 44 percent of workers had been trained as apprentices in their fields, and that 52 percent of firms were training apprentices at the time of the survey. Studies in other countries confirm that skill deficiencies are rarely cited as a major problem confronting small-scale entrepreneurs.

Training in the informal sector may be sufficient for perpetuating current activities, but lack of knowledge about marketing, new technologies, and general business skills may constrain the expansion of informal sector firms. Training services targeted at small enterprises and aimed at remedying these deficiencies have shown some promise. One example is Mexico's Multiple Support Service Program (known by its Spanish acronym CIMO), which provides technical assistance and training services to micro- and small enterprises. Numerous case studies document cost-effective improvements in productivity and increases in employment and profitability among CIMO participants. The scope for replicating and expanding such programs, however, is limited. For many public interventions aimed at microenterprises, costs are high because of program administrative expenses and the high failure rate of small enterprises.

In many countries, governments use training to address such problems as low skill levels among the employed work force, high youth unemployment, displacement of workers during economy-wide transitions, and the structural unemployment and poverty associated with disadvantaged workers. But whether public expenditures on training are warranted depends on the underlying cause of the problem, and on the opportunity cost of public resources.

Low work force skill levels appear to be less the result of failures in the market for training than of a generally low level of labor demand. The same may hold true for youth unemployment. But the rationale for government involvement in training displaced workers is more compelling. Displacement due to major economic transitions or aggregate shocks may call for government support of retraining, because of absent markets, excessive risk, and the need to ensure social stability and public support for the broader reform program; unfortunately, the direct economic benefits often are limited (see Chapter 17).

Enterprise-led training is usually the most cost-effective means of developing worker skills. By comparison, government delivery in most countries, in state-sponsored training centers and especially in vocational education, has proved expensive and often has provided trainees with few marketable skills. Ways must be found to reorient public training institutions to respond to consumer and market demands. The best way is often to shift public financing from providers of training to the demand side of the market, enabling targeted workers to purchase training within a competitive environment of alternative suppliers.

This shift has happened in some Latin American countries. Training institutions had been guaranteed financing from payroll levies to perform preemployment training, even though frequently they were unable to place their graduates. But with the right incentives many of these same institutions have evolved and now sell valued services directly to private enterprises and individuals. Chile's use of training vouchers for workers and tax credits for employers is one example of successful reform in this area. Vouchers are distributed to targeted groups—young, unemployed workers, usually women. At the same time, rights to offer training courses are auctioned by a government agency to a competitive market of training organizations, both public and private; their cost recovery is conditional on a minimum rate of trainees finding jobs after completing training. In this way the burden of designing successful training programs is shifted to where it belongs—the training institutions themselves.

Private training providers are also emerging in the transitional economies of Eastern Europe and Asia, for example in foreign language, education, and computer skills. Prior to the transition all training institutions were public, and few were oriented to the new skills required by a modern market economy. Government can support private sector initiatives by removing prohibitions on the private supply of training: price controls on tuition fees, excessive regulation of curricula, and competition with subsidized public institutions all limit the private sector's response.

• • •

Households and firms need an environment that encourages good decisionmaking with respect to investing in skills. What should governments do? Where private returns to human capital are high but the investments are not being undertaken, government must first try to understand why before designing and implementing interventions, especially pricing strategies. In primary education, free public provision usually makes sense, to reap the gains to society as a whole and reach the poor. But for most other human resources programs, free provision more often is not justified. Especially in the area of training, governments should focus more on financing and less on production. Government intervention, whatever its form, should avoid benefiting the privileged few. The highest priority should be placed on investing in children, because their health, nutrition, and basic education are the foundation of a nation's future.

CHAPTER 6

Markets, Labor, and Inequality

ECONOMIC GROWTH GENERALLY BENEFITS the majority of a country's population as the economy becomes more efficient, creates more jobs, and raises incomes. Yet while most households gain, inequality between individuals and groups often persists: between men and women, between ethnic groups, or indeed between households. And growth fails to reach some groups at all. The disabled, the economically disadvantaged, and those living in poor, lagging regions are among those most at risk of getting left behind. Lacking equal access to assets—and especially to education and skill training—and often faced with other obstacles such as ethnic or sex discrimination, these groups may be unable to take advantage of the new opportunities generated by economic change.

Growth does not necessarily mean greater inequality. Long-term growth has often reduced inequality, for example in Colombia, Indonesia, and Malaysia. And growth almost always reduces poverty, sometimes despite rising inequality, as in Brazil between 1960 and 1980. But societies need to worry about the distribution of income if for no other reason than that a more equal distribution of income ensures that the benefits of growth get spread more evenly and reach the poor.

This chapter examines the distribution of the income that people derive from their labor—whether from wage-paying employment or from self-employment on a farm or as a trader. It examines the dimensions of and reasons for persisting inequality across individuals, regions, and gender and ethnic groups. And it asks what governments can do to spread opportunities and to help those who get left behind.

What determines inequality of labor incomes?

In all countries the wages paid to workers in different sectors and occupations vary widely. Even in formerly socialist Poland, average wages in 1993 in the highest-paid occupations—engineers and extractive occupations—were nearly 80 percent higher than those in the lowest-paid—personal services. Skilled white-collar workers in the financial services industry could earn three times the wage of an unskilled worker in retail trade. Differences in wages across individuals reflect, to a large extent, different talents and skill endowments, as well as differences in working conditions or job requirements. Difficult jobs, and jobs per-

formed in risky or dirty environments, are likely to pay higher wages than jobs of equivalent skill that are easier, safer, and cleaner.

Even when all these factors are taken into account, however, some differences in wages remain. These may reflect unobservable individual ability, discrimination, or other forms of market failure. Even in the highly integrated labor market of the United States, detailed studies of wage differentials find that individual characteristics and industry-, occupation-, and firm-related factors explain only between 50 and 70 percent of the observed variance. Comparisons of wage dispersion across countries indicate that although inequality tends to decline as economies grow richer, it can vary greatly between countries at similar income levels.

A market-based distribution of labor income can be more or less equal or can leave many workers living in poverty. Two factors are especially important in determining the degree of inequality. The more powerful influence is the initial distribution of assets, especially of education (Table 6.1). The poorest members of society are usually those with less access to land, credit, and social services and fewer of the skills that allow poor workers to move into high-productivity, higher paying sectors. The second determinant of inequality is in the way that similar assets are rewarded differently across sectors and occupations. These differences exist not only between jobs in the formal modern sector, but also between returns to labor in the wage sector and in self-employment, and between outcomes within self-employment.

Inequalities in the distribution of assets

Income inequality across workers is strongly associated with inequality of education and skills. Educational attainment is the single most important predictor of individual labor incomes. Combined with other human capital variables such as experience and occupation, skills account for one-third to one-half of the variation in earnings observed across individuals within countries. Not surprisingly, policies that increase the education of the poor can have a dramatic impact on wage inequality. Educational inequality in Brazil continues to far exceed that in the Republic of Korea and explains more than one-fourth of the much greater earnings inequality there. In Colombia the expansion of

The poor are usually those with less access to education.

Table 6.1 Average years of schooling by per capita income quintile in selected developing countries

Country	Lowest	Second	Third	Fourth	Highest	All
Brazil	2.1	3.1	4.3	5.7	8.7	5.2
Costa Rica	4.8	5.6	6.2	7.1	9.4	6.8
Guatemala	1.0	1.5	2.3	3.5	7.0	3.2
Viet Nam[a]	5.1	5.7	6.1	6.5	8.0	6.4

Note: Data are for all persons fifteen years and over.
a. Data are by expenditure quintile.
Source: Viet Nam poverty assessment; Psacharopoulos and others 1993.

education reduced wage differentials between top and bottom by 20 percent, despite rising demand for skilled workers. In both Malaysia and Costa Rica increased educational opportunities were associated with sharp reductions in wage inequality. As Figure 6.1 illustrates, the expansion of education generally works to reduce wage dispersion. But there are exceptions: in countries such as Chile and Mexico the positive effects of increased education have been swamped by strong shifts in demand against unskilled workers.

Inequality between rural and urban incomes is particularly pervasive. Much of this inequality has its origins in decades of policies that favored cities over the countryside. Although in many countries these have been partly or wholly abandoned, in others—especially in Africa—they remain in place. Antirural policy biases have included discrimination against agriculture arising from overvalued currencies and industrial protection, and from the taxation of export commodities. These were aggravated by biases in favor of cities in the allocation of physical and social infrastructure, and by land policies that made it difficult for the poor to acquire land, sharply reducing self-employment opportunities in rural areas. Compensation for these adverse policies, where it was given, largely benefited richer, larger farmers and left poor rural workers and small-scale farmers to bear the brunt of discrimination. As discussed in Chapter 4, these policy biases led to a premature movement of workers into the cities, before the cities were able to gainfully employ them, and to the depression of wages in the urban informal sector.

Inequality can show remarkable persistence across generations, as the benefits of physical and educational assets and positions of power are transmitted from parents to children, and cultural norms that perpetuate inequality become embedded in economic systems. Altering the distribution of assets is crucial to breaking these circles of poverty and reducing income inequality. But this is not easily accomplished. Large redistributions of land (or of capital) have seldom occurred except in times of great political upheaval. In parts of East Asia where reforms put land securely in the hands of small farmers, they have led to accelerated rural growth, employment, and political stability. Where the land was collectivized, or where small farmers did not receive secure rights to the land, as in Mexico, reforms were associated with stagnation and social distress. Nevertheless, where much land remains inefficiently used in large holdings, further land reform will be needed.

An easier way to reduce poverty and increase equality of incomes is to change the distribution of human capital. Unlike with physical capital or land, this can be done by adding to the existing stock rather than through redistribution. Investing in the *human* capital of the poor, through primary health care and education, has been an important part of successful strategies of poverty alleviation in countries such as Indonesia and Colombia.

Inequalities in the returns to assets

Increasing the returns to the few assets that poor workers hold also has an important influence on the distribution of income. Since the main asset of the poor is their labor, this means, above all, removing biases that tend to depress returns to labor.

Shifting to a less distorted and more formalized labor market can function as an equalizing mechanism. In the absence of market failures such as discrimination, the wage labor market ensures that similarly productive workers employed in comparable jobs receive similar pay. As a result, outcomes in the wage labor market are less tied to workers' initial endowments of assets than are the outcomes from self-employment.

Formal labor markets, however, are often distorted and biased against the poor. In many countries urban development has encouraged the growth of groups of protected

The wage gap between workers at differing levels of education has narrowed, except where labor demand has shifted strongly against the unskilled, as in Chile.

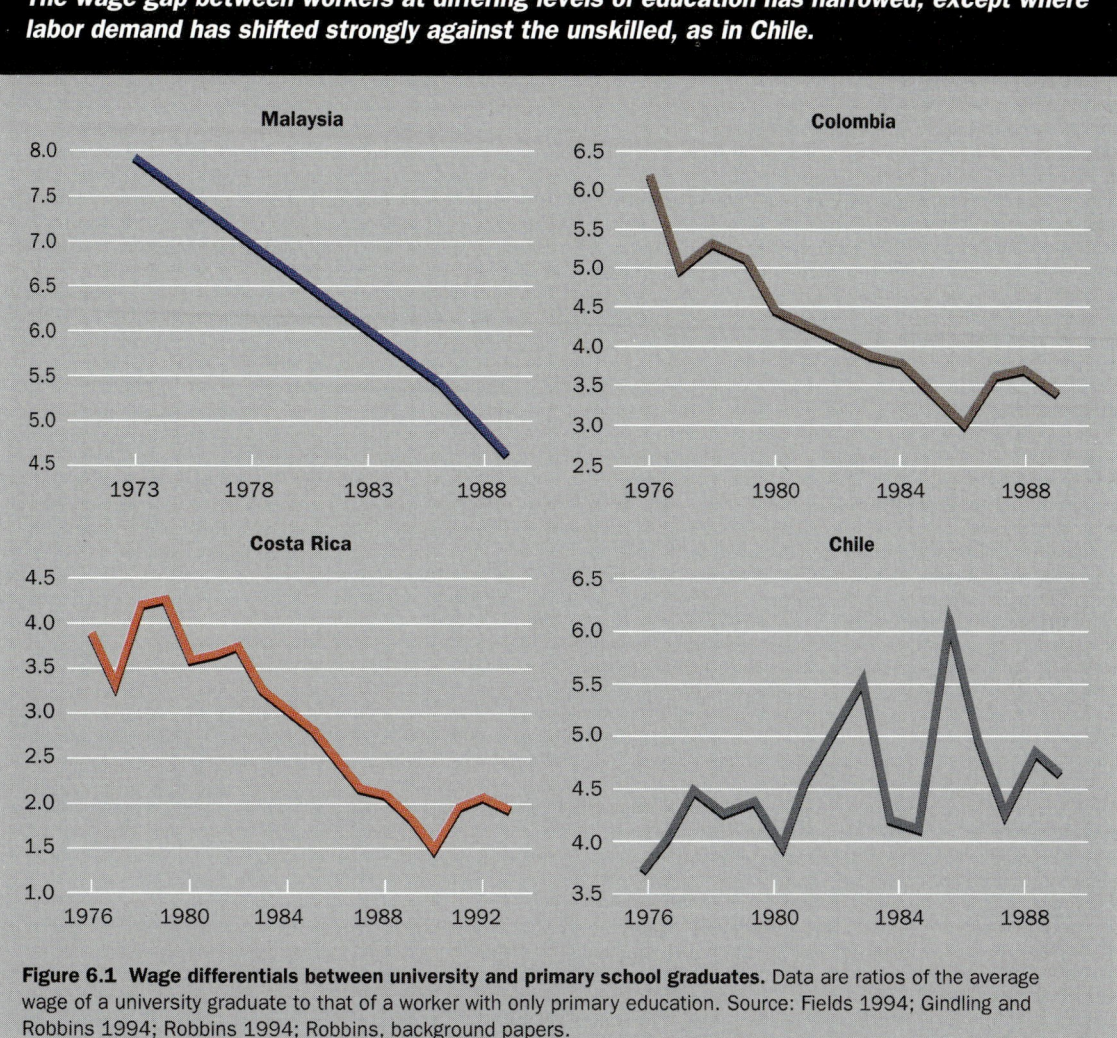

Figure 6.1 Wage differentials between university and primary school graduates. Data are ratios of the average wage of a university graduate to that of a worker with only primary education. Source: Fields 1994; Gindling and Robbins 1994; Robbins 1994; Robbins, background papers.

formal sector workers. Outsiders, including most of the poor in the rural sector and the urban informal sector, lack access to the high-wage jobs with greater job security and better working conditions that privileged workers enjoy.

Dimensions of inequality

Even in the absence of distortions, labor market outcomes can be inequitable because of discrimination—for example, against women or ethnic groups. Labor outcomes may also be conditioned by regional differences, making households victims of the accidents of geography. Three types of in-

equality have proved particularly difficult to resolve through market forces alone: inequalities between men and women, inequalities between ethnic and social groups, and inequalities across regions.

Inequalities between men and women

In almost all societies women have less power than men, receive less for their work, and have less control over household resources, and in many countries they receive less education. Women have less access to better paying jobs in the formal sector and are disproportionately represented among unpaid family workers and in the informal sector.

When women are allowed to enter the same markets as men, they often face discrimination.

Although women work fewer hours on average in market activities than men, this difference is more than offset by their greater hours of effort in household activities. In almost every country, women are responsible for a disproportionate share of work within the household. In Bangladesh men and women were found to work approximately the same number of hours per week. But whereas men devoted 90 percent of their work hours to income-generating activities, women allocated 80 percent of their work time to household chores. This division of labor continues to hold even when women work outside the home. Argentine women work on average seventy-three hours a week in the home if they are not employed, and fifty-six hours if they are—far more than men. These differences between men and women in the allocation of effort affect the distribution of power within the household. Where women earn little in the cash economy, they have less say in the allocation of family income and in strategic household decisions, such as those about schooling. The evidence shows that this distribution of power has detrimental effects on children, especially daughters.

Some division of labor between men and women flows from the dominant role of women in childrearing. Especially when lives are relatively short and fertility is high, women tend to be tied to home-based activities for a significant fraction of their working lives. Sometimes a premium on physical strength, as in most unskilled work, can reinforce the economics of the traditional gender-based division of labor. But such a division becomes more and more inefficient as development and technological change result in longer working lives for women, fewer children, and a higher premium on skills.

The differences in the returns to work for men and women stem from two factors. First, most women are less proficient in marketable skills because of biases against women in education and skill training. Educational biases are severe in Asia and the Middle East and significant in Africa, but insignificant in Latin America and the countries of the former Soviet bloc. Second, women often face a narrower range of job opportunities, and so attain worse labor market outcomes than men with the same endowments. In many countries large female-male wage differentials remain even after controlling for differences in education and experience (Box 6.1). In India women's real wages are 51 percent of men's, and only 34 percentage points of the gap can be explained by differences in worker characteristics. In Kenya women's wages are 18 percent lower than men's after adjusting for skill and experience. In Latin America average female wages are 71 percent of average male wages, and only 20 percentage points of the differential can be explained by differences in human capital. Even in the former Soviet Union, women earned on average 30 percent less

than men. Less than one-tenth of this differential was due to differences in endowments.

Economic growth has proved a slow instrument of change in the status of women. Among the industrial countries inequality between men and women remained remarkably stable for nearly two centuries before declining sharply over the last thirty years. Shifts from agriculture into industry and services have not always had much impact on occupational biases against women—occupational segregation in Russia, for example, remains severe, explaining much of the observed wage differentials between men and women there. But there is hope that in the developing countries change will come faster. Recent evidence for six developing countries in East Asia, Latin America, and Sub-Saharan Africa indicates that growth has increased female wages and reduced wage differentials in all but one country. Employment segregation, on the other hand, has remained largely unchanged.

These lags flow from a number of factors. Men's greater power in most societies affects whether women participate in the labor force—when men prefer that their wives not work outside the household, for example. Discrimination in the workplace, stemming in part from cultural norms, is widespread. And there are many associated institutional and legal factors that tend to reduce demand for women workers, especially in formal jobs—for example, paternalistic discrimination may prevent women from working in "dangerous" occupations or at night.

Weaker labor market opportunities produce weaker incentives to educate girls; this creates a vicious cycle, since less educated women are much less likely to educate their daughters. Breaking this cycle can be difficult. Increasing pressures and incentives to educate girls is essential, and support for childcare and legal reforms can also play a role. Measures to reduce discrimination in the workplace and to avoid raising the cost to employers of hiring women through paternalistic attempts to protect them also are important (see Chapter 11).

Inequalities between ethnic and social groups

Indigenous people of Latin America, African Americans and Native Americans in the United States, gypsies in Central and Eastern Europe, scheduled castes in India, and blacks in South Africa have in common a relatively low status in the labor market associated with their ethnicity or the group in society into which they were born. These inequalities are between households, not within them, but here too the story is one of individuals whose futures are determined by the accident of their birth.

Groups such as Andean Indians and South African blacks typically earn less than other workers in the same economies. Indigenous male workers in Bolivia earn on average 60 percent of what a nonindigenous worker earns. The wages of Guarani speakers in Paraguay are 64 percent

Box 6.1 Do lower wages for women indicate discrimination?

Not all of the observed gender wage gap necessarily represents discrimination in the labor market. A lower wage for women in a given economy may reflect their lower productivity in wage employment. Women in developing countries often have less schooling and on-the-job experience than men, and estimates of wage discrimination need to account for such factors. One method is to estimate returns to certain attributes and characteristics, such as schooling, experience, and occupation, separately for males and females, and then decompose the observed wage differential into two parts. The first shows the component of the wage differential due to women actually having "worse" attributes and characteristics than men, whereas the second addresses what women would be earning if they had the *same* attributes as the men in the economy. This second measure points to discrimination, if women's earnings are still less than those of men.

The most striking examples of the use of this methodology come from countries such as Ecuador, Jamaica, and the Philippines. Women in those countries actually have more education and experience, on average, than men but get paid between 20 and 30 percent less. In these countries, women would actually have higher wages than men were their contributions valued equally by the labor market.

The decomposition analysis has some problems: for example, using "years since school" as a measure of experience may misstate the nature of women's experience, or the use of broad occupational categories may obscure a tendency for women to hold lower status jobs than men within the same occupation. Nevertheless, results from a wide range of developing countries make it clear that labor markets do discriminate against women workers.

of those of Spanish speakers. And in Brazil, blacks earn only 50 percent as much as whites. But, as with that between men and women, not all of the wage gap reflects discrimination. About 70 percent of the difference in earnings between indigenous and nonindigenous workers in Bolivia, for instance, can be attributed to differences in schooling attainment and experience. The remaining 30 percent is unexplained, reflecting unaccounted-for factors such as differences in ability or quality of education, and labor market discrimination.

Every seventh person in India—about 2 percent of the world's population—is a member of a scheduled caste. These lowest-caste individuals are born into families whose traditional occupations—scavenging, tanning leather, working in agriculture—yield little return to education or skill acquisition. Tradition also used to dictate that these families could not change their occupations—a street cleaner's son also became a street cleaner. This extreme labor market inflexibility provided few incentives for members of the lower castes to educate themselves. The custom of inherited occupations has been relaxed in recent years, but in 1988–89 a third of workers in the informal sector in the Indian state of Bihar belonged to scheduled castes.

In South Africa, white colonialism and then apartheid rule actively created differences in assets and power between whites and blacks. Democracy finally brought political power to the black majority, but the government now faces the tough problem of reversing the results of many decades of discrimination, most of all in education and skills. For the group that attended school in the 1970s and 1980s the situation is particularly severe. Schools for blacks were of poor quality in any case, but in addition many schoolchildren resisted apartheid through school boycotts. Most enter the new era with a strong political consciousness but a weak ability to gain from expanding economic opportunities.

Members of groups with little economic, social, and political power are vulnerable to self-reinforcing cycles of low education and low returns in the labor market feeding back into lower incentives to acquire human capital. These cycles make it increasingly difficult to overcome relative—and sometimes absolute—poverty and alienation from the increasing prosperity in which others in the economy participate. Intergenerational issues again matter, particularly where groups get stuck in complex cycles of dependency and inferiority.

One group that has expressly used government policy to pull itself into the economic mainstream is the *bumiputeras,* or ethnic Malays, in Malaysia. Literally "sons of the soil," most *bumiputeras* were confined for most of this century to traditional small-scale agriculture and rice cultivation. At independence, even though they were the ethnic majority and controlled the public sector, their economic role was limited, with industry and finance mostly in the hands of the ethnic Chinese middle class. To increase their role in the economy the Malaysian government undertook a number of concerted policies, including targeted and subsidized education and preferential treatment in an expanding public sector. These policies succeeded in raising the educational attainment and the average incomes of the *bumiputeras.* As a result, inequality of incomes between the *bumiputeras* and the rest of the population, mainly Chinese and Indians, declined significantly: between 1970 and 1984 the average incomes of the *bumiputeras* rose 40 percent more than the incomes of other groups. However, these policies have not contributed as much to reducing overall inequality, because inequality of incomes *within* each ethnic group has increased.

Inequalities across regions

Inequality often has a regional dimension. Almost all countries manifest regional disparities in resource endowments, incomes, and growth rates, and these are known to persist over time. Some regions' relative disadvantages are so extreme as to constrain the opportunities of individuals born there. A child born in the Mexican state of Chiapas, for example, has much bleaker prospects than a child born in Mexico City: the child from Chiapas is twice as likely to die before age five, less than half as likely to complete primary school, and ten times as likely to live in a house without access to running water. Assuming that he or she does not migrate, such an individual will earn 20 to 35 percent less than a comparable worker living in Mexico City and 40 to 45 percent less than one living in northern Mexico.

Initial conditions are a crucial determinant of regional performance. Scarce resources, a history of neglect, lack of investment, and a concentration of low-skilled people who may be ethnically distinct from the rest of the population combine to explain the lagging performance of certain areas. Gansu, with an income per capita 40 percent below the national average, is one of the poorest regions in China. Unfavorable geography, poor soil that is highly susceptible to erosion, low and erratic rainfall, and limited off-farm employment opportunities underlie its high poverty levels. Chaco Province in Argentina has a GDP per capita that is only 38 percent of the national average. Low educational attainment and lack of infrastructure, especially roads, explain much of this deviation.

Relative and absolute regional poverty can persist for long periods even when growth in other parts of the economy is strong. The crash of the sugar economy in the seventeenth century, for instance, pushed northeastern Brazil into a decline from which it has never fully recovered. In the United States the fortunes of coal-mining West Virginia waned with the collapse of the coal industry and the increased importance of oil and gas in energy production. It remains one of the poorest areas in the United States to this day. In Thailand rapid development failed to reach the northern hill people. Fewer than 30 percent of their villages have schools, and only 15 percent of the hill people can read and write Thai. Their average annual income is less than a quarter of GNP per capita.

What can be done to help those left behind?

Market-based growth that makes efficient use of labor and encourages a large wage employment sector can be good for achieving equality. But market-based development alone is a weak instrument for reducing inequalities between the sexes, between ethnic groups, or between otherwise similar people. Improving the distribution of initial endowments, especially by promoting access to education for the poor, is crucial for realizing improvements in the distribution of incomes. Public action can play a role in accelerating change by pushing to improve the human endowments of those worse off and by acting to reduce discrimination. But tackling the problems of those left out is a formidable challenge for policy, in industrial as well as in developing countries. Investment in these individuals often has a low return, either because they are old and have relatively few years of work left, or because they lack the basic skills necessary to function in a work environment, or because they are stuck in backward regions.

• • •

A fifty-three-year-old widow of the Kapu caste from the Chintapalli village of Raole Mandal in India lives alone in a mud hut. She was married to an older, propertyless cousin, whose death has left her without independent resources. She survives on lacemaking. Working for ten hours a day on 5,000 meters of thread, she earns the equivalent of $0.30 per day. Old age, ill health, and strong caste identification preclude her from participating in other remunerated activities.

• • •

An underemployed agricultural laborer living near Tamale in Ghana's savanna region works on average less than four days a week. When employed, he gets paid around $0.80 a day. During the cotton harvest there is enough work, but in winter jobs are scarce. He, his wife, and their five children live in a mud hut. His wife and ten-year-old daughter help care for their small vegetable garden, which supplies food for the family dinner table even when the father is not working. The parents worry about their children's future. They would like to move to an area with more job opportunities but cannot afford to lose the family's only asset, their small plot of land.

• • •

What can governments do about cases such as these? Policies to help those left out must combine special measures to reintegrate able-bodied individuals into the world of work, transfers to sustain their living standards above a certain minimum, and interventions to reach their children and give the next generation the opportunity to escape poverty.

Targeted investments

Society can attempt to integrate disadvantaged workers into the mainstream through retraining programs that give them basic skills or through programs that help them become self-employed. Targeted training programs for disadvantaged groups—whose focus is on reducing poverty rather than retooling the unemployed—are relatively rare in the developing countries but have a longer history in the industrial world. The United States, for example, has had publicly sponsored programs to aid the disadvantaged since 1964. Many of these programs have been tied to transfer schemes such as the Aid to Families with Dependent Children program. These programs have been only moderately successful: training services have sometimes, but not always, raised participants' earnings. In general, training for the disadvantaged in the United States has been much more effective in helping adult women than in helping men or youths.

Deprivation and poverty usually go hand in hand with lack of access to both physical and social infrastructure. The allocation of government expenditures on social services is often biased against the poor, and especially against those in rural areas and lagging regions. The result is usually a lack of adequate sewerage, roads, and health and school facilities to serve poor communities. Redressing the balance through public infrastructure investment in these disadvantaged areas can be crucial to helping poor households pull themselves out of poverty. Since 1988, Mexico's Solidaridad program has provided poor municipalities with funds to finance small subprojects linked to school rehabilitation, improvement of rural water supply, and rural road rehabilitation and maintenance.

Transfers

Sometimes there may be little scope for investment, either in skills or in infrastructure, to help those left behind. Poverty relief policies or transfers will then be necessary. These transfers can be integrated with more permanent income security mechanisms (see Chapter 13) or can be part of special transition measures (see Chapter 17). Whether permanent or temporary, the type of safety net chosen is usually a function of the country's income and traditions. In low- and middle-income countries public employment schemes can deliver these transfers cost-effectively. In recent years several countries have experimented with approaches that combine poverty relief with reintegration into the labor market for those displaced during adjustment episodes. For example, Bolivia, Honduras, Egypt, Guinea, and Senegal have all established social funds to encourage income-generating activities and the formation of microenterprises. These funds usually finance small-scale infrastructure projects, technical assistance, training, and micro credit schemes. However, not all those left out can be reintegrated into the labor market. For those unable to work—because of old age or disability, for example—complementary transfers of either cash or food may be necessary.

Reaching the next generation

Policies aimed at reaching the children of those left behind are more likely to be effective. Breaking intergenerational cycles of poverty means giving children access to opportunities that have passed their parents by. Investing in the human capital of these children is key, but education alone is usually not enough: investing in their health and nutrition is also necessary. Chapter 5 noted, and previous editions of *World Development Report* have examined in some detail, the complementarities between these different types of interventions: better nutrition and health improve children's capacity to learn while in school and increase their productivity at work when they are older.

A number of countries are making efforts to improve the delivery of social services to the poor and their children. Colombia's community childcare and nutrition program, for example, provides preschool care that includes meals and health monitoring. Participating children benefit from exposure to preschool learning activities, improved nutrition, and health care. Families—especially mothers—benefit from the opportunity to seek paid employment outside the home. Mexico's Basic Health Care Program for the Uninsured Population (PASSPA) extends both basic health care services and targeted nutrition assistance to the uninsured poor. Bangladesh's general education program aims at increasing equitable access to primary and secondary schooling for poor children, especially girls. It focuses on expanding education services to poor, underserved communities, increasing the share of female teachers, and extending a successful pilot scholarship program for girls. El Salvador is experimenting with a targeted nutrition program that distributes food supplements to schoolchildren.

• • •

Market-based development can reduce both inequality and poverty in developing countries. Ensuring that poor workers have access to education, and that labor markets are not so distorted that formal wage employment growth is stunted, is crucial to encouraging faster growth and reducing inequality. But inequalities persist even in growing economies, because of discrimination based on gender or ethnicity or because particular individuals or regions are excluded from the fruits of growth. Government policy should, wherever possible, fight discrimination and draw these excluded groups back into the mainstream. But above all, governments should ensure that the children of disadvantaged households do not remain trapped in poverty but instead have the chance to fulfill their potential.

PART TWO

Is International Integration an Opportunity or a Threat to Workers?

THE LIVES OF WORKERS around the world are increasingly connected through international trade, capital flows, and migration. This expands opportunities, but it also raises fears that international competition and free-wheeling capital will cost workers jobs or impair their standards of living, and that some groups of workers or countries will be left out of expanding international markets altogether. In Chapter 7 we outline the channels of interaction in an integrating world, and we assess in the remaining three chapters of this part of the Report how trade, capital flows, and migration affect workers in both rich and poor countries.

CHAPTER 7

The Emerging Global Labor Market

J OE LIVES IN A SMALL TOWN IN SOUTHERN *Texas. His old job as an accounts clerk in a textile firm, where he had worked for many years, was not very secure. He earned $50 a day, but promises of promotion never came through, and the firm eventually went out of business as cheap imports from Mexico forced textile prices down. Joe went back to college to study business administration and was recently hired by one of the new banks in the area. He enjoys a more comfortable living even after making the monthly payments on his government-subsidized student loan.*

• • •

Maria recently moved from her central Mexican village and now works in a U.S.-owned firm in Mexico's maquiladora sector. Her husband, Juan, runs a small car upholstery business and sometimes crosses the border during the harvest season to work illegally on farms in California. Maria, Juan, and their son have improved their standard of living since moving out of subsistence agriculture, but Maria's wage has not increased in years: she still earns about $10 a day, and her wage is likely to decline following the recent capital outflows.

• • •

Xiao Zhi is an industrial worker in Shenzhen, a Special Economic Zone in southern China. After three difficult years on the road as part of China's floating population, fleeing the poverty of nearby Sichuan Province, he has finally settled with a new firm from Hong Kong that produces garments for the U.S. market. He can now afford more than a bowl of rice for his daily meal. He makes $2 a day and is hopeful for the future.

• • •

Workers around the world are living increasingly intertwined lives. Most of the world's population now lives in countries that are either integrated into world markets for goods and finance, or rapidly becoming so. Not so long ago, in the late 1970s, only a few developing countries, led by some in East Asia, were opening their borders to flows of trade and investment capital. About a third of the world's labor force lived in countries with centrally planned economies, and at least another third lived in countries insulated from international markets by prohibitive trade barriers and capital controls. Today, three giant population blocs—China, the republics of the former Soviet Union, and India—with nearly half the world's labor force among them, are entering the global market, and many other countries from Mexico to Indonesia have already established deep linkages. By the year 2000 fewer than 10 per-

cent of the world's workers are likely to be cut off from the economic mainstream.

But are workers better off as a result of these globalizing trends? Stories about losers from integration often make headlines: how Joe lost his job because of competition from poor Mexicans like Maria, and how her wage is held down by cheaper exports from China. But Joe now has a better job, and the U.S. economy has gained from expanding exports to Mexico. Maria's standard of living has improved, and her son can hope for a better future. The productivity of both workers is rising with increased investment, financed partly by the savings of workers in other countries, and Joe's pension fund is earning higher returns through diversification and new investment opportunities. Juan is looking forward to the day when he will no longer need to travel north—Xiao Zhi, meanwhile, would jump at the opportunity to make the wages Juan earns in California.

The complexity of these economic relationships would have been unthinkable just ten or twenty years ago. And as new opportunities for trade and interaction have grown, so too have attitudes shifted. In the 1950s and 1960s most developing countries regarded world market forces as a threat to their industrialization and development. Today they see them as a source of new opportunities. There is greater recognition that exports create good jobs, external capital flows spur accumulation and growth, and migration brings mutual gains.

But not everyone has benefited, and the international system has come under attack by some in industrial countries where rising unemployment and wage inequality are making people feel less secure about the future. Some workers in the industrial world are fearful of losing their jobs because of cheap exports from lower cost producers. Others worry about companies relocating abroad in search of low wages and lax standards, or fear that hordes of poor migrants will soon be at the door, offering to work for lower wages. The response has been a proliferation of protectionist demands, many of them under the guise of demands for fair trade and a level playing field.

Driving forces of global integration

Technological change and continually falling communications and transport costs have been a major factor behind global integration. Cross-border transport and trade are also easier today because of progress in resolving many of the political conflicts that have divided the economic world for decades, such as the cold war, the apartheid system in South Africa, and the volatile situation in the Middle East. Most important, however, have been the actions of developing countries themselves. By rejecting the failed development strategies of the past based on insulation from world economic events, more countries than ever before have joined the economic mainstream.

Development strategies are changing fast all over the world. Central planning has been abandoned in the former Soviet Union and in Eastern Europe, and countries throughout Latin America, South Asia, and the Middle East are reversing policies of import substitution designed to prevent the need for trade. This development revolution is most apparent in the area of trade policies. Since 1986 more than sixty developing countries have reported unilateral liberalization measures to the General Agreement on Tariffs and Trade (GATT), twenty-four have joined GATT, and twenty are in the process of joining its successor the World Trade Organization. Barriers to trade should fall further now that the Uruguay Round is complete, and with the enlargement of the North American Free Trade Agreement (NAFTA) and the European Union.

Governments are increasingly seeking to improve the international competitiveness of their economies rather than shield them behind protective walls. Developing countries have made tremendous progress in education and steady improvements in physical capital and infrastructure, boosting their productive capacity and enabling them to compete in world markets. Between 1970 and 1992 the low- and middle-income countries' share of the world's work force rose from 79 percent to 83 percent, but their share of the world's skilled work force (those workers with at least a secondary education) jumped from a third to nearly a half. Their share in total capital stocks also grew but remains small, rising from 9 percent to 13 percent of the world total.

This shift in development strategy has been reinforced by technological changes that have made the world easier to navigate—goods, capital, people, and ideas travel faster and cheaper today than ever before. Underlying these changes have been huge reductions in transport and communications costs. By 1960 maritime transport costs were less than a third of their 1920 level, and costs have continued to fall (Figure 7.1). Communications costs are falling even more dramatically—the cost of an international telephone call fell sixfold between 1940 and 1970 and tenfold between 1970 and 1990.

Channels of global interactions

International trade is the first avenue by which most countries feel the impact of economic integration. Volumes of goods and services traded across borders have grown tremendously in recent years, accounting for about 45 percent of world GDP in 1990, up from 25 percent in 1970

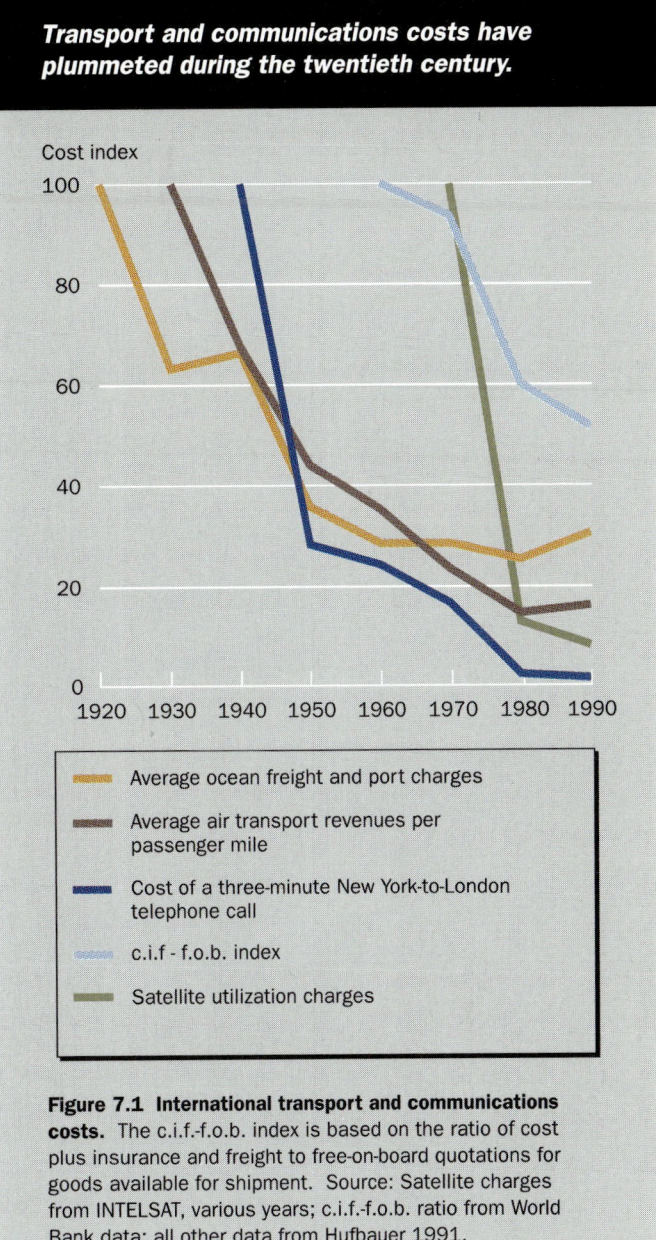

Transport and communications costs have plummeted during the twentieth century.

Cost index

Legend:
- Average ocean freight and port charges
- Average air transport revenues per passenger mile
- Cost of a three-minute New York-to-London telephone call
- c.i.f - f.o.b. index
- Satellite utilization charges

Figure 7.1 International transport and communications costs. The c.i.f.-f.o.b. index is based on the ratio of cost plus insurance and freight to free-on-board quotations for goods available for shipment. Source: Satellite charges from INTELSAT, various years; c.i.f.-f.o.b. ratio from World Bank data; all other data from Hufbauer 1991.

(Figure 7.2). In 1990, 17 percent of the labor force in developing and former centrally planned economies worked directly or indirectly in the export sector, with exports to the richer countries accounting for two-thirds of this employment effect. There was also a rapid shift to higher-value-added activities: the share of manufactures in developing countries' exports tripled between 1970 and 1990, from 20 percent to 60 percent. This rise marks a radical change in the international division of labor since the 1960s, when developing countries exported primary commodities almost exclusively. With the expansion of labor-intensive exports of manufactures, trade has come of age.

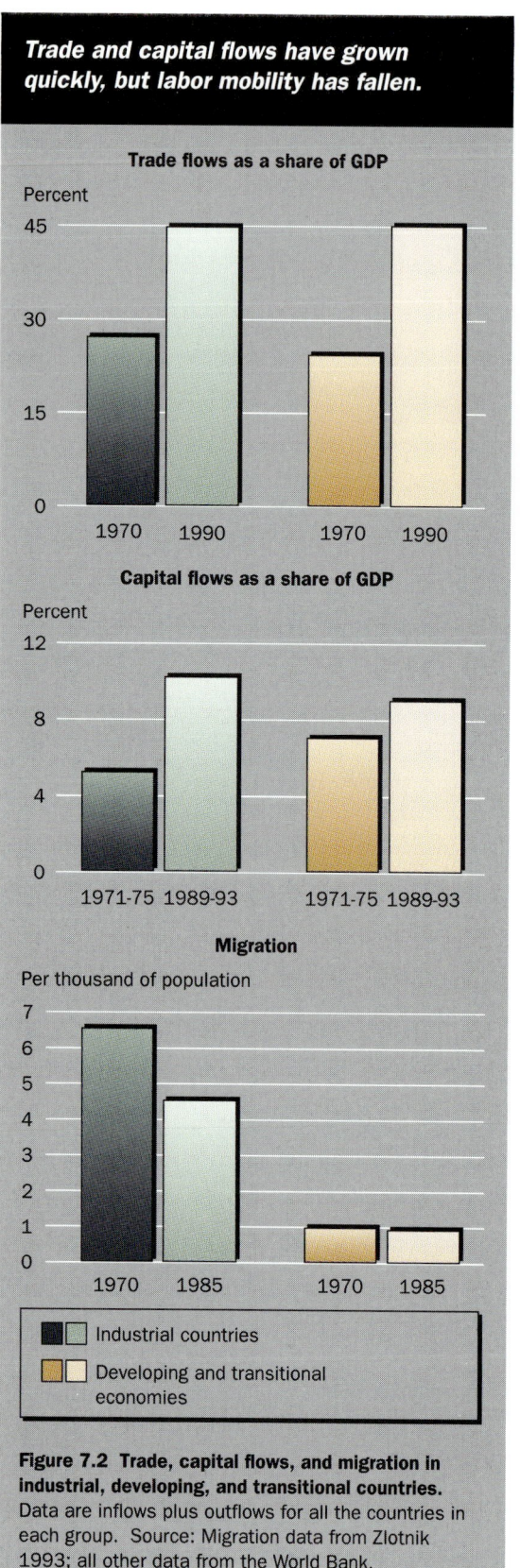

Trade and capital flows have grown quickly, but labor mobility has fallen.

Trade flows as a share of GDP

Capital flows as a share of GDP

Migration

Industrial countries

Developing and transitional economies

Figure 7.2 Trade, capital flows, and migration in industrial, developing, and transitional countries. Data are inflows plus outflows for all the countries in each group. Source: Migration data from Zlotnik 1993; all other data from the World Bank.

International trade is booming—but it has not affected all regions evenly. The East Asian economies were the first to demonstrate the dynamic effects on economic growth when open trade is coupled with government expenditures directed at human and physical capital infrastructure and heavy imports of capital and technology. Several middle-income economies from Chile to Turkey followed suit in exploiting export-led growth. As the successful newly industrializing economies have climbed the quality ladder and moved out of products based on unskilled labor, poorer countries such as China and India have moved in. Trailing the other regions are Sub-Saharan Africa and the Middle East, which did not expand their exports of manufactures. Both regions remain producers of primary commodities, and their terms of trade have continued to fall.

Capital has also become increasingly mobile, ever in search of the best returns. Gross capital flows (inflows plus outflows), an admittedly imperfect measure of capital mobility, rose from 7 percent to 9 percent of GDP in developing and transitional economies during the past two decades (Figure 7.2). Capital controls have been relaxed and are easily evaded anyway. Today capital moves more readily into successful countries and out of those countries where returns on investment are outweighed by the risks.

But capital does not always flow toward poorer countries. Although overall capital flows have grown steadily, net flows (total inflows minus total outflows) have remained small and unstable. Net flows rose in the 1970s, fell sharply in the 1980s as the debt crisis brought rising debt service burdens and massive capital flight, and then started to rise again at the end of the decade. By 1992 net capital flows to developing countries had returned to earlier levels. Overall, the transfer of resources from rich to poor countries has played only a moderate role in complementing domestic saving in developing countries: under the extreme assumption that domestic saving rates have not been affected by these flows, about 11 percent of capital formation in developing countries during the 1970–90 period could be attributed to the cumulative effect of capital mobility (an amount equivalent to only about 2 percent of the combined capital stocks of the industrial countries).

Regions have fared unequally in attracting capital inflows. Latin America has long been an important participant in international capital markets. Countries there were hit hard by the 1980s debt crisis but witnessed major reflows after the debt reductions of late in that decade. The Mexican crisis of 1994–95 shows how fickle these flows can be when confidence in economic management disappears. In the past, capital flows played a less important role in Asia, but this asymmetry is fading fast with rising involvement of foreign capital in China and the progressive liberalization of capital markets in India and East Asia. Most of the capital going to Sub-Saharan Africa and the Middle

East is from official sources, but capital flight from these regions has been large.

International migration of people in search of work is the laggard in this story. Annual migratory flows from developing countries (total inflows and outflows) are no greater now, relative to population size, than in the early 1970s, at about one emigrant per thousand inhabitants (Figure 7.2). The overall effect of international migration is much smaller than that of capital or trade: only about 2 percent of people born in low- and middle-income countries do not live in their country of origin. Migrants send home about $75 billion a year, about one-third the volume of net capital flows. Some 2 million to 3 million new migrants now leave developing countries each year (both legally and illegally), about half of whom go to industrial countries. For the latter, migration from developing countries translates into 1.5 new immigrants per thousand inhabitants per year, the same as in 1970. Migration between industrial countries has fallen since 1970 from 2.5 migrants per thousand inhabitants in 1970 to 1.5 per thousand in 1990. The foreign-born share of the population in industrial countries—currently about 5 percent—has been rising, however, because of the slower growth of the native population.

Nor is international migration yet a global business. Most migrants still stay within their regions: African migrants most often go to other African countries, and those from Asia and the Middle East mainly to the Arab Gulf countries. Recently migration within Asia has picked up. In Europe migrants are typically from former colonies or neighboring countries. Migration to the United States differs from this pattern: its immigrants come not only from nearby Mexico but from a variety of far-flung countries including the Philippines, the Republic of Korea, Viet Nam, India, and China.

Will a new golden age bring convergence?

Most workers in poorer countries are only just beginning to feel the benefits—and costs—of global integration. Participation by developing countries in the earlier globalization of 1850 to 1900 was shallow and often based on unfavorable terms, especially in Asia and Africa. They exported exclusively primary products, and capital flowed in mainly to support such enterprises—to develop capacity in natural resource extraction and maintain the support of friendly governments. Today, developing countries have the opportunity to play a far more active role. The potential for large gains is enormous. Whether they are realized will depend on the policy choices made by developing country governments and on the reactions of industrial countries.

The combination of powerful, cost-reducing technological change, policy change, and political developments is forging ever-stronger links within the global labor market. But it would be foolish to predict that the differences between rich and poor countries will rapidly disappear through convergence, either upward (of poorer countries'

Box 7.1 Are poorer countries catching up with richer ones?

Are there advantages to backwardness? Or are richer countries getting richer while the poor get poorer? And what is the role of international integration in allowing the poorer countries to catch up? The debate about convergence is based on a search for such historical regularities. Careful empirical work suggests that absolute divergence in output per person is a dominant feature of the world economic scene, but that "conditional convergence" forces are also at work.

Divergence in incomes per capita is the dominant feature of modern economic history. By one estimate, the ratio of income per capita in the richest to that in the poorest countries has increased from eleven in 1870, to thirty-eight in 1960, and to fifty-two in 1985. This divergent relation between growth performance and the initial level of income per capita not only applies to those extreme cases but is empirically valid on average over a sample of 117 countries. Statistical analysis of growth in income per capita confirms the importance of initial levels: on average, countries that started richer grew faster.

But although absolute divergence appears to be the rule, cross-country econometric work also finds "conditional convergence" occurring. When growth in income per capita is regressed not only on the initial level of income but also on the main determinants of growth—investment rates and the stock of human capital—a lower initial level predicts a faster growth rate. This means that if all countries had similar investment rates and similar levels of human capital, poor countries would grow faster than rich ones (but only slightly), and therefore differences in income per capita would fall over time. This weaker type of convergence is generally attributed to the advantage conferred by backwardness: technical innovations developed in rich countries benefit poorer ones.

How should divergence and conditional convergence be reconciled? Countries that are initially poor tend to invest less and to have less educated populations. This closes the circle. Poor countries tend to grow more slowly than richer countries in spite of the (small) advantages conferred by backwardness, because their poverty does not allow them to invest in human and physical capital as much as the richer countries do.

wages and living standards toward those in the rich countries) or downward (the reverse). Convergence is a notion both dear to economists, who like its close fit with theory, and abhorred by populists in rich countries, who see it as a threat to their incomes. Past experience, however, supports neither the hopes of the former nor the fears of the latter (Box 7.1). Wages have converged within Europe and the United States, where integration has been deep and the initial conditions were not too different, but even there convergence has been slow and incomplete .

But while some poorer countries—most notably the East Asian stars—are catching up with the richer ones, just as many have failed to narrow the gap, and some are losing ground. Overall, divergence, not convergence, has been the rule: the ratio of income per capita in the richest countries to that in the poorest increased fivefold between 1870 and 1985, and global inequality rose slightly between 1960 and 1986 (the output share of the poorest 50 percent of the world population shrank from 7.3 percent to 6.3 percent, while that of the richest 20 percent rose from 71.3 percent to 74.1 percent), before improving more recently as a result of faster growth in the poor countries of Asia.

• • •

Globalization is unavoidable—the welfare of Joe, Maria, and Xiao Zhi is now more closely linked than ever before. But growth prospects remain dominated by the effects of national economic policies. The forces of globalization increase both the benefits of good policies and the cost of failure. Although no group of workers can rely on the forces of convergence to raise their wages automatically, neither need they fear that such forces will unavoidably pull their wages down. Whether a new golden age arrives for all depends mostly on the responses of individual countries to the new opportunities offered by this increasingly global economy.

CHAPTER 8

A Changing International Division of Labor

TOYS FROM CHINA, COPPER FROM CHILE, rice from Thailand—trade in goods and increasingly in services is the most important and most stable form of economic contact with the rest of the world for Joe, Maria, and Xiao Zhi. It also promises great opportunities for lowering consumption and investment costs and speeding the growth of output and wages. But countries must undergo considerable and often painful adjustments before reaping these rewards, especially if their economies have been heavily protected. Changes in the pattern of trade bring about social transformations, hurting those workers who lack the flexibility or the skills to leave decaying sectors previously propped up by trade barriers.

So there are also reasons to worry—despite the promise of the Uruguay Round agreement and the proliferation of regional free trade accords. To reap the gains that freer trade offers, policy frameworks, both national and international, must be supportive of change. This chapter considers how the changing international division of labor affects different groups of workers, what the future holds for international trade and trade relations, and how policy can support the kind of change that improves the lot of workers.

Trade increases most workers' welfare

International trade benefits most workers: because workers are also consumers, it brings them immediate gains through cheaper imports, and it enables most workers to become more productive as the goods they produce increase in value. One statistic powerfully makes the case for an export-led strategy: during the past two decades real wages rose at an average annual rate of 3 percent in those developing countries where the growth of exports as a share of GNP was above the median, but wages stagnated in those where exports expanded least (Figure 8.1). This does not necessarily mean that increased exports are a sufficient condition for faster economic growth, but it does suggest that they are part of the story. Trade helps workers in two ways:

■ It allows workers to shop for consumption goods where they are cheapest and allows employers to buy the equipment and technologies that best complement their workers' skills. The rapid industrialization of East Asia has been built to a large extent on massive imports of the West's best technologies and machinery. In industrial countries, imports from cheaper producers have reduced the price of labor-intensive consumer goods.

■ More important, the global market frees workers from the constraints imposed by domestic demand. This is of special importance for those countries seeking to move into the higher productivity activities that are key to development. Labor-intensive manufactures took off in the East Asian economies, not by selling to domestic markets, which remained primarily agrarian, but by accessing international markets. In protected South Asia, meanwhile, manufacturing faltered at least until recently. Global markets are not only larger than any single domestic market but generally more stable as well—and still have room to accommodate newcomers. Although developing country exports of primary and manufactured goods have grown by more than 5 percent a year in recent years and now total $900 billion annually, they

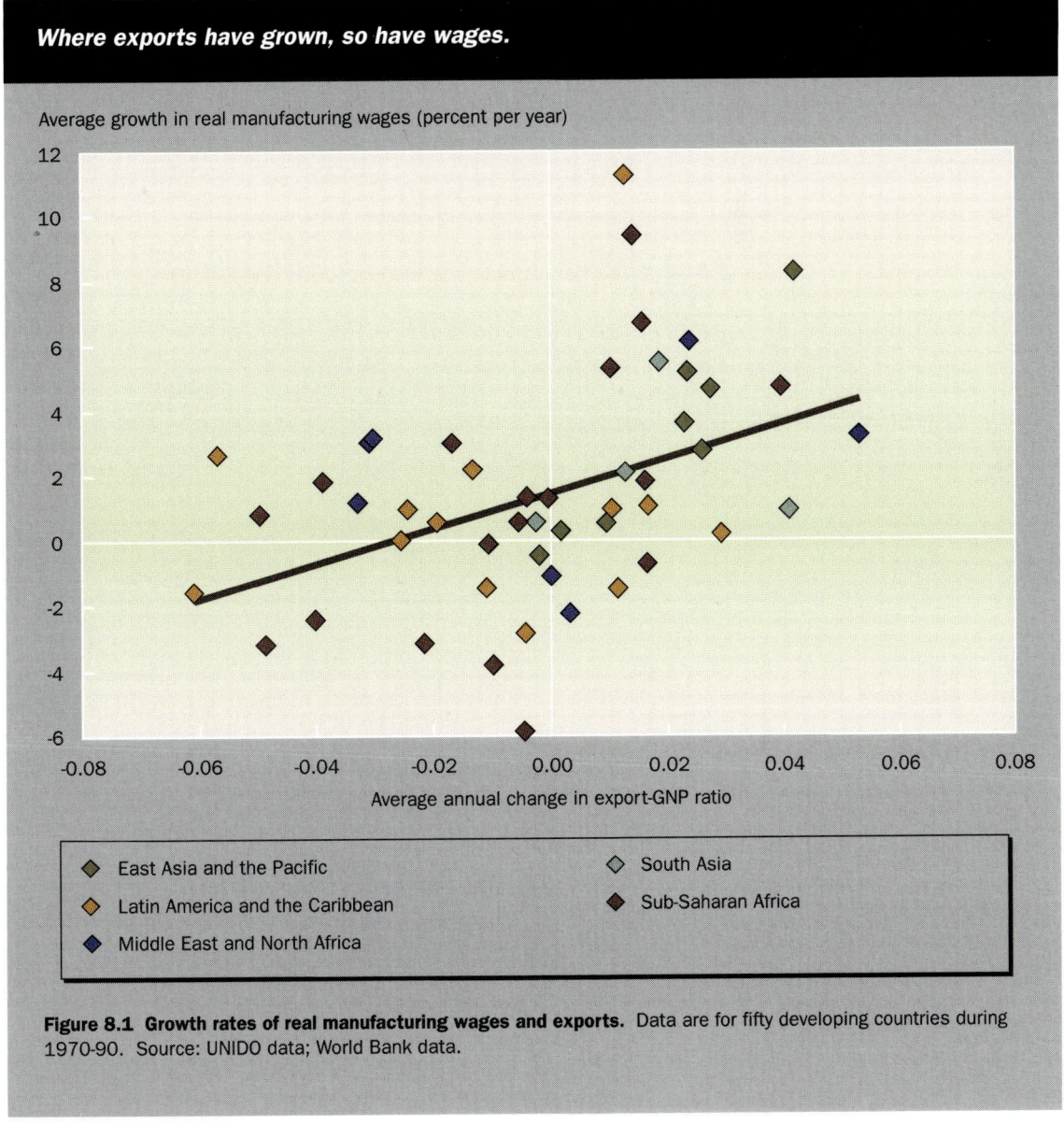

Where exports have grown, so have wages.

Average growth in real manufacturing wages (percent per year)

Average annual change in export-GNP ratio

◆ East Asia and the Pacific
◆ Latin America and the Caribbean
◆ Middle East and North Africa
◇ South Asia
◆ Sub-Saharan Africa

Figure 8.1 Growth rates of real manufacturing wages and exports. Data are for fifty developing countries during 1970-90. Source: UNIDO data; World Bank data.

still account for only 3.5 percent of rich countries' combined GDP.

Trade brings mutual gains to all countries, but it can also have important distributional effects within national boundaries, benefiting some workers like Maria and Xiao Zhi, whose products become more in demand, and hurting others who lose out to new competitors. Trade with poorer countries hurts unskilled workers in industrial countries, like Joe—although most economists believe that it explains only a relatively small part of their labor market difficulties (Box 8.1). It has also hurt those workers in developing and former centrally planned economies hit hard by the demise of previously protected sectors. But since society as a whole gains, the challenge for policymakers is to ease the transition to free trade by encouraging the labor force to upgrade their skills, as happened with Joe, and by compensating the losers (see Part Four)—and to avoid protection, which only makes the national pie smaller.

Increased openness to trade has been strongly associated with the reduction of poverty in most developing countries. In Morocco, for example, the incidence of poverty fell by half, from 26 percent to 13 percent of the population, in just five years after trade was liberalized in the mid-1980s. New jobs—most of them connected to a booming garment manufacturing sector geared to the European market—drew unskilled workers from rural areas to the cities. Export-led growth has also been associated with poverty reduction in East Asia, Chile, Mauritius, and Turkey.

The impact of increased trade on income distribution in developing countries has been much more varied than the impact on poverty. In Morocco trade was equalizing. In East Asia, too, income distribution became more equal as trade expanded. But in some Latin American countries, such as Chile and Mexico, a more recent wave of trade liberalization has coincided with increased wage *and* income inequalities. In Mexico's maquiladora enterprises the ratio of nonproduction (white-collar) to production wages rose

Box 8.1 How does trade with developing countries affect the unskilled in industrial countries?

Many in the industrial countries are concerned with the shrinking of labor-intensive activities, including whole sectors such as garments and footwear, in the face of increased competition from low-wage producers and the parallel relocation of jobs by multinational corporations. Industrial countries have undergone pronounced shifts since 1970 in key aspects of their employment and wage structures. In some, especially the United States, wage inequality rose sharply in the 1980s: average real wages of young American men with college degrees rose by 11 percent between 1979 and 1987, while the wages of those with only a secondary education fell by 20 percent. In Europe, wage-setting mechanisms meant to reduce inequality have contributed to high unemployment: there were 8 million unemployed in the countries of the Organization for Economic Cooperation and Development (OECD) in 1970; now there are 35 million, or 8 percent of the labor force—most of them unskilled workers.

There is no doubt that part of these developments is related to increased competition from developing countries' imports—the difficult question is how much. Most analyses conclude that trade with developing countries can explain only 10 to 30 percent of the industrial countries' labor market difficulties, but some studies come up with more extreme results—on both sides of the argument. Imports of manufactures from developing countries were only about 2 percent of GDP in industrial countries in 1992. Even allowing for the unusually labor-intensive nature of the goods concerned, the direct effect

of this trade on workers in industrial countries must have been limited. Factor content calculations suggest that trade with developing countries during the past two decades reduced the demand for unskilled workers by 3 million to 9 million, or 1 to 3 percent of total employment (2 to 5 percent of the unskilled labor force), depending on whether the factor proportions used in the computations are those of industrial or developing countries.

But these estimates do not account for the additional job loss due to either defensive labor-saving innovation by firms or the displacement of unskilled labor in services and nontraded-goods sectors that supply intermediate inputs to manufacturing. There is no precise way of quantifying these effects. But for trade with developing countries to account for all of the labor market developments in the industrial countries, the estimated upper range of the direct impact of trade would have to be quadrupled.

The effect of trade also seems modest when compared with other changes in labor markets. In the United States alone, for example, employment in services (mainly retail trade, hotels, and restaurants) grew by over 6 million workers during the 1970–90 period. Rising wage inequality within skill groups, and increases in the ratio of skilled to unskilled employment in all sectors, also suggest that some other force is at play. In particular, technological change seems to be increasingly labor-saving—perhaps partly because of increased international competition.

from 2 to 2.5 between 1985 and 1988. And in Chile the wages of university graduates rose by 56 percent relative to those of high school graduates between 1980 and 1990. These trends may be linked to the introduction of new labor-saving technologies, particularly the computer revolution, which have increased inequality in industrial countries. But a number of other factors could also explain the phenomenon: well-trained white-collar workers are often scarce immediately after liberalization; some of the industries that were previously protected were themselves labor-intensive; some of the activities that are moving from industrial to developing countries along with capital are skill-intensive by developing countries' standards; and in some middle-income countries unskilled workers are facing greater competition from workers in poorer countries.

The future of trade

These trends in the international division of labor are likely to accelerate over the coming decades. Changes will be driven by two policy-related forces, namely, trade liberalization and changes in the international distribution of skilled labor, and an exogenous one, technological change, especially falling communications costs. If managed effectively, these changes should lead to rising real incomes for most workers, although they will also mean ups and downs in employment levels in different activities within countries. Deepening integration has raised the issue—which we discuss in Chapter 11—of linking trade to enforcement of national labor standards.

One-time gains from liberalization

The 1994 Uruguay Round accord is the widest-ranging and most ambitious multilateral trade agreement ever negotiated. Its centerpiece is a new multilateral organization, the World Trade Organization, which will bring under one roof all the separate agreements negotiated during the round. Earlier rounds of trade liberalization had brought industrial countries' average tariffs on industrial products down to 6.3 percent, from more than 40 percent in 1947. The recent round has reduced tariffs to an average of 3.9 percent. Average tariffs remain higher on imports from developing countries because tariffs on such common developing country exports as textiles, clothing, and fish products remain generally higher. Other concrete benefits of the round are the phased removal of all quantitative restrictions and subsidies on agriculture, textiles, and clothing, although the phaseout will be slow.

Reductions in trade barriers change domestic prices and push workers into sectors in which their country is best able to trade internationally. With many countries set to relax trade barriers at the same time, the pattern of international supply will gradually but profoundly change. Snapshot estimates of the effects of full implementation of the Uruguay

The purchasing power of wages will rise with full implementation of the Uruguay Round.

Table 8.1 Estimates of changes in wages and prices resulting from the Uruguay Round agreement by 2005
(percent)

Country or region	Change in unadjusted wages	Change in consumer prices	Change in wages adjusted for price changes
Industrial countries			
European Union	−1.8	−2.1	0.3
Japan	−0.1	−0.8	0.7
North America	−1.6	−2.0	0.4
Developing countries			
ASEAN	5.0	1.1	3.8
Asian NIEs	−0.1	−1.3	1.2
China	5.6	2.8	2.9
Latin America	−0.7	−0.9	0.2
South Asia	7.2	5.4	1.8
Sub-Saharan Africa	−1.5	−1.5	0.0

Source: Hertel and others 1995.

Round, holding each region's factor endowments at current levels, point to modest but not inconsequential global welfare gains. Once all the market access provisions are in place, global gains will total some $100 billion to $200 billion a year. Roughly one-third of these gains will go to developing and transitional countries. The purchasing power of wages will rise in all regions except Africa (Table 8.1). Nominal wage incomes will rise in those countries with advantage in labor-intensive goods—the ASEAN countries, China, and South Asia—and fall in all others because of increased competition in the goods in which they now specialize. But this fall in incomes will be more than compensated for by price reductions.

The elimination of the Multi-Fibre Arrangement represents a clear gain for low-skill producers. Under the old arrangement industrial countries were able to impose quotas on their imports of finished garments—the one item in which low-skill producers have a sure comparative advantage and which, along with textiles, accounts for more than half of their exports of manufactures. The entry of new producers in these sectors will increase employment in textiles and garments in the ASEAN countries, China, and South Asia. Their entry will lower prices, benefiting consumers worldwide but hurting established producers in the industrial countries, the Asian NIEs, and Latin America. In the industrial countries employment losses in labor-intensive activities will be made up for by employment gains in higher wage, skill-intensive industries such as machinery and transport equipment, and in services.

The Uruguay Round agreement in agriculture is a mixed blessing for poor countries. In the short term the elimination of industrial country export subsidies will worsen the terms of trade for food-importing developing countries, mainly Sub-Saharan Africa, the ASEAN countries, and the Middle East. But new market opportunities will open up for food exporters. Land-rich countries in Sub-Saharan Africa and Latin America will be encouraged to increase food production and exports if food price rises are passed on to farmers.

Dynamic gains from liberalization

The dynamic effects of liberalization on world trade are likely to far exceed the one-time effects. As the East Asian experience shows, countries able to expand domestic capacity by investing in human and physical capital can grow by moving up the product ladder, shifting from low-value products into higher value exports. This strategy would be severely restricted if, in the absence of expanding export markets, production were constrained by domestic demand.

But an export-led growth strategy does not mean similar product mixes for all developing countries. The growth path that each country takes will depend on its initial endowments and strategic choices. For many, a move up the product ladder involves shifting from agriculture and primary production to manufacturing—first of labor-intensive goods and then of increasingly skill-intensive products (Box 8.2). But countries that are richer in natural resources will remain net exporters of primary products longer: they will have to attain a higher average skill level and accumulate more capital per worker before they start to specialize in manufactures. Many countries in Latin America, and New Zealand and the United States earlier in their history, are good examples. In many Sub-Saharan African countries the accumulation of skills and capital may first raise the efficiency of primary commodity production before feeding into growth in manufacturing. In contrast, in resource-poor countries—the East Asian NIEs in the past, India and China now—skill acquisition and capital deepening will translate into rapid manufacturing growth. Other countries with poor supplies of natural resources, however, may remain net exporters of primary products if their supply of skilled labor is even more meager—as in Nepal, for example. Finally, some countries will manage to find a niche in services, as have Singapore and Lebanon, which specialize in the supply of financial services to their neighbors, or the many small islands around the world that specialize in tourism.

Who gets hurt and what should be done

Free trade produces losers as well as winners as a result of international price changes, both within countries and between them. Globalization affects the relative scarcity of various types of skills and the wages workers can command. As an economy opens up, domestic prices become more aligned with international prices, and wages rise for workers whose skills are more scarce internationally than at home and fall for those who encounter greater competition. As other economies open as well, the relative scarcity of various skills in the global marketplace changes still further, hurting those countries with an abundance of workers who have the skills that are becoming less scarce. Increased competition also means that unless countries are able to match the productivity gains of their competitors, the wages of their workers will be eroded. In the coming decade the most vulnerable groups are likely to be:

- unskilled workers in middle-income and rich countries, like Maria and Joe, as they face more competition from low-cost producers; and
- some entire countries (especially in Sub-Saharan Africa) that lack the dynamism needed to compensate for rising competition and match the efficiency gains achieved by their competitors, or the flexibility to move into other products.

Dealing with increased competition

Countries that do not keep pace with change can be hurt by their competitors' improvements in efficiency. For example, as China becomes a more effective exporter of garments and a larger importer of other goods, the international price of garments relying on low-skilled labor will fall relative to the prices of the products that China imports, especially primary products and high-technology goods. Other countries that specialize in the production of garments, such as Mexico and other NIEs, will lose unless they upgrade their own production and move into higher-value-added activities. The entry of the former centrally planned economies into the global market may likewise reduce prices and wages in the medium-technology sectors. Consumers will benefit in all cases, but workers in the decaying sectors will lose out unless they can move to higher-value-added activities or to nontradables.

Protectionism, on the other hand, is a self-defeating response. Imposing trade or capital restrictions to help those who lose out will only make the domestic economic pie smaller. By preventing society from moving forward, these policies result in lower welfare for workers over the long term. At best, trade restrictions can protect the domestic market at a high cost to consumers. But because such restrictions do not improve competitiveness, they hasten the fall in exports and, over time, in real wages.

Similarly counterproductive would be a policy of taxing multinational corporations in an attempt to keep low-skill jobs from migrating to developing countries. Shifting production abroad is an effective strategy for enlarging a

Box 8.2 Heckscher-Ohlin, skills, and comparative advantage

The celebrated Heckscher-Ohlin model of trade stresses the relation between endowments and comparative advantage: countries tend to export goods whose production makes intensive use of their more abundant factors. Whereas its usual forms have emphasized relative endowments of capital, labor, and natural resources, recent variations on the model focus increasingly on the importance of skills in the trade equation, a view strongly supported by empirical evidence. A simple trade model based on the presumption that an important determinant of a country's comparative advantage is its relative endowments of skills and land illustrates this well.

In the figure below, the regression line relates the split of each country's exports between manufactures and primary products to its relative supplies of skills and land. The regional averages also are plotted. The largest contrast is between Africa and the industrial world, which lie toward opposite ends of the regression line; in between lie Latin America, South Asia, and East Asia, in that order. The ranking of Latin America and South Asia is instructive: South Asia and Africa both have low levels of schooling, and Latin America and East Asia intermediate levels. But the two Asian regions have little land compared with Africa and Latin America.

Skill accumulation increases growth by changing the nature of comparative advantage. Although the figure was estimated on the basis of cross-sectional data for 1985, it can also be used to describe the dynamics of development. Progress in the diagram consists of movement upward and to the right, reflecting a higher average skill level in a country's labor force and an increase in its comparative advantage in manufacturing over primary commodities.

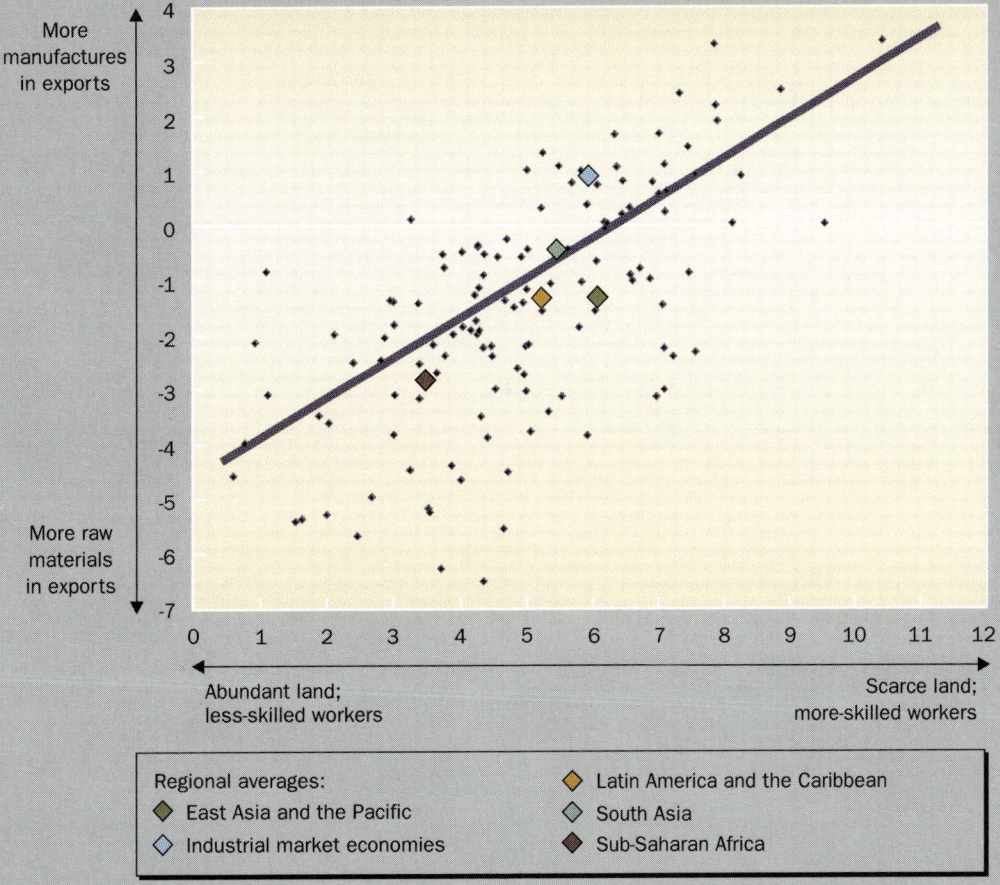

Skill intensity of exports and human capital endowment. Data are for 126 industrial and developing countries in 1985. Values along the horizontal axis are logarithms of the ratio of the country's average educational attainment to its land area; vertical axis values are logarithms of the ratio of manufactured to primary-products exports. Source: Export data from United Nations Statistical Office COMTRADE data base; education data from UNDP 1990; land data from the World Bank.

firm's market share in a competitive world—or for minimizing its losses. For example, while the U.S. share in world exports of manufactures declined over the past three decades from 17 percent to 12 percent, the share of U.S. multinational corporations and their affiliates fell only from 18 percent to 16 percent. This relative success was due largely to growing overseas operations (production by foreign affiliates of U.S. multinational firms rose from 37 percent to 54 percent). This globalization of operations prevented further declines in these firms' exports due to competitive pressures and instead allowed them to generate extra exports and better jobs at home (especially in highly skilled research and development and supervisory activities).

The countries that have gained the most from an export-led development strategy over long periods are those that have responded flexibly to changing circumstances. This flexibility shows up in sharper reactions to price changes. The terms of trade for developing countries have fluctuated greatly but have been on a steady downward trend for several decades, particularly for primary products. The remarkable performance of those countries whose growth in exports relative to GDP was above international averages during 1970–90 occurred despite terms-of-trade losses to these economies of about 1 percent a year—a drag on income growth of about 0.3 percent a year. The wage increases of about 3 percent a year that these economies enjoyed must have been the result of an even larger rise in labor productivity, both within sectors and through intersectoral shifts. In contrast, workers stuck in the weak trading group—on the half of the trade growth scale where wages did not grow—experienced larger terms-of-trade losses, averaging nearly 2 percent a year, which because of the smaller export base also resulted in a 0.3 percent drag on income growth.

Ensuring that a commitment to open trade remains politically acceptable sometimes requires policy measures to ease the plight of the minority that loses out. But over the longer term, public policies that encourage workers to upgrade their skills, educate their children, and support the mobility of workers into new jobs are clearly to be preferred over programs that create a dependence on welfare (see Part Four).

Countries left behind

The plight of countries left behind is increasingly at the center of the development agenda. In most cases, countries with weak political structures have been further weakened by unfavorable international developments. In many Sub-Saharan African countries, large declines in commodity prices not only have led to lower wages and incomes but also have weakened the ability of policymakers to respond. Prices fell because of metal- and energy-saving technical progress and industrial countries' subsidies to agriculture, but also because of efficiency improvements by some producers, especially in Asia. Most Sub-Saharan African commodity exporters were not able to keep up with the competition—for example, cocoa, rubber, and coffee trees, many of them planted in the 1950s, have become less productive. And new sectors did not emerge as price structures changed: in fact, Sub-Saharan African manufacturing exports have fallen over the past two decades. The situation in many Middle Eastern countries, although not as dramatic, is similar.

In Sub-Saharan Africa and much of the Middle East, this failure is related to a pervasive uncertainty that is self-reinforcing. Despite the opportunities for profit offered by current policy regimes, private investments have not picked up, and this failure compounds the risk of policy reversals. As the number of new competitors proliferates, entry into international markets will become more difficult. In both regions, strategies are needed now that can generate an export push. Countries with small formal sectors might gain by eliminating corporate and export taxation altogether.

• • •

Trade benefits most, but not all, workers. As trade becomes increasingly open, the poor in developing countries benefit because the demand for their labor goes up. Skilled workers in industrial economies also gain because the demand for their skills rises. But the welfare of unskilled workers in rich and middle-income countries can fall. Competition by low-cost producers should boost welfare by encouraging labor in richer countries to shift from low-productivity to high-productivity activities. But these gains cannot be realized if workers remain unemployed. Policies to compensate those hurt by change and help them shift to new occupations are essential so that trade can deliver higher incomes for all, and protectionism can be defeated.

CHAPTER 9

Capital Mobility: Blessing or Curse?

THE GLOBALIZATION OF FINANCIAL MARkets means gains for private capital, which can now flow around the world in search of the highest returns. But how has it affected workers such as Joe, Maria, and Xiao Zhi? Optimists stress the possibilities for mutual gains—capital and labor need each other to produce goods and services of higher value. Where domestic policy is sound, capital flows should follow, reinforcing the effects of open trade in allowing countries to exploit their competitive advantages. Pessimists emphasize the risks and dangers—rich countries fear that an alliance between capital and cheap labor in developing countries will lower wages and living standards at home. Meanwhile poorer countries fear exploitation—that capital will come only when wages are low and leave when wages rise. Both rich and poor countries worry about the limited ability of government to tax capital and about the instability that footloose capital can generate.

Both the optimistic and the pessimistic view have elements of truth. But one fact is indisputable: capital crosses borders more easily than labor and despite the best efforts of national governments to control it. Rising capital mobility intensifies the impact of domestic policy on labor outcomes: success will breed success because it will attract capital, but failure will mean labor is punished harder as capital flees the scene.

This chapter addresses three related issues. First, how can developing and transitional economies attract more private capital? Second, what can policymakers do to maximize the benefits for workers and minimize the risks? And third, could private capital flows out of rich countries hurt workers there?

How to attract capital

The industrial countries have always used the lion's share of global savings. Average capital per worker is $13,000 in developing countries and $150,000 in industrial countries—close to twelve times more. There was some convergence in the 1970s, but the gap grew in the 1980s. For most developing countries the share of foreign inflows in investment is small, averaging 11 percent of the capital stock and ranging between 20 percent for poorer countries (mostly in the form of official debt) and 5 percent for middle-income countries (mainly in the form of private capital).

Recently, however, the picture has been changing: private capital has been flowing to low- and middle-income countries at record levels. These flows are estimated to have totaled $175 billion in 1994, more than four times the 1989 figure of $42 billion, all on a net basis. There are a number of reasons why these flows have accelerated: economic reforms in many countries, the debt reductions of the early 1990s, and the fall in world interest rates. The composition of these flows has also changed dramatically. About two-thirds of recent total long-term flows have gone to the private sector, compared with only 44 percent in 1990. But more than a decade after the onset of the debt crisis, net commercial bank financing continues to be negative. Instead, foreign direct investment (FDI) has surged ahead, to about $67 billion in 1993 (with China alone receiving $26 billion), followed by sharply higher portfolio investments ($47 billion) and a burst of bond issuance by both private firms and governments ($42 billion).

Policies to attract private capital

Workers have an interest in attracting capital to complement their labor and raise their productivity and wages. The recent upsurge in private flows to the developing world has been concentrated in a few successful countries. How can others reap similar gains? Must they grant special favors to capital, and is it necessary to hold wages down or restrict union activity? Although many countries have indeed offered tax breaks and other enticements, and some authoritarian governments have repressed labor, these are not the primary attractions for capital, and over the long term they are more likely to reduce net capital inflows.

Capital holders are, first and foremost, looking for good returns, and they are deeply concerned with risk. The key attractions are good infrastructure, a reliable and skilled work force, guarantees of their right to repatriate both income and capital, and social and political stability. A tradition of prudent fiscal management and deep links with global markets that would be costly to break have more influence on the investment decisions of both multinationals and portfolio investors than special deals. When domestic markets are distorted for the sake of attracting capital, workers end up sharing the excess profits with foreigners. A small minority of workers may gain, but most lose out from the increased labor market dualism. Countries such as

Brazil and Egypt, which in the past offered favors and protected markets, suffered from this syndrome. Similarly, labor repression is unlikely to be sustainable, since sooner or later it leads to social instability. South Africa under apartheid represents an extreme case of a repressive country that at first succeeded in attracting foreign capital but ended up only scaring it away.

Some may take the lesson from Mexico's 1994–95 currency crisis that deep, NAFTA-style integration heightens a country's vulnerability. But this would be a misreading of that episode. NAFTA provided an impetus for investors to move in to Mexico, but there were also huge capital inflows to other Latin American countries during that period of enthusiasm for emerging markets and low U.S. interest rates. Mexico went into crisis, but Chile did not, because Mexico's macroeconomic and financial sector policy was poor, while Chile's was robust. Moreover, Mexico's involvement in NAFTA undoubtedly helped the situation once the crisis broke, both by facilitating the preparation of a rescue package and by preventing a major policy reversal. Such a reversal would have had much worse consequences for labor.

The potential for capital flight is, however, a fact of life—for both governments and workers. Capital controls are generally impotent to stop most forms of capital mobility. The capital controls that most Latin American, Middle Eastern, and Sub-Saharan African countries had in place during the 1980s debt crisis failed to prevent massive capital flight—equivalent to 10 to 20 percent of their total capital stocks—which led to deeper domestic recessions and sharper wage declines than would otherwise have occurred.

Multinational corporations as agents of change

Multinational corporations have been a major vehicle for the globalization of manufacturing, in which relatively cheap labor in developing countries has been equipped with capital and modern techniques—of storage management and telecommunications, as well as of production. Recently most of the expansion of multinational corporations has occurred in developing countries: 5 million of the 8 million jobs created by multinationals between 1985 and 1992 were in the developing world. The number of workers employed by multinationals in developing countries now stands at 12 million, but the true number who owe their livelihood to multinationals may be twice that, given the prevalence of subcontracting.

FDI flows now respond rapidly to new profit opportunities, shifting production to places where wages are low relative to potential productivity. It is important for countries to attract capital on the basis of sound economic fundamentals, rather than through protection of domestic markets, which multinationals are only too happy to exploit. In the past FDI flowed mainly to countries with large, rich domestic markets such as the United States and the United Kingdom, as evidenced by a strong correlation between FDI stocks and income per capita. More recent flows have tended to be searching for cheaper export platforms, and the relation between the size of FDI flows (as a share of investment) and income per capita has nearly disappeared. Cross-border trade flows within companies now account for roughly a third of world trade and perhaps as much as 15 percent of world GNP.

Multinational corporations account for a sizable share of modern sector manufacturing employment in both small countries and large—more than a fifth in Argentina, Barbados, Botswana, Indonesia, Malaysia, Mauritius, Mexico, the Philippines, Singapore, and Sri Lanka. But many developing countries fear that increased competition for funds by other developing countries will lead to a rise in footloose investments, prone to leave at the slightest shock and unlikely to establish strong links with the rest of the economy. Investment in export processing zones—designated duty-free areas that account for about 45 percent of total employment by multinational corporations in developing countries—is a case in point, with benefits to the recipient country restricted to labor receipts. This problem is especially acute in low-skill industries such as garments and footwear, where firm-specific knowledge is slight and exit costs are low. These fears may be legitimate, but the alternative of multinationals creating no new jobs is even less attractive. Rather, low-skill jobs must be seen as just one step in the growth dynamic. In several successful cases, such as Mauritius, the Philippines, and the Republic of Korea, FDI flows into low-skill sectors have now ceased as domestic wages have risen and domestic firms have matured, and foreign firms in those sectors have moved on to a new generation of export processing zones with cheaper labor—in China, Sri Lanka, and Morocco.

How can workers gain from capital inflows?

Workers can benefit from capital inflows, but they are almost always hit hardest by capital flight. During the debt crisis of the 1980s, adjustment costs were high and workers paid a large share of the adjustment burden (see Part Four). In Latin America wages fell an average of 25 percent during this period, even as the regional stock market index rose enormously (Table 9.1). Financial crises are bad for workers for several reasons:

■ *Capital is more mobile than labor*, making it harder to tax, so workers normally end up footing the bill. Much of the burden of servicing high levels of public debt falls on labor in the form of reduced social services, less public investment, or higher taxes. The necessary movement of labor toward tradable sectors entails real costs—in transitory unemployment and loss of human capital—that can only be partly compensated by transfers financed by taxes on capital. Sometimes overindebted firms end up being bailed out by public funds. Such bailouts occurred throughout most of Latin America in the early 1980s and explain part of the debt crisis. In Chile, for example, the majority of public debt was originally contracted by the private sector, especially banks. But workers, through their taxes, picked up the bill when these private debtors went bankrupt.

- *Capital is cautious.* Capital can take a long time to flow back into a country following a crisis, leaving labor short of capital in the meantime. It is not enough for countries to make the needed adjustments in their internal and external accounts—investors must believe these changes to be sustainable. Building this trust may take a while—five years or more—and even then it remains fragile. When risks rise, the expectation of failure can become self-fulfilling, precipitating a financial crisis, especially when the level of indebtedness approaches the danger level. The recent devaluation in Mexico shows how dramatic the influence of expectations can be in an environment with extremely mobile capital.

Making sure that workers gain from capital inflows, and that the risks of capital flight are minimized, requires policy action on a number of fronts, concerning the type of international borrowing and the scope for capital controls and other kinds of domestic action. Investment is a risky business, and as much of this risk as possible should be shifted away from the government budget and onto lenders and private borrowers and markets. Publicly owned external debt is the worst form of finance from the point of view of labor. It tends to crowd out more useful and productive private investment from which workers have more to gain, and, if things go wrong, the burden of debt repayment tends to fall on labor—a burden usually exacerbated by the devaluation required to generate the necessary foreign exchange for debt service. Market-intermediated finance that is allocated through the domestic banking sector and securities markets is better at shifting risk away from labor—so long as the state does not bail out failures. FDI is the best instrument from a risk-sharing perspective.

Recently some countries have become wary of large capital inflows returning in the wake of debt reduction agreements or financial liberalization. But while controls on capital inflows, especially short-term and liquid flows, can be useful, they have become increasingly less so. The fear of hot money is greater when the efficiency of financial intermediation is low and potential losses are likely to be passed on to taxpayers. Workers are more exposed to the effects of excessive risk taking and costly bailouts by the existence of implicit or explicit deposit insurance, excessive borrowings by firms too large to be allowed to fail, or lending by banks that are hostage to weak borrowers. Good financial intermediation requires good intermediaries. Without them, market-based flows will lead to financial blowouts, as has happened many times in the past.

Wages in the major Latin American debtors have fallen since the debt crisis, but stock markets have risen.

Table 9.1 Indebtedness, stock market performance, and wages in the five largest Latin American debtor countries

Country	Debt-GNP ratio in 1982	Ratio of 1991 real stock market index to 1982 index	Ratio of 1991 real wages to 1982 wages[a]
Argentina	0.55	25	1.02
Brazil	0.35	4	0.69
Chile	0.78	15	0.85
Mexico	0.53	47	0.78
Venezuela	0.41	9	0.60

a. In manufacturing.
Source: UNIDO and International Finance Corporation data.

The difficulty of controlling the level and composition of private capital inflows makes prudent macroeconomic policies all the more important—particularly for workers. That means maintaining the right exchange rate, interest rates, and level of reserves to discourage sudden capital outflows.

There are also things that industrial countries can do to keep international interest rates low. In the medium term there are reasons to believe that the supply of global saving may increase in the next decade as demographic factors cause saving in rich countries first to rise and then to fall as their populations age. Between now and 2010 the share of the industrial countries' population between the ages of forty and sixty-five—a cohort of net savers—is expected to rise from 40 percent to 45 percent, while the proportion of those between twenty and thirty years old—net borrowers—is expected to fall from 42 percent to 34 percent. Over the coming decade, however, what happens to industrial country budget deficits could make all the difference. A rise in deficits could easily offset the expected movement in private saving and send interest rates upward. Unless the recent trend of lower U.S. deficits is sustained, and unless deficits fall further in other industrial countries, interest rates will keep going up—at the expense of workers throughout the developing world. Workers in industrial countries, who own at least 25 percent of financial capital through pension funds, will be partly compensated by higher returns on their savings, but workers in developing countries, whose savings are meager, will not.

The outlook for capital flows

The globalization of capital is likely to usher in a long and mutually beneficial period of large capital flows from industrial to developing countries. Equipping the increasingly skilled work force in developing countries with more sophisticated capital will boost workers' productivity, while good long-term investments in those countries will help the aging work forces of the industrial countries get the most out of their retirement funds. The coincidence of increased trade and capital flows is also virtuous; capital flows will help developing countries take advantage of new trade opportunities and increase their incentive to follow sound domestic policies. But capital relocation will not occur overnight, and for industrial countries it will not lead to measurable social dislocations.

Capital flows will remain constrained by country risk and can grow only as fast as the developing countries' creditworthiness improves. These are severe constraints. In the average creditworthy country the ratio of foreign liabilities to exports is two to one, and in the best of cases it has reached three to one; the latter can be taken as an upper bound of the speed at which developing countries' debts can safely grow. Even if all developing countries borrowed enough to reach that limit within a five-year span, the maximum flows would be $500 billion a year. (Actual effective demand for funds is likely to be much smaller because several of the most creditworthy countries, such as Korea, Malaysia, Portugal, and Thailand, have reached a point in

their saving-investment cycles where they are becoming capital exporters themselves.) Yet even this amount is small by industrial country standards. During the past twenty-five years the accumulated (net) flows to developing countries were only 2 percent of the industrial countries' capital stock. These rough estimates would at most double the level of the average historical flows.

These capital flows, while having little impact on workers in industrial countries, could have much larger effects in developing countries. These estimates, assuming normal responses, imply a boost to GDP growth of 0.5 to 1 percent a year. But for workers in developing countries the discipline imposed by the mobility of savings—on macroeconomic policy, governance, and institutions—may even be more important than the direct gains involved.

• • •

The global capital market is making the differences between winners and losers much starker. The future will be brighter for Maria and Xiao Zhi if their governments manage to strike the right balance between fiscal prudence, reliance on markets, and stabilizing social policies. But capital outflows will tend to reduce investment and growth in those countries that fail to get the balance right—and even to exclude them from the economic mainstream altogether.

CHAPTER 10

International Migration

Like trade and capital flows, international labor flows offer great potential for benefit for both the home and the host country. Migrants are often more productive—and reduce labor costs—in the host country, and they send remittances to relatives back home, boosting incomes in the (usually poorer) home country. But migration also raises concerns. Not everyone will gain: unskilled workers in host countries are most likely to suffer as jobs are lost to immigrants or wages fall, and, as with capital movements, greater mobility—in this case of highly skilled workers—tends to reward success but punish domestic policy failures severely.

International migration remains much more politically charged than trade and capital flows. In the host countries public opposition to unskilled migrants has risen sharply,

exacerbated by domestic employment difficulties not necessarily of the migrants' causing. This chapter investigates whether migrants do take jobs from native workers and contribute to wage inequalities. Do they represent a net burden on government budgets? And can something be done to stop the exodus of trained workers from poorer countries?

Dimensions of migration

Throughout history there have been periods when migration has been an important economic and social safety valve, allowing labor to relocate to areas where it was more scarce. Usually the cost and difficulty of travel were a serious limitation, but a major break occurred in the twentieth century, when lower transportation costs made possible a

Most migrants live in developing countries, but a much larger share of the industrial countries' population is foreign-born.

Table 10.1 The world's foreign-born population by region

Region	Millions of persons		Percentage of total population	
	1965	1985	1965	1985
World	75.9	105.5	2.3	2.2
Industrial countries, Eastern Europe,				
* and the former Soviet Union*	31.0	47.4	3.5	4.5
Europe	15.6	23.0	3.5	4.7
Former Soviet Union	0.1	0.2	0.1	0.1
North America	12.7	20.4	6.0	7.8
Oceania	2.6	3.9	14.8	16.0
Low- and middle-income countries	45.0	58.1	1.9	1.5
Caribbean and Central America	0.5	0.9	2.0	2.7
China	0.3	0.3	0.0	0.0
East and Southeast Asia	7.6	7.5	1.9	1.2
North Africa and West Asia	5.5	13.4	4.0	5.7
Gulf Cooperation Council states	0.7	5.8	11.0	34.2
South America	5.4	5.6	2.4	1.5
South Asia	18.7	19.2	2.8	1.8
Sub-Saharan Africa	7.1	11.3	3.0	2.7

Source: United Nations 1994b.

sharp increase in labor mobility, even as the rise of the nation-state increased controls on migration. Today the number of both sending and receiving nations has increased—at least 125 million people now live outside their country of origin. Migrants today increasingly come from poor countries, and their stay in the host countries is becoming shorter. The number of highly skilled workers on the move has increased as well. There has also been a sharp rise in the number of refugees, a consequence of regional conflicts and the breakup of the old East-West order.

More than half the global flow of migrants is now between developing countries—examples include South Asians going to oil-rich countries in the Middle East and newly industrializing economies in East Asia, and relatively successful countries in Sub-Saharan Africa attracting workers from their poorer neighbors. Côte d'Ivoire, Nigeria, and South Africa have received about half of Africa's large migratory flow. But many migrants returned to their home countries during the 1980s, at a time when economic crisis led to antimigrant behavior. The demand for temporary migrants in the Gulf countries rose sharply during the 1970s and early 1980s before tapering off with the decline in oil prices after 1982. The 1991 Gulf war saw a radical change in the migrant population, with 1 million Egyptians leaving Iraq, 800,000 Yemenis leaving Saudi Arabia, and about 500,000 Palestinian and Jordanian workers being replaced by Asians and Egyptians in Kuwait. Most re-

cently there has been a rising demand for temporary workers in the successful Asian economies, particularly Japan, the Republic of Korea, and Malaysia. Fears of massive population movement following the dissolution of the Soviet Union have not materialized, either within the region or from East to West.

The flow of migrants to industrial countries has risen (Table 10.1), and its composition has shifted to developing country sources. In Australia, Canada, and the United States inflows from developing countries have risen slowly, reaching about 900,000 a year by 1993. In Western Europe large-scale labor recruitment began during the boom years of the 1960s. After the oil shock of 1973 and the ensuing recession, foreign workers were encouraged to return home. A dip in the early 1980s was soon followed by a rise in the growth of the foreign population to about 180,000 a year. Unlike that of the 1960s, however, this latest burst of growth is occurring in an environment of rising unemployment that is exacerbating social tensions and increasing xenophobia—both in the United States and across Europe.

Who gains and who loses?

Migration creates efficiency gains when workers move to where they are more productive. These gains can be widely distributed: to the migrants as higher earnings, to their countries of origin through remittances, and to the destination country through lower production costs. But not everyone necessarily gains, particularly if unskilled migrants displace native workers with similar skills. In the short to medium term, however, the effects depend on whether the migrants' skills complement or substitute for the skills of native workers and of those left behind.

Sending countries

Migration generally leads to important gains for the sending country, primarily through remittances. For some countries, remittances represent a sizable share of GNP—between 10 and 50 percent in Jordan, Lesotho, Yemen, and the West Bank and Gaza. Ratios of remittances to exports can reach as high as 25 to 50 percent—as in Bangladesh, Burkina Faso, Egypt, Greece, Jamaica, Malawi, Morocco, Pakistan, Portugal, Sri Lanka, Sudan, and Turkey. Because international wage differences are so large, the amounts remitted are often a multiple of what the migrants could have earned at home—about double in the case of Filipino and Korean emigrants, for example. But remittances tend to decline as migrants become integrated into the host country.

At the household level, migration decisions are often part of strategies to diversify risk. In war-torn Lebanon the outflow of skilled labor allowed those left behind to get by: remittances amounted to an estimated 50 percent of national income in 1980. In countries with active welfare policies, outmigration reduces budgetary pressures. The Egyptian employment guarantee scheme could not have worked in the 1970s without the massive migrations to the Gulf countries. In Puerto Rico the U.S. minimum wage law would have led to high unemployment in the absence of a pull effect from markets abroad (one-third of the labor force migrated to the United States).

The effect of migration on income inequality is complex. Because migrating is costly, migrants rarely come from among the poorest households. As a result, remittances often increase income inequality, as they have in Egypt and the Philippines. There are, however, offsetting effects—as migration networks develop and costs fall, poorer workers can afford to migrate. In a study of two Mexican villages, remittances were found to be equalizing in the village with the more established networks abroad but to increase inequality in the other. Remittances are usually found to be equalizing when second-round effects are considered—remittances increased investment in rural areas in Pakistan, boosting the demand for unskilled workers.

The fear of brain drain is receding in many countries where the supply of skills is no longer constrained by the lack of highly educated nationals. Brain drain remains a problem, however, where there are distortions in the labor market or in the education system. In some countries with stagnant modern sectors, generous subsidies to higher education are producing more graduates than the economy can absorb, imposing large fiscal costs and creating pressures to

migrate. Migration of skilled workers is also sometimes due to a lack of demand, as when government policies depress capital formation and the demand for skilled labor. On both these scores, many African countries have been hit hard. Like that for capital, the market for skills is becoming globalized, and this increases the costs associated with policy failures: the exodus of university professors, doctors, and other professionals in scarce supply has been enormous in Malawi, Sudan, Zaire, and Zambia. But migrants are likely to return when conditions at home improve. Indian returnees from Silicon Valley and similar areas in the United States, for example, have been the main force behind the growth of the software industry in India since liberalization.

Receiving countries

Receiving countries, particularly industrial economies, also usually gain from migration. Indeed, virtually all the labor flows to industrial countries have been deliberately initiated by them. Skilled migrants bring gains because of economies of agglomeration. Inflows of unskilled migrants benefit capital holders and the more skilled segment of the labor force, but they can hurt unskilled native workers by depressing their wages.

On the other hand, populist fears about migrants stealing jobs from natives are too simplistic. Social gains to host country workers are greatest when migrants bring characteristics that complement the existing national mix of skills. The United States, Canada, and Australia have economies and cultures based on migrants. Elsewhere, migrants and their descendants often constitute an important source of dynamism; examples are Chinese industrialists in Indonesia and Malaysia, Hong Kong businessmen in Canada, Indian and Lebanese entrepreneurs in Africa, and Jordanian and Palestinian civil servants in the oil-rich countries of the Gulf. Increasingly, workers migrate to fill unskilled manual jobs that native workers try to avoid—this type of migration accounts for perhaps as much as 70 percent of recent flows. In France and Germany unskilled migrants, mainly from North Africa and Turkey, make up 60 and 80 percent of total migrant flows, respectively. Palestinians in Israel, Pakistanis in the Gulf, Indonesians in Malaysia, and Bolivians in Argentina are other examples. Often these migrants fill jobs that would otherwise disappear, and even create jobs for natives. The production of palm oil and rubber in Malaysia would probably not survive without Indonesian workers. Migrants working in mines, as in South Africa, or on plantations, as in the Dominican Republic, Malaysia, and Spain, keep these industries from extinction in the face of competition from lower cost producers.

Unskilled migrants could hurt the native unskilled population if the demand for unskilled work that they generate indirectly—through their demand for goods and services—

is less than their own labor supply, since that would put downward pressure on the wages of unskilled workers. The pressure introduced by migrants on the unskilled segment of the labor market in the United States and Europe is comparable with that created by their trade with developing countries, augmenting the labor force by about 5 percent and affecting mainly unskilled workers. For example, one in four workers in the United States with less than twelve years of education was born outside the country: some studies estimate that migration explains about 30 percent of the rise in U.S. wage inequality over the past two decades. The effects of migration are also more potent than those of trade, in that migrants can enter nontradable sectors in which workers displaced by trade could otherwise find refuge.

Managing migration

Many countries have liberalized their trade, but nearly all stick to the notion that governments should manage migration. At first glance, the case for freer labor mobility seems as compelling from an economic standpoint as the case for free trade. Both lead to aggregate gains, but both can also create social dislocations that require a policy response. The main difference between the two seems to be noneconomic: large migrations disturb the way a society thinks of itself as a unified cultural or ethnic entity. Japan, for example, favors immigration by ethnic Japanese from Brazil, and Germany that of Germans from Eastern Europe, over entry by members of other ethnic groups.

But there are also economic considerations that make migration different from trade. One difference is that some migrants may seek to increase their incomes by moving, even if they are no more productive in the host than in the home country. An extreme example is the Gulf countries. Because of their oil reserves these countries tend to restrict ownership rights by not allowing migrants to become citizens. In industrial countries the fear is that migrants will be attracted by the spoils of the welfare state. Welfare states are especially vulnerable when they have poor neighbors: the United States faces pressure from Mexico and the Caribbean, France from the Maghreb countries, and Germany from Turkey. But while the evidence is mixed, there is scant indication that migrants constitute a large fiscal burden—perhaps precisely because most rich countries, especially those with developed welfare systems, try to exercise some control over the characteristics of the migrants they admit. All industrial countries have admitted migrants selectively, using instruments ranging from visa restrictions and border controls to legislated criteria for admission—age, wealth, education, national origin, and family ties. The strongest evidence for migrants acting as a budget drain is in the United States, a country in which unskilled migration has recently increased. On a per capita basis, the new

waves of migrants seem to be drawing more welfare benefits than previous cohorts and slightly more than the population as a whole.

Whereas these arguments support the case for controls on the quality of migrants, other reasons are usually offered to support quantitative restraints. The pervasiveness of international poverty and falling transportation and communications costs mean that free labor mobility could lead to large immigrations to rich countries, producing equally large social dislocations there. These effects would be much larger than those from open trade, and they would be more diffused, affecting the services sector as well as the tradable-goods sector. The redistributions required to preserve social stability would be massive and costly. Targeting of special industries, through farm income support programs, for example, would have to give way to more wholesale and less efficient policies. In that case the alternative of slowing migration to the rate at which labor scarcities appear, as native skills get upgraded, may make sense. Europe applied this type of policy during the reconstruction boom of the 1960s.

But policies to restrict migration are a tricky matter. They may result in bad outcomes of their own if they encourage illegality and exploitation. The main challenge is finding ways to ration what is an attractive alternative for many would-be migrants without creating incentives for illegal activities. The United States has the greatest number of illegal immigrants—perhaps as many as 4 million—because of its long border with Mexico. Western Europe has about 3 million, mainly from Africa. Illegal migrants are in the most precarious position because they can be deported at any time, which creates incentives for their exploitation by unscrupulous employers. When labor markets are competitive, as in the United States, part of the scarcity rent can be paid up front: for example, illegal Chinese immigrants must often provide three years of unpaid work to a middleman in return for passage, yet the enormous wage differentials still provide incentives to migrate.

It is rarely feasible to use migration as a tool to fine tune the business cycle. Temporary work arrangements do provide flexibility from the host country's perspective and can be desirable from the migrant's viewpoint if the alternative is illegality. But ensuring that temporary workers remain temporary requires rapid rotation, and that involves costs in terms of management time and the loss of country-specific or job-specific skills. Some successful programs rely on self-management by migrants. The demand for Filipino nurses, Sri Lankan maids, and Korean construction workers has risen since organizations (sometimes backed by the state) have begun to manage temporary migration on a more formal basis. A few countries—for example, Switzerland and the Gulf countries—have succeeded in keeping temporary workers temporary, but more often such schemes have tended to become permanent, as they have in

France and Germany. To reduce the attachment of migrants to the host country (and the urge to bring dependents along), several countries encourage rotation of migrants. In Saudi Arabia, for example, the cost of a work permit rises sharply when it is renewed.

• • •

Migration is usually beneficial to both sending and receiving countries. But it is unlikely to become as important as trade and capital movements as a form of economic interaction between richer and poorer countries. Some level of migratory flows is mutually beneficial, but unrestricted migration of unskilled workers is likely to be counterpro-

ductive. Possible economic costs to unskilled native workers and cultural resistance mean that migration will have to be managed to ensure its own sustainability. But managing migratory flows is difficult because restrictions can create scarcity rents that encourage illegal flows. Migrants' basic human rights should be protected, and they should be subject to the same labor laws and regulations as citizens. In addition, in many countries migrants do not have access to social services and other entitlements at par with citizens. At the margin, temporary programs can be useful both in stabilizing the host country labor market and in reducing the pressure for illegal migration.

PART THREE

How Should Governments Intervene in Labor Markets?

GOVERNMENTS INTERVENE in the workplace and in the lives of workers in many ways. But there is a growing debate over whether such interventions are really in workers' best interest. One side calls for aggressive action to protect workers, through regulations on minimum wages, restrictions on firing, and the like. The other side argues against such meddling, because it discourages job creation and helps only a privileged subset of workers, while hurting or, at best, neglecting the most vulnerable. This part of the Report analyzes the role of government in labor markets. Chapter 11 examines labor standards and their impact. Chapter 12 reviews the role of labor unions and their relation to government. Chapter 13 considers policies designed to deal with income insecurity. And Chapter 14 takes up the role of government itself as an employer.

CHAPTER 11

Public Policy and Labor Standards

L ABOR MARKETS ARE DIFFERENT FROM MARkets for commodities. The wages they set and the employment conditions they determine profoundly affect the quality of life of workers and their families, often in ways that may seem harsh or unfair. Not surprisingly, societies, and the governments that represent them, are heavily involved in labor markets the world over. Nearly all governments set workplace standards, such as minimum wages and special protections for working women and minorities. Standards differ in their objectives (Table 11.1). Some aim at protecting vulnerable workers and eliminating injustices, others at helping the market work better. Not all legislated standards achieve their objectives, however. Some end up protecting a group of relatively well-off workers at the cost of limiting employment in the modern sector. In transitional economies some standards introduce rigidities and hinder the redeployment of labor. In many developing countries with limited administrative capacity, standards are often unenforced.

How should governments determine workplace standards? And is linking standards to international trade an efficient way of improving enforcement in low- and middle-income countries? This chapter analyzes the rationale for government intervention in labor markets, the costs and benefits of different types of legislated standards, and the case for international action to improve enforcement.

Why do societies intervene in labor markets?

Societies intervene when unfettered labor markets fail to deliver the most efficient outcomes, or when they want to move market outcomes into line with their preferences and values. Four reasons are often given for intervention: uneven market power, discrimination, insufficient information, and inadequate insurance against risk.

All four reasons raise considerations of efficiency and equity. When market power is uneven, it is usually workers who find themselves in a weak position relative to firms, unable to protect themselves from unjust treatment. This also leads to efficiency losses as workers become less likely to invest in firm-specific skills. Uneven market power becomes an even greater problem for workers belonging to groups that traditionally have had little voice in society— children, women, and ethnic and religious minorities. Dis-

crimination leads to market outcomes that are not only inequitable but inefficient: it limits the contribution of women and minority groups to economic development. Inefficiencies increase when workers and some employers are poorly informed about their work environment, particularly in regard to health and safety hazards. Finally, workers and their families are typically unable to insure themselves adequately against the risk of income loss due to unemployment, disability, or old age.

Societies usually respond to these market failures or injustices in three ways: by establishing informal arrangements, by empowering labor unions to bargain on behalf of workers, and by direct government legislation or intervention. Informal labor market arrangements can be very effective. Although labor contracts rarely offset basic differences in wealth and power between employers and employees, in traditional societies employers usually respect certain norms of justice and avoid exploitative behavior, or face social sanctions. Most informal employment contracts involve some form of risk sharing. For example, sharecropping, in which landless peasants share their output with the landlord, is a common risk-sharing arrangement in Asia and Africa. Informal arrangements can also help provide income security. Private saving is an important mechanism for dealing with risks, such as unemployment, that are not easily insured against. For the poor who have little or no savings, private transfers between households—within extended families or local communities—are often the recourse.

Informal arrangements are by far the dominant solution to labor market problems in low- and middle-income countries. As Table 11.2 shows, over 80 percent of workers in low-income countries, and more than 40 percent of those in middle-income countries are nonwage workers who typically operate in informal and rural labor markets, beyond the reach of trade unions and direct government intervention. Even these figures may overestimate the number of workers covered by formal sector employment protection. Weak administrative capacity and restrictions on trade union freedom mean that, in many countries, labor regulations are not enforced even in large urban firms. But informal arrangements are intrinsically limited. They tend to break down as enterprises grow and as the social and communal links between workers and employers diminish.

Governments intervene in labor markets in a variety of ways.

Table 11.1 Types of government intervention in labor markets

Type of intervention	Specific guarantees and policies	Examples
Establishment and protection of workers' rights	Right to associate and organize	Workers can form labor unions.
	Right to bargain collectively	Unions can negotiate wages and working conditions with employers.
	Right to engage in industrial action (strike)	Workers can strike or use other nonviolent means to achieve their demands.
Protection for the vulnerable	Minimum working age	Children under fifteen may not be employed; the minimum age of work is eighteen if the work is hazardous to health, safety, or morals.
	Equality of wages and employment opportunities	No worker can be paid a lower wage than others or be excluded from employment for reasons of gender, race, religion, ethnic background, national origin, or sexual orientation. Affirmative action may be used for disadvantaged groups.
	Special provisions for women	Women workers need to be provided with maternity leave; they may not be compelled to work during the night.
Establishment of minimum compensation for work	Minimum wages	Workers are to be paid a minimum hourly wage.
	Minimum nonwage benefits and overtime pay	Workers are to be provided with housing or medical benefits, a minimum number of holidays in a year, and specified overtime wages for work beyond the maximum hours.
Assurance of decent working conditions	Minimum occupational health and safety	Workplaces must have proper light and ventilation, and workers must have protection from hazardous activity.
	Maximum hours of work	Workers cannot ordinarily be required to work more than a certain number of hours in a week; they must have at least one rest day a week.
Provision of income security	Social security	Workers who are out of work because of disability, layoff, or old age are entitled to transfer payments based on their prior work experience.
	Job security and severance pay	Workers have some rights not to be dismissed at will, and a right to compensation when laid off.
	Public works	Temporary employment is provided for those willing to work in times of weak labor demand.

A key problem in modern firms is that of coordinating the actions of a large number of workers to bargain with employers and improve the quality of their workplace. The organization of labor, usually into trade unions, is a response to this problem of collective action. Collective bargaining by labor unions can help solve problems of unequal market power, discrimination, and insufficient information. Unions provide their members with important services, negotiating on their behalf for better working conditions, protecting them from unfair treatment, and dividing the cost of obtaining information among a large number of workers.

Governments have an important role even where there are worker organizations. They set the rules within which formal economic transactions are consummated. For informal employment these rules are usually implicit, flowing from social custom and the personal character of the employment relationship, whereas formal sector employment is governed by an explicit legal framework that provides the basis for either individual or collective contracts. The rules governing formal labor markets usually define the rights of workers, unions, and employers; the conditions for collective bargaining; and a system for settling disputes (see Chapter 12). Governments also intervene directly in the labor market to achieve particular social goals. Some of the more common interventions include bans on child labor, protection for women and minority workers, setting of minimum wages, and legislation on workplace safety and health standards.

Employment for wages is a less important share of the total in poorer countries.

Table 11.2 Wage employment as a share of total employment, by sector and country income group
(percentage of total)

Sector	Low-income	Middle-income	High-income
Agriculture	3.6	25.6	38.2
Industry	29.8	76.7	89.1
Services	46.4	68.2	85.6
All sectors	17.1	57.4	84.4

Note: Data are projected from a sample of countries in each income group. See Appendix tables for countries and years.
Source: ILO 1986 with ILO data updates.

Child labor

Most countries have laws against child labor. Yet perhaps 100 million or more children in the world below the age of fifteen participate in substantial economic activity at some point during the year. The United Nations Children's Fund (UNICEF) calculates that, in 1991, 80 million children between ten and fourteen years old were engaged in work so arduous for so much of the day that it interfered with their development.

• • •

A ten-year-old girl in rural Maharashtra State, India, attends primary school. Every afternoon after school she and her two brothers help their father with farm work. The work interferes with their studies, and her elder brother had to repeat seventh grade. Without their work, however, the family could not afford to send them to school.

• • •

A thirteen-year-old boy working in a Bogotá quarry lives with his parents in a squatter settlement and has never been to school. His job is to separate rocks by size after they have been extracted by bulldozers and explosives and pulverized by mechanical crushers. His parents argue that without his wages the family would starve and that he is better off in the quarry than on the streets, where he would fall into a life of crime and other dangerous activities.

• • •

Some types of child labor are considered more harmful than others. The girl in Maharashtra and her brothers are representative of the vast majority of working children in the world. They are unpaid helpers on the family farm. Most people would not condemn such work provided the children continue to attend school. The boy in Bogotá is one of a minority of child laborers engaged in casual wage work in urban areas. But most people imagine a child like him when they hear the term "child labor," evoking dis-

turbing images reminiscent of the "dark Satanic mills" of the industrial revolution.

Causes of child labor

A high prevalence of child labor is linked to poverty and to poor quality or availability of education. Children in poor families work because the family needs the extra income, especially if the parents' major source of revenue is uncertain. Surveys in rural India indicate that poor households, with no savings or current assets and unable to borrow, have no choice but to send their children out to work, to minimize the potential impact of a parent's loss of a job or of a failed harvest on the family farm. As parents' incomes rise they are able to send their children to school rather than to work. In Egypt a 10 percent increase in mothers' wages was found to result in a 15 percent decline in labor among children ages twelve to fourteen, and a 27 percent decline among six- to eleven-year-olds. In India the same increase would lower girls' labor force participation by 9 to 10 percent.

Low-cost schooling of good quality can reduce child labor. The Indian state of Kerala provides an example. Around 25 percent of the state's budget goes to education—compared with an average of 17 percent for other Indian states. The state has achieved excellent results. One hundred percent of pupils entering first grade complete the fifth grade, and the state has twice the national literacy rate. Access to education in Kerala is unparalleled in India. Anthropological research in a Kerala fishing village indicates that school attendance does not eliminate child labor, but it does prevent its worst forms, which can be found elsewhere in India. Work can often be coordinated with the school day. This research found that poor village children do attend school but continue to work part-time to help support their families. Their paid out-of-school activities typically include looking after smaller children, foraging, petty trading, domestic chores, and fishing.

Toward eradicating child labor

National legislation and international conventions banning child labor have symbolic value as an expression of society's desire to eradicate this practice. But they cannot deliver results unless accompanied by measures to shift the balance of incentives away from child labor and toward education. The most important ways in which governments can shift this balance are by providing a safety net to protect the poor, expanding opportunities for quality education, and gradually increasing institutional capacity to enforce legislated bans. Programs that provide income security for poor households, such as food-for-work or other public works programs, will have beneficial effects on child labor. Measures to reduce the cost of school attendance (subsidies, construction of schools closer to children's homes) and improve the quality of education (changes in curricula, more and better teachers) could also help. As the incidence of poverty falls and education improves, child labor will decline. That in turn will make enforcement of legislated bans easier, starting with such universally abhorred forms of child labor as prostitution and hazardous work.

Cooperation between local communities, nongovernmental organizations (NGOs), and government can also help. An example of such cooperation involves the deep-sea fishing industry on the Philippine island of Cebu, where large numbers of young boy divers were being hired in an extremely dangerous occupation called Muro-ami fishing. The local community refrained from acting against this practice because parents had no other way to sustain their families. The initiative for change came from national civic groups based in Manila, which applied pressure on the government and mobilized the community. A special Muro-ami task force was created, including representatives of both government and NGOs. Under pressure, employers agreed not to recruit boys less than eighteen years old. To obtain the community's support, and especially that of the children's families, priority was given to creating alternative sources of income through the establishment of soapmaking, weaving, and pig-rearing projects, and the extension of soft loans and training to the boys' mothers.

Standards affecting working women and minorities

Women and ethnic minorities are also protected by special regulations in many countries. Standards to help these workers can be divided into two groups. The first provide women with special rights and protections in the workplace because of their role in bearing and raising children. An example is maternity benefits. The second seek to end discrimination in the labor market by establishing equal pay for work of equal value or prohibiting the exclusion of women or minorities from certain jobs. The use of antidiscrimination standards is not limited to the protection of women workers—in many countries they also cover ethnic and religious minorities.

Workplace protection for women

Nearly all countries have legislation establishing standard periods of maternity leave and other special benefits for women. Typically, such legislation requires employers to provide these benefits to female workers, effectively increasing the cost of hiring them. So there is a risk that legislation aimed at protecting women will end up depressing their wages or discouraging their employment. Sometimes this type of standard has other unwelcome effects. For example, the ILO's committee of experts noted that many Austrian firms employ young women only on fixed-term contracts in order to avoid paying maternity benefits. Some garment manufacturers in Bangladesh hire young women only on a

daily, casual basis for the same reason. Some firms in Latin America take more extreme precautions, requiring women to produce medical certificates attesting to their sterilization before hiring them.

Women in developing countries are often overrepresented in the informal sector (Table 11.3) and are so eager for jobs in the modern sector that they willingly ignore an employer's failure to meet government-legislated standards. Many are not even aware that the standards exist: a survey of female garment workers in Bangladesh found that very few knew that they had a legal right to paid maternity leave. Yet these workers are much better off with jobs in the modern sector than without them—their wages, although low by formal sector standards, are more than double what they could earn in the informal sector or in rural areas. Perhaps more important, having a stable source of income can change their status within the household. Female rural workers in Bangladesh work 5 to 30 percent longer hours than do men, because they have household responsibilities in addition to their work in the fields. These women rarely have a say in the allocation of household expenditures. But surveys indicate that the husbands of garment workers contribute 1.3 to 3.7 hours a day to household work, and that 57 percent of female workers determine how their own salaries are spent. It appears, therefore, that women as a group gain much more from better access to modern sector jobs than from special standards to protect those who already have good employment.

One way to provide women workers with special benefits, without risk of reducing their wages or the number

Women workers tend to be concentrated in the informal sector.

Table 11.3 Shares of men and women workers in nonwage employment
(percentage of total)

Country	Year	Men	Women
Bolivia	1991	42	70
Cape Verde	1990	42	54
Egypt	1989	46	74
El Salvador	1991	28	48
Ghana	1989	69	92
Indonesia	1989	70	79
Korea, Rep. of	1991	38	43
Pakistan	1992	66	77
Peru	1991	39	55
Tanzania	1988	84	95
Thailand	1989	71	76
Tunisia	1989	36	51
Turkey	1991	55	80

Source: ILO, various years; World Bank data.

employed, is for society as a whole to bear the cost of those benefits rather than require those employers who hire women to pay the cost alone. This is the approach adopted in many of the former centrally planned economies. Under such a system maternity benefits are usually financed through a payroll tax—although they could also be financed from general revenues. Thus the link between hiring a female worker and paying the cost of providing her with special benefits is broken, removing an important disincentive to hiring women. As long as the payroll tax is the same for all workers, this arrangement in effect transfers resources from men to women. But it will often pose difficulties in practice, especially for low-income countries. Administrative requirements are high, and there are significant risks of abuse. Moreover, a scheme financed by general revenues would partly finance benefits for women employees in the formal sector at the expense of poorer men and women in rural and informal work.

Antidiscrimination policies

DISCRIMINATION AGAINST WOMEN. Standards designed to protect women from job discrimination are often difficult to enforce. Enforcing a standard of equal remuneration for work of equal value, not merely work of the same kind, requires a sophisticated job evaluation system. This has proved very difficult even in industrial countries and is a virtual impossibility for many low- and middle-income countries with limited expertise and resources. In any case, unless accompanied by a prohibition on discrimination in hiring, equal-remuneration legislation is unlikely to have much of an impact. Governments should not give up efforts to end discrimination in the workplace. But the focus of those efforts will need to change, with greater emphasis on policies to improve women's access to modern sector jobs—for example, through merit-based hiring of more women in the public sector.

Egypt provides an example of how government employment policies can help improve women's labor market situation. Although Egypt's policy of guaranteeing employment for graduates has led to an unsustainable growth in government employment and overstaffing, it may have had a positive impact on the role of women in the labor market. Like their counterparts in many other countries, women in Egypt have very limited access to modern sector jobs: the unemployment rate for women with a secondary education or above was estimated in 1988 at 31 percent, compared with 10 percent for men. Moreover, their wages in the private sector are only about half those of comparable males. Public employment policies help offset the impact of this discrimination in two ways. First, government provides more employment opportunities for women than does the nonagricultural private sector. In 1986, 26 percent of all government employees were women, versus only 8 percent in the private sector. Moreover, nearly 95 percent of female government workers have at least completed secondary school. Second, women in government jobs are paid the same as men.

OTHER TYPES OF DISCRIMINATION. Governments also set standards to eliminate ethnic and religious discrimination. Countries as different as the United States and India are attempting to eradicate discrimination from their labor markets. The U.S. Civil Rights Act of 1964 outlawed all forms of discrimination in employment, including discrimination based on gender or ethnicity. Enforcement depends upon lawsuits against discriminators, which can be quite difficult given the high cost of litigation and the fact that women or minorities excluded from certain jobs rarely are in a position to file a complaint or even know that they have been discriminated against. These difficulties have given rise to affirmative action plans, which focus on results and try to increase the proportion of minorities and women employed in certain positions. However, affirmative action is usually too costly and difficult to implement in the private sector. In the United States, affirmative action plans—generally specifying numerical targets and timetables for hiring—are required of firms with federal government contracts. The Indian government has an affirmative action program in the public sector favoring lower castes. The impact of affirmative action is still being debated. Opponents argue that it generates a backlash against minorities and enmity between social groups. Proponents, however, consider it useful for getting government and its private contractors to hire more women and minority workers.

Minimum wages

Whether or not to set a minimum wage remains one of the most controversial labor market policy dilemmas governments face. Proponents believe that, appropriately applied, minimum wage legislation can raise the incomes of the most poverty-stricken workers at little or no cost to overall employment. Opponents argue that minimum wages make things worse for poor workers by raising production costs in the formal sector and reducing employment. More workers are then forced to seek jobs in the unregulated informal sector, pushing the wages of the working poor lower.

Both sides are partly right. Whether minimum wages have an overall positive or negative impact depends on their effect on employment, which in turn depends on the market structure, the level at which the minimum is set, and government's ability to enforce it. In a fully competitive labor market a binding minimum wage will always reduce employment. But if employers have some market power, a small increase in the minimum wage could actually raise employment. Of course, if the minimum is too high, employers with market power will choose to hire fewer workers. In low- and middle-income countries, raising the minimum wage often increases employers' and workers' incentive to avoid it, so that there is little effect on employment—or on wages.

Empirical evidence and country experiences

Evidence exists to support either side of the debate. High minimum wages for male workers in Mauritius's export processing zone prior to 1984 may have discouraged their employment. The government eliminated the male minimum wage in December 1984, after noticing that demand for female workers in the zone (for whom the minimum wage was lower) exceeded supply, while male unemployment was high. Male recruitment rose sharply, and more than 95 percent of workers recruited in January 1985 were paid less than the former minimum. On the other hand, recent evidence from the United States supports the view that small increases in the minimum do not hurt employment. The 1992 increase in the minimum wage in the state of New Jersey did not reduce employment in the fast-food industry. Similarly, a cross-state analysis found that the 1990 and 1991 increases in the federal minimum wage did not hurt teenage employment.

It is unlikely that increases in minimum wages would have the same impact on employment in low- and middle-income countries as in the United States. In many countries the minimum is already too high relative to the country's income and to other wages in the economy, so that even a small increase would lower employment. The level of the minimum wage relative to the average income tends to be higher in poorer countries, and to fall as national income rises (Figure 11.1). Some of Bangladesh's sectoral minimum wages are more than double GNP per capita, whereas in Canada, for example, the minimum is only one-fourth of GNP per capita. In Russia the ratio of the minimum wage to the average wage fell from more than 40 percent in 1990 to around 20 percent in 1993. In Kazakhstan the ratio fell from nearly 50 percent to around 20 percent over the same period.

Distributional impact

Minimum wages may help protect the most poverty-stricken workers in industrial countries, but they clearly do not in developing nations. Those affected by minimum wage provisions in low- and middle-income countries are rarely the most needy. Most of the real poor operate in rural and informal markets in such countries and are not protected by minimum wages. The workers whom minimum wage legislation tries to protect—urban formal workers—already earn much more than the less favored majority. Sometimes the differences are extreme—an urban construction worker in Côte d'Ivoire earns 8.8 times the rural wage rate, and a steelworker in India earns 8.4 times the rural wage (Table 11.4). And inasmuch as minimum wage

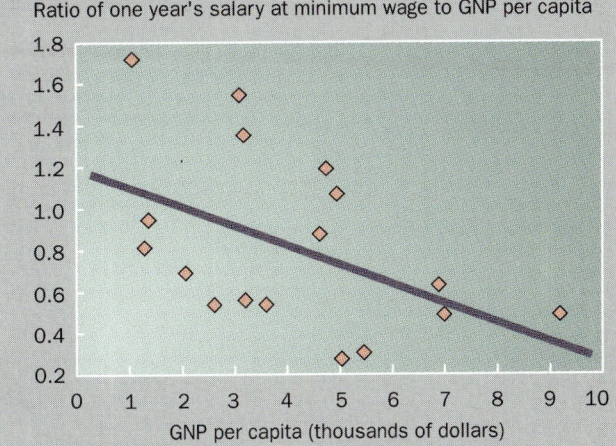

The relative level of the minimum wage declines as income rises.

Ratio of one year's salary at minimum wage to GNP per capita

GNP per capita (thousands of dollars)

Figure 11.1 The minimum wage and GNP per capita. The sample consists of seventeen developing countries. Years vary by country from 1988 to 1992. Data are in international prices. Source: World Bank data.

and other regulations discourage formal employment by increasing wage and nonwage costs, they hurt the poor who aspire to formal employment. Hence it is difficult to argue for minimum wages in low- and middle-income countries on equity grounds.

Enforceability

Whatever their potential impact, minimum wages in many countries are often not enforced (Figure 11.2). Household surveys indicate that 16 percent of Mexico's full-time male workers and 66 percent of female workers were paid less than the minimum wage in 1988. In Morocco half the firms surveyed in 1986 paid their unskilled workers below the minimum. Few low- and middle-income nations have the administrative capacity to police minimum wage regulations, especially when the minimum is set so high as to discourage hiring—creating strong incentives for employers and workers alike to ignore the regulations. Employers clearly benefit from a lower minimum, which reduces costs. Workers will also gain as long as the wage being offered is above what they could earn in informal sector activities.

When economic and financial crises hit the developing world in the 1980s, most governments let real minimum wages fall rapidly. Between 1980 and 1987 the real minimum wage in Mexico tumbled 43.2 percent and average real wages fell 43.3 percent; meanwhile Chile's real mini-

Urban wages are much higher than rural wages in many developing countries.

Table 11.4 Ratios of wages in selected urban industrial occupations to rural wages

Country	Iron and steel laborer	Construction laborer
Cameroon	1.52	1.52
Costa Rica	1.09	1.10
Côte d'Ivoire	3.95	8.80
Fiji	1.46	1.17
India	8.43	1.70
Indonesia	1.50	1.34
Jordan	1.32	1.23
Kenya	1.37	1.87
Peru	1.63	1.43
Philippines	1.96	1.67
Trinidad and Tobago	2.19	1.54
Tunisia	1.79	1.56

Source: ILO and World Bank data.

Small firms often disregard labor regulations.

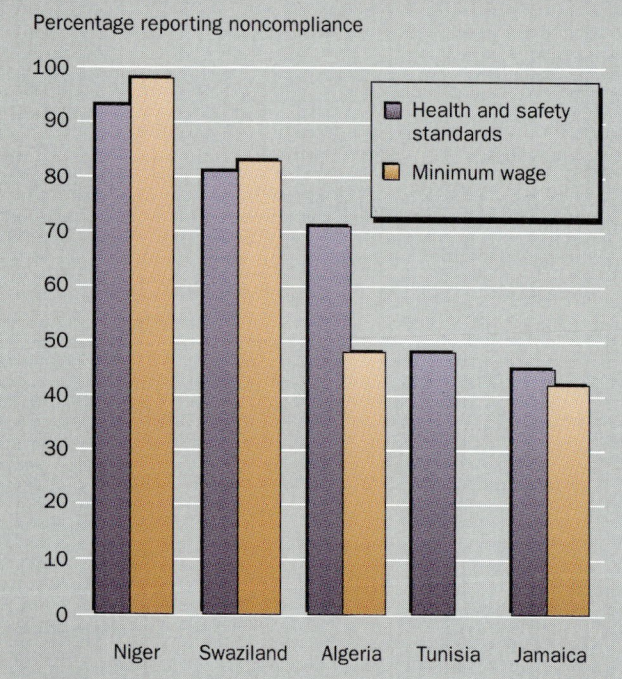

Percentage reporting noncompliance

- Health and safety standards
- Minimum wage

Niger Swaziland Algeria Tunisia Jamaica

Figure 11.2 Compliance by microenterprises with national labor standards. Data on minimum wage compliance in Tunisia were unavailable. Source: Morrisson, Lecomte, and Oudin 1994.

mum wage plunged 42.4 percent, but its average real wage fell only 6 percent. In Kenya between 1980 and 1986 real minimum wages fell 41.2 percent and the average real wage 22.8 percent. Falling real wages have welfare costs, but since employers and workers ignore minimum wage regulation when jobs are at stake, attempting to hold the line on minimum wages would have been fruitless. Similarly, in most transitional economies minimum wages have fallen faster than average wages and are unlikely to have impeded labor reallocation. Discussions of minimum wages in transitional economies focus on their impact on the process of economic restructuring and the reallocation of labor from declining sectors to more dynamic ones. Minimum wage regulations could slow adjustments in relative wages and distort market signals during transitions. In practice, however, these regulations did not hinder the adjustment process, especially in the former Soviet Union, because all the transitional economies substantially lowered the real minimum wage.

Safety and health standards

Workers often encounter health risks on the job. The World Health Organization has estimated that nearly 3 percent of the global burden of disease is caused each year by preventable injuries and deaths in high-risk occupations, and by chronic illness stemming from exposure to toxic substances, noise, and hazardous work patterns. According to the ILO, the cost of occupational injuries and deaths in the industrial countries is between 1 and 4 percent of GNP. For low- and middle-income countries these costs are surely greater still, because occupational accident rates are higher. Rates of fatal occupational injuries among construction workers in Guatemala are six times those in Switzerland. Fatalities among workers in the transport industry in Kenya are nine times those in Denmark. And a manufacturing worker in Pakistan is nearly eight times more likely to die in an accident on the job than a worker in France.

• • •

In 1994 a lawsuit was filed in Texas on behalf of 16,000 farm laborers who claimed that exposure to a pesticide proven to cause reproductive problems had made them sterile. In Costa Rica banana workers and their families suffer from an array of medical problems ranging from cancer to higher than average rates of birth defects; health experts argue that these problems are caused by the potent pesticides used on plantations. The World Health Organization estimates that more than 1 million agricultural workers across Latin America are poisoned every year and that 10,000 die from exposure to chemicals.

• • •

On March 25, 1911, a fire swept through the Triangle Shirtwaist Company in the Greenwich Village section of New York City. One hundred and forty-six workers, mostly women, died in a burning building whose doors had been locked to keep employees at their work. A similar accident occurred eighty-two years later, on May 11, 1993, in a toy factory west of Bangkok. One hundred and two workers died, eighty-seven of them women.

Agricultural and other informal sector workers

Most workers in low- and middle-income countries operate in rural and informal markets where legislated labor standards are usually useless for dealing with their health and safety concerns. Societies try to improve health and safety conditions for agricultural and informal sector workers through general policies aimed at improving the overall environment within which they have to work, rather than through labor legislation. The use of dangerous chemicals in agriculture, for example, is usually best controlled by regulations affecting their import or production. Similarly, efforts at providing clean drinking water in rural areas and improving sanitary conditions in villages and urban slums can have a profound impact on the welfare of the majority of workers in low- and middle-income countries.

The Onchocerciasis Control Program in West Africa is one of the most successful programs ever implemented for improving the health standards of rural workers. Onchocerciasis, or river blindness, has long been described as a "plague upon the land" because of its devastating impact on rural workers' health and well-being. Twenty years ago the sight of abandoned villages in West Africa often meant that river blindness had struck and the farmers had fled to unaffected areas. Eradicating onchocerciasis was viewed as the best way to improve rural workers' health standards.

Started in 1974 by seven African countries—later expanded to eleven—with support from over twenty bilateral and multilateral donors, the onchocerciasis program has now succeeded in eliminating the disease-causing parasites in the human population throughout more than 60 percent of the eleven-country area. The program protects more than 30 million people from contracting the disease. Roughly one and a half million people who were infected but not yet blinded have completely recovered. It is estimated that by 1995 the program had prevented over 250,000 more cases of blindness; had freed 25 million hectares of land from the disease, making it available for resettlement and cultivation; and had made 1 million worker-years of additional productive labor available.

Formal sector workers

Nearly all countries legislate minimum safety and health standards aimed at protecting formal sector workers. They are usually justified on the grounds that employers are aware of workplace dangers but workers may not be, and even if workers are aware of occupational risks, they may accept dangerous jobs because they have few or no alternative employment opportunities. Some arguments for standards thus fall into the category of preventing workers from consciously doing harm to themselves by agreeing to dangerous work. Legislated standards are also defended on the grounds that there are externalities to the risks that workers take—for example, if the costs of medical treatment of those who are injured or fall ill are subsidized by taxpayers.

One difficulty in setting standards is how to determine their level or stringency. Reducing hazards in the workplace is costly, and typically the greater the reduction, the more it costs. Moreover, the costs of compliance often fall largely on employees through lower wages or reduced employment. As a result, setting standards too high can actually lower workers' welfare, but setting them too low may fail to deal adequately with the risk that workers face. The appropriate level is therefore that at which the costs are commensurate with the value that informed workers place on improved working conditions and reduced risk. There is no magic formula. In many countries the determination of this level involves consultations between government, employers, and workers.

Enforcement of health and safety standards is often a problem, particularly in small enterprises in low- and middle-income countries (Figure 11.2). Employers sometimes try to avoid health and safety regulations, and workers in need of a job may accept the risk and tacitly agree to ignore the regulations. In a survey of health and safety conditions in the Philippines, 81 percent of inspected establishments violated one or more standards. In many countries enforcement is so weak that employers have little incentive to comply. Labor departments in low- and middle-income countries often lack the personnel and equipment for regular inspections, and when inspections do occur, they can be occasions for collecting bribes rather than enforcing the law. In 1984 there were only fifty staff members assigned to conduct inspections and enforce labor standards in all of metropolitan Manila, covering nearly 30,000 enterprises.

Toward better enforcement

As a nation's income rises, it is able to devote more resources to building up administrative capacity to ensure that workplace standards are respected. Poorer countries will be unable to enforce labor standards at the same level as richer economies, so they usually need to focus their limited administrative capacity where it will do the most good. For example, standards on the accessibility of fire escapes are simple to develop and monitor. Recent tragedies in Thailand and China might have been avoided if those standards had been enforced. Providing information to workers—and to worker organizations—on the risks of certain toxic chemicals and other workplace hazards is also relatively cheap and can be very effective in helping workers negotiate for better working conditions.

Labor unions in the United States play an important role in enforcing health and safety standards.

Table 11.5 Enforcement of health and safety standards in unionized and nonunionized firms in the United States, by firm size

Firm size (number of employees)	Probability of inspection (percent)		Percentage of inspections with employee walkaround[a]	
	Union	Nonunion	Union	Nonunion
1–99	6	14	47.8	2.7
100–249	37	22	59.3	2.6
250–499	51	19	63.7	2.6
500+	95	16	69.8	3.7

Note: Data are for 1985.
a. In a walkaround, employees accompany government inspectors during a tour of the workplace.
Source: Weil 1991.

Trade unions and other civic organizations can play an important role in enforcing health and safety standards. Individual workers may find it too costly to obtain information on health and safety risks on their own, and they usually want to avoid antagonizing their employers by insisting that standards be respected. The benefits from compliance with standards are not limited to any individual but are enjoyed by all workers. A union can spread the cost of obtaining information on health and safety issues among all workers, bargain with employers on the level of standards to be observed, and monitor their enforcement without putting any individual worker at risk of losing his or her job.

Studies in industrial countries indicate that the role of labor unions in ensuring compliance with health and safety standards is often an important one. If trade union monitoring has a positive impact on compliance in industrial countries where public enforcement capacity is already high, their contribution could be even greater in low- and middle-income countries with weaker administrations. A 1991 study, using U.S. data, found that unions dramatically increased enforcement of the Occupational Safety and Health Act in the manufacturing sector. Unionized firms had a higher probability of having a health and safety inspection, and their inspections tended to be more probing, as employees exercised their "walkaround rights"—the right to accompany a government inspector during a workplace tour (Table 11.5).

Labor standards and international trade

Some members of the international community argue that the present system of developing and monitoring labor standards is inadequate and needs to be complemented with linkages between labor standards and multilateral trade or lending agreements. Countries that fail to meet a minimum set of standards would sooner or later face sanctions in the form of trade restrictions or reduced access to capital. This chapter has concluded that some standards do make sense within countries. But linking them to international transactions—trade or financial—raises two complex sets of issues: Which standards are basic, and which are a function of the stage of development? And what are the costs of such linkages, both for the economic development of the countries targeted by sanctions and for the workers whom sanctions are intended to help? These are important issues, especially since some of the pressure for sanctions comes from protectionist groups.

Labor conditions, like poverty reduction and overall development, have always been important areas of international concern. Until now, international action to improve labor standards in the developing world has focused on support of domestic efforts, especially through the work of the ILO. Countries have adopted various ILO conventions and have set a wide range of workplace standards, whose implementation the ILO has monitored. But most low- and middle-income countries are unable to enforce all the standards that they have introduced into their legal systems. And in many cases the standards are set so high—at levels more appropriate for a rich country—that even if implemented they could have untoward effects on employment and economic growth.

Failure to ensure implementation of a minimal set of labor standards in poorer nations has prompted several groups to call for international sanctions, to force low- and middle-income countries to monitor compliance with their own labor regulations. Conclusion of the NAFTA accord depended on Mexico's agreement to better enforce its own standards (environmental as well as labor). The international labor confederations, many NGOs, France, and the United States all argued for linking labor standards to the Uruguay Round agreement and for addressing them within the new World Trade Organization.

Proponents of linking labor standards and international transactions distinguish between core standards, which they argue are basic rights and should be subject to linkage, and standards that should rise with development and need not be linked to international transactions. Core standards usually include freedom of association and the right to collective bargaining, the elimination of forced labor (the only area already addressed in GATT), exploitative forms of child labor, and discrimination. It is argued that these basic human rights are absolute moral concerns and that the international community should exert trade pressure on countries that violate them, because those violations reduce the legitimacy of the trading system. Standards whose level typically rises with development include minimum wages and health standards. Many advocates of linkage acknowledge that using trade sanctions to raise this second group of standards could seriously reduce world trade and may actually hurt the very people it aims to help.

Countries that do not respect core standards pose a serious dilemma for the international community. Trade sanctions against them could be justified on moral grounds—and on economic grounds, for example because free trade unions bargaining collectively with employers can help ensure that labor conditions reflect the country's income level. However, such sanctions will hurt the entire global community and not just the country in question, and the cost to the rest of the world will rise with the offending country's size and importance. There is a risk that sanctions will only be applied to small countries, while large violators of basic rights go unpunished.

The real danger of using trade sanctions as an instrument for promoting basic rights is that the trade-standards link could become hijacked by protectionist interests attempting to preserve activities rendered uncompetitive by cheaper imports. The history of antidumping—the practice of retaliating against countries that sell their goods in another country's market at a price below their production cost, or below the price in other markets—shows that discretionary trade protection, even when both rational and well-intended, is highly vulnerable to misuse. Low-cost unskilled labor is the main comparative advantage of poor countries. Differences in endowments are the very basis of international trade and, as was argued in Part Two of this Report, are not a source of general declines in employment in richer countries—even though they may contribute to

changes in employment structure and contraction of employment in certain activities. Where jobs are lost, there is a case for public action, but trade protection is a blunt instrument, taxing others in the society and delaying the structural change that will be the foundation of future growth and jobs.

• • •

Because the formal sector is typically very small and enforcement capacity weak, labor standards in many low- and middle-income countries apply either only to a fraction of the labor force, or not at all. Needy workers in those countries often are not reached by protective labor legislation. They benefit from public action that attempts to improve the working environment in the rural and informal sectors—for example, through the provision of drinking water, improved sanitary conditions, or eradication of infectious diseases. This does not mean that governments should not try to set standards for formal sector workers. But standards that aim at protecting the vulnerable or those who face discrimination—for example, bans on child labor or equal-pay legislation—need to be complemented by other actions such as subsidies for education or greater access for women to modern sector jobs. Health and safety standards can also improve workers' welfare, but compliance increases when it is monitored by labor unions or other civic organizations. Minimum wages may be useful under some circumstances in industrial countries, but they are difficult to justify in low- and middle-income nations. And the costs of trying to link national labor standards to international trade relations will almost certainly outweigh any benefits.

CHAPTER 12

The Role of Unions

FREE TRADE UNIONS ARE A CORNERSTONE OF any effective system of industrial relations that seeks to balance the need for enterprises to remain competitive with the aspirations of workers for higher wages and better working conditions. Unions act as agents for labor, organizing large numbers of workers into a single entity whose collective bargaining power matches that of the employer. Trade unions can also monitor employers' compliance with government regulations (Chapter 11), and they can help raise workplace productivity and reduce workplace discrimination. They have a noneconomic role as well—some unions have contributed significantly to their countries' political and social development. Nations that, usually for political reasons, limit the freedom of unions to organize and operate are left without a mechanism that allows workers and firms to negotiate wages and working conditions equitably. The result has tended to be excessive intervention and regulation as governments try to pacify workers and gain support for state-controlled unions. But unions can also have negative economic effects. In some countries they behave as monopolists, protecting a minority group of relatively well-off unionized workers at the expense of the unemployed and those in rural and informal markets, whose formal sector employment opportunities are correspondingly reduced.

On balance, do free trade unions help or hinder the functioning of labor markets? This chapter examines the economic and political roles of labor unions and identifies the legislative and broader economic framework under which unions work best.

The economic role of unions

There are two very different views about the economic impact of labor unions. Supporters see them as giving workers a collective voice and enhancing productivity and equality. Opponents see them as monopolists, limiting employment in order to raise members' wages. Do economic analyses and country experiences allow us to make such generalizations? The answer is no. Unions can have positive or negative effects, depending upon the incentives they face and the regulatory environment within which they operate.

Positive effects

IMPROVED PRODUCTIVITY. Trade union activities can be conducive to higher efficiency and productivity. Unions provide their members with important services. At the plant level, unions provide workers with a collective voice. By balancing the power relationship between workers and managers, unions limit employer behavior that is arbitrary, exploitative, or retaliatory. By establishing grievance and arbitration procedures, unions reduce turnover and promote stability in the work force—conditions which, when combined with an overall improvement in industrial relations, enhance workers' productivity.

In many jobs workers are better informed than management about how to improve productivity. They will be more willing to share this information if they are confident of benefiting from any resulting change in organization. The presence of an agent on the workers' behalf, the union, may make them less suspicious that any information they reveal will benefit only management. If the union involves workers in activities that improve efficiency, unionism can be associated with a more productive organization.

Working conditions in some enterprises exhibit the characteristics of nonrival public goods: their "consumption" by one worker does not reduce their availability to another. Job safety is an example. Workers could shop for the level of workplace safety they want by changing jobs until they find one whose conditions suit them, but frequent worker turnover is inefficient and costly for employers as well as for labor. Those costs can be avoided by a union that efficiently communicates workers' preferences.

There are very few studies of the relationship between trade unions and productivity in low- and middle-income countries, but a recent analysis of Malaysian data provides some support for the view that unions can enhance productivity and efficiency (Table 12.1). Unionized Malaysian firms tended to train their workers more and to use job rotation to enhance flexibility and efficiency. They were also more likely to adopt productivity-raising innovations relating to technological change, changing product mix, and reorganization of work.

INCREASED EQUALITY AND REDUCED DISCRIMINATION. Trade unions tend to increase wage disparities between union and nonunion workers, but they usually push for greater wage equality for their own members. When union members are women or belong to ethnic minorities, unions also fight against discrimination. Although sometimes desirable, the compression of wage differences due to union activity may reduce efficiency, by sending wrong signals to

Unionized firms in Malaysia stress the importance of raising productivity.

Table 12.1 Effect of unionization on productivity-enhancing initiatives by firms in Malaysia
(percentage of firms taking action indicated)

Type of firm	Implementation of job rotation policy[a]	Reorganization of work	Upgrading of technology	Extension of product range
Plant union	30	29	40	20
Industrial union	31	32	37	26
Nonunion	22	18	26	20

a. Firms with more than 1,000 workers only.
Source: Standing 1992.

workers about which skills are most needed and which industries and occupations have the highest productivity.

The reduction in wage dispersion within unionized firms is well documented for industrial countries, and there are indications that the same effect occurs in low- and middle-income countries as well. A study in the Republic of Korea in 1988–90 found that unions there placed great value on wage equalization and that the degree of wage dispersion in the unionized sector was 5.2 percent lower than in the nonunionized sector. In Mexico union action appears to have helped reduce discrimination. A study using wage data for 1989 concluded that, in the nonunion sector, men enjoyed a 17.5 percent wage advantage over women with identical skills and experience, but the study found no significant wage differential between men and women in the unionized sector. Similarly, the study found a significant wage disadvantage for indigenous peoples in the nonunionized sector but no discrimination in firms covered by trade unions.

Negative effects

MONOPOLISTIC BEHAVIOR. Unions do often act as monopolists, improving wages and working conditions for their members at the expense of capital holders, consumers, and nonunion (unorganized) labor. The higher wages unions win for their members either reduce business profits or get passed on to consumers in the form of higher prices. Either result leads unionized firms to hire fewer workers, increasing the supply of labor to the unorganized sector and depressing wages there. The size of the union wage effect—the difference in compensation between otherwise similar workers that is attributed to union membership—has been studied in several countries. Results indicate that it can reach up to 31 percent in developing countries, 10 percent in Europe, and around 20 percent in North America (Table 12.2).

Where wages for the relatively few workers who are unionized are pushed up, the actions of unions can adversely affect the distribution of income. In most developing economies only a small fraction of the working population belong to trade unions. For example, union coverage is less than 4 percent of the labor force in Pakistan, 5 percent in Kenya, and 10 percent in Malaysia (Figure 12.1). In such settings unions can play an important role in determining pay differentials between workers in the small formal economy and the vast informal and rural working population. If the formal economy is unionized, the distributional outcome is likely to be regressive. Where formal sector production also enjoys trade protection, unions are likely to share the spoils with capital holders at the expense of consumers and the masses of workers in the nonunionized sectors.

But the existence of a union wage premium is not always proof of negative distributional effects, even in developing

Unions are usually able to raise their members' wages above levels prevailing in the overall labor market.

Table 12.2 Union wage premiums in selected countries

Country	Year	Estimated difference between union and nonunion wages (percent)
South Africa[a]	1985	10–24
Mexico	1989	10
Malaysia	1988	15–20
Ghana	1992–93	31
United States	1985–87	20
United Kingdom	1985–87	10
Germany	1985–87	5

a. Black unions only.
Source: Blanchflower and Freeman 1990; Moll 1993; Panagides and Patrinos 1994; Standing 1992; Teal 1994.

countries. The actions of black unions in South Africa implied a union wage premium of 10 to 24 percent in 1985. But by raising the wages of unionized black workers and bringing them closer to those of white workers, union action may have helped improve the distribution of income.

There are situations where the union wage premium is very small or even nonexistent. A 1991 study in Korea estimated that the wages of unionized production workers were only 2 to 4 percent higher than those of nonunion workers. Failure to detect a strong positive union wage differential is sometimes due to union influence extending beyond the unionized sector—there is often another relatively high-wage sector in the economy that is affected by the unions' wage-setting practices. Obvious examples can be found in some industrial countries, where the coverage of union agreements is automatically extended by law to nonunion workers—in Spain 75 percent of employees are covered by some collective agreement, although only 10 to 15 percent are union members. Where such laws do not exist, nonunionized firms are often under political pressure to pay union-negotiated wages, or they may choose to pay higher wages to head off unionization of their work forces.

OPPOSITION TO REFORM. Trade unions have sometimes wielded their political power against structural adjustment. India's unions continue to criticize the government's recent liberalization efforts, despite the apparent success of many of these initiatives since 1991. The unions have organized nationwide general strikes to oppose incipient industrial restructuring measures aimed in part at increasing India's outward orientation and the reform of state enterprises. India's unions are propping up the part of the economy most in

Trade union membership rarely includes a majority of workers.

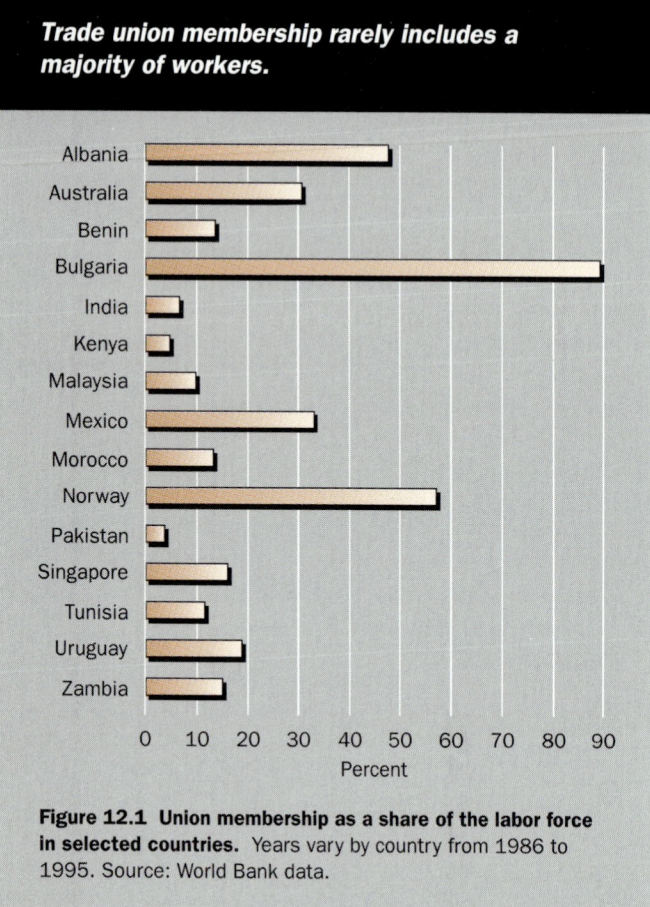

Figure 12.1 Union membership as a share of the labor force in selected countries. Years vary by country from 1986 to 1995. Source: World Bank data.

members. Raising wages would force unionized establishments out of business unless the higher wages could be justified by increased productivity. In less competitive environments unions will attempt to capture economic rents and will ally themselves politically with their employers and with politicians who promise to perpetuate those rents. This kind of behavior is evident in industrial countries, where union wage premiums are greatest in regulated sectors and in concentrated industries. In many countries union opposition to trade liberalization and privatization is a rational strategy for maintaining higher wages for unionized workers in the short run at the expense of nonunion workers. Promoting domestic competition and openness to international markets will therefore help curtail these negative effects.

LABOR REGULATIONS AND THE SYSTEM OF INDUSTRIAL RELATIONS. The structure of union organization and the coverage of collective agreements condition union behavior. A key principle in industrial relations is to ensure that the parties engaged in bargaining absorb the costs of their actions rather than shift them to third parties. But in some countries legislation requires that workers be paid even when they are on strike—a clear disincentive to compromise. In contrast, many governments refrain from providing loans or deferring tax payments for firms during strikes or lockouts. Negotiations between unions and public enterprises show starkly how unions are able to achieve distorted outcomes when third parties bear the cost of negotiated agreements. If a public enterprise can turn to the government for subsidies or easy credit when it is in financial difficulty, or if its monopoly status allows it to raise prices at will, the burden of high settlements falls on those who pay the resulting higher prices or higher taxes, not on the workers or the enterprise managers who negotiated the increase.

Legislation in many countries stipulates the right to join a union of one's own choice as a basic human freedom. This is the legal foundation for the emergence of unions that are free and independent. Such unions are able to act as genuine representatives of workers and thus to bargain with employers to the extent that the competitive environment allows. Such legislation usually allows more than one union to be established to represent a given group of workers; this is a strong incentive for established unions to maintain the quality of their services. Legislation of limits on the number of unions per enterprise is viewed as an infringement on workers' rights. Union fragmentation and interunion rivalry are sometimes disruptive, however, and bargaining costs rise if workers have many representatives. These issues are often dealt with through cooperation, with employers offering unions incentives to join together for bargaining. Freedom of association also encompasses the right not to be forced into a union. In economic terms, a competitive nonunion labor market could exert discipline on the mo-

need of reform. Latin America also has a long history of union opposition to adjustment. In the 1980s organized labor opposed such comprehensive reform programs as the Cruzado Plan in Brazil and the Austral Plan in Argentina.

Improving the economic impact of unions

How can policymakers create an environment that minimizes the negative effects trade unions can have, while encouraging them to make a positive contribution to economic growth and equity? Experience indicates that such an environment will usually include competitive product markets and regulatory and institutional frameworks designed to protect workers' freedom of association and organization, including their right to join the union of their choice or not to join any union. Many countries' regulations also seek to support the process of collective bargaining in the private and the public sector.

Encouraging unions' positive contributions

COMPETITION ON THE OUTPUT SIDE. Competitive product markets limit unions' ability to obtain higher wages for their nopolistic wage practices of unionism. If, however, the state encumbers the nonunion sector with regulations on minimum wages and restrictions on hiring and firing, the sector will operate much less effectively as a constraint on unions' wage demands.

The importance of competitive output markets and of the principle of internalizing bargaining outcomes is illustrated by two contrasting examples. A survey of twenty industrial firms in Brazil found that increased competition in the output market caused those firms to introduce productivity-enhancing techniques and processes such as quality controls and quality circles. Labor, keen to ensure continued competitiveness, did not insist on past privileges but instead cooperated with management in this process. This indicates that there is more to industrial relations than bargaining over wages and other conditions. In many countries labor and management get together to consider ways of increasing competitiveness. Coal miners in India, in contrast, have been shielded from competition ever since the government takeover of the industry in 1973. The highly unionized coal workers exert political pressure to obtain wage increases that are unrelated to market realities. As a result, their wages have been mainly based on political considerations, without regard to the country's economic interests and development objectives: the real wages of coal miners have jumped noticeably in the years just before national elections (Figure 12.2).

Collective bargaining in the private sector

THE LEVEL AT WHICH BARGAINING TAKES PLACE. The experience of several countries indicates that bargaining at the enterprise level can be an appropriate framework for achieving positive economic effects. At the other extreme is bargaining at the national level, common in Northern and Western Europe. Although these systems have fallen out of favor as Europeans grapple with rising unemployment and inflexible labor markets, they are associated with decades of positive industrial relations and good wage and employment outcomes for European workers. But national-level bargaining requires that most workers be covered by union agreements. If they are not, as is the case in most countries, national agreements will benefit the unionized sector at the expense of the unorganized and poorer groups in society. That has been the result in Latin America, where centralized approaches to industrial relations have fared poorly.

If collective bargaining takes place at the enterprise or the plant level, the union's ability to effect monopolistic wage increases is tempered by the strong competitive pressures on the firm from the product market. In Malaysia it has been calculated that the wage premium for plant-level unions is around 15 percent, whereas sectoral, or industrywide, unions are associated with a wage premium of nearly 20 percent.

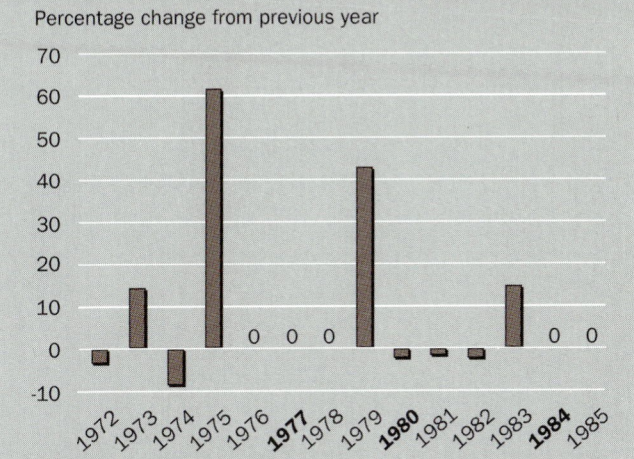

Indian coal miners have often seen their wages jump before national elections.

Percentage change from previous year

Figure 12.2 Real wages of coal miners in India. Election years are indicated in bold type. Source: Banerji and Sabot 1993.

Examples of how decentralized bargaining can achieve good results are found in certain industrial countries (Canada, the United States, and Japan) and in some of the newly industrializing East Asian economies (Hong Kong and Korea after 1987). The system of collective bargaining in transitional economies is still being developed. In Canada and the United States collective bargaining is mostly at the enterprise level, although there are some multiemployer arrangements. There is no tradition of involvement by central organizations in bargaining in most sectors, and there are no central employer organizations. Enterprise unions have been heralded as one of the pillars of industrial relations supporting Japan's economic achievements. In Japan collective bargaining takes place at the enterprise level, but confederations of labor unions play an important coordinating role during the annual bargaining exercises. In Hong Kong unions are also organized along enterprise lines, although as in Japan there is some coordination by trade union federations. Hong Kong's unions operate in an environment of strong competition in the output market, as well as in the labor market because of migration from China. This weakens their bargaining position, and most unions are in the business of providing insurance and social assistance to their members rather than fighting for higher wages.

Recent developments in Korea's system of industrial relations provide useful lessons for other countries. Trade union freedom increased as part of the process of political liberalization that started in 1987. The number of unions and their membership rose rapidly (Table 12.3). In 1992 Korea had 7,676 firm-level unions and 21 industrial federations. After a chaotic beginning, with conflict-ridden labor-management relations in 1987–89, collective bargaining is now becoming an established institutional arrangement. Bargaining is decentralized and is conducted at the enterprise level, except in a few cases, such as textiles and banking, where bargaining occurs at the industry level or through a multiemployer arrangement. Korean industrial relations are still evolving, but the tradition of enterprise-level bargaining has not been significantly modified in the new collective bargaining experiments since 1987, and a restructuring of bargaining patterns appears unlikely in the near future.

The system of industrial relations in the countries of Eastern Europe and the former Soviet Union is also still evolving. Transitional economies inherited heavily unionized labor markets, with more than 90 percent of workers belonging to unions sponsored and supported by the state and the communist party. Economic and political transformation has led to a decline in union membership, even as unions were gaining their independence. But unionization—estimated in 1990 at around 80 percent in Russia and 60 percent in Poland—remains much higher than in most high-income industrial or developing countries. Unions in transitional economies are still trying to adapt to new realities and to develop their own approach to bargaining. Experiences have been mixed. Countrywide bargaining between unions and employers in the Czech Republic—a relatively small country with a tradition of coordination at the national level—appears to be achieving good results.

This was not the case in Ukraine, however, where centralized bargaining in 1993 led to an unsustainable agreement whereby wages rose faster than inflation.

That plant-level collective bargaining may be better suited to conditions in many countries does not mean that consultations at the sectoral or the national level should not take place, or that national trade union federations have no role. In nearly all of the country examples presented here, enterprise-level bargaining is complemented by sectoral or national coordination. And multiemployer agreements may under certain circumstances be more efficient than enterprise bargaining, as in the construction sector in some areas of the United States, where the nature of the work is such that workers change employers very often. Trade union federations can be important when large-scale structural adjustment and rapid disinflation are needed. In Israel and Mexico, organized labor rallied behind governments committed to adjustment programs and agreed to social pacts that have facilitated stabilization, but instances of this constructive role of labor confederations have been rare. It is difficult to persuade a powerful pressure group to help design and implement a stabilization plan, and eschew general strikes against restructuring measures aimed at increasing the outward orientation and privatization of industry, when the result is likely to be to reduce the relative wages of its members.

SUPPORTIVE LEGISLATION AND THE ROLE OF EMPLOYERS. Decentralized bargaining requires strong guarantees of union rights. A system of industrial relations based on enterprise-level unions can be open to abuse by employers. Some employers try to use their relative market power to discourage the organization of labor unions in their enterprises. Employer abuse can lead to deteriorating industrial relations and unrest, which are hardly conducive to investment and growth. Labor legislation must try to strike a difficult balance, protecting unions' rights while limiting their potential monopoly power.

The content of enterprise-level collective bargaining is usually determined by the parties themselves, obviating the need for legislation to spell out what contracts may or may not cover. If management is willing to enter into agreements about capital-labor ratios, apprenticeship programs, and the conditions under which temporary workers are hired, the law should not forbid it. In a competitive product market the costs of such agreements will fall mainly on the firm and the union, which should deter them from reaching unrealistic agreements.

Nor is there usually a need to legislate a limit of one union per enterprise. If management wants to minimize bargaining costs by having just one union to deal with, it is up to management to persuade the unions to join together for collective bargaining. Allowing other unions to form

---

The number of Korean trade unions has risen sharply since 1987, with most organized at the firm level.

Table 12.3 Types of labor organization in the Republic of Korea

Year	Total	Industrial federations	Local branches[a]	Firm-level unions
1965	2,634	16	362	2,255
1975	4,091	17	488	3,585
1986	2,635	16	0	2,618
1988	2,742	16	0	2,725
1990	6,164	21	0	6,142
1992	7,698	21	0	7,676

a. Local branches were transformed into individual unions in the 1980 labor law revision.
Source: Krause and Park 1993. Reprinted with permission.

provides a check against an established union serving only the interests of a small group of workers. Alternatively, some labor regulations—for example, in Bangladesh—stipulate that only one union may act as a "collective bargaining agent" and call for the election of this agent from among all unions in the enterprise at regular intervals.

Unions in the public sector and natural monopolies

Ensuring that unions play a positive role is more difficult when they operate in noncompetitive markets, such as the public sector and natural monopolies (electric utilities, telephone companies, and others). The costs to society of an interruption of work by firefighters, police officers, teachers, nurses, utility workers, or public transport operators can be very high. Consumers have limited scope to look elsewhere for these services. As a result, a large part of the costs of a strike or lockout is borne by parties not represented in the negotiations.

The special features of labor negotiations in the public sector create a difficult dilemma. Should laws protect public sector workers' rights to freedom of association and organization and their right to strike? Or should they protect the general public's right to uninterrupted essential services and protect society from being held hostage by a small group of civil servants?

Societies' responses to these questions vary. Public sector workers in Bangladesh are allowed to form unions but are not permitted to bargain collectively. Salaries and wages of civil servants and workers in public enterprises are determined by government-appointed commissions. However, this arrangement has not stopped public workers from going on illegal nationwide strikes to exert political pressure on the government to raise their wages. In Malaysia collective bargaining is allowed in the public sector, but the central government has the authority to accept or reject the final agreement—in addition, Malaysian public sector unions tend to be less independent from government pressures than unions in South Asia. Federal workers in the United States were denied the right to form unions until 1962, and even now they do not have the right to strike. In many U.S. states, state workers are also prohibited from going on strike. Spanish public workers, on the other hand, are allowed to form unions, bargain collectively, and strike, provided they continue supplying a minimum level of "essential services," defined by law.

Dealing successfully with the problems raised by public sector unions depends upon the quality of labor legislation and dispute settlement procedures. Effective labor legislation for the public sector tries to set up alternative mechanisms to strikes and lockouts for the settlement of disputes—arbitration by third parties is an obvious example. Chile's labor law provides for a special type of arbitration to deal with disputes involving public workers. Called "final offer arbitration," the arrangement requires the arbitrator to choose either management's final offer or the union's final offer. This encourages the two parties to present reasonable demands and thus to design their own contract.

Unions and politics

All pluralistic societies consider freedom of association and organization a basic human right, and organized labor is often in the vanguard of the movement toward greater political openness and democracy. But many countries still restrict trade union activities. How have constraints on freedom of association and organization affected labor market outcomes? In countries without free unions, collective bargaining is unavailable to determine wages and other working conditions; governments therefore perceive a need to intervene and set those conditions administratively. As a result, many countries that have repressed unions have had highly distorting labor policies.

Polish workers' struggle for freedom in the 1980s was a dramatic reminder that free labor unions are mostly democratic institutions. Solidarity's leaders believed that pluralistic labor unions could be the catalyst for a pluralistic political system and that free trade unions were a prerequisite for a free society. Negotiations in the city of Gdansk in August 1980, which focused on labor issues, led to the creation of the first free trade union in a communist country. But it quickly became obvious that authoritarian rule and a free trade union could not coexist: the communist leadership outlawed Solidarity in 1982.

South Africa's black labor unions, like Solidarity, gave powerless people a chance to make their voices heard. Although the unions were concerned mainly with organizing workers to bargain over workplace issues, their political activities have received far more attention. The South African government's original intention was to develop a pluralistic system of industrial relations that confined unions to workplace issues and left political issues to political parties. But South Africa's experience also showed that free trade unions are inconsistent with nondemocratic practices—the black union movement became a leader in the struggle against apartheid.

Many governments continue for political reasons to exercise strict control over labor movements. Although a large number of nations have ratified Convention 87 of the ILO guaranteeing freedom of association and organization, its full application has proved elusive. Many countries deny workers the right to organize outside officially recognized and controlled structures. Responding to ILO inquiries, governments have given different explanations for this situation, not all of them convincing. A Nigerian government argued that its imposition of a single trade union center "responded to the desires of the workers to amalgamate the many trade unions and four central organizations which had existed." Egypt's government sought to justify the trade union monopoly conferred by law on the Egyptian Trade Union Federation by declaring that it "represents the wish of the workers and corresponds to the needs of many countries, including developing countries." And the Seychelles government told the ILO that the legal monopoly of the National Workers Union was established "after the voluntary dissolution of all trade unions."

In the absence of free unions and collective bargaining, many governments feel obliged to reach out to formal sector workers through labor regulations and special privileges. This is particularly true when the government needs the political support of strong urban groups in order to remain in power. One result is that labor market distortions are particularly severe in many countries that repressed labor unions. Overstaffing in the public sector, high minimum wages, and restrictions on firing—policies introduced in Congo, Kenya, Sudan, Tanzania, and Zambia in the 1960s—reflected political realities for the governments that took power and repressed labor unions after independence. In Egypt in the 1950s and 1960s President Gamal Abdel Nasser, needing the support of the urban middle class, promised their children public sector jobs upon graduation from college. In Bangladesh during the 1980s General Hussain Mohammad Ershad, likewise needing the support of urban labor, negotiated with the country's federation of labor unions and agreed to increase public sector wages, severance pay, allowances, and nonwage benefits.

Not all countries that repressed unions adopted inefficient labor policies—Korea before 1987 is a notable example—and not all countries that allowed unions to operate freely had good labor outcomes. But the probability of governments passing inefficient labor legislation may be higher when workers' right to representation is not protected. Empirical analysis finds that political liberties, which almost always go hand in hand with the freedom of unions to organize, are associated with less dualism in labor markets and a larger formal sector. Some East Asian countries both restricted union activity and achieved rapid growth in formal employment with only a moderate tendency toward dualism. But they appear to be exceptions.

• • •

Denial of workers' rights is not necessary to achieve growth of incomes. It is possible to identify the conditions and policies under which free trade unions can advance rather than impede development. Unions are likely to have positive effects on efficiency and equity, and their potential negative effects are likely to be minimized, when they operate in an environment in which product markets are competitive, collective bargaining occurs at the enterprise or the plant level, and labor laws protect the right of individual workers to join the union of their choosing, or none at all.

CHAPTER 13

Dealing with Income Insecurity

Sharp drops in income from work can have a profound impact on the living standards of workers and their families. Unemployment, disability, and old age are all important causes of poverty in industrial and developing countries alike, and of deeper poverty for those already poor. Dealing with these risks is particularly important in transitional economies. Most societies have developed ways of coping with the threat to living standards from both expected and unexpected falls in income. Often this involves some combination of private saving, informal support mechanisms, and obligations on employers. Governments step in when these informal or private solutions prove insufficient. Households may find it difficult to borrow to cover temporary falls in labor income. Community support mechanisms break down when there is a community- or economy-wide shock, and they tend to decline with urbanization and the diminishing importance of the extended family. Private markets for unemployment and disability insurance and old age pensions are limited or absent, in part because they can suffer from perverse incentive effects such as adverse selection (only those likely to need insurance buy it) and moral hazard (once insured, individuals are less likely to avoid risky behavior).

How can governments best fill the gaps that traditional and market-driven arrangements leave? This chapter examines the ways in which governments of low- and middle-income countries can help households deal with labor market risks in both the informal and the formal sector. It also identifies the pitfalls that governments face in trying to do so.

Income security for informal sector workers

Informal sector workers in rural and urban areas face a much greater risk of income loss than those in the modern sector. But they are also the group for whom it is most difficult to provide greater security through public intervention. Income loss is mostly associated with loss of employment, which can occur either because no jobs are available—because of seasonal or more permanent changes in labor demand—or because of incapacity to work as a result of physical disability, sickness, or old age. The vast majority of workers in low- and middle-income countries depend upon informal arrangements to provide insurance against these risks, but governments often intervene to complement them. Public works programs, when well designed, avoid crowding out private transfers, and have often been used to reduce the risks informal sector workers face.

Community support and private transfers

Employer-worker relations in the informal sector are governed by social customs and traditions. For wage earners the informal employment arrangement often includes an element of insurance and risk sharing, with employers agreeing to pay workers a fixed wage while they remain employed, regardless of seasonal or other fluctuations in demand. It is also common for employers to provide loans to workers who face unexpected expenses, or to support older workers or those unable to work for health reasons. This type of support is never formally agreed upon in advance. But in many countries informal commitments by employers are an important part of socially acceptable codes of conduct, especially in rural areas.

Financial help from relatives remains the principal form of income support and redistribution in developing countries. The extended family system is an important way of providing extra income and security to individual workers and their immediate households. For example, among a sample of urban poor in El Salvador, 33 percent reported receiving private transfers, which on average accounted for 39 percent of their total income (Table 13.1). In Malaysia private transfers accounted for almost half the income of the poorest fifth of households. Nearly three-quarters of rural households in Java, Indonesia, gave private transfers to other households.

Private transfers play an important insurance function in addition to reducing income inequality: they provide old age support and ameliorate the effects of disability, illness, and unemployment. In most developing countries, especially in rural areas, older generations rely on the young to supplement their income. Indeed, ensuring support in old age is one of the reasons for having children. Studies in Kenya and Peru found that more than a quarter of private transfers were given to parents by their children. There is also evidence that households struck with disability, illness, or unemployment receive increased transfers. A study in Peru indicated that the sick receive larger transfers, and studies in both Peru and Indonesia showed that being unemployed significantly increases both the probability of receiving a transfer and its amount.

Public works programs

Public works programs can complement private efforts to help the unemployed poor, provided the recipients are willing to work for low wages. The low wages act as a self-targeting mechanism, because only the truly needy will accept them. These schemes are particularly appropriate during recessions, when other job opportunities are unavailable. They are also well suited for rural areas during the slack season and can have a secondary benefit of building or maintaining important infrastructure assets. In Ethiopia, for example, program participants have been employed building roads and preventing soil erosion. In the United States, in what was perhaps the most significant use of public works programs as relief among industrial countries to date, the Works Progress Administration provided employment for up to a fifth of all U.S. workers during the Great Depression of the 1930s.

Many developing countries have also made extensive use of public works programs. The Food for Work Program in Zimbabwe and the Emergency Social Fund in Bolivia provide a basic level of employment and consumption for some of the poor. The Employment Guarantee Scheme in the Indian state of Maharashtra uses taxes to redistribute income from the wealthier urban areas, particularly Bombay, to the poor who work in rural areas. Chile introduced large government-financed urban public works programs during the recessions of the mid-1970s and early 1980s. Like the Indian scheme, the Chilean programs' main objective was to create employment: at the bottom of the recession of the early 1980s they absorbed more than 10 percent of the labor force. By December 1988, a year after Chile's vigorous economic recovery, that share had fallen to less than 0.1 percent.

Public works programs tend to have a greater chance of success where labor is more mobile and where there is a tradition of community work. When workers are able to move, the location of the program can be determined

Private transfers are large in many countries.

Table 13.1 Prevalence and amounts of private transfers in selected countries

Country	Year	GNP per capita (1986 dollars)	Percentage of households receiving or giving transfers		Average transfer as a percentage of average income[a]	
			Receiving households	Giving households	Receiving households	Giving households
El Salvador (urban poor)	1976	820	33	..	11	..
India	1975–83	290	93	..	8	..
Indonesia (Java)	1982	490				
Rural			31	72	10	8
Urban			44	45	20	3
Kenya		300				
Urban (recent migrants)	1968		..	59	..	13
Nairobi (urban poor)	1971		..	89	..	21
Nationwide	1974		..	27	3	4
Rural			..	19	2	3
Urban			..	62	4	6
Malaysia	1977–78	1,830	19–30[b]	33–47[b]	11[c]	..
Mexico (two villages)	1982	1,860	..	..	16–21[b]	..
Peru[a]	1985	1,090	22	23	2	1
Philippines[d]	1978	560	47	..	9	..
United States	1979	17,480	15	..	1	..

.. Not available.

a. Average income includes the incomes of those who did not receive or give transfers. The average transfer received as a percentage of recipients' income is much larger: 39 percent in El Salvador and 9 percent in Peru. Similarly, the average transfer is computed as a proportion of total consumption expenditures.

b. Averages not available; figures denote upper and lower bounds.

c. The average transfer was 46 percent of income for households in the lowest income quintile.

d. Cash gifts in a large informal housing area.

Source: Cox and Jimenez 1990.

mainly by the quality of projects. Poor laborers looking for public jobs are usually willing to relocate, at least temporarily, to obtain them. But low labor mobility makes these programs less effective—some studies have indicated that obstacles to mobility in China have made it more difficult for that country's public works programs to reach the poor. Community participation greatly enhances the probability of success. Studies from Niger and Senegal indicate that communities with a strong tradition of employment pooling can assist in the mobilization of workers and facilitate the production of public goods, for example through local production on common fields for common stockholding or simple neighborhood assistance schemes.

The level of wages in such programs is important in determining their success at targeting the needy. High wages may attract better-off workers and, given limited budgets, lead to fewer jobs being created for the truly destitute. The importance of wage determination for the success of public works programs is demonstrated by the Maharashtra program in India, which seeks to guarantee employment on demand. In its initial fifteen years the program maintained

wages on a par with prevailing wages for unskilled casual agricultural labor. But in 1988 wages were increased sharply, in line with a doubling of the statutory minimum wage. The higher wage, combined with budgetary pressures, effectively eliminated the employment guarantee in the year after the wage increase.

Most public works programs have two objectives: providing relief to laborers in distress and creating a public asset. To achieve both, programs must be managed flexibly, to respond to changes in the labor market, and, especially, must have the capacity to expand employment rapidly in time of crisis. This implies the need for a large pipeline of well-prioritized projects. In normal times only a core program of high-return investments should be undertaken. Employment can then be expanded during crises by implementing some of the lower priority projects in the pipeline.

Income security for the formal sector

Risk-sharing provisions are common in formal labor contracts. But private solutions are often inadequate because they cannot insure against economy-wide shocks, and because of insurance market failures; therefore most governments are involved in the provision of income security to formal sector workers. Getting the design of these programs right is very important. There is great risk that the initial beneficiaries of social insurance—usually the relatively well-off—will gain at the expense of other workers.

Unemployment benefits

Nearly all the industrial market economies, as well as the countries of Eastern Europe and the former Soviet Union, have unemployment benefit systems. These countries face two important questions: how should the systems be financed? and what steps can be taken to ensure that they do not distort incentives and discourage unemployed workers from seeking a job?

From an efficiency perspective, an unemployment benefit scheme should ideally require all workers to pay for their own insurance, by taxing them—or their employers, who would then shift the burden to the workers through lower wages—at different rates related to the probability of their losing their jobs. In practice, however, most countries finance unemployment benefits through a flat payroll tax, which implies that stable employers and their workers finance benefits for more unstable employers. The United States tries to address this problem by using an experience rating system: unemployment insurance is funded through a payroll tax rate that varies according to the likelihood that the employer will cause the benefits to be used, subject to a lower and an upper limit. By raising the cost of unemployment insurance for activities that create more unemployment, an experience rating system provides an automatic link between its outlay and its income and encourages more stable employment patterns. But such schemes are administratively complex.

Generous unemployment benefits may discourage some workers from seriously seeking work or from accepting job offers that fail to meet their aspirations. Countries deal with this problem by changing the time profile and amount of unemployment compensation. The fraction of the salary that is replaced often decreases over the benefit period, gradually increasing the worker's incentive to find a job. Unemployment insurance offices may require beneficiaries to accept job offers, take training courses, or collect benefits in person, and some make voluntary quitters ineligible for benefits.

Two principles have emerged from the experience of industrial countries with unemployment benefits: benefits should, as far as possible, be tied to job search, and permanent dependency on unemployment benefits should be avoided. Most countries limit the duration of benefits, in the hope that this will shorten unemployment spells and reduce dependency. They usually continue to provide people with basic levels of social assistance when they are no longer eligible for benefits, to ensure that they are not simply thrown into poverty. This type of assistance is sometimes combined with some form of training, in an effort to simultaneously provide income support for the unemployed and increase their probability of reemployment.

Job security regulations

Unemployment benefit schemes are rarely used in developing countries because they are complicated and costly to administer. Instead, many developing countries have introduced job security regulations to make it difficult for firms to lay off workers. Some regulation may be needed to limit unfair practices, but too much can discourage employment creation. Some observers argue that job security regulations in Brazil, India, Peru, and Zimbabwe have made formal sector employers more cautious about hiring permanent workers, slowing the rate of formal job creation. By creating impediments to formal job creation, excessive job security regulation may protect those who are in wage employment at the expense of outsiders—the unemployed and those in the informal and rural sectors.

Job security legislation often tries to discourage arbitrary dismissals by establishing a liability for employers who fire workers without just cause. Mexican law requires employers to give one month's notice to workers being dismissed and to pay three months' wages as a minimum severance. In the absence of just cause, the severance increases by twenty days' wages for each year on the job. This type of formula may create a problem if, as in many countries, the interpretation of just cause extends only to serious misconduct, not to economic causes. In these countries the restructuring of firms tends to lead to sharp labor-management disputes and a significant waste of resources. Disputes often end up in court, introducing uncertainty about the benefits that dismissed workers will actually receive.

Sri Lanka provides another example of job security regulations that may undermine the efficient functioning of the labor market. In addition to requiring employers to make severance payments and provident fund contributions, Sri Lanka's laws impose tight restrictions on firms' ability to lay off workers. Firms with more than fifteen workers may not shed labor on nondisciplinary grounds without the concerned workers' written consent. Firms usually must make large severance payments, beyond what is required by law, to obtain this consent. Under these circumstances it is not surprising that many firms hire workers on a casual or daily basis or rely on subcontracting.

Severance pay

Instead of restrictive income security regulations, many countries address the real concerns of formal sector workers by having firms make lump-sum severance payments to laid-off employees. Ideally, the precise amount should be negotiated between workers and employers, with some government oversight to ensure equity. The workers benefiting from this insurance would normally pay at least part of the costs, either directly or indirectly through lower wages. But this arrangement is rarely seen; instead most countries have administratively fixed severance payments, which often are too high. If wages are fully flexible, these high payments may not be a problem, because employers will offset the high cost of firing by lowering wages. If wages are rigid, however, the additional cost may discourage employment. In some countries, employers and workers try to avoid the requirement through fixed-term or daily contracts, which defeat the purpose of the legislation.

The problem with severance pay lies in determining the level of payment that would provide adequate protection to workers without excessively taxing firms that need to shed labor. There is no magic formula for striking this balance, but collective bargaining between employers and free labor unions may achieve a more desirable result than government fiat. Employers and worker representatives should be allowed to bargain over the entire remuneration package and be able to trade more severance pay for lower wages or less agreeable working conditions. Under this framework, labor laws would announce the principle of income security through severance payments and perhaps define a maximum level, leaving the actual amounts to differ across firms. Government's role would be to ensure that workers' rights to collective bargaining are protected and help settle disputes. Agreements reached in this way would have a better chance of balancing workers' desire for security with market realities and would be easier to enforce than legislated severance payments.

Alternatively, governments may decide to make the severance payments themselves and finance them through general revenue. The level at which severance payments are set then have no effect on firms' employment and wage levels—instead, taxpayers subsidize the affected workers. But this approach has major problems. It provides an incentive for firms and workers to engage in high turnover. It could, for example, encourage firms to fire workers during the slack season and rehire them when activity picks up, letting government pay the firing costs.

Empirical evidence

Many observers believe that the regulations on job security and severance pay adopted in many European and low- and middle-income countries have reduced employment creation. But there are very few empirical studies that substantiate this belief, and fewer still have tried to estimate the magnitude of the effect. Evidence from industrial countries where these regulations are strictly enforced is inconclusive. A 1991 analysis of the declining European steel industry found that stringent job security guarantees on the conti-

nent led to fewer job losses than in the more laissez-faire United Kingdom. On the other hand, Spain's experience with job security regulation provides a strong case in which relaxation led to an expansion of employment. The introduction of a fixed-term employment contract option in 1980 and its expansion in 1984 were associated with faster aggregate employment growth, consisting almost exclusively of people on fixed contracts, than was expected on the basis of past productivity trends and output expansion.

Stringent job security regulations that require firms to obtain prior government consent before laying off workers have been analyzed in India and Zimbabwe. This analysis found that firms in the formal sector could not pass on the cost of job security to their workers because of wage rigidities. Instead they adjusted to the cost of this regulation by employing fewer workers. The study estimated that, on average, these regulations reduced formal employment in thirty-five Indian industries by 18 percent and in twenty-nine industries in Zimbabwe by 25 percent.

A study of rural labor markets in northeastern Brazil provides further evidence of the possible negative impact of job security legislation. The Brazilian Rural Labor Statute of 1963 required agriculture labor contracts to meet certain minimum standards, including severance pay. This may have led firms to hire temporary (casual) rather than permanent workers. Although total employment in the region increased in the 1960s, permanent employment declined from 45 percent to 39 percent of peak-season employment. The decline was reversed in the 1970s, and the ratio rebounded to 65 percent by 1980. But the study argued that, in the absence of the severance pay regulations, permanent employment would have risen throughout the period. It concludes that the Brazilian legislation may have been counterproductive because it led to a significant reduction in permanent contracts.

Not all studies detect a negative impact of job security and severance pay regulations on formal employment in developing countries. For example, almost all Malaysian firms in an ILO survey stated that job security laws had no impact on their employment. But the potential for negative effects on formal sector employment from high costs of shedding labor has led several countries to reconsider their job security and severance pay legislation. Senegal has revised its labor code, lowering the cost of labor shedding. Argentina added "economic cause" to the list of allowable reasons for dismissal in its job security legislation. In a series of reforms begun in 1978, Chile has consistently limited the payoff workers may receive under court verdicts.

Programs to help those who cannot work

Public works employment and unemployment insurance are irrelevant for those whom disability or old age prevents from working. Disabled and elderly individuals without a history of formal sector employment rely primarily on family and community-based support mechanisms in most societies. However, some more-formal programs providing transfers to the nonworking poor have had success. Bangladesh's Vulnerable Groups Development program supplies grain to some half a million rural women and children, focusing on high-risk regions and relying on local leaders to identify the needy. A means-tested scheme for agricultural workers in India's Kerala State provides a modest pension that supports the cost of home care for the elderly without supplanting strong informal support arrangements.

For formal sector workers and in richer societies, including many transitional countries, formal schemes of social assistance, disability payment, and pensions are often a major source of support for those who cannot work. Disability and pension systems in part take the form of insurance programs, linked to the labor contract by payments made by employers or workers. This linkage of benefits to contributions made by or on behalf of the individual is important; otherwise there are incentives to avoid payments, for example through going informal or casual. This can lead to insolvent schemes and redistributive transfers. Generous pension and disability plans can also provide incentives for individuals to withdraw from work earlier than they otherwise would. A recent World Bank study assessed the problems of linkage and distorted incentives with respect to pensions. It found that many schemes are unviable

and that evasion is a major problem in countries such as Jamaica, Rwanda, Uruguay, and Turkey. Many countries in Eastern Europe and the former Soviet Union may be at the beginning of such crises. Another issue is targeting benefits to the truly needy. Means-tested benefits are often used in rich countries but impose heavy administrative burdens. More practical for most low- and middle-income countries are schemes that target an attribute closely associated with need, such as widowhood, single-parenthood, or the presence of a handicap or severe disability.

• • •

Most governments are heavily involved in providing income security, despite the risk of discouraging the expansion of formal employment. Many have had good results. Public works programs are often a powerful instrument for providing income security to unemployed informal sector and rural workers, and for complementing community-based arrangements and other basic safety nets for the poor. Low- and middle-income countries with limited administrative capacity do best with schemes based on severance pay for formal workers, preferably negotiated through collective bargaining, rather than unemployment insurance. Experience shows that these different types of schemes, as well as pension systems, are successful when they are largely self-financed, with a close correspondence between those who pay and those who benefit, and when they are designed to minimize incentives to leave the labor force or shift to informal or casual labor contracts.

CHAPTER 14

The Government as an Employer

BIG GOVERNMENT IS OUT OF FASHION. AS countries around the world move toward open markets and less regulation, many are also reconsidering the role of the state in economic life. Although active government is necessary to support market-oriented, labor-demanding development, often this means less government, doing different things than in the past, and doing them better. The size

of the government's work force varies significantly across countries (Figure 14.1). But whereas every country has individual teachers, police officers, bureaucrats, and government clerks who are dedicated and efficient, the civil service as a whole is often regarded as poorly motivated and unproductive. Inspired by the East Asian economies, where efficient civil services have contributed to economic development, developing countries in Africa and Latin America as

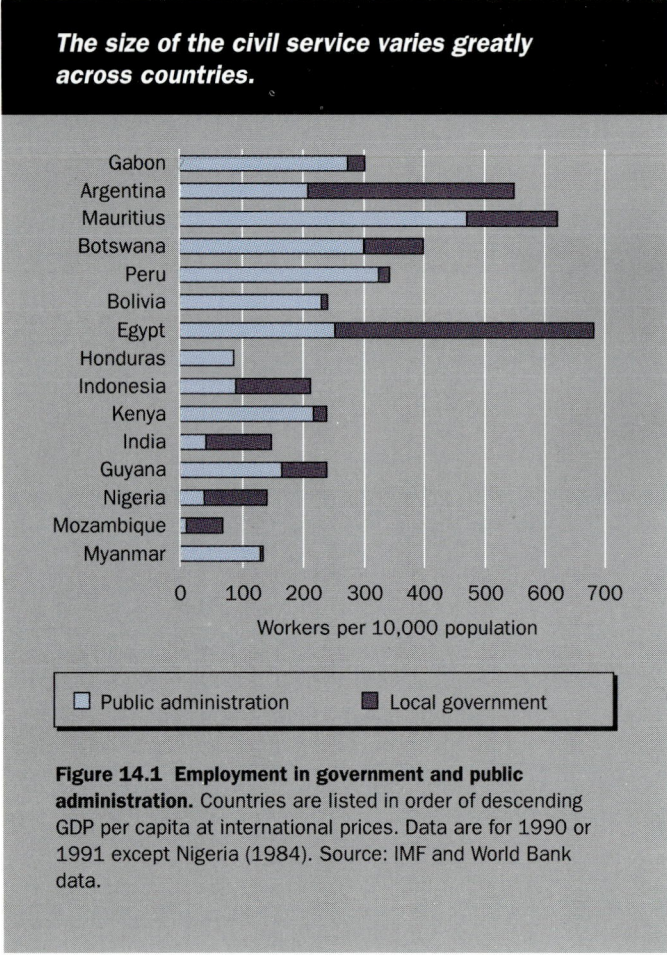

The size of the civil service varies greatly across countries.

Workers per 10,000 population

Public administration   Local government

Figure 14.1 Employment in government and public administration. Countries are listed in order of descending GDP per capita at international prices. Data are for 1990 or 1991 except Nigeria (1984). Source: IMF and World Bank data.

inadequate public salaries and so are unavailable for poor patients. And some bureaucrats are more interested in receiving commissions on procurement contracts than in ensuring the efficient execution of vital infrastructure projects.

Measuring the quality and quantity of public service provision is difficult, as is evaluating workers on the basis of their personal achievements. In such areas as health and education, public service providers are encumbered by multiple objectives—ensuring equity, addressing poverty—that their private counterparts may not face. And, as in other "street-level" bureaucracies—the police force, courts, agricultural extension agents, and irrigation—direct, continuous supervision is impossible because these workers interact with the public on a daily, one-to-one basis. Therefore it is hard to measure and reward each worker's contribution. The problem is compounded by the fact that public workers have enormous opportunities for rent-seeking behavior and shirking of responsibilities (Box 14.1).

Poor government wage and employment policies exacerbated these problems during the economic crises of the 1970s and 1980s. Many governments used their limited resources to hire more people rather than ensure adequate pay and other resources for those already on the public payroll. Often the basic pay systems collapsed, and public sector workers were forced to live on nontransparent sources of remuneration, from benefits in kind and perks to moonlighting and corruption. In some cases, foreign donors supporting particular project staff have compounded the problem by bypassing civil service rules and offering special remuneration packages. Low pay reduced the loyalty and dedication of many civil servants and lowered the incentive for talented and honest workers to apply for, or remain in, public sector jobs. Low pay also led many public workers to try to exploit their positions for financial gain, while overstaffing made it even harder to monitor effort. Lack of complementary inputs and supplies provided an excuse for poor performance. The problems of many countries' public sectors were summarized in a 1982 report by a Ugandan government commission: "The civil servant had either to survive by lowering his standard of ethics, performance, and dutifulness or remain upright and perish. He chose to survive."

Low public sector wages are a relatively new phenomenon. Government workers in many countries once earned more than their urban private sector counterparts. In Tanzania in 1971 a government worker earned about 14 percent more than a private sector employee with the same schooling and work experience, while in Kenya in 1970 the estimated differential ranged from 11 to 16 percent. The fall in the real pay of civil servants was caused by the fiscal crises that affected most low- and middle-income countries in the late 1970s and the 1980s. Faced with mounting constraints on resources, governments should have lowered or

well as the former centrally planned economies are seeking to improve the quality of their public sectors to make them more accountable, transparent, and responsive to the needs of society.

How can public services be improved? To answer that question, this chapter studies government pay and employment policies and incentive structures. It then discusses the kinds of reform that can improve the efficiency and responsiveness of public sector workers, and why economic and political barriers can make it hard to implement them.

Why do public agencies perform poorly?

Poor provision of essential public goods and services is widespread. Why are public employees, especially those in low- and middle-income countries, often so unproductive? Most of the answers lie in the connection between the special character of public service, which makes monitoring hard and output difficult to measure, and the history of ill-chosen and shortsighted personnel policies adopted by governments. Demoralized school teachers do not provide quality education. Doctors often have to supplement

Box 14.1 How does the principal-agent problem apply to public employment?

Why are public employees more likely to shirk or be inefficient than employees in the private sector? One set of explanations falls under the general heading of the "principal-agent problem." When any economic actor (the principal) employs others (agents) to carry out tasks on his or her behalf, the principal faces the challenge of ensuring that the agents work in a way that fulfills not just their own personal objectives but that of the principal as well. Private organizations tackle the principal-agent problem using four broad methods—identification, authority, peer pressure, and rewards—but many governments find it difficult to adopt and adapt these methods.

The identification method, important for organizations in Japan and other East Asian countries, relies on convincing individuals to take the goals of the firm as their own—to identify with the firm. But for identification to work with civil servants, a level of social cohesiveness and belief in the value of public service is required. The authority method relies on employees agreeing to do as they are ordered. Since this only works when the results to be achieved are very specific, and when management is indifferent about the method used to achieve them, this method is inapplicable for most government activities. Peer pressure relies on transferring responsibility for monitoring from the management to workers in groups, by making payment to each member of a group partly a function of the whole group's performance. Finally, the reward method, widely used in Western economies, relies on management inducing workers to advance the organization's objectives through personal incentives such as raises, bonuses, and promotions.

The peer pressure method, and to some extent the reward method, both require that the principal be able to evaluate group performance and identify individual contributions. This is a daunting task even in a private firm. For the civil service the problem is magnified by the difficulty of measuring productivity—ensuring that individual judges are supplying adequate justice, or that policemen are providing good security, poses unique problems.

The examples of successful civil services in East Asia and many industrial countries have shown that the principal-agent problem is not insurmountable. Most successful public sectors have relied on a mixture of the identification and reward methods. Where a public sector ethos has collapsed, however, it will often be difficult to restore identification in the short run, although this will probably be part of the long-run solution. Tackling problems of rewards will be necessary for both short- and medium-term gains.

frozen public employment. Many did the opposite. Worried that rising urban unemployment would create serious economic and political problems, they responded to economic slowdowns by trying to absorb larger numbers into the public sector. Somalia's per capita GDP fell between 1975 and 1990, but the number of Somali civil servants rose from 20,000 to 44,000 during the same period. Although Ghana's government revenue fell from 15 percent of GDP in 1970 to 6 percent in 1983, public employment more than doubled. The problem was made worse in several countries by guarantees of public sector employment for university graduates, those discharged from military service, or graduates of certain training institutions.

This combination of falling government revenues and increasing government employment meant that real earnings had to fall. Declines in the real salaries of government workers became a widespread phenomenon in countries with macroeconomic difficulties (Figure 14.2). In Zambia the salary of an undersecretary in 1986 commanded just 22 percent of its 1976 purchasing power. In El Salvador during the 1980s, real salaries of civil servants declined by 48 to 89 percent, depending on rank. Although some reduction in government pay was warranted to bring salaries in line with the market and to reflect macroeconomic adjust-

ments, such enormous declines undoubtedly reduced the quality of public services.

The quality of public services deteriorated further because of salary compression, as the salaries of professional and skilled staff were allowed to fall more quickly in real terms than the earnings of those in lower grades. Tanzania provides an example. In 1969 the top public sector salary was thirty times the lowest government wage. By the mid-1980s this ratio had collapsed to six to one. Similarly, a Zambian assistant director received seventeen times what the lowest-paid public employee earned in 1971, but only 3.7 times as much in 1986. This was not the result of any market evaluation of experience or education. Rather it was a reflection of policymakers' sense of fairness and of political realities that made higher salaries easier to cut. Drastic changes in relative pay had significant consequences for the hiring, retention, and performance of senior civil servants and the most highly skilled employees, and hence for the productivity of those under their supervision.

Reductions in expenditures on materials and supplies led to a further deterioration in the quality of public services. Civil servants were not provided with the tools they needed to carry out their work. Many public hospitals in low- and middle-income countries have excellent physi-

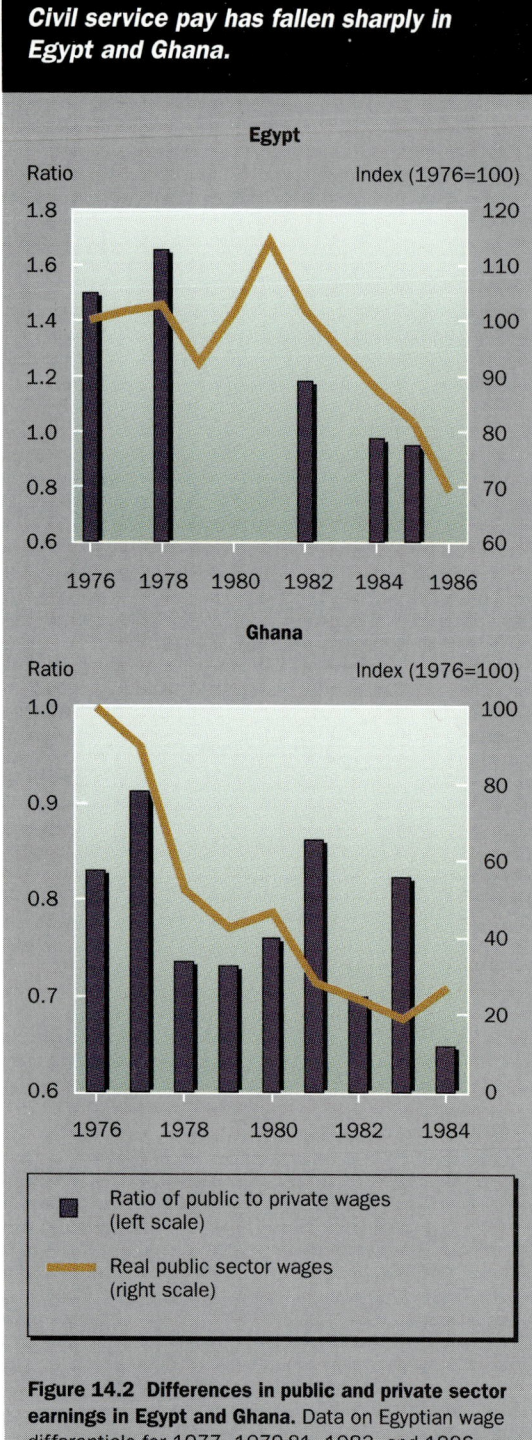

Civil service pay has fallen sharply in Egypt and Ghana.

Egypt

Ghana

Ratio of public to private wages (left scale)

Real public sector wages (right scale)

Figure 14.2 Differences in public and private sector earnings in Egypt and Ghana. Data on Egyptian wage differentials for 1977, 1979-81, 1983, and 1986 were unavailable. Source: Banerji and Sabot, forthcoming; Zaytoun 1991.

cians but lack medicines and surgical supplies, severely limiting their ability to serve patients. Teachers in public schools are not provided with books, blackboards, or chalk, and agriculture extension agents receive salaries but lack the vehicles and fuel needed to visit farms. Faced with a choice between cutting the public sector's wage bill and reducing spending on operations and maintenance, governments chose the politically easy route.

Poor working conditions in the public sector have led the best and the brightest members of the labor force in many countries—in Africa, Eastern Europe, and South Asia—to look for jobs in the private sector, or even to leave their countries. Most recently, civil service employment has declined—by 36 percent in Jamaica between 1982 and 1988 and by as much as 23 percent in Guinea between 1985 and 1989. But the quality of civil servants may be declining as well. A root cause is the inability of public employment structures to adequately reward the most highly skilled workers. Reductions in employment also often fail to protect the most able, relying instead on across-the-board cuts.

Improving the quality and accountability of public workers

Improving the performance of government workers, although difficult, is not impossible, as the well-functioning bureaucracies of some East Asian and industrial countries prove. Some of the issues and the different approaches used to tackle them can be illustrated by considering government irrigation workers in India and the Republic of Korea.

• • •

Being an irrigation patroller is a full-time job in India. Selected by the engineer in charge of the project, the patroller supervises canal gates far from his own village and knows that, although he will be transferred to another posting within six years, he cannot be fired easily. Suspicious that the patroller is not performing his duties, his supervisor takes every occasion to berate him and the five other patrollers under his supervision.

• • •

The Korean patroller is a farmer from one of the villages served by the canal. He supervises the canal gates part-time for six months during the year. Selected by his village chief, the patroller knows that his daily wage depends on his being renominated by the chief. He has one supervisor, who is from the same locality but works in another part of the Farmland Improvement Organization. The supervisor drops by unannounced once or twice a week for lunch, to see whether the patroller is having any problems.

• • •

Irrigation patrollers are crucial for the functioning of canal irrigation systems in both countries. Patrolling canal banks, they open and shut water gates, diverting the flow of water to the areas that most need it. The nature of the job makes it practically impossible to monitor performance in any direct, objective way. But shirking or corruption on the patroller's part can have serious consequences for the local harvest. The Korean and Indian approaches to monitoring effort have very different results. The Korean civil servant operates under a number of checks and balances, lacking in the case of his Indian counterpart, that control any desire to shirk responsibilities. As part of the local farming network, the Korean patroller is directly accountable to his chief and to his peers—if he slips up, his own family and friends will suffer, and he will lose his job. He is further discouraged from shirking by the random pattern of monitoring and by his desire to meet his colleague's expectations. The Indian worker, on the other hand, has no real disincentive to shirk his duties. Not a farmer himself, he works for a community that is not his own, and he can only be fired for major transgressions. Moreover, his adversarial relationship with his supervisor encourages him to malinger.

The quantity and pay of civil servants are not, therefore, the only variables that affect the quality of public services. Governments also need to ensure that they select the right people, reward them for hard work, and hold them fully accountable for their actions, and that the quality of civil servants' work is subjected, whenever possible, to the discipline of the marketplace.

One way of ensuring that the civil service attracts the best employees is to combine good salaries with an objective, merit-based selection procedure, such as a system of entrance examinations and interviews. India does well in this regard. University graduates are recruited into officer ranks by national and state public service commissions, which interview candidates and design examinations for different government departments. Although the large number of applicants means that some interviews take less than five minutes, the examination and the interview add a merit-based element to recruitment.

Public sector workers also need to be rewarded for their achievements and held accountable for their failures. One powerful way of motivating public sector workers involves linking promotion to performance—this runs directly counter to the tradition of civil service promotions being unrelated to merit. The Indian civil service is typical. Promotion within the officer cadre is based solely on seniority. Officers are recruited in groups, and within each group seniority is determined by the ranking assigned by the public service commission on the basis of the initial examination and interview. This seniority ranking is carried by officers for the rest of their careers, and it is rare for an officer to be promoted out of order.

Bureaucracies in the successful East Asian countries have introduced merit as a basis for determining promotion, linking incentives for individual performance with en-

couragement for teamwork. Promotion of officers in the Korean civil service is based on a formula that assigns weight to both length of service and individual merit. The judgment of merit is partly subjective and partly objective and includes test scores from training courses, performance assessments by supervisors, and records of awards for outstanding job performance or other public service. In addition, assemblies, group meetings, sports, and competitions among units are used to strengthen teamwork. Such actions reinforce the sense of each administrative unit as a group.

Promotion systems based on merit have traditionally been difficult to organize in the public sector, because managers cannot objectively measure the performance of individuals or groups who provide public services for which no standard of market value exists. One solution is to decentralize some public activities and encourage the private sector to provide public goods. Not all public goods can be supplied in this way, but it is often important to subject civil servants to some form of market discipline. Reforms of the Chilean education system provide an example. Ownership of public schools was first transferred to the municipalities, which were given full responsibility for managing them and paying the teachers. This decentralization made the civil servants more directly accountable to the populations they served. Next, central government support to public schools and subsidized private schools was reformed, with amounts based on the number of students enrolled. By setting the payment per student 10 percent higher than before the reform, the government ensured that private schools were able to provide free education and that the public schools had to compete for central government financing. School administrators and teachers, who remained public employees, could now be easily monitored, and the improved schools attracted more students and more government funds. However, this reform program was imposed by a military government against a backdrop of repressive labor policies, so its implementation involved a high social cost.

Politics and public employment reforms

The need for public employment reform is recognized in many countries. Yet governments are often reluctant to undertake serious changes. Governments oppose reforms that include laying off redundant public employees and decompressing wages, on the grounds that they are not politically feasible, since lower level workers are usually the main losers. Some governments also argue that, because urban unskilled public workers constitute an essential part of the regime's support, penalizing them would have great political cost. There are several examples of strong political opposition to civil service reforms. Efforts to downsize the Brazilian civil service, for example, have met with formidable opposition and have been constrained by constitutionally guaranteed employee rights. Jamaica's powerful civil service union successfully opposed significant pay restructuring that would have rewarded the upper tiers at the expense of lower ones.

In many cases, however, the political risks incurred by regimes undertaking public pay and employment reforms have been overstated. Argentina, Ghana, and Guinea have lowered public employment by 16 to 23 percent without much political opposition, regime destabilization, or social upheaval. Why is there often surprisingly little opposition to reform? One reason is that wages and benefits in public employment have already fallen dramatically in countries that are in particular need of reform. The less the job is worth, the less the opposition to retrenchment—the costs of adjustment have, by and large, already been borne. Thus even modest severance pay may be adequate to compensate for large-scale retrenchments. In addition, evidence indicates that the usual targets of civil service reforms are the large number of unskilled workers occupying the lower ranks of the civil service, who are relatively powerless. In most countries public workers are insufficiently organized to mount a viable protest to proposed cuts.

Some governments avoid reforming the civil service for fear of disrupting their system of patronage, which is sometimes necessary for their political survival. The organization and functioning of bureaucracies are usually closely related to the generation and distribution of the economic privileges required for politicians to stay in power. Governments often rely on the resources they command in the civil service to fragment opposition and build patron-client linkages of support. Civil service reforms are perceived by these governments as a serious threat.

• • •

Many governments are realizing that increasing exposure to international competition requires well-functioning, flexible bureaucracies. To be an effective employer and ensure public services of high quality, governments need to reform their pay, recruitment, and promotion policies and make more extensive use of the private sector in delivering services. However, implementing these reforms, which often imply downsizing the public work force, is difficult because political and economic needs often conflict. Success requires a high degree of political commitment.

PART FOUR

How Can Policy Choices Help Workers in Periods of Major Change?

STRUCTURAL ADJUSTMENT and the transition from central planning often bring wrenching changes for workers and their families. But is the pain they bear due to the faulty design of reform policy, or to the failed development strategy that reform is now in the process of uprooting? Are workers suffering a disproportionate burden of the costs of adjustment? We look at these questions in this part of the Report. Chapter 15 surveys the similarities and differences of the difficult adjustments that many countries are now going through, and how labor fares in each case. Chapter 16 analyzes who gains and who loses during these episodes of major economic upheaval. Chapter 17 considers a menu of microeconomic choices that can both speed the transition and ease its impact on workers.

CHAPTER 15

Patterns of Reform

THE CONTOURS OF THE WORLD ECONOMY have changed radically over the past few years as a whole series of countries have embarked upon dramatic transformations. Almost every region of the world has been affected: Latin America and the Middle East, in response to the debt crisis and oil price shocks; China and Viet Nam, as they undertake market reforms; Sub-Saharan Africa, as the continent struggles to restore growth; and Central and Eastern Europe and the former Soviet Union, as they make their epic transition to a market system.

Most of these transformations involve a shift from a failed development strategy to a new one. They often occur in a context of crisis: in response to external shocks, as in Latin America after the debt crisis and in Sub-Saharan Africa following the slump in commodity prices, or to a general collapse of the previous system, as in the former centrally planned economies. But international shocks often simply bring the problems of failed growth into the open and expose the internal inconsistencies of the system in place.

Whatever the cause, the collapse of a development strategy forces countries to undergo reform. Some countries, like the Democratic People's Republic of Korea, resist and try to stay with the old strategy as long as possible. Others, such as Nigeria and Venezuela, get stuck for a time between strategies. But more and more countries, from Poland to Chile, are taking the need for change head-on, rapidly adjusting to new realities and switching to new development paths. This switch typically involves turmoil and potentially high adjustment costs but, if successful, leads the economy onto a path of faster growth.

The wide variety of causes of change and the different starting points of countries facing similar shocks make it difficult to generalize about their impact on workers and

the appropriate policy response. But the experience of the past decade makes clear that workers suffer more when necessary reforms are delayed or aborted, that restoring sustained growth is the key to a successful transformation, and that there is an important role for government policy in easing the transition for workers and equipping them to succeed in new circumstances.

This chapter maps out a taxonomy of economic transformations and highlights the implications of each type for the labor market. It then focuses on how differing initial conditions affect the overall reform strategy and the role of macroeconomic policy.

Major features of reform

No one country's experience in managing transformation is exactly like another's. But each involves some combination of macroeconomic stabilization, liberalization of trade and internal markets, and institutional reform. The last two are part and parcel of the strategic shift to greater international integration and a reduced role of the state. All three have an impact on labor. We distinguish four broad patterns that transformation takes in different countries; Table 15.1 summarizes how these patterns differ on each of the three dimensions of reform:

- *The industrial postsocialist pattern.* Typical of the industrial former centrally planned economies, these transitions are characterized by radical institutional reform, huge drops in GDP, and substantial redeployment of labor across sectors and from the state to the private sector. Nearly 195 million workers in these economies are struggling with transition.
- *The Latin American pattern.* These transformations combine stabilization and substantial liberalization, especially of trade. They are associated with moderate rede-

Patterns of reform are distinguished by their differences in emphasis.

Table 15.1 Characteristics of the four major patterns of reform

| Pattern | Scope of reform | | |
	Stabilization	Liberalization	Institutional reform
Industrial postsocialist	Major	Major	Major
Latin American	Moderate to major	Moderate	Moderate
Sub-Saharan African	Minor to moderate	Moderate to major	Moderate
Asian agrarian	Minor	Moderate to major	Moderate to major

In reforming economies in Latin America and Africa, real wages often fell sharply and then recovered, while unemployment often remained moderate.

Table 15.2 Real wages and unemployment in four reforming countries in Latin America and Sub-Saharan Africa

Country	1978	1979	1980	1981	1982	1983	1984	1985	1986	1987	1988	1989	1990
Real wages (index)[a]													
Bolivia	196.4	200.0	181.8	145.5	101.8	76.4	65.5	100.0	61.8	76.4	..	..	..
Chile	82.0	94.3	100.9	105.6	116.1	97.3	100.0	94.2	94.5	93.9	99.3	104.0	105.2
Mexico	..	..	129.4	135.5	133.5	93.6	100.0	94.4	66.5	66.2	81.2	93.7	103.3
Ghana	275.6	226.8	243.9	143.9	129.3	100.0	146.3	212.2	218.8	254.3	254.3	295.7	379.3
Unemployment rate (percent)													
Bolivia	..	..	7.5	6.2	7.5	8.2	6.6	5.7	4.2	5.9	11.5	10.7	..
Chile	14.0	14.0	10.0	11.0	20.0	15.0	14.0	12.0	9.0	8.0	6.0	5.0	6.0
Mexico	..	..	4.7	4.2	4.2	6.1	5.6	4.4	4.3	3.9	3.5	2.9	2.8
Ghana	..	..	..	..	..	0.5	0.4	0.5	0.5	1.8	1.2	..	..

.. Not available.
a. The index is set equal to 100 in the initial year of adjustment.
Source: World Bank staff estimates.

ployment of labor and some decline in GDP. This pattern is consistent with the experiences of most Latin American countries, but also of some economies in the Middle East and North Africa, and that of the Philippines. About 155 million workers in those regions are affected.

■ *The Sub-Saharan African pattern.* Macroeconomic decline typically precedes reform in these adjustment episodes, which are characterized by profound restructuring within a small modern sector and by a relatively weak rural supply response (due to weak infrastructure and continuing policy biases). There are approximately 70 million workers in Sub-Saharan African countries struggling with adjustment.

■ *The Asian agrarian pattern.* These transitions in primarily agricultural economies are marked by steady growth in GDP, some institutional reform, and (over time) potentially a large redeployment of labor. This is the pattern in China, India, and Viet Nam. Slightly over a billion workers, well over a third of the world's work force, live in the Asian agrarian economies.

The impact of reform on the labor market

The labor market plays an important role in determining the success of adjustment and reform and their impact on living standards. The response of real wages to economy-wide drops in the demand for labor, and the ease with which labor can be redeployed from collapsing sectors, together have a large impact on the welfare of the working population during transitions. Different patterns of employment losses, real wage declines, and unemployment increases have very different implications for the distribution of income and the welfare of the population.

Real wages and unemployment

Most adjustment involves a fall in the aggregate demand for labor as a result of macroeconomic decline and institutional reform. Adjusting to this fall in labor demand usually requires a decline in the real wage. Many countries that went through severe macroeconomic adjustment in Latin America and Sub-Saharan Africa experienced dramatic fluctuations in real wages, which at their lowest fell to 30 percent of their peak levels—a far greater decline than that of GDP (Table 15.2). Real wages fell because nominal wage increases typically lagged behind inflation. In all successful adjustment episodes, however, wages recovered as macroeconomic adjustment curbed inflation, but sometimes not to their former levels. This pattern is visible in Bolivia, Ghana, and Mexico, among others. Large real wage declines usually reduced the need for absolute falls in employment, and unemployment in these countries remained moderate throughout—with Bolivia a possible exception. In a few Latin American and Sub-Saharan African countries, real wage fluctuations were less extreme; an example is Chile, where wage declines were moderated by institutional mechanisms such as the indexation of wages to prices, but at the cost of much higher unemployment.

Patterns of wage and employment adjustment among former centrally planned countries fit into two distinct groups. China and Viet Nam, which weathered the transition to the market without macroeconomic decline, showed fairly steady growth in real wages and negligible unemployment. Industrial postsocialist economies such as Latvia, Poland, and Russia, on the other hand, all suffered a combination of sharp drops in real wages and falls in employment (Table 15.3). In Poland wage declines were less severe and the rise in unemployment was sharper, whereas in Russia real wages fell by more, but open unemployment has remained low. These differences reflect both the influence of institutional factors, such as the level of unemployment benefits, and choices by firms and workers about labor shedding versus reductions in hours worked per employee.

Relative wages and the redeployment of labor

All transformations involve the reallocation of labor from unviable jobs to higher productivity sectors and activities. What matters here is not the aggregate response of wage levels, but whether the labor market can send the signals that attract labor to those markets where demand is high. The labor market performs this task primarily though changes in relative wages, with wages in expanding sectors rising relative to those in contracting ones. A temporary increase in wage differentials encourages labor to flow out of unviable jobs into new jobs in the growing sectors. The faster the flow of labor to the growing sectors, the faster the desired adjustment in national output. If that flow is sluggish—because relative wages are not changing, because adjustment costs are high, or because old jobs become unviable before new ones are created—the economy may experience larger transitory declines in employment and parallel rises in unemployment.

Two indicators of the impact on labor are the aggregate change in the openness of the economy (for centrally planned economies, in the openness to trade with market economies) and the rise in the share of private employment. For developing countries already oriented to markets, the increase in openness appears more important; for some industrial postsocialist countries, both shifts can be very large (Figure 15.1).

Most reforming economies show significant shifts in relative wages. In Ghana relative wages increased in both agriculture and mining, the two sectors favored by the reform program. In Mexico intersectoral wage differentials were compressed initially but later widened, with wages in growing, export-oriented industries such as transport equipment rising relative to those in contracting, import-substituting sectors. In Chile manufacturing wages rose relative to the average wage, and within manufacturing, wage differentials across sectors and by skill level also increased. Sizable changes in relative wages are also evident among the industrial postsocialist countries. Sectoral wage dispersion in the Czech and Slovak republics has risen, and a similar increase in the variance of wages across industries has occurred in Bulgaria.

Employment usually shifts in parallel to these movements in relative wages. Bolivia, Côte d'Ivoire, and Ghana all experienced shifts back into agriculture as a result of movements in relative prices and wages. In Costa Rica employment moved into industries producing exportable goods. And in the Czech and Slovak republics, Poland, and

---

Economies in transition show a variety of labor market adjustment patterns.

Table 15.3 Real wages and unemployment in five former centrally planned economies

Economy	1984	1985	1986	1987	1988	1989	1990	1991	1992	1993
Real wages (index)[a]										
China[b]	82.7	94.9	100.0	108.2	109.1	108.3	103.1	112.6	117.2	..
Hungary	..	..	..	..	99.3	100.0	98.7	96.6	97.9	96.8
Latvia	..	..	..	..	90.3	94.9	100.0	73.9	49.6	54.7
Poland	..	..	..	81.4	93.6	100.0	75.7	75.5	73.4	71.2
Russia	..	..	..	..	90.0	95.3	103.5	100.0	70.0	73.4
Unemployment rate (percent)										
China	1.9	1.8	2.0	2.0	2.0	2.6	2.5	3.0	..	..
Hungary	..	..	..	..	0.3	0.4	1.9	7.8	13.2	12.6
Latvia	..	..	..	..	0.0	0.0	0.0	0.1	2.3	5.7
Poland	..	..	..	0.1	0.1	0.1	6.3	11.8	13.6	15.7
Russia	..	..	..	..	0.0	0.0	0.0	0.1	4.8	5.5

.. Not available.
a. The index is set equal to 100 in the initial year of adjustment.
b. In 1986 the first major attempts to reform the state enterprise sector were made.
Source: World Bank staff estimates.

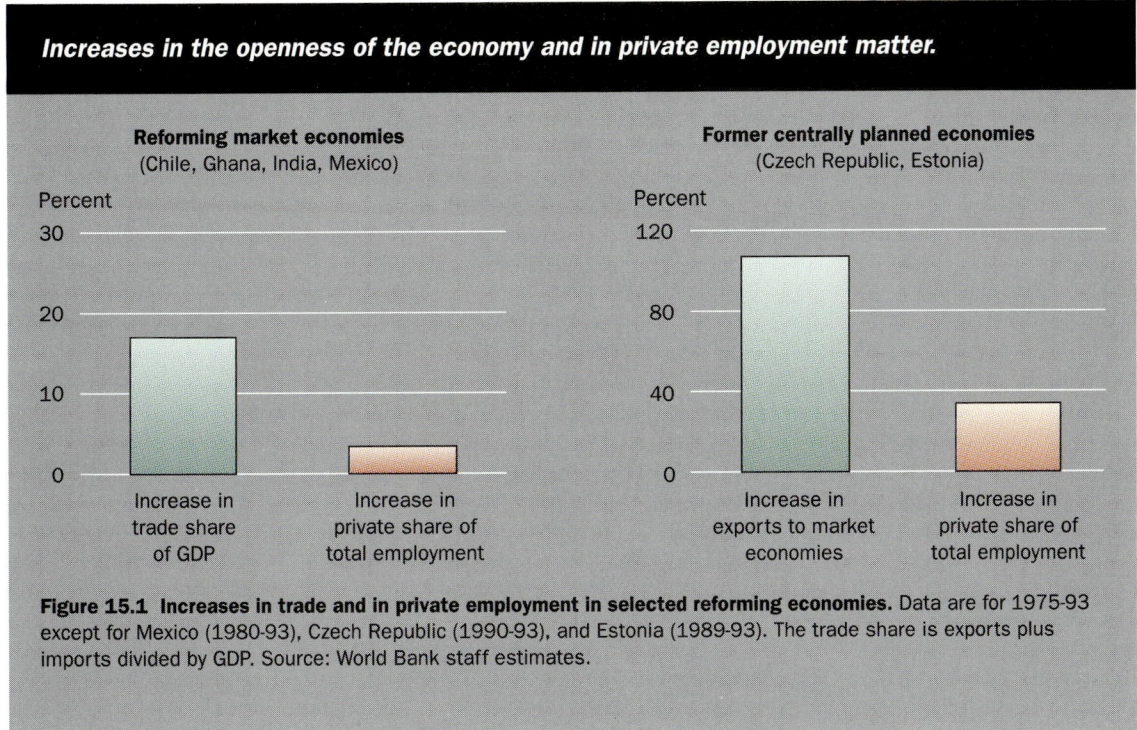

Increases in the openness of the economy and in private employment matter.

Reforming market economies
(Chile, Ghana, India, Mexico)

Former centrally planned economies
(Czech Republic, Estonia)

Figure 15.1 Increases in trade and in private employment in selected reforming economies. Data are for 1975-93 except for Mexico (1980-93), Czech Republic (1990-93), and Estonia (1989-93). The trade share is exports plus imports divided by GDP. Source: World Bank staff estimates.

Russia, labor flowed from industry to services, and from the public to the private sector. In Russia, for example, the share of state employment declined from nearly 83 percent in 1990 to 67 percent in 1993.

The constraints imposed by initial conditions

Initial conditions are an important influence on the scope and pace of reform. The pace of job destruction, for example, can be managed only if the formerly protected sector is small relative to the rest of the economy. Similarly, a gradualist approach to reform is easier in an economy that starts from macroeconomic equilibrium than in one plagued by high inflation or shortages of foreign exchange. A comparison of China and Russia illustrates this. China chose a two-track approach to reform: it continued state control of existing enterprises while permitting growth of a new, nonstate sector largely outside government control. This strategy was possible because the inefficient state sector accounted for a relatively small share of the economy. And because China had a far larger informal agricultural sector than more heavily industrialized Russia (Figure 15.2), it had experienced less misallocation of resources.

These different initial conditions constrained both the path of transition and the strategic choices open to policymakers. China's large rural supply potential gave a powerful initial spurt to growth and employment creation in the nonstate sector and allowed the government to take a gradualist approach to reform of inefficient state enterprises.

Lacking such supply potential, the countries of Central and Eastern Europe and the former Soviet Union had to reform their state sectors and accept the destruction of state employment rather than postpone reforms as China did. As a general proposition, initial conditions are more advantageous when labor and capital are highly mobile, and where there are viable sectors with a strong potential for increasing supply. Countries with a developed formal private sector and only moderate protection required less sectoral reallocation of labor than did the former centrally planned economies. In contrast, massive labor reallocation is required in the countries of Central and Eastern Europe and the former Soviet Union. Many Sub-Saharan African countries had little misallocated labor but experienced weak short-run output responses because of inadequate infrastructure and institutional support and continued policy biases against agriculture.

The role of policy

The choice and sequencing of policies can also have a big impact on the speed of transition and the welfare of workers. The key policy concern in managing structural reform is how to facilitate the flow of workers from unviable jobs to new ones without raising the short-term costs of adjustment. Policy choices involve several dimensions.

The first policy choice is *when to start adjustment*. There is sometimes room for discretion: Peru could have initiated reform in the mid-1980s but chose to delay—at great cost

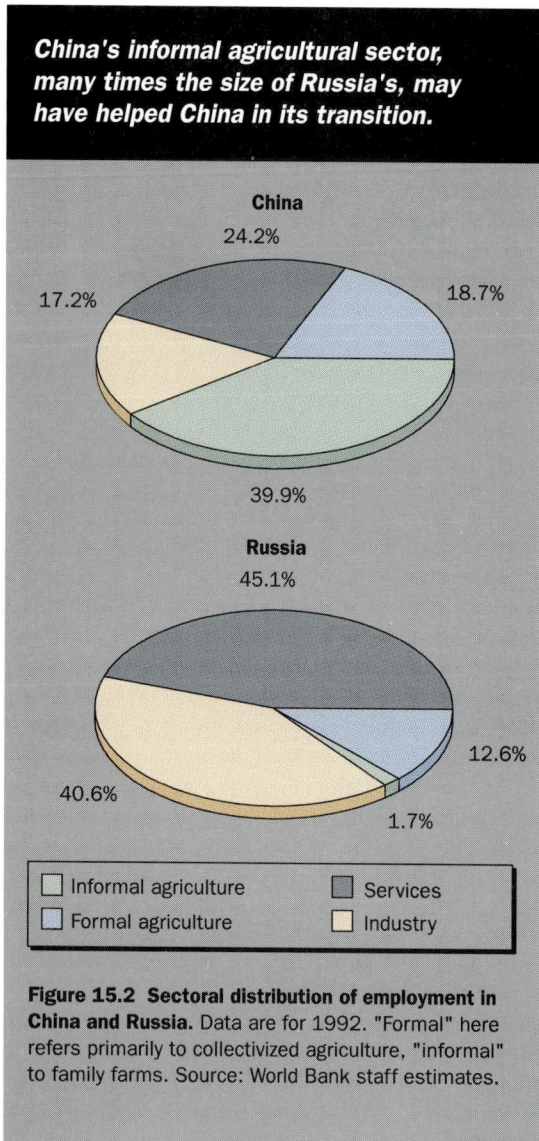

China's informal agricultural sector, many times the size of Russia's, may have helped China in its transition.

China
24.2%
17.2%
18.7%
39.9%

Russia
45.1%
40.6%
1.7%
12.6%

☐ Informal agriculture   ■ Services
☐ Formal agriculture   ☐ Industry

Figure 15.2 Sectoral distribution of employment in China and Russia. Data are for 1992. "Formal" here refers primarily to collectivized agriculture, "informal" to family farms. Source: World Bank staff estimates.

in terms of increasing poverty. But it is generally better to tackle reform as soon as trust in the government's commitment has been established. If policymakers wait until the economy collapses, they will have fewer options and probably a more painful transition. Tackling reform before the government has established its commitment and credibility, however, can backfire and set back the cause of reform, with disastrous consequences for growth, as is evident from the experience of Côte d'Ivoire in the 1980s.

Second, policymakers have to decide the *speed of reform*. Should reform be gradual, with slow destruction of unviable jobs? Or should it be rapid, even at the risk of encouraging a sharp initial fall in aggregate employment? From labor's perspective the ideal is to phase out jobs only as new jobs are created, and thus to minimize the drop in total

labor demand. This strategy has been used by such countries as China and India, which have chosen to protect unviable jobs to avoid social and political difficulties, even though the inefficiency of the protected sector will at some point have to be addressed. For most countries, however, a gradualist approach is rarely an option. Most economies begin reform in the midst of a macroeconomic crisis, with accelerating inflation and an unsustainable current account deficit. Tackling stabilization and liberalization simultaneously is then the only option. Rapid stabilization can only work if the government's stated intention to be tough on inflation is believed. Most often this calls for rapid disinflation to establish credibility, precluding a gradualist approach. The more aggressive and comprehensive the reform package, the more credible the government's intentions, and the sharper the change in people's expectations and behavior.

The third dimension of policy design concerns the *sequencing of reforms*. An important lesson of both failed and successful reform attempts in Sub-Saharan Africa and Latin America is that governments must take into account the interdependence of markets in the transition process and their different speeds of adjustment. Reform must not stop with goods and capital markets, especially because labor market adjustment is almost always slower than that of goods and capital markets anyway. Labor market reform is often the missing ingredient that can hamper the process, as a sluggish labor market response leaves the partially reformed economy vulnerable to shocks during the transition. The collapse of the Chilean program in 1982 illustrates this point. By 1980 Chile had liberalized both its external and its financial markets, but it had only partially reformed the labor market and had left wage indexation mechanisms intact. A sudden increase in capital inflows during 1979–81 led to an overappreciation of the peso, compounded by the indexation of wages to past inflation. The peso appreciated further in real terms. In 1982 the currency collapsed, depreciating by nearly 90 percent in just a year; output contracted by 14 percent; and the unemployment rate increased to a quarter of the work force.

The *level of the real exchange rate* is the fourth crucial element of policy design, and one that Chile's 1982 experience highlights. Large real overvaluations of a country's currency can have significant adverse effects on tradable-goods industries and can weaken the response of exports and the creation of new jobs. Ultimately, real overvaluation of the currency can undermine the whole reform process. Côte d'Ivoire in the mid-1980s attempted to liberalize while sustaining a fixed exchange rate and a large fiscal deficit: the result was real appreciation of the currency, an enlarged import bill, and a balance of payments crisis. Failed adjustment translated into stagnant growth and declining GDP per capita for most of the decade. In contrast, Ghana's liberalization was accompanied by several large devaluations of the cedi and by an adjustment in macroeconomic policies so as to reduce inflation. The result was a real devaluation, which provided a major impetus for the growth of exports and cushioned the impact of reduced protection on the import-competing sector.

A fifth dimension of policy design concerns the *political economy of reform*. Experience shows that the key to successful adjustment is a credible commitment to moving away from an old, bad development path to a new, growth-friendly equilibrium. Governments must gain this credibility, not simply by repeating the mantras of the International Monetary Fund and the World Bank, but by following a consistent approach to reform.

A credible and sustainable reform program requires that government, capital, and labor perceive a common interest. Winning the support of organized labor is critical, especially if, as is sometimes the case, unions represent only that part of the labor force that was relatively privileged before the transition and may have a vested interest in impeding reform. Making the long-term gains from reform explicit can help build support for change, as can mechanisms that precommit the government to follow through with the reforms and prevent it from reneging on its promises. In Israel and Mexico during the 1980s, all-encompassing social pacts helped gain broad support for reform. Such pacts may also play an important role in South Africa in the 1990s. Social pacts can provide a vehicle for labor, employers, and governments to reach some consensus on the reform package as a whole and on the tradeoffs involved. They can also help break nominal price-wage inertia. But social pacts have important drawbacks. In particular, there is a conflict between the coordinated wage adjustments that social pacts bring and the strong need for relative wage flexibility and labor reallocation during restructuring. To resolve this conflict, countries that have centralized union bargaining may want to move quickly to a decentralized arrangement once they achieve stabilization. In early 1995 Mexico moved in that direction—perhaps belatedly—by terminating centralized wage agreements in favor of decentralized bargaining.

• • •

Over the past two decades many developing and former centrally planned countries have undertaken major shifts in their development strategies. Two features have dominated these shifts: a move toward export-oriented policies and open markets, and a reassessment of the role of the state. These long-term changes pose unique challenges to the functioning of labor markets. They require an acceleration of the redeployment of labor from unviable sectors to expanding ones. And they involve coping with sharp, transitory drops in the demand for labor nationwide. How labor fares during these periods of major change depends on how successfully countries manage these two tasks. Although initial conditions matter greatly in easing the adjustment process, so do policy choices about the timing, pace, and sequencing of reform.

CHAPTER 16

Winners and Losers

Workers suffer during the wrenching transition from a failed development strategy, even if in the long run they benefit from the change. The poor may find it especially difficult to cope with the falls in wages and employment that tend to occur during the transition. Sometimes women are disproportionately affected. And the pain can be deeply felt if the transition is accompanied by recession or if the renewal of growth takes longer than expected.

Are the burdens that stabilization and reform programs place on workers an inevitable cost, or are they evidence of the programs' flawed design? Many observers—from union spokespersons to some international and nongovernmental organizations—argue that, in developing market economies and former centrally planned economies alike, structural adjustment policies are too preoccupied with inflation and fiscal balance, and with deregulating and liberalizing markets, and too little concerned about the immediate impact on workers. A review of the evidence certainly suggests that labor does suffer during adjustment, and maybe worse than other groups. But are there effective alternative policies that would better suit the interests of workers? This chapter examines the distribution of the burdens of transition and the claim that adjustment policies are not in labor's best interest.

Adjustment, labor, and the poor

Transformations involve profound structural reforms. They create new opportunities as well as new risks, which will necessarily generate winners and losers. But in moving labor to more productive uses, structural change eventually increases output and the returns to labor.

Labor does tend to suffer during the initial period of adjustment, and possibly more than capital. But most often it is not because the design of the adjustment policies is flawed, but because adjustment occurs simultaneously with—or is triggered by—a macroeconomic crisis, followed by a sharp drop in aggregate demand. Labor is less internationally mobile than capital and thus less able to leave when the domestic economy declines (see Chapter 9). So when an economy crashes, labor is likely to bear the brunt of the shock, while capital flees. But it is usually the aggregate demand shock, not the ensuing adjustment, that hurts labor.

Adjustment can pay off for labor, despite temporary declines in employment and real wages, as the experience of adjusting African countries during the 1980s demonstrates. Of twenty-nine Sub-Saharan African countries examined in a recent World Bank study, the six that went furthest in undertaking and sustaining major policy reforms enjoyed the strongest resurgence in economic growth. Between 1981–86 and 1987–91 these six countries experienced a median increase in annual growth of GDP per capita of 2 percentage points. The countries that did not undertake adjustment saw their median growth rate fall to −2 percent a year. Although data on wage and employment trends in Africa are scarce, evidence from two adjusting countries—Ghana and Tanzania—reveals that both employment and wage performance improved following structural reform. During 1985–92, employment in Tanzania grew at an average annual rate of 6.1 percent, up from −1.5 percent during the first half of the decade. In Ghana real earnings in the private sector almost tripled between 1983 and 1988, following the reforms.

In Latin America the poor certainly suffered during the macroeconomic crisis, but largely because of past policy mistakes, not because of the adjustment policies themselves. Rising poverty in Brazil and Peru in the 1980s was due to lack of adjustment and economic decline. In some Latin American countries there is evidence that inequality rose in recessions and fell in recoveries (Figure 16.1), but this appears to be an inherent feature of the business cycle—as it is in some industrial countries—and not of reform. In Chile there is some evidence of rising wage differentials among workers of different educational attainments until 1992, but rapid growth in wages and employment clearly brought substantial benefits for all Chilean workers.

The transition has been associated with rising inequality in the former centrally planned economies. Inequality under socialism was very low, but market economies require some inequality to function efficiently: wages must differ if investments in skills and experience are to be rewarded. An increase in inequality was thus an unavoidable—and indeed a desirable—consequence of the move from central planning toward a market system. In the Czech Republic, Poland, Slovenia, and eastern Germany increased inequality has largely resulted from rising relative returns to the highly educated. There has been little or no change in the ratio between the wages of the lowest-paid 10 percent of workers and those of the median worker.

The transition to the market has meant an increase in the ranks of the poor in all the former centrally planned economies. Increases in poverty have been large in Belarus, Lithuania, Moldova, and Russia. The incidence of poverty is likely to fall with economic growth, which has already resumed in several transitional economies. The poverty that occurs during the transition should thus not become permanent for most of those who fell into it. Only those with poor educational qualifications that prevent them from adapting to the new system are likely to remain poor.

The worst scenario for poor workers is a reform that starts and then falters. In countries that abandon reform midway or get stuck between paths, living standards often fall dramatically and stay low. In Côte d'Ivoire in 1984–86, sustained economic growth resulting from an attempt at structural reform and from buoyant cocoa and coffee prices led to substantial reductions in poverty. But when the country's terms of trade collapsed in 1986 and the government abandoned reform, GDP growth plummeted and poverty soared, erasing the earlier gains. Between 1985 and 1988 the share of the population living below the poverty line increased from 30 percent to 46 percent. Another example is the Philippines in the early 1980s, where inflation and a misaligned exchange rate caused the poor to suffer and prevented them from achieving any gains. And in Ukraine in the early 1990s, hyperinflation, continued restrictions on foreign trade, and a sluggish response in the private sector pummeled the poor without delivering on the promise of quick improvement.

Recession, unemployment, and falling wages all hit the poor very hard in the early phase of transition, but the structural reforms that constitute the real transformation are good for poor workers, even in the short run. Trade liberalization and real depreciation of the currency together promote exports, which tend in developing countries to be intensive in less skilled labor. And private sector development often means the growth of new businesses in labor-intensive sectors. Because tradable goods account for a smaller part of the consumption baskets of most poor people than of the well-off, the rising relative prices of imports affect them less.

In former centrally planned economies, however, these short-run effects can work against the poor. Housing, utilities, and public transport were almost free under the previous system, and food was subsidized, whereas most imported goods were unavailable or available only at very high prices in the black market. With trade liberalization, exchange rate adjustment, and cuts in subsidies, imported goods become less expensive or available for the first time, while prices of utilities, food, and housing increase.

Who bears the burden of major changes?

Most households depend largely on their incomes from work. Therefore household living standards during periods of major change are closely—although not exclusively—tied to what happens in the labor market. But looking at wages alone can be deceptive, because a number of other factors influence current standards of living, such as labor force participation rates, rates of personal saving, the variety and quality of products consumed, and formal and informal income transfers (Box 16.1).

The demand for labor has fallen in almost all episodes of transition and adjustment (except perhaps in those of China and Viet Nam) as a result of some combination of macroeconomic decline and labor redeployment. The reduction is most pronounced in sectors that are no longer economically viable. Almost no adjusting economy entirely escapes a temporary decline in real wages and increase in unemployment, but the size and duration of both effects differ from country to country. What ultimately makes the difference is how many new jobs are created and how quickly—and that depends on the speed and credibility of reform.

How workers and households react to the shift in the pattern of labor demand depends on the age, sources of income, and employment status of the worker and on the size of the household. Where there is support for workers during spells out of work, whether in the form of income transfers from the state, from other household members, or from other households, the proportion of the working-age population that is out of work typically rises. The rise in the number of people out of work can take the form of increased unemployment, early retirement, or other withdrawal from the labor force (for example, the discouraged-worker effect).

In most countries in Central and Eastern Europe unemployment has reached levels well above 10 percent (it has risen above 15 percent in Bulgaria and Poland). At first in-

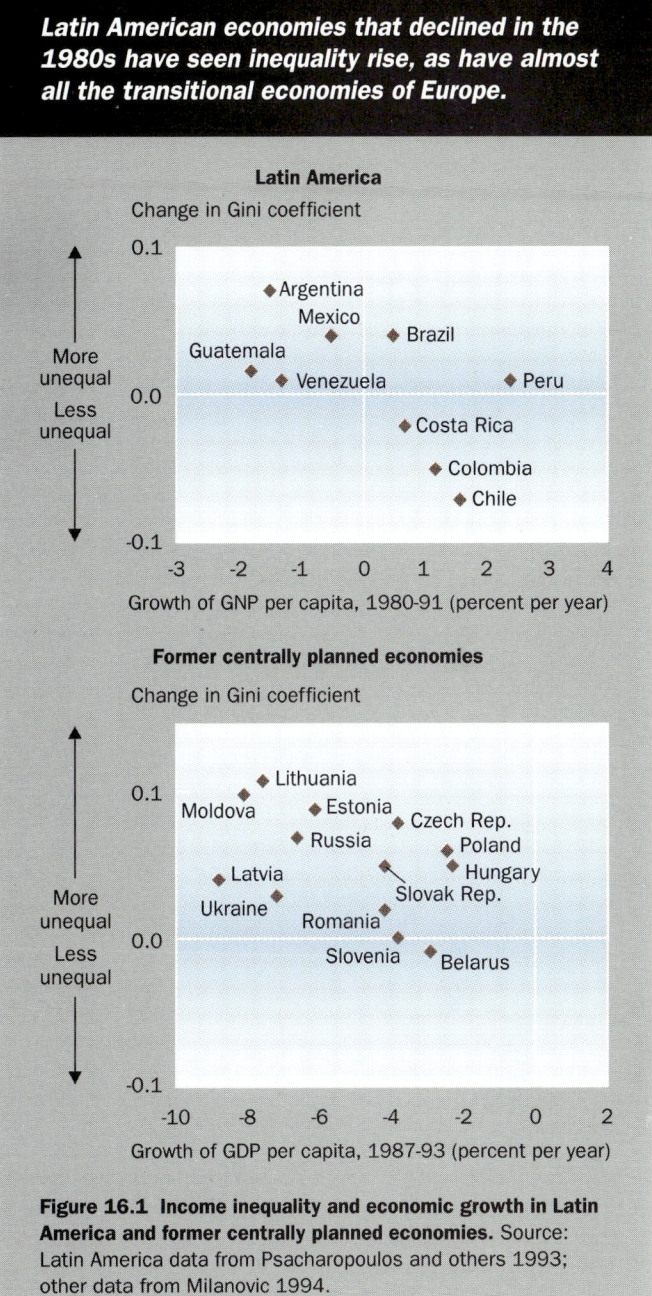

Latin American economies that declined in the 1980s have seen inequality rise, as have almost all the transitional economies of Europe.

Figure 16.1 Income inequality and economic growth in Latin America and former centrally planned economies. Source: Latin America data from Psacharopoulos and others 1993; other data from Milanovic 1994.

spection these levels do not appear much higher than those in many Western European economies, none of which have suffered equivalent transitional shocks in recent years. But unemployment in Central and Eastern Europe would be much higher still but for the fact that large numbers of workers have dropped out of the formal labor force. Even in those countries that cut subsidies to public enterprises, forcing them to shed workers, there was little movement

Box 16.1 Do we know how much household welfare declines in periods of major change?

Households in reforming economies can face crippling losses in welfare as both real wages and employment decline. But households do not absorb these shocks passively; they try to adapt. Households switch from wage to nonwage sources of income, particularly through increased participation in the informal sector. More women join the labor force, and other household members work extra hours to bring in supplementary income. In some countries additional income earners join the household to pool incomes and risks. And because households affected by the shocks accompanying transformation alter their consumption patterns as well, measurement problems arise in estimating wage declines. As a result, aggregate estimates of the decline in wages and employment may be inaccurate barometers of how households are faring. Studies from Ecuador, Mexico, Poland, and Zambia illustrate why this is so.

A simple way to see the discrepancy between changes in wages and changes in welfare is to look at how consumption is modified during periods of major change. In Mexico real wages dropped by 8.6 percent a year between 1983 and 1988, but private consumption fell by a more moderate 1.9 percent a year. The 32 percent drop in real wages in Poland during 1990 should be evaluated alongside the smaller 14 percent decline in

consumption, according to official estimates, or the 5 percent fall derived from consumer expenditure data. In both Ecuador and Zambia, participation in the informal sector increased—from 3 percent of employment in 1988 to 21 percent in 1992 for Ecuador, and from 19 percent in 1978 to 52 percent in 1992 for Zambia. And in Ecuador, Mexico, and Zambia more women entered the labor force: in Guayaquil, Ecuador, for example, the proportion of wives working outside the household jumped from 45 percent to 90 percent during the transition years. Mean household size also increased from 4.3 to 5.3 percent in Zambia, while in Ecuador the proportion of extended households rose from 33 percent to 38 percent.

Welfare is notoriously difficult to measure. The Polish data do not account for the improvement in product variety and quality during the transition or for the relief from long waiting lines. On the other hand, the data for Ecuador and Zambia cannot capture the increased crime and violence, even within households, that accompanied the fall in living standards. None of the data reveal the extent to which household members, especially women, have to work longer hours (in and outside the home) to make ends meet. Certainly, formal wage and employment data reveal only a small part of the picture.

---

either into or out of unemployment. But while unemployment became an increasingly stagnant pool, there was significant growth in self-employment and informal sector employment.

These shifts in employment have profound effects on households. Most formal sector workers who lose their jobs or suffer steep cuts in real wages do not come from households that were poor before the changes occurred, but some fall into poverty as a result of those changes. Where unemployment has increased significantly, it has contributed strongly to driving households below the poverty line. In 1993 Polish households with two or more unemployed members were three times more likely to fall into poverty than the average household. Unemployed urban workers in Mexico in 1992 were 20 percent more likely to be poor than employed ones. And in the late 1980s the incidence of poverty among urban households in Peru was highest among the unemployed. However, in most adjusting countries—including Bolivia, Brazil, Ghana, and even Mexico and Peru—those working for declining wages account for most of the increase in the number of poor. This is also true in some industrial former centrally planned countries, such as Russia, where firms have relied on furloughs, reductions in hours, and lower wages to keep workers on the payroll.

Among workers who remain employed, the effects of reforms can vary greatly. Table 16.1 looks at who wins and who loses in transitions. Workers are grouped by their participation in the formal or the informal labor market, place of residence (urban or rural), sex, and skill level. The effects of transition on each group are compared with the effects on the average worker across the four broad categories of countries identified in Chapter 15.

Formal and informal sectors

Shifts from formal into informal employment are as important a feature of labor market adjustment as the increase in unemployment rates, especially in countries with no safety net or unemployment insurance. Informal employment tends to swell during adjustment, as workers laid off in the formal sector seek new jobs, and women and other household members find outside employment to help offset declines in household income. This informalization of employment has characterized both former centrally planned economies, where the informal sector was underdeveloped, and Sub-Saharan African and Latin American market economies, where the informal sector was already highly developed but the formal sector suffered steep declines. Surveys in September 1994 showed that more than a third of the Polish labor force worked full- or part-time in the informal sector and that 46 percent of the unemployed were in fact employed full- or part-time in informal sector activities. Conservative estimates for Mexico place informal sector employment at 25 to 40 percent of total employment, and growing 9.5 percent a year between 1983 and 1988. Similarly, in Brazil employment in the informal sector swelled by nearly 30 percent during the recession of 1981–83, while private formal sector employment declined.

Workers in the informal sector have generally fared better than those in formal employment during major transformations. Evidence from former centrally planned economies suggests that informal sector workers did better during the initial stages of transition. In Poland, for example, informal sector wages were initially several times higher than formal sector wages—in part because workers and employers operating in the informal sector were earning high profits outside the taxed economy, and in part because these workers were moving into new, profitable sectors where demand was extremely high. This differential has since shrunk, and informal sector wages are now heading below those in the formal sector. In parts of Sub-Saharan Africa, too—for example, in Côte d'Ivoire—adjustment hit workers in the formal public sector harder than those in agriculture and informal urban employment. But in much of Latin America self-employed urban workers—particularly those in the informal sector—saw their position erode relative to that of formal wage workers. During the 1981–83 recession in Brazil, for example, the ratio of formal to informal sector incomes increased by 7 percent. In the Asian agrarian countries the picture is more diverse. At one extreme is China, which has protected workers in the formal sector and postponed reform of state-owned enterprises. At the other extreme, Viet Nam has gone through a dramatic state enterprise reform since 1989, shifting about one-third of the 2.4 million employees in that sector to the private sector. Overall, even though formal sector workers in the Asian countries may have lost ground relative to informal sector workers, the welfare of both groups has risen in absolute terms.

Rural and urban areas

In almost all countries the poor are most numerous—and poorest—in rural areas. But poor rural households have often benefited from adjustment. Although workers in agriculture are affected by macroeconomic decline, they are typically better shielded from the effects of a shrinking public sector than workers in urban areas. And in many countries they have benefited greatly from the removal of the pro-urban biases that pervaded the old, protected, import-substituting regimes. Where price changes improved the terms of trade for rural workers, rural households gained even before the overall economy started to grow. In Ghana

Unskilled urban workers tend to lose ground in periods of major change.

Table 16.1 Impact of reform on workers in the four major reform patterns

Type of worker	Industrial postsocialist	Latin American	Sub-Saharan African	Asian agrarian
Formal sector	−	+	−	−
Informal sector	+	−	+	+
Urban	+	−	−	+
Rural	−	+	+	+
Women	+/−	−	−	+
Skilled urban	+	+	+	+
Unskilled urban	−	−	−	−

Note: The four patterns are described in Chapter 15. A plus sign indicates a gain, and a minus sign a loss, relative to the average worker. A plus/minus sign indicates an ambiguous outcome.

agricultural real wages rose by 27 percent, whereas wages in nontradable-goods sectors (mainly commerce) declined by about 22 percent following adjustment. In Latin America and Asia the rural population also benefited in relative terms during the adjustment period, even though poverty remains concentrated in rural areas. Only in the former centrally planned economies of Europe do rural households appear to have suffered more in relative terms during the transition, as policies of agricultural protection were discontinued.

Women

The position of women in periods of major change deserves special attention because of the increased demands they face in periods of crisis. On top of their usual household responsibilities, women are typically called upon to help sustain household incomes when the wages of male heads of household fall. When employed, women are often more vulnerable than men, disproportionately concentrated in low-wage sectors or occupations and often segregated into the informal sector. Not surprisingly, their relative position has often deteriorated during structural adjustment.

In Latin American adjustment episodes the hourly earnings of women declined even more dramatically than those of men, partly because women were concentrated in the informal sector and in hard-hit low-paying sectors such as apparel. But women in poor households also exhibited strong increases in labor force participation—what is often called the "added worker" effect. In Ghana women working in the informal sector also saw their wages decline, as excess labor released from formal employment moved into informal activities. Women were further affected by a shift in resources away from food crop agriculture—where women predominate—toward cash crops. In Côte d'Ivoire women's relative lack of education placed them at a disadvantage, and in Egypt women were hurt by lengthening waiting lists for government employment and by their more limited private sector alternatives. Women played a distinct role during the transition in Asian countries as well. Although Vietnamese women faced particular challenges resulting from the collapse of childcare services provided by cooperatives, their overall position improved in line with economic growth, and female-headed households are now no poorer than those headed by men.

The evidence on the effect of adjustment on women in the former centrally planned economies is mixed, but their situation is clearly not as gloomy as is usually portrayed. On the one hand, women have shifted out of the labor force at a higher rate than men, starting from very high participation levels compared with other countries. They also exhibit slower transition rates out of unemployment. On the other hand, studies in the Czech Republic and Slovenia indicate that, when individual characteristics are controlled for, women have actually gained relative to men in both wages and employment, either because women are better educated (and returns to education have risen) or because they disproportionately occupy jobs in sectors that have been hurt less by labor demand shocks, especially services and labor-intensive industries.

Skilled and unskilled workers

The burden of adjustment falls most heavily on the unskilled and uneducated in both former centrally planned and market economies in transition. These workers are more vulnerable to structural change because they are less able to adjust to a changing environment and to take advantage of new job opportunities. In former centrally planned economies there is a strong inverse correlation between skill levels and the probability of sliding into poverty. The relative position of manual workers and low-skilled clerical staff, often with only a vocational education or less, has deteriorated more than any other group during the transition, whereas returns to education increased sharply in Slovenia and Poland. In some market economies such as Chile and Mexico the relative wage structure has also shifted in favor of the more highly skilled, possibly as a consequence of trade liberalization. In Viet Nam and Mongolia the largest wage gains have taken place in the booming services sector, which employs increasing numbers of skilled workers who have moved out of the shrinking industrial sector.

• • •

Severe shocks to the economy can create opportunities for some workers and have wrenching effects on others. Transformation follows diverse patterns in different countries, but it always involves a marked acceleration in the destruction of unviable jobs and the creation of new ones. That process is almost always accompanied by macroeconomic decline, requiring a reduction in the demand for labor and a fall in real wages. The net effects are often large drops in labor incomes, rising unemployment, and a shift from the formal to the informal sector. Even the best-designed reform produces gainers and losers in the short term, with losers particularly concentrated among the unskilled and formal sector workers in urban areas. Moving the economy as quickly as possible to the new growth path is key to limiting welfare losses, whereas giving up halfway hits poor workers hardest.

CHAPTER 17

Employment Restructuring

MAJOR TRANSFORMATIONS ARE ASSOciated with massive employment restructuring—many jobs must be destroyed and many new ones created. Both hires and separations increase dramatically during periods of major change, creating turmoil in the labor market and uncertainty for workers. In former centrally planned economies, as well as in many adjusting Latin American and Middle Eastern countries, formal employment has fallen by 5 to 15 percent, and real wages by more than 40 percent in extreme cases, before recovering. Some workers can gain immediately if they move quickly to expanding sectors. But many suffer losses associated with falls in wages, shifts into lower paying jobs in the informal sector, or unemployment. The shock is short-lived for those who regain employment and wages when the economy takes off. But other workers suffer permanent losses, either because they lack skills or because they were earning high wages in protected sectors before reform.

From the perspective of workers, regaining and sustaining growth are key to a successful transformation. And although the timing and design of macroeconomic reform have a powerful influence on the speed at which labor demand recovers, labor market policies can also have a big impact. What can government do to speed the transition and ease the plight of displaced workers, both those looking to move into new sectors and those who risk permanent

losses? This chapter examines the effectiveness of four types of policy response: those aimed at reducing the labor market rigidities that can stall recovery; those that assist workers by equipping them to adapt to change; those that provide transfers to reduce income losses; and those designed to deal with mass layoffs.

Increasing labor market adaptability

Adaptable labor markets are essential if workers are to benefit quickly from economic recovery (Table 17.1). Increasing labor market flexibility—despite the bad name it has

Governments can facilitate labor market restructuring and dampen the cost of adjustment for workers.

Table 17.1 Policies that ease employment restructuring

Policy	Effectiveness and recommendations
Increasing labor market adaptability	
Facilitating labor mobility	Residence permits and restrictive job security regulations should be lifted.
Wage flexibility	Increased relative wage flexibility is key to sectoral employment adjustment and can reduce the decline in aggregate employment.
Reducing disincentives to change jobs	Delinking social services from employment is important in former centrally planned economies. Reform of other markets, especially housing, is essential.
Equipping workers for change (active policies)	
Retraining	Robust evaluations of its effectiveness are few, even in industrial countries. State financing (but rarely provision) is desirable in some cases for those hurt by changes, at least on welfare and political grounds.
Job search assistance	Inexpensive and often effective in industrial countries in increasing job placements, although relevant only for a fraction of job seekers. May help in former centrally planned economies.
Wage subsidies	Expensive and often risky, with only minor net effects in industrial countries. Can risk undermining reforms. May make sense if tightly targeted, for example to one-company towns.
Allowances (grants, loans, or prepayment of benefits) to support business start-ups	Administratively intensive. Net employment effects have rarely been properly evaluated. Can only reach a small minority of workers.
Public employment for disadvantaged youth and public support of apprenticeships	Mixed results. Programs have rarely been properly evaluated. Some positive effects have been found for programs carefully targeted to dropout minorities, when combined with on-the-job training. Administratively intensive and difficult to implement outside industrial countries.
Providing transfers (passive policies)	
Unemployment benefits	Useful in first stages of transition from central planning. Disincentive effects of long-duration benefits have been found in industrial countries. Benefit administration should be simple.
Severance pay	Often part of formal sector labor contracts; can be key to downsizing public sector.
Old age and disability pensions	Constitute a major cash benefit scheme in former centrally planned economies. Often used in lieu of unemployment benefits. Often require immediate cost containment on fiscal grounds. Long-term reform toward funded arrangement is desirable.
Social assistance and family benefits	Can reduce the poverty of those hurt in transition. Means testing can be difficult. Family benefits are generous in former centrally planned economies and may need to be cut back on fiscal grounds.
Public works	Effective antipoverty and relief measure if wages are kept low.

acquired as a euphemism for pushing wages down and workers out—is essential in all regions of the world undergoing major reforms. In the former centrally planned economies there are still large groups of workers stuck in unviable jobs—estimates put this labor hoarding at 20 percent of the work force or higher. China and the South Asian countries have rigid and highly protected public sectors, although they are small compared with the economy as a whole. In Latin America, and in the Middle East and North Africa, numerous regulatory restrictions impede labor adjustment. And most Sub-Saharan African countries have overstaffed, underpaid, and unproductive public sectors. Many of the necessary reforms will involve large, one-time layoffs or liberalization of complementary markets, especially the housing market. But the most important reforms involve lifting constraints on labor mobility and wage flexibility, as well as breaking the ties between social services and labor contracts.

Facilitating labor mobility

Substantial constraints on labor mobility hamper labor markets in many reforming countries. Most of these constraints originate outside the labor market: in legal restrictions still in place in many parts of the former Soviet Union, in well-entrenched habits, in poorly functioning housing markets, or in the idiosyncrasies of land tenancy institutions in, for example, Mexico. Lifting these restrictions and reforming other markets can provide a boost to labor mobility. China's recent economic growth was fueled by millions of rural workers moving to take advantage of new employment opportunities. Liberalization of hiring and firing practices in Peru in the early 1990s markedly increased job creation.

Greater labor mobility is also important for overcoming geographical imbalances. Labor markets are usually geographically segmented, and different regions fare differently. Regional unemployment in 1993 ranged from 7 to 46 percent in Hungary, and from 3 to 22 percent even in small Latvia. In Mexico in 1992 the unemployment rate in the city of Matamoros was twice the national average and nearly five times that in Orizaba. In extreme cases, when long-lasting regional disparities are reinforced by a major regional shock, even high mobility may not be enough, and public investment may be needed to aid the regional economy, especially in areas with great potential but weak infrastructure.

Making relative wages more flexible

Inflexible relative wages can undermine employment restructuring, even if other markets function well. When wages for different industries and occupations and in different regions are not free to vary, wage structures cannot provide the right incentives for labor to move from less productive to more productive jobs. Prior to reform, the former centrally planned economies had very rigid wage structures. This is changing, but even in a liberalized environment there are often constraints on wage flexibility that can seriously slow down employment restructuring. These constraints can be the result of collective agreements with unions, as in Mexico in the early 1980s, or of penalty tax–based incomes policies aimed at containing nominal wage growth in a period of stabilization, as in a number of Central and Eastern European countries (for example, in the former Czechoslovakia, Latvia, and Poland). In Mexico relative wage inflexibility probably delayed employment restructuring compared with Chile, which had a more flexible wage-setting mechanism after the removal of generalized wage indexation in 1982. In Central and Eastern Europe there was a conflict between wage flexibility and stabilization objectives in 1990–92, which was rightly solved in favor of the latter. Since then, however, most of the Central and Eastern European countries have replaced the penalty tax on excess wage fund growth with other, more flexible mechanisms, such as negotiated average wage increases, or have abolished incomes policies altogether. The Czech Republic has been particularly successful in retaining relative wage flexibility within a centralized bargaining framework. This has helped contain unemployment at low levels.

Minimum wage policy is also important. Too high a minimum wage puts a floor beneath the wage distribution and prevents wages from being set at market-clearing levels. That can price low-skilled or young workers out of a formal sector job. In practice, however, most reforming governments, particularly in the former Soviet Union, have allowed minimum wages to drop faster than average wages (Figure 17.1).

Breaking the link between social services and employment

Enterprises in former centrally planned economies, and large public enterprises elsewhere, provide extensive nonwage social benefits such as housing and some education and health care. Some enterprises, in particular in the former Soviet Union and China, also supply services and infrastructure such as sewerage and hospital buildings to the entire local community. In extreme cases nonwage benefits and services may amount to some 35 percent of total enterprise labor costs. Nonwage benefits hinder labor mobility, because changing jobs means losing access to many of these benefits, at least temporarily, and because enterprises are reluctant to hire workers from certain groups, such as women with children. Competition is distorted because the net burden of services falls differently on different enterprises.

Governments can help by transferring provision of social services and benefits from enterprises to local governments. The gains in labor market efficiency from such a

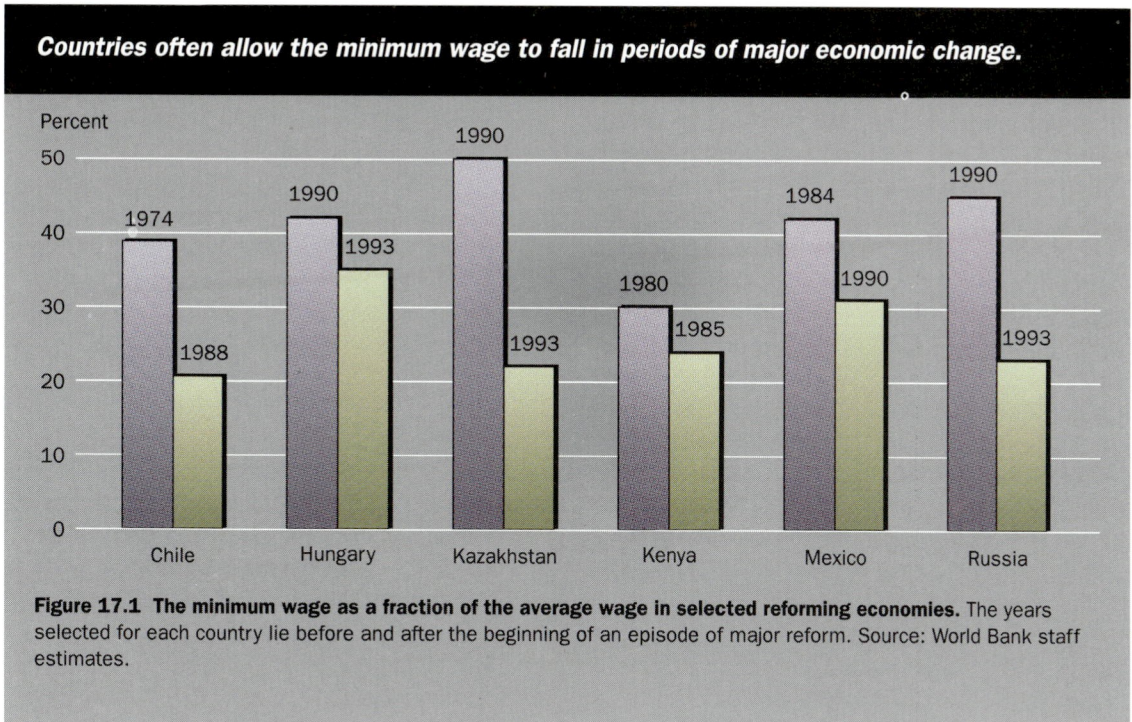

Countries often allow the minimum wage to fall in periods of major economic change.

Figure 17.1 The minimum wage as a fraction of the average wage in selected reforming economies. The years selected for each country lie before and after the beginning of an episode of major reform. Source: World Bank staff estimates.

move depend heavily on reforms in the complementary markets, especially the housing market. Without them, enterprises will have to pay as much in local taxation to the government as they previously paid in direct costs.

Measures to increase flexibility can influence the overall trajectory and speed of recovery. They are therefore especially helpful for those workers who can expect to move into new employment and are unlikely to suffer permanent long-term losses. These measures are likely to be insufficient, however, for workers who are not prepared for change because of their inadequate skills or well-entrenched habits, or simply because the speed with which skills and habits change lags that of the changing pattern of labor demand.

Equipping workers for change

Making labor markets efficient and adaptable involves more than simply removing systemic barriers to mobility and ensuring that wages adjust quickly. Workers must also have the resources—the appropriate skills and job habits—to take advantage of new opportunities as they arise in fast-changing labor markets.

Skills imbalances

Jobs differ greatly in the skills they require, and often workers whose jobs disappear find that they lack the right skills for the jobs being created, or lack the basic education necessary to learn new skills quickly. Poorly educated workers often get stuck in unemployment or must compete for a shrinking set of low-skill jobs, even when there are unfilled vacancies elsewhere.

The secular worldwide trend in labor demand toward workers with greater general skills and higher education is reinforced during major transformations. This means that the unskilled have less chance of escaping unemployment. For some—displaced rural Mexican laborers moving to Mexico City, for example—the skills required to find a new job are simply basic literacy and numeracy. Without these skills the migrant faces few job prospects outside the informal sector. This pattern holds throughout much of Latin America, where the unskilled account for the bulk of the unemployed. In former centrally planned economies the roots of the problem lie in premature and narrow specialization and in the inability of inherited vocational training to adapt to rapidly changing labor markets. Unemployment is already higher among semiskilled workers than among professional and managerial workers.

Most industrial countries run public retraining programs, as do many former centrally planned economies. Evidence of their effectiveness should be viewed with caution, because only a few thorough evaluations—based on controlled experiments with a random selection of participants or on carefully constructed comparison groups—have been done (Box 17.1). Overall, the evidence on public retraining is mixed. Results should in any case be interpreted as very country-specific, since retraining schemes

Box 17.1 How effective is public retraining?

Many countries operate public retraining programs, but only a few programs have been properly evaluated. Results are mixed. The bulk of the evidence from the industrial countries, mainly Canada and the United States, suggests that retraining can be modestly effective for some groups, such as disadvantaged adult women in the United States, but is completely ineffective for others, such as male youths. Recent evaluations of retraining schemes for displaced workers in Mexico and Hungary are equally ambiguous.

Mexico's PROBECAT program has provided short-term skills training to unemployed workers since 1984. Originally designed for displaced workers, the program has also attracted a large share of first-time job seekers. A recent evaluation found the program to be effective in shortening the duration of unemployment for trainees with previous work experience. The program has also helped raise the earnings of adult male trainees, especially those with six to twelve years of schooling, but it was completely ineffective for trainees with no previous work experience and for women who had reentered the labor force.

Hungary's retraining program appears to have had no significant impact on either the probability of reemployment or the earnings of the average trainee, once differences in observable characteristics of trainees and nontrainees are controlled for. However, the program appears to have been more effective in helping certain problem groups, such as older workers and those with less education, find a steady job. A possible conclusion from this experience is that public programs should target disadvantaged groups, while letting the private sector take over retraining for those displaced workers for whom the potential returns to training are higher.

Taken together, these evaluations show that public retraining programs have helped some groups of workers in some countries escape from unemployment. Such programs are unlikely, however, to help the majority of workers. Careful targeting, monitoring, and evaluation of retraining schemes are key to ensuring their effectiveness and preventing the waste of scarce public resources.

---

seem to work differently for different groups of workers in different countries. Continuous evaluation of these programs—preferably through controlled experiments—is essential to ensure that they are cost-effective. Programs should be evaluated both for their relative efficiency, in increasing earnings or the probability of employment, and for their overall efficiency, that is, whether the benefits outweigh the costs.

Strengthening the private sector as a training provider can improve the effectiveness of retraining. As the Chilean experience demonstrates, systems based on distributing vouchers to targeted groups so that they can then buy training services in a competitive market can work well. But such a system may initially be less useful in former centrally planned economies that have no recent experience with private sector retraining. Government involvement may in any case be desirable to maintain support for reform and social stability. Where retraining is required because of a once-and-for-all aggregate shock to the economy, there may also be a public policy argument for government to take on some of the cost. Where banking systems and capital markets are inefficient, households and producers may be unable to finance labor retraining, and here too government support may be indicated.

Retraining of disadvantaged workers is one area where private provision and financing of retraining are unlikely to suffice. The economic returns to such training may be low,

even though the benefits to society in terms of improved social cohesion can be high. Governments should concentrate on supporting and regulating the private markets that provide retraining for displaced workers for whom the returns are potentially high, and reserve their direct involvement (and major subsidies) for disadvantaged groups such as single women with children and persons with disabilities.

Lack of information

Workers cannot take advantage of new job opportunities unless they know what jobs are available and the wages they pay. In developing countries workers rely almost entirely on informal exchange of information to find new jobs. In industrial and former centrally planned economies, however, job search assistance is often provided by a formal network of public and sometimes private offices. A limited number of evaluations of job search assistance in industrial countries suggest that it is quite effective. In the United States, for example, job search assistance has proved to be as effective as retraining in helping displaced workers find jobs, and much less costly.

Job search assistance, however, is an administration-intensive activity and is unlikely to be a solution for low- and many middle-income countries. Even in the industrial market economies only a small percentage of job seekers—usually no more than 10 to 15 percent—get their jobs through public employment offices. In Poland the share is only 3 to 5 percent. But even if it turns out that *public* employment services are relevant only in industrial countries, allowing private employment services to operate makes sense under all circumstances.

Supporting entrepreneurship

Countries have often tried to assist job losers by providing support to those wishing to start their own businesses. Many countries have experimented with special credit schemes and other programs to encourage the development of microenterprises. Such schemes have seldom been evaluated rigorously, but experience with government-run special credit programs in Sub-Saharan Africa and Latin America suggests that they have rarely brought benefits. Privately run micro credit schemes have proved more effective, especially in rural communities. And in Poland a recent experiment with a start-up loan program seems to be functioning well. Nevertheless, these schemes have been shown to be of interest only to a very small subgroup of the unemployed (about 3 percent in industrial countries and about 1 percent in Poland).

Wage subsidies

Wage subsidies must be limited and well controlled if they are to play a positive role. In the industrial countries they have proved ineffective in speeding up adjustment, although they can help the long-term unemployed. There are substitution effects whereby workers whose wages are subsidized replace those whose wages are not. Moreover, wage subsidies can easily undermine reform by keeping unprofitable firms afloat. Wage subsidies should be considered only in special cases where targeting is easy, for example in one-company towns (see below). When they are well controlled, they can be a less expensive alternative to transfers and yield a better outcome in terms of social cohesion in isolated areas.

Reducing insecurity through transfer programs

Workers face substantial risks during major transformations, the greatest being the risk of losing a job and a source of income. Even in stable industrial economies the risk of unemployment is very difficult to fully insure against (see Chapter 13). During periods of major change the operation of private insurance schemes is even more difficult, because with the fall in labor demand occurring throughout the economy, the probability of losing a job rises for all simultaneously. There is, therefore, a case for public action in providing some form of insurance and income security.

Permanent income security mechanisms such as those discussed in Chapter 13 can quickly become insufficient in transitions because of huge—albeit temporary—increases in the number of people unemployed or in the number of

households in poverty. Governments may also be concerned about losing political support for reforms if incomes fall too far, especially among the politically influential. Both considerations can lead to increased transfers. In those former centrally planned economies that have drastically cut subsidies to enterprises, increases in transfers are aimed at partially offsetting these cuts. In extreme cases—Bulgaria and Poland, for example—subsidies came down from a range of 12 to 15 percent of GDP to 1 to 2 percent. Meanwhile transfers increased by 5 to 8 percent of GDP.

Different countries are likely to implement different strategies, since they start out with huge differences in the importance of family support mechanisms and the size of the informal sector, as well as in expectations about state intervention. In general, the more industrialized the economy, the stronger the case for more use of public benefits, because of the greater availability of resources and the weakness of alternative informal support mechanisms. Not surprisingly, transfers are higher in Slovenia than in Uzbekistan, and higher in Argentina than in Bolivia.

Poverty relief is best accomplished by simple targeting mechanisms to reach those who lose out. Since unemployment and family status are most likely to be linked to poverty, former centrally planned economies in transition use both of them widely to alleviate the adverse effects of transition. More industrialized transitional economies try to supplement this targeting with a formal social assistance system based on means testing. But means testing has high administrative requirements and is difficult, and hence unlikely to work well outside the industrial world. Some countries use various forms of self-targeting, for example by conditioning benefits on participation in public employment. Although such schemes do not improve the long-term job prospects of participants, they can be useful during transitions not only as an effective self-selection mechanism, making targeting to the poorest possible, but also as a bridge between jobs. For instance, targeting of unemployment benefits in Estonia improved substantially when they were made conditional upon participation in part-time public employment schemes. Only the truly poor came forward to claim the benefits. In Albania public employment schemes are being widely used to cushion the transition between jobs. As discussed in Chapter 13, there are numerous other examples of public employment schemes working well in developing countries.

A second reason for increasing transfers is to maintain popular support for reform—which usually means ensuring support from the most influential groups. In many countries, and particularly in industrial former centrally planned economies, old age pensioners are a much more influential group than the unemployed. Social insurance schemes therefore played an important role as transfer mechanisms in Central and Eastern Europe, and most reform strategies in these countries had to balance short-term objectives of poverty alleviation during the transition, which call for severance pay and unemployment benefits, against longer term objectives and permanent transfers such as pensions.

Income transfers to mitigate income and employment losses, especially unemployment benefits, are often labeled "passive" labor market policies, whereas those designed to equip workers for change are called "active" policies. In industrial countries the two types of measures are often considered substitutes for each other, with some studies claiming that increased spending on active measures is more efficient, because by getting people back to work it allows savings on transfers. However, active and passive measures are unlikely to be substitutes in transitional economies, where most people are likely to be unemployed because of low labor demand rather than ineffective supply.

Mass layoffs

Massive reductions in and restructuring of the public sector are common during major transformations. Large layoffs are expensive in the short run. If enterprises are potentially viable and can sooner or later be privatized, reforms can be relatively easy. In most cases, however, large state enterprises or even whole industries have to be downsized or closed. Examples include the downsizing of the Chilean public sector, the gradual retrenchment of workers in Spain's state-owned steel company, and Mexico's trimming of public enterprise employment before privatization. An example in the making is the restructuring of Russia's coal sector, where it is estimated that a viable industry would employ only 50 percent of the almost 800,000 mineworkers. The common denominator in these examples is that large numbers of workers are affected, often in one city or region, making it difficult for displaced workers to move easily into new occupations.

Best practice in the area of mass layoffs varies with countries' level of development and the type of enterprise and its work force. In some cases governments should lay off redundant workers before privatization, as was done in Spain, to allow the new owners the greatest possible flexibility in restructuring the enterprise. Otherwise privatization can come first, leaving restructuring to the new owners. Often constraints on firing or on the level of wages will remain— this is generally the case in Central and Eastern Europe. In low- and middle-income countries, unions are rarely involved—exceptions are Ghana's public bus service and the preparation of the schemes in the transport sector in Mauritius and Yugoslavia, where union involvement was crucial for success. In contrast, in industrial countries such as Canada and Sweden, numerous cutbacks were carried out in close cooperation between unions, workers, and local communities. This appears to work best for more industrialized countries with stable and well-educated work forces.

Advance notice, choices for workers who lose their jobs, and a restructuring of pay systems for those who remain have been essential for efficiency in the wake of layoffs. Opposition can be reduced where the scheme is part of a broader effort at structural reform. In former centrally planned economies that had already experienced a few mass layoffs, the larger effort came in the form of a comprehensive shift from a socialist to a market economy. In the Ghanaian transportation sector it was part of a widespread reduction of excess labor in the civil and educational services and in some state-owned enterprises. In the bus sector in Sri Lanka it was part of a general reduction in the size of government.

There is no definitive evidence on whether the optimal severance payment should be a lump-sum payment, which laid-off workers can use to start their own businesses, or take the form of long-term periodic payments, thus providing sustenance over a longer period. The former is better for enterprising individuals, and the latter for those who are risk-averse. Allowing workers to self-select into one of these schemes may be the best general approach.

The following basic principles should guide retrenchment schemes. The less developed the economy, the simpler and more transparent the mechanisms should be. A special severance scheme that adds to existing nationwide severance schemes is better than an extension of unemployment benefits, because it is administratively simpler. To avoid introducing biases against labor demand, such special schemes ought not to be financed through payroll taxes. For reasons of fairness and efficiency, employees to be laid off should be offered a choice among several exit options. To reduce the danger that the best workers will leave, wage structures should be reformed in coordination with layoffs to tighten the link between performance and pay. Finally, rules requiring advance notice of layoffs may help workers adjust—but because advance notice can slow voluntary exit and encourage workers to wait for retrenchment packages, it may be appropriate to accompany the notice with lower remuneration for workers who remain. Other components of these schemes, popular in the industrial countries, such as on-site employment services, can only work if administrative capacity exists. They are unlikely to be useful in most developing countries but may prove relevant to some former centrally planned economies.

One-company towns pose a particular problem because of the lack of alternative opportunities. In the Russian coal sector, for example, a number of mines are located in isolated areas and often sustain the bulk of employment there. Ideally, governments should encourage change—migration, creation of new jobs and new firms—but this rarely solves the problem in the short run. When the prospects for change are limited, or when adjustment is bound to be slow, temporary policies aimed at sustaining existing enterprises may make sense under certain conditions. First, if the social or political costs of job destruction are high, maintaining the subsidies may actually hasten rather than impede the broader transition. Second, if the value of the firm's output exceeds the value of the inputs used, the scheme can be cost-saving if unemployment or social assistance benefits would otherwise have to be paid. The biggest problem in designing schemes to support enterprises in isolated areas is avoiding perverse incentives for more workers or companies to move there. Any industrial support scheme must be instituted for a limited period to ensure that enterprises use the support to restructure their activities rather than to perpetuate inefficiency.

● ● ●

Adaptable labor markets are essential for a successful transition. Reforms to promote labor mobility, transfer programs, and policies to equip workers for change are all necessary to increase adaptability. Support for labor mobility is key, while transfers serve a dual role of cushioning falls in consumption and reducing the risk associated with job cuts. Active labor market measures to encourage job search are less useful in the early stages of transitions. But once the major shock is over, there is likely to be some substitution in resources from transfers to active policies, particularly in countries with the higher levels of administrative capability needed to run these programs successfully.

PART FIVE

The Outlook for Workers in the Twenty-First Century

THE PAST CENTURY has witnessed more divergence than convergence in the fortunes of workers in different parts of the world. Can the twenty-first century be different? Will it bring in an era of inclusion, in which economic integration continues and spreads, raising the incomes of workers in all regions—and especially the poorest? Chapter 18 relates the themes articulated in the preceding chapters to the outlook for workers in the principal regions of the world. It develops both a pessimistic scenario for the future, in which workers' living standards in the various regions drift further apart, and an optimistic one, in which countries seize the opportunities that global integration presents to better the lives of their working populations.

CHAPTER 18

Policy Choices and the Prospects for Workers

FOR THE PAST CENTURY RISING INEQUALITY of incomes has been a dominant trend in the world economy. The most prosperous group of workers in the world—the skilled workers of the industrial countries—now earn on average some sixty times more than the poorest group—the farmers of Sub-Saharan Africa. The past fifteen to twenty years have seen rapid advancement for large numbers of Asian workers, but stagnation or decline for many in the Middle East, Latin America, Sub-Saharan Africa, and, most recently, the former centrally planned economies of Europe and Central Asia. Can the twenty-first century usher in an era of converging incomes? The stakes are high. There is the potential for great advances on all fronts: robust job creation, rising productivity, and improvements in job quality. But there is also the risk that progress will leave some out, from unemployed workers in the industrial countries to much of the population in Sub-Saharan Africa, and will fail to reduce severe inequalities in Latin America and elsewhere.

Conditions both in individual domestic economies and in the international economic environment matter to the outcome. The potential for deeper international integration expands opportunities for those countries and groups of workers with the capacity to respond. The actions of rich countries—in particular with respect to trade policy and fiscal deficits—will make a difference. Unless deficits fall, all will pay the price in the form of lower productivity and slower growth. International assistance is also vital in supporting the inclusion of all groups of workers in the global economy. But probably of greatest importance are the conditions prevailing within developing and transitional economies, in particular in the four areas discussed in the preceding parts of this Report:

- whether countries succeed in getting onto market-based growth paths that both generate rapid demand for labor and raise the productivity of the work force
- whether they succeed in taking advantage of changes at the international level, be it in reacting to new market opportunities or in attracting capital—or in managing the dislocations that changing trade patterns bring
- whether governments succeed in putting in place a framework for labor policy that complements informal and rural labor markets, supports an effective system of industrial relations in the formal sector, provides safeguards for the vulnerable, and avoids biases that favor relatively well-off insiders, and
- whether the countries struggling with the transition to more market-based and internationally integrated patterns of development succeed in this move without large or permanent costs for labor.

Two global scenarios

Two global scenarios, developed for this Report, illustrate the extent of what is possible and the magnitude of the dangers ahead for workers in each of the world's principal regions. The first scenario is one of muddling through and is largely based on persistence of past trends. Because there is the distinct possibility that this path would lead to widening differences between some regions and widening inequality in labor income within some countries, we call this a scenario of slow growth and divergence—the "divergent" scenario. The second scenario explores the potential implications of strong policy action at the domestic level in all parts of the world, combined with deeper international integration. This we term a scenario of inclusion and convergence—the "convergent" scenario. Both scenarios are only illustrative—the numbers are projections based on many assumptions, and certainly not a forecast. But they are a plausible guide to the consequences of success and failure and take into account likely future trends in both economy-wide effects and international integration.

The principal determinant of the outlook for workers is domestic investment—in capital, education, infrastructure, and technology. The divergent scenario assumes that recent trends in investments continue or deteriorate, that a sizable share of those already enrolled in schools drop out prematurely, and that the overall productivity of labor does not rise rapidly (Table 18.1). The convergent scenario assumes that investment rates pick up, that enrollment rates stabilize at current levels and dropout rates decline, and that investments in infrastructure, technological transfers, and improvements in the quality of governance contribute to rising labor productivity. The convergent scenario must be supported by at least slight rises in saving rates, lower fiscal deficits in the rich countries, and reasonable amounts of international capital flows, including development assistance. The effort in Sub-Saharan Africa must be especially strong.

The international scene also matters greatly. In the divergent scenario, we assume that protectionism does not go

The convergent scenario will require high rates of investment in human and physical capital, as well as overall productivity gains.

Table 18.1 Assumptions underlying the projections

Region	Investment share of GDP (percent)			Average years of schooling			Annual growth of total factor productivity (percentage per year)		
	Actual 1992	1994–2010 Divergent	Convergent	Actual 1992	2010 Divergent	Convergent	Actual 1960–87	1994–2010 Divergent	Convergent
China[a]	30	22	26	5.0	5.4	6.1	..	0.7	1.7
East Asia	28	22	28	6.5	7.3	7.9	1.9	1.0	1.8
Former CMEA	19	18	22	8.2	9.1	10.5	..	0.5	2.1
Latin America	20	22	15	4.9	5.5	6.1	0.0	0.6	1.6
Middle East and North Africa	23	20	25	3.6	4.5	5.5	1.4	0.5	1.5
South Asia	23	23	26	3.4	4.2	5.1	0.6	0.7	1.5
Sub-Saharan Africa	17	16	25	2.3	2.6	2.8	0.0	0.5	1.4
OECD[b]	20	20	22	9.6	10.5	11.1	1.1	0.9	1.3

.. Not available.
a. Includes Hong Kong.
b. Includes Australia, Canada, European Union, Japan, New Zealand, and United States only.
Source: World Bank staff estimates.

away and that countries either drag their feet in implementing the Uruguay Round agreement or offset gains in one area with protectionism of another sort. In the convergent scenario the Uruguay Round is fully implemented and there is further progress in trade liberalization—including in agriculture—at both the regional and the multilateral levels. In the divergent scenario, export growth is slow and there is little change in the international division of labor. In contrast, global integration interacts with domestic investment in capital and people to bring large net gains in the convergent scenario (Table 18.2). The developing regions capitalize on their workers' improved skills in an expanding global market, and all move up the technological ladder: workers in the industrial market economies continue to move out of medium-skill products and into high-technology goods and services; the Asian newly industrializing economies and the former centrally planned economies master the production of medium-skill products and start moving into high-technology goods; Latin America and the Middle East extend their lead in mining and agriculture and start moving into the production of technologically more demanding goods; China and India become steadily larger exporters of labor-intensive products; and Sub-Saharan Africa regains its advantages in natural resources and becomes a large exporter of agricultural products.

How does labor fare? We assume in both scenarios that the technological bias favoring skilled workers that characterized the past two decades continues. Under the divergent scenario, this bias interacts with slow capital accumulation and stagnating world trade. The result is slow GDP growth in most regions and rising inequality among and within re-

gions. In contrast, the convergent scenario finds incomes rising and inequality falling across most countries and within most regions (Table 18.3). In poorer developing countries the rise of globalization helps by increasing the demand for low-skilled workers. In the middle-income and wealthier countries the negative effects of globalization are swamped by the effects of skill improvement, which reduces the pool of unskilled workers and so increases the relative demand for their services.

International inequality will change only slowly under any realistic scenario. But the scenario of convergence and inclusion could start to reduce the immense differences that now exist. The ratio between the wages of the richest and the poorest groups in the international wage hierarchy—skilled industrial country workers and African farmers—could fall from an estimated sixty to one in 1992 to fifty to one by 2010 (Figure 18.1). This would begin to reverse the large gap that has emerged over the past century, as workers in industrial countries reaped the benefits of economic takeoff, but those in Sub-Saharan Africa did not. Under the divergent scenario things could actually get worse—the ratio of labor incomes between these two groups could rise to about seventy to one. We now turn to a region-by-region account of the main constraints to improvements in labor conditions.

Industrial countries

The industrial countries have been struggling with their employment problem for some fifteen years. Its key features are rising inequality in North America and the United Kingdom, stubbornly high unemployment in continental

Europe, and in both a growing underclass with few opportunities for employment. Despite persistent attention from governments, international agencies, and academics, deep questions remain about what can be done. There clearly has been a shift in the pattern of labor demand against unskilled and manual workers and in favor of college-educated and white-collar workers, and from full-time work, dominated by men, to more flexible or temporary work, with rising participation of women. As was discussed in Part Two, international trade, migration, and capital have had some influence, and their impact may be on the rise as much larger population blocs become integrated into world markets; but technological changes, in particular those associated with the information revolution, have probably been more important.

In the more flexible labor market of the United States a major question is whether the supply response to the shift in demand toward higher skills, already under way—as reflected in the recent rise in enrollments of adults in community colleges—will be sufficient to reverse the trend toward rising inequality and reach those left out in the 1980s. In Europe the issue is much more one of how to increase com-

---

Both incomes per capita and exports grow much more rapidly under the scenario of convergence and inclusion.

Table 18.2 Projections of growth in GDP per capita and exports by region
(percent)

| Region | Annual average growth in GDP per capita | | | Annual average growth in exports | | |
| | Actual 1970–90 | 1994–2010 | | Actual 1980–90 | 1994–2010 | |
		Divergent	Convergent		Divergent	Convergent
China[a]	4.6	2.3	3.9	11.3	4.7	6.6
East Asia	5.5	3.0	4.4	10.2	5.3	6.5
Former CMEA	–3.0	0.9	3.5	2.1	2.2	5.6
Latin America	1.7	1.4	3.3	2.4	3.8	7.0
Middle East and North Africa	0.8	1.4	3.4	4.2	3.3	5.5
South Asia	2.0	2.4	4.0	6.3	6.6	8.9
Sub-Saharan Africa	–0.3	–0.3	1.7	3.1	3.6	6.7
OECD[b]	1.9	1.6	2.3	1.5	2.9	3.7

a. Includes Hong Kong.
b. Includes Australia, Canada, European Union, Japan, New Zealand, and United States only.
Source: World Bank staff estimates.

Wage gains for unskilled workers are dramatically higher in the convergent scenario, reducing inequality.

Table 18.3 Projections of wages of skilled and unskilled workers by region
(percentage change from 1994 to 2010)

| Region | Divergent scenario | | Convergent scenario | |
	Unskilled	Skilled	Unskilled	Skilled
China[a]	19	35	65	72
East Asia	41	54	63	81
Former CMEA	3	29	61	74
Latin America	–3	45	58	62
Middle East and North Africa	–2	27	63	39
South Asia	15	49	81	56
Sub-Saharan Africa	6	9	44	49
OECD[b]	15	47	47	45

a. Includes Hong Kong.
b. Includes Australia, Canada, European Union, Japan, New Zealand, and United States only.
Source: World Bank staff estimates.

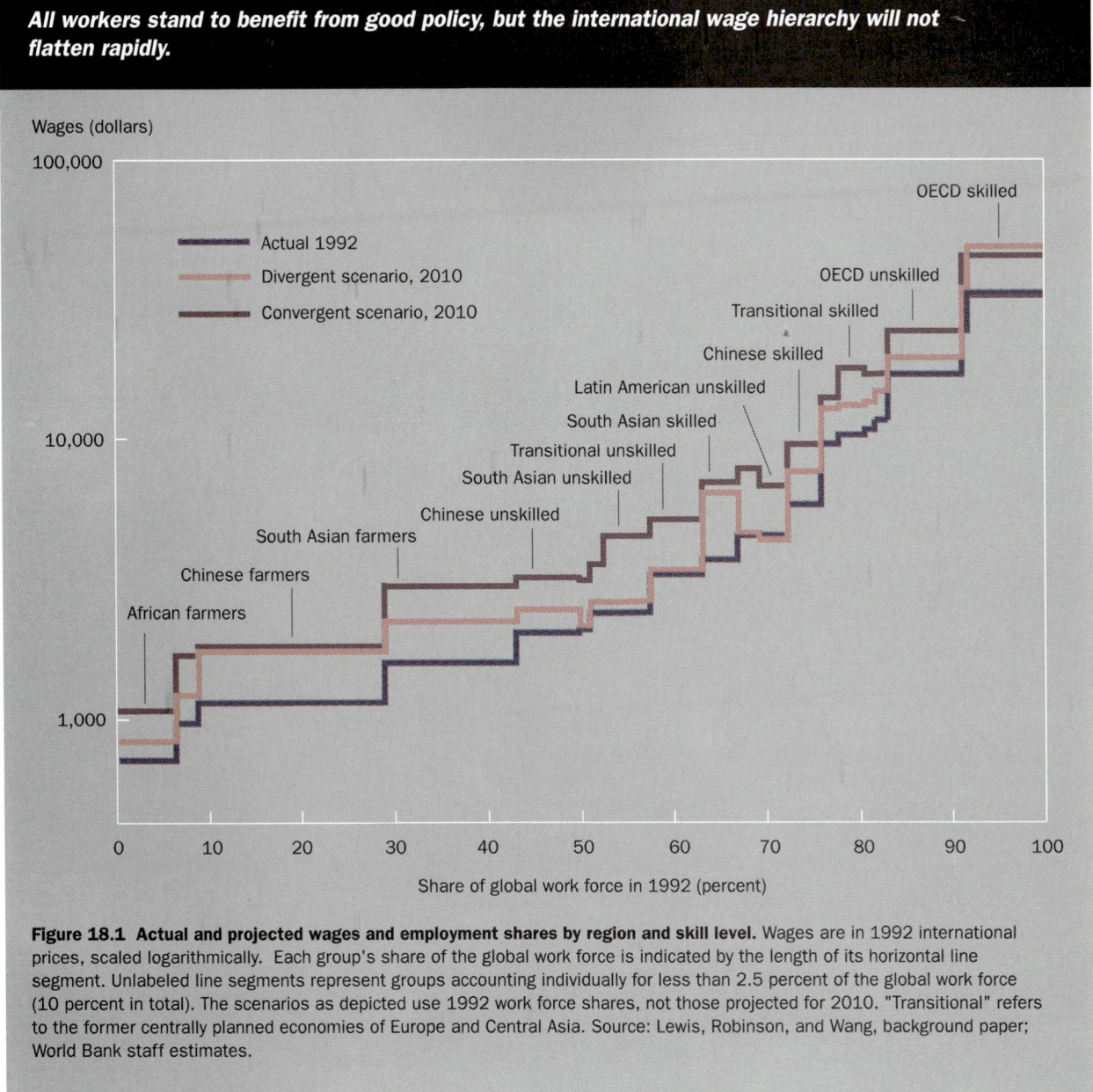

All workers stand to benefit from good policy, but the international wage hierarchy will not flatten rapidly.

Wages (dollars)

Legend:
- Actual 1992
- Divergent scenario, 2010
- Convergent scenario, 2010

Labels (bottom to top by wage): African farmers, Chinese farmers, South Asian farmers, Chinese unskilled, South Asian unskilled, Transitional unskilled, South Asian skilled, Latin American unskilled, Chinese skilled, Transitional skilled, OECD unskilled, OECD skilled

X-axis: Share of global work force in 1992 (percent)

Figure 18.1 Actual and projected wages and employment shares by region and skill level. Wages are in 1992 international prices, scaled logarithmically. Each group's share of the global work force is indicated by the length of its horizontal line segment. Unlabeled line segments represent groups accounting individually for less than 2.5 percent of the global work force (10 percent in total). The scenarios as depicted use 1992 work force shares, not those projected for 2010. "Transitional" refers to the former centrally planned economies of Europe and Central Asia. Source: Lewis, Robinson, and Wang, background paper; World Bank staff estimates.

petition in service industries to allow more labor demand growth, and in some countries, notably Spain, how to shift from patterns of collective bargaining that favor insiders at the expense of outsiders. But increased flexibility in wage structures will only significantly reduce unemployment in the context of strong overall growth in labor demand.

The history of the past decade or so makes it difficult to be optimistic that there will be a swift resolution of the employment problems in the industrial countries. A critical question is what action in the industrial countries may mean for the rest of the world. Under the divergent sce-

nario there is a significant probability that employment concerns and fears of competition will lead to a stalling of the potential gains from greater openness. As noted in Chapter 8, the Uruguay Round agreement is too limited to bring large gains by itself, and what gains it achieves are vulnerable to substitution with contingent protection—whether through antidumping or through the capture of labor and environmental standards by protectionists. Under the convergent scenario, however, progress in domestic action helps support a faster pace of integration, although with continued management of migration flows to limit the pressure of migrants on the unskilled domestic labor market.

South Asia, China, and Viet Nam

Are China, Viet Nam, and the countries of South Asia poised for an East Asian–style takeoff and engagement in the international economy, or will their transitions stall? Their performance is key to the largest single groups of poor workers in the world—the rural farmers and laborers of the Indian subcontinent and China. At present, the countries of this region are weakly integrated into international trade; the unfolding export boom in labor-intensive products offers the best hope of raising the incomes of these workers. Their rising involvement will send positive ripple effects throughout the world in the form of higher demand from global markets, but also increased competitive pressures on unskilled workers elsewhere, with the attendant risks of protectionist backlash.

These countries have seen average incomes steadily rising, together with labor productivity. The accumulation of capital and skills has also been steady, but relatively slow outside China. There is good potential for rapid accumulation in the future. Agriculture has done well and explains a large part of past success. But in the subcontinent industrial labor absorption has been weak, and agriculture remains heavily protected. The liberalization of agriculture and the takeoff in manufacturing must go hand in hand in the future. In the absence of a strong pull of labor demand from manufacturing, there is a real risk of rising inequality and stalled reforms. In the convergent scenario there is steady growth in incomes and falling poverty. But reductions in inequality are likely to remain limited, especially in China and Viet Nam where rising agricultural wages could be offset by widening inequality elsewhere—some of it desirable because of decompression of earnings schedules in state enterprises, some less so where people are stuck in stagnating regions.

Labor policy remains in need of reform in both South Asia and China. Each has a small group of workers who are relatively well paid and enjoy high job security and, especially in China, generous nonwage benefits, but are stuck in activities that need to be restructured. Regulation is excessive, and workers have substantial political power—manifested in South Asia in independent and highly politicized unions, in China in the potential for industrial action. Resistance to change could threaten the transition to an open economy and the integration of the domestic labor market. The strong tradition of support for income stabilization in informal and rural labor needs to be maintained and supported, especially in terms of public works and basic safety nets.

Although the transition to new forms of governance is advancing fast, China and India, the two giants of the region, face internal difficulties. Managing the decline of public enterprises and the protected private sector is the key issue in the transition. In China social responsibilities must ultimately be shifted out of the state enterprise sector. In India the challenges are to raise rural incomes to reduce poverty, and to restructure inefficient enterprises with powerful unions. Under the divergent scenario, public sector retrenchment weakens and exacerbates the risk of slow growth, partial international integration, continued sharp dualism, and weak growth in unskilled labor demand; inequalities rise, especially in the subcontinent. Under the convergent scenario there is both rapid and equalizing growth prompted by rural-urban migration, skill accumulation, and rising rural productivity.

Sub-Saharan Africa

The plight of the African continent remains the most serious challenge for the emerging world order. International prospects are mixed. The Uruguay Round agreement will raise food prices, which will hurt the urban poor in the short term but create important opportunities for peasants down the road. The agreement will also erode the region's trade preferences in the markets of some European states, and greater global competition will reduce the returns to low-skill manufacturing activities. Even in primary commodities, an area of comparative advantage, Sub-Saharan Africa must raise productivity in order to compete with the resource-rich countries of Southeast Asia and Latin America.

The ingredients of any movement forward must include, first and foremost, greater accumulation of capital and improvements in efficiency. Investment rates have fallen to less than 16 percent of GDP. Given the high rate of population growth, standards of living cannot improve unless investment rises dramatically. Until this happens, the quantity of education is unlikely to present an important constraint, although raising its quality is vital; in the divergent scenario enrollment rates are actually assumed to continue to decline, as they did in many countries in the 1980s. Unless the strategic risks faced by investors, especially in terms of possible policy reversals, are reduced, investment is unlikely to rise sufficiently. To achieve the dramatic turnaround in overall efficiency that is required, there must be a great effort on many fronts, from an acceleration of the still-unfinished reform agenda to improvements in basic infrastructure and better governance. For the great majority of poor farmers, agricultural reforms are the most pressing concern. To take advantage of the potential gains offered by higher international food prices, this growth potential must be passed on to small farmers; this may require well-structured land reforms in some countries, such as South Africa and Zimbabwe, and better access of farmers to financing.

Interventions in labor markets must mainly reduce the bias against small and informal businesses and agriculture. Public sector reforms are crucial for increasing the quality of the services offered. This should entail a simultaneous reduction in public employment and a more competitive wage structure.

The risks are high and are exacerbated by globalization. In the divergent scenario Africa continues to fall into a poverty trap and becomes increasingly marginalized from the world economy. A credible strategy will require rising global demand for agricultural products and mining, as well as bold international actions that are commensurate with the challenge at hand. Measures such as greater and faster opening of agricultural markets in the industrial countries, debt reductions with strong conditionality, and a stronger anchor to the rest of the world—perhaps in the context of free trade agreements with Europe—must be considered seriously. The goal should be partly to secure markets with some degree of temporary preferences so as to offset the losses due to the Uruguay Round. Much more important, however, such agreements need to emphasize internal reforms and a clear time frame. This could help boost the credibility of the reform agenda and reduce its uncertainty by locking governments into a process they cannot afford to tamper with. If such a strategy is followed, South Africa, Francophone West Africa, and even Nigeria could emerge as important regional growth poles.

East Asia

The East Asian region, with a few exceptions, has been a paradigm of investment and international engagement bringing large gains, at least in wage incomes, to workers. Export-led growth is likely to continue with increasing insertion into the international economy at increased skill levels—and with deepening intraregional links. There is, however, a risk of backlash from the industrial countries, possibly linked with concerns over labor standards, and a risk of rising competition—from China, Viet Nam, and the countries of South Asia for the poorer members of the group, and from Central and Eastern Europe for the richer ones. These risks are exacerbated by the expected opening up in agriculture, a highly protected sector: this is likely to hurt farm workers and lead to increased inequality.

There is a high probability of continued robust capital investment, but in the region's middle-income countries there is an emerging issue of skill shortages. In some countries, notably Thailand, education systems have lagged the growth of demand. Responses to these emerging constraints to development include faster growth of higher education, the return of highly skilled migrants from the industrial countries, and the use of highly skilled imported labor. All of these are happening in various degrees and are important components of a strategy to keep inequalities

from rising rapidly in the face of reduced agricultural protection.

Labor policy is in transition. In the past, many of the countries of the region repressed independent unions and preferred to substitute mandated standards for bargained solutions, albeit at relatively moderate, market-related levels. But as incomes continue to grow and these countries become middle-income economies, important questions about more modern management approaches and the development of democratic systems will increasingly come into play. Past development success has created a need to upgrade labor standards, and in particular to develop rational forms of formal job security. Korea has already started on this road, initiating in 1995 a major revision of its labor code and unemployment law.

Central and Eastern Europe and the former Soviet Union

The development path of the past has bequeathed to this region a rich stock of human capital and a developed but aging infrastructure. But the transition to the market has started with a collapse in production that has resulted in high unemployment. The key to renewed growth is a successful reorganization of labor out of the public sector and into higher productivity activities. This involves mass privatizations, falling trade protection, and a more workable financial system. The implied structural change will hurt some workers, either temporarily when reallocations are involved, or permanently when labor productivity is below the old wage. The main challenge is to allow the transformation to a private economy to proceed while minimizing social dislocations and transitional costs in unemployment.

Wages have exhibited a fair degree of downward flexibility; the challenge is to increase mobility across sectors. Nonwage labor costs are high and should be reduced in the context of a comprehensive reform of social insurance schemes. Unions are expected to continue playing a positive role at the firm level. However, they are likely to continue opposing rapid reforms unless the workers that stand to lose receive proper support and compensation.

External conditions appear favorable, especially for the countries of Central and Eastern Europe and the Baltic states, which have recently acquired preferential access to the markets of the European Union. This provides both new opportunities and a credible anchor for macroeconomic policies and reforms. The inflow of complementary capital will be important in generating growth, allowing the twin processes of job creation and job destruction to proceed smoothly, and retraining existing human capital.

There is, however, a serious risk of a stalled or incomplete transition if social tensions are not addressed. The main risks are of slow overall engagement in the international economy, led by difficulties in internal structural reforms; rising macroeconomic imbalances, prompted by high transfers and subsidies; and the creation of a new underclass of up to 10 to 20 percent of the population, hurt by passage through long-term unemployment and widening regional disparities. Managing the social dimension of the transition, keeping up the quality of social services, creating the conditions for rapid job creation, and avoiding the creation of new poverty are all key goals, but they must also be balanced with fiscal probity to ensure both social and macroeconomic stability. Success is likely to breed success by attracting foreign capital. But failure to jointly address these economic and social concerns risks prolonging the transition, at a high cost in human suffering and in lost opportunities.

Middle East and North Africa

Changing international conditions in this region make a shift from a state-led to a market-led and from a closed to an internationally oriented economy only more pressing. With the old sources of foreign exchange—aid and workers' remittances—unlikely to grow, export growth is key for the future. Globalization offers opportunities but also exacerbates risks. More than ever before, a credible and realistic strategy is needed to link the region with the world economy. The possibility of reduced regional tensions and the potential for deeper links with the European Union offer important opportunities. But entry could be tough, given the region's weak industrial history, and will require serious programs of internal liberalization.

The countries of the Middle East and North Africa have been on a roller coaster of boom and bust, driven by oil and a strong public sector. The combination of declining public sector revenues and rising urbanization and education have by now rendered the old social contract unaffordable, and the conditions must be put in place to allow the private sector to become the engine of growth. However, entrepreneurs are unlikely to take chances until strategic risk is reduced, and this will require progress toward regional peace and resolving internal conflicts, as well as resolute action on the economic policy front.

Public sector employment remains a major source of distortion, leading to macroeconomic fragility and reducing the credibility of other reforms. Together with an extensive web of regulations in the modern sector, this has resulted in a growing split between a regulated sector on the decline and an expanding low-productivity informal economy, with a small labor elite hanging on to its relative position at the expense of the majority. This may fuel social instability. There is an urgent need to revisit the social contract and redefine the role of the state, from an engine of growth to a regulator that allows markets to work and deliver socially acceptable outcomes. Labor policy also needs major reforms: unions are repressed and only weakly

perform their role, or do so in a highly politicized fashion. There is a need to rationalize their function.

The divergent scenario could be gloomy. Lack of resolute reforms will lead to rising poverty and social polarization. The fickleness of private capital and the bumpy peace process heighten the risks, and rapid labor supply growth complicates the transition. However, the convergent scenario offers rosier prospects, with capital inflows allowing for a fuller use of existing skills. Credibility and domestic politics are the main issues. Mechanisms to facilitate the transfer of laid-off workers to new jobs, compensation for those hurt, and an overall policy framework supportive of reductions in poverty will be important ingredients of a successful transition.

Latin America and the Caribbean

The integration of this region with the global economy is proceeding apace, especially in trade and capital markets, and in Central America through international migration. The international environment is promising, because the natural resource base leaves the region less exposed to international competition in labor-intensive products. Rapid growth is possible. The hope is of diversifying exports away from natural resources and into medium-skill products. An important issue for the future is whether NAFTA will be extended to the rest of the hemisphere or get hamstrung by the standards debate.

Most Latin American countries have been taking off, with some recovery in wages. Although it would be wrong to overreact to Mexico's recent financial trouble, there is a broader risk that the takeoff will fail to resolve the problems of inequality, and that countries will get caught in a vise of low-wage competition from Asia and fail to achieve the human capital accumulation appropriate for the region's level of income. Accumulation is already rising fast in countries, such as Chile, that implemented robust reforms. The main problems that need to be addressed are the weakness of skill formation and the remaining biases against labor in countries where land distribution is unequal, such as Colombia and Brazil. Land reform and removal of policy biases against labor use in agriculture will be required.

Labor policy is a major piece of the unfinished agenda. Although some progress has been achieved in deregulating labor markets, distorted labor markets continue to lead to excessively large informal sectors in countries such as Ecuador and Peru. Unions have become weaker, except in the public sector, but independent unions have an important role to play and in some countries need to be strengthened, especially in their role in decentralized bargaining. There is also a need to reform hiring and firing rules, deal with public sector problems, and deepen the reform of systems of social security.

Transitional problems remain: issues of state enterprise

layoffs in Argentina, relative wage flexibility in Mexico, and special social safety nets. Under the divergent scenario there is a distinct possibility of only modest growth with widening inequality. This would ultimately threaten the social fabric. But concerted action could lead to recovery of labor demand in agriculture, easing the formal-informal divide and preventing inequality from rising further.

Slow growth or inclusion?

Governments have to work with the legacies of past policies and development structures. Workers have to live with the opportunities at hand. These are molded by the structure of the economies and societies in which they live and by the capabilities formed by their personal histories—what they have received from their parents and from their schooling. But for both governments and workers, that is just the starting point. Both are agents of change. Good choices by governments, in the domestic and the international realms, can lead to advances in the living standards of all groups of workers in the world and help bring back into the fold those who are unable to keep up or adjust on their own. If international conditions are favorable and governments do their part to create the right environment, workers will be able to make the job choices, negotiate the conditions of work, and make the schooling decisions for their children that will improve the welfare of all groups of workers. That could begin to reverse the long-run trend of widening international inequality between workers that has been so marked a feature of the past century, and bring new hope and opportunities to millions currently trapped in poverty. And that would set the stage for a truly global golden age in the twenty-first century.

Bibliographical Note

THIS REPORT HAS DRAWN ON A WIDE range of World Bank reports and on numerous outside sources. World Bank sources include ongoing research as well as country economic, sector, and project work. These and other sources are listed alphabetically by author or organization in two groups: background papers commissioned for this Report and a selected bibliography. The background papers, some of which will be available through the Policy Research Working Paper series, and the rest through the *World Development Report* office, synthesize relevant literature and Bank work. The views they express are not necessarily those of the World Bank or of this Report.

In addition to the principal sources listed, many persons, both inside and outside the World Bank, helped with the Report. In particular, the core team wishes to thank Paul Collier, Richard Freeman, John Pencavel, Christopher Pissarides, Lyn Squire, David Turnham, and Adrian Wood for their extensive support.

Others who provided substantial inputs or comments include Arvil V. Adams, Nisha Agrawal, Jane Armitage, Jere Behrman, Hans Binswanger, Peter Fallon, Keith Griffin, Stephan Haggard, James Harrison, Shigeru Ishikawa, Ravi Kanbur, Homi Kharas, Dipak Mazumdar, Guy Pfefferman, Lant Pritchett, Martin Rama, Richard Sabot, and Paulo Vieira da Cunha. Bruce Ross-Larson and Meta de Coquereaumont provided valuable editorial advice and assistance at various points. Those who commented on particular parts of the Report are noted below.

Special thanks go to Katherine Hagen as well as others at the International Labour Office (ILO) for their comments at various stages, and to Stephen Pursey of the International Confederation of Free Trade Unions and Eddy Peeters of the World Confederation of Labor for their comments throughout the process, as well as their organization of a consultation meeting with union representatives.

Contributors and attendees at the consultation with union representatives included Alan Abrahart, Gemma Adaba, Victor Baez-Mosqueira, Ching Chabo, Jorgen Eckeroth, Hans Engelberts, Seyhan Erdogdu, John Evans, David Fowler, Reynaldo Geronimo, Ronald Hansen, Robert Harris, Craig Hill, Anne Knipper, David Lambert, Janusz Michalski, Agnes Mukupa, Eddy Peeters, Stephen Pursey, Markley Roberts, Michael Sebastian, Alione Sow, Peter Unterweger, Dirk Uyttenhove, Nazaryo Vivero, and Mike Waghorne.

Contributors and attendees at the consultation with government, multilaterals, and NGO representatives included Rolf Alter, Philip Barry, Joan Boer, Jacques Bugnicourt, Marion Crawshaw, Rudy Delarue, Walter Dhondt, Georg Fischer, Jean-Baptiste de Foucault, Sakiko Fukuda-Parr, Katherine Hagen, Anne Kristin Hermansen, Roy Jones, Nicholas Karavitis, Martin Khor, Horst Kleinschmidt, Marc de Lamotte, Anna Lekwall, John Martin, Ruth Mayne, Merje Mikkola, Christopher Moir, Guy de Monchy, John Morley, Jorgen Ohlsson, David Ould, Anders Serup Rasmussen, Anne Richards, Fabrice Ritchie, John Roberts, Gregory Schoepfle, Takemichi Shirai, Rudiger Sielaff, Matti Sihto, Naresh C. Singh, James F. Steel, Arne Strom, Stanley Taylor, Christine Toetzke, Kazuto Tsuji, David Turnham, Roberto Urmenenta, Jan Vandemoortle, Laurent Vernière, Philip R. Wall, Thomas Weiss, Dominique Welcomme, and Peter Whitney.

Informal focus groups were formed in the following countries to comment on the Report: Bangladesh, Belarus, Ghana, Hungary, Indonesia, Poland, South Africa, and Venezuela.

The data underlying this Report come from a wide variety of sources. Particular use was made of the ILO's data bases, a compilation of data on labor being undertaken in the World Bank (see Topel, Levy, and Rama 1994), household survey data, especially from the Living Standards Measurement Study project, and country sources.

The persons and events described in the short biographical sketches in the Overview and elsewhere in the Report are fictitious. The characters are composites based on information from household surveys and published and unpublished case studies and hence may be considered typical of persons in their circumstances.

Part One benefited from valuable comments by Arvil V. Adams, Harold Alderman, Jere Behrman, Alan Berg, Hans Binswanger, William Easterly, Alison Evans, Richard Freeman, David Fretwell, James Harrison, Stephen Heyneman, Keith Hinchcliffe, Emmanuel Jimenez, Robert Lalonde, Matthew McMahan, Tom Merrick, John Middleton, Minh Chau Nguyen, Harry Anthony Patrinos, Guy Pfefferman, Lant Pritchett, George Psacharopoulos, Martin Ravallion, David Turnham, and Zafiris Tzannatos.

Part Two benefited from contributions by Jean Baneth, Barry Chiswick, Stijn Claessens, Daniel Cohen, Paul Collier, Richard Freeman, Will Martin, Guy Pfefferman, Christopher Pissarides, Lant Pritchett, Dani Rodrik, Sharon Russell, Frances Stewart, David Turnham, and Adrian Wood.

Part Three drew on background papers and a range of academic sources. The principal commentators were Richard Freeman and John Pencavel. Useful material and comments were also provided by Arvil V. Adams, Mark Blackden, Daniel Cohen, Paul Collier, Alison Evans, Peter Fallon, Homi Kharas, Elizabeth Morris-Hughes, Stephen Pursey, Martin Ravallion, Martin Rama, and Dominique Van de Walle.

Valuable contributions to Part Four came from many sources, both in and outside the World Bank, including Christine Allison, Nicholas Barr, Maurice Boissiere, Jeanine Braithwaite, Mary Cannings, Carlos Cavalcanti, Simon Commander, Saul Estrin, Monica Fong, David Fretwell, Alan Gelb, Marek Góra, Ralph W. Harbison, Christine Kessides, Timothy King, Kathie Krumm, Robert Liebenthal, Dipak Mazumdar, Michael Mertaugh, Branko Milanovic, Michael Mills, Caroline Moser, Kyle Peters, Martin Rama, Paolo Roberti, Jan Rutkowski, Martin Schrenk, Mark Sundberg, and Milan Vodopivec.

Chapter 1

The empirical profile of world labor market outcomes is drawn from many sources. The estimate of the increase in income inequality since the nineteenth century is from Pritchett 1994. The distribution of the working-age population by economic activity is based on estimates of participation rates reported in ILO 1986 and ILO data updates as applied to recent UN age-specific population estimates. These are combined with employment data by economic sector from ILO, various years, further supplemented with data from country sources. For details, see the Filmer background paper.

The international wage hierarchy is drawn from data published in Union Bank of Switzerland 1994. GDP growth rates for different regions are from World Bank estimates of GDP growth at market prices minus estimates of labor force growth from ILO 1986 and ILO data updates. Regional growth rates are derived from country-specific growth rates weighted by ILO estimates of the working-age population in 1995. Data from the former Soviet Union and elsewhere in the region are drawn from EBRD 1994 and Kornai 1992.

The review of alternative development strategies and their consequences for labor is drawn from many sources including Easterly and Fischer 1994, Lindauer and Roemer 1994, and World Bank 1993.

Chapter 2

The section on growth patterns and labor outcomes relies on data from the Ghana Living Standards Measurement Study survey of 1989 and the Malaysian Labor Force Survey of 1989 as well as data from various official publications.

There is a vast literature on the determinants of economic growth. This chapter draws on the background paper by Spiegel as well as on detailed econometric work found in Barro 1991, Levine and Renelt 1992, and Mankiw, Romer, and Weil 1992.

The literature on population growth and economic development is equally vast. The discussion here draws from Kelley 1994, Pritchett 1994, and World Bank 1994d.

Chapter 3

The section on household decisions is inspired by the model of time allocation in Becker 1965. The discussion on labor force participation by age and sex draws on the Behrman and Zhang background paper, Goldin 1990, Horton 1994b, Horton, Kanbur, and Mazumdar 1994a and 1994b, Psacharopoulos and Tzannatos 1992, and Schultz 1990. Labor force information on hours worked is from the Malaysian Labor Force Survey of 1989 and the Ghana Living Standards Measurement Study survey of 1988–89. Trends in hours worked in high-income OECD economies are reported in Maddison 1989.

The section on unemployment draws from Commander and Coricelli 1994, OECD 1994a, and Turnham 1993. Unemployment data are from a variety of sources, including EBRD 1994, ILO 1994b, OECD 1994a, and Topel, Levy, and Rama 1994, as well as country sources.

Chapter 4

The section on changing patterns of employment by sector draws on Krueger 1983, Schiff and Valdes 1992, and Syrquin and Chenery 1989. The section on nonfarm rural employment draws on the Lanjouw and Lanjouw background paper and on Turnham 1993. The discussion of the informal sector draws on background papers by Banerji and Banerji, Campos, and Sabot. Box 4.1 was prepared by Hans Binswanger.

Chapter 5

Reviews of the literature on nutrition and productivity include Behrman 1993 and Pinstrup-Andersen and others 1993. The specific evidence on nutritional status and farm output in southern India is from Deolalikar 1988 and in the Philippines from Haddad and Bouis 1991.

Evidence on education and the adoption of high-yielding varieties of rice is presented in Lin 1994 for China and in Foster and others 1994 for India.

Evidence on training in Taiwan, China, is from Aw and Tan 1993. The impact of improved nutrition on education in Guatemala is from Pollitt and others 1995. Complementarity of education and training in Peru is drawn from Arriagada 1989. Data for Slovenia are from Orazem and Vodopivec 1994. In the discussion of education and human capital the data on trends in world enrollments are as reported in Barro and Lee 1993 and Tilak 1989. Valuable overviews of education as an investment are provided in Becker 1995, Schultz 1994, and World Bank 1995a.

Alida Castillo-Freeman provided the results on the United States for the figure in Box 5.1. Care has been taken to ensure comparability among the studies mentioned in the figure, but because each study employs a different specification for the earnings function, this is not guaranteed. Starting from log wage equations, which for the most part deal with selection into wage employment and individual characteristics, the premiums to each educational level are imputed from either (i) the implied return to a level obtained by multiplying the return to a year at that level by the number of years at that level in the country's school system; or (ii) the implied return to a level by converting a school-level dummy variable into its percentage effect on earnings.

Training as a human capital investment is described in Middleton, Adams, and Ziderman 1993 and in World Bank 1991. Training data for Mexico are from World Bank internal documents as is the discussion of Mexico's CIMO program. Training data for Japan are reported in Lynch 1994. Turnover rates in Korean manufacturing are from the Republic of Korea 1987. An analysis of apprenticeship programs in Ghana appears in Velenchik forthcoming. Chile's training system is described in King and Hill 1993.

Chapter 6

The discussion of growth and earnings inequality is based on Dickens and Katz 1987, Freeman 1993b, Krueger and Summers 1987, Rutkowski 1993 and 1994, and World Bank 1990. The section on inequality and schooling draws on Gindling and Robbins 1994, Park, Ross, and Sabot 1992, Psacharopoulos and others 1993, Robbins 1994, and the Robbins background papers. The discussion pertaining to Mexico draws on the Hanson and Harrison background paper and Revenga 1994.

The discussion of rural-urban inequality benefited greatly from comments by Hans Binswanger and also draws on some of the material presented in Chapter 4. The discussion of the equalizing role of the formal labor market uses numbers taken from Bell 1994. The section on inequalities among ethnic groups is based on Psacharopoulos and Patrinos 1994 and on the background paper by Banerji. The discussion of preferential policies in Malaysia draws heavily from Tzannatos 1994.

Data on regional inequality in Mexico come from World Bank 1994c, whereas the reference to Gansu, China, is drawn from World Bank 1992b. The reference to the northern hill people in Thailand comes from Oomen 1992. The discussion of regional inequality in Argentina is based on the work of Estache and Fay 1995.

The analysis of wage differentials between men and women is based on Horton 1994b, Newell and Reilly 1995, and Tzannatos 1995. Box 6.1 also draws on Oaxaca 1973 and Psacharopoulos and Tzannatos 1992. Some of the country references come from Birdsall and Sabot 1991.

Chapter 7

The discussion on globalization draws from Rodrik 1994 and World Bank 1992a. The discussion on convergence draws on Berry, Bourguignon, and Morrisson 1989 and on recent work by Ben-David 1994, the Pritchett background paper, and Quah 1994. For more comment on the golden age of capitalism, see Maddison 1982, Neal 1985, and Zevin 1989; for migration history see Hatton and Williamson 1994 and Stalker 1994.

Chapter 8

The analysis of the Uruguay Round draws on Goldin and van der Mensbrugghe 1995, Harrison, Rutherford, and Tarr 1995, Hathaway and Ingco 1995, Hertel and others 1995, and Rodrik 1994. The discussion on trade and wages in industrial market economies follows Bhagwati and Kosters 1994, Cooper 1994, Freeman 1995, Krugman and Lawrence 1993, Lawrence and Slaughter 1993, Neven and Wyplosz 1994, Sachs and Shatz 1994, Stolper and Samuelson 1941, Wood 1994a, and Wood and Berge 1994. Discussion of the effects in developing countries draws on results in Davis 1992, Feenstra and Hanson 1994, Krueger 1978, the Robbins background papers, and Wood 1994a. The demographic projections for the rich countries are from McKinsey Global Institute 1994. The figure in Box 8.2 follows the methodology of Wood 1994b.

Chapter 9

The material on saving-investment correlations relies on Montiel 1993 and Schmidt-Hebbel, Servén, and Solimano 1994. The material on multinational corporations and foreign direct investment is based on Feldstein 1994, Lawrence 1994, Lipsey 1994, and United Nations 1994a. The effect of private flows and instability draws from Calvo, Leiderman, and Reinhart 1992, Chuhan, Claessens, and Mamingi 1993, Claessens, Dooley, and Warner 1995, Dadush, Phareshwan, and Johannes 1994, and Schadler and others 1993.

Chapter 10

For more on migration theory, see Bhagwati 1991, Massey 1990, Massey and others 1993, Razin and Sadka 1994, and Stark 1991. On broad migration issues, see Russell and Teitelbaum 1992, Stalker 1994, and Zlotnik 1993. The treatment of the effect of migration on countries that send workers abroad is based on work by Abella and Mori 1994, Adams 1989 and 1992, Findley 1994, and Rodriguez and

Horton 1994. The effect on countries taking in workers is based on Borjas 1994, Borjas and Freeman 1993, Overbeek 1994, and Zimmermann 1995. Kwong 1994 reports on illegal practices involving Chinese immigrants in the United States.

Chapter 11

Solow 1980 discusses why labor markets are different from other markets and why governments intervene in labor markets. A survey of the reasons for government interventions in labor markets is in Kaufman 1991. Mazumdar 1989 presents a survey of labor market problems in developing countries and policies to deal with them.

An overview of the key workplace standards and their usefulness and objectives can be found in ILO 1994a and the Robinson background paper. The background paper by Grootaert and Kanbur provided the organizing framework for the section on child labor and many of the empirical arguments. A typology of child labor is presented in Rodgers and Standing 1981. Galbi 1994 presents the problem of child labor in a historical perspective; Nichols 1993 presents some real-life examples from South Asia and the dilemma facing foreign firms; and Boyden 1988 describes the situation in Lima, Peru. The discussion of the experience in the Indian state of Kerala and of the Philippine island of Cebu is from Boyden and Myers 1994. The analysis in Patrinos and Psacharopoulos 1995 shows that family size is an important determinant of child labor, and Siddiqi and Patrinos 1994 argue that schooling problems contribute to child labor. The link between the failure of the education system in Africa and child labor is explored in Bonnet 1993, and further evidence on the negative correlation between child labor and education is presented in Rivera-Batiz 1985. The data on Egypt are from Levy 1985, and the discussion on India is from Rosenzweig 1981 and Rosenzweig and Evenson 1977. A discussion of the relationship between the uncertainty of household income and child labor can be found in Jacoby and Skoufias 1994. A description of child labor in Bogotá's quarries can be found in Salazar 1988.

A cross-country description of the patterns of female employment is in the Behrman and Zhang background paper. A historical perspective on women in the labor market in America is in Goldin 1990 and for women in Asia in Horton 1994b. The discussion of maternity leave is from the Robinson background paper, and arguments for why benefits should not be employer-financed can be found in Tzannatos 1995. References to female employment in Bangladesh are from Chaudhuri and Paul-Majumder 1991 and the Rahman background paper. The discussion of the impact of Egyptian public employment policies on female workers is based on the Assaad background paper. Patrinos 1994 presents arguments that investments in education for members of indigenous, ethnic, racial, and linguistic mi-

norities will result in eliminating most of the observed wage differentials. The review of discrimination and affirmative action in industrial countries relied on Becker 1957, Beller 1979, Bergmann 1989, Brown 1982, Edwards 1994, Gold 1983, Goldstein and Smith 1976, Hill 1984, Leonard 1984a, 1984b, and 1989, and Smith and Welch 1984.

The Azam background paper presents a survey of the arguments about the impact of minimum wages and some empirical evidence. Arguments for why minimum wages may not have much of an impact on employment, with evidence from industrial countries, are from Card and Krueger 1995 and Krueger 1994. Rama and Tabellini 1995 present a model where minimum wages are used for creating rents for some groups of workers, and Freeman 1993c describes how minimum wages may be regarded as a budget-neutral tool for redistributing income. The Mauritius example is from the Robinson background paper. Explanations for why compliance with minimum wages is low in developing countries, together with some evidence of noncompliance, can be found in the Squire and Suthiwart-Narueput background paper. Evidence of noncompliance with labor regulations in small enterprises in developing countries is from Morrisson, Solignac Lecomte, and Oudin 1994. Data on Mexico are from Bell 1994; data for Morocco come from Harrison 1993 and for Kenya from Freeman 1993b.

The discussion of safety and health regulations is based on several sources. Comparative data on health hazards and workplace injuries are from the International Labour Office and the World Health Organization. The description of the impact of exposure to pesticides on the health of agricultural workers is from *Boston Globe* 1994. The description of particular factory fires is from Foner and Garraty 1991 and newspaper sources. The discussion of the enforcement of safety regulations in the Philippines is from Laboj 1988. Description of the labor market implications of the river blindness program is from Cooley and Benton 1995. Reviews of studies of health and safety regulations can be found in both Currington 1988 and Viscusi 1986. The evidence that the presence of unions may change this result is from Weil 1991.

The question of whether labor standards should be linked to trade agreements is widely debated. U.S. Department of Labor 1994 presents the different points of view and their supporting arguments.

Chapter 12

This chapter is based on background papers that defined the analytical framework and provided some empirical evidence: by Banerji and Ghanem, Ghanem, Devarajan, and Thierfelder, and Pencavel. The analysis in this chapter also benefited from the work of Freeman 1992, Freeman and Medoff 1984, Katz, Kuruvilla, and Turner 1993, Pencavel

1991, and Rees 1989. A description of the functions of trade unions can be found in Sugeno 1994.

The data and country examples are from many sources. Evidence on the union wage premiums is from Blanchflower and Freeman 1990, Moll 1993, Panagides and Patrinos 1994, Park 1991, Standing 1992, and Teal 1994. Data on unionization in India are from Joshi and Little 1994, for East Asia from Frenkel 1993, and for Spain from ILO 1985 and Jimeno and Toharia 1993. Arguments and data on the positive impact of unions on income distribution are from Freeman 1980, Lee and Nam 1994, and Panagides and Patrinos 1994. Data on the positive impact of Malaysian unions are from Standing 1992. The example of industrial unions in Brazil is from Fleury and Humphrey 1993, and that of Indian coal miners is from Banerji and Sabot 1993. Discussion of the level at which collective bargaining takes place can be found in Calmfors and Driffil 1988 and Freeman 1988. Freeman 1993a describes and analyzes industrial relations in East Asia, and Krause and Park 1993 provide a detailed analysis for Korea. The analysis of public sector unions is based on the Pencavel background paper and benefited greatly from discussions with trade union representatives. The quotes of country responses to ILO queries on freedom of association are from Botswana Federation of Trade Unions and International Federation of Trade Unions 1991.

The chapter benefited from other case studies of the role of unions in developing countries, including Bhattacherjee 1987 and Bhattacherjee and Chaudhuri 1994 on India, Manning 1993 on Indonesia, McCoy 1989 on Venezuela, and Mondal 1992 on Bangladesh.

Chapter 13

The discussion of income security for informal workers deals with community support and private transfers, public works programs, and safety nets for the rural poor. A survey of the literature on community support and private transfers is presented by Cox and Jimenez 1990. The specific example of Peru is from Cox and Jimenez 1989. A review of the issues surrounding public works programs is presented in the Mukherjee background paper. Von Braun 1994 presents many case studies, summarizes lessons from experience, and is the source for the references to the programs in Bolivia, China, Ethiopia, Niger, Senegal, Zimbabwe, and Maharashtra, India. Datt and Ravallion 1994 also present a detailed empirical analysis of the impact of the Maharashtra State scheme. A description of the Chilean public works program can be found in Edwards and Cox Edwards 1991 and Hudson 1994.

A description of the experience with rating unemployment benefit systems in the United States can be found in Hamermesh 1991 or Topel and Welch 1980, and an analysis of the link between unemployment duration and unemployment benefits is in Pujol 1994. The discussion of the

link between job security and employment draws heavily on Freeman 1993b. It also uses the work of Bertola 1990, Blank and Freeman 1993, and Lazear 1990. The discussion of the European steel industry is from Houseman 1991, and the reference to Spain is from Alba-Ramirez 1991. Schaffner 1993 presents an analysis of income security regulations in northeast Brazil, and Marshall 1991 studies Peru. All other references to cases in Latin America are from Cox Edwards 1993 and 1994. The reference to Sri Lanka is based on the work of Rama 1994, and the Malaysia example is from Standing 1989. The analysis of job security regulations in India and Zimbabwe is from Fallon and Lucas 1991. The discussion of social assistance schemes is based on Milanovic 1995.

Chapter 14

The economic arguments in this chapter relied heavily on the work of Lindauer and Nunberg 1994 and Wade 1994. The latter is the source of the argument using the principal-agent presentation and is the source for Box 14.1 and the comparison between the Indian and Korean irrigation services. Reviews of the issues that need to be addressed by policymakers embarking on civil service reforms are presented in Dia 1993, Gregory and Perlman 1994, Lindauer and Nunberg 1994, Nunberg 1993, Reid 1992, and Reid and Scott 1994. Kraay and van Rijckeghem 1994 present a cross-country empirical analysis of the determinants of public sector wages and employment.

Description of public sector hiring and compensation policies in Egypt is from the Assaad background paper, and the data for the Egypt and Ghana comparison are from Banerji and Sabot forthcoming. Some of the Ghana data are also from Lindauer, Meesook, and Suebsaeng 1988. The quotation on the Ugandan civil service is from Republic of Uganda 1992. Discussion of Tanzania is based partly on Lindauer and Sabot 1983, and some of the Kenyan data are from Johnson 1971. Some of the discussion of Zambia is based on the work of Colclough 1989, and the data on El Salvador are from Gregory 1991. Knight and Sabot 1987, Terrell 1993, and van der Gaag, Stelcner, and Vijverberg 1989 present estimates of private-public wage differentials. The description of reforms in Chile's education sector is from Castaneda 1992.

The section on the political economy of civil service reforms used the analysis of Kenya in Cohen 1993 as well as by some recent work on the issue of governance and the political economy of development, including Boeninger 1991, Landell-Mills and Serageldin 1992, Martin 1991, Nelson 1994, and Rodrik 1992.

Chapter 15

The discussion of the collapse of different development strategies and the move to a new growth path relies on Estrin 1994, Hierro and Sanginés 1991, Lustig 1992, World

Bank 1994a, and internal World Bank documents. The analysis of the major features of reform is drawn from a combination of internal Bank documents and outside sources, including Bosworth, Dornbusch, and Laban 1994, Chamley and Ghanem 1994, Cooper 1994, Gelb and Gray 1991, Husain and Faruqee 1994, Larraín and Selowsky 1991, and World Bank 1994a. The discussion of partial reforms in centrally planned economies is based on Kornai 1992.

Estimates of patterns of macroeconomic decline and job turbulence indices come from World Bank staff estimates, government sources, and internal World Bank documents and also draw on the Jackman background paper. Estimates of the number of workers associated with each regional pattern of structural reform are based on work force data from ILO, various years (for specific countries see the Appendix).

The discussion of real wages and unemployment draws heavily from Horton, Kanbur, and Mazumdar 1994a and 1994b. The material on adjustment in Sub-Saharan Africa also draws on the Mazumdar background paper and World Bank 1994a.

The section on relative wages and the redeployment of labor relies on Beaudry and Sowa 1994, Gindling and Berry 1994, Horton 1994a, Horton, Kanbur, and Mazumdar 1994b, Mazumdar 1994, Riveros 1994, and Revenga and Montenegro 1995 for the discussion of the experience of developing market economies; and on Beleva, Jackman, and Nenova-Amar 1994, Commander, McHale, and Yemtsov 1994, Ham, Svejnar, and Terrell 1994, and Rutkowski 1994 for the discussion of the former centrally planned economies.

The discussion of how initial conditions have affected reform paths in Russia and China comes from Sachs and Woo 1994 and takes into account arguments developed by McKinnon 1994.

The section on macroeconomic policy draws on Bruno 1988, Chamley and Ghanem 1994, Easterly and Schmidt-Hebbel 1994, and World Bank 1994a. The discussion of the role of speed and credibility in reforming centrally planned economies is based on Balcerowicz and Gelb 1995 and Kornai 1995.

Chapter 16

This chapter draws heavily on several assessments of adjustment programs throughout the world. The analysis of the results of adjustment programs in Sub-Saharan Africa, Latin America, and the Middle East and North Africa draws heavily on Horton, Kanbur, and Mazumdar 1994a and 1994b, Mazumdar 1994, and World Bank 1994a. The data on income inequality for Latin America come from Psacharopoulos and others 1993, while those for Africa and Asia come from Sen 1994. This section also relies on Fox and Morley 1990, World Bank 1990, and poverty assessments for Indonesia, Mexico, Peru, and Viet Nam.

The income inequality data for transitional economies are drawn from Atkinson and Micklewright 1992 and Kornai 1992, who describe initial conditions, and Milanovic 1994 and 1995, which examine the effects of transition. Data on wage differentials for Poland are based on Rutkowski 1994, for eastern Germany on the Lehmann background paper, and for the Czech Republic on Chase 1994. Changes in the incidence of poverty are described in Milanovic forthcoming.

Box 16.1 is based on Lustig 1992, Moser 1994, and Moser and others 1994, as well as on Berg and Sachs 1992, which contains an analysis of the welfare measurement problems in transition economies. Information on workers leaving the labor force is taken from Flanagan 1995. The section on the probabilities of falling into poverty for different groups of the population draws heavily on World Bank internal documents, especially poverty assessments and studies on women in development, and on Milanovic forthcoming. This section also makes use of Fox and Morley 1990, Horton, Kanbur, and Mazumdar 1994a and 1994b, and World Bank 1990. Data on shares of the informal labor market were taken from the Banerji background paper, Braithwaite 1994, Dallago 1995, and national sources.

The section on skills draws heavily on studies of rates of return to education: on Robbins 1994 for the discussion of Chile; on the Hanson and Harrison background paper and Revenga 1994 for the discussion of Mexico; and on Chase 1994, Orazem and Vodopivec 1994, and World Bank 1994e for the discussion of Eastern European countries, as well as on country economic memoranda for Viet Nam and Mongolia.

Chapter 17

The discussion of employment hires and separations draws on Roberts forthcoming and the Rutkowski and Sinha background paper. The analysis of real wage declines is based on national statistical yearbooks, the Commander and McHale background paper, and Horton, Kanbur, and Mazumdar 1994a and 1994b. The evaluation of initial conditions of workers and their response to shocks draws from Jackman and Rutkowski 1994.

The section on labor market adaptability and labor mobility draws on the Knight and Song background paper. Discussion of Peru is based on the Bank's poverty assessment and conversations with Edgardo Favaro. The analysis of regional unemployment rates is based on numbers taken from internal World Bank documents and draws on Boeri and Scarpetta 1994, Commander and Coricelli 1994, Erbenova 1994, Góra and Lehmann 1995, and Scarpetta 1994. Data on wage differentials come from Rutkowski 1993 and 1994. The comments on labor hoarding draw on the Commander and McHale background paper and Rutkowski 1990. Information on excess wage taxes comes from numerous Bank documents and from the analysis of Commander, Coricelli, and Staehr 1991, Coricelli and Revenga 1992, and Rostowski 1994. Data on minimum wages come from CIS 1994 and statistical yearbooks covering Chile and Mexico. The analysis of social services provided by public enterprises benefits from observations by many World Bank staff members and draws on results of empirical investigations in Commander and Jackman 1993 and Estrin, Schaffer, and Singh 1994, as well as on internal World Bank documents on China.

The section on equipping workers for change, including Box 17.1, is based on a variety of sources, especially Burda 1993, Fretwell and Goldberg 1993, Fretwell and Jackman 1994, Ham, Svejnar, and Terrell 1993 and 1994, Jacobson 1994, Johnson, Dickinson, and West 1985, the Lehmann background paper, Leigh 1992, Micklewright and Nagy 1995, OECD 1993 and 1994b, O'Leary 1995, Orr and others 1994, Revenga, Riboud, and Tan 1994, Sohlman and Turnham 1994, and Wilson and Adams 1994. Box 17.1 is based on Fretwell and Jackman 1994 and on the analysis in OECD 1993.

Most of the discussion on reducing insecurity through transfer programs is based on Barr 1994 and Krumm, Milanovic, and Walton 1994. Data on shares of social expenditures in GDP come from internal Bank documents. The discussion of the difficulties of means testing and designing targeting mechanisms is based on insights in Barr forthcoming and Sipós 1994. The discussion of the role of older workers draws from Jimeno and Toharia 1994 and Revenga and Riboud 1993.

Most of the examples on mass layoff schemes come from Chaudhry, Reid, and Malik 1994, Hess 1994, and Svejnar and Terrell 1991. Conceptual insights in the discussion on the basic principles guiding retrenchment schemes and on policies toward one-company towns were inspired by Diwan 1994 and Jackman and Rutkowski 1994, as well as by internal World Bank documents on Sri Lanka and the Russia Coal Projects.

Chapter 18

The projections presented are based on a simulation model developed by Sherman Robinson and Jeff Lewis, with the assistance of Zhi Wang. Adrian Wood provided helpful suggestions.

Background papers

Agrawal, Nisha. "Indonesia—Labor Market Policies and International Competitiveness."

Ahuja, Vinod, and Deon Filmer. "Educational Attainment in Developing Countries: New Estimates and Projections Disaggregated by Gender."

Appleton, Simon, John Hoddinott, Pramila Krishnan, and Kerry Max. "Gender Differences in the Returns to Schooling in Three African Countries."

Assaad, Ragui. "The Effects of Public Sector Hiring and Compensation Policies on the Egyptian Labor Market."

Azam, Jean-Paul. "Effects of Minimum Wages in Developing Countries: An Exploration."

Banerji, Arup. "Workers in the 'Informal Sector' in Developing Countries."

Banerji, Arup, J. Edgardo Campos, and Richard Sabot. "The Political Economy of Formal Sector Pay and Employment in Developing Countries."

Banerji, Arup, and Hafez Ghanem. "Political Regimes and Labor Policies in Developing Countries."

Behrman, Jere, and Zheng Zhang. "Women's Employment: Patterns Across Countries and Over Time."

Collier, Paul, John Hoddinott, and Francis Teal. "African Labor Markets."

Commander, Simon, and John McHale. "Labor Markets in the Transition in East Europe and Russia: A Review of Experience."

Filmer, Deon. "Estimating the World at Work."

Ghanem, Hafez, Shantayanan Devarajan, and Karen Thierfelder. "Trade Reform and Labor Unions: A General-Equilibrium Analysis Applied to Bangladesh and Indonesia."

Grootaert, Christian, and Ravi Kanbur. "Child Labor."

Hanson, Gordon, and Ann Harrison. "Trade, Technology, and Wage Inequality: Evidence from Mexico."

Jackman, Richard. "Coping with Job Destruction in Economies in Transition."

Knight, John, and Lina Song. "Towards a Labor Market in China."

Lanjouw, Peter, and Jean O. Lanjouw. "Rural Nonfarm Employment: A Survey."

Lehmann, Hartmut. "Active Labour Market Policies in the OECD and in Selected Transition Economies."

Lewis, Jeffrey, Sherman Robinson, and Zhi Wang. "General Equilibrium Analysis of Effects of Human Capital and Trade on the International Distribution of Labor."

Mazumdar, Dipak. "The Structure of Wages in African Manufacturing."

Mukherjee, Anindita. "Public Work Programs: A Review."

Pencavel, John. "The Role of Labor Unions in Fostering Economic Development."

Pissarides, Christopher. "Trade and the Returns to Human Capital in Developing Economies."

Pritchett, Lant. "Divergence, Big Time."

Rahman, Rushidan Islam. "Formal Sector Employment Among Women in Bangladesh and Gender Composition of Industrial Workers."

Ravallion, Martin, and Gaurav Datt. "Growth and Poverty in Rural India."

Revenga, Ana, and Adrian Wood. "International Trade, Inequality, and Human Capital: A Review and Synthesis of Theoretical and Empirical Work."

Robbins, Donald. "Earnings Inequality, Structural Adjustment, and Trade Liberalization in Costa Rica."

———. "Summary of Preliminary Analysis of Malaysia Wage Structure 1973–1989."

———. "Wage Dispersion in Argentina 1986–1993."

———. "Wage Dispersion and Trade in Colombia—An Analysis of Greater Bogotá 1976–1989."

Robinson, Derek. "Do Standards for the Workplace Help or Hurt?"

Rutkowski, Michal, and Sarbajit Sinha. "Employment Flows and Sectoral Shifts during the Transition Shock in Post-Socialist Countries."

Spiegel, Mark. "Determinants of Long-Run Labor Productivity Growth: Selective Survey with Some New Empirical Results."

Squire, Lyn, and Sethaput Suthiwart-Narueput. "The Impact of Labor Market Regulations."

Tan, Hong, and Geeta Batra. "Technology and Industry Wage Differentials: Evidence from Three Developing Countries."

Turnham, David. "What Can We Learn from Past Efforts to Encourage Employment-Intensive Development?"

Vashishtha, Prem. "Informal Sector Workers in India."

Selected bibliography

Abella, Manolo, and Hiromi Mori. 1994. "Structural Change and Labor Migration in East Asia." Paper presented at the OECD Conference on Development Systems, Employment, and International Migration, Paris, July 11–13.

Adams, Richard, Jr. 1989. "Worker Remittances and Inequality in Rural Egypt." *Economic Development and Cultural Change* 38 (October): 45–71.

———. 1992. "The Effects of Migration and Remittances on Inequality in Rural Pakistan." *The Pakistan Development Review* 31 (Winter): 1189–1203.

Alba-Ramirez, Alfonso. 1991. "Fixed-Term Employment Contracts in Spain: Labor Market Flexibility or Segmentation?" Paper presented at EALE Conference, Spain, September.

Appleton, Simon, Paul Collier, and Paul Horsnell. 1990. *Gender, Education, and Employment in Côte d'Ivoire*. SDA Working Paper No. 8. Washington, D.C.: World Bank.

Arriagada, Ana-Maria. 1989. "Occupational Training Among Peruvian Men: Does It Make a Difference?" Policy Research Working Paper No. 207. World Bank, Washington, D.C.

Atkinson, Anthony B., and John Micklewright. 1992. *Economic Transformation in Eastern Europe and the Distribution of Income*. Cambridge, U.K.: Cambridge University Press.

Aw, Bee-Yan, and Hong Tan. 1993. "Training, Technology, and Firm-Level Productivity." PSD Working Paper. World Bank, Private Sector Development Department, Washington, D.C.

Balcerowicz, Leszek, and Alan Gelb. 1995. "Macropolicies in Transition to a Market Economy: A Three-Year Perspective." *Proceedings of the World Bank Annual Conference on Development Economics 1994*. Washington, D.C.

Banerji, Arup, and Richard H. Sabot. 1993. "Wage Distortions, Overmanning, and Reform in Developing Country Public Enterprises." World Bank, Policy Research Department, Washington, D.C.

———. Forthcoming. "Barriers to Labor Reform in Developing Country Public Enterprises." *World Development*.

Barr, Nicholas. 1994. "Income Transfers: Social Insurance." In Nicholas Barr, ed., *Labor Markets and Social Policy in Central and Eastern Europe: The Transition and Beyond*. New York: Oxford University Press.

———. Forthcoming. "On the Design of Social Safety Nets." HRO Discussion Paper. World Bank, Human Resources Development and Operations Policy, Washington, D.C.

Barro, Robert J. 1991. "Economic Growth in a Cross Section of Countries." *The Quarterly Journal of Economics* 106 (2): 407–43.

Barro, Robert J., and Jong-Wha Lee. 1993. "International Comparisons of Educational Attainment." *Journal of Monetary Economics* 32 (3): 363–94.

Beaudry, P., and N. K. Sowa. 1994. "Ghana." In Susan Horton, Ravi Kanbur, and Dipak Mazumdar, eds., *Labor Markets in an Era of Adjustment*. Volume 2: Case Studies. EDI Development Study. World Bank, Washington, D.C.

Becker, Gary S. 1957. *The Economics of Discrimination*. Chicago, Ill.: University of Chicago Press.

———. 1965. "A Theory of the Allocation of Time." *Economic Journal* 75 (299): 493–517.

———. 1995. "Human Capital and Poverty Alleviation." HRO Working Paper No. 52. World Bank, Human Resources Development and Operations Policy, Washington, D.C.

Behrman, Jere R. 1993. "The Economic Rationale for Investing in Nutrition in Developing Countries." *World Development* 21 (11): 1749–71.

Behrman, Jere R., and Anil B. Deolalikar. 1994. "Are There Differential Returns to Schooling by Gender? The Case of Indonesian Labor Markets." University of Pennsylvania, Philadelphia.

Beleva, Iskra, Richard Jackman, and Mariela Nenova-Amar. 1994. "Bulgaria." In Simon Commander and Fabrizio Coricelli, eds., *Unemployment, Restructuring, and the Labor Market in Eastern Europe and Russia*. EDI Development Studies. Washington, D.C.: World Bank.

Bell, Linda A. 1994. "The Impact of Minimum Wages in Mexico and Colombia." Paper presented at World Bank Labor Markets in Developing Countries Workshop, Washington, D.C., July 6–8.

Beller, Andrea H. 1979. "The Economics of Enforcement of an Antidiscrimination Law: Title VII of the Civil Rights Act of 1964." *Journal of Law and Economics*.

Ben-David, Dan. 1994. "Convergence Clubs and Diverging Economies." University of Houston, Department of Economics, Houston, Tex.

Berg, Andrew, and Jeffrey Sachs. 1992. "Structural Adjustment and International Trade in Eastern Europe: The Case of Poland." *Economic Policy: A European Forum* 14 (April): 117–73.

Bergmann, Barbara. 1989. "Does the Market for Women's Labor Need Fixing?" *Journal of Economic Perspectives* 3 (Winter) 43–60.

Berry, Albert, François Bourguignon, and Christian Morrisson. 1989. "The World Distribution of Income: Evolution over the Recent Period and Effects of Population Growth." Paper prepared for the Conference on the Consequences of Rapid Population Growth, United Nations, New York, August 23–25.

Bertola, Giuseppe. 1990. "Job Security, Employment and Wages." *European Economic Review* 34 (June): 851–86.

Bhagwati, Jagdish. 1991. "Free Traders and Free Immigrationists: Strangers or Friends?" Russell Sage Foundation Working Paper No. 20. New York.

Bhagwati, Jagdish, and Marvin Kosters. 1994. *Trade and Wages*. Washington, D.C.: American Enterprise Institute.

Bhattacherjee, Debashish. 1987. "Union-Type Effects on Bargaining Outcomes in Indian Manufacturing." *British Journal of Industrial Relations*.

Bhattacherjee, Debashish, and Tamal Datta Chaudhuri. 1994. "Unions, Wages and Labour Markets in Indian Industry, 1960–86." *Journal of Development Studies* 30 (2): 443–65.

Birdsall, Nancy, and Richard Sabot, eds. 1991. *Unfair Advantage: Labor Market Discrimination in Developing Countries*. World Bank Regional and Sectoral Studies. Washington, D.C.

Blanchflower, David G., and Richard B. Freeman. 1990. "Going Different Ways: Unionism in the U.S. and Other Advanced OECD Countries." NBER Working Paper No. 3342. National Bureau of Economic Research, Cambridge, Mass.

Blank, Rebecca M., and Richard B. Freeman. 1993. "Evaluating the Connection Between Social Protection and Economic Flexibility." NBER Working Paper No. 4338. National Bureau of Economic Research, Cambridge, Mass.

Boeninger, Edgardo. 1991. "Governance and Development: Issues, Challenges, Opportunities, and Constraints." *Proceedings of the World Bank Annual Conference on Development Economics 1991*. Washington, D.C.

Boeri, Tito, and Stefano Scarpetta. 1994. "Convergence and Divergence of Regional Labour Market Dynamics in Central and Eastern Europe." Paper presented at the Technical Workshop on Regional Unemployment in Central and Eastern Europe. Organization for Economic Cooperation and Development, Institute for Advanced Studies, Vienna, Austria, November 3–5.

Bonnet, M. 1993. "Child Labor in Africa." *International Labour Review* 132 (3): 371–89.

Borjas, George J. 1994. "The Economics of Immigration." *Journal of Economic Literature* 32 (December): 1667–1717.

Borjas, George J., and Richard B. Freeman. 1993. *Immigration and the Work Force: Economic Consequences for the United States and Source Areas*. Chicago, Ill.: University of Chicago Press.

Boston Globe. 1994. "Harvesting Bananas, and Poison, from the Rain Forest." July 11 (p. 7).

Bosworth, Barry, Rudiger Dornbusch, and Raul Laban. 1994. *The Chilean Economy: Policy Lessons and Challenges*. Washington, D.C.: Brookings Institution.

Botswana Federation of Trade Unions and International Confederation of Free Trade Unions. 1991. *Democracy Development and the Defence of Human and Trade Union Rights in Africa*. Brussels: ICFTU.

Boyden, Jocelyn. 1988. "Working Children in Lima, Peru." In Assefa Bekele and Jo Boyden, eds., *Combating Child Labor*. Geneva: International Labour Office.

Boyden, Jo, and William Myers. 1994. "Exploring Alternative Approaches to Combating Child Labour: Case Studies from Developing Countries." Innocenti Occasional Papers, Child Rights Series No. 8. International Labour Office, Geneva, and the UNICEF International Child Development Centre, Florence.

Braithwaite, Jeanine. 1994. "From Second Economy to Informal Sector: The Russian Labor Market in Transition." World Bank, Education and Social Policy Department, Washington, D.C.

Brown, Charles. 1982. "The Federal Attack on Labor Market Discrimination: The Mouse that Roared?" In R. G. Ehrenberg, ed., *Research in Labor Economics* 5. Greenwich, Conn.: JAI Press.

Bruno, Michael. 1988. "Opening Up: Liberalization and Stabilization." In Rudiger Dornbusch, F. Leslie, and C. H. Helmers, eds., *The Open Economy: Tools for Policymakers in Developing Countries*. New York: Oxford University Press.

Burda, Michael. 1993. "Unemployment, Labour Market Institutions and Structural Change in Eastern Europe." *Economic Policy: A European Forum* 8 (April): 101–37.

Calmfors, Lars, and John Driffil. 1988. "Centralization of Wage Bargaining and Macroeconomic Performance." *Economic Policy* April.

Calvo, Guillermo A., Leonardo Leiderman, and Carmen M. Reinhart. 1992. "Capital Inflows and Exchange Rate Appreciation in Latin America: The Role of External Factors." *International Monetary Fund Staff Papers* 40 (March): 108–51.

Card, David, and Alan Krueger. 1995. *Myth and Measurement: The New Economics of the Minimum Wage*. Princeton, N.J.: Princeton University Press.

Castaneda, Tarsicio. 1992. *Combating Poverty: Innovative Social Reforms in Chile during the 1980s*. San Francisco, Calif.: ICS Press.

Chamley, Christophe, and Hafez Ghanem. 1994. "Côte d'Ivoire: Fiscal Policy with Fixed Nominal Exchange Rates." In William Easterly, Carlos Alfredo Rodríguez, and Klaus Schmidt-Hebbel, eds., *Public Sector Deficits and Macroeconomic Performance*. New York: Oxford University Press.

Chase, Robert S. 1994. "Returns to Education and Experience in Transition Czech Republic and Slovakia: Research in Progress." Yale University, Department of Economics, New Haven, Conn.

Chaudhry, Shahid Amjad, Gary James Reid, and Waleed Haider Malik, eds. 1994. *Civil Service Reform in Latin America and the Caribbean: Proceedings of a Conference*. Technical Paper No. 259. World Bank, Washington, D.C.

Chaudhuri, Salma, and Pratima Paul-Majumder. 1991. "The Conditions of Garment Workers in Bangladesh—An Appraisal." Bangladesh Institute of Development Studies, Dhaka.

Chuhan, Punam, Stijn Claessens, and Nlandes Mamingi. 1993. "Equity and Bond Flows to Latin American and Asia: The Role of Global and Country Factors." Policy Research Working Paper No. 1160. World Bank, Washington, D.C.

CIS (Commonwealth of Independent States). 1994. *Statistical Yearbook*. Moscow: Statistical Committee of the CIS.

Claessens, Stijn, Michael Dooley, and Andrew Warner. 1995. "Portfolio Capital Flows: Hot or Cold." *World Bank Economic Review* 9 (1): 153–74.

Cohen, John M. 1993. "Importance of Public Service Reform: the Case of Kenya." *Journal of Modern African Studies* 31 (3; September): 449–76.

Colclough, Christopher. 1989. "The Labor Market and Economic Stabilization in Zambia." Working Paper Series No. 222. World Bank, Country Economics Department, Washington, D.C.

Commander, Simon, and Fabrizio Coricelli, eds. 1994. *Unemployment, Restructuring, and the Labor Market in Eastern Europe and Russia*. EDI Development Studies. Washington, D.C.: World Bank.

Commander, Simon, Fabrizio Coricelli, and Karsten Staehr. 1991. "Wages and Employment in the Transition to a Market Economy." Policy Research Working Paper No. 736. World Bank, Washington, D.C.

Commander, Simon, and Richard Jackman. 1993. "Providing Social Benefits in Russia: Redefining the Roles of Firms and Government." Policy Research Working Paper No. 1184. World Bank, Washington, D.C.

Commander, Simon, John McHale, and Ruslan Yemtsov. 1994. "Russia." In Simon Commander and Fabrizio Coricelli, eds. *Unemployment, Restructuring, and the Labor Market in Eastern Europe and Russia*. EDI Development Studies. Washington, D.C.: World Bank.

Cooley, Laura, and Bruce Benton. 1995. "Controlling Riverblindness in West Africa." In *Investing in People: The World Bank in Action*. Directions in Development. Washington, D.C.: World Bank.

Cooper, Richard N. 1994. "Foreign Trade, Wages, and Unemployment." Harvard University, Department of Economics, Cambridge, Mass.

Coricelli, Fabrizio, and Ana Revenga, eds. 1992. "Wage Policy during the Transition to a Market Economy: Poland 1990–91." Discussion Paper No. 158. World Bank, Washington, D.C.

Cox, Donald, and Emmanuel Jimenez. 1989. "Private Transfers and Public Policy in Developing Countries: A Case Study for Peru." Policy, Planning and Research Working Paper No. 345. World Bank, Washington, D.C.

———. 1990. "Achieving Social Objectives Through Private Transfers: A Review." *The World Bank Research Observer* 5 (2): 205–18.

Cox Edwards, Alejandra. 1993. "Labor Market Legislation in Latin America and the Caribbean." World Bank Regional Studies Program, Washington, D.C.

———. 1994. "Poverty Alleviation and the Labor Market in Ecuador." World Bank, Washington, D.C.

Currington, W. P. 1988. "Federal vs. State Regulation: The Early Years of OSHA." *Social Science Quarterly* 69 (2).

Dadush, Uri, Ashok Phareshwan, and Ronald Johannes. 1994. "Are Private Capital Flows to Developing Countries Sustainable?" Policy Research Working Paper No. 1397. World Bank, Washington, D.C.

Dallago, Bruno. 1995. "The Irregular Economy in Transition: Features, Measurement and Scope." In Robert Holzman, Janos Gacs, and Georg Windkler, eds., *Output Decline in Eastern Europe: Unavoidable, External Influence, or Homemade.* International Studies in Economics and Econometrics 34: 31–60.

Datt, Gaurav, and Martin Ravallion. 1994. "Transfer Benefits from Public-Works Employment: Evidence for Rural India." *Economic Journal: The Journal of the Royal Economic Society* 104 (November): 1346–69.

Davis, Steven J. 1992. "Cross-Country Patterns of Change in Relative Wages." In *NBER Macroeconomics Annual 1992.* London: MIT Press.

Deolalikar, Anil B. 1988. "Nutrition and Labor Productivity in Agriculture: Estimates for Rural South India." *The Review of Economics and Statistics* 70 (3): 406–13.

Dia, Mamadou. 1993. *A Governance Approach to Civil Service Reform in Sub-Saharan Africa.* World Bank Technical Paper No. 225. Washington, D.C.

Dickens, William T., and Lawrence F. Katz. 1987. "Inter-Industry Wage Differences and Industry Characteristics." NBER Working Paper Reprint No. 894. National Bureau of Economic Research, Cambridge, Mass.

Diwan, Ishac. 1994. "Public Sector Retrenchment and Severance Pay: Nine Propositions." In World Bank Technical Paper No. 259. Washington, D.C.

Easterly, William, and Stanley Fischer. 1994. "The Soviet Economic Decline: Historical and Republican Data." NBER Working Paper Series No. 4735. National Bureau of Economic Research, Cambridge, Mass. Forthcoming in *World Bank Economic Review.*

Easterly, William, and Klaus Schmidt-Hebbel. 1994. "Fiscal Adjustment and Macroeconomic Performance: A Synthesis." In William Easterly, Carlos Alfredo Rodríguez, and Klaus Schmidt-Hebbel, eds., *Public Sector Deficits and Macroeconomic Performance.* New York: Oxford University Press.

EBRD (European Bank for Reconstruction and Development). 1994. "Economic Transition in Eastern Europe and the Former Soviet Union." *Transition Report* (October). London.

Edwards, Linda N. 1994. "The Status of Women in Japan: Has the Equal Employment Opportunity Law Made a Difference?" *Journal of Asian Economics* 5 (2; Summer): 217–40.

Edwards, Sebastian, and Alejandra Cox Edwards. 1991. *Monetarism and Liberalization: The Chilean Experience.* Chicago, Ill.: The University of Chicago Press.

Ehrenberg, Ronald G., and Robert S. Smith. 1994. *Modern Labor Economics: Theory and Public Policy,* 5th ed. New York: Harper Collins College Publishers.

Erbenova, Michaela. 1994. "Regional Unemployment and Geographical Labour Mobility: A Case Study of the Czech Republic." Paper presented at the Technical Workshop "Regional Unemployment in Central and Eastern Europe." Organization for Economic Cooperation and Development, Institute for Advanced Studies, Vienna, Austria, November 3–5.

Estache, Antonio, and Marianne Fay. 1995. "What Should Regional Policy in Argentina Focus On?" World Bank, Latin America and Caribbean Country Department I, Washington, D.C.

Estrin, Saul. 1994. "The Inheritance." In Nicholas Barr, ed., *Labor Markets and Social Policy in Central and Eastern Europe: The Transition and Beyond.* New York: Oxford University Press.

Estrin, Saul, Mark Schaffer, and Inderjit Singh. 1994. "The Provision of Social Benefits in State-Owned, Privatized and Private Firms in Poland." Paper presented at the Workshop on Enterprise Adjustment in Eastern Europe, World Bank, Policy Research Department, Washington, D.C., Sept. 22–23.

Fallon, Peter R., and Robert E. B. Lucas. 1991. "The Impact of Changes in Job Security Regulations in India and Zimbabwe." *World Bank Economic Review* 5 (3): 395–413.

Feenstra, Robert C., and Gordon H. Hanson. 1994. "Foreign Direct Investment and Relative Wages: Evidence from Mexico's *Maquiladoras.*" University of Texas, Department of Economics, Austin.

Feldstein, Martin. 1994. "The Effects of Outbound Foreign Direct Investment on the Domestic Capital Stock." NBER Working Paper No. 4668. National Bureau of Economic Research, Cambridge, Mass.

Fields, Gary S. 1994. "Changing Labor Market Conditions and Economic Development." Cornell University, Economics Department, Ithaca, N.Y.

Findley, Sally E. 1994. *To Go But Not to Go: Migration and Family Interactions in Africa.* New York: Columbia University.

Flanagan, Robert J. 1995. "Labor Market Responses to a Change in Economic System." *Proceedings of the World Bank Annual Bank Conference on Development Economics 1994.* Washington, D.C.

Fleury, Alfonso, and John Humphrey. 1993. "Human Resources and the Diffusion and Adaptation of New Quality: Methods in Brazilian Manufacturing." Institute of Development Studies, Research Report 24. Sussex, U.K.

Foner, Eric, and John A. Garraty, eds. 1991. *The Reader's Companion to American History.* Boston: Houghton-Mifflin.

Foster, Andrew D., Mark R. Rosenzweig, and the Rural Indian Economic Growth Research Group. 1994. "Technical Change and Human Capital Returns and Investments: Consequences of the Green Revolution." University of Pennsylvania, Philadelphia, and National Council of Applied Economic Research, Washington, D.C.

Fox, M. Louise, and Samuel A. Morley. 1990. "Who Paid the Bill? Adjustment and Poverty in Brazil, 1980–90." Policy Research Working Paper No. 648. World Bank, Washington, D.C.

Freeman, Richard B. 1980. "Unionism and the Dispersion of Wages." *Industrial and Labor Relations Review.*

———. 1988. "Labour Market Institutions and Economic Performance." *Economic Policy: A European Forum* 3 (April): 63–80.

———. 1992. "Is Declining Unionization of the U.S. Good, Bad, or Irrelevant?" In Lawrence Mishel and Paula B. Voos, eds., *Unions and Economics Competitiveness.* Armonk, N.Y.: M. E. Sharpe.

———. 1993a. "Does Suppression of Labor Contribute to Economic Success? Labor Relations and Markets in East Asia." Harvard University, Department of Economics, Cambridge, Mass.

———. 1993b. "Labor Market Institutions and Policies: Help or Hindrance to Economic Development?" *Proceedings of the World Bank Annual Conference on Development Economics 1992.* Washington, D.C.

———. 1993c. "Minimum Wages—Again?" Paper presented at the Conference on *Analyse Economique des bas Salaires et des Effets du Salaire Minimum,* CER/GRIFE, University of Aix-en-Provence, Arles, France.

———. 1995. "Will Globalization Dominate U.S. Labor Market Outcomes?" Paper prepared for the conference on "Imports, Exports, and the American Worker." Brookings Institution, Washington, D.C., February 2–3.

Freeman, Richard B., and James L. Medoff. 1984. *What Do Unions Do?* New York: Basic Books.

Frenkel, Stephen, ed. 1993. *Organized Labor in the Asia-Pacific Regions: A Comparative Study of Unionism in Nine Countries.* Cornell International Industrial and Labor Relations Report No. 24. Ithaca, N.Y.: ILR Press.

Fretwell, David, and Susan Goldberg. 1993. "Developing Effective Employment Services." World Bank Discussion Paper No. 208. Washington, D.C.

Fretwell, David, and Richard Jackman. 1994. "Labor Markets: Unemployment." In Nicholas Barr, ed., *Labor Markets and Social Policy in Central and Eastern Europe: The Transition and Beyond.* New York: Oxford University Press.

Galbi, Douglas. 1994. "Child Labor and the Division of Labor." King's College Centre for History and Economics, Cambridge, U.K.

Gelb, Alan H., and Cheryl W. Gray. 1991. "The Transformation of Economies in Central and Eastern Europe: Issues, Progress, and Prospects." Policy, Research and External Affairs Paper No. 17. World Bank, Washington, D.C.

Ghana Statistical Service. Various years. *Ghana Quarterly Digest of Statistics.* Accra.

Gindling, T. H., and Albert Berry. 1994. "Costa Rica." In Susan Horton, Ravi Kanbur, and Dipak Mazumdar, eds., *Labor Markets in an Era of Adjustment.* Volume 2: Case Studies. EDI Development Studies. Washington, D.C.: World Bank.

Gindling, T. H., and Donald Robbins. 1994. "Earnings Inequality, Structural Adjustment, and Trade Liberalization in Costa Rica." Harvard Institute for International Development, Cambridge, Mass.

Gold, Michael Evans. 1983. *A Debate on Comparable Worth.* Ithaca, N.Y.: Industrial and Labor Relations Press.

Goldin, Claudia. 1990. *Understanding the Gender Gap: An Economic History of American Women.* New York: Oxford University Press.

Goldin, Ian, and Dominique van der Mensbrugghe. 1995. "The Uruguay Round: An Assessment of Economywide and Agricultural Reforms." Paper presented at the Conference on the Uruguay Round and the Developing Economies. World Bank, Washington, D.C., January 26–27.

Goldstein, Morris, and Robert S. Smith. 1976. "The Estimated Impact of the Antidiscrimination Program Aimed at Federal Contractors." *Industrial and Labor Relations Review* July (24).

Góra, Marek, and Hartmut Lehmann. 1995. "How Divergent is Regional Labour Market Adjustment in Poland?" Working Paper No. 1. IFO Institute for Economic Research, Munich, Germany.

Gregory, Peter. 1991. "Increasing the Efficiency of the Public Sector." A report prepared for USAID/El Salvador. U.S. Agency for International Development, Washington, D.C.

Gregory, Peter, and Bruce J. Perlman. 1994. "Civil Service Diagnostic Review: Nicaragua." World Bank, Latin American and the Caribbean Country Department II, Washington, D.C.

Haddad, Lawrence, and Howarth Bouis. 1991. "The Impact of Nutritional Status on Agricultural Productivity: Wage Evidence from the Philippines." *Oxford Bulletin of Economics and Statistics* 53 (1): 45–68.

Ham, John, Jan Svejnar, and Katherine Terrell. 1993. "The Emergence of Unemployment in the Czech and Slovak Republics." *Comparative Economic Studies* 35 (4): 121–34.

———. 1994. "Czech Republic and Slovakia." In Simon Commander and Fabrizio Coricelli, eds., *Unemployment, Restructuring, and the Labor Market in Eastern Europe and Russia.* EDI Development Studies. Washington, D.C.: World Bank.

Hamermesh, Daniel. 1991. "Unemployment Insurance: Goals, Structure, Economic Impacts, and Transferability to Developing Countries." World Bank, Population and Human Resouces Department, Washington, D.C.

Harrison, Ann. 1993. "Morocco Private Sector Assessment: The Labor Market, 1993." World Bank, Washington, D.C.

Harrison, Glenn, Thomas Rutherford, and David Tarr. 1995. "Quantifying the Uruguay Round." Paper presented at the Conference on the Uruguay Round and the Developing Economies, World Bank, Washington, D.C., January 26–27.

Hathaway, Dale E., and Merlinda D. Ingco. 1995. "Agricultural Liberalization and the Uruguay Round." Paper presented at the Conference on the Uruguay Round and the Developing Economies, World Bank, Washington, D.C., January 26–27.

Hatton, Timothy J., and Jeffrey G. Williamson, eds. 1994. *Migration and the International Labor Market, 1850–1939: An Economic Survey.* London and New York: Rutledge Press.

Hertel, Thomas, Will Martin, Koji Yanagishima, and Betina Dimaranan. 1995. "Liberalizing Manufactures Trade in a Changing World Economy." Paper presented at the Conference on the Uruguay Round and the Developing Economies, World Bank, Washington, D.C., January 26–27.

Hess, Jolanta. 1994. "Managing Large Scale Labor Restructuring." World Bank, Washington, D.C.

Hierro, Jorge, and Allen Sanginés. 1991. "Public Sector Behavior in Mexico." In Felipe Larraín and Marcelo Selowsky, eds., *The Public Sector and the Latin American Crisis.* San Francisco, Calif.: Institute for Contemporary Studies Press.

Hill, Herbert. 1984. "Race and Ethnicity in Organized Labor: The Historical Sources of Resistance to Affirmative Action." *The Journal of Intergroup Relations* Winter: 12.

Horton, Susan. 1994a. "Bolivia." In Susan Horton, Ravi Kanbur, and Dipak Mazumdar, eds., *Labor Markets in an Era of Adjustment.* Volume 2: Case Studies. EDI Development Studies. Washington, D.C.: World Bank.

———, ed. 1994b. "Women and Industrialization in Asia." Institute for Policy Analysis, University of Toronto.

Horton, Susan, Ravi Kanbur, and Dipak Mazumdar. 1994a. *Labor Markets in an Era of Adjustment.* Volume 1: Issues Papers. EDI Development Studies. Washington, D.C.: World Bank.

———. 1994b. *Labor Markets in an Era of Adjustment.* Volume 2: Case Studies. EDI Development Studies. Washington, D.C.: World Bank.

Houseman, Susan. 1991. *Industrial Restructuring with Job Security.* Cambridge, Mass.: Harvard University Press.

Hudson, Rex. 1994. "Chile: A Country Study." Library of Congress, Federal Research Division, Washington, D.C.

Hufbauer, Gary. 1991. "World Economic Integration: The Long View." *International Economic Insights* May/June: 26–27.

Husain, Ishrat, and Rashid Faruqee, eds. 1994. *Adjustment in Africa: Lessons from Country Case Studies.* A World Bank Regional and Sectoral Study. Washington, D.C.

IFC (International Finance Corporation). 1992. *Emerging Stock Markets Factbook 1992.* Washington, D.C.

ILO (International Labour Office). 1985. *The Trade Union Situation and Industrial Relations in Spain.* Geneva.

———.1986. *Economically Active Population Estimates and Projections: 1950–2025.* Geneva.

———.1994a. *Defending Values, Promoting Change: Social Justice in a Global Economy: An ILO Agenda.* Report of the Director-General (Part I), International Labour Conference, 81st Session. Geneva.

———. 1994b. *World Labour Report 1994.* Geneva.

———. 1995a. *World Employment 1995.* Geneva.

———. 1995b. *World Labour Report 1995.* Geneva.

———. Various years. *Yearbook of Labor Statistics.* Geneva.

INTELSAT. Various years. *International Telecommunications Satellite Report.* Washington, D.C.

Jackman, Richard, and Michal Rutkowski. 1994. "Labor Markets: Wages and Employment." In Nicholas Barr, ed., *Labor Markets and Social Policy in Central and Eastern Europe: The Transition and Beyond.* New York: Oxford University Press.

Jacobson, Louis. 1994. Evaluating Policy Resources Aimed at Reducing the Costs to Workers of Increased Import Competition." Paper presented at the conference on "Imports, Exports and the American Worker," Brookings Institution, Washington, D.C., February 2–3.

Jacoby, H., and E. Skoufias. 1994. "Risk, Financial Markets and Human Capital in a Developing Country." World Bank, Policy Research Department, Washington, D.C.

Jimeno, Juan F., and Luis Toharia. 1994. "Unemployment and Labour Market Flexibility: The Case of Spain." Geneva: International Labour Office.

———. 1993. "Spanish Labor Markets: Institutions and Outcomes." In J. Hartog and J. Theemuwes, eds., *Labor Market Contracts and Institutions: A Cross-National Comparison.* Amsterdam: North-Holland.

Johnson, G. E. 1971. "The Determination of Individual Hourly Earnings in Urban Kenya." Intitute for Development Studies, Discussion Paper No. 115. University of Nairobi.

Johnson, Terry R., Katherine P. Dickinson, and Richard W. West. 1985. "An Evaluation of the Impact of ES Referrals on Applicant Earnings." *Journal of Human Resources* 20 (Winter): 117–37.

Joshi, Vijay, and I. M. D. Little. 1994. *India: Macroeconomics and Political Economy 1964–91.* A World Bank Comparative Macroeconomic Study. Washington, D.C.

Katz, Harry C., Sarosh Kuruvilla, and Lowell Turner. 1993. "Trade Unions and Collective Bargaining." Policy Research Working Paper No. 1099. World Bank, Education and Social Policy Department, Washington, D.C.

Kaufman, Bruce E. 1991. *The Economics of Labor Markets,* 3d ed. Chicago, Ill.: Dryden Press.

Kelley, Allen C. 1994 "The Consequences of Rapid Population Growth on Human Resource Development: The Case of Education." In Dennis A. Ahlburg, Allen C. Kelley, and Karen Oppenheim Mason, eds., *The Impacts of Population Growth in Developing Countries.* Berlin: Springer-Verlag.

Khandker, Shahidur R. 1991. "Labor Market Participation, Returns to Education, and Male-Female Wage Differences in Peru." In Barbara Herz and Shahidur R. Khandker, eds., *Women's Work, Education, and Family Welfare in Peru.* World Bank Discussion Paper No. 116. Washington, D.C.

King, Elizabeth M., and M. Anne Hill. 1993. *Women's Education in Developing Countries: Barriers, Benefits, and Policies.* Baltimore, Md.: Johns Hopkins University Press.

Knight, J. B., and Richard H. Sabot. 1987. "Educational Expasion, Government Policy and Wage Compression." *Journal of Development Economics* 26 (August): 201–21.

Kornai, János. 1992. *The Socialist System: The Political Economy of Communism.* Princeton, N.J.: Princeton University Press.

———. 1995. *Highways and Byways: Studies on Reform and Postcommunist Transition.* Cambridge, Mass.: MIT Press.

Kraay, Aart, and Caroline van Rijckeghem. 1994. "Employment and Wages in the Public Sector—A Cross-Country Study." International Monetary Fund, Fiscal Affairs Department, Washington, D.C.

Krause, Lawrence B., and Fun-Koo Park, eds. 1993. *Social Issues in Korea: Korean and American Perspectives.* Seoul: Korea Development Institute.

Krueger, Alan B. 1994. "The Effect of the Minimum Wage When It Really Bites: A Reexamination of the Evidence from Puerto Rico." NBER Working Paper No. 4757. National Bureau of Economic Research, Cambridge, Mass.

Krueger, Alan B., and Lawrence H. Summers. 1987. "Reflections on the Inter-Industry Wage Structure." In Kevin Lang and Jonathan S. Leonard, eds., *Unemployment and the Structure of Labor Markets.* New York: Basil Blackwell.

Krueger, Anne O. 1978. "Foreign Trade Regimes and Economic Development: Liberalization Attempts and Consequences." NBER Working Paper. National Bureau of Economic Research, Cambridge, Mass.

———. 1983. *Trade and Employment in Developing Countries.* Volume 3: Synthesis. Chicago, Ill.: University of Chicago Press.

Krugman, Paul, and Robert Lawrence. 1993. "Trade, Jobs and Wages." NBER Working Paper No. 4478. National Bureau of Economic Research, Cambridge, Mass.

Krumm, Kathie, Branko Milanovic, and Michael Walton. 1994. "Transfers and the Transition from Socialism: Key Tradeoffs." Policy Research Working Paper No. 1380. World Bank, Europe and Central Asia Regional Office, Washington, D.C.

Kwong, Peter. 1994. "China's Human Traffickers." *The Nation.* October 17: 422–25.

Laboj, Elmer. 1988. "Occupational Health and Hazards in the Philippines." *Labour, Capital, and Society* (Special issue on health and safety) 21 (November): 294–306.

Lalonde, Robert S. 1992. "The Earnings Impact of U.S. Employment and Training Programs." University of Chicago, Department of Economics, Chicago, Ill.

Landell-Mills, Pierre, and Ismaïl Serageldin. 1992. "Governance and the External Factor." *Proceedings of the World Bank Annual Bank Conference on Development Economics 1991.* Washington, D.C.

Larraín, Felipe, and Marcelo Selowsky, eds. 1991. *The Public Sector and the Latin American Crisis.* San Francisco, Calif.: Institute for Contemporary Studies Press.

Lawrence, Robert Z. 1994. "Trade, Multinationals, and Labor." NBER Working Paper No. 4836. National Bureau of Economic Research, Cambridge, Mass.

Lawrence, Robert, and Mathew Slaughter. 1993. "International Trade and American Wages in the 1980s: Giant Sucking Sound or Small Hiccup?" *Brookings Papers on Economic Activity: Microeconomics* 2: 161–226.

Lazear, Edward. 1990. "Job Security Provisions and Employment." *Quarterly Journal of Economics* 105 (August): 699–726.

Lee, Joung-Woo, and Sang-Sup Nam. 1994. "The Effect of Labor Unions on the Wage Dispersion in Korea." *Korean Economic Journal* 41 (3): 251–77 (in Korean).

Leigh, Duane E. 1992. "Retraining Displaced Workers: What Can Developing Countries Learn from OECD Nations?" Policy Research Working Paper No. 946. World Bank, Population and Human Resources Department, Washington, D.C.

Leonard, Jonathan S. 1984a. "The Impact of Affirmative Action on Employment." *Journal of Labor Economics* 2 (October): 439–63.

———. 1984b. "Employment and Occupational Advances Under Affirmative Action." *Review of Economics and Statistics* 66 (August): 377–85.

———. 1989. "Women and Affirmative Action." *Journal of Economic Perspectives* 3 (1).

Levine, Ross, and David Renelt. 1992. "A Sensitivity Analysis of Cross-Country Growth Regressions." *American Economic Review* 82 (September): 942–63.

Levy, Victor. 1985. "Cropping Pattern, Mechanization, Child Labor, and Fertility Behavior in a Farming Economy: Rural Egypt." *Economic Development and Cultural Change* 33 (July): 777–91.

Lin, Justin Y. 1994. "The Nature and Impact of Hybrid Rice in China." In Cristina C. David and Keijiro Otsuka, eds., *Modern Rice Technology and Income Distribution in Asia.* Boulder, Colo.: Lynne Rienner Publishers.

Lindauer, David L., O. A. Meesook, and Parita Suebsaeng. 1988. "Government Wage Policy in Africa: Some Findings and Policy Issues." *World Bank Research Observer* 3 (1; January): 1–25.

Lindauer, David L., and Barbara Nunberg, eds. 1994. *Rehabilitation Government: Pay and Employment Reform in Africa.* A World Bank Regional and Sectoral Study. Washington, D.C.

Lindauer, David L., and Michael Roemer, eds. 1994. *Asia and Africa: Legacies and Opportunities in Development.* San Francisco, Calif.: Institute for Contemporary Studies Press.

Lindauer, David L., and Richard Sabot. 1983. "The Public/Private Wage Differential in a Poor Urban Economy." *Journal of Development Economics* 12 (Feb./Apr.): 137–52.

Lipsey, Robert. 1994. "Outward Direct Investment and the U.S. Economy." NBER Working Paper No. 4691. National Bureau of Economic Research, Cambridge, Mass.

Lustig, Nora. 1992. *Mexico: The Remaking of an Economy.* Washington, D.C.: Brookings Institution.

Lynch, Lisa M., ed. 1994. *Training and The Private Sector.* Chicago, Ill.: University of Chicago Press.

Maddison, Angus. 1982. *Phases of Capitalist Development.* New York: Oxford University Press.

———. 1989. *The World Economy in the 20th Century.* Development Centre Studies. Paris: OECD.

Malaysia (Jabatan Perangkaan). Various years. *Rubber Statistics Handbook.* Kuala Lumpur.

Mankiw, N. Gregory, David Romer, and David N. Weil. 1992. "A Contribution to the Empirics of Economic Growth." *Quarterly Journal of Economics* 107 (May): 407–37.

Manning, Chris. 1993. "Structural Change and Industrial Relations during the Soeharto Period: An Approaching Crisis." *Bulletin of Indonesian Economic Studies* 29 (2): 59–95.

Marshall, Adrian. 1991. "The Impact of Labor Law on Employment Practices: Temporary and Part-Time Employment in Argentina and Peru." ILO DP/38. Labor Market Program, International Labour Office, Geneva.

Martin, Denis-Constant. 1991. "The Cultural Dimensions of Governance." *Proceedings of the World Bank Annual Conference on Development Economics 1991.* Washington, D.C.

Massey, Douglas S. 1990. "The Social and Economic Origins of Immigration." *Annals of the American Academy of Political and Social Science* 510 (July): 60–72.

Massey, Douglas S., Joaquin Arango, Graeme Hugo, Ali Kouaouci, Adela Pellegrino, and J. Edward Taylor. 1993. "Theories of International Migration: A Review and Appraisal." *Population and Development Review* 19 (3): 431–66.

Mazumdar, Dipak. 1989. "Microeconomic Issues of Labor Markets in Developing Countries: Analysis and Policy Implications." EDI Seminar Paper No. 40. World Bank, Washington, D.C.

———. 1994. "Wages in Africa." World Bank, Office of the Chief Economist, Africa Regional Office, Washington, D.C.

McCoy, Jennifer. 1989. "Labor and the State in a Party-Mediated Democracy: Institutional Change in Venezuela." *Latin American Research Review* 24 (2): 35–67.

McKinnon, Ronald I. 1994. *Gradual versus Rapid Liberalization in Socialist Economies: Financial Policies in China and Russia Compared.* San Francisco, Calif.: Institute for Contemporary Studies Press.

McKinsey Global Institute. 1994. *The Global Capital Market: Supply, Demand, Pricing, and Allocation.* Washington, D.C.

Micklewright, John, and Gyula Nagy. 1995. "Unemployment Insurance and Incentives in Hungary." *Centre for Economic Policy Research Discussion Paper Series* 1118 (January): 1–42.

Middleton, John, Arvil Van Adams, and Adrian Ziderman. 1993. *Skills for Productivity: Vocational Education and Training in Developing Countries.* New York: Oxford University Press.

Milanovic, Branko. 1994. "Poverty in Transition." World Bank, Policy Research Department, Washington, D.C.

———. 1995. "Poverty, Inequality and Social Policy in Transition Economies." World Bank, Policy Research Department, Washington, D.C.

Moll, P. G. 1993. "Black South African Unions: Relative Wage Effects in International Perspective." *Industrial and Labor Relations Review* 46 (2).

Mondal, Abdul Hye. 1992. "Trade Unionism, Wages and Labour Productivity in the Manufacturing Sector of Bangladesh." Research Report No. 133. Bangladesh Institute of Development Studies, Dhaka.

Montiel, Peter J. 1993. "Capital Mobility in Developing Countries: Some Measurement Issues and Empirical Estimates." Policy Research Working Paper No. 1103. World Bank, International Economics Department, Washington, D.C. Reprinted in *World Bank Economic Review* 8(3): 311–50.

Morrisson, Christian, Henri-Bernard Solignac Lecomte, and Xavier Oudin. 1994. *Micro-Enterprises and the Institutional Framework in Developing Countries.* Paris: OECD Development Centre.

Moser, Caroline. 1994."Poverty and Vulnerability in Chawama, Lusaka, Zambia 1978–1992." World Bank, Transportation, Water, and Urban Development Department, Washington, D.C.

Moser, Caroline, Cathy McIlwaine, Helen Garcia, and Cecilia Zanetta. 1994. "Poverty and Vulnerability in Guayaquil, Ecuador." World Bank, Transportation, Water, and Urban Development Department, Washington, D.C.

Neal, Larry. 1985. "Integration of International Capital Markets: Quantitative Evidence from the Eighteenth to Twentieth Centuries." *Journal of Economic History* 45 (2): 219–26.

Nehru, Vikram, and Ashok Dhareshwar. 1991. "A New Database on Physical Capital Stock: Sources, Methodology and Results." *Revista de Analisis Económico* 8 (1): 37–59.

Nehru, Vikram, Eric Swanson, and Ashutosh Dubey. 1993. "A New Database on Human Capital Stock: Sources, Methodology and Results." Policy Research Working Paper No. 1124. World Bank, Washington, D.C.

Nelson, Joan M. 1994. "Organized Labor, Politics, and Labor Market Flexibility in Developing Countries." In Susan Horton, Ravi Kanbur, and Dipak Mazumdar, eds., *Labor Markets in an Era of Adjustment.* Volume 1: Issues Papers. EDI Development Studies, Washington, D.C.: World Bank.

Neven, Damien, and Charles Wyplosz. 1994. "Trade and European Labor Markets." University of Lausanne, Department of Economics, Lausanne, Switzerland.

Newell, Andrew, and Barry Reilly. 1995. "The Gender Wage Gap in Russia." Paper presented at seminar on "Gender in Transition." Bucharest, Romania.

New York Times. 1993. "102 Dead in Thai Factory Fire: Higher Toll Seen." May 11, p. 3.

Nichols, Martha. 1993. "Third-World Families at Work: Child Labor or Child Care?" *Harvard Business Review.*

Nunberg, Barbara. 1993. "Public Sector Pay and Employment Reform: A Review of World Bank Experience." World Bank Discussion Paper 68. Washington, D.C.

Oaxaca, R. L. 1973. "Male-Female Wage Differences in Urban Labor Markets.*" International Economic Review* 14 (1): 693–701.

OECD (Organization for Economic Cooperation and Development). 1993. "Active Labour Market Policies: Assessing Macroeconomic and Microeconomic Effects." Paris.

———. 1994a. *The Jobs Study—Facts, Analysis, Strategies.* Paris.

———. 1994b. "Review of the Labour Market in the Czech Republic." Paris.

O'Leary, Christopher J. 1995. "An Impact Analysis of Employment Programs in Hungary." Staff Working Paper No. 95-30. W. E. Upjohn Institute for Employment Research, Kalamazoo, Mich.

Oomen, Joep. 1992. "Hill Tribes in Thailand: Victims of Development?" *International Work Group for Indigenous Affairs Newsletter* 4 (Oct.–Dec.): 38–40.

Orazem, Peter F., and Milan Vodopivec. 1994. "Winners and Losers in Transition: Returns to Education, Experience, and Gender in Slovenia." Policy Research Working Paper No. 1342. World Bank, Washington, D.C. Reprinted in *World Bank Economic Review* 9(2): 201–30.

Orr, Larry L., Howard S. Bloom, Stephen H. Bell, Winston Lin, George Cave, and Fred Doolitle. 1994. "The National JTPA Study: Impacts, Benefits, and Costs of Title II-A." A Report to the U.S. Department of Labor. ABT Associates, Inc., Bethesda, Md.

Overbeek, Henk. 1994. "Globalisation and the Restructuring of the European Labor Market: The Role of Migration." Department of International Relations, University of Amsterdam.

Panagides, Alexis, and Harry Anthony Patrinos. 1994. "Union-Nonunion Wage Differentials in the Developing World: A Case Study of Mexico." Policy Research Working Paper No. 1269. World Bank, Education and Social Policy Department, Washington, D.C.

Park, Young-Bum. 1991. "Union/Minimum Wage Differentials in the Korean Manufacturing Sector." *International Economic Journal* 5(4).

Park, Young-Bum, David R. Ross, and Richard Sabot. 1992. "Educational Expansion and the Inequality of Pay in Brazil and Korea." International Food Policy Research Institute, Washington, D.C.

Patrinos, Harry Anthony. 1994. "The Costs of Discrimination in Latin America." World Bank, Education and Social Policy Department, Washington, D.C.

Patrinos, Harry Anthony, and George Psacharopoulos. 1995. "Schooling and Non-Schooling Activities of Peruvian Youth: Indigenous Background, Family Composition and Child Labor." World Bank, Education and Social Policy Department, Washington, D.C.

Pencavel, John. 1991. *Labor Markets under Trade Unionism: Employment, Wages, and Hours.* Cambridge, Mass.: Basil Blackwell.

Pinstrup-Andersen, Per, Susan Burger, Jean-Pierre Habicht, and Karen Peterson. 1993. "Protein-Energy Malnutrition." In Dean Jamison and others, eds., *Disease Control Priorities in Developing Countries.* New York: Oxford University Press.

Pollitt, Ernesto, Kathleen S. Gorman, Patrice L. Engle, Juan A. Rivera, and Reynaldo Martorell. 1995. "Nutrition in Early Life and the Fulfillment of Intellectual Potential." *Journal of Nutrition* 125 (4S): 1111S–1118S.

Pritchett, Lant. 1994. "Population, Factor Accumulation, and Productivity." World Bank, Policy Research Department, Washington, D.C.

Psacharopoulos, George, Samuel Morley, Ariel Fiszbein, Haeduck Lee, and Bill Wood. 1993. "Poverty and Income Distribution in Latin America: The Story of the 1980s." Regional Studies Program, Report No. 27. World Bank, Latin America and the Caribbean Technical Department, Washington, D.C.

Psacharopoulos, George, and Harry Anthony Patrinos, eds. 1994. *Indigenous People and Poverty in Latin America: An Empirical Analysis.* A World Bank Regional and Sectoral Study. Washington, D.C.

Psacharopoulos, George, and P. Zafiris Tzannatos, eds. 1992. *Women's Employment and Pay in Latin America: Overview and Methodology.* A World Bank Regional and Sectoral Study. Washington, D.C.

Pujol, Thierry. 1994. "Unemployment Duration and the Welfare Impact of Unemployment Benefits." International Monetary Fund, Washington, D.C.

Quah, Danny. 1994. "Empirics for Economic Growth and Convergence." *Centre for Economic Policy Research Discussion Paper Series* 954 (May): 1–50.

Rama, Martin. 1994. "Flexibility in Sri Lanka's Labor Market." Policy Research Working Paper No. 1262. World Bank, Policy Research Department, Washington, D.C.

Rama, Martin, and Guido Tabellini. 1995. "Endogenous Distortions in Product and Labor Markets." World Bank, Poverty and Human Resources Division, Washington, D.C.

Razin, Assaf, and Efraim Sadka. 1994. *Population Economics.* Cambridge, Mass.: MIT Press.

Rees, Albert. 1989. *The Economics of Trade Unions,* 3d ed. Chicago, Ill.: University of Chicago Press.

Reid, Gary. 1992. "Civil Service Reform in Latin America: Lessons from Experience." LATPS Occasional Paper Series. World Bank, Latin America and the Caribbean Region Technical Department, Washington, D.C.

Reid, Gary J., and Graham Scott. 1994. "Public Sector Human Resource Management: Experience in Latin America and the Caribbean and Strategies for Reform." Report No. 12839. World Bank, Latin America and the Caribbean Region Technical Department, Washington, D.C.

Republic of Korea. 1987. *Yearbook of Labor Statistics.* Seoul: Ministry of Labor.

———. Various years. *Report on Mining and Manufacturing Survey.* Seoul: National Statistical Office.

Republic of Uganda. 1982. *Report of the Public Service Salaries Review Commission 1980–82.* Kampala.

Revenga, Ana. 1994. "Employment and Wage Effects of Trade Liberalization: The Case of Mexican Manufacturing." Paper presented at the World Bank Labor Markets Workshop, Washington, D.C., July 6–8.

Revenga, Ana, and Claudio Montenegro. 1995. "North American Integration and Factor Price Equalization: Is There Evidence of Wage Convergence between Mexico and the U.S.?" Paper prepared for the conference on "Imports, Exports, and the American Worker," Brookings Institution, Washington, D.C., February 2–3.

Revenga, Ana, and Michelle Riboud. 1993. "Unemployment in Mexico: Its Characteristics and Determinants." Policy Research Working Paper No. 1230. World Bank, Latin America and Caribbean Country Department II, Washington, D.C.

Revenga, Ana, Michelle Riboud, and Hong Tan. 1994. "The Impact of Mexico's Retraining Program on Employment and Wages." *World Bank Economic Review* 8 (2): 247–77.

Rivera-Batiz, T. L. 1985. "Child Pattern and Legislation in Relation to Fertility." Indiana University, Department of Economics, Bloomington, Ind.

Riveros, Luis A. 1994. "Chile." In Susan Horton, Ravi Kanbur, and Dipak Mazumdar, eds., *Labor Markets in an Era of Adjustment.* Volume 2: Case Studies. EDI Development Studies. Washington, D.C.: World Bank.

Robbins, Donald J. 1994. "Worsening Relative Wage Dispersion in Chile During Trade Liberalization, and Its Causes: Is Supply at Fault?" *Harvard Institute for International Development Discussion Papers* 1 (April): 60.

Roberts, Mark J. Forthcoming. "Employment Flows and Producer Turnover in Three Developing Countries." In Mark J. Roberts and James R. Tybout, eds., *Producer Heterogeneity and Performance in Semi-Industrialized Countries.*

Rodgers, Gerry, and Guy Standing, eds. 1981. *Child Work, Poverty and Underdevelopment.* Geneva: International Labour Office.

Rodriguez, Edgar, and Susan Horton. 1994. "International Return Migration and Remittances in the Philippines." University of Toronto, Department of Economics, Toronto.

Rodrik, Dani. 1992. "Political Economy and Development Policy." *European Economic Review* 36 (April): 329–36.

———. 1994. "Developing Countries After the Uruguay Round." Columbia University, Department of Economics, New York.

Rosenzweig, Mark R. 1981. "Household and Nonhousehold Activities of Youths: Issues of Modeling, Data and Estimation Strategies." In Gerry Rodgers and Guy Standing, eds., *Child Work, Poverty and Underdevelopment."* Geneva: International Labour Office.

Rosenzweig, Mark R., and R. Evenson. 1977. "Fertility, Schooling, and the Economic Contribution of Children in Rural India: An Economic Analysis." *Econometrica* 45 (5).

Rostowski, Jacek. 1994. "Labour Markets and Wages Policies During Economic Transition." Center for Social and Economic Research, Warsaw.

Russell, Sharon Stanton, and Michael S. Teitelbaum. 1992. "International Migration and International Trade." World Bank Discussion Paper No. 160. Washington, D.C.

Rutkowski, Jan. 1993. "Wage Determination in Historically Planned Economies: The Case of Poland." Centre for Economic Performance Discussion Paper No. 164. London School of Economics, London.

———. 1994. "Labor Market Transition and Changes in the Wage Structure: The Case of Poland." Polish Policy Research Group Discussion Paper No. 32. Warsaw University, Warsaw.

Rutkowski, Michal. 1990. "Labour Hoarding and Future Open Unemployment in Eastern Europe: The Case of Polish Industry." Centre for Economic Performance Discussion Paper No. 6. London School of Economics, London.

Sachs, Jeffrey D., and Howard J. Shatz. 1994. "Trade and Jobs in U.S. Manufacturing." *Brookings Papers on Economic Activity* 1: 1–84.

Sachs, Jeffrey D., and Wing Thye Woo. 1994. "Experiences in the Transition to a Market Economy." *Journal of Comparative Economics* 18 (June): 271–75.

Salazar, M. C. 1988. "Child Labor in Colombia: Bogotá's Quarries and Brickyards." In Assefa Bekele and Jo Boyden, eds., *Combating Child Labor.* Geneva: International Labour Office.

Scarpetta, Stefano. 1994. "Spatial Variations in Unemployment in Central and Eastern Europe: Underlying Reasons and Labour Market Policy Options." Paper presented at the technical workshop on "Regional Unemployment in Central and Eastern Europe," Organization for Economic Cooperation and Development, Institute for Advanced Studies, Vienna, Austria, November 3–5.

Schadler, Susan, Maria Carkovic, Adam Bennet, and Robert Kahn. 1993. "Recent Experiences with Surges in Capital Inflows." International Monetary Fund Occasional Paper No. 108. Washington, D.C.

Schaffner, Julie Anderson. 1993. "Rural Labor Legislation and Permanent Agricultural Employment in Northeastern Brazil." *World Development* 21(5): 705–19.

Schiff, Maurice, and Alberto Valdes. 1992. *The Plundering of Agriculture in Developing Countries.* Washington, D.C.: World Bank.

Schmidt-Hebbel, Klaus, Luis Servén, and Andrés Solimano. 1994. "Saving, Investment and Growth in Developing Countries: An Overview." Policy Research Working Paper No. 1382. World Bank, Policy Research Department, Washington, D.C. Forthcoming in *World Bank Research Observer*.

Schultz, T. Paul. 1990. "Women's Changing Participation in the Labor Force: A World Perspective." *Economic Development and Cultural Change* 38 (April): 457–88.

_____. 1993. "Investments in the Schooling and Health of Women and Men." *Journal of Human Resources* 28 (4): 694–734.

_____. 1994. "Integrated Approaches to Human Resources Development." Human Resources Development and Operation Policy Working Paper No. 44. World Bank, Washington, D.C.

Sen, Binayak. 1994. "Adjustment, Poverty and Inequality: Insights from a Cross-Country Analysis with Household Expenditure Survey Data." World Bank, Operations Evaluation Department, Washington, D.C.

Siddiqi, Faraaz, and Harry Anthony Patrinos. 1994. "Child Labor: Issues, Causes and Interventions." World Bank, Washington, D.C.

Sipós, Sándor. 1994. "Income Transfer: Family Support and Poverty Relief." In Nicholas Barr, ed., *Labor Markets and Social Policy in Central and Eastern Europe*. New York: Oxford University Press.

Smith, James, and Finnis Welch. 1984. "Affirmative Action and Labor Markets." *Journal of Labor Economics* April (2).

Sohlman, Asa, and David Turnham. 1994. "What Can Developing Countries Learn from OECD Labour Market Programmes and Policies?" OECD Technical Paper No. 9. Organization for Economic Cooperation and Development, Paris.

Solow, R. M. 1980. "On Theories of Unemployment." *American Economic Review* 70 (1).

Stalker, Peter. 1994. *The Work of Strangers: A Survey of International Labour Migration*. Geneva: International Labour Office.

Standing, Guy. 1989. "The Growth of External Labor Flexibility in a Nascent NIC: A Malaysian Labor Flexibility Survey." ILO Working Paper 35. International Labour Office, Geneva.

_____. 1992. "Do Unions Impede or Accelerate Structural Adjustment? Industrial Versus Company Unions in an Industrialising Labour Market." *Cambridge Journal of Economics* 16 (Sept.): 327–54.

Stark, Oded. 1991. *The Migration of Labor*. Cambridge, Mass.: Basil Blackwell.

Statistical Yearbook for Poland. 1993. Warsaw: Central Statistical Office (in Polish).

Stolper, Wolfgang, and Paul A. Samuelson. 1941. "Protection and Real Wages." *Review of Economic Studies* 9: 58–73.

Sugeno, Kazuo. 1994. "Unions as Social Institutions in Democratic Market Economies." *International Labour Review* 133 (4): 511–22.

Summers, Robert, and Alan Heston. 1991. "The Penn World Table (Mark 5): An Expanded Set of International Comparisons, 1950–1988." *Quarterly Journal of Economics* 106 (May): 327–68.

Svejnar, Jan, and Katherine Terrell. 1991. "Reducing Labor Redundancy in State-Owned Enterprises." Policy Research Working Paper No. 792. World Bank, Infsrastructure and Urban Development Department, Washington, D.C.

Syrquin, Moshe, and Hollis B. Chenery. 1989. *Patterns of Development, 1950 to 1983*. World Bank Discussion Paper No. 41. Washington, D.C.

Teal, Francis. 1994. "The Size and Sources of Economic Rents in a Developing Country Manufacturing Labor Market." St. John's College, Oxford, Center for the Study of African Economics, Oxford, U.K.

Terrell, Katherine. 1993. "Public-Private Wage Differentials in Haiti: Do Public Servants Earn a Rent?" *Journal of Development Economics* 42.

Tilak, Jandhyala B. G. 1989. *Education and Its Relation to Economic Growth, Poverty, and Income Distribution: Past Evidence and Further Analysis*. World Bank Discussion Paper No. 46. Washington, D.C.

Topel, Robert, and Finnis Welch. 1980. "Unemployment Insurance: Survey and Extensions." *Economica* 47: 351–79.

Topel, Robert, Anat Levy, and Martin Rama. 1994. "A Labor Market Cross-Country Database." Paper presented at the Labor Markets in Developing Countries Workshop, World Bank, Washington, D.C., July 6–8.

Turnham, David. 1993. *Employment and Development: A New Review of Evidence*. Paris: OECD.

Tzannatos, P. Zafiris. 1994. "Reverse Discrimination in Higher Education: A Framework of Analysis and Country Experience." World Bank, Education and Social Policy Department, Washington, D.C.

_____. 1995. "Economic Growth and Gender Equity in the Labor Market." World Bank, Education and Social Policy Department, Washington, D.C.

UNDP (United Nations Development Programme). 1990. *Human Development Report 1990*. New York: Oxford University Press.

UNIDO (United Nations Industrial Development Organization). Various years. *Industrial Statistics Yearbook*. New York: United Nations.

Union Bank of Switzerland. 1994. *Prices and Earnings Around the Globe*. Zurich.

United Nations. 1994a. "Transnational Corporations, Employment and the Workplace." *World Investment Report*. New York and Geneva.

_____. 1994b. "Trends in Total Migrant Stock." Department of Economic and Social Information and Policy Analysis, New York.

U.S. Department of Labor. 1994. *Proceedings of the Labor Department Symposium on International Labor Standards*, Yale University, April 25, New Haven, Conn.

van der Gaag, Jacob, Morton Stelcner, and WimVijverberg. 1989. "Wage Differentials and Moonlighting by Civil Servants: Evidence from Côte d'Ivoire and Peru." *World Bank Economic Review* 3 (1; January): 67–95.

Velenchik, Ann D. Forthcoming. "Apprenticeship Contracts, Small Enterprises and Credit Markets in Africa." *World Bank Economic Review*.

Viscusi, W. K. 1986. "The Impact of Occupational Safety and Health Regulation 1973–83." *Journal of Economics* 17 (4).

Von Braun, Joachim. 1994. "Employment for Poverty Reduction and Food Security." International Food Policy Research Institute, Washington, D.C.

Wade, Robert. 1994. "Organizational Determinants of a 'High-Quality Civil Service': Bureaucratic and Technological Incentives in Canal Irrigation in India and Korea." Sussex University, Institute of Development Studies, Brighton, U.K.

Weil, David. 1991. "Enforcing OSHA: The Role of Labor Unions." *Industrial Relations* 30 (1; Winter): 20–36.

141

Wilson, Sandra, and Arvil V. Adams. 1994. "Promotion of Self-Employment for the Unemployed: Experience in OECD and Transitional Economies." World Bank, Education and Social Policy Department, Washington, D.C.

Wood, Adrian. 1994a. *North-South Trade, Employment and Inequality: Changing Fortunes in a Skill-Driven World.* Oxford, U.K.: Clarendon Press.

———. 1994b. "Skill, Land, and Trade: A Simple Analytical Framework." Working Paper No. 1. Institute of Development Studies, University of Sussex, Brighton, U.K.

Wood, Adrian, and Kersti Berge. 1994. "Export Manufactures: Trade Policy or Human Resources?" Institute of Development Studies Working Paper No. 4. University of Sussex, Brighton, U.K.

World Bank. 1990. *World Development Report 1990: Poverty.* New York: Oxford University Press.

———. 1991. *Vocational and Technical Education and Training.* A World Bank Policy Paper. Washington, D.C.

———. 1992a. *Global Economic Prospects and the Developing Countries.* Washington, D.C.

———. 1992b. *Poverty Reduction Handbook.* Washington, D.C.

———. 1992c. *World Development Report.* New York: Oxford University Press.

———. 1993. *The East Asian Miracle: Economic Growth and Public Policy.* A World Bank Policy Research Report. New York: Oxford University Press.

———. 1994a. *Adjustment in Africa: Reforms, Results, and the Road Ahead.* A World Bank Policy Research Report. New York: Oxford University Press.

———. 1994b. *Averting the Old Age Crisis: Policies to Protect the Old and Promote Growth.* A World Bank Policy Research Report. New York: Oxford University Press.

———. 1994c. "Mexico: Second Decentralization and Regional Development Report." Staff Appraisal Report No. 13032-ME. World Bank, Latin America and Caribbean Regional Office, Washington, D.C.

———. 1994d. *Population and Development: Implications for the World Bank.* Development in Practice Series. Washington, D.C.

———. 1994e. "Poverty in Poland." World Bank, Central Europe Department, Washington, D.C.

———. 1995a. "Priorities and Strategies for Education." A World Bank Sector Review. Education and Social Policy Department, Washington, D.C.

———. 1995b. *Social Indicators of Development 1995.* Baltimore, Md.: Johns Hopkins University Press.

———. Various years. *World Debt Tables.* Washington, D.C.

———. Various years. *World Tables.* Baltimore, Md.: Johns Hopkins University Press.

Zaytoun, Mohaya A. 1991. "Earnings and the Cost of Living: An Analysis of Recent Developments in the Egyptian Economy." In Heba Jandouss and Gillian Potters, eds., *Employment and Structural Adjustment: Egypt in the 1990s.* Cairo: American University in Cairo Press.

Zevin, Robert B. 1989. "Are World Financial Markets More Open? If So, Why and with What Effects?" WIDER Working Paper No. 75. World Institute for Development Economics Research, United Nations University, Helsinki.

Zimmermann, Klaus F. 1995. "European Migration: Push and Pull." *Proceedings of the World Bank Annual Bank Conference on Development Economics 1994.* Washington, D.C

Zlotnik, Hania. 1993. "International Migration: Causes and Effects." In Laurie Ann Mazur, ed., *Beyond the Numbers: A Reader on Population, Consumption, and the Environment.* Covelo, Calif.: Island Press.

International Labor Statistics

Table A-1 Labor supply

Table A-1 presents data on labor supply for countries with an estimated labor force of over 400,000 people. Data are derived from ILO 1986 and ILO data updates through 1994. The labor force is equal to the economically active population reported by the ILO minus those ages ten to fourteen and those over sixty-five. ILO 1986 defines the economically active population as all persons in employment (employers, own-account workers, salaried employees, wage earners, unpaid family workers, members of producer cooperatives, and members of the armed forces) as well as all the unemployed (both those with previous job experience and those seeking work for the first time). Labor force participation rates for working-age adults (ages fifteen to sixty-four) and youths (ages ten to nineteen) are the percentages of those age groups that are economically active.

Table A-2 Distribution of the work force

Table A-2 presents data on the distribution of the work force across six categories: wage and nonwage employment in each of the three sectors of agriculture, industry, and services. Data are drawn primarily from ILO, various issues. For China, India, and Indonesia the data are from country sources (government statistics offices). Included are those countries for which data were available in any year since 1980. ILO data by sector are aggregated as follows: agricul-

ture, industry (mining and quarrying, manufacturing, gas, electricity and water, and construction), services (trade, transport, banking, commercial services, and "not adequately defined/described"). Within each sector the share classified by the ILO as employees is reported here in wage employment. Nonwage employment refers to those classified as employers or own-account workers, unpaid family workers, and "not classifiable by status."

Table A-3 Growth in GDP per capita and wages

Table A-3 presents the data underlying Figure 2.2. Since the years over which the wages are observed vary by country and industry, each wage growth rate is matched with the real GDP per capita growth rate for the corresponding period from a data base compiled by Nehru and Dhareshwar (Nehru and Dhareshwar 1991). Wages in agriculture are generally from country sources. Wages in manufacturing correspond to average earnings in manufacturing from UNIDO, various years. Wage data are adjusted for inflation using consumer price index data from IMF, various years.

Table A-4 Ratification of basic ILO conventions

Table A-4 lists countries that have ratified basic ILO conventions relating to freedom of association, forced labor, discrimination, child labor, and employment policy. Data are reprinted with the permission of the ILO.

Table A-1 Labor supply

	Labor force in 1995				Labor force participation rate in 1995 (percent)			
	Thousands of workers ages 15–64		Average annual growth rate (percent)		Ages 15–64		Ages 10–19	
Country	Male	Female	1965–95	1995–2025	Male	Female	Male	Female
East Asia and the Pacific								
Cambodia	2,319	1,395	1.32	2.28	95	50	31	36
China	406,660	316,623	2.60	0.41	96	80	45	43
Hong Kong	1,905	995	2.55	−0.17	86	50	24	23
Indonesia	52,766	24,161	2.48	1.50	85	38	29	16
Korea, Democratic Rep. of	5,945	5,140	2.61	1.65	75	65	21	21
Korea, Rep. of	12,413	6,505	2.48	0.55	76	41	14	16
Lao PDR	1,228	981	2.00	2.54	98	76	41	37
Malaysia	5,365	3,004	3.49	2.01	91	52	20	13
Mongolia	630	526	2.81	2.63	89	75	31	26
Myanmar	12,529	6,983	2.33	1.90	93	51	38	32
Papua New Guinea	1,156	691	2.08	2.22	89	58	44	36
Philippines	17,426	7,644	2.85	1.91	85	38	25	16
* Singapore	812	500	1.82	..	84	53	15	15
Thailand	16,542	13,084	2.66	0.63	86	67	39	37
Viet Nam	19,299	16,996	2.53	2.05	92	77	37	33
Europe and Central Asia								
* Albania	908	623	2.78	..	86	63	27	15
* Armenia	837	754	2.71	..	79	69	13	12
* Azerbaijan	1,670	1,278	2.23	..	78	56	15	14
* Belarus	2,671	2,551	1.42	..	82	73	13	12
* Bosnia-Herzegovina	1,183	717	0.83	..	79	47	12	9
Bulgaria	2,225	2,007	0.00	−0.07	76	68	11	14
* Croatia	1,177	874	0.54	..	77	56	11	9
* Czech Rep.	2,784	2,530	0.54	..	82	74	17	17
Estonia	394	372	0.76	0.09	78	71	17	15
* Georgia	1,381	1,179	1.13	..	80	64	14	13
Greece	2,711	1,021	0.56	−0.03	79	30	21	11
Hungary	2,878	2,398	0.34	−0.15	82	67	31	24
* Kazakhstan	4,192	3,608	2.30	..	82	68	16	12
* Kyrgyz Rep.	962	827	2.41	..	78	65	13	12
Latvia	660	631	0.62	0.02	79	71	17	15
Lithuania	953	888	0.87	0.20	79	70	18	15
* Macedonia, FYR of	535	357	1.64	..	78	53	11	9
* Moldova	1,081	1,025	1.13	..	81	70	13	14
Poland	10,583	9,081	0.88	0.34	84	71	21	14
Portugal	2,736	1,616	1.03	0.08	84	48	38	21
Romania	6,112	5,373	0.43	0.42	78	69	20	18
* Russian Fed.	39,212	36,613	1.04	..	82	72	15	12
* Slovak Rep.	1,372	1,208	1.13	..	82	71	17	16
* Slovenia	500	424	1.06	..	77	65	13	10
* Tajikistan	1,082	792	2.70	..	78	56	14	15
Turkey	17,067	8,856	2.36	1.65	87	48	37	26
* Turkmenistan	816	663	2.95	..	81	64	17	16
* Ukraine	13,060	12,496	0.66	..	80	70	14	13
* Uzbekistan	4,240	3,644	2.83	..	76	64	14	15
* Yugoslavia, Fed. Rep. of	2,625	1,868	0.88	..	77	55	12	9
Latin America and the Caribbean								
Argentina	8,472	3,442	1.25	1.28	80	32	25	13
Bolivia	1,734	589	2.37	2.36	78	25	26	12
Brazil	41,470	16,551	2.90	1.31	82	33	31	14
Chile	3,682	1,508	2.37	1.11	83	33	13	6
Colombia	8,788	2,553	2.72	1.52	81	23	18	9
Costa Rica	908	263	3.59	1.99	87	26	28	8
Cuba	3,153	1,591	2.32	0.40	84	42	15	7
Dominican Rep.	2,113	411	3.24	1.93	87	18	27	5
Ecuador	2,774	686	2.96	1.99	79	20	24	7

	Labor force in 1995				Labor force participation rate in 1995 (percent)			
	Thousands of workers ages 15–64		Average annual growth rate (percent)		Ages 15–64		Ages 10–19	
Country	Male	Female	1965–95	1995–2025	Male	Female	Male	Female
El Salvador	1,322	486	2.44	2.29	87	29	33	13
Guatemala	2,359	525	2.83	3.46	85	19	34	8
Haiti	1,536	1,059	1.12	2.07	79	51	33	29
Honduras	1,400	385	3.52	3.07	87	24	41	8
Jamaica	682	596	2.19	1.45	86	75	23	17
Mexico	23,132	8,937	3.58	1.83	83	32	26	12
Nicaragua	942	384	3.48	3.33	88	32	32	12
Panama	691	276	2.90	1.62	83	34	22	8
Paraguay	1,257	328	3.27	2.49	89	24	36	10
Peru	5,656	1,833	2.80	2.16	78	26	17	9
Puerto Rico	867	365	1.75	0.93	75	29	13	4
Trinidad and Tobago	358	157	1.90	1.21	92	39	22	8
Uruguay	826	397	0.59	0.74	83	39	28	12
Venezuela	5,351	2,154	3.73	1.75	81	33	21	6
Middle East and North Africa								
Algeria	5,926	676	3.06	3.32	76	8	15	3
Egypt, Arab Rep. of	14,430	1,687	2.70	2.35	84	10	22	4
Iran, Islamic Rep. of	15,765	3,737	3.86	3.74	93	23	24	11
Iraq	4,495	1,327	3.84	3.61	78	24	17	8
Israel	1,503	799	3.23	1.28	84	44	17	9
Jordan	954	123	2.82	3.90	72	10	18	2
Kuwait	439	114	4.03	1.90	94	25	16	3
Lebanon	676	256	1.88	1.81	77	27	17	10
Libya	1,177	132	3.95	3.88	79	10	15	3
Morocco	7,100	1,893	3.39	2.52	88	23	28	15
Oman	434	44	4.02	3.99	87	10	23	3
Saudi Arabia	4,625	385	4.78	3.25	81	10	23	4
Syrian Arab Rep.	2,911	634	3.69	4.46	79	17	18	10
Tunisia	2,237	747	3.26	1.90	83	28	25	14
United Arab Emirates	799	64	9.89	0.45	90	19	23	4
Yemen, Rep. of	2,877	419	2.52	4.25	90	12	36	8
High-income OECD								
Australia	5,333	3,318	2.15	0.94	86	55	28	25
Austria	2,108	1,436	0.55	..	80	55	28	24
Belgium	2,760	1,393	0.59	−0.44	82	42	12	11
Canada	8,353	5,607	2.24	0.65	87	58	27	21
Denmark	1,589	1,294	0.99	−0.36	89	75	34	26
Finland	1,359	1,219	0.71	−0.31	80	73	17	13
France	15,641	10,721	0.95	−0.07	83	57	19	14
Germany	24,381	15,493	0.52	−0.31	87	57	27	24
Ireland	920	397	0.90	0.36	82	36	22	17
Italy	15,653	7,469	0.45	−0.41	79	37	26	20
Japan	36,799	23,025	0.83	−0.35	84	53	10	10
Netherlands	4,497	1,976	1.38	−0.06	83	38	11	13
New Zealand	1,040	571	1.67	0.49	89	49	27	23
Norway	1,280	930	1.48	0.19	90	68	20	17
Spain	10,741	3,527	0.84	0.08	80	26	23	15
Sweden	2,538	2,066	1.04	0.02	89	75	19	18
Switzerland	2,176	1,233	0.92	−0.06	91	53	27	25
United Kingdom	17,290	10,941	0.45	−0.04	91	59	28	25
United States	73,443	52,242	1.70	0.44	86	60	24	20
South Asia								
Afghanistan	5,791	612	2.15	3.07	85	9	39	6
Bangladesh	31,458	2,723	2.57	2.75	84	8	45	4
Bhutan	468	207	1.96	2.64	96	43	54	38
India	260,802	83,502	2.09	1.61	90	31	30	16

(Table continues on the following page)

Table A-1 *(Continued)*

Country	Labor force in 1995				Labor force participation rate in 1995 (percent)			
	Thousands of workers ages 15–64		Average annual growth rate (percent)		Ages 15–64		Ages 10–19	
	Male	Female	1965–95	1995–2025	Male	Female	Male	Female
Nepal	5,532	2,516	2.18	2.52	91	43	46	37
Pakistan	34,008	5,344	3.29	3.21	90	16	34	5
Sri Lanka	4,763	1,806	1.93	1.35	82	30	20	10
Sub-Saharan Africa								
Angola	2,466	1,512	2.06	3.32	91	54	41	28
Benin	1,166	1,051	2.21	3.24	88	77	44	40
Botswana	274	156	2.68	2.97	79	39	37	19
Burkina Faso	2,504	2,107	2.05	2.63	94	77	60	53
Burundi	1,487	1,316	1.81	2.93	96	79	62	54
Cameroon	2,999	1,431	2.09	3.10	87	41	43	20
Central African Rep.	771	635	1.69	2.76	92	70	46	42
Chad	1,500	399	1.81	2.98	90	23	51	13
Congo	560	364	2.53	3.32	88	53	29	18
Côte d'Ivoire	3,314	1,718	2.98	3.91	93	51	40	25
Ethiopia	13,425	7,777	2.17	2.86	91	53	53	35
Gabon	310	181	2.71	2.72	78	45	30	23
Ghana	3,491	2,254	2.15	3.18	78	49	21	16
Guinea	1,616	991	1.77	2.84	96	59	51	34
Guinea-Bissau	259	169	1.87	2.10	91	57	51	35
Kenya	5,631	3,546	3.16	3.45	82	51	53	36
Lesotho	468	339	1.96	2.27	89	60	47	15
Liberia	660	273	2.58	3.30	85	36	46	19
Madagascar	3,242	2,023	2.34	3.27	90	55	48	33
Malawi	2,479	1,604	3.05	3.00	94	57	45	34
Mali	2,417	434	2.28	3.56	92	16	65	14
Mauritania	506	158	4.68	3.16	85	26	39	13
Mauritius	322	120	2.46	0.74	85	31	28	8
Mozambique	3,877	3,381	1.79	2.92	93	78	51	47
Namibia	369	114	2.61	3.35	85	26	24	11
Niger	2,096	1,825	2.54	3.02	95	80	62	55
Nigeria	26,686	13,993	2.73	3.19	85	43	44	22
Rwanda	1,879	1,623	2.81	3.34	96	80	56	54
Senegal	1,901	1,157	2.45	2.56	87	52	54	35
Sierra Leone	1,075	503	1.80	2.87	89	40	29	16
Somalia	2,302	1,407	2.47	3.10	92	55	43	29
South Africa	9,275	5,250	2.56	2.40	75	42	16	12
Sudan	6,630	2,045	2.87	3.42	87	27	38	9
Tanzania	6,430	5,680	2.65	3.21	86	73	49	46
Togo	922	495	2.72	3.17	88	46	48	31
Uganda	4,553	3,029	2.75	2.97	92	60	58	40
Zaire	9,530	5,128	2.45	3.54	90	47	36	21
Zambia	1,997	867	3.11	3.45	89	36	36	22
Zimbabwe	2,464	1,257	2.74	2.66	82	41	45	28

.. Not available.

Note: Asterisks before country names indicate that labor force and participation rates are for 1990 and growth rates for 1960–90. Comparable data are not available for 1995–2025 but were estimated to be 0.28 for the former Czechoslovakia, 0.48 for the former Soviet Union, and 0.18 for the former Yugoslavia.

Source: ILO 1986 with ILO data updates.

Table A-2 Distribution of the work force
(percent)

Country	Year	Agriculture		Industry		Services		Income group
		Wage	Nonwage	Wage	Nonwage	Wage	Nonwage	
East Asia and the Pacific								
Brunei	1981	2.5	2.5	29.9	1.3	59.3	4.5	High
China	1993	1.0	60.0	4.0	14.0	11.0	10.0	Low
French Polynesia	1988	1.3	11.5	8.8	1.4	56.1	21.0	High
Guam	1980	0.8	0.1	14.7	0.3	81.3	2.9	Middle
Hong Kong	1991	0.3	0.5	32.1	2.8	55.8	8.5	High
Indonesia	1993	6.5	43.9	10.0	5.8	14.3	19.5	Middle
Korea, Rep. of	1991	1.2	15.5	30.5	5.1	29.0	18.7	Middle
Macao	1990	0.0	0.2	39.9	2.5	47.3	10.0	Middle
Malaysia	1988	8.8	21.8	19.0	3.6	34.0	12.7	Middle
Philippines	1991	9.6	35.7	12.3	3.7	23.6	15.1	Middle
Singapore	1991	0.2	0.1	32.6	2.6	53.9	10.7	High
Thailand	1989	6.6	59.7	8.7	3.2	11.6	10.2	Middle
Europe and Central Asia								
Bulgaria	1985	26.4	0.2	13.9	0.0	59.2	0.3	Middle
Cyprus	1989	2.2	11.8	24.1	3.9	47.7	10.2	High
Czechoslovakia (former)	1980	9.5	12.1	15.4	0.2	62.2	0.6	Middle
Greece	1990	1.0	22.2	19.6	8.1	32.0	17.0	Middle
Hungary	1991	17.1	21.4	11.6	3.9	37.3	8.6	Middle
Malta	1983	0.8	4.1	34.8	3.5	49.0	7.8	Middle
Poland	1988	6.0	21.9	34.5	1.8	34.7	1.2	Middle
Portugal	1990	3.4	14.5	30.0	4.5	37.3	10.4	Middle
Romania	1990	5.2	23.3	41.1	2.0	26.6	1.8	Middle
Turkey	1991	1.4	47.4	15.3	4.8	19.5	11.5	Middle
Yugoslavia[a]	1981	4.8	36.1	9.9	0.6	45.5	3.2	Middle
Latin America and the Caribbean								
Argentina	1980	6.4	5.7	23.6	7.9	41.6	14.9	Middle
Bahamas, The	1980	3.3	2.4	13.2	3.3	71.3	6.6	High
Barbados	1982	8.6	1.5	9.1	1.8	71.1	8.0	Middle
Bolivia	1991	0.5	0.7	15.2	9.6	34.1	39.9	Middle
Brazil	1988	9.4	14.8	19.4	4.0	37.3	15.1	Middle
Chile	1991	10.5	8.6	20.5	5.8	38.0	16.6	Middle
Costa Rica	1991	14.5	10.5	20.0	6.9	36.3	11.7	Middle
Cuba	1981	25.2	7.0	39.6	0.4	27.0	0.9	Middle
Dominican Rep.	1981	4.6	19.0	14.1	4.0	36.4	21.9	Middle
Ecuador	1990	8.2	23.0	8.4	9.7	26.4	24.4	Middle
El Salvador	1991	7.0	3.7	19.6	9.6	38.0	22.2	Middle
Falkland Islands	1986	14.3	5.6	17.2	1.2	58.9	2.8	Middle
Guatemala	1989	17.2	32.7	11.1	7.2	20.3	11.5	Middle
Haiti	1990	4.1	61.6	4.7	4.1	10.2	15.4	Low
Honduras	1991	11.9	25.0	13.5	7.4	21.0	21.3	Low
Mexico	1990	9.3	13.3	23.2	4.6	35.6	14.0	Middle
Panama	1989	7.9	19.1	11.3	4.7	44.8	12.3	Middle
Puerto Rico	1992	2.1	1.5	24.6	1.7	58.4	11.8	Middle
Suriname	1980	5.8	3.5	19.1	2.7	58.1	10.9	Middle
Trinidad and Tobago	1991	5.5	4.9	29.9	2.6	43.8	13.3	Middle
Uruguay	1985	8.3	6.3	20.1	5.7	43.5	16.1	Middle
Venezuela	1991	4.7	6.7	18.7	9.0	38.4	22.6	Middle
Middle East and North Africa								
Algeria	1987	6.2	11.1	27.2	4.0	40.4	11.1	Middle
Bahrain	1981	1.2	1.5	32.7	2.2	54.6	7.8	Middle
Egypt, Arab Rep. of	1989	6.3	36.2	15.6	5.1	27.2	9.6	Low
Iran, Islamic Rep. of	1986	3.0	26.1	15.0	10.3	30.3	15.3	Middle
Israel	1990	1.5	3.8	6.1	2.2	67.1	19.3	High
Kuwait	1985	1.7	0.2	26.2	2.4	65.6	3.9	High
Qatar	1986	3.1	0.1	31.8	0.4	63.3	1.4	High
Syrian Arab Rep.	1989	3.5	19.3	20.6	8.3	32.2	16.1	Middle

(Table continues on the following page)

Table A-2 *(Continued)*

Country	Year	Agriculture Wage	Agriculture Nonwage	Industry Wage	Industry Nonwage	Services Wage	Services Nonwage	Income group
Tunisia	1989	9.2	16.6	26.0	7.7	30.7	9.9	Middle
United Arab Emirates	1980	3.9	0.7	37.3	0.9	51.9	5.4	High
High-income OECD								
Australia	1991	1.8	3.5	18.6	5.8	57.0	13.4	High
Austria	1990	1.0	6.7	35.2	1.9	49.7	5.5	High
Belgium	1990	0.5	2.2	25.1	2.6	55.4	14.3	High
Canada	1991	1.5	2.0	22.9	1.5	66.2	5.9	High
Denmark	1990	2.0	3.4	25.5	2.2	61.6	5.3	High
Finland	1991	2.3	5.9	27.7	2.5	56.2	5.5	High
France	1991	1.2	4.5	26.4	2.4	57.5	8.0	High
Ireland	1990	2.1	12.8	25.2	3.2	48.2	8.6	High
Italy	1991	3.4	5.0	26.5	5.5	41.7	17.8	High
Japan	1991	0.7	6.0	29.5	5.0	48.4	10.4	High
Luxembourg	1991	0.5	3.0	27.5	1.5	61.2	6.4	High
Netherlands	1991	1.6	2.9	24.2	1.1	63.1	7.2	High
New Zealand	1991	4.1	6.0	19.1	4.6	55.1	11.1	High
Norway	1991	1.4	4.3	21.0	2.7	64.0	6.6	High
Spain	1991	4.5	6.2	28.3	4.4	41.9	14.7	High
Sweden	1991	1.3	1.9	26.3	1.9	63.5	5.0	High
Switzerland	1980	3.5	2.8	36.8	2.2	50.0	4.8	High
United Kingdom	1990	1.1	1.0	24.9	3.8	60.2	9.1	High
United States	1991	1.6	1.3	24.2	1.6	65.5	5.8	High
South Asia								
Bangladesh	1989	0.6	64.9	2.0	13.5	7.0	12.6	Low
India	1991	1.5	61.7	3.7	10.5	9.4	13.2	Low
Maldives	1990	3.6	21.6	7.3	15.1	38.8	13.5	Middle
Pakistan	1992	4.5	42.9	13.8	6.1	16.2	16.5	Low
Sri Lanka	1986	21.5	27.6	13.2	4.9	23.8	9.1	Low
Sub-Saharan Africa								
Botswana	1981	2.9	51.1	12.0	0.4	30.7	2.9	Middle
Cameroon	1982	2.5	74.2	2.6	4.2	10.3	6.3	Middle
Cape Verde	1990	9.1	15.7	21.7	2.8	22.9	27.8	Middle
Central African Rep.	1988	0.7	79.5	1.2	2.1	6.8	9.7	Low
Comoros	1980	9.4	43.9	3.5	3.9	12.7	26.5	Low
Ghana	1984	3.2	57.8	3.2	9.6	9.7	16.5	Low
Liberia	1984	6.7	72.7	3.7	2.1	5.0	9.8	Low
Malawi	1987	5.3	81.2	3.6	1.4	5.2	3.3	Low
Nigeria	1986	1.1	43.9	1.4	5.2	17.0	31.4	Low
Reunion	1982	6.5	9.1	9.5	1.1	65.7	8.0	Middle
São Tomé and Principe	1981	52.7	7.1	6.4	1.2	25.8	6.8	Low
Seychelles	1981	7.2	2.8	17.1	3.4	54.6	14.8	Middle
Togo	1981	0.7	65.8	1.9	7.3	8.2	16.1	Low
Zambia	1980	22.5	29.8	11.9	1.6	24.2	10.0	Low

Note: Income groups are from World Bank 1995.

a. Data refer to the pre-1991 federation.

Sources: ILO, various years; country sources.

Table A-3 Growth in output per capita and wages

(percentage per year)

Country	Period	GDP per capita	Agricultural wages	Period	GDP per capita	Manufacturing wages
Bangladesh	1960–91	0.81	−0.73	1967–89	0.74	−1.05
Brazil	..	..	..	1963–91	3.19	1.64
Chile	..	..	..	1963–92	1.17	2.10
Colombia	1960–88	2.32	2.17	1968–92	2.45	0.35
Côte d'Ivoire	..	..	..	1966–82	2.27	0.66
Egypt, Arab Rep. of	1970–88	4.45	5.20	1970–87	4.62	0.85
Ghana	1969–88	−1.20	−4.03	1964–87	−1.27	−3.55
India	1960–90	1.93	1.82	1963–90	1.94	1.74
Indonesia	1976–88	3.96	3.74	1970–91	4.21	5.52
Jordan	..	..	..	1983–91	−1.64	−4.34
Kenya	1964–92	2.13	−0.92	1963–91	2.11	−0.98
Korea, Rep. of	1960–78	6.90	7.06	1966–91	7.44	9.09
Malawi	1968–89	0.98	−3.68	1968–86	1.18	0.20
Malaysia	1971–92	4.35	3.96	1968–92	4.14	2.18
Mexico	1962–85	2.93	1.25	1970–91	1.56	−1.20
Nigeria	..	..	..	1963–85	−0.04	−1.40
Pakistan	1970–92	2.32	2.94	1963–88	3.00	4.89
Peru	1960–86	1.00	−2.03	1963–86	0.68	−0.97
Philippines	1960–77	2.37	−1.10	1963–91	1.20	0.89
Sri Lanka	1980–90	2.76	−1.06	1966–90	2.91	1.03
Thailand	..	..	..	1970–90	4.89	3.00
Turkey	..	..	..	1960–85	2.75	2.64

.. Not available.

Note: Data are averages for the period indicated.

Source: UNIDO data; country sources; Nehru and Dhareshwar 1991.

Table A-4 Ratification of basic ILO conventions

| Country | Total number of ratifications | Freedom of association | | Forced labor | | Discrimination | | | | Tripartite Consultation (Stand.) (No. 144) |
		Right to Organize (No. 87)	Collective Bargaining (No. 98)	Forced Labor (No. 29)	Abolition (No. 105)	Employment and Occupation (No. 111)	Equal Remuneration (No. 100)	Employment Policy (No. 122)	Minimum Age (No. 138)	
East Asia and the Pacific										
Cambodia	5			x				x		
China	17						x			x
Indonesia	10		x	x			x			x
Korea, Rep. of	4							x		
Lao PDR	4			x						
Malaysia	11		x	x	x					
Mongolia	8	x	x			x	x	x		
Myanmar	21	x		x						
Papua New Guinea	19		x	x	x			x		
Philippines	26	x	x		x	x	x	x		x
Singapore	21		x	x	x					
Thailand	11			x	x			x		
Viet Nam	22		x	x		x		x		
Europe and Central Asia										
Albania	17	x	x	x			x	x		
Armenia	5					x	x	x		
Azerbaijan	50	x	x	x		x	x	x	x	x
Belarus	40	x	x	x		x	x	x	x	x
Bosnia-Herzegovina	66	x	x	x		x	x	x	x	
Bulgaria	80	x	x	x		x	x		x	
Croatia	34	x	x	x		x		x	x	
Czech Rep.	57	x	x	x		x	x	x		
Estonia	24	x	x							x
Greece	66	x	x	x	x	x	x	x	x	x
Hungary	63	x	x	x	x	x	x	x		x
Kyrgyz Rep.	42	x	x	x		x	x	x	x	
Latvia	43	x	x		x	x	x	x		
Lithuania	30	x	x	x	x	x	x			x
Moldova	1				x					
Poland	78	x	x	x	x	x	x	x	x	x
Portugal	68	x	x	x	x	x	x	x		x
Romania	42	x	x	x		x	x	x	x	x
Russian Fed.	50	x	x	x		x	x	x	x	
Slovak Rep.	57	x	x	x		x	x	x		
Slovenia	66	x	x	x		x	x	x	x	
Tajikistan	42	x	x	x		x	x	x	x	
Turkey	35	x	x		x	x	x			x
Ukraine	50	x	x	x		x	x	x	x	x
Yugoslavia, Fed. Rep. of	76	x	x	x		x	x	x	x	
Latin America and the Caribbean										
Argentina	67	x	x	x	x	x	x			x
Bolivia	43	x	x		x	x	x	x		
Brazil	76		x	x	x	x	x	x		x
Chile	41			x		x	x			x
Colombia	52	x	x	x	x	x	x			
Costa Rica	48	x	x	x	x	x	x	x	x	x
Cuba	86	x	x	x	x	x	x	x	x	
Dominican Rep.	28	x	x	x	x	x	x			
Ecuador	56	x	x	x	x	x	x	x		x
El Salvador	6				x					
Guatemala	67	x	x	x	x	x	x	x	x	x
Haiti	23	x	x	x	x	x	x			
Honduras	20	x	x	x	x	x	x	x	x	
Jamaica	25	x	x	x	x	x	x	x		

Country	Total number of ratifi-cations	Freedom of association		Forced labor		Discrimination		Employ-ment Policy (No. 122)	Minimum Age (No. 138)	Tripartite Consulta-tion (Stand.) (No. 144)
		Right to Organize (No. 87)	Collec-tive Bar-gaining (No. 98)	Forced Labor (No. 29)	Abolition (No. 105)	Employ-ment and Occupa-tion (No. 111)	Equal Remun-eration (No. 100)			
Mexico	76	x		x	x	x	x			x
Nicaragua	58	x	x	x	x	x	x	x	x	x
Panama	70	x	x	x	x	x	x	x		
Paraguay	35	x	x	x	x	x	x	x		
Peru	67	x	x	x	x	x	x	x		
Trinidad and Tobago	12	x	x	x	x	x				
Uruguay	97	x	x		x	x		x	x	x
Venezuela	52	x	x	x	x	x	x	x	x	x
Middle East and North Africa										
Algeria	53	x	x	x	x	x	x	x	x	x
Egypt, Arab Rep. of	60	x	x	x	x	x	x			x
Iran, Islamic Rep. of	11			x	x	x	x	x		
Iraq	64		x	x	x	x	x	x	x	x
Israel	44	x	x	x	x	x	x	x	x	
Jordan	17		x	x	x	x	x	x		
Kuwait	14	x		x	x	x				
Lebanon	37		x	x	x	x	x	x		
Libya	27		x	x	x	x	x	x	x	
Morocco	41		x	x	x	x	x	x		
Saudi Arabia	13			x	x	x	x			
Syrian Arab Rep.	46	x	x	x	x	x	x			x
Tunisia	55	x	x	x	x	x	x	x		
United Arab Emirates	4		x							
Yemen, Rep. of	26	x	x	x	x	x	x	x		
High-income OECD										
Australia	54	x	x	x	x	x	x	x		x
Austria	48	x	x	x	x	x	x	x		x
Belgium	85	x	x	x	x	x	x	x	x	x
Canada	28	x			x	x	x	x		
Denmark	62	x	x	x	x	x	x	x		x
Finland	86	x	x	x	x	x	x	x	x	x
France	115	x	x	x	x	x	x	x	x	x
Germany	75	x	x	x	x	x	x	x	x	x
Ireland	60	x	x	x	x		x	x	x	x
Italy	102	x	x	x	x	x	x	x	x	x
Japan	41	x	x	x			x	x		
Netherlands	94	x	x	x	x	x	x	x	x	x
New Zealand	56			x	x	x	x	x		x
Norway	99	x	x	x	x	x	x	x	x	x
Spain	124	x	x	x	x	x	x	x	x	x
Sweden	84	x	x	x	x	x	x	x	x	x
Switzerland	51	x		x	x	x	x			
United Kingdom	80	x	x	x	x		x	x		x
United States	11				x					x
South Asia										
Afghanistan	15				x	x	x			
Bangladesh	31	x	x	x	x	x				x
India	36			x		x	x			x
Nepal	4					x	x			
Pakistan	31	x	x	x	x	x				x
Sri Lanka	33		x	x			x			x
Sub-Saharan Africa										
Angola	30		x	x	x	x	x			
Benin	18	x	x	x	x	x	x			

(Table continues on the following page)

Table A-4 *(Continued)*

| Country | Total number of ratifications | Freedom of association | | Forced labor | | Discrimination | | | | |
		Right to Organize (No. 87)	Collective Bargaining (No. 98)	Forced Labor (No. 29)	Abolition (No. 105)	Employment and Occupation (No. 111)	Equal Remuneration (No. 100)	Employment Policy (No. 122)	Minimum Age (No. 138)	Tripartite Consultation (Stand.) (No. 144)
Botswana	2									
Burkina Faso	31	x	x	x		x	x			
Burundi	26	x		x	x	x	x			
Cameroon	47	x	x	x	x	x	x	x		
Central African Rep.	35	x	x	x	x	x	x			
Chad	19	x	x	x	x	x	x			
Congo	17	x		x						
Côte d'Ivoire	31	x	x	x	x	x	x			x
Ethiopia	15	x	x			x				
Gabon	34	x	x	x	x	x	x			x
Ghana	45	x	x	x	x	x	x			
Guinea	53	x	x	x	x	x	x	x		
Kenya	46		x	x	x				x	x
Lesotho	11	x	x	x						
Liberia	20	x	x	x	x	x				
Madagascar	30	x		x		x	x	x		
Malawi	23		x			x	x			x
Mali	21	x	x	x	x	x	x			
Mauritania	37	x		x		x		x		
Mauritius	34		x	x	x			x		x
Mozambique	11				x	x	x			
Niger	32	x	x	x	x	x	x		x	
Nigeria	30	x	x	x	x		x			x
Rwanda	25	x	x		x	x	x		x	
Senegal	34	x	x	x	x	x	x	x		
Sierra Leone	33	x	x	x	x	x	x			x
Somalia	14			x	x	x				
South Africa	12									
Sudan	12		x	x	x	x	x	x		
Tanzania	28		x	x	x					x
Togo	18	x	x	x		x	x		x	x
Uganda	26		x	x	x			x		x
Zaire	30		x	x			x			
Zambia	38			x	x	x	x	x	x	x
Zimbabwe	9									x

Note: Ratifications are as of October 31, 1994.

Source: *World Labour Report 1995* (ILO 1995b), pages 108–09. Copyright © 1995, International Labour Organization, Geneva.

WORLD DEVELOPMENT INDICATORS

Contents

Key

In each table, economies are listed within their groups in ascending order of GNP per capita, except those for which no GNP per capita can be calculated; these are italicized, in alphabetical order, at the end of their group. The ranking below refers to the order in the tables.

Figures in colored bands in the tables are summary measures for groups of economies. The letter w means weighted average; m, median value; t, total.

All growth rates are in real terms.

Data cutoff date is April 30, 1995.

The symbol . . means not available

The figures 0 and 0.0 mean zero or less than half the unit shown.

A blank means not applicable.

Figures in italics indicate data that are for years or periods other than those specified.

The symbol † indicates economies classified by the United Nations or otherwise regarded by their authorities as developing.

Country	Country ranking in tables	Country	Country ranking in tables	Country	Country ranking in tables
Albania	22	Guinea	34	Oman	99
Algeria	73	Guinea-Bissau	14	Pakistan	31
Argentina	103	Honduras	38	Panama	82
Armenia	42	†Hong Kong	114	Papua New Guinea	59
Australia	113	Hungary	95	Paraguay	70
Austria	125	India	20	Peru	69
Azerbaijan	46	Indonesia	47	Philippines	53
Bangladesh	12	*Iran, Islamic Rep.*	86	Poland	80
Belarus	88	Ireland	110	Portugal	106
Belgium	123	†Israel	112	Puerto Rico	102
Benin	29	Italy	118	Romania	61
Bolivia	49	Jamaica	68	Russian Federation	81
Botswana	84	Japan	131	Rwanda	11
Brazil	89	Jordan	62	*Saudi Arabia*	107
Bulgaria	60	Kazakhstan	71	Senegal	48
Burkina Faso	19	Kenya	15	Sierra Leone	4
Burundi	6	Korea, Rep.	105	†Singapore	119
Cameroon	50	†Kuwait	117	Slovak Republic	75
Canada	120	Kyrgyz Republic	52	Slovenia	101
Central African Republic	28	Lao PDR	18	South Africa	90
Chad	10	Latvia	76	Spain	111
Chile	94	Lesotho	41	Sri Lanka	39
China	33	Lithuania	66	Sweden	127
Colombia	67	Macedonia, FYR	51	Switzerland	132
Congo	54	Madagascar	13	Tajikistan	32
Costa Rica	78	Malawi	9	Tanzania	2
Côte d'Ivoire	40	Malaysia	93	Thailand	77
Czech Republic	83	Mali	16	Togo	24
Denmark	130	Mauritania	35	Trinidad and Tobago	97
Dominican Republic	64	Mauritius	91	Tunisia	72
Ecuador	63	Mexico	96	Turkey	85
Egypt, Arab Rep.	43	Moldova	57	*Turkmenistan*[c]	108
El Salvador	65	Mongolia	27	Uganda	7
Estonia	92	Morocco	56	Ukraine	79
Ethiopia[a]	3	Mozambique	1	†United Arab Emirates	122
Finland	116	*Myanmar*	44	United Kingdom	115
France	124	Namibia	74	United States	128
Gabon	100	Nepal	8	Uruguay	98
Gambia, The	25	Netherlands	121	Uzbekistan	55
Georgia	37	New Zealand	109	Venezuela	87
Germany[b]	126	Nicaragua	23	Viet Nam	5
Ghana	30	Niger	17	*Yemen, Rep.*	45
Greece	104	Nigeria	21	Zambia	26
Guatemala	58	Norway	129	Zimbabwe	33

Note: Economies with sparse data or with population of more than 30,000 and fewer than 1 million are shown in Table 1a; however, data for these economies are included in the country groups calculations of totals and weighted averages in the main tables. For data comparability and coverage throughout the tables, see the technical notes.

a. In all tables, data exclude Eritrea unless otherwise noted.

b. In all tables data refer to the unified Germany, unless otherwise noted.

c. In all tables, Turkmenistan should be classified as lower-middle-income.

Introduction to World Development Indicators

THIS EIGHTEENTH EDITION OF THE WORLD Development Indicators provides economic, social, and natural resource indicators for selected periods or years for 209 economies and various analytical and geographic groups of economies. Although most of the data collected by the World Bank are on low- and middle-income economies, comparable data for high-income economies are readily available and are also included in the tables. Additional information may be found in *The World Bank Atlas, World Tables, World Debt Tables,* and *Social Indicators of Development.* These data are now also available on diskettes in the World Bank's Socioeconomic Time-series Access and Retrieval System—☆STARS☆.

Changes in this edition

Unlike previous years, in this edition the demographic data are from the U.N. Population Division, although supplemented in a few cases from national sources. Since these data do not include *hypothetical stationary population* and *projected year of reaching net reproduction rate (NRR) of 1,* these columns have been dropped from Tables 25 and 26 respectively. In Table 32, the *percentage of households with electricity* has been replaced with *per capita electricity production in kwh.* Trade data presented in tables 13 to 15 are from the United Nations Conference on Trade and Development (UNCTAD); therefore, coverage, growth rates, shares, etc. differ from previous editions.

Classification of economies

As in the Report itself, the main criterion used to classify economies and broadly distinguish different stages of economic development is GNP per capita. This year the per capita income groups are low-income, $695 or less in 1993 (45 economies); middle-income, $696 to $8,625 (63 economies); and high-income, $8,626 or more (24 economies). Economies with populations of fewer than 1 million and those with sparse data are not shown separately in the main tables but they are included in the aggregates. Basic indicators for these economies may be found in Table 1a.

Further classification of economies is by geographic location. For a list of economies in each group, see the tables on classification of economies at the back of this book. Aggregates for severely indebted middle-income economies are also presented.

Methodology

The World Bank continually reviews methodology in an effort to improve the international comparability and analytical significance of the indicators. Differences between data in this year's and last year's editions reflect not only updates for the countries but also revisions to historical series and changes in methodology.

All dollar figures are current U.S. dollars unless otherwise stated. The various methods used for converting from national currency figures are described in the technical notes.

Summary measures

The summary measures in the colored bands on each table are totals (indicated by *t*), weighted averages (*w*), or median values (*m*) calculated for groups of economies. Countries for which individual estimates are not shown, because of size, nonreporting, or insufficient history, have been implicitly included by assuming they follow the trend of reporting countries during such periods. This gives a more consistent aggregate measure by standardizing country coverage for each period shown. Group aggregates include countries for which country-specific data do not appear in the tables. Where missing information accounts for a third or more of the overall estimate, however, the group measure is reported as not available. The weightings used for computing the summary measures are stated in each technical note.

Terminology and data coverage

In these notes the term "country" does not imply political independence but may refer to any territory whose authorities present for it separate social or economic statistics.

The unified Germany does not yet have a fully merged statistical system. Throughout the tables, data for Germany are footnoted to explain coverage; most economic data before 1990 refer to the former Federal Republic, but demographic and social data generally refer to the unified Germany. The data for China do not include Taiwan, China, but footnotes to Tables 13, 14, 15, and 17 provide estimates of international transactions for Taiwan, China. Data presented for Ethiopia exclude Eritrea, unless otherwise stated.

Table content

The indicators in Tables 1 and 1a give a summary profile of economies. Data in the other tables fall into the following broad areas: production, domestic absorption, fiscal and monetary accounts, core international transactions, external finance, human resources development, and environmentally sustainable development. The table format of this edition follows that used in previous years. In each group, economies are listed in ascending order of GNP per capita, except that those for which no such figure can be calculated are italicized and listed in alphabetical order at the end of the group deemed appropriate. This order is used in all tables except Table 18, which covers only high-income OPEC and OECD countries. The alphabetical list in the key shows the reference number for each economy; here, too, italics

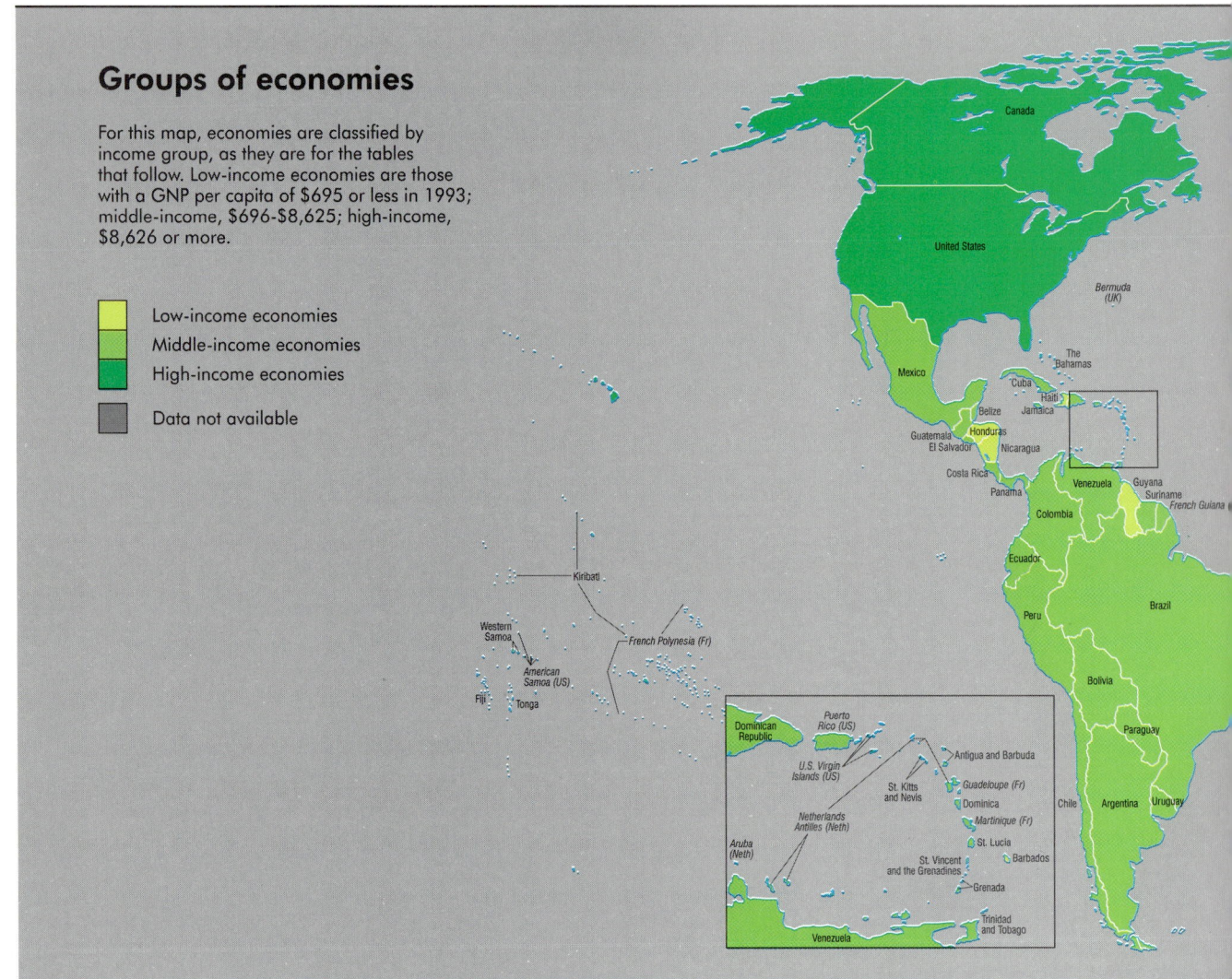

Groups of economies

For this map, economies are classified by income group, as they are for the tables that follow. Low-income economies are those with a GNP per capita of $695 or less in 1993; middle-income, $696-$8,625; high-income, $8,626 or more.

- Low-income economies
- Middle-income economies
- High-income economies
- Data not available

indicate economies with no current estimates of GNP per capita. Economies in the high-income group marked by the symbol † are those classified by the United Nations or otherwise regarded by their authorities as developing.

Technical notes

The technical notes and the footnotes to tables should be referred to in any use of the data. The notes outline the methods, concepts, definitions, and data sources used in compiling the tables. A bibliography at the end of the notes lists the data sources, which contain some of the comprehensive definitions and descriptions of the concepts used. Country notes to the *World Tables* provide additional explanations of sources used, breaks in comparability, and other exceptions to standard statistical practices that World Bank staff have identified in national accounts and international transactions.

Comments and questions relating to the World Development Indicators should be addressed to: Development Data Group, International Economics Department, The World Bank, 1818 H Street, N.W., Washington, D.C. 20433.

Population density

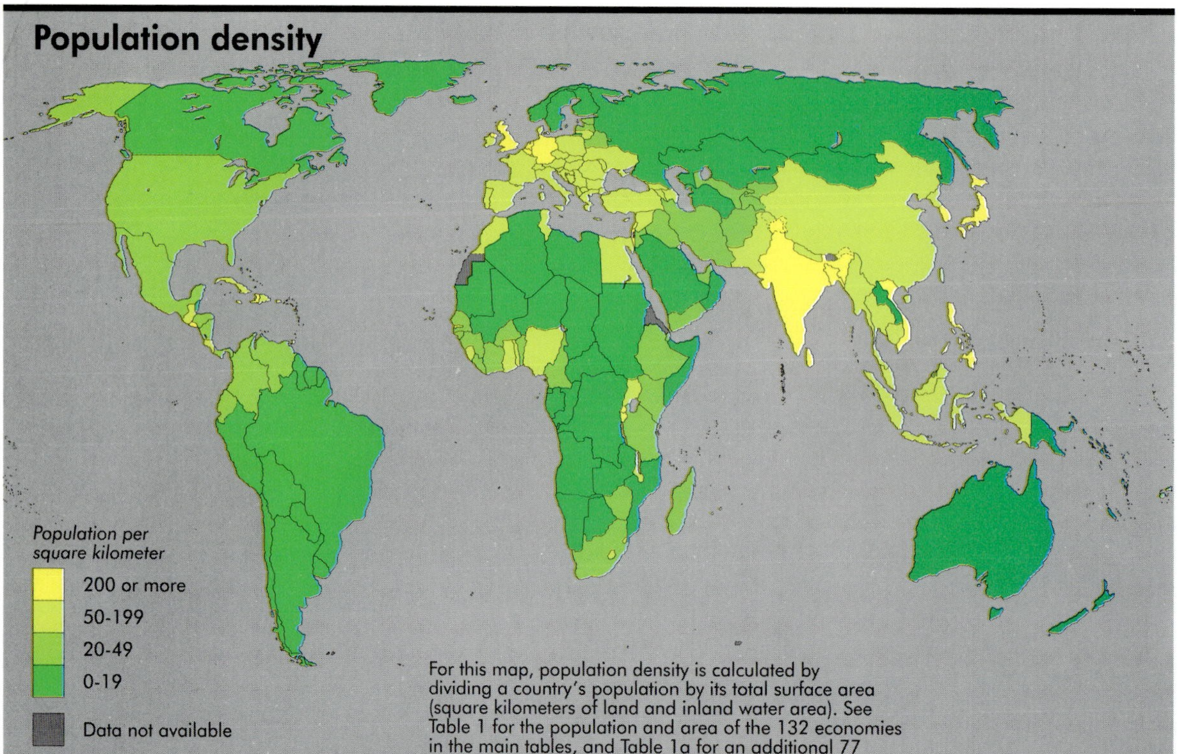

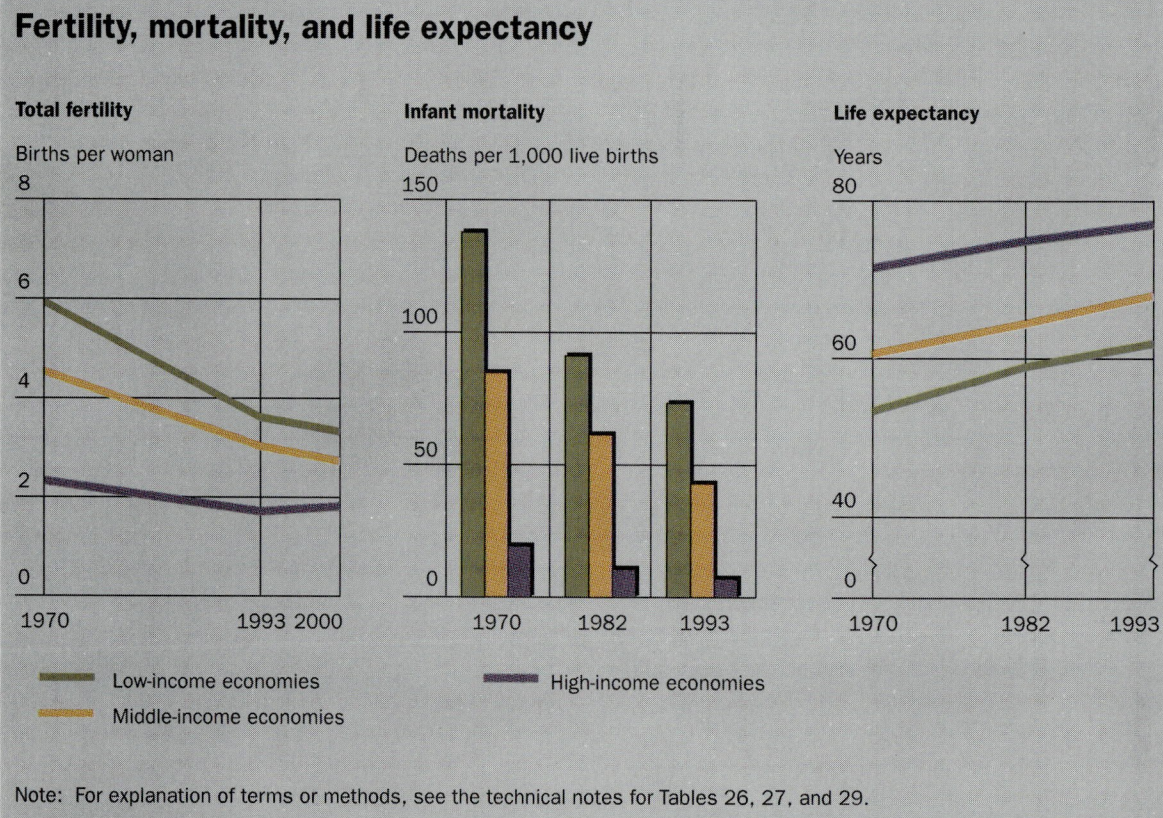

Population per square kilometer

- 200 or more
- 50-199
- 20-49
- 0-19
- Data not available

For this map, population density is calculated by dividing a country's population by its total surface area (square kilometers of land and inland water area). See Table 1 for the population and area of the 132 economies in the main tables, and Table 1a for an additional 77 economies.

Fertility, mortality, and life expectancy

Total fertility

Births per woman

1970 — 1993 2000

Infant mortality

Deaths per 1,000 live births

1970 — 1982 — 1993

Life expectancy

Years

1970 — 1982 — 1993

Legend:
- Low-income economies
- Middle-income economies
- High-income economies

Note: For explanation of terms or methods, see the technical notes for Tables 26, 27, and 29.

Female labor force participation rate

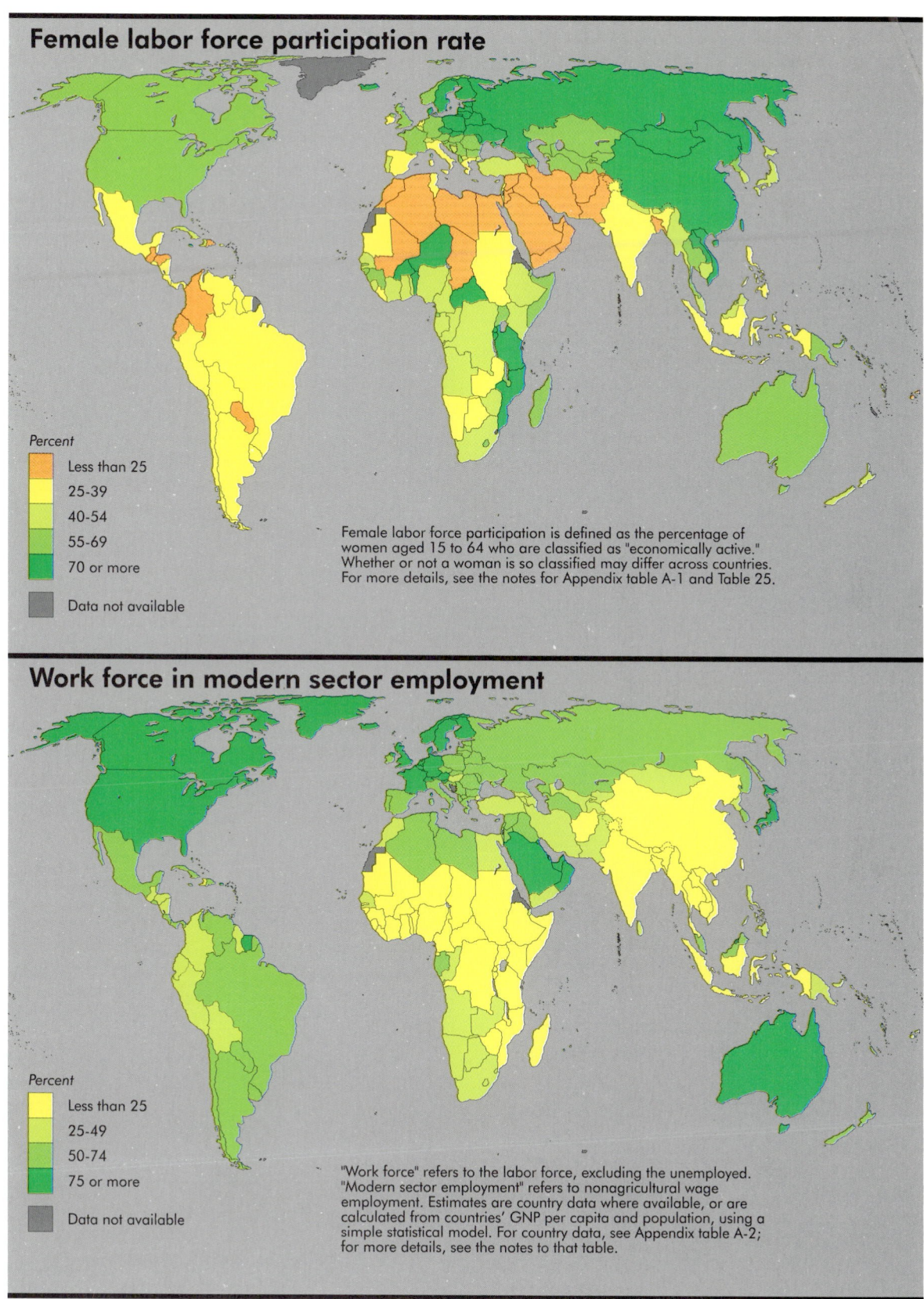

Percent

- Less than 25
- 25-39
- 40-54
- 55-69
- 70 or more
- Data not available

Female labor force participation is defined as the percentage of women aged 15 to 64 who are classified as "economically active." Whether or not a woman is so classified may differ across countries. For more details, see the notes for Appendix table A-1 and Table 25.

Work force in modern sector employment

Percent

- Less than 25
- 25-49
- 50-74
- 75 or more
- Data not available

"Work force" refers to the labor force, excluding the unemployed. "Modern sector employment" refers to nonagricultural wage employment. Estimates are country data where available, or are calculated from countries' GNP per capita and population, using a simple statistical model. For country data, see Appendix table A-2; for more details, see the notes to that table.

Table 1. Basic indicators

		Population (millions) mid-1993	Area (thousands of sq. km)	GNP per capita[a]		Avg. annual rate of inflation (%)		Life expect. at birth (years) 1993	Adult illiteracy (%)	
				Dollars 1993	Avg. ann. growth (%), 1980–93	1970–80	1980–93		Female 1990	Total 1990
	Low-income economies	3,092.7 t	39,093 t	380 w	3.7 w	7.3 w	14.1 w	62 w	53 w	41 w
	Excluding China & India	1,016.1 t	26,244 t	300 w	0.1 w	13.4 w	27.1 w	56 w	61 w	49 w
1	Mozambique	15.1	802	90	−1.5	. .	42.3	46	79	67
2	Tanzania[b]	28.0	945	90	0.1	14.1	24.3	52	. .	. .
3	Ethiopia	51.9	1,097	100	. .	. .	. .	48	. .	. .
4	Sierra Leone	4.5	72	150	−1.5	12.5	61.6	39	89	79
5	Viet Nam	71.3	332	170	. .	. .	. .	66	16	12
6	Burundi	6.0	28	180	0.9	11.8	4.6	50	60	50
7	Uganda	18.0	236	180	. .	. .	. .	45	65	52
8	Nepal	20.8	141	190	2.0	8.5	11.5	54	87	74
9	Malawi	10.5	118	200	−1.2	8.8	15.5	45	. .	. .
10	Chad	6.0	1,284	210	3.2	7.7	0.7	48	82	70
11	Rwanda	7.6	26	210	−1.2	14.3	3.4	. .	63	50
12	Bangladesh	115.2	144	220	2.1	20.8	8.6	56	78	65
13	Madagascar	13.9	587	220	−2.6	9.9	16.1	57	27	20
14	Guinea-Bissau	1.0	36	240	2.8	5.7	58.7	44	76	64
15	Kenya	25.3	580	270	0.3	10.1	9.9	58	42	31
16	Mali	10.1	1,240	270	−1.0	9.9	4.4	46	76	68
17	Niger	8.6	1,267	270	−4.1	10.9	1.3	47	83	72
18	Lao PDR	4.6	237	280	. .	. .	. .	52	. .	. .
19	Burkina Faso	9.8	274	300	0.8	8.6	3.3	47	91	82
20	India	898.2	3,288	300	3.0	8.4	8.7	61	66	52
21	Nigeria	105.3	924	300	−0.1	15.2	20.6	51	61	49
22	Albania	3.4	29	340	−3.2	. .	5.6	72	. .	. .
23	Nicaragua	4.1	130	340	−5.7	12.6	664.6	67	. .	. .
24	Togo	3.9	57	340	−2.1	8.9	3.7	55	69	57
25	Gambia, The	1.0	11	350	−0.2	10.6	16.2	45	84	73
26	Zambia	8.9	753	380	−3.1	7.6	58.9	48	35	27
27	Mongolia	2.3	1,567	390	0.2	. .	13.8	64	. .	. .
28	Central African Republic	3.2	623	400	−1.6	12.1	4.2	50	75	62
29	Benin	5.1	113	430	−0.4	10.3	1.4	48	84	77
30	Ghana	16.4	239	430	0.1	35.2	37.0	56	49	40
31	Pakistan	122.8	796	430	3.1	13.4	7.4	62	79	65
32	Tajikistan[c]	5.8	143	470	−3.6	1.4	26.0	70	. .	2
33	China	1,178.4	9,561	490[d]	8.2	0.6	7.0	69	38	27
34	Guinea	6.3	246	500	. .	. .	. .	45	87	76
35	Mauritania	2.2	1,026	500	−0.8	9.9	8.2	52	79	66
36	Zimbabwe	10.7	391	520	−0.3	9.4	14.4	53	40	33
37	Georgia[c]	5.4	70	580	−6.6	. .	40.7	73	. .	1
38	Honduras	5.3	112	600	−0.3	8.1	8.2	68	29	27
39	Sri Lanka	17.9	66	600	2.7	12.3	11.1	72	17	12
40	Côte d'Ivoire	13.3	322	630	−4.6	13.0	1.5	51	60	46
41	Lesotho	1.9	30	650	−0.5	9.7	13.8	61	. .	. .
42	Armenia[c]	3.7	30	660	−4.2	0.7	26.9	73	. .	1
43	Egypt, Arab Rep.	56.4	1,001	660	2.8	9.6	13.6	64	66	52
44	*Myanmar*	44.6	677	. .	. .	11.4	16.5	58	28	19
45	*Yemen, Rep.*	13.2	528	. .	. .	. .	. .	51	74	62
	Middle-income economies	1,596.3 t	62,452 t	2,480 w	0.2 w	22.1 w	90.1 w	68 w	. .	17 w
	Lower-middle-income	1,095.8 t	40,604 t	1,590 w	−0.5 w	8.3 w	35.2 w	67 w	. .	19 w
46	Azerbaijan	7.4	87	730	−3.5	1.7	28.2	71	. .	3
47	Indonesia	187.2	1,905	740	4.2	21.5	8.5	63	32	23
48	Senegal	7.9	197	750	0.0	8.5	4.9	50	75	62
49	Bolivia	7.1	1,099	760	−0.7	21.0	187.1	60	29	23
50	Cameroon	12.5	475	820	−2.2	9.0	4.0	57	57	46
51	Macedonia, FYR	2.1	26	820	. .	. .	. .	72	. .	. .
52	Kyrgyz Republic[c]	4.6	199	850	0.1	0.8	28.6	69	. .	3
53	Philippines	64.8	300	850	−0.6	13.3	13.6	67	11	10
54	Congo	2.4	342	950	−0.3	8.4	−0.6	51	56	43
55	Uzbekistan[c]	21.9	447	970	−0.2	1.0	24.5	69	. .	3
56	Morocco	25.9	447	1,040	1.2	8.3	6.6	64	62	51
57	Moldova[c]	4.4	34	1,060	−2.0	0.9	32.4	68	. .	4
58	Guatemala	10.0	109	1,100	−1.2	10.5	16.8	65	53	45
59	Papua New Guinea	4.1	463	1,130	0.6	9.1	4.8	56	62	48
60	Bulgaria	8.9	111	1,140	0.5	. .	15.9	71	. .	. .
61	Romania	22.8	238	1,140	−2.4	. .	22.4	70	. .	. .
62	Jordan[e]	4.1	89	1,190	. .	. .	. .	70	30	20
63	Ecuador	11.0	284	1,200	0.0	13.8	40.4	69	16	14
64	Dominican Republic	7.5	49	1,230	0.7	9.1	25.0	70	18	17
65	El Salvador	5.5	21	1,320	0.2	10.7	17.0	67	30	27
66	Lithuania[c]	3.7	65	1,320	−2.8	. .	35.2	70	. .	. .
67	Colombia	35.7	1,139	1,400	1.5	22.3	24.9	70	14	13
68	Jamaica	2.4	11	1,440	−0.3	17.0	22.4	74	1	2
69	Peru	22.9	1,285	1,490	−2.7	30.1	316.1	66	21	15
70	Paraguay	4.7	407	1,510	−0.7	12.7	25.0	70	12	10
71	Kazakhstan[c]	17.0	2,717	1,560	−1.6	0.7	35.2	70	. .	3
72	Tunisia	8.7	164	1,720	1.2	8.7	7.1	68	44	35

Note: For other economies see Table 1a. For data comparability and coverage, see the technical notes. Figures in italics are for years other than those specified.

		Population (millions) mid-1993	Area (thousands of sq. km)	GNP per capita[a]		Avg. annual rate of inflation (%)		Life expect. at birth (years) 1993	Adult illiteracy (%)	
				Dollars 1993	Avg. ann. growth (%), 1980–93	1970–80	1980–93		Female 1990	Total 1990
73	Algeria	26.7	2,382	1,780	−0.8	14.5	13.2	67	55	43
74	Namibia	1.5	824	1,820	0.7	..	11.9	59	..	..
75	Slovak Republic	5.3	49	1,950	..	..	..	71	..	..
76	Latvia[c]	2.6	65	2,010	−0.6	..	23.8	69	..	..
77	Thailand	58.1	513	2,110	6.4	9.2	4.3	69	10	7
78	Costa Rica	3.3	51	2,150	1.1	15.3	22.1	76	7	7
79	Ukraine[c]	51.6	604	2,210	0.2	0.1	37.2	69	..	2
80	Poland	38.3	313	2,260	0.4	..	69.3	71	..	..
81	Russian Federation[c]	148.7	17,075	2,340	−1.0	−0.1	35.4	65	..	2
82	Panama	2.5	76	2,600	−0.7	7.7	2.1	73	12	12
83	Czech Republic	10.3	79	2,710	..	..	..	71	..	..
84	Botswana	1.4	582	2,790[f]	6.2	11.6	12.3	65	35	26
85	Turkey	59.6	779	2,970[f]	2.4	29.6	53.5	67	29	19
86	*Iran, Islamic Rep.*	64.2	1,648	..	..	..	*17.1*	68	57	46
	Upper-middle-income	500.5 t	21,848 t	4,370 w	0.9 w	36.3 w	158.7 w	69 w	17 w	14 w
87	Venezuela	20.9	912	2,840	−0.7	14.0	23.9	72	17	8
88	Belarus[c]	10.2	208	2,870	2.4	0.0	30.9	70	..	2
89	Brazil	156.5	8,512	2,930	0.3	38.6	423.4	67	20	19
90	South Africa	39.7	1,221	2,980	−0.2	13.0	14.7	63	..	..
91	Mauritius	1.1	2	3,030	5.5	15.3	8.8	70	..	..
92	Estonia[c]	1.6	45	3,080	−2.2	..	29.8	69	..	..
93	Malaysia	19.0	330	3,140	3.5	7.3	2.2	71	30	22
94	Chile	13.8	757	3,170	3.6	186.2	20.1	74	7	7
95	Hungary	10.2	93	3,350	1.2	3.4	12.8	69	..	..
96	Mexico	90.0	1,958	3,610	−0.5	18.1	57.9	71	15	13
97	Trinidad and Tobago	1.3	5	3,830	−2.8	18.5	4.8	72	..	..
98	Uruguay	3.1	177	3,830	−0.1	63.7	66.7	73	4	4
99	Oman	2.0	212	4,850	3.4	28.0	−2.3	70	..	..
100	Gabon	1.0	268	4,960	−1.6	17.5	1.5	54	52	39
101	Slovenia	1.9	20	6,490	..	..	..	73	..	..
102	Puerto Rico	3.6	9	7,000	1.0	6.5	3.2	75	..	..
103	Argentina	33.8	2,767	7,220	−0.5	134.2	374.3	72	5	5
104	Greece	10.4	132	7,390	0.9	14.3	17.3	78	11	7
105	Korea, Rep.	44.1	99	7,660	8.2	19.5	6.3	71	7	g
106	Portugal	9.8	92	9,130[f]	3.3	16.9	16.4	75	19	15
107	*Saudi Arabia*	17.4	2,150	..	−3.6	24.5	*−2.1*	70	52	38
108	*Turkmenistan[c]*	3.9	488	..	..	2.4	*16.5*	65	..	2
	Low- and middle-income	4,689.0 t	101,544 t	1,090 w	0.9 w	18.5 w	72.8 w	64 w	..	33 w
	Sub-Saharan Africa	559.0 t	24,274 t	520 w	−0.8 w	13.8 w	16.1 w	52 w	62 w	50 w
	East Asia & Pacific	1,713.9 t	16,369 t	820 w	6.4 w	9.7 w	7.1 w	68 w	34 w	24 w
	South Asia	1,194.4 t	5,133 t	310 w	3.0 w	9.7 w	8.6 w	60 w	69 w	54 w
	Europe and Central Asia	494.6 t	24,242 t	2,450 w	−0.3 w	4.6 w	35.3 w	69 w	..	5 w
	Middle East & N. Africa	262.5 t	11,015 t	..	−2.4 w	16.9 w	10.7 w	66 w	57 w	..
	Latin America & Caribbean	466.3 t	20,507 t	2,950 w	−0.1 w	46.7 w	245.0 w	69 w	18 w	15 w
	Severely indebted	385.8 t	17,968 t	2,640 w	−1.1 w	52.4 w	302.7 w	67 w	27 w	23 w
	High-income economies	812.4 t	32,145 t	23,090 w	2.2 w	9.5 w	4.3 w	77 w	..	..
109	New Zealand	3.5	271	12,600	0.7	12.5	8.5	76	g	g
110	Ireland	3.5	70	13,000	3.6	14.2	4.8	75	g	g
111	Spain	39.5	505	13,590	2.7	16.1	8.4	78	7	5
112	† Israel	5.2	21	13,920	2.0	39.6	70.4	77	..	..
113	Australia	17.6	7,713	17,500	1.6	11.8	6.1	78	g	g
114	† Hong Kong	5.8	1	18,060[h]	5.4[h]	9.2	7.9	79	..	..
115	United Kingdom	57.9	245	18,060	2.3	14.5	5.6	76	g	g
116	Finland	5.1	338	19,300	1.5	12.3	5.8	76	g	g
117	† Kuwait	1.8	18	19,360	−4.3	21.9	..	75	33	27
118	Italy	57.1	301	19,840	2.1	15.6	8.8	78	g	g
119	† Singapore	2.8	1	19,850	6.1	5.9	2.5	75	g	g
120	Canada	28.8	9,976	19,970	1.4	8.7	3.9	78	g	g
121	Netherlands	15.3	37	20,950	1.7	7.9	1.7	78	g	g
122	† United Arab Emirates	1.8	84	21,430	−4.4	..	..	74	..	..
123	Belgium	10.0	31	21,650	1.9	7.8	4.0	77	g	g
124	France	57.5	552	22,490	1.6	10.2	5.1	77	g	g
125	Austria	7.9	84	23,510	2.0	6.5	3.6	76	g	g
126	Germany	80.7	357	23,560	2.1[i]	5.1[i]	2.8[i]	76	g	g
127	Sweden	8.7	450	24,740	1.3	10.0	6.9	78	g	g
128	United States	257.8	9,809	24,740	1.7	7.5	3.8	76	g	g
129	Norway	4.3	324	25,970	2.2	8.4	4.6	77	g	g
130	Denmark	5.2	43	26,730	2.0	10.1	4.6	75	g	g
131	Japan	124.5	378	31,490	3.4	8.5	1.5	80	g	g
132	Switzerland	7.1	41	35,760	1.1	5.0	3.8	78	g	g
	World	5,501.5 t	133,690 t	4,420 w	1.2 w	11.4 w	19.6 w	66 w	..	33 w

† Economies classified by the United Nations or otherwise regarded by their authorities as developing.   a. See the technical notes.   b. In all tables GDP and GNP data cover mainland Tanzania only.   c. Estimates for economies of the former Soviet Union are preliminary, and their classification will be kept under review. Note that in all tables, Turkmenistan should be classified as lower-middle-income.   d. Preliminary estimate, see the technical note to Table 1, paragraph 8.   e. In all tables, data for Jordan cover the East Bank only.   f. Reflect recent revision of 1993 GNP per capita from $2,590 to $2,790 for Botswana; from $2,120 to $2,970 for Turkey; and from $7,890 to $9,130 for Portugal.   g. According to UNESCO, illiteracy is less than 5 percent.   h. Data refer to GDP.   i. Data refer to the Federal Republic of Germany before unification.

Table 2. Growth of production

		GDP		Agriculture		Industry		Manufacturing[a]		Services, etc.[b]	
		1970–80	1980–93	1970–80	1980–93	1970–80	1980–93	1970–80	1980–93	1970–80	1980–93
	Low-income economies	4.3 w	5.7 w	2.0 w	3.4 w	6.3 w	7.6 w	7.3 w	8.6 w	5.5 w	6.3 w
	Excluding China & India	4.4 w	2.9 w	..	2.2 w	5.3 w	2.2 w	..	..	6.5 w	3.8 w
1	Mozambique	..	1.0	..	1.4	..	–4.4	..	..	..	3.4
2	Tanzania	3.0	3.6	0.7	4.9	2.6	2.5	3.7	0.9	9.0	1.6
3	Ethiopia	..	1.8	..	..	..	..	..	..	..	..
4	Sierra Leone	1.6	1.1	6.0	2.8	–3.2	–1.5	–2.1	–4.2	2.3	1.8
5	Viet Nam[c]	..	..	..	..	..	..	..	..	..	..
6	Burundi	3.1	*3.6*	2.2	*2.7*	10.5	*4.4*	2.7	*0.5*	2.5	*4.9*
7	Uganda	..	3.8	..	..	..	..	..	..	..	..
8	Nepal	2.0	5.0	0.5	3.6	..	..	..	..	..	..
9	Malawi	5.8	3.0	4.4	2.1	*6.3*	3.3	..	3.6	*7.1*	3.5
10	Chad[c]	0.1	4.8	*–0.4*	4.0	*–2.1*	5.0	..	..	*2.2*	5.8
11	Rwanda	..	1.1	..	–0.2	..	0.6	..	1.7	..	3.5
12	Bangladesh[c]	2.3	4.2	0.6	2.6	5.2	5.2	5.1	3.4	3.8	5.4
13	Madagascar	0.5	0.9	0.4	2.4	0.6	1.0	..	..	0.6	0.3
14	Guinea-Bissau	*2.4*	4.8	*–1.2*	6.1	*2.1*	0.0	..	..	*11.8*	4.9
15	Kenya	6.4	3.8	4.8	2.6	8.6	3.8	9.9	4.7	6.8	4.7
16	Mali[c]	4.7	1.9	4.2	4.2	2.0	2.8	..	..	5.9	–0.3
17	Niger[c]	0.6	–0.6	3.7	..	11.3	..	..	..	1.4	..
18	Lao PDR[c]	..	4.8	..	..	..	..	..	..	..	..
19	Burkina Faso	*4.4*	3.7	*1.0*	2.8	*2.5*	3.8	*4.1*	3.1	*19.7*	4.8
20	India	3.4	5.2	1.8	3.0	4.5	6.2	4.6	6.3	4.6	6.4
21	Nigeria	4.6	2.7	–0.1	3.6	7.3	0.8	5.2	..	9.6	4.2
22	Albania	..	–1.8	..	–0.2	..	–4.0	..	..	..	–0.4
23	Nicaragua[c]	1.2	–1.8	1.9	–1.8	1.1	–2.9	2.8	–3.1	0.6	–1.4
24	Togo[c]	4.0	0.7	1.9	4.9	7.7	0.0	..	1.2	3.6	–2.2
25	Gambia, The	4.5	2.4	1.6	0.8	6.7	5.5	..	..	6.4	3.0
26	Zambia[c]	1.4	0.9	2.1	*2.5*	1.5	*1.3*	2.4	*4.2*	1.2	*0.0*
27	Mongolia[c]	..	3.8	..	..	..	..	..	..	..	..
28	Central African Republic	2.4	1.0	1.9	2.0	4.1	2.4	..	..	2.4	–0.5
29	Benin[c]	2.2	*2.7*	*1.8*	*4.9*	*1.4*	*1.7*	..	*5.1*	*2.8*	*1.5*
30	Ghana[c]	–0.1	3.5	–0.3	1.3	–1.0	4.2	–0.5	4.1	1.1	6.8
31	Pakistan	4.9	6.0	2.3	4.4	6.1	7.2	5.4	7.3	6.3	6.3
32	Tajikistan	–5.1	–0.8	..	..	..	..	..	..	..	..
33	China[c]	5.5	9.6	2.6	5.3	8.9	11.5	10.8	11.1	5.3	11.1
34	Guinea[c]	..	3.7	..	..	..	..	..	0.4	..	..
35	Mauritania	1.3	2.0	–1.0	1.7	0.5	3.6	..	..	3.6	1.3
36	Zimbabwe	1.6	2.7	*0.6*	1.5	*1.1*	2.8	*2.8*	2.2	*2.5*	3.0
37	Georgia[c]	6.5	–6.1	..	0.8	..	–1.8	..	–2.2	..	–2.3
38	Honduras	5.8	2.9	2.2	3.1	6.7	3.6	6.9	3.6	7.1	2.5
39	Sri Lanka	4.1	4.0	2.8	2.1	3.4	5.0	1.9	6.7	5.7	4.6
40	Côte d'Ivoire	6.8	0.1	2.7	–0.1	9.1	2.5	..	..	10.3	–1.3
41	Lesotho	8.6	5.5	*0.2*	–0.5	*27.8*	9.3	*18.0*	12.2	*13.6*	5.0
42	Armenia[c]	7.3	–2.8	..	–5.2	..	3.0	..	..	..	5.4
43	Egypt, Arab Rep.	9.5	4.3	2.8	1.3	9.4	1.6	..	..	17.5	6.9
44	*Myanmar*	4.7	*0.8*	4.3	*0.6*	4.7	*1.4*	4.2	*0.1*	5.4	*0.9*
45	*Yemen, Rep.*	..	..	..	..	..	..	..	..	..	..
	Middle-income economies	5.5 w	2.1 w	..	1.6 w	..	2.0 w	..	..	..	2.8 w
	Lower-middle-income	5.1 w	1.6 w	..	1.4 w	..	1.8 w	..	..	..	2.9 w
46	Azerbaijan[c]	6.9	–2.2	..	..	..	..	..	..	..	..
47	Indonesia[c]	7.2	5.8	4.1	3.2	9.6	6.3	14.0	11.8	7.7	6.9
48	Senegal[c]	2.3	2.8	1.3	2.1	5.3	3.6	2.4	4.2	2.0	2.7
49	Bolivia[c]	4.5	1.1	3.9	..	2.6	..	6.0	..	7.6	..
50	Cameroon[c]	8.0	0.0	4.0	–1.1	10.9	–0.3	7.0	9.0	9.9	1.0
51	Macedonia, FYR	..	..	..	..	..	..	..	..	..	..
52	Kyrgyz Republic[c]	4.4	1.9	..	..	..	..	..	..	..	..
53	Philippines[c]	6.0	1.4	4.0	1.2	8.2	–0.1	6.1	0.8	5.1	2.9
54	Congo[c]	5.8	2.7	2.5	2.6	10.3	4.3	..	5.1	4.5	1.6
55	Uzbekistan[c]	6.3	2.2	..	0.2	..	4.3	..	5.6	..	5.1
56	Morocco[c]	5.6	3.7	1.1	4.1	6.5	2.8	..	3.9	7.0	4.1
57	Moldova[c]	5.1	–1.3	..	–5.1	..	–1.3	..	..	..	3.9
58	Guatemala[c]	5.8	1.7	4.6	1.8	7.7	1.0	6.2	–1.1	5.6	1.9
59	Papua New Guinea[c]	2.2	3.1	2.8	1.9	..	5.1	..	0.7	..	2.1
60	Bulgaria	..	0.9	..	–2.0	..	1.1	..	..	..	2.4
61	Romania	..	*–2.5*	..	0.6	..	–4.4	..	..	..	*1.1*
62	Jordan	..	*1.2*	..	..	..	..	..	..	..	..
63	Ecuador[c]	9.5	2.4	2.8	4.5	13.9	1.4	10.5	0.3	9.4	2.4
64	Dominican Republic[c]	6.5	2.8	3.1	0.4	8.3	1.6	6.5	1.0	7.2	4.1
65	El Salvador[c]	4.2	1.6	3.4	0.4	5.2	1.9	4.1	*2.1*	4.0	1.7
66	Lithuania[c]	4.9	–2.2	..	..	..	..	..	..	..	..
67	Colombia	5.4	3.7	4.6	3.2	5.1	4.5	5.8	3.5	5.9	3.4
68	Jamaica[c]	–1.3	2.3	0.3	1.5	–3.4	2.7	–2.1	2.0	1.2	2.1
69	Peru[c]	3.5	–0.5	..	..	..	..	..	..	..	..
70	Paraguay[c]	8.5	2.8	6.2	3.4	11.2	0.7	7.9	2.3	8.6	3.6
71	Kazakhstan[c]	4.6	–0.6	..	0.7	..	1.2	..	0.1	..	5.5
72	Tunisia	6.8	3.7	4.1	4.8	8.7	3.4	10.4	7.3	6.6	3.5

Note: For data comparability and coverage, see the technical notes. Figures in italics are for years other than those specified.

		Average annual growth rate (%)									
		GDP		Agriculture		Industry		Manufacturing[a]		Services, etc.[b]	
		1970–80	1980–93	1970–80	1980–93	1970–80	1980–93	1970–80	1980–93	1970–80	1980–93
73	Algeria	4.6	2.1	7.5	4.5	3.8	0.8	7.6	–2.2	4.8	2.7
74	Namibia	..	1.3	..	–0.1	..	–0.5	..	5.4.	2.6	3.5
75	Slovak Republic [c]	..	..	..	..	..	..	..	..	..	..
76	Latvia	..	–0.3	..	–0.9	..	–1.7	..	–2.4	..	0.9
77	Thailand [c]	7.1	8.2	4.4	3.8	9.7	11.0	10.5	10.8	7.0	7.7
78	Costa Rica [c]	5.7	3.6	2.5	3.6	8.2	3.3	..	3.6	5.8	3.7
79	Ukraine [c]	4.5	0.5	..	–0.9	..	0.5	..	3.4	..	1.3
80	Poland	..	0.7	..	–0.5	..	–3.2	..	..	..	2.7
81	Russian Federation [c]	5.6	–0.5	..	–0.9	..	0.2	..	..	..	2.0
82	Panama [c]	4.4	1.3	1.8	2.6	3.9	0.3	2.8	0.7	5.0	1.5
83	Czech Republic [c]	..	..	..	..	..	..	..	..	..	..
84	Botswana [c]	14.5	9.6	8.3	3.5	17.6	9.2	22.9	8.6	14.8	11.6
85	Turkey	5.7	4.6	3.4	2.6	6.6	5.9	6.1	7.0	6.3	4.6
86	*Iran, Islamic Rep.*	..	2.6	..	4.6	..	4.6	..	6.0	..	0.9
	Upper-middle-income	5.9 w	2.7 w	3.2 w	1.8 w	6.1 w	2.3 w	6.6 w	2.5 w	6.3 w	2.9 w
87	Venezuela [c]	3.5	2.1	3.4	2.3	0.5	2.5	5.7	1.3	6.3	1.6
88	Belarus [c]	6.9	2.9	..	–0.8	..	4.7	..	5.0	..	2.7
89	Brazil	8.1	2.1	4.2	2.5	9.4	0.7	9.0	0.2	7.8	3.3
90	South Africa	3.2	0.9	3.2	1.8	2.7	–0.2	4.7	–0.4	3.7	1.9
91	Mauritius	6.8	6.0	–3.3	1.9	10.4	8.8	7.1	9.8	10.9	5.5
92	Estonia [c]	..	–2.6	..	–2.9	..	–0.6	..	..	..	–2.6
93	Malaysia [c]	7.9	6.2	5.0	3.5	8.7	8.2	11.7	10.3	9.1	5.5
94	Chile [c]	1.8	5.1	3.1	5.5	0.2	4.5	–0.8	4.4	2.9	5.4
95	Hungary [c]	4.6	–0.1	2.8	–0.8	4.5	–1.6	..	..	5.3	1.5
96	Mexico [c]	6.3	1.6	3.2	0.6	7.2	1.7	7.0	2.1	6.3	1.6
97	Trinidad and Tobago	5.9	–3.6	–1.4	–3.0	5.6	–4.1	1.7	–6.7	7.3	–3.3
98	Uruguay [c]	3.1	1.3	0.8	1.0	4.1	0.2	..	0.3	3.0	2.1
99	Oman [c]	6.2	7.6	..	6.9	..	9.2	..	17.2	..	6.2
100	Gabon [c]	9.0	1.2	..	1.3	..	2.5	..	8.7	..	0.1
101	Slovenia	..	..	..	..	..	..	..	..	..	..
102	Puerto Rico [c]	3.9	4.1	2.3	2.2	5.0	3.6	7.9	1.0	3.2	4.7
103	Argentina	2.5	0.8	2.5	1.4	1.9	0.4	1.3	0.4	2.9	1.0
104	Greece	4.9	1.3	1.9	0.2	5.0	1.2	6.0	0.3	6.4	2.0
105	Korea, Rep. [c]	10.1	9.1	2.7	2.0	16.4	12.1	17.7	12.3	10.4	8.3
106	Portugal [c]	4.3	3.0	..	..	..	..	..	..	..	..
107	*Saudi Arabia* [c]	9.0	0.4	5.7	..	8.6	..	6.9	..	9.7	..
108	*Turkmenistan*	4.1	2.6	..	1.0	..	1.6	..	..	..	6.9
	Low- and middle-income	5.2 w	2.9 w	..	2.2 w	..	3.0 w	..	4.6 w	..	3.4 w
	Sub-Saharan Africa	3.8 w	1.6 w	1.7 w	1.7 w	3.8 w	0.9 w	4.3 w	0.9 w	4.9 w	2.2 w
	East Asia & Pacific	6.9 w	7.8 w	3.1 w	4.0 w	10.1 w	10.0 w	11.3 w	10.6 w	7.5 w	8.2 w
	South Asia	3.5 w	5.2 w	1.8 w	3.1 w	4.6 w	6.3 w	4.6 w	6.3 w	4.7 w	6.3 w
	Europe and Central Asia	5.4 w	0.4 w	..	–0.2 w	..	0.7 w	..	..	..	2.5 w
	Middle East & N. Africa	..	2.2 w	..	4.4 w	..	..	..	..	..	..
	Latin America & Caribbean	5.4 w	1.9 w	3.4 w	2.1 w	5.7 w	1.4 w	6.2 w	0.8 w	5.7 w	2.4 w
	Severely indebted	5.8 w	1.5 w	3.6 w	1.6 w	..	0.6 w	..	0.5 w	5.9 w	2.5 w
	High-income economies	3.2 w	2.9 w	..	..	..	..	..	..	..	..
109	New Zealand [c]	1.9	1.5	..	3.9	..	0.8	..	0.3	..	1.7
110	Ireland	4.9	3.8	..	..	..	..	..	..	..	..
111	Spain [c]	3.5	3.1	..	..	..	..	..	..	..	..
112	† Israel	4.8	4.1	..	..	..	..	..	..	..	..
113	Australia [c]	3.0	3.1	..	2.9	..	2.1	..	1.4	..	3.6
114	† Hong Kong	9.2	6.5	..	..	..	..	..	..	..	..
115	United Kingdom	2.0	2.5	..	..	..	..	..	..	..	..
116	Finland	3.0	2.0	0.0	–0.7	2.6	2.2	3.0	2.3	3.7	2.4
117	† Kuwait [c]	–0.2	..	7.5	..	–2.4	..	..	..	3.9	..
118	Italy [c]	3.8	2.2	0.9	0.8	3.6	2.2	5.8	2.8	4.0	2.5
119	† Singapore [c]	8.3	6.9	1.4	–6.4	8.6	6.2	9.7	7.2	8.3	7.4
120	Canada	4.6	2.6	1.2	1.7	3.2	2.2	3.5	2.3	6.1	2.8
121	Netherlands [c]	2.9	2.3	..	..	..	..	..	..	..	..
122	† United Arab Emirates	..	0.3	..	9.7	..	–1.5	..	2.7	..	3.6
123	Belgium [c]	3.0	2.1	..	2.0	..	..	..	..	..	..
124	France [c]	3.2	2.1	..	1.8	..	1.2	..	0.9	..	2.7
125	Austria [c]	3.4	2.3	2.6	0.5	3.1	2.2	3.2	2.6	3.6	2.5
126	Germany [c] [d]	2.6	2.6	1.1	..	1.7	..	2.0	..	3.5	..
127	Sweden	1.9	1.7	..	1.0	..	2.1	..	1.8	..	1.4
128	United States [c]	2.8	2.7	..	..	..	..	..	..	..	..
129	Norway	4.8	2.6	1.3	1.2	7.1	5.3	1.2	0.4	4.4	1.5
130	Denmark	2.2	2.0	2.3	2.5	1.1	2.3	2.6	1.0	2.6	2.1
131	Japan [c]	4.3	4.0	–0.2	0.6	4.0	5.0	4.7	5.6	4.8	3.7
132	Switzerland [c]	0.5	1.9	..	..	..	..	..	..	..	..
	World	3.6 w	2.9 w	..	..	..	..	..	..	..	..

a. Because manufacturing is generally the most dynamic part of the industrial sector, its growth rate is shown separately.   b. Services, etc. includes unallocated items.   c. GDP and its components are at purchaser values.   d. Data refer to the Federal Republic of Germany before unification.

Table 3. Structure of production

| | | GDP (million $) | | Distribution of gross domestic product (%) | | | | | | | |
| | | | | Agriculture | | Industry | | Manufacturing[a] | | Services, etc.[b] | |
		1970	1993	1970	1993	1970	1993	1970	1993	1970	1993
	Low-income economies	246,551 t	990,262 t	37 w	28 w	28 w	35 w	19 w	25 w	33 w	38 w
	Excluding China & India	96,886 t	339,816 t	31 w	37 w	35 w	22 w	..	13 w	34 w	42 w
1	Mozambique	..	1,367	..	33	..	12	..	..	..	55
2	Tanzania	1,174	2,086	41	56	17	14	10	5	42	30
3	Ethiopia	..	5,750	..	60	..	10	..	4	..	29
4	Sierra Leone	383	660	28	38	30	16	6	5	42	46
5	Viet Nam[c]	..	12,834	..	29	..	28	..	22	..	42
6	Burundi	225	855	71	52	10	21	7	11	19	27
7	Uganda	..	3,037	..	53	..	12	..	5	..	35
8	Nepal	861	3,551	67	43	12	21	4	9	21	36
9	Malawi	271	1,810	44	39	17	18	..	12	39	43
10	Chad[c]	302	1,133	47	44	18	22	17	16	35	35
11	Rwanda	..	1,359	..	41	..	21	..	14	..	38
12	Bangladesh[c]	6,664	23,977	55	30	9	18	6	10	37	52
13	Madagascar	995	3,126	24	34	16	14	..	..	59	52
14	Guinea-Bissau	79	241	47	45	21	19	21	8	31	36
15	Kenya	1,453	4,691	33	29	20	18	12	10	47	54
16	Mali[c]	338	2,662	61	42	11	15	7	9	28	42
17	Niger[c]	647	2,220	65	39	7	18	5	7	28	44
18	Lao PDR[c]	..	1,334	..	51	..	18	..	13	..	31
19	Burkina Faso	335	2,698	42	..	21	..	14	..	37	..
20	India	52,949	225,431	45	31	22	27	15	17	33	41
21	Nigeria	11,594	31,344	41	34	14	43	4	7	45	24
22	Albania	..	692	..	40	..	13	..	..	..	47
23	Nicaragua[c]	786	1,800	25	30	26	20	20	17	49	50
24	Togo[c]	253	1,249	34	49	21	18	10	7	45	33
25	Gambia, The	49	303	33	28	9	15	3	7	58	58
26	Zambia[c]	1,789	3,685	11	34	55	36	10	23	35	30
27	Mongolia[c]	..	539	..	21	..	46	..	..	..	33
28	Central African Republic	169	1,172	35	50	26	14	7	..	38	36
29	Benin[c]	332	2,125	36	36	12	13	..	8	52	51
30	Ghana[c]	2,214	6,084	47	48	18	16	11	8	35	36
31	Pakistan	9,102	46,360	37	25	22	25	16	17	41	50
32	Tajikistan	..	2,520	..	33	..	35	..	..	..	32
33	China[c]	93,244	425,611	34	19	38	48	30	38	28	33
34	Guinea[c]	..	3,172	..	24	..	31	..	5	..	45
35	Mauritania	197	859	29	28	38	30	5	12	32	42
36	Zimbabwe	1,415	4,986	15	15	36	36	21	30	49	48
37	Georgia[c]	..	2,994	..	58	..	22	..	21	..	20
38	Honduras	654	2,867	32	20	22	30	14	18	45	50
39	Sri Lanka	2,215	9,377	28	25	24	26	17	15	48	50
40	Côte d'Ivoire	1,147	8,087	40	37	23	24	13	..	36	39
41	Lesotho	67	609	35	10	9	47	4	16	56	43
42	Armenia[c]	..	2,190	..	48	..	30	..	..	..	22
43	Egypt, Arab Rep.	6,598	35,784	29	18	28	22	..	16	42	60
44	*Myanmar*	..	..	38	63	14	9	10	7	48	28
45	*Yemen, Rep.*	..	11,958	..	21	..	24	..	11	..	55
	Middle-income economies	..	3,884,168 t	..	..	..	..	..	..	..	..
	Lower-middle-income	..	1,697,910 t	..	..	..	..	..	..	..	..
46	Azerbaijan[c]	..	4,992	..	22	..	52	..	..	..	26
47	Indonesia[c]	9,657	144,707	45	19	19	39	10	22	36	42
48	Senegal[c]	865	5,770	24	20	20	19	16	13	56	61
49	Bolivia[c]	1,020	5,382	20	..	32	..	13	..	48	..
50	Cameroon[c]	1,160	11,082	31	29	19	25	10	11	50	47
51	Macedonia, FYR	..	1,704	..	..	..	..	..	..	..	..
52	Kyrgyz Republic[c]	..	3,915	..	43	..	35	..	..	..	22
53	Philippines[c]	6,691	54,068	30	22	32	33	25	24	39	45
54	Congo[c]	274	2,385	18	11	24	35	..	8	58	53
55	Uzbekistan[c]	..	20,425	..	23	..	36	..	..	..	41
56	Morocco[c]	3,956	26,635	20	14	27	32	16	18	53	53
57	Moldova[c]	..	4,292	..	35	..	48	..	..	..	18
58	Guatemala[c]	1,904	11,309	..	25	..	19	..	..	..	55
59	Papua New Guinea[c]	646	5,091	37	26	22	43	5	9	41	31
60	Bulgaria	..	10,369	..	13	..	38	..	..	..	49
61	Romania	..	25,969	..	21	..	40	..	36	..	40
62	Jordan	..	4,441	..	8	..	26	..	15	..	66
63	Ecuador[c]	1,674	14,421	24	12	25	38	18	22	51	50
64	Dominican Republic[c]	1,485	9,510	23	15	26	23	19	12	51	62
65	El Salvador[c]	1,029	7,625	28	9	23	25	19	19	48	66
66	Lithuania[c]	..	4,335	..	21	..	41	..	..	..	38
67	Colombia	7,199	54,076	25	16	28	35	21	18	47	50
68	Jamaica[c]	1,405	3,825	7	8	43	41	16	18	51	51
69	Peru	7,234	41,061	19	11	32	43	20	21	50	46
70	Paraguay[c]	595	6,825	32	26	21	21	17	15	47	53
71	Kazakhstan[c]	..	24,728	..	29	..	42	..	..	..	30
72	Tunisia	1,244	12,784	20	18	24	31	10	19	56	51

Note: For data comparability and coverage, see the technical notes. Figures in italics are for years other than those specified.

| | | GDP (million $) | | Distribution of gross domestic product (%) | | | | | | | |
| | | | | Agriculture | | Industry | | Manufacturing[a] | | Services, etc.[b] | |
		1970	1993	1970	1993	1970	1993	1970	1993	1970	1993
73	Algeria	4,541	39,836	11	13	41	43	15	11	48	43
74	Namibia	..	2,109	..	10	..	27	..	9	..	63
75	Slovak Republic[c]	..	11,076	..	7	..	44	..	..	..	49
76	Latvia	..	4,601	..	15	..	32	..	22	..	53
77	Thailand[c]	7,087	124,862	26	10	25	39	16	28	49	51
78	Costa Rica[c]	985	7,577	23	15	24	26	..	19	53	59
79	Ukraine[c]	..	109,078	..	35	..	47	..	45	..	18
80	Poland	..	85,853	..	6	..	39	..	..	..	55
81	Russian Federation[c]	..	329,432	..	9	..	51	..	..	..	39
82	Panama[c]	1,016	6,565	14	10	22	18	13	8	64	72
83	Czech Republic[c]	..	31,613	..	6	..	40	..	..	..	54
84	Botswana[c]	84	3,813	33	6	28	47	6	4	39	47
85	Turkey	11,400	156,413	30	15	27	30	17	19	43	55
86	*Iran, Islamic Rep.*	..	*107,335*	..	*24*	..	*29*	..	*14*	..	*47*
	Upper-middle-income	**205,283 t**	**2,161,066 t**	**12 w**	..	**38 w**	..	**25 w**	..	**49 w**	..
87	Venezuela[c]	13,432	59,995	6	5	39	42	16	14	54	53
88	Belarus[c]	..	27,545	..	17	..	54	..	44	..	29
89	Brazil	35,550	444,205	12	*11*	38	*37*	29	*20*	49	*52*
90	South Africa	16,293	105,636	8	5	40	39	24	23	52	56
91	Mauritius	184	2,780	16	10	22	33	14	23	62	57
92	Estonia[c]	..	5,092	..	8	..	29	..	19	..	63
93	Malaysia[c]	4,200	64,450	29	..	25	..	12	..	46	..
94	Chile[c]	8,426	43,684	7	..	40	..	25	..	53	..
95	Hungary[c]	5,543	38,099	18	6	45	28	..	19	37	66
96	Mexico[c]	38,318	343,472	12	8	29	28	22	20	59	63
97	Trinidad and Tobago	775	4,487	5	3	44	43	26	9	51	55
98	Uruguay[c]	2,313	13,144	16	9	31	27	..	19	53	64
99	Oman[c]	256	11,686	16	*3*	77	*53*	0	*4*	7	*44*
100	Gabon[c]	322	5,420	19	8	48	45	7	12	34	47
101	Slovenia	..	10,337	..	6	..	36	..	30	..	58
102	Puerto Rico[c]	5,035	35,834	3	1	34	42	24	39	62	57
103	Argentina	30,660	255,595	10	6	44	31	32	*20*	47	63
104	Greece	8,600	63,240	22	*18*	37	*32*	23	*20*	41	*50*
105	Korea, Rep.[c]	9,025	330,831	25	7	29	43	21	29	46	50
106	Portugal[c]	7,031	85,665	..	..	..	..	..	..	..	..
107	*Saudi Arabia* [c]	5,094	*121,530*	4	..	69	..	9	..	26	..
108	*Turkmenistan*	..	*5,156*	..	*32*	..	*31*	..	..	..	*37*
	Low- and middle-income	..	**4,865,030 t**	..	..	..	..	..	..	..	..
	Sub-Saharan Africa	**57,268 t**	**269,414 t**	**27 w**	**20 w**	**28 w**	**33 w**	**13 w**	**16 w**	**46 w**	**47 w**
	East Asia & Pacific	**158,653 t**	**1,285,142 t**	**34 w**	**17 w**	**35 w**	**41 w**	**24 w**	**30 w**	**31 w**	**41 w**
	South Asia	**73,654 t**	**313,869 t**	**44 w**	**30 w**	**21 w**	**26 w**	**14 w**	**17 w**	**34 w**	**44 w**
	Europe and Central Asia	..	**1,094,235 t**	..	..	..	..	..	..	..	..
	Middle East & N. Africa	..	..	..	..	..	..	..	..	..	..
	Latin America & Caribbean	**165,819 t**	**1,406,254 t**	**12 w**	..	**35 w**	..	**25 w**	..	**53 w**	..
	Severely indebted	**119,492 t**	**1,054,063 t**	**14 w**	..	**41 w**	..	**28 w**	..	**47 w**	..
	High-income economies	**2,083,094 t**	**18,247,536 t**	**4 w**	..	**38 w**	..	**28 w**	..	**60 w**	..
109	New Zealand[c]	6,415	43,699	*12*	..	*33*	..	*24*	..	55	..
110	Ireland	3,501	42,962	..	8	..	*10*	..	*3*	..	82
111	Spain[c]	37,569	478,582	..	..	..	..	..	..	..	..
112	† Israel	5,603	69,739	..	..	..	..	..	..	..	..
113	Australia[c]	39,324	289,390	6	*3*	39	*29*	24	*15*	55	*67*
114	† Hong Kong	3,463	89,997	2	*0*	36	*21*	29	*13*	62	*79*
115	United Kingdom	106,502	819,038	3	*2*	45	*33*	33	*25*	52	*65*
116	Finland	9,762	74,124	12	*5*	40	*31*	27	*28*	48	*64*
117	† Kuwait	2,874	22,402	0	*0*	67	*55*	4	*9*	33	*45*
118	Italy[c]	107,485	991,386	8	*3*	41	*32*	27	*25*	51	*65*
119	† Singapore[c]	1,896	55,153	2	*0*	30	37	20	28	68	63
120	Canada	73,847	477,468	4	..	36	..	23	..	59	..
121	Netherlands[c]	34,049	309,227	..	*4*	..	28	..	*19*	..	68
122	† United Arab Emirates	..	34,935	..	*2*	..	57	..	8	..	40
123	Belgium[c]	25,242	210,576	..	..	..	..	..	..	..	..
124	France[c]	142,869	1,251,689	..	*3*	..	*29*	..	*22*	..	69
125	Austria[c]	14,457	182,067	7	*2*	45	*35*	34	*26*	48	*62*
126	Germany[c]	184,508[d]	1,910,760	3[d]	*1*	49[d]	38	38[d]	27	47[d]	*61*
127	Sweden	30,013	166,745	..	*2*	..	31	..	26	..	67
128	United States[c]	1,011,563	6,259,899	3	..	34	..	25	..	63	..
129	Norway	11,183	103,419	6	*3*	32	*35*	22	*14*	62	62
130	Denmark	13,511	117,587	7	*4*	35	*27*	22	*20*	59	69
131	Japan[c]	203,736	4,214,204	6	*2*	47	*41*	36	*24*	47	*57*
132	Switzerland[c]	20,733	232,161	..	..	..	..	..	..	..	..
	World	..	**23,112,566**	..	..	..	..	..	..	..	..

a. Because manufacturing is generally the most dynamic part of the industrial sector, its share is shown separately. b. Services, etc. includes unallocated items. c. GDP and its components are at purchaser values. d. Data refer to the Federal Republic of Germany before unification.

Table 4. Agriculture and food

		Value added in agriculture (million $)		Cereal imports (thousand t)		Food aid in cereals (thousand t)		Fertilizer consumption (hundred grams per hectare of arable land)		Food production per capita (avg. ann. growth rate, %)	Fish products (% of total daily protein supply)	
		1980	1993	1980	1993	1979/80	1992/93	1979/80	1992/93	1979–93	1980	1990
	Low-income economies	86,936 t	245,475 t	32,801 t	34,420 t	6,101 t	8,334 t	528 w	1,028 w		4.5 w	4.6 w
	Excluding China & India	30,083 t	124,490 t	19,425 t	26,394 t	5,745 t	7,951 t	196 w	352 w		4.6 w	4.7 w
1	Mozambique	*722*	453	368	507	151	958	90	15	−2.1	3.9	3.0
2	Tanzania	2,030	1,168	399	215	89	35	125	137	−1.3	6.3	7.8
3	Ethiopia	*2,617*	3,476	397[a]	. .	111[a]	. .	31[a]	95[a]	−1.2[a]	0.0[a]	0.0[a]
4	Sierra Leone	334	. .	83	136	36	29	36	26	−1.2	15.2	10.8
5	Viet Nam	. .	3,759	1,160	289	184	84	236	1,347	2.2	. .	6.6
6	Burundi	530	443	18	22	8	4	8	34	−0.3	1.6	1.3
7	Uganda	893	1,599	52	76	17	59	1	1	0.3	7.6	7.2
8	Nepal	1,127	1,532	56	27	21	15	97	391	1.2	0.2	0.3
9	Malawi	413	709	36	514	5	635	250	434	−4.2	4.3	5.1
10	Chad[b]	388	494	16	59	16	3	3	26	0.3	9.4	9.9
11	Rwanda	*533*	551	16	115	14	82	1	6	−2.5	0.2	0.2
12	Bangladesh[b]	6,429	7,306	2,194	1,175	1,480	719	455	1,032	−0.1	5.0	4.8
13	Madagascar	1,078	1,062	110	111	14	58	29	25	−1.5	2.9	4.4
14	Guinea-Bissau	47	108	21	70	18	9	7	10	0.9	3.1	2.1
15	Kenya	2,019	1,357	387	569	86	287	271	410	−0.4	1.4	2.9
16	Mali[b]	951	1,128	87	83	22	34	69	103	−0.9	6.0	3.5
17	Niger	1,080	855	90	136	9	26	8	4	−1.8	0.9	0.2
18	Lao PDR[b]	. .	685	121	8	3	8	58	42	−0.2	2.9	2.1
19	Burkina Faso	548	. .	77	121	37	30	15	60	2.5	0.7	0.9
20	India	59,102	70,702	424	694	344	276	329	720	1.5	1.7	1.6
21	Nigeria	24,673	10,505	1,828	1,584	. .	. .	57	175	2.1	7.5	3.5
22	Albania	*455*	*277*	44	647	. .	513	1,335	338	−2.3	1.2	1.1
23	Nicaragua[b]	497	545	149	125	70	85	435	246	−2.7	0.5	0.4
24	Togo	312	607	41	63	7	3	43	183	−0.6	6.9	8.4
25	Gambia, The	64	83	47	87	7	6	130	44	−4.0	6.3	8.9
26	Zambia[b]	552	1,242	498	353	167	535	154	160	−0.3	5.0	4.3
27	Mongolia[b]	*231*	112	70	182	. .	9	69	108	−2.5	0.4	0.5
28	Central African Republic	300	584	12	32	3	5	7	5	−1.0	4.0	3.0
29	Benin[b]	498	760	61	134	5	19	5	82	1.9	7.5	4.8
30	Ghana[b]	2,575	2,893	247	396	110	75	43	38	0.3	17.4	18.7
31	Pakistan	6,279	11,500	613	2,893	146	188	532	1,015	1.2	0.9	0.8
32	Tajikistan	. .	. .	. .	450	. .	72	. .	1,618		. .	. .
33	China[b]	60,670	82,918	12,952	7,332	12	107	1,497	3,005	3.0	2.2	3.9
34	Guinea[b]	. .	759	171	335	24	30	4	47	−0.3	4.2	4.5
35	Mauritania	202	238	166	286	26	42	67	82	−1.6	3.6	3.3
36	Zimbabwe	702	757	156	538	. .	900	683	481	−3.0	1.4	1.1
37	Georgia[b]	. .	1,738	. .	500	. .	170	. .	680	. .	. .	. .
38	Honduras	544	566	139	197	27	64	162	210	−1.3	0.8	1.8
39	Sri Lanka	1,037	2,311	884	1,149	170	248	882	964	−1.8	11.6	9.9
40	Côte d'Ivoire	2,633	3,026	469	590	2	41	172	132	−0.1	9.1	8.7
41	Lesotho	75	61	107	131	29	45	154	178	−2.2	0.9	0.8
42	Armenia[b]	. .	1,051	. .	350	. .	143	. .	436	. .	. .	. .
43	Egypt, Arab Rep.	3,993	6,396	6,028	7,206	1,758	482	2,714	3,392	1.3	2.0	2.4
44	*Myanmar*	. .	. .	16	. .	11	. .	100	69	−1.3	6.7	6.2
45	Yemen, Rep.	. .	2,511	596	1,843	19	21	77	99	−0.5	. .	. .
	Middle-income economies	. .	. .	. .	115,228 t	. .	6,021 t	682 w	603 w		8.6 w	7.8 w
	Lower-middle-income	. .	. .	. .	66,281 t	. .	5,477 t	650 w	554 w		8.0 w	7.5 w
46	Azerbaijan[b]	. .	*1,304*	. .	480	. .	12	. .	395	. .	. .	. .
47	Indonesia[b]	18,701	27,189	3,534	3,105	831	40	600	1,147	2.2	8.1	8.7
48	Senegal[b]	568	1,126	452	579	61	71	83	72	0.0	9.7	9.8
49	Bolivia[b]	564	. .	263	298	150	227	14	58	0.7	1.9	0.6
50	Cameroon[b]	2,089	3,170	140	281	4	1	46	30	−1.9	6.4	6.7
51	Macedonia, FYR	. .	. .	. .	117	. .	. .	. .	248	. .	. .	. .
52	Kyrgyz Republic[b]	. .	. .	. .	120	. .	91	. .	242	. .	. .	. .
53	Philippines[b]	8,150	11,723	1,053	2,036	95	53	383	540	−1.3	21.6	20.9
54	Congo[b]	199	273	88	148	4	7	35	118	−1.5	21.1	22.8
55	Uzbekistan[b]	. .	4,693	. .	4,151	. .	. .	. .	1,566	. .	. .	. .
56	Morocco[b]	3,468	3,809	1,821	3,653	119	234	258	326	2.3	2.8	2.8
57	Moldova[b]	. .	1,485	. .	200	. .	72	. .	612	. .	. .	. .
58	Guatemala[b]	. .	2,845	204	486	10	109	489	833	−0.5	0.4	0.4
59	Papua New Guinea[b]	844	1,321	152	227	. .	0	148	308	−0.2	13.1	11.8
60	Bulgaria	*2,889*	1,346	693	241	. .	. .	1,986	663	−1.9	2.0	1.7
61	Romania	. .	5,327	2,369	2,649	. .	180	1,165	423	−2.4	2.7	3.3
62	Jordan	. .	353	505	1,596	72	254	427	398	0.2	1.5	1.2
63	Ecuador[b]	1,423	1,746	387	428	8	14	295	380	0.6	7.6	6.8
64	Dominican Republic[b]	1,336	1,473	365	961	120	7	363	694	−0.9	5.4	2.8
65	El Salvador[b]	992	654	144	286	3	131	832	1,073	0.7	1.1	0.7
66	Lithuania[b]	. .	890	. .	. .	. .	407	. .	545	. .	. .	. .
67	Colombia	6,466	*7,607*	1,068	1,702	3	17	601	1,032	1.0	2.5	1.4
68	Jamaica[b]	220	321	469	429	117	206	729	973	1.0	8.1	8.9
69	Peru[b]	2,113	4,518	1,309	1,920	109	378	336	216	−0.4	8.9	10.6
70	Paraguay[b]	1,311	1,802	75	82	11	. .	36	96	1.3	0.4	1.0
71	Kazakhstan[b]	. .	. .	. .	100	. .	3	. .	134	. .	. .	. .
72	Tunisia	1,235	2,287	817	1,044	165	100	132	223	1.5	3.1	3.7

Note: For data comparability and coverage, see the technical notes. Figures in italics are for years other than those specified.

		Value added in agriculture (million $)		Cereal imports (thousand t)		Food aid in cereals (thousand t)		Fertilizer consumption (hundred grams per hectare of arable land)		Food production per capita (avg. ann. growth rate, %)	Fish products (% of total daily protein supply)	
		1980	1993	1980	1993	1979/80	1992/93	1979/80	1992/93	1979–93	1980	1990
73	Algeria	3,453	5,366	3,414	5,821	19	15	314	123	1.2	1.2	2.1
74	Namibia	237	207	54	141	..	26	..	..	–2.0	3.4	3.5
75	Slovak Republicb	813	741	..	..	..	..	..	..	..	..	..
76	Latvia	..	685	..	11	..	390	..	982	..	..	..
77	Thailandb	7,519	12,441	213	638	3	60	150	544	0.0	11.1	12.0
78	Costa Ricab	860	1,158	180	535	1	95	1,453	2,354	0.7	4.6	2.2
79	Ukraineb	..	37,873	..	1,500	..	197	..	841	..	..	..
80	Poland	..	5,434	7,811	3,142	..	200	2,339	811	0.7	4.8	4.8
81	Russian Federationb	..	35,553	..	11,238	..	1,124	..	417	..	..	..
82	Panamab	354	667	87	159	2	3	551	476	–1.2	8.4	7.4
83	Czech Republicb	2,104	1,952	..	519	..	..	..	..	..	..	..
84	Botswanab	126	216	68	133	20	10	14	9	–2.1	1.6	1.3
85	Turkey	12,165	23,609	6	2,107	16	2	511	702	0.3	2.9	2.3
86	Iran, Islamic Rep.	16,268	25,653	2,779	4,840	..	31	447	755	1.0	0.5	1.6
	Upper-middle-income	23,940 t	..	34,308 t	48,947 t	..	..	722 w	728 w		9.4 w	8.2 w
87	Venezuelab	3,363	3,024	2,484	2,314	..	..	642	874	0.2	..	6.7
88	Belarusb	..	4,643	..	1,250	..	246	..	2,228	..	..	..
89	Brazil	23,373	..	6,740	7,848	3	11	855	608	1.2	3.1	2.6
90	South Africa	5,027	4,815	159	2,275	..	..	803	596	–2.0	3.6	3.8
91	Mauritius	119	274	181	240	22	5	2,492	2,512	0.0	9.7	8.5
92	Estoniab	..	411	..	46	..	231	..	1,229	..	..	..
93	Malaysiab	5,365	..	1,336	3,288	..	4	944	1,977	4.3	18.4	13.8
94	Chileb	1,992	..	1,264	983	22	3	314	849	1.9	6.0	7.8
95	Hungaryb	3,796	2,135	155	137	..	..	2,624	292	–0.7	1.1	1.3
96	Mexicob	16,036	29,037	7,226	6,223	..	45	505	653	–0.9	3.3	3.3
97	Trinidad and Tobago	140	114	252	232	..	..	688	801	–0.6	4.8	3.6
98	Uruguayb	1,371	1,187	45	110	7	..	558	608	0.3	1.9	1.1
99	Omanb	152	374	120	369	..	..	259	1,270	..	..	..
100	Gabonb	289	447	27	77	..	..	2	11	–1.4	19.2	12.9
101	Slovenia	..	583	..	549	..	..	..	2,306	..	..	..
102	Puerto Ricob	380	410	..	..	..	..	..	..	–0.3	..	..
103	Argentina	4,890	15,312	8	8	..	..	42	78	–0.3	1.5	1.7
104	Greece	7,224	12,014	1,199	708	..	..	1,342	1,309	0.0	4.5	4.8
105	Korea, Rep.b	9,250	23,403	5,143	11,271	184	..	3,657	4,656	0.5	12.4	15.8
106	Portugalb	2,950	..	3,372	2,147	267	..	824	813	2.6	10.4	15.0
107	Saudi Arabiab	1,675	..	3,061	5,186	..	..	209	1,438	9.1	3.1	2.3
108	Turkmenistan	..	..	..	940	..	2	..	1,204	..	..	..
	Low- and middle-income	..	..	105,595 t	149,648 t	..	..	594 w	790 w		7.2 w	6.7 w
	Sub-Saharan Africa	14,945 t	54,381 t	8,647 t	13,157 t	1,601 t	5,079 t	138 w	149 w		6.7 w	6.1 w
	East Asia & Pacific	50,344 t	219,191 t	26,646 t	30,036 t	1,535 t	447 t	1,079 w	2,055 w		12.6 w	11.4 w
	South Asia	32,720 t	94,968 t	4,211 t	6,211 t	2,339 t	1,624 t	346 w	737 w		11.5 w	14.4 w
	Europe and Central Asia	..	..	15,752 t	34,452 t	..	4,392 t	1,304 w	570 w		4.0 w	4.1 w
	Middle East & N. Africa	..	..	24,557 t	38,092 t	..	..	400 w	641 w		1.9 w	1.7 w
	Latin America & Caribbean	20,444 t	..	25,782 t	27,700 t	..	1,565 t	542 w	524 w		7.5 w	6.7 w
	Severely indebted	17,265 t	..	26,690 t	24,753 t	681 t	1,747 t	719 w	446 w		4.7 w	4.9 w
	High-income economies	88,458 t	..	79,799 t	77,530 t	..	..	1,294 w	1,115 w		8.4 w	8.6 w
109	New Zealandb	2,425	..	63	282	..	..	10,247	12,745	0.0	5.5	8.5
110	Ireland	2,036	..	553	409	..	..	5,414	7,021	1.9	4.0	3.9
111	Spainb	..	20,295	6,073	4,955	..	..	811	769	1.1	9.1	9.8
112	† Israel	976	..	1,601	2,293	31	..	1,919	2,253	–1.8	4.5	5.0
113	Australiab	8,454	9,404	5	32	..	..	263	265	0.3	3.7	4.1
114	† Hong Kong	223	190	812	640	..	..	..	..	1.4	16.0	16.9
115	United Kingdom	10,106	16,383	5,498	3,534	..	..	2,936	3,205	0.0	4.0	5.1
116	Finland	4,523	4,717	367	108	..	..	1,908	1,363	–0.3	8.9	8.7
117	† Kuwaitb	52	110	340	251	..	..	4,400	1,600	..	3.6	4.5
118	Italyb	26,044	38,380	7,629	6,249	..	..	1,698	1,560	–0.3	4.1	5.6
119	† Singaporeb	150	103	1,324	798	..	..	5,500	56,000	–6.4	9.5	9.2
120	Canada	10,005	..	1,383	1,095	..	..	424	479	0.6	4.6	6.6
121	Netherlandsb	..	11,636	5,246	4,431	..	..	8,262	5,889	0.4	3.1	2.9
122	† United Arab Emirates	223	773	426	583	..	..	1,328	4,436	..	5.2	6.4
123	Belgiumb	2,500	3,644	5,599c	5,291c	..	..	5,773c	4,246c	2.2c	4.7c	5.0c
124	Franceb	28,168	37,337	1,570	1,188	..	..	2,969	2,354	0.1	5.0	5.8
125	Austriab	3,423	4,491	131	184	..	..	2,491	1,773	0.2	2.0	2.7
126	Germanyb	16,791 d	23,267	9,500 d	3,533	..	..	4,126 d	2,387	0.5 d	..	4.0 d
127	Sweden	4,238	5,208	124	202	..	..	1,624	1,077	–1.4	9.6	9.3
128	United Statesb	70,320	..	199	4,684	..	..	1,127	1,011	–0.3	3.5	4.3
129	Norway	2,221	..	725	302	..	..	3,174	2,276	0.2	14.7	15.2
130	Denmark	3,161	4,360	355	579	..	..	2,364	2,088	2.0	8.3	10.5
131	Japanb	39,022	80,528	24,473	28,035	..	..	3,721	3,951	–0.3	26.6	28.0
132	Switzerlandb	..	..	1,247	455	..	..	4,409	3,340	–0.3	3.0	3.7
	World	..	..	185,394 t	227,178 t	..	..	817 w	874 w		7.5 w	7.2 w

a. Includes Eritrea. b. Value added in agriculture data are at purchaser values. c. Includes Luxembourg. d. Data refer to the Federal Republic of Germany before unification.

Table 5. Commercial energy

		Average annual growth rate (%)				Energy use (oil equivalent)				Energy imports as a % of merchandise exports	
		Energy production		Energy consumption		Per capita (kg)		GDP output per kg ($)			
		1971–80	1980–93	1971–80	1980–93	1971	1993	1971	1993	1970	1993
	Low-income economies	**6.6 w**	**4.9 w**	**6.6 w**	**5.4 w**	**174 w**	**353 w**	**0.7 w**	**0.9 w**		
	Excluding China & India	**4.6 w**	**3.9 w**	**5.0 w**	**5.2 w**	**83 w**	**136 w**	**2.1 w**	**2.5 w**		
1	Mozambique	22.9	–15.6	–1.7	–3.0	103	43	..	2.2	17	..
2	Tanzania	4.5	5.1	2.2	0.6	53	35	1.9	2.4	11	..
3	Ethiopia[a]	6.4	6.5	0.8	6.0	19	23	..	..	11	..
4	Sierra Leone	..	..	0.4	0.4	133	74	1.2	2.3	5	..
5	Viet Nam	10.9	9.7	–9.2	2.6	165	77	..	2.4	..	..
6	Burundi	..	6.9	7.6	7.0	8	24	9.4	6.7	10	..
7	Uganda	–4.0	2.1	–7.0	3.3	58	21	0.0	7.7	1	..
8	Nepal	11.9	14.1	7.3	8.1	6	22	12.6	6.5	..	..
9	Malawi	11.4	3.6	7.6	1.5	37	35	2.1	5.4	8	..
10	Chad	..	..	4.1	0.5	18	16	5.2	12.1	32	..
11	Rwanda	3.3	3.4	18.2	–0.1	11	27	5.2	7.2	6	..
12	Bangladesh	11.4	12.2	9.0	7.9	18	59	5.2	3.5	..	26
13	Madagascar	–0.8	5.7	–3.7	1.7	64	34	2.7	7.1	9	..
14	Guinea-Bissau	..	..	4.1	2.1	35	37	4.1	6.4	47	..
15	Kenya	15.9	15.6	4.2	2.9	114	99	1.3	2.2	15	..
16	Mali	8.4	5.2	7.9	1.9	16	20	4.2	13.1	13	..
17	Niger	..	8.5	11.9	2.2	17	38	9.6	6.8	7	..
18	Lao PDR	40.0	–1.2	–3.4	2.6	55	39	..	7.4	..	..
19	Burkina Faso	..	..	12.7	1.1	9	16	7.4	17.7	22	..
20	India	5.3	6.6	4.7	6.7	111	242	1.0	1.2	8	36
21	Nigeria	2.5	2.4	18.7	1.9	39	141	6.6	2.1	3	..
22	Albania	5.0	–5.4	10.1	–3.1	604	455	..	..	..	..
23	Nicaragua	2.8	2.7	3.5	2.4	248	241	1.6	1.8	7	61
24	Togo	8.4	..	9.0	0.9	51	47	2.7	6.9	5	..
25	Gambia, The	..	..	14.5	0.8	35	57	3.4	6.1	4	..
26	Zambia	6.5	–3.0	0.9	–2.5	335	146	1.1	2.8	5	..
27	Mongolia	10.3	4.6	10.4	2.2	632	1,089	..	0.2	..	..
28	Central African Republic	4.8	2.5	–0.5	2.9	40	29	2.5	13.4	2	..
29	Benin	..	11.2	1.6	–3.3	39	20	3.1	20.4	7	..
30	Ghana	7.1	2.1	3.3	2.7	107	96	2.6	3.8	5	..
31	Pakistan	6.9	7.3	5.8	6.8	103	209	1.5	1.9	11	24
32	Tajikistan	..	..	..	..	..	634	..	0.7	..	31
33	China	7.8	4.9	7.4	5.1	278	623	0.4	0.6	..	6
34	Guinea	14.1	3.8	2.3	1.4	69	66	..	7.7	..	..
35	Mauritania	..	..	5.0	0.4	105	105	1.7	4.2	5	..
36	Zimbabwe	0.2	7.1	1.1	5.5	442	471	0.7	1.1	..	15
37	Georgia	..	..	..	..	..	891	..	0.6	..	..
38	Honduras	13.1	3.3	6.3	1.7	185	180	1.5	3.5	8	16
39	Sri Lanka	8.1	6.7	2.1	1.9	80	110	2.3	5.3	..	13
40	Côte d'Ivoire	21.8	–6.1	6.3	0.3	152	109	1.8	6.4	4	..
41	Lesotho	..	..	..	..	..	..	..	..	..	..
42	Armenia	..	..	..	..	..	958	..	0.7	..	..
43	Egypt, Arab Rep.	14.2	4.1	8.9	5.8	200	539	1.2	1.2	10	6
44	*Myanmar*	8.0	–1.5	2.7	–0.8	56	39	1.4	..	9	..
45	*Yemen, Rep.*	..	..	7.6	7.8	111	285	..	3.4	9	..
	Middle-income economies	..	..	..	..	..	**1,563 w**	..	**1.6 w**		
	Lower-middle-income	..	..	..	..	..	**1,531 w**	..	**1.0 w**		
46	Azerbaijan	..	..	..	..	..	2,470	..	0.3	..	3
47	Indonesia	7.7	3.7	12.5	7.5	71	321	1.1	2.3	30	6
48	Senegal	..	..	5.3	0.4	121	115	1.7	6.3	6	..
49	Bolivia	3.6	0.8	10.4	0.9	173	310	1.5	2.5	1	8
50	Cameroon	46.6	5.3	8.3	1.6	59	87	3.1	10.2	6	..
51	Macedonia, FYR	..	..	..	..	..	..	..	..	..	..
52	Kyrgyz Republic	..	..	..	..	..	965	..	0.9	..	41
53	Philippines	30.9	5.6	5.3	3.5	222	328	0.9	2.5	14	19
54	Congo	33.2	6.9	1.4	1.5	176	165	1.4	5.9	4	..
55	Uzbekistan	..	..	..	..	..	2,033	..	0.5	..	30
56	Morocco	2.9	–2.7	8.3	3.8	155	299	1.8	3.4	8	24
57	Moldova	..	..	..	..	..	1,345	..	0.7	..	..
58	Guatemala	21.4	3.8	6.6	1.8	155	159	2.4	7.1	2	26
59	Papua New Guinea	12.0	20.1	6.7	2.4	136	238	2.1	5.2	9	..
60	Bulgaria	4.2	0.4	5.2	–3.0	2,223	1,954	..	0.6	..	..
61	Romania	2.7	–4.6	5.7	–2.7	1,955	1,765	..	0.6	..	34
62	Jordan	..	..	14.2	5.0	228	766	..	1.4	31	37
63	Ecuador	28.6	3.9	16.0	2.8	202	561	1.3	2.3	9	1
64	Dominican Republic	22.3	3.7	5.0	1.3	235	340	1.6	3.7	9	..
65	El Salvador	16.7	3.5	7.8	2.3	160	222	1.8	6.2	2	39
66	Lithuania	..	..	..	..	..	2,596	..	0.4	..	43
67	Colombia	–1.7	11.9	4.0	4.0	444	694	0.8	2.3	1	5
68	Jamaica	0.0	–5.6	–0.2	1.9	996	1,096	0.8	1.4	10	..
69	Peru	12.9	–3.9	3.6	–0.6	429	332	1.4	5.4	1	8
70	Paraguay	14.1	45.5	10.3	5.9	94	214	2.9	6.8	15	30
71	Kazakhstan	..	..	..	..	..	4,435	..	0.3	..	..
72	Tunisia	4.5	–0.8	9.5	4.0	262	582	1.2	2.9	8	13

Note: For data comparability and coverage, see the technical notes.   Figures in italics are for years other than those specified.

		Average annual growth rate (%)				Energy use (oil equivalent)				Energy imports as a % of merchandise exports	
		Energy production		Energy consumption		Per capita (kg)		GDP output per kg ($)			
		1971–80	1980–93	1971–80	1980–93	1971	1993	1971	1993	1970	1993
73	Algeria	5.0	4.6	14.9	5.0	255	955	1.4	1.9	3	*1*
74	Namibia	..	..	..	..	..	..	..	..	..	..
75	Slovak Republic	..	..	..	..	..	..	..	..	..	..
76	Latvia	..	..	..	..	..	1,717	..	1.0	..	..
77	Thailand	10.1	26.0	6.8	10.5	178	678	1.1	3.2	16	9
78	Costa Rica	6.8	5.8	5.8	3.6	443	558	1.4	4.2	5	12
79	Ukraine	..	..	..	..	..	3,960	..	0.5	..	..
80	Poland	3.5	−2.2	5.1	−2.0	2,493	2,390	..	0.9	..	20
81	Russian Federation	..	..	..	..	..	4,438	..	0.5	..	..
82	Panama	17.2	10.4	−0.3	0.3	834	599	0.9	4.3	63	51
83	Czech Republic	..	..	..	..	..	..	..	..	..	..
84	Botswana	9.2	−0.2	10.6	2.7	243	388	0.7	7.0	..	..
85	Turkey	5.8	3.5	7.7	5.1	377	983	0.9	3.0	11	26
86	*Iran, Islamic Rep.*	−7.7	6.8	8.3	6.7	714	1,235	..	..	..	..
	Upper-middle-income	**4.1 w**	**2.1 w**	**6.6 w**	**4.4 w**	**831 w**	**1,632 w**	**0.9 w**	**2.8 w**		
87	Venezuela	−4.7	1.8	4.8	2.3	2,072	2,369	0.6	1.2	1	*1*
88	Belarus	..	..	..	..	..	3,427	..	0.8	..	*11*
89	Brazil	6.1	7.5	8.4	3.7	361	666	1.4	4.9	13	11
90	South Africa	8.1	3.1	3.5	3.0	1,993	2,399	0.4	1.2	9	0
91	Mauritius	1.8	7.1	4.6	3.0	225	391	1.3	7.7	8	*11*
92	Estonia	..	..	..	..	..	..	..	..	..	..
93	Malaysia	19.2	11.6	8.4	9.8	436	1,529	0.9	2.2	10	*4*
94	Chile	0.3	1.5	0.8	4.7	709	911	1.5	3.5	5	11
95	Hungary	2.4	−0.3	4.6	−0.6	1,872	2,385	0.3	1.6	10	19
96	Mexico	16.6	1.8	10.3	3.1	653	1,439	1.2	2.7	6	4
97	Trinidad and Tobago	5.8	−0.3	4.4	3.4	2,735	4,696	0.3	0.8	60	14
98	Uruguay	0.8	6.5	0.8	1.0	749	715	1.3	5.8	15	12
99	Oman	1.0	8.3	41.2	9.7	119	2,408	3.4	2.4	0	*1*
100	Gabon	5.7	5.7	4.8	1.8	805	769	0.9	5.6	1	..
101	Slovenia	..	..	..	..	..	1,531	..	4.0	..	..
102	Puerto Rico	−3.9	1.9	−2.6	0.7	3,862	2,018	0.5	4.9	..	..
103	Argentina	2.7	2.5	2.6	1.1	1,282	1,351	1.1	5.6	4	3
104	Greece	7.8	6.2	6.0	3.4	1,034	2,160	1.2	3.3	21	24
105	Korea, Rep.	5.2	7.5	11.1	9.5	507	2,863	0.6	2.6	16	18
106	Portugal	2.3	2.4	5.2	4.8	721	1,781	1.2	4.9	15	*13*
107	*Saudi Arabia*	7.5	0.7	21.0	5.3	1,061	4,552	1.0	..	0	69
108	*Turkmenistan*	..	..	..	..	..	2,268	..	..	..	..
	Low- and middle-income	..	..	..	..	..	**760 w**	..	**1.4 w**		
	Sub-Saharan Africa	**4.5 w**	**3.6 w**	**4.1 w**	**2.7 w**	**224 w**	**250 w**	**1.0 w**	**1.9 w**		
	East Asia & Pacific	**7.6 w**	**5.0 w**	**7.2 w**	**5.6 w**	**268 w**	**620 w**	**0.5 w**	**1.2 w**		
	South Asia	**5.3 w**	**6.6 w**	**4.9 w**	**6.7 w**	**98 w**	**213 w**	**1.2 w**	**1.3 w**		
	Europe and Central Asia	..	..	..	..	..	**2,934 w**	..	**0.8 w**		
	Middle East & N. Africa	**2.7 w**	**2.3 w**	**11.6 w**	**5.4 w**	**404 w**	**1,098 w**	**1.3 w**	**1.9 w**		
	Latin America & Caribbean	**2.0 w**	**2.8 w**	**5.8 w**	**2.6 w**	**640 w**	**915 w**	**1.1 w**	**3.5 w**		
	Severely indebted	**5.6 w**	**1.3 w**	**5.7 w**	**0.7 w**	**791 w**	**871 w**	**1.2 w**	**3.4 w**		
	High-income economies	**1.7 w**	**1.8 w**	**2.0 w**	**1.6 w**	**4,495 w**	**5,245 w**	**0.8 w**	**4.4 w**		
109	New Zealand	5.4	7.5	2.5	4.6	2,434	4,299	1.1	2.9	7	6
110	Ireland	1.8	2.7	2.2	2.1	2,357	3,016	0.7	4.5	12	4
111	Spain	4.5	5.1	5.2	2.9	1,264	2,373	1.0	5.1	26	13
112	† Israel	−46.1	−10.4	2.7	4.4	2,073	2,607	1.0	5.1	9	11
113	Australia	5.0	5.6	3.4	2.3	4,079	5,316	0.9	3.1	5	6
114	† Hong Kong	..	..	6.6	6.6	850	2,278	1.2	8.3	3	2
115	United Kingdom	8.4	0.1	−0.3	1.0	3,790	3,718	0.7	4.4	12	6
116	Finland	3.2	2.7	2.8	1.7	3,982	5,635	0.7	2.9	13	10
117	† Kuwait	−5.8	−2.3	6.6	−4.2	7,264	4,217	0.7	3.0	0	*1*
118	Italy	−0.5	2.4	1.8	1.5	2,141	2,697	1.0	6.4	16	9
119	† Singapore	..	..	7.7	7.7	1,396	5,563	0.8	3.6	21	13
120	Canada	2.8	3.7	4.0	1.5	6,233	7,821	0.7	2.4	5	4
121	Netherlands	6.4	−0.1	2.3	1.3	3,900	4,533	0.8	4.5	12	8
122	† United Arab Emirates	6.7	5.9	27.3	10.5	4,151	16,878	..	1.2	2	..
123	Belgium	2.9	3.0	1.3	1.6	4,127	4,989	0.7	4.2	..	..
124	France	1.4	6.7	1.9	2.0	3,025	4,031	1.0	5.4	13	9
125	Austria	0.2	1.4	2.0	1.4	2,557	3,277	0.9	7.1	10	6
126	Germany[b]	0.6	−1.3	1.7	0.0	3,953	4,170	..	5.7	8	7
127	Sweden	9.5	4.5	1.8	1.3	4,521	5,385	1.0	4.0	11	8
128	United States	0.7	0.7	1.7	1.4	7,633	7,918	0.7	3.1	7	13
129	Norway	30.1	9.0	3.7	1.5	3,565	5,096	0.9	4.7	12	2
130	Denmark	14.3	24.1	0.7	0.7	3,866	3,861	0.9	6.8	14	*5*
131	Japan	2.6	4.6	2.5	2.7	2,553	3,642	0.9	9.3	20	14
132	Switzerland	8.8	2.6	1.7	1.8	2,742	3,491	1.5	9.4	7	4
	World	..	..	..	..	..	**1,421 w**	..	**3.1 w**		

a. Includes Eritrea.   b. Data refer to Federal Republic of Germany before unification.

Table 6. Structure of manufacturing

| | | Value added in manufacturing (million $) | | Distribution of manufacturing value added (%) | | | | | | | | | |
| | | | | Food, beverages, and tobacco | | Textiles and clothing | | Machinery, transport equipment | | Chemicals | | Other[a] | |
		1970	1992	1970	1992	1970	1992	1970	1992	1970	1992	1970	1992
	Low-income economies	47,123 t	237,098 t										
	Excluding China & India	..	41,279 t										
1	Mozambique	..	..	51	..	13	..	5	..	3	..	28	..
2	Tanzania	118	121	36	..	28	..	5	..	4	..	26	..
3	Ethiopia	..	210	..	62[b]	..	21[b]	..	1[b]	..	2[b]	..	14[b]
4	Sierra Leone	22	*34*	..	..	..	..	..	..	..	..	..	..
5	Viet Nam[c]	..	2,139	..	..	..	..	..	..	..	..	..	..
6	Burundi	16	93	*53*	*83*	*25*	*9*	*0*	*0*	*6*	*2*	*16*	*7*
7	Uganda	..	155	*40*	..	*20*	..	*2*	..	*4*	..	*34*	..
8	Nepal	32	322	..	*31*	..	*39*	..	*1*	..	*4*	..	*25*
9	Malawi	..	244	51	..	17	..	3	..	10	..	20	..
10	Chad[c]	51	198	..	..	..	..	..	..	..	..	..	..
11	Rwanda[c]	..	180	86	..	0	..	3	..	2	..	8	..
12	Bangladesh[c]	387	2,164	30	*24*	47	*38*	3	*7*	11	*17*	10	*15*
13	Madagascar	..	..	36	..	28	..	6	..	7	..	23	..
14	Guinea-Bissau	17	19	..	..	..	..	..	..	..	..	..	..
15	Kenya	174	764	33	39	9	9	16	10	9	9	33	33
16	Mali[c]	25	234	36	..	40	..	4	..	5	..	14	..
17	Niger[c]	30	151	..	..	..	..	..	..	..	..	..	..
18	Lao PDR[c]	..	149	..	..	..	..	..	..	..	..	..	..
19	Burkina Faso	47	..	69	..	9	..	2	..	1	..	19	..
20	India	7,928	41,558	13	12	21	15	20	25	14	14	32	35
21	Nigeria	426	2,012	36	..	26	..	1	..	6	..	31	..
22	Albania	..	..	..	*24*	..	*33*	..	..	..	*8*	..	*36*
23	Nicaragua[c]	159	306	53	..	14	..	2	..	8	..	23	..
24	Togo[c]	25	161	..	..	..	..	..	..	..	..	..	..
25	Gambia, The	2	21	..	..	..	..	..	..	..	..	..	..
26	Zambia[c]	181	1,057	49	*45*	9	*12*	5	*7*	10	*11*	27	*26*
27	Mongolia[c]	..	..	..	..	..	..	..	..	..	..	..	..
28	Central African Republic	12	..	..	75	..	3	..	2	..	8	..	12
29	Benin[c]	*38*	170	..	..	..	..	..	..	..	..	..	..
30	Ghana[c]	252	598	34	..	16	..	4	..	4	..	41	..
31	Pakistan	1,462	7,538	24	..	38	..	6	..	9	..	23	..
32	Tajikistan			..	..	..	..	..	..	..	..	..	..
33	China[c]	27,555	147,302	..	13	..	13	..	27	..	12	..	35
34	Guinea[c]	..	135	..	..	..	..	..	..	..	..	..	..
35	Mauritania	10	115	..	..	..	..	..	..	..	..	..	..
36	Zimbabwe	293	1,379	24	34	16	14	9	11	11	5	40	36
37	Georgia[c]	..	861	..	..	..	..	..	..	..	..	..	..
38	Honduras	91	510	58	49	10	9	1	3	4	6	28	32
39	Sri Lanka	369	1,354	26	40	19	29	10	4	11	5	33	22
40	Côte d'Ivoire	149	..	27	..	16	..	10	..	5	..	42	..
41	Lesotho	3	97	..	..	..	..	..	..	..	..	..	..
42	Armenia	..	..	..	29	..	46	..	16	..	−1	..	10
43	Egypt, Arab Rep.	..	5,747	17	15	35	23	9	6	12	9	27	48
44	*Myanmar*	..	..	..	..	..	..	..	..	..	..	..	..
45	*Yemen, Rep.*	..	977	..	..	..	..	..	..	..	..	..	..
	Middle-income economies	..	..										
	Lower-middle-income	..	..										
46	Azerbaijan[c]	..	2,557	..	..	..	..	..	..	..	..	..	..
47	Indonesia[c]	994	27,854	65	23	14	16	2	14	6	7	13	40
48	Senegal[c]	141	809	51	..	19	..	2	..	6	..	22	..
49	Bolivia[c]	135	..	47	*21*	28	*3*	1	*0*	6	*2*	19	*73*
50	Cameroon[c]	119	1,384	50	*61*	15	*−13*	4	*5*	3	*5*	27	*42*
51	Macedonia, FYR	..	..	..	25	..	28	..	15	..	9	..	24
52	Kyrgyz Republic[c]	..	..	..	..	..	..	..	..	..	..	..	..
53	Philippines[c]	1,665	12,811	39	37	8	13	8	11	13	12	32	27
54	Congo[c]	..	228	65	..	4	..	1	..	8	..	22	..
55	Uzbekistan[c]	..	5,494	..	..	..	..	..	..	..	..	..	..
56	Morocco[c]	641	5,118	..	25	..	18	..	6	..	15	..	35
57	Moldova[c]	..	..	..	..	..	..	..	..	..	..	..	..
58	Guatemala[c]	..	..	*42*	*42*	*14*	*9*	*4*	*3*	*12*	*16*	*27*	*28*
59	Papua New Guinea[c]	35	404	23	..	1	..	35	..	4	..	37	..
60	Bulgaria	..	..	..	..	..	..	..	..	..	..	..	..
61	Romania	..	10,623	..	*19*	..	*15*	..	*12*	..	*6*	..	*47*
62	Jordan	..	598	21	20	14	6	7	4	6	20	52	50
63	Ecuador[c]	305	2,790	43	29	14	10	3	7	8	12	32	42
64	Dominican Republic[c]	275	1,094	74	..	5	..	1	..	6	..	14	..
65	El Salvador[c]	194	1,238	40	*36*	30	*14*	3	*4*	8	*24*	18	*23*
66	Lithuania[c]	..	..	..	..	..	..	..	..	..	..	..	..
67	Colombia	1,487	9,618	31	29	20	14	8	10	11	16	29	31
68	Jamaica[c]	221	620	46	44	7	6	11	9	5	7	30	34
69	Peru[c]	1,430	..	25	..	14	..	7	..	7	..	47	..
70	Paraguay[c]	99	1,103	56	*55*	16	*16*	1	..	5	*12*	21	*17*
71	Kazakhstan[c]	..	10,571	..	..	..	..	..	..	..	..	..	..
72	Tunisia[c]	121	2,576	29	..	18	..	4	..	13	..	36	..

Note: For data comparability and coverage, see the technical notes. Figures in italics are for years other than those specified.

		Value added in manufacturing (million $)		Distribution of manufacturing value added (%)									
				Food, beverages, and tobacco		Textiles and clothing		Machinery, transport equipment		Chemicals		Other[a]	
		1970	1992	1970	1992	1970	1992	1970	1992	1970	1992	1970	1992
73	Algeria	682	4,010	32	22	20	19	9	11	4	3	35	45
74	Namibia	..	173	..	..	..	..	..	..	..	..	..	..
75	Slovak Republic[c]	..	..	..	..	..	..	..	..	..	..	..	..
76	Latvia	..	1,738	..	..	..	..	..	..	..	..	..	..
77	Thailand[c]	1,130	31,185	23	16	14	16	4	40	25	5	34	23
78	Costa Rica[c]	203	1,380	48	47	12	8	6	8	7	10	28	27
79	Ukraine[c]	..	48,872	..	..	..	..	..	..	..	..	..	..
80	Poland	..	..	20	21	19	9	24	26	8	7	28	37
81	Russian Federation[c]	..	200,237	..	..	..	..	..	..	..	..	..	..
82	Panama[c]	127	502	41	51	9	5	1	3	5	9	44	32
83	Czech Republic[c]	..	..	..	..	..	..	..	..	..	..	..	..
84	Botswana[c]	5	161	..	..	..	..	..	..	..	..	..	..
85	Turkey	1,930	27,465	26	18	15	14	8	19	7	9	45	40
86	*Iran, Islamic Rep.*	..	15,363	30	14	20	17	18	26	6	6	26	37
	Upper-middle-income	**50,427**	..										
87	Venezuela[c]	2,163	8,838	30	22	13	5	9	9	8	12	39	52
88	Belarus[c]	..	12,179	..	..	..	..	..	..	..	..	..	..
89	Brazil	10,422	90,062	16	15	13	11	22	22	10	14	39	38
90	South Africa	3,892	26,050	15	17	13	8	17	19	10	10	45	47
91	Mauritius	26	602	75	23	6	51	5	3	3	5	12	19
92	Estonia[c]	..	1,265	..	..	..	..	..	..	..	..	..	..
93	Malaysia[c]	500	..	26	10	3	6	8	34	9	11	54	39
94	Chile[c]	2,088	..	17	29	12	7	11	5	5	11	55	49
95	Hungary[c]	..	7,381	12	11	13	9	28	27	8	14	39	40
96	Mexico[c]	8,449	67,157	..	24	..	5	..	25	..	17	..	30
97	Trinidad and Tobago	198	496	18	..	3	..	7	..	2	..	70	..
98	Uruguay[c]	619	2,476	34	33	21	18	7	8	6	9	32	32
99	Oman[c]	0	495	..	..	..	..	..	..	..	..	..	..
100	Gabon[c]	22	653	37	..	7	..	6	..	6	..	44	..
101	Slovenia	..	3,670	..	16	..	16	..	23	..	10	..	35
102	Puerto Rico[c]	1,190	13,392	..	16	..	5	..	13	..	50	..	16
103	Argentina	9,963	50,009	18	21	17	10	17	13	8	12	40	44
104	Greece	1,952	12,398	19	26	19	17	13	12	9	9	41	35
105	Korea, Rep.[c]	1,880	85,454	26	10	17	12	11	30	11	10	36	37
106	Portugal[b]	..	..	18	20	19	23	13	12	10	10	39	35
107	*Saudi Arabia[c]*	435	..	..	..	..	..	..	..	..	..	..	..
108	*Turkmenistan*	..	..	..	..	..	..	..	..	..	..	..	..
	Low- and middle-income	..	..										
	Sub-Saharan Africa	**7,233 t**	**45,698 t**										
	East Asia & Pacific	**37,886 t**	**343,419 t**										
	South Asia	**10,362 t**	**53,889 t**										
	Europe and Central Asia	..	..										
	Middle East & N. Africa	..	..										
	Latin America & Caribbean	**41,601 t**	..										
	Severely indebted	**33,568 t**	..										
	High-income economies	**568,236 t**	..										
109	New Zealand[c]	1,809	..	24	27	13	8	15	14	4	6	43	45
110	Ireland	786	1,511	31	27	19	3	13	27	7	21	30	22
111	Spain[c]	..	100,672	13	18	15	8	16	26	11	10	45	38
112	† Israel	..	..	15	13	14	9	23	32	7	8	41	38
113	Australia[c]	9,551	43,679	16	18	9	6	24	20	7	8	43	48
114	† Hong Kong	1,013	12,020	4	11	41	35	16	21	2	2	36	32
115	United Kingdom	35,540	201,859	13	15	9	5	31	30	10	13	37	37
116	Finland	2,588	20,785	13	14	10	3	20	23	6	8	51	51
117	† Kuwait[c]	120	1,731	5	4	4	3	1	2	4	3	86	88
118	Italy[c]	29,093	250,345	10	10	13	14	24	33	13	6	40	38
119	† Singapore[c]	379	13,568	12	4	5	3	28	54	4	9	51	30
120	Canada	16,782	..	16	17	8	5	23	26	7	10	46	41
121	Netherlands[c]	..	58,476	17	21	8	3	27	24	13	16	36	36
122	† United Arab Emirates	..	2,708	..	..	..	..	..	..	..	..	..	..
123	Belgium[c]	1,425	..	17	17	13	8	25	22	9	14	37	39
124	France[c]	..	271,133	12	14	10	6	26	30	8	9	44	42
125	Austria[c]	4,873	46,739	16	15	13	6	20	28	7	8	45	43
126	Germany[c]	70,888[d]	565,603	13[d]	..	8[d]	..	31[d]	..	10[d]	..	39[d]	..
127	Sweden	..	43,605	10	11	6	2	30	33	5	10	49	44
128	United States[c]	254,115	..	12	13	8	5	31	31	10	12	39	38
129	Norway	2,416	*14,282*	15	23	7	2	23	27	7	8	49	40
130	Denmark	2,929	23,478	20	23	8	4	24	23	8	12	40	38
131	Japan[c]	73,342	1,023,048	8	10	8	5	34	38	11	10	40	38
132	Switzerland[c]	..	..	..	10	..	4	..	14	..	..	..	72
	World	..	..										

a. Includes unallocated data; see the technical notes. b. Includes Eritrea. c. Value added in manufacturing data are at purchaser values. d. Data refer to the Federal Republic of Germany before unification.

Table 7. Manufacturing earnings and output

		Earnings per employee					Total earnings as % of value added				Gross output per employee (1980=100)			
		Avg. annual growth rate (%)		Index (1980=100)										
		1970–80	1980–92	1990	1991	1992	1970	1990	1991	1992	1970	1990	1991	1992
Low-income economies														
Excluding China & India														
1	Mozambique	..	..	..	..	..	29	..	..	..	..	..	..	..
2	Tanzania	..	..	..	..	..	42	..	..	..	122	..	..	..
3	Ethiopia[a]	..	..	..	..	..	..	22	..	..	..	..	..	..
4	Sierra Leone	..	..	..	..	..	..	..	..	..	..	..	..	..
5	Viet Nam	..	..	..	..	..	..	..	..	..	..	..	..	..
6	Burundi	−7.5	..	129	123	..	..	21	19	..	..	75	71	..
7	Uganda	..	..	..	..	..	..	..	..	..	..	..	..	..
8	Nepal	..	..	..	..	..	..	23	25	..	..	..	..	..
9	Malawi	..	..	..	..	..	36	..	..	..	126	..	..	..
10	Chad	..	..	..	..	..	..	..	..	..	..	..	..	..
11	Rwanda	..	..	..	..	..	22	..	..	..	..	..	..	..
12	Bangladesh	−3.0	−0.7	86	..	..	26	39	..	..	..	..	..	..
13	Madagascar	−0.8	..	..	..	..	36	..	..	..	106	..	..	..
14	Guinea-Bissau	..	..	..	..	..	..	..	..	..	..	..	..	..
15	Kenya	−3.4	−2.1	91	83	69	50	43	40	42	43	233	247	235
16	Mali	..	..	..	..	..	46	..	..	..	139	..	..	..
17	Niger	..	..	..	..	..	..	..	..	..	..	..	..	..
18	Lao PDR	..	..	..	..	..	..	..	..	..	..	..	..	..
19	Burkina Faso	..	..	..	..	..	..	..	..	..	..	..	..	..
20	India	0.4	2.5	134	130	129	46	39	38	38	83	212	214	217
21	Nigeria	−0.8	..	..	..	..	18	..	..	..	182	..	..	..
22	Albania	..	..	..	..	..	..	36	..	..	..	..	..	..
23	Nicaragua	−2.0	..	..	..	..	16	..	..	..	210	..	..	..
24	Togo	..	..	..	..	..	..	..	..	..	..	..	..	..
25	Gambia, The	..	..	..	..	..	..	..	..	..	..	..	..	..
26	Zambia	−3.2	3.8	122	130	..	34	26	26	..	109	129	132	..
27	Mongolia	..	..	..	..	..	..	..	..	..	..	..	..	..
28	Central African Republic	..	..	..	..	..	..	41	..	36	..	142	..	122
29	Benin	..	..	..	..	..	..	..	..	..	..	..	..	..
30	Ghana	−14.8	..	..	..	..	23	..	..	..	193	..	..	..
31	Pakistan	3.4	..	..	..	..	21	..	..	..	50	..	..	..
32	Tajikistan	..	..	..	..	..	..	..	..	..	..	..	..	..
33	China	..	..	..	..	..	..	..	..	..	..	243	269	318
34	Guinea	..	..	..	..	..	..	..	..	..	..	..	..	..
35	Mauritania	..	..	..	..	..	..	..	..	..	..	..	..	..
36	Zimbabwe	1.6	0.1	106	108	106	43	33	29	27	98	127	132	132
37	Georgia	..	..	..	..	..	..	..	..	..	..	..	..	..
38	Honduras	..	..	..	..	..	..	37	35	36	..	..	..	..
39	Sri Lanka	..	1.4	95	..	..	..	18	..	..	70	138	..	..
40	Côte d'Ivoire	−0.9	..	..	..	..	27	..	..	..	71	..	..	..
41	Lesotho	..	..	..	..	..	..	..	..	..	..	..	..	..
42	Armenia	..	..	..	..	..	..	..	..	..	..	..	..	..
43	Egypt, Arab Rep.	4.1	−3.6	82	80	73	54	33	30	29	89	215	234	209
44	*Myanmar*	..	..	..	..	..	..	..	..	..	..	..	..	..
45	*Yemen, Rep.*	..	..	..	..	..	..	..	..	..	..	..	..	..
Middle-income economies														
Lower-middle-income														
46	Azerbaijan	..	..	..	..	..	..	..	..	..	..	..	..	..
47	Indonesia	5.2	4.3	164	171	172	26	20	20	19	42	206	214	214
48	Senegal	..	..	..	..	..	..	..	..	..	..	..	..	..
49	Bolivia	1.7	−0.8	74	78	..	37	9	8	..	50	..	..	..
50	Cameroon	..	..	88	..	..	29	45	..	..	80	189	..	..
51	Macedonia, FYR	..	..	..	..	..	..	48	49	28	..	..	..	..
52	Kyrgyz Republic	..	..	..	..	..	..	..	..	..	..	..	..	..
53	Philippines	−3.7	5.2	161	180	181	21	27	27	26	104	111	122	128
54	Congo	..	..	..	..	..	34	..	..	..	..	..	..	..
55	Uzbekistan	..	..	..	..	..	..	..	..	..	..	..	..	..
56	Morocco	..	−2.5	76	78	78	..	37	37	37	..	91	90	89
57	Moldova	..	..	..	..	..	..	..	..	..	..	..	..	..
58	Guatemala	−3.2	−1.6	97	..	..	..	20	..	..	..	..	..	..
59	Papua New Guinea	2.9	..	..	..	..	40	..	..	..	..	..	..	..
60	Bulgaria	..	..	..	..	..	..	..	..	..	..	128	138	132
61	Romania	..	..	..	..	..	..	42	39	..	..	..	..	..
62	Jordan	..	−3.3	79	73	70	37	24	26	29	..	..	..	..
63	Ecuador	3.3	−0.7	91	98	105	27	39	38	38	83	116	123	124
64	Dominican Republic	−1.1	..	..	..	..	35	..	..	..	63	..	..	..
65	El Salvador	2.4	..	..	..	..	28	..	20	..	71	..	..	..
66	Lithuania	..	..	..	..	..	..	..	..	..	..	..	..	..
67	Colombia	−0.2	1.0	116	115	111	25	15	15	15	86	168	160	167
68	Jamaica	−0.2	−1.5	90	89	87	43	32	33	34	99	76	72	75
69	Peru	..	..	..	..	..	..	..	..	..	80	..	..	..
70	Paraguay	..	..	..	..	..	..	..	22	..	..	..	..	..
71	Kazakhstan	..	..	..	..	..	..	..	..	..	..	..	..	..
72	Tunisia	..	..	..	..	..	44	..	..	..	94	..	..	..

Note: For data comparability and coverage, see the technical notes. Figures in italics are for years other than those specified.

		Earnings per employee					Total earnings as % of value added				Gross output per employee (1980=100)			
		Avg. annual growth rate (%)		Index (1980=100)											
		1970–80	1980–92	1990	1991	1992	1970	1990	1991	1992	1970	1990	1991	1992
73	Algeria	−1.3	..	..	..	..	45	..	..	..	121	..	..	..
74	Namibia	..	..	..	..	..	..	..	..	..	..	..	..	..
75	Slovak Republic	..	..	..	..	..	..	..	..	..	..	..	..	..
76	Latvia	..	..	..	..	..	..	..	..	..	..	..	..	..
77	Thailand	..	..	..	..	..	26	16	12	..	..	..	..	..
78	Costa Rica	..	..	..	..	..	41	38	36	..	..	..	..	..
79	Ukraine	..	..	..	..	..	..	..	..	..	..	..	..	..
80	Poland	5.6	−0.8	83	78	74	24	16	..	..	..	..	..	..
81	Russian Federation	..	..	..	..	..	..	..	..	..	..	..	..	..
82	Panama	0.2	2.0	129	134	139	32	36	36	37	67	91	93	95
83	Czech Republic	..	..	..	..	..	..	..	..	..	..	..	..	..
84	Botswana	..	..	..	..	..	..	..	..	..	..	..	..	..
85	Turkey	6.1	3.0	122	158	154	26	22	25	25	108	173	200	204
86	*Iran, Islamic Rep.*	..	−6.8	45	59	..	25	32	35	..	..	110	118	..
Upper-middle-income															
87	Venezuela	4.9	−5.4	58	61	57	31	16	21	19	102	121	118	122
88	Belarus	..	..	..	..	..	..	..	..	..	..	..	..	..
89	Brazil	5.0	−2.4	81	80	..	22	23	23	..	82	95	97	..
90	South Africa	2.7	0.2	107	105	107	46	51	51	51	64	81	78	75
91	Mauritius	1.8	0.4	101	107	..	34	46	48	..	139	76	76	..
92	Estonia	..	..	..	..	..	..	..	..	..	..	..	..	..
93	Malaysia	2.0	2.3	129	135	138	28	27	27	27	96	..	..	..
94	Chile	8.1	−0.3	105	111	116	19	17	18	18	60	..	..	..
95	Hungary	3.6	1.7	122	115	118	28	41	43	..	46	94	106	85
96	Mexico	..	..	..	..	..	..	21	22	..	..	..	..	..
97	Trinidad and Tobago	..	..	..	..	..	..	..	..	..	..	..	..	..
98	Uruguay	..	−2.3	84	81	74	..	23	23	23	..	109	110	112
99	Oman	..	..	..	..	..	..	2	..	..	..	..	..	..
100	Gabon	..	..	..	..	..	..	..	..	..	..	..	..	..
101	Slovenia	..	..	..	..	..	..	76	80	74	..	..	..	..
102	Puerto Rico	..	..	..	..	..	..	..	..	..	..	..	..	..
103	Argentina	−2.1	−2.2	82	69	..	28	20	19	..	75	113	120	..
104	Greece	4.9	0.8	114	114	111	32	43	41	39	55	113	114	110
105	Korea, Rep.	10.0	8.4	209	231	237	25	28	26	26	34	223	249	270
106	Portugal	1.8	0.5	103	..	..	34	36	..	..	..	125	..	..
107	*Saudi Arabia*	..	..	..	..	..	..	..	..	..	..	..	..	..
108	*Turkmenistan*	..	..	..	..	..	..	..	..	..	..	..	..	..
Low- and middle-income															
Sub-Saharan Africa															
East Asia & Pacific															
South Asia															
Europe and Central Asia															
Middle East & N. Africa															
Latin America & Caribbean															
Severely indebted															
High-income economies															
109	New Zealand	1.2	0.1	95	102	108	62	57	56	56	..	144	..	..
110	Ireland	4.1	2.0	112	116	123	49	27	27	26	..	..	..	..
111	Spain	4.1	1.2	111	115	..	52	41	42	..	..	..	..	..
112	† Israel	8.8	−1.6	94	91	86	36	60	59	..	..	..	..	..
113	Australia	2.9	0.5	104	110	112	52	39	39	35	..	149	164	163
114	† Hong Kong	..	4.8	153	157	158	..	55	52	52	..	..	..	..
115	United Kingdom	1.7	2.5	125	128	131	52	42	44	44	..	..	..	..
116	Finland	2.6	2.6	130	129	130	47	47	52	48	74	143	144	160
117	† Kuwait	7.0	−1.6	64	..	..	12	19	..	..	..	..	..	..
118	Italy	4.1	5.8	177	179	173	41	67	69	69	50	151	152	152
119	† Singapore	3.0	5.1	176	187	200	36	32	33	34	72	130	128	132
120	Canada	1.8	0.1	101	99	102	53	46	48	47	68	113	..	..
121	Netherlands	2.5	1.7	137	138	..	52	61	60	..	..	..	..	..
122	† United Arab Emirates	..	..	..	..	..	..	..	..	..	..	..	..	..
123	Belgium	4.7	0.5	104	105	108	46	39	42	42	..	166	..	..
124	France	..	..	..	..	..	..	..	..	..	..	122	122	124
125	Austria	3.5	2.0	120	126	127	47	53	54	54	62	134	138	139
126	Germany	..	..	..	..	..	..	..	..	..	..	..	..	..
127	Sweden	0.4	1.2	106	108	113	52	35	52	53	..	134	150	159
128	United States	0.1	0.4	103	103	105	47	36	36	35	..	..	..	..
129	Norway	2.6	2.3	112	115	142	50	59	60	71	74	135	133	..
130	Denmark	2.5	−0.3	90	92	97	56	61	59	58	69	81	82	85
131	Japan	3.1	1.9	120	122	123	32	33	33	35	48	136	141	138
132	Switzerland	..	..	..	..	..	..	..	..	..	..	..	..	..
World															

a. Includes Eritrea.

Table 8. Growth of consumption and investment

		Average annual growth rate (%)					
		General government consumption		Private consumption, etc.		Gross domestic investment	
		1970–80	1980–93	1970–80	1980–93	1970–80	1980–93
	Low-income economies	**5.1 w**	**6.0 w**	**4.1 w**	**4.7 w**	**6.4 w**	**6.1 w**
	Excluding China & India	..	**2.7 w**	..	**2.1 w**	**7.4 w**	**–0.2 w**
1	Mozambique	..	–1.5	..	3.5	..	3.3
2	Tanzania	..	..	..	..	3.1	5.6
3	Ethiopia	..	..	..	..	..	..
4	Sierra Leone	a	–2.4	5.3	–0.1	–1.2	–1.9
5	Viet Nam	..	..	..	..	..	..
6	Burundi	2.0	3.3	3.7	4.1	16.1	3.2
7	Uganda	..	3.9	..	3.2	..	7.1
8	Nepal	..	..	..	..	..	..
9	Malawi	7.9	5.0	3.4	3.0	4.2	–2.3
10	Chad	..	..	..	..	..	..
11	Rwanda	7.5	7.3	5.3	0.9	10.4	0.0
12	Bangladesh	a	a	2.3	2.7	4.8	1.6
13	Madagascar	1.5	–0.1	–0.2	–0.7	0.4	2.5
14	Guinea-Bissau	1.3	5.0	–3.2	2.9	–1.7	9.1
15	Kenya	9.2	3.4	6.4	4.7	2.4	–0.7
16	Mali	4.0	5.4	5.2	1.0	4.9	5.1
17	Niger	3.0	1.7	–1.7	–0.2	7.6	–6.8
18	Lao PDR	..	..	..	..	..	..
19	Burkina Faso	6.6	5.5	4.7	2.5	4.4	7.9
20	India	4.1	6.2	2.8	4.7	4.5	5.7
21	Nigeria	11.4	0.3	7.8	–0.9	11.4	–5.5
22	Albania	..	a	..	4.1	..	–11.8
23	Nicaragua	10.7	–3.0	1.1	–1.2	..	–5.5
24	Togo	10.2	–1.9	2.6	2.5	11.9	–1.4
25	Gambia, The	8.5	2.4	6.3	5.6	31.4	2.5
26	Zambia	1.4	–0.1	0.2	0.8	–10.9	2.5
27	Mongolia	..	..	..	..	..	..
28	Central African Republic	–2.4	–6.0	5.2	2.0	–9.7	0.6
29	Benin	–1.9	0.6	3.1	1.5	11.4	–3.0
30	Ghana	5.1	1.1	1.7	3.1	–2.5	9.8
31	Pakistan	4.1	8.0	4.2	4.8	3.7	5.6
32	Tajikistan	..	1.2	..	3.8	..	4.2
33	China	6.3	10.8	5.3	7.9	7.6	11.1
34	Guinea	..	..	..	..	..	..
35	Mauritania	11.4	–2.6	2.7	3.2	8.3	–2.8
36	Zimbabwe	12.1	3.4	2.6	2.7	–4.2	3.0
37	Georgia	..	–1.3	..	3.0	..	–9.2
38	Honduras	6.5	2.1	5.9	2.5	9.1	5.5
39	Sri Lanka	0.3	5.6	5.0	3.5	13.8	2.4
40	Côte d'Ivoire	9.6	–1.2	6.6	0.3	10.1	–9.5
41	Lesotho	17.8	2.9	10.6	0.3	23.4	9.4
42	Armenia	..	4.0	..	2.3	..	4.5
43	Egypt, Arab Rep.	a	2.8	7.4	2.3	18.7	1.2
44	Myanmar	a	a	4.1	0.5	8.0	–0.7
45	Yemen, Rep.	..	..	..	..	..	..
	Middle-income economies	..	**1.4 w**	..	**2.2 w**	..	**1.3 w**
	Lower-middle-income	..	**0.2 w**	..	**1.6 w**	..	**0.8 w**
46	Azerbaijan	..	1.5	..	2.9	..	0.4
47	Indonesia	13.1	4.8	6.5	4.4	14.1	7.1
48	Senegal	5.9	1.9	3.0	2.6	0.3	3.4
49	Bolivia	7.9	–1.7	4.5	2.8	2.3	–4.3
50	Cameroon	5.2	5.1	7.4	–1.6	11.2	–4.0
51	Macedonia, FYR	..	..	..	..	..	..
52	Kyrgyz Republic	..	1.7	..	1.9	..	4.5
53	Philippines	6.8	1.0	4.3	2.4	11.3	–0.1
54	Congo	4.1	2.2	1.5	1.8	1.5	–11.1
55	Uzbekistan	..	3.5	..	1.7	..	0.9
56	Morocco	14.0	5.0	5.5	3.7	9.9	2.6
57	Moldova	..	3.9	..	6.2	..	3.6
58	Guatemala	6.5	3.4	5.3	2.1	7.9	1.7
59	Papua New Guinea	–1.3	0.6	4.5	0.9	–5.4	0.3
60	Bulgaria	..	9.9	..	0.3	..	–2.3
61	Romania	..	..	..	..	..	–3.8
62	Jordan	..	..	..	..	..	..
63	Ecuador	14.5	–1.3	8.1	2.1	11.0	–1.7
64	Dominican Republic	2.7	2.0	5.6	0.5	9.4	3.5
65	El Salvador	6.8	2.5	4.2	1.0	7.3	3.9
66	Lithuania	..	..	..	..	..	..
67	Colombia	5.4	4.5	5.3	3.1	5.0	2.1
68	Jamaica	6.5	5.0	7.5	4.6	–9.6	0.7
69	Peru	4.0	–0.9	2.2	0.3	6.5	–2.3
70	Paraguay	4.8	4.0	8.7	2.3	18.6	0.8
71	Kazakhstan	..	2.2	..	2.4	..	1.9
72	Tunisia	7.8	3.7	8.9	3.2	6.1	1.2

Note: For data comparability and coverage, see the technical notes. Figures in italics are for years other than those specified.

		Average annual growth rate (%)					
		General government consumption		Private consumption, etc.		Gross domestic investment	
		1970–80	1980–93	1970–80	1980–93	1970–80	1980–93
73	Algeria	11.5	4.9	3.6	2.1	13.6	–3.6
74	Namibia	..	4.5	..	2.6	..	–6.5
75	Slovak Republic	..	..	..	..	..	..
76	Latvia	..	..	..	..	..	..
77	Thailand	9.8	4.6	6.4	7.0	7.2	11.4
78	Costa Rica	6.6	1.5	4.8	3.7	9.2	5.5
79	Ukraine	..	–0.2	..	1.5	..	–4.4
80	Poland	..	–0.1	..	1.6	..	–1.1
81	Russian Federation	..	–2.0	..	–3.5	..	–0.1
82	Panama	5.8	–0.4	3.9	1.3	0.3	–1.5
83	Czech Republic	..	..	..	..	..	..
84	Botswana	..	..	..	..	..	..
85	Turkey	6.3	3.3	4.7	5.1	6.9	5.6
86	*Iran, Islamic Rep.*	..	–2.5	..	4.5	..	0.4
	Upper-middle-income	6.4 w	3.8 w	6.2 w	3.1 w	6.4 w	2.1 w
87	Venezuela	..	2.8	..	2.2	7.1	–1.1
88	Belarus	..	1.9	..	1.1	..	3.3
89	Brazil	6.0	5.2	8.0	1.8	8.9	–0.3
90	South Africa	5.5	3.1	3.4	1.5	0.9	–4.7
91	Mauritius	9.8	3.5	9.2	5.5	10.0	11.1
92	Estonia	..	4.1	..	0.4	..	–6.9
93	Malaysia	9.3	3.9	7.5	5.5	10.8	6.3
94	Chile	2.4	0.9	0.7	3.2	–2.1	9.6
95	Hungary	2.5	1.8	3.0	0.0	6.7	–1.6
96	Mexico	8.3	1.9	5.9	2.6	8.3	0.1
97	Trinidad and Tobago	9.0	–4.5	6.4	–0.7	14.2	–8.9
98	Uruguay	4.0	2.1	0.1	*1.7*	10.7	–3.4
99	Oman	..	..	..	..	..	..
100	Gabon	10.2	–0.4	7.3	0.5	13.6	–5.3
101	Slovenia	..	..	..	..	..	..
102	Puerto Rico	..	4.5	..	3.1	..	6.8
103	Argentina	a	a	2.3	1.1	3.1	–1.3
104	Greece	6.9	2.4	4.5	3.3	2.1	0.4
105	Korea, Rep.	7.4	6.1	8.2	8.6	14.1	11.8
106	Portugal	8.7	4.5	4.4	2.9	2.7	4.1
107	*Saudi Arabia*	..	..	..	..	..	..
108	*Turkmenistan*	..	5.7	..	3.6	..	–0.9
	Low- and middle-income	..	2.4 w	..	2.8 w	..	2.4 w
	Sub-Saharan Africa	5.8 w	1.9 w	4.5 w	1.2 w	4.3 w	–2.8 w
	East Asia & Pacific	7.7 w	6.8 w	6.2 w	6.9 w	9.8 w	9.6 w
	South Asia	4.0 w	7.0 w	3.0 w	4.6 w	4.6 w	5.5 w
	Europe and Central Asia	..	–0.2 w	..	0.3 w	..	–0.1 w
	Middle East & N. Africa	..	..	..	..	..	..
	Latin America & Caribbean	6.2 w	3.3 w	6.3 w	2.1 w	6.6 w	0.1 w
	Severely indebted	..	3.6 w	..	1.7 w	6.7 w	–1.0 w
	High-income economies	2.6 w	2.1 w	3.5 w	3.0 w	2.3 w	3.4 w
109	New Zealand	3.6	1.0	1.6	1.5	–1.0	2.4
110	Ireland	6.0	0.2	4.3	3.3	5.2	–0.3
111	Spain	5.8	5.4	3.8	2.7	1.5	5.1
112	† Israel	3.9	0.9	5.8	5.4	0.6	5.8
113	Australia	5.1	3.4	3.2	3.2	1.9	1.2
114	† Hong Kong	8.3	5.7	9.0	7.1	12.1	5.0
115	United Kingdom	2.4	1.2	2.0	3.3	0.2	4.0
116	Finland	5.2	2.7	2.8	3.3	0.6	–1.0
117	† Kuwait	10.7	..	8.7	..	19.4	..
118	Italy	3.0	2.3	4.1	2.7	1.6	1.5
119	† Singapore	6.2	6.3	5.9	6.3	7.8	5.7
120	Canada	3.8	2.5	5.1	2.8	5.7	3.6
121	Netherlands	2.9	1.5	3.9	2.0	0.1	2.7
122	† United Arab Emirates	..	..	..	..	..	..
123	Belgium	4.1	0.7	3.5	1.9	2.1	3.7
124	France	3.4	2.2	3.3	2.2	1.4	2.1
125	Austria	3.8	1.4	3.7	2.5	2.7	3.0
126	Germanyb	3.3	1.3	3.2	2.6	0.5	2.4
127	Sweden	3.3	1.6	1.9	1.5	–0.6	1.8
128	United States	1.1	2.4	3.1	2.9	2.8	2.5
129	Norway	5.4	2.8	4.1	1.6	3.3	–1.0
130	Denmark	4.1	0.9	2.0	1.7	–0.8	1.2
131	Japan	4.9	2.3	4.7	3.5	2.5	5.5
132	Switzerland	1.8	2.7	1.0	1.4	–1.8	3.1
	World	..	2.3 w	..	3.1	..	3.2 w

a. General government consumption figures are not available separately; they are included in private consumption, etc.   b. Data refer to the Federal Republic of Germany before unification.

Table 9. Structure of demand

		Distribution of gross domestic product (%)													
		General govt. consumption		Private consumption,etc.		Gross domestic investment		Gross domestic savings		Exports of goods & nonfactor services		Resource balance	
		1970	1993	1970	1993	1970	1993	1970	1993	1970	1993	1970	1993
Low-income economies		9 w	10 w	74 w	63 w	20 w	30 w	19 w	27 w	7 w	20 w	−1 w	−3 w
Excluding China & India		11 w	12 w	76 w	81 w	14 w	17 w	12 w	10 w	13 w	19 w	−3 w	−8 w
1	Mozambique	..	17	..	94	..	41	..	−11	..	21	..	−53
2	Tanzania	11	9	69	82	23	51	20	10	26	31	−2	−41
3	Ethiopia	..	11	..	86	..	12	..	3	..	..	..	−9
4	Sierra Leone	12	11	74	84	17	9	15	5	30	22	−2	−4
5	Viet Nam	..	a	..	84	..	21	..	..	..	28	..	−4
6	Burundi	10	13	87	90	5	18	4	−3	11	9	−1	−21
7	Uganda	a	14	84	89	13	15	..	−2	22	5	3	−18
8	Nepal	a	9	97	80	6	21	3	11	5	18	−3	−10
9	Malawi	16	17	73	81	26	12	11	2	24	17	−15	−10
10	Chad	27	17	64	93	18	9	10	−10	23	13	−8	−19
11	Rwanda	9	22	88	87	7	15	3	−10	12	7	−4	−25
12	Bangladesh	13	14	79	79	11	14	7	8	8	12	−4	−6
13	Madagascar	13	7	79	91	10	12	7	2	19	14	−2	−10
14	Guinea-Bissau	20	7	77	93	30	26	3	0	4	11	−26	−26
15	Kenya	16	13	60	66	24	16	24	21	30	42	−1	5
16	Mali	10	13	80	81	16	22	10	7	13	16	−6	−15
17	Niger	9	17	89	82	10	6	3	1	11	13	−7	−4
18	Lao PDR	..	..	..	..	..	..	..	..	..	21	..	−10
19	Burkina Faso	9	17	92	81	12	22	−1	2	7	12	−12	−20
20	India	9	11	75	66	17	24	16	24	4	11	−1	0
21	Nigeria	8	18	80	63	15	15	12	19	8	36	−3	3
22	Albania	..	a	..	170	..	10	..	−70	..	12	..	−81
23	Nicaragua	9	17	75	91	18	17	16	−8	26	20	−2	−25
24	Togo	16	17	58	86	15	6	26	−2	50	23	11	−8
25	Gambia, The	11	18	84	74	5	20	5	8	33	53	0	−12
26	Zambia	16	11	39	75	28	15	45	14	54	35	17	−1
27	Mongolia	..	18	..	66	..	19	..	16	..	63	..	−3
28	Central African Republic	21	10	75	89	19	9	4	1	28	15	−15	−7
29	Benin	10	11	85	85	12	15	5	3	22	22	−6	−12
30	Ghana	13	12	74	90	14	15	13	−1	21	20	−1	−16
31	Pakistan	10	14	81	74	16	21	9	12	8	16	−7	−9
32	Tajikistan	..	..	..	..	..	..	..	..	..	..	..	..
33	China	8	9	64	51	28	41	29	40	3	24	0	−1
34	Guinea	..	7	..	84	..	16	..	9	..	21	..	−7
35	Mauritania	14	10	56	79	22	24	30	11	41	46	8	−14
36	Zimbabwe	12	19	67	64	20	22	21	17	..	34	..	−6
37	Georgia	..	9	..	89	..	32	..	2	..	36	..	−30
38	Honduras	11	12	74	70	21	27	15	19	28	32	−6	−8
39	Sri Lanka	12	9	72	75	19	25	16	16	25	33	−3	−9
40	Côte d'Ivoire	14	20	57	63	22	9	29	16	36	34	7	7
41	Lesotho	12	30	120	112	12	76	−32	−42	11	15	−44	−118
42	Armenia	..	22	..	91	..	14	..	−14	..	..	..	−28
43	Egypt, Arab Rep.	25	14	66	80	14	17	9	6	14	25	−5	−11
44	*Myanmar*	a	a	89	89	14	12	11	11	5	2	−4	−1
45	*Yemen, Rep.*	..	29	..	68	..	20	..	3	..	15	..	−17
Middle-income economies		..	..	..	..	..	23 w	..	22 w	..	22 w	..	−1 w
Lower-middle-income		..	14 w	..	64 w	..	23 w	..	22 w	..	28 w	..	−1 w
46	Azerbaijan	..	20	..	54	..	14	..	26	..	..	..	12
47	Indonesia	8	10	78	60	16	28	14	31	13	28	−2	2
48	Senegal	15	12	74	80	16	14	11	7	27	22	−5	−7
49	Bolivia	10	13	66	81	24	15	24	6	25	17	0	−9
50	Cameroon	12	12	70	73	16	15	18	15	26	19	2	0
51	Macedonia, FYR	..	..	..	..	..	..	..	..	..	..	..	..
52	Kyrgyz Republic	..	16	..	52	..	25	..	32	..	..	..	7
53	Philippines	9	9	69	76	21	24	22	16	22	32	1	−9
54	Congo	17	22	82	70	24	14	1	8	35	44	−23	−7
55	Uzbekistan	..	22	..	44	..	29	..	34	..	..	..	5
56	Morocco	12	18	73	65	18	23	15	17	18	23	−4	−6
57	Moldova	..	a	..	104	..	7	..	−4	..	31	..	−11
58	Guatemala	8	6	78	85	13	17	14	9	19	18	1	−8
59	Papua New Guinea	30	21	64	51	42	20	6	29	18	49	−35	9
60	Bulgaria	..	17	..	66	..	20	..	17	..	50	..	−3
61	Romania	..	12	..	66	..	27	..	22	..	23	..	−5
62	Jordan	..	24	..	90	..	30	..	−13	..	38	..	−43
63	Ecuador	11	8	75	71	18	21	14	22	14	26	−5	1
64	Dominican Republic	12	5	77	77	19	22	12	18	17	24	−7	−4
65	El Salvador	11	10	76	88	13	17	13	2	25	14	0	−14
66	Lithuania	..	13	..	76	..	18	..	11	..	71	..	−7
67	Colombia	9	12	72	70	20	22	18	18	14	17	−2	−4
68	Jamaica	12	13	61	61	32	35	27	26	33	60	−4	−8
69	Peru	12	8	70	76	16	19	17	16	18	10	2	−2
70	Paraguay	9	9	77	77	15	22	14	14	15	27	−1	9
71	Kazakhstan	..	28	..	62	..	31	..	10	..	..	..	−21
72	Tunisia	17	16	66	63	21	29	17	20	22	40	−4	−9

Note: For data comparability and coverage, see the technical notes. Figures in italics are for years other than those specified.

		Distribution of gross domestic product (%)																					
		General govt. consumption		Private consumption,etc.		Gross domestic investment		Gross domestic savings		Exports of goods & nonfactor services		Resource balance											
		1970	1993	1970	1993	1970	1993	1970	1993	1970	1993	1970	1993										
73	Algeria	15	17	56	54	36	29	29	28	22	22	–7	–1										
74	Namibia	..	33	..	63	..	10	..	4	..	59	..	6										
75	Slovak Republic	..	23	..	54	..	25	..	22	..	67	..	–2										
76	Latvia	..	19	..	57	..	11	..	24	..	67	..	14										
77	Thailand	11	10	68	54	26	40	21	36	15	37	–4	–4										
78	Costa Rica	13	17	74	59	21	30	14	25	28	40	–7	–6										
79	Ukraine	..	13	..	80	..	8	..	7	..	17	..	–1										
80	Poland	..	22	..	65	..	16	..	13	..	19	..	–3										
81	Russian Federation	..	15	..	52	..	26	..	32	..	39	..	7										
82	Panama	15	17	61	59	28	25	24	24	38	37	–4	–1										
83	Czech Republic	..	26	..	54	..	17	..	20	..	55	..	3										
84	Botswana	20	..	78	..	42	..	2	..	23	61	–41	–3										
85	Turkey	13	13	70	65	20	27	17	22	6	14	–2	–5										
86	*Iran, Islamic Rep.*	..	15	..	55	..	29	..	30	..	24	..	1										
	Upper-middle-income	**11** w	**..**	**65** w	**..**	**24** w	**23** w	**23** w	**21** w	**15** w	**21** w	**–1** w	**–2** w										
87	Venezuela	11	9	52	73	33	19	37	18	21	26	4	–1										
88	Belarus	..	22	..	51	..	35	..	27	..	46	..	–8										
89	Brazil	11	a	69	79	21	19	20	21	7	8	0	2										
90	South Africa	12	21	61	60	30	15	27	19	22	23	–4	4										
91	Mauritius	14	11	75	65	10	29	11	24	43	63	1	–5										
92	Estonia	..	19	..	57	..	26	..	23	..	57	..	–3										
93	Malaysia	16	13	58	49	22	33	27	38	42	80	4	5										
94	Chile	12	10	68	66	19	26	20	24	15	28	1	–2										
95	Hungary	10	27	58	62	34	20	31	11	30	30	–2	–9										
96	Mexico	7	9	75	75	21	22	19	16	6	13	–3	–6										
97	Trinidad and Tobago	13	12	60	66	26	13	27	22	43	38	1	9										
98	Uruguay	15	14	74	72	11	16	10	14	13	20	–1	–1										
99	Oman	13	39	19	*34*	14	*17*	68	*27*	74	..	54	*10*										
100	Gabon	20	16	37	48	32	22	44	36	50	47	12	15										
101	Slovenia	..	23	..	56	..	20	..	21	..	63	..	1										
102	Puerto Rico	15	14	74	63	29	17	10	23	44	..	–18	6										
103	Argentina	10	a	67	84	25	18	23	..	7	6	a	–2										
104	Greece	13	19	68	71	28	20	20	10	10	22	–8	–10										
105	Korea, Rep.	10	11	76	54	24	34	15	35	14	29	–10	0										
106	Portugal	13	17	64	65	28	27	23	18	21	24	–6	*–9*										
107	*Saudi Arabia*	17	*33*	28	*40*	12	*24*	55	*27*	66	*43*	44	*3*										
108	*Turkmenistan*	..	*23*	..	*44*	..	*46*	..	*33*	..	..	..	*–13*										
	Low- and middle-income	**..**	**..**	**..**	**..**	**..**	**24** w	**..**	**23** w	**..**	**22** w	**..**	**–1** w										
	Sub-Saharan Africa	**13** w	**18** w	**69** w	**67** w	**21** w	**16** w	**18** w	**15** w	**20** w	**27** w	**–3** w	**–1** w										
	East Asia & Pacific	**8** w	**10** w	**64** w	**55** w	**27** w	**36** w	**28** w	**35** w	**6** w	**30** w	**1** w	**–1** w										
	South Asia	**9** w	**11** w	**76** w	**68** w	**16** w	**23** w	**15** w	**21** w	**5** w	**13** w	**–1** w	**–2** w										
	Europe and Central Asia	**..**	**20** w	**..**	**63** w	**..**	**21** w	**..**	**17** w	**..**	**30** w	**..**	**–4** w										
	Middle East & N. Africa	**..**	**22** w	**..**	**51** w	**..**	**28** w	**..**	**27** w	**..**	**32** w	**..**	**–1** w										
	Latin America & Caribbean	**10** w	**..**	**69** w	**..**	**22** w	**20** w	**20** w	**19** w	**13** w	**14** w	**–2** w	**–1** w										
	Severely indebted	**12** w	**..**	**72** w	**..**	**23** w	**18** w	**16** w	**19** w	**..**	**15** w	**–7** w	**1** w										
	High-income economies	**16** w	**17** w	**60** w	**63** w	**23** w	**19** w	**24** w	**20** w	**14** w	**20** w	**1** w	**1** w										
109	New Zealand	13	15	65	60	25	21	22	24	23	31	–3	3										
110	Ireland	14	16	70	56	24	14	16	28	35	68	–8	14										
111	Spain	9	18	65	63	27	20	26	19	13	19	–1	–1										
112	† Israel	34	27	58	59	27	22	8	14	25	31	–20	–9										
113	Australia	14	18	59	63	27	20	27	19	14	19	0	0										
114	† Hong Kong	7	9	68	60	21	27	25	31	92	143	4	4										
115	United Kingdom	18	22	62	64	20	15	21	14	23	25	1	–1										
116	Finland	14	23	57	57	30	14	29	20	26	33	–1	6										
117	† Kuwait	14	32	39	37	12	23	48	30	60	53	36	7										
118	Italy	13	18	60	62	27	17	28	20	16	23	0	4										
119	† Singapore	12	9	70	43	39	44	18	47	102	169	–20	4										
120	Canada	19	22	57	61	22	18	24	18	23	30	3	–1										
121	Netherlands	15	15	58	61	28	19	27	24	43	51	–2	5										
122	† United Arab Emirates	..	18	..	49	..	25	..	33	..	68	..	9										
123	Belgium	13	15	60	62	24	18	27	23	52	69	2	5										
124	France	15	19	58	61	27	18	27	20	16	23	1	2										
125	Austria	15	19	55	55	30	25	31	26	31	38	1	1										
126	Germany	16 b	20	55 b	58	28 b	22	30 b	22	21 b	22	2 b	0										
127	Sweden	22	28	53	55	25	13	25	17	24	33	–1	4										
128	United States	19	17	63	68	18	16	18	15	6	10	0	–1										
129	Norway	17	22	54	52	30	20	29	26	42	43	–1	7										
130	Denmark	20	26	57	52	26	14	23	21	28	35	–3	8										
131	Japan	7	10	52	58	39	30	40	33	11	9	1	2										
132	Switzerland	10	14	59	59	32	22	31	27	33	36	–2	5										
	World	**..**	**..**	**..**	**..**	**..**	**22** w	**..**	**22** w	**..**	**21** w	**..**	**1** w										

a. General government consumption figures are not available separately; they are included in private consumption etc. b. Data refer to the Federal Republic of Germany before unification.

Table 10. Central government expenditure

		Percentage of total expenditure												Total expenditure (% of GNP)		Overall surplus/deficit (% of GNP)	
		Defense		Education		Health		Housing, etc., soc. sec., welfare		Economic services		Other[a]					
		1980	1993	1980	1993	1980	1993	1980	1993	1980	1993	1980	1993	1980	1993	1980	1993
Low-income economies																	
Excluding China & India																	
1	Mozambique	..	..	..	..	..	..	..	..	..	..	..	..	..	..	..	..
2	Tanzania	9.2	..	13.3	..	6.0	..	2.5	..	42.9	..	26.1	..	28.8	..	-8.4	..
3	Ethiopia[b]	*34.0*	..	*10.7*	..	*4.0*	..	*6.5*	..	*24.7*	..	*20.1*	..	..	..	..	..
4	Sierra Leone[c]	*4.1*	..	*14.9*	..	*9.1*	..	*3.6*	..	..	..	*68.3*	..	29.8	23.0	-13.2	-5.0
5	Viet Nam	..	..	..	..	..	..	..	..	..	..	..	..	..	..	..	..
6	Burundi	..	..	..	..	..	..	..	..	..	..	..	..	21.7	..	-3.9	..
7	Uganda	25.2	..	14.9	..	5.1	..	4.2	..	11.1	..	39.5	..	6.1	..	-3.1	..
8	Nepal	6.7	*5.9*	9.9	*10.9*	3.9	*4.7*	1.7	*6.8*	58.8	*43.0*	19.1	*28.8*	14.2	*18.7*	-3.0	*-6.3*
9	Malawi[c]	12.8	..	9.0	..	5.5	..	1.6	..	43.7	..	27.3	..	37.6	..	-17.3	..
10	Chad	..	..	..	..	..	..	..	..	..	..	..	..	..	*32.0*	..	*-7.5*
11	Rwanda	..	..	..	..	..	..	..	..	..	..	..	..	14.3	31.9	-1.7	-9.1
12	Bangladesh[c]	9.4	..	11.5	..	6.4	..	5.3	..	46.9	..	20.4	..	10.0	..	2.5	..
13	Madagascar	..	*7.5*	..	*17.2*	..	*6.6*	..	*1.5*	..	*36.0*	..	*31.2*	..	*16.1*	..	*-5.9*
14	Guinea-Bissau	..	..	..	..	..	..	..	..	..	..	..	..	..	..	..	..
15	Kenya[c]	16.4	6.2	19.6	18.8	7.8	5.4	5.1	1.9	22.7	14.9	28.2	52.8	26.1	28.9	-4.6	-3.8
16	Mali	11.0	..	15.7	..	3.1	..	3.0	..	11.2	..	56.0	..	21.6	..	-4.7	..
17	Niger	3.8	..	18.0	..	4.1	..	3.8	..	32.4	..	38.0	..	18.7	..	-4.8	..
18	Lao PDR	..	..	..	..	..	..	..	..	..	..	..	..	..	..	..	..
19	Burkina Faso	17.0	..	15.5	..	5.8	..	7.6	..	19.3	..	34.8	..	14.1	..	0.3	..
20	India	19.8	14.5	1.9	2.2	1.6	1.9	4.3	7.1	24.2	16.2	48.3	58.0	13.2	16.9	-6.5	-4.8
21	Nigeria[c]	..	..	..	..	..	..	..	..	..	..	..	..	..	..	..	..
22	Albania	..	..	..	..	..	..	..	..	..	..	..	..	..	..	..	..
23	Nicaragua	11.0	6.8	11.6	14.2	14.6	13.0	7.4	15.8	20.6	18.0	34.9	32.2	32.3	39.5	-7.3	0.5
24	Togo	*7.1*	..	*22.9*	..	*6.1*	..	*11.0*	..	*22.2*	..	*30.8*	..	31.9	..	-2.0	..
25	Gambia, The	0.0	..	12.3	..	7.4	..	3.3	..	44.9	..	32.2	..	33.7	..	-4.7	..
26	Zambia	0.0	..	11.4	..	6.1	..	3.4	..	32.6	..	46.6	..	40.0	..	-20.0	..
27	Mongolia	..	10.7	..	2.7	..	2.3	..	19.1	..	23.8	..	41.3	..	25.3	..	-2.0
28	Central African Republic	*9.7*	..	*17.6*	..	*5.1*	..	*6.3*	..	*19.6*	..	*41.7*	..	21.9	..	-3.5	..
29	Benin	..	..	..	..	..	..	..	..	..	..	..	..	..	..	..	..
30	Ghana[c]	3.7	4.9	22.0	22.0	7.0	7.0	6.8	9.9	20.7	15.9	39.8	40.3	10.9	21.0	-4.2	-2.5
31	Pakistan	30.6	26.9	2.7	1.1	1.5	0.4	4.1	2.8	37.2	6.5	23.9	62.4	17.7	24.0	-5.8	-7.4
32	Tajikistan	..	..	..	..	..	..	..	..	..	..	..	..	..	..	..	..
33	China[c]	..	*16.4*	..	*2.2*	..	*0.4*	..	*0.2*	..	*39.5*	..	*41.3*	..	*9.2*	..	*-2.3*
34	Guinea	..	..	..	..	..	..	..	..	..	..	..	..	..	*21.9*	..	*-3.3*
35	Mauritania	..	..	..	..	..	..	..	..	..	..	..	..	..	..	..	..
36	Zimbabwe	25.0	..	15.5	..	5.4	..	7.8	..	18.1	..	28.2	..	35.3	*36.2*	-11.1	*-7.0*
37	Georgia	..	..	..	..	..	..	..	..	..	..	..	..	..	..	..	..
38	Honduras	..	..	..	..	..	..	..	..	..	..	..	..	..	..	..	..
39	Sri Lanka	1.7	11.4	6.7	10.4	4.9	5.2	12.7	16.6	15.9	20.8	58.2	35.5	41.6	26.9	-18.4	-6.4
40	Côte d'Ivoire	3.9	..	16.3	..	3.9	..	4.3	..	13.4	..	58.1	..	33.3	..	-11.4	..
41	Lesotho	*0.0*	*6.5*	*15.3*	*21.9*	*6.2*	*11.5*	*1.3*	*5.5*	*35.9*	*31.6*	*41.2*	*23.1*	*22.7*	*32.1*	-3.7	*-0.3*
42	Armenia	..	..	..	..	..	..	..	..	..	..	..	..	..	..	..	..
43	Egypt, Arab Rep.	11.4	*8.2*	8.1	*10.3*	2.4	*2.1*	13.1	*14.7*	7.2	*6.7*	57.7	*57.9*	53.7	*46.6*	-12.5	*-4.1*
44	*Myanmar*	21.9	*32.7*	10.6	*17.0*	5.3	*7.4*	10.6	*5.5*	33.7	*18.7*	17.9	*18.8*	15.9	*12.1*	1.2	*-3.1*
45	*Yemen, Rep.*	33.2[d]	*30.7*	12.6[d]	*19.2*	4.0[d]	*4.1*	0.0[d]	*2.4*	13.0[d]	6.0	37.2[d]	*37.6*	..	*50.7*	..	*-20.6*
Middle-income economies																	
Lower-middle-income																	
46	Azerbaijan	..	..	..	..	..	..	..	..	..	..	..	..	..	..	..	..
47	Indonesia	13.5	6.2	8.3	10.0	2.5	2.7	1.8	1.6	40.2	27.3	33.7	52.2	23.1	18.9	-2.3	0.7
48	Senegal	16.8	..	23.0	..	4.7	..	9.5	..	14.4	..	31.6	..	23.9	..	0.9	..
49	Bolivia	..	8.2	..	11.0	..	6.6	..	13.5	..	32.7	..	28.0	..	26.6	..	-2.1
50	Cameroon	9.1	9.4	12.4	18.0	5.1	4.8	8.0	2.8	24.0	10.2	41.4	54.8	15.5	18.3	0.5	-2.0
51	Macedonia, FYR	..	..	..	..	..	..	..	..	..	..	..	..	..	..	..	..
52	Kyrgyz Republic	..	..	..	..	..	..	..	..	..	..	..	..	..	..	..	..
53	Philippines[c]	15.7	10.6	13.0	15.9	4.5	3.0	6.6	5.0	56.9	27.8	3.4	37.7	13.4	18.1	-1.4	-1.5
54	Congo	*9.7*	..	*11.0*	..	*5.1*	..	*7.0*	..	*34.2*	..	*33.0*	..	54.6	..	-5.8	..
55	Uzbekistan	..	..	..	..	..	..	..	..	..	..	..	..	..	..	..	..
56	Morocco	17.9	..	17.3	..	3.4	..	6.5	..	27.8	..	27.1	..	34.2	..	-10.0	..
57	Moldova	..	..	..	..	..	..	..	..	..	..	..	..	..	..	..	..
58	Guatemala	..	..	..	..	..	..	..	..	..	..	..	..	14.4	..	-3.9	..
59	Papua New Guinea[c]	4.4	4.2	16.5	15.0	8.6	7.9	2.6	1.4	22.7	21.6	45.1	49.9	35.2	35.8	-2.0	-6.4
60	Bulgaria	..	6.3	..	3.4	..	3.3	..	34.2	..	10.2	..	42.5	..	47.8	..	-12.9
61	Romania	..	*8.1*	..	*9.0*	..	*7.9*	..	*24.5*	..	*31.9*	..	*18.6*	..	*40.4*	..	*-4.7*
62	Jordan[c]	*25.3*	*22.1*	*7.6*	*14.3*	*3.7*	*6.3*	*14.5*	*16.3*	*28.3*	*12.8*	*20.6*	*28.2*	..	*36.0*	..	*6.0*
63	Ecuador[c]	12.5	..	34.7	..	7.8	..	1.3	..	21.1	..	22.6	..	15.0	15.4	-1.5	0.5
64	Dominican Republic	7.8	..	12.6	..	9.3	..	13.8	..	37.1	..	19.3	..	17.5	..	-2.7	..
65	El Salvador[c]	8.8	*16.0*	19.8	*12.8*	9.0	*7.3*	5.5	*4.7*	21.0	*19.4*	36.0	*39.7*	17.6	*11.2*	-5.9	*-0.8*
66	Lithuania	..	3.5	..	7.2	..	5.0	..	37.0	..	18.2	..	29.2	..	20.4	..	0.6
67	Colombia	6.7	..	*19.1*	..	*3.9*	..	*21.4*	..	*27.1*	..	*21.8*	..	13.5	..	-1.8	..
68	Jamaica	..	..	..	..	..	..	..	..	..	..	..	..	45.7	..	-17.1	..
69	Peru[c]	21.0	..	15.6	..	5.6	..	0.0	..	22.1	..	35.7	..	20.4	14.0	-2.5	-1.8
70	Paraguay	12.4	10.7	12.9	22.1	3.6	7.3	19.2	16.7	18.9	16.5	33.0	26.7	9.8	13.0	0.3	1.2
71	Kazakhstan	..	..	..	..	..	..	..	..	..	..	..	..	..	..	..	..
72	Tunisia	12.2	*5.4*	17.0	*17.5*	7.2	*6.6*	13.4	*18.6*	27.8	*22.5*	22.4	*29.3*	32.5	*33.2*	-2.9	*-2.6*

Note: For data comparability and coverage, see the technical notes. Figures in italics are for years other than those specified.

		Percentage of total expenditure												Total expenditure (% of GNP)		Overall surplus/deficit (% of GNP)	
		Defense		Education		Health		Housing, etc., soc. sec., welfare		Economic services		Other[a]					
		1980	1993	1980	1993	1980	1993	1980	1993	1980	1993	1980	1993	1980	1993	1980	1993
73	Algeria	..	..	..	..	..	..	..	..	..	..	..	..	..	..	..	..
74	Namibia	..	6.6	..	22.6	..	9.9	..	15.1	..	17.7	..	28.1	..	40.2	..	−4.8
75	Slovak Republic	..	..	..	..	..	..	..	..	..	..	..	..	..	..	..	..
76	Latvia	..	..	..	..	..	..	..	..	..	..	..	..	..	..	..	..
77	Thailand	21.7	17.2	19.8	21.1	4.1	8.2	5.1	6.7	24.2	26.2	25.1	20.7	19.0	16.3	−4.9	2.1
78	Costa Rica	2.6	..	24.6	22.3	28.7	28.5	9.5	10.8	18.2	9.7	16.4	28.7	26.3	26.7	−7.8	−0.2
79	Ukraine	..	..	..	..	..	..	..	..	..	..	..	..	..	..	..	..
80	Poland	..	..	..	..	..	..	..	..	..	..	..	..	..	..	..	..
81	Russian Federation	..	..	..	..	..	..	..	..	..	..	..	..	..	..	..	..
82	Panama	0.0	4.2	13.4	15.9	12.7	24.5	13.5	23.3	21.9	6.4	38.4	25.7	33.4	32.1	−5.7	4.4
83	Czech Republic	..	6.3	..	11.0	..	18.1	..	28.3	..	12.5	..	23.8	..	41.7	..	2.6
84	Botswana[c]	9.8	11.9	22.2	20.4	5.4	4.9	7.9	16.2	26.9	15.5	27.9	31.2	36.5	40.2	−0.2	11.2
85	Turkey	15.2	8.9	14.2	16.8	3.6	3.0	6.1	6.0	34.0	18.5	26.9	46.7	26.3	25.9	−3.8	−7.0
86	Iran, Islamic Rep.	15.9	..	21.3	..	6.4	..	8.6	..	24.0	..	23.7	..	35.5	20.1	−13.7	−1.4
Upper-middle-income																	
87	Venezuela	5.8	..	19.9	..	8.8	..	9.5	..	20.2	..	35.7	..	18.7	19.2	0.0	−3.0
88	Belarus	..	6.2	..	10.1	..	5.6	..	37.2	..	23.7	..	17.3	..	33.1	..	−2.9
89	Brazil	4.0	2.6	4.0	3.6	4.0	5.2	32.0	30.0	20.0	7.5	36.0	51.1	20.9	25.6	−2.6	−1.0
90	South Africa	..	..	..	..	..	..	..	..	..	..	..	..	23.1	32.6	−2.5	−4.4
91	Mauritius	0.8	1.5	17.6	15.0	7.5	9.4	21.4	22.3	11.7	15.5	41.0	36.3	27.4	22.2	−10.4	..
92	Estonia	..	2.7	..	9.1	..	18.1	..	35.0	..	11.3	..	23.9	..	26.7	..	−2.0
93	Malaysia	14.8	11.8	18.3	20.3	5.1	5.7	7.0	11.4	30.0	18.5	24.7	32.4	29.6	26.7	−6.2	1.7
94	Chile	12.4	9.1	14.5	13.4	7.4	11.5	37.1	39.3	13.8	14.6	14.8	12.2	29.1	22.6	5.6	2.1
95	Hungary	4.4	..	1.8	..	2.7	..	22.3	..	44.0	..	24.7	..	58.3	..	−2.9	..
96	Mexico	2.3	..	18.0	..	2.4	..	18.5	..	31.2	..	27.6	..	17.4	..	−3.1	..
97	Trinidad and Tobago	1.7	..	11.6	..	5.8	..	15.9	..	43.5	..	21.5	..	32.0	..	7.6	..
98	Uruguay	13.4	8.0	8.8	6.6	4.9	5.6	48.5	56.0	11.4	8.2	13.0	15.6	22.7	29.2	0.0	0.6
99	Oman	51.2	34.7	4.8	12.6	2.9	6.3	2.0	11.5	18.4	11.8	20.8	23.1	43.1	63.9	0.5	−17.4
100	Gabon[c]	..	..	..	..	..	..	..	..	..	..	..	..	40.5	33.8	6.8	−1.8
101	Slovenia	..	..	..	..	..	..	..	..	..	..	..	..	..	..	..	..
102	Puerto Rico	..	..	..	..	..	..	..	..	..	..	..	..	..	..	..	..
103	Argentina	..	..	..	..	..	..	..	..	..	..	..	..	18.4	..	−2.6	..
104	Greece	12.6	8.9	10.0	8.5	10.3	7.4	31.3	14.7	16.6	9.4	19.2	51.0	34.4	43.1	−4.8	−15.6
105	Korea, Rep.	34.3	20.1	17.1	16.8	1.2	1.0	7.5	11.2	15.6	18.8	24.3	32.1	17.6	17.1	−2.3	0.6
106	Portugal	7.4	..	11.2	..	10.3	..	27.0	..	19.9	..	24.2	..	34.1	42.3	−8.7	−2.2
107	Saudi Arabia	..	..	..	..	..	..	..	..	..	..	..	..	..	..	..	..
108	Turkmenistan	..	..	..	..	..	..	..	..	..	..	..	..	..	..	..	..
Low- and middle-income																	
Sub-Saharan Africa																	
East Asia & Pacific																	
South Asia																	
Europe and Central Asia																	
Middle East & N. Africa																	
Latin America & Caribbean																	
Severely indebted																	
High-income economies																	
109	New Zealand	5.1	3.8	14.7	14.1	15.2	12.3	31.1	39.7	15.0	5.8	18.9	24.4	39.0	36.6	−6.8	0.1
110	Ireland	3.4	3.2	11.4	12.8	13.7	14.0	27.7	30.3	18.4	12.8	25.4	26.9	46.5	47.0	−12.9	−2.3
111	Spain	4.3	4.2	8.0	4.7	0.7	6.1	60.3	38.8	11.9	8.9	14.8	37.4	27.0	35.1	−4.2	−3.7
112	† Israel	39.8	20.3	9.9	11.9	3.6	4.1	14.4	31.3	13.4	10.6	19.0	21.8	72.4	44.2	−16.1	−1.7
113	Australia	9.4	7.9	8.2	7.2	10.0	12.6	28.5	33.7	8.2	8.0	35.8	30.5	23.1	28.2	−1.5	−2.3
114	† Hong Kong	..	..	..	..	..	..	..	..	..	..	..	..	..	..	..	..
115	United Kingdom	13.8	9.9	2.4	3.3	13.5	14.0	30.0	32.5	7.5	6.6	32.9	33.7	38.2	43.4	−4.6	−5.1
116	Finland	5.6	4.4	14.7	13.2	10.5	0.1	28.2	51.9	27.0	17.6	14.0	12.8	28.6	44.5	−2.2	−15.4
117	† Kuwait	12.2	20.2	9.2	10.4	5.1	5.7	12.2	25.8	20.3	8.6	40.9	29.3	23.7	54.6	50.2	−26.1
118	Italy	3.4	..	8.4	..	12.6	..	29.6	..	7.2	..	38.7	..	41.0	53.4	−10.7	−10.1
119	† Singapore	25.2	24.5	14.6	22.3	7.0	6.1	7.6	9.0	17.7	11.5	27.9	26.6	20.8	19.7	2.2	12.6
120	Canada	7.7	6.8	3.8	2.7	6.7	4.6	35.1	41.9	19.4	8.7	27.3	35.3	21.8	25.8	−3.6	−3.8
121	Netherlands	5.6	4.2	13.1	10.2	11.7	13.7	39.5	41.5	10.9	5.6	19.2	24.7	52.7	53.9	−4.5	−0.9
122	† United Arab Emirates[c]	47.5	37.8	11.7	16.7	7.9	7.4	5.3	5.3	6.1	4.5	22.9	28.3	11.6	11.4	2.0	−0.2
123	Belgium	5.7	..	15.0	..	1.6	..	44.7	..	16.0	..	17.0	..	51.3	50.9	−8.2	−7.0
124	France	7.4	6.0	8.6	7.0	14.8	16.1	46.8	45.5	6.8	5.0	15.6	20.4	39.3	45.5	−0.1	−3.8
125	Austria	3.0	2.3	9.7	9.4	13.3	13.4	48.7	47.5	11.7	8.9	13.5	18.4	37.7	39.7	−3.4	−3.9
126	Germany[e]	9.1	6.4	0.9	0.8	19.0	16.8	49.6	45.9	8.7	9.7	12.6	20.4	..	33.6	..	−2.4
127	Sweden	7.7	5.3	10.4	7.3	2.2	0.4	51.5	53.3	10.9	16.2	17.3	17.4	39.5	53.9	−8.1	−12.2
128	United States	21.2	19.3	2.6	2.0	10.4	17.1	37.8	31.7	9.7	6.2	18.2	23.7	21.7	23.8	−2.8	−4.0
129	Norway	7.7	..	8.7	..	10.6	..	34.7	..	22.7	..	15.6	..	39.2	..	−2.0	..
130	Denmark	6.5	5.0	10.4	9.8	1.8	1.1	44.7	41.3	6.5	7.2	30.0	35.7	40.4	45.5	−2.7	−2.4
131	Japan[c]	..	..	..	..	..	..	..	..	..	..	..	..	18.4	..	−7.0	..
132	Switzerland	10.2	..	3.4	..	11.7	..	49.3	..	14.2	..	11.2	..	19.5	..	−0.2	..
World																	

a. See the technical notes.   b. Includes Eritrea.   c. Data are for budgetary accounts only.   d. Data refer to the former Yemen Arab Republic only.   e. Data prior to 1991 refer to the Federal Republic of Germany before unification.

Table 11. Central government current revenue

		Percentage of total current revenue													
		Tax revenue												Total current revenue (% of GNP)	
		Income, profit, capital gains		Social security		Goods & services		Intl. trade & transactions		Other[a]		Nontax revenue			
		1980	1993	1980	1993	1980	1993	1980	1993	1980	1993	1980	1993	1980	1993
	Low-income economies														
	Excluding China & India														
1	Mozambique	..	..	0.0	..	40.8	..	17.3	..	1.6	..	7.8	..	..	..
2	Tanzania	32.5	..	0.0	..	40.8	..	17.3	..	1.6	..	7.8	..	17.6	..
3	Ethiopia[b]	*24.6*	21.7	0.0	..	*22.5*	..	*28.4*	..	*3.5*	47.4	*20.9*	30.9	..	..
4	Sierra Leone[c]	22.4	24.3	0.0	0.0	16.3	36.2	49.6	34.6	1.5	0.0	10.1	4.9	16.9	15.8
5	Viet Nam	..	..	..	..	..	..	..	..	..	..	..	..	..	..
6	Burundi	19.3	..	1.0	..	25.3	..	40.4	..	8.4	..	5.6	..	14.0	..
7	Uganda	11.5	..	0.0	..	41.0	..	44.3	..	0.2	..	3.1	..	3.1	..
8	Nepal	5.5	*9.9*	0.0	0.0	*36.8*	*36.7*	33.2	*30.8*	8.2	*5.5*	16.2	*17.1*	7.8	*9.6*
9	Malawi[c]	33.9	..	0.0	..	30.9	..	22.0	..	0.3	..	12.9	..	20.7	..
10	Chad[c]	..	*22.6*	..	*0.0*	..	*33.7*	..	*15.3*	..	*6.6*	..	*21.8*	..	*9.1*
11	Rwanda	17.8	*15.6*	4.1	2.4	19.3	*34.7*	42.4	*31.1*	2.4	*4.2*	14.0	*12.0*	12.8	*13.2*
12	Bangladesh[c]	10.1	..	0.0	..	25.5	..	28.6	..	3.9	..	31.9	..	11.3	..
13	Madagascar	16.6	*15.3*	11.3	*0.0*	39.3	*19.5*	27.6	*44.5*	2.7	*1.1*	2.4	*19.5*	13.4	*9.1*
14	Guinea-Bissau	..	..	..	..	..	..	..	..	..	..	..	..	..	..
15	Kenya[c]	29.1	29.6	0.0	0.0	38.8	47.5	18.5	10.6	1.0	1.1	12.6	11.2	22.6	22.5
16	Mali	17.9	..	0.0	..	36.8	..	17.9	..	19.5	..	8.0	..	11.0	..
17	Niger	23.8	..	4.0	..	18.0	..	36.4	..	2.6	..	15.3	..	14.7	..
18	Lao PDR	..	..	..	..	..	..	..	..	..	..	..	..	..	..
19	Burkina Faso	17.8	..	7.8	..	15.9	..	43.7	..	4.3	..	10.5	..	13.6	..
20	India	18.3	18.7	0.0	0.0	42.5	32.1	22.0	24.9	0.6	0.4	16.6	23.9	11.7	14.4
21	Nigeria[c]	..	..	..	..	..	..	..	..	..	..	..	..	..	..
22	Albania	..	..	..	..	..	..	..	..	..	..	..	..	..	..
23	Nicaragua	7.8	11.3	8.9	10.9	37.3	44.3	25.2	21.1	10.7	5.8	10.1	6.5	24.7	29.8
24	Togo	34.4	..	5.8	..	15.3	..	32.0	..	-1.7	..	14.2	..	31.4	..
25	Gambia, The	15.5	..	0.0	..	3.2	..	65.3	..	1.5	..	14.5	..	24.5	..
26	Zambia	38.1	..	0.0	..	43.1	..	8.3	..	3.1	..	7.3	..	27.0	..
27	Mongolia	..	48.4	..	5.7	..	24.9	..	14.5	..	0.0	..	6.4	..	25.7
28	Central African Republic	*16.1*	..	*6.4*	..	*20.8*	..	*39.8*	..	*7.8*	..	*9.1*	..	*16.4*	..
29	Benin	..	..	..	..	..	..	..	..	..	..	..	..	..	..
30	Ghana[c]	20.5	16.8	0.0	0.0	28.2	33.9	44.2	26.8	0.2	0.0	6.9	22.6	6.9	16.9
31	Pakistan	13.8	13.9	0.0	0.0	33.6	29.1	34.4	26.3	0.2	0.5	17.9	30.2	16.4	18.4
32	Tajikistan	..	..	..	..	..	..	..	..	..	..	..	..	..	..
33	China[c]	..	*36.9*	..	*0.0*	..	*15.3*	..	*16.9*	..	*0.0*	..	*30.9*	..	*5.2*
34	Guinea	*28.1*	*14.6*	*1.0*	*0.0*	*6.4*	*27.2*	*27.9*	*47.5*	*0.7*	*0.6*	*35.8*	*10.0*	..	*14.0*
35	Mauritania	..	..	..	..	..	..	..	..	..	..	..	..	..	..
36	Zimbabwe	46.2	*44.4*	0.0	*0.0*	27.9	*26.3*	4.4	*19.0*	1.2	*1.0*	20.2	*9.3*	24.4	*31.8*
37	Georgia	..	..	..	..	..	..	..	..	..	..	..	..	..	..
38	Honduras	30.8	..	0.0	..	23.8	..	37.2	..	1.8	..	6.5	..	15.4	..
39	Sri Lanka	15.5	13.9	0.0	0.0	26.8	50.3	50.5	21.0	1.9	3.5	5.3	11.3	20.3	19.7
40	Côte d'Ivoire	13.0	..	5.8	..	24.8	..	42.8	..	6.1	..	7.5	..	24.0	..
41	Lesotho	13.4	*16.9*	0.0	*0.0*	10.2	*16.7*	61.3	*51.8*	*1.2*	*0.1*	13.9	*14.5*	*17.1*	*27.1*
42	Armenia	..	..	..	..	..	..	..	..	..	..	..	..	..	..
43	Egypt, Arab Rep.	16.2	*22.0*	9.1	*9.8*	15.1	*14.2*	17.3	*10.9*	7.7	*9.5*	34.6	*33.6*	47.1	*38.7*
44	*Myanmar*	2.9	*16.4*	0.0	*0.0*	42.3	*33.3*	14.9	*15.0*	0.0	*0.0*	39.9	*35.3*	16.1	*8.4*
45	*Yemen, Rep.*	6.8[d]	*19.3*	0.0[d]	*0.0*	7.5[d]	*12.4*	58.8[d]	*20.5*	4.4[d]	*5.1*	22.5[d]	*42.7*	..	*29.9*
	Middle-income economies														
	Lower-middle-income														
46	Azerbaijan	..	..	..	..	..	..	..	..	..	..	..	..	..	..
47	Indonesia	78.0	49.3	0.0	0.0	8.6	26.4	7.2	5.2	1.2	3.2	4.9	15.9	22.2	19.4
48	Senegal	18.4	..	3.7	..	26.0	..	34.2	..	11.4	..	6.3	..	24.9	..
49	Bolivia	..	6.0	..	8.3	..	38.5	..	7.1	..	10.1	..	30.1	..	15.6
50	Cameroon	21.7	19.9	8.0	0.0	18.0	19.9	38.4	19.6	5.9	10.5	7.9	30.2	16.2	16.3
51	Macedonia, FYR	..	..	..	..	..	..	..	..	..	..	..	..	..	..
52	Kyrgyz Republic	..	..	..	..	..	..	..	..	..	..	..	..	..	..
53	Philippines[c]	21.1	29.1	0.0	0.0	41.9	27.5	24.2	30.1	2.2	2.8	10.6	10.5	14.0	17.1
54	Congo	48.8	..	4.4	..	7.6	..	13.0	..	2.7	..	23.5	..	39.1	..
55	Uzbekistan	..	..	..	..	..	..	..	..	..	..	..	..	..	..
56	Morocco	19.2	..	5.4	..	34.7	..	20.8	..	7.4	..	12.5	..	24.0	..
57	Moldova	..	..	..	..	..	..	..	..	..	..	..	..	..	..
58	Guatemala	11.2	..	11.2	..	26.4	..	30.2	..	11.1	..	9.9	..	11.3	..
59	Papua New Guinea[c]	60.5	49.6	0.0	0.0	12.1	10.0	16.4	24.1	0.6	1.9	10.5	14.3	23.5	25.4
60	Bulgaria	..	12.7	..	29.8	..	18.3	..	9.1	..	5.5	..	24.6	..	35.6
61	Romania	..	35.6	..	29.5	..	19.2	..	3.6	..	3.7	..	8.4	..	36.5
62	Jordan[c]	13.2	*9.7*	0.0	*0.0*	7.3	*18.6*	47.8	*35.9*	9.5	*9.5*	22.2	*26.2*	..	*37.4*
63	Ecuador[c]	44.6	..	0.0	..	17.4	..	30.8	..	3.0	..	4.3	..	13.5	15.9
64	Dominican Republic	19.3	..	3.9	..	21.6	..	31.2	..	1.7	..	22.4	..	14.7	..
65	El Salvador[c]	23.2	*20.4*	0.0	*0.0*	29.8	*49.5*	37.0	*17.0*	5.6	*6.7*	4.5	*6.5*	11.7	*9.7*
66	Lithuania	..	27.2	..	27.6	..	31.2	..	3.9	..	0.4	..	9.7	..	21.4
67	Colombia	24.9	..	11.3	..	22.6	..	20.6	..	6.8	..	13.9	..	12.1	..
68	Jamaica	33.7	..	3.7	..	49.3	..	3.1	..	6.3	..	4.0	..	31.9	..
69	Peru[c]	25.9	18.3	0.0	0.0	37.2	52.3	27.1	11.0	2.2	4.6	7.7	13.8	17.9	10.8
70	Paraguay	15.2	10.3	13.1	0.0	17.7	35.8	24.8	12.5	20.5	5.9	8.8	35.5	10.6	14.1
71	Kazakhstan	..	..	..	..	..	..	..	..	..	..	..	..	..	..
72	Tunisia	14.6	*12.6*	9.3	*12.4*	23.9	*23.7*	24.7	*28.5*	5.6	*4.5*	22.0	*18.3*	32.3	*29.9*

Note: For data comparability and coverage, see the technical notes. Figures in italics are for years other than those specified.

		Percentage of total current revenue														
		Tax revenue													Total current revenue (% of GNP)	
		Income, profit, capital gains		Social security		Goods & services		Intl. trade & transactions		Other[a]		Nontax revenue				
		1980	1993	1980	1993	1980	1993	1980	1993	1980	1993	1980	1993		1980	1993
73	Algeria	..	..	..	..	..	..	..	..	..	..	..	..		..	..
74	Namibia	..	28.6	..	0.0	..	28.7	..	30.5	..	1.3	..	10.9		..	34.9
75	Slovak Republic	..	..	..	..	..	..	..	..	..	..	..	..		..	..
76	Latvia	..	..	..	..	..	..	..	..	..	..	..	..		..	..
77	Thailand	17.7	27.9	0.2	1.1	46.0	39.8	26.2	18.2	1.8	3.0	8.1	9.9		14.4	18.3
78	Costa Rica	13.7	9.7	28.9	27.7	30.4	33.2	18.9	15.0	2.3	1.2	5.8	13.2		18.7	26.5
79	Ukraine	..	..	..	..	..	..	..	..	..	..	..	..		..	..
80	Poland	..	..	..	..	..	..	..	..	..	..	..	..		..	..
81	Russian Federation	..	..	..	..	..	..	..	..	..	..	..	..		..	..
82	Panama	21.2	*16.9*	21.2	*19.0*	16.7	*15.7*	10.3	*9.8*	3.8	*2.9*	26.7	*35.7*		27.7	*32.7*
83	Czech Republic	..	18.8	..	34.9	..	31.6	..	3.9	..	3.7	..	7.0		..	41.9
84	Botswana[c]	33.3	29.0	0.0	0.0	0.7	3.0	39.1	22.3	0.1	0.1	26.7	45.6		36.6	56.1
85	Turkey	49.1	35.6	0.0	0.0	19.7	32.4	6.0	4.3	4.6	2.5	20.7	25.3		22.3	18.7
86	Iran, Islamic Rep.	3.9	*12.4*	7.4	*6.0*	3.6	*5.4*	11.7	*15.0*	5.3	*4.0*	68.2	*57.2*		21.4	*18.3*
Upper-middle-income																
87	Venezuela	67.4	51.8	4.6	6.6	4.2	12.5	6.8	10.5	1.8	0.7	15.2	17.8		22.2	18.0
88	Belarus	..	12.4	..	27.7	..	31.6	..	17.1	..	8.2	..	3.0		..	30.0
89	Brazil	10.7	*16.5*	25.0	28.6	32.1	*17.6*	7.1	*1.7*	3.6	5.5	21.4	*30.0*		23.2	26.6
90	South Africa	55.8	*52.7*	1.1	*1.7*	23.8	*33.2*	3.3	*3.8*	3.2	*2.5*	12.7	*6.0*		24.6	28.3
91	Mauritius	15.3	11.8	0.0	5.4	17.2	23.8	51.6	41.4	4.3	6.5	11.6	11.1		21.0	22.6
92	Estonia	..	16.5	..	37.7	..	39.1	..	1.9	..	0.5	..	4.3		..	27.6
93	Malaysia	37.5	34.5	0.4	0.8	16.8	22.0	33.0	13.8	1.8	3.5	10.5	25.4		27.3	28.7
94	Chile	17.6	19.3	17.4	6.6	35.8	45.8	4.3	9.9	4.9	5.9	19.9	12.4		33.2	24.4
95	Hungary	*18.5*	..	*15.3*	..	*38.3*	..	*6.9*	..	*4.8*	..	*16.1*	..		*55.5*	..
96	Mexico	36.7	..	14.1	..	28.9	..	27.6	..	−12.6	..	5.3	..		15.6	..
97	Trinidad and Tobago	72.7	..	..	..	3.9	..	6.7	..	0.6	..	16.1	..		44.7	..
98	Uruguay	10.9	*6.9*	23.4	*30.2*	43.3	*35.8*	14.2	*7.1*	2.7	*14.8*	5.5	*5.2*		23.1	*29.9*
99	Oman	26.0	16.8	0.0	0.0	0.5	1.0	1.4	3.2	0.3	0.8	71.8	78.1		42.9	46.1
100	Gabon[c]	39.9	*27.6*	0.0	*0.8*	4.8	*23.7*	19.7	*17.4*	2.0	*1.2*	33.7	*29.3*		39.4	*32.0*
101	Slovenia	..	..	..	..	..	..	..	..	..	..	..	..		..	..
102	Puerto Rico	..	..	..	..	..	..	..	..	..	..	..	..		..	..
103	Argentina	..	..	..	..	..	..	..	..	..	..	..	..		15.8	..
104	Greece	17.4	29.8	25.8	1.5	31.6	68.3	5.0	0.1	9.6	−5.9	10.6	6.2		29.7	24.3
105	Korea, Rep.	22.3	31.4	1.1	8.3	45.9	34.2	15.0	5.8	3.2	7.6	12.5	12.6		18.0	18.9
106	Portugal	19.4	*26.2*	26.0	*24.3*	33.7	*34.3*	5.1	*0.3*	8.7	*2.8*	7.1	*12.2*		26.8	*34.3*
107	*Saudi Arabia*	..	..	..	..	..	..	..	..	..	..	..	..		..	..
108	*Turkmenistan*	..	..	..	..	..	..	..	..	..	..	..	..		..	..
Low- and middle-income																
Sub-Saharan Africa																
East Asia & Pacific																
South Asia																
Europe and Central Asia																
Middle East & N. Africa																
Latin America & Caribbean																
Severely indebted																
High-income economies																
109	New Zealand	67.3	59.1	0.0	0.0	18.0	27.6	3.2	2.2	1.3	2.3	10.3	8.9		34.9	34.2
110	Ireland	34.3	*37.9*	13.4	*14.8*	30.1	*30.5*	9.2	*6.9*	1.9	*3.1*	11.1	*6.7*		35.8	*42.0*
111	Spain	23.2	32.2	48.0	37.9	12.6	21.7	3.8	1.1	4.4	0.4	8.0	6.8		24.4	31.4
112	† Israel	40.7	37.2	10.1	6.7	24.5	35.3	3.6	1.0	7.0	4.1	14.1	15.7		52.0	38.3
113	Australia	60.8	*63.8*	0.0	0.0	23.4	*19.7*	5.4	*3.5*	0.3	*1.4*	10.1	*11.6*		22.1	*25.3*
114	† Hong Kong	..	..	..	..	..	..	..	..	..	..	..	..		..	..
115	United Kingdom	37.7	*35.3*	15.6	*16.4*	27.8	*32.1*	0.1	*0.1*	5.7	*7.6*	13.1	*8.5*		35.2	*36.2*
116	Finland	28.5	*32.1*	9.7	*9.4*	49.1	*44.3*	2.0	*0.9*	3.0	*3.0*	7.7	*10.2*		27.6	*34.1*
117	† Kuwait	1.9	0.7	0.0	0.0	0.2	0.0	0.8	2.7	0.1	0.1	97.0	96.5		76.4	28.3
118	Italy	30.0	37.6	34.7	30.5	24.7	27.1	0.1	0.0	2.5	2.6	8.1	2.2		31.2	41.8
119	† Singapore	32.5	*30.0*	0.0	*0.0*	15.8	*16.7*	6.9	*2.0*	13.9	*15.1*	30.9	*36.1*		26.3	*26.6*
120	Canada	52.6	*52.7*	10.4	*16.7*	16.6	*17.7*	7.0	*2.9*	−0.2	*0.0*	13.6	*10.0*		19.2	*22.1*
121	Netherlands	29.6	30.7	36.3	36.8	20.8	21.0	0.0	0.0	2.7	3.2	10.6	8.3		49.3	50.7
122	† United Arab Emirates[c]	..	..	..	..	..	..	..	..	..	..	..	..		..	..
123	Belgium	38.5	*33.1*	30.6	*36.8*	24.2	*23.9*	0.0	*0.0*	2.5	*2.6*	4.3	*3.6*		44.0	*43.9*
124	France	17.7	*17.3*	41.2	*44.5*	30.9	*27.0*	0.1	*0.0*	2.7	*4.1*	7.4	*7.1*		39.4	*40.7*
125	Austria	21.1	*20.1*	35.0	*36.7*	25.6	*24.5*	1.6	*1.4*	9.1	*8.5*	7.7	*8.8*		34.9	*36.6*
126	Germany[e]	18.7	15.0	54.2	46.2	23.1	24.5	0.0	0.0	0.1	7.9	3.9	6.4		..	31.6
127	Sweden	18.2	5.8	33.2	36.7	29.1	32.7	1.2	0.9	4.3	6.7	14.1	17.2		35.2	40.1
128	United States	56.6	50.7	28.2	34.2	4.4	3.8	1.4	1.6	1.2	1.0	8.2	8.7		19.9	19.7
129	Norway	27.4	..	22.3	..	39.6	..	0.6	..	1.1	..	8.9	..		42.4	..
130	Denmark	35.9	37.8	2.3	3.8	46.9	38.3	0.1	0.1	3.3	4.1	11.6	16.0		36.4	42.1
131	Japan[c]	70.8	..	0.0	..	20.8	..	2.4	..	0.8	..	5.2	..		11.6	..
132	Switzerland	14.0	..	48.0	..	19.3	..	9.5	..	2.0	..	7.3	..		18.9	..
World																

a. See the technical notes.   b Includes Eritrea   c. Data are for budgetary accounts only.   d. Data refer to the former Yemen Arab Republic only.   e. Data prior to 1991 refer to the Federal Republic of Germany before unification.

Table 12. Money and interest rates

		Money, broadly defined					Avg. annual inflation (GDP deflator)	Nominal interest rates of banks (avg. annual %)			
		Avg. annual nominal growth rate (%)		Average outstanding as a percentage of GDP				Deposit rate		Lending rate	
		1970–80	1980–93	1970	1980	1993	1980–93	1980	1993	1980	1993
Low-income economies											
Excluding China & India											
1	Mozambique	..	..	..	..	..	42.3	..	..	..	..
2	Tanzania	22.6	..	22.9	37.2	33.2	24.3	4.0	..	11.5	31.0
3	Ethiopia[a]	14.4	13.0	..	..	..	2.8	..	11.5	..	14.0
4	Sierra Leone	19.9	57.2	12.6	20.6	11.7	61.6	9.2	27.0	11.0	62.8
5	Viet Nam	..	..	..	..	..	..	..	..	..	..
6	Burundi	20.1	..	9.1	13.5	..	4.6	2.5	..	12.0	..
7	Uganda	28.1	..	16.2	12.7	8.3	..	6.8	16.3	10.8	..
8	Nepal	19.9	19.9	10.6	21.9	..	11.5	4.0	..	14.0	..
9	Malawi	14.7	18.6	21.7	20.5	21.8	15.5	7.9	21.8	16.7	29.5
10	Chad	15.2	5.6	9.4	20.0	16.8	0.7	5.5	7.5	11.0	16.3
11	Rwanda	21.5	8.1	10.7	13.6	17.8	3.4	6.3	5.0	13.5	15.0
12	Bangladesh	..	18.0	..	18.4	33.1	8.6	8.3	8.2	11.3	15.0
13	Madagascar	13.8	16.4	17.3	22.3	22.5	16.1	5.6	..	9.5	..
14	Guinea-Bissau	..	59.8	..	..	12.5	58.7	..	53.9	..	63.6
15	Kenya	19.8	16.4	31.2	36.8	45.7	9.9	5.8	13.7	10.6	18.8
16	Mali	18.5	7.7	13.8	17.9	21.7	4.4	6.2	7.8	14.5	16.8
17	Niger	23.9	3.9	5.2	13.3	19.2	1.3	6.2	7.8	14.5	16.8
18	Lao PDR	..	..	..	..	..	..	7.2	14.0	4.8	15.0
19	Burkina Faso	21.5	9.8	9.3	15.9	21.8	3.3	6.2	7.8	14.5	16.8
20	India	17.5	16.7	23.6	36.2	44.1	8.7	..	..	16.5	16.3
21	Nigeria	34.3	18.0	9.2	23.8	..	20.6	5.3	23.2	8.4	31.7
22	Albania	..	..	..	..	..	5.6	2.0	..	2.0	..
23	Nicaragua	19.3	..	14.1	24.5	..	664.6	7.5	..	..	..
24	Togo	22.2	3.2	17.2	29.0	34.9	3.7	6.2	7.8	14.5	17.5
25	Gambia, The	18.3	19.0	15.6	21.1	23.0	16.2	5.0	13.0	15.0	26.1
26	Zambia	10.7	..	29.9	32.6	..	58.9	7.0	48.5	9.5	113.3
27	Mongolia	..	..	..	..	..	13.8	..	..	..	..
28	Central African Republic	15.8	3.5	16.3	18.9	17.4	4.2	5.5	7.5	10.5	16.3
29	Benin	19.0	6.3	10.1	17.1	28.8	1.4	6.2	7.8	14.5	16.8
30	Ghana	36.4	42.0	18.0	16.2	15.1	37.0	11.5	23.6	19.0	..
31	Pakistan	17.1	14.2	41.2	38.7	41.9	7.4	..	..	..	..
32	Tajikistan	..	..	..	..	..	26.0	..	..	..	..
33	China	..	25.7	..	33.5	79.7	7.0	5.4	..	5.0	..
34	Guinea	..	..	..	..	..	..	..	19.8	..	24.5
35	Mauritania	21.5	10.9	9.5	21.3	24.0	8.2	5.5	5.0	12.0	10.0
36	Zimbabwe	..	..	..	..	35.5	14.4	3.5	29.5	17.5	36.3
37	Georgia	..	..	..	..	..	40.7	..	..	..	..
38	Honduras	16.0	14.3	19.5	22.6	31.2	8.2	7.0	11.6	18.5	22.1
39	Sri Lanka	23.1	15.6	22.0	35.3	36.3	11.1	14.5	18.4	19.0	16.4
40	Côte d'Ivoire	22.6	2.5	24.7	26.7	31.5	1.5	6.2	7.8	14.5	16.8
41	Lesotho	..	16.3	..	..	33.5	13.8	..	8.1	11.0	15.8
42	Armenia	..	..	..	..	..	26.9	..	..	..	..
43	Egypt, Arab Rep.	26.0	21.4	33.5	52.2	95.6	13.6	8.3	..	13.3	..
44	*Myanmar*	15.1	15.8	23.9	23.9	27.9	16.5	1.5	..	8.0	..
45	*Yemen, Rep.*	..	18.7	..	..	..	..	9.3	..	..	..
Middle-income economies											
Lower-middle-income											
46	Azerbaijan	..	..	..	..	..	28.2	..	..	..	..
47	Indonesia	35.9	26.3	7.8	13.2	48.2	8.5	6.0	20.4	..	20.2
48	Senegal	19.6	4.7	14.0	26.6	22.1	4.9	6.2	7.8	14.5	16.8
49	Bolivia	29.4	207.1	14.8	16.2	39.0	187.1	18.0	22.2	28.0	53.9
50	Cameroon	22.5	3.1	14.2	19.4	19.5	4.0	7.5	8.0	13.0	16.3
51	Macedonia, FYR	..	..	..	..	..	..	..	..	..	..
52	Kyrgyz Republic	..	..	..	..	..	28.6	..	..	..	..
53	Philippines	19.2	17.4	29.9	26.4	37.9	13.6	12.3	9.6	14.0	14.7
54	Congo	15.4	4.9	17.1	14.8	21.7	–0.6	6.5	..	11.0	..
55	Uzbekistan	..	..	..	..	..	24.5	..	..	..	..
56	Morocco	18.7	13.7	31.1	42.4	64.5	6.6	4.9	8.5	7.0	9.0
57	Moldova	..	..	..	..	..	32.4	..	..	..	..
58	Guatemala	18.6	19.3	17.1	20.5	24.0	16.8	9.0	12.6	11.0	24.7
59	Papua New Guinea	..	8.7	..	32.9	31.3	4.8	6.9	5.0	11.2	11.3
60	Bulgaria	..	..	..	..	..	15.9	..	54.5	..	64.1
61	Romania	..	18.8	..	33.4	16.0	22.4	..	..	..	..
62	Jordan	24.2	12.4	..	..	122.1	..	..	3.3	..	9.0
63	Ecuador	24.2	38.8	20.0	20.2	..	40.4	..	33.8	9.0	47.0
64	Dominican Republic	18.3	29.3	17.9	22.0	25.5	25.0	..	..	..	..
65	El Salvador	17.3	18.5	22.5	28.1	32.2	17.0	..	15.3	..	19.4
66	Lithuania	..	..	..	..	..	35.2	..	..	..	..
67	Colombia	32.7	..	20.0	23.7	30.1	24.9	..	25.8	..	35.8
68	Jamaica	15.7	27.3	31.4	35.4	48.3	22.4	10.3	36.2	13.0	50.1
69	Peru	33.6	296.6	17.8	16.4	..	316.1	..	44.1	..	97.4
70	Paraguay	27.0	36.9	7.7	10.1	24.7	25.0	..	22.1	..	30.8
71	Kazakhstan	..	..	..	..	..	35.2	..	..	..	..
72	Tunisia	20.3	15.5	33.0	42.1	..	7.1	2.5	7.4	7.3	9.9

Note: For data comparability and coverage, see the technical notes. Figures in italics are for years other than those specified.

		Money, broadly defined					Avg. annual inflation (GDP deflator)	Nominal interest rates of banks (avg. annual %)			
		Avg. annual nominal growth rate (%)		Average outstanding as a percentage of GDP				Deposit rate		Lending rate	
		1970–80	1980–93	1970	1980	1993	1980–93	1980	1993	1980	1993
73	Algeria	24.1	..	52.6	58.5	..	13.2	..	..	..	..
74	Namibia	..	..	..	..	..	11.9	..	9.6	..	18.0
75	Slovak Republic	..	..	..	..	..	..	..	8.0	..	14.4
76	Latvia	..	..	..	..	..	23.8	..	..	..	..
77	Thailand	19.1	19.2	29.7	37.1	77.3	4.3	12.0	..	18.0	..
78	Costa Rica	30.6	25.5	18.9	38.8	37.1	22.1	..	16.9	..	30.0
79	Ukraine	..	..	..	..	..	37.2	..	..	..	..
80	Poland	..	64.1	..	57.0	31.1	69.3	..	34.0	8.0	35.3
81	Russian Federation	..	..	..	..	..	35.4	..	..	..	..
82	Panama	..	..	..	..	..	2.1	..	5.9	..	10.1
83	Czech Republic	..	..	..	..	..	..	..	7.0	..	14.1
84	Botswana	..	25.2	..	28.2	34.2	12.3	5.0	13.5	8.5	14.9
85	Turkey	32.9	60.6	27.9	17.2	21.2	53.5	8.0	64.6	25.7[b]	..
86	*Iran, Islamic Rep.*	33.2	18.4	26.1	54.4	39.1	17.1	..	..	..	..
Upper-middle-income											
87	Venezuela	26.4	22.7	24.1	43.0	32.7	23.9	..	53.7	..	48.9
88	Belarus	..	..	..	..	..	30.9	..	..	..	..
89	Brazil	52.7	..	23.0	18.4	..	423.4	115.0	3,293.5	..	..
90	South Africa	15.6	*16.6*	59.9	50.1	*56.2*	14.7	5.5	*13.8*	9.5	16.2
91	Mauritius	25.9	21.6	32.5	41.1	69.3	8.8	..	8.4	..	16.6
92	Estonia	..	..	..	..	..	29.8	..	..	..	..
93	Malaysia	25.2	*12.6*	34.4	69.8	107.2	2.2	6.2	*7.2*	7.8	*8.1*
94	Chile	194.2	29.1	12.1	21.0	36.9	20.1	37.7	18.2	47.1	24.3
95	Hungary	..	..	..	..	..	12.8	3.0	13.4	9.0	25.4
96	Mexico	26.6	57.8	26.9	27.5	31.9	57.9	20.6	15.5	28.1	..
97	Trinidad and Tobago	27.1	5.5	28.2	30.5	49.7	4.8	..	7.1	10.0	15.5
98	Uruguay	80.8	70.1	18.5	31.2	37.2	66.7	50.3	39.4	66.6	97.3
99	Oman	*29.4*	9.6	..	13.8	28.8	−2.3	..	4.2	..	8.5
100	Gabon	31.3	3.1	14.8	15.3	15.6	1.5	7.5	*8.8*	12.5	*12.5*
101	Slovenia	..	..	..	..	..	..	..	..	..	..
102	Puerto Rico	..	..	..	..	..	3.2	..	..	..	..
103	Argentina	143.4	356.7	21.6	19.0	15.0	374.3	79.6	11.3	86.9	6.3
104	Greece	23.9	*22.3*	42.9	61.6	..	17.3	14.5	19.3	21.3	28.6
105	Korea, Rep.	30.4	21.9	31.6	31.2	62.7	6.3	19.5	8.6	18.0	8.6
106	Portugal	20.2	18.5	77.0	69.9	73.6	16.4	19.0	11.1	18.8	16.5
107	*Saudi Arabia*	43.7	7.1	13.3	13.8	..	*−2.1*	..	..	..	..
108	*Turkmenistan*	..	..	..	..	..	16.5	..	..	..	..
Low- and middle-income											
Sub-Saharan Africa											
East Asia & Pacific											
South Asia											
Europe and Central Asia											
Middle East & N. Africa											
Latin America & Caribbean											
Severely indebted											
High-income economies											
109	New Zealand	15.1	..	51.4	51.0	..	8.5	..	6.2	12.6	10.3
110	Ireland	19.1	7.4	60.9	55.2	48.3	4.8	12.0	2.3	16.0	*10.6*
111	Spain	20.1	11.6	69.5	75.4	77.7	8.4	13.1	9.3	16.9	12.8
112	† Israel	35.2	78.6	45.1	14.7	62.2	70.4	..	10.4	176.9	16.4
113	Australia	16.8	*11.5*	43.6	46.5	..	6.1	8.6	..	10.6	*12.0*
114	† Hong Kong	..	..	..	69.5	..	7.9	..	..	..	..
115	United Kingdom	15.2	..	49.2	46.0	..	5.6	14.1	3.8	16.2	5.9
116	Finland	15.4	11.4	39.8	39.8	61.7	5.8	..	4.8	9.8	9.9
117	† Kuwait	24.3	..	36.1	33.1	80.8	..	4.5	7.1	6.8	7.9
118	Italy	20.4	*10.5*	79.3	83.1	*72.9*	8.8	12.7	6.1	19.0	13.9
119	† Singapore	17.1	13.5	66.2	74.4	119.3	2.5	9.4	2.3	11.7	5.4
120	Canada	17.5	8.1	48.4	65.0	78.6	3.9	12.9	4.9	14.3	5.9
121	Netherlands	14.6	..	54.3	77.7	..	1.7	6.0	3.1	13.5	10.4
122	† United Arab Emirates	..	8.0	..	19.0	53.1	..	9.5	..	12.1	..
123	Belgium	10.8	..	56.7	57.0	..	4.0	7.7	7.1	..	11.8
124	France	15.6	..	57.8	69.7	..	5.1	6.3	..	18.7	..
125	Austria	13.7	7.3	54.0	72.6	89.8	3.6	5.0	3.0	..	..
126	Germany	9.4[b]	6.8[b]	*52.8*[b]	*60.7*[b]	66.1	*2.7*[b]	8.0[b]	6.3	12.0[b]	12.9
127	Sweden	11.5	6.9	55.2	53.9	48.7	6.9	11.3	5.1	15.2	11.4
128	United States	9.9	7.2	61.1	58.7	63.7	3.8	..	..	15.3	6.0
129	Norway	12.8	9.5	54.6	51.6	65.7	4.6	5.0	5.5	12.6	9.2
130	Denmark	12.4	9.8	44.8	42.6	62.6	4.6	10.8	6.5	17.2	10.5
131	Japan	16.0	8.2	94.7	134.1	188.8	1.5	5.5	2.1	8.4	4.4
132	Switzerland	5.4	6.2	109.8	107.4	117.7	3.8	..	3.5	..	6.4
World											

a. Includes Eritrea. b. Data refer to the Federal Republic of Germany before unification.

Table 13. Growth of merchandise trade

		Merchandise trade (million $)		Average annual growth rate (%)				Terms of trade (1987=100)	
				Exports		Imports			
		Exports 1993	Imports 1993	1970–80	1980–93	1970–80	1980–93	1985	1993
	Low-income economies	**156,474 t**	**188,764 t**	**2.7 w**	**6.4 w**	**6.5 w**	**2.4 w**	**111 m**	**94 m**
	Excluding China & India	**43,177 t**	**62,914 t**	**0.4 w**	**1.4 w**	**5.7 w**	**−2.6 w**	**112 m**	**93 m**
1	Mozambique	132	955	−10.6	−6.9	−7.3	0.0	113	122
2	Tanzania	420	1,523	−6.8	−0.4	0.4	−1.1	126	85
3	Ethiopia[a]	199	787	−0.7	−2.2	1.2	−1.3	119	67
4	Sierra Leone	118	147	−5.2	−0.1	−1.3	−7.4	109	76
5	Viet Nam	..	..	..	..	..	..	..	..
6	Burundi	68	212	0.1	5.6	5.1	−0.4	133	52
7	Uganda	179	516	−10.5	−1.4	−9.1	−2.3	149	49
8	Nepal	390	880	..	..	..	..	..	..
9	Malawi	320	546	5.5	2.1	3.9	4.0	99	86
10	Chad	176	300	−1.6	5.5	−4.4	8.6	99	101
11	Rwanda	68	288	2.6	2.5	12.1	−0.4	136	73
12	Bangladesh	2,272	4,001	−2.4	9.8	2.9	4.8	126	94
13	Madagascar	267	452	−2.5	0.4	−0.9	−3.3	124	68
14	Guinea–Bissau	16	62	11.1	−5.7	−5.8	−0.4	91	92
15	Kenya	1,374	1,711	−2.2	3.3	1.2	−0.8	124	81
16	Mali	342	477	8.2	4.2	8.9	0.5	100	102
17	Niger	283	331	23.3	−5.5	13.3	−4.3	91	105
18	Lao PDR	80	353	..	..	..	..	..	..
19	Burkina Faso	145	642	7.2	4.1	8.2	3.4	103	106
20	India	21,553	22,761	5.9	7.0	4.5	4.2	92	96
21	Nigeria	11,886	8,276	1.4	−0.6	18.8	−11.2	167	99
22	Albania	..	..	..	..	..	..	..	..
23	Nicaragua	266	727	2.0	−4.7	−0.5	−3.3	111	94
24	Togo	322	418	1.5	5.2	11.8	0.3	139	97
25	Gambia, The	80	234	1.2	3.9	10.5	3.4	137	95
26	Zambia	1,168	870	−0.5	−2.6	−6.4	−3.2	89	98
27	Mongolia	..	..	..	..	..	..	..	..
28	Central African Republic	124	165	−1.6	−1.1	−2.9	2.1	109	91
29	Benin	115	360	−5.3	4.8	5.5	−4.8	111	133
30	Ghana	1,051	1,728	−8.0	5.3	−1.1	2.7	93	65
31	Pakistan	6,636	9,500	3.1	10.1	5.4	3.0	112	100
32	Tajikistan[b]	263	374	..	..	..	..	..	..
33	China*	91,744	103,088	8.7	11.5	11.1	9.7	109	101
34	Guinea	440	600	12.2	−4.5	4.1	−3.2	120	84
35	Mauritania	450	670	−5.3	5.1	4.6	5.1	110	115
36	Zimbabwe	1,180	1,500	2.8	−1.1	−4.1	0.2	100	89
37	Georgia[b]	222	460	..	..	..	..	..	..
38	Honduras	814	1,059	3.4	1.4	3.6	−1.5	118	73
39	Sri Lanka	2,896	4,227	−1.4	7.3	2.6	4.0	106	86
40	Côte d'Ivoire	2,880	1,663	3.2	2.7	9.8	−4.2	109	79
41	Lesotho	109	933	..	..	..	..	..	..
42	Armenia[b]	29	188	..	..	..	..	..	..
43	Egypt, Arab Rep.	2,244	8,175	−1.7	0.8	9.6	−1.5	147	99
44	Myanmar	583	814	0.2	−2.5	−4.2	−1.0	128	111
45	Yemen, Rep.	650	2,400	5.7	1.2	16.0	−5.3	131	88
	Middle-income economies	**648,218 t**	**724,625 t**	..	..	..	..	..	..
	Lower-middle-income	**280,438 t**	**333,510 t**	..	..	..	..	..	..
46	Azerbaijan[b]	351	241	..	..	..	..	..	..
47	Indonesia	33,612	28,086	6.5	6.7	12.1	4.5	145	90
48	Senegal	740	1,262	−1.3	2.9	4.5	1.8	107	106
49	Bolivia	728	1,206	−4.0	1.7	7.1	−0.1	130	78
50	Cameroon	1,815	1,108	2.0	6.8	7.3	−2.5	113	77
51	Macedonia, FYR	..	..	..	..	..	..	..	..
52	Kyrgyz Republic[b]	112	112	..	..	..	..	..	..
53	Philippines	11,089	18,757	7.2	3.4	5.3	4.5	99	117
54	Congo	1,116	541	−1.6	3.0	7.0	−4.4	150	98
55	Uzbekistan[b]	1,466	1,280	..	..	..	..	..	..
56	Morocco	3,991	6,760	−0.6	3.9	7.4	4.0	99	114
57	Moldova[b]	174	210	..	..	..	..	..	..
58	Guatemala	1,340	2,599	6.0	−0.1	6.2	1.4	114	93
59	Papua New Guinea	1,790	1,299	8.8	6.0	0.1	1.2	111	91
60	Bulgaria	4,071	4,239	..	..	..	..	95	..
61	Romania	4,892	6,404	6.3	−10.8	7.5	−3.0	66	111
62	Jordan	1,232	3,539	18.0	5.8	15.2	−2.4	127	123
63	Ecuador	2,904	2,562	0.1	3.4	10.3	−2.2	143	90
64	Dominican Republic	555	2,125	6.2	−3.5	3.9	2.4	115	130
65	El Salvador	555	1,919	6.0	−2.8	4.6	2.0	122	88
66	Lithuania[b]	696	486	..	..	..	..	..	..
67	Colombia	7,052	9,841	2.6	11.0	5.2	−0.9	124	68
68	Jamaica	1,047	2,097	−3.9	2.1	−6.2	2.6	89	109
69	Peru	3,463	3,389	5.0	−0.3	1.6	−1.6	111	90
70	Paraguay	695	1,689	6.2	8.6	8.8	7.5	110	112
71	Kazakhstan[b]	1,529	1,269	..	..	..	..	..	..
72	Tunisia	3,802	6,214	0.2	7.2	11.2	3.0	123	100
*	Data for Taiwan, China, are:	84,678	77,099	16.5	10.0	12.4	13.2	85	112

Note: For data comparability and coverage, see the technical notes. Figures in italics are for years other than those specified.

		Merchandise trade (million $)		Average annual growth rate (%)				Terms of trade (1987=100)	
		Exports 1993	Imports 1993	Exports		Imports		1985	1993
				1970–80	1980–93	1970–80	1980–93		
73	Algeria	10,230	7,770	1.1	3.0	13.1	–5.1	173	95
74	Namibia	..	..	..	..	..	..	..	..
75	Slovak Republic	5,451	6,345	..	..	..	..	..	..
76	Latvia[b]	460	339	..	..	..	..	..	..
77	Thailand	36,800	46,058	8.9	15.5	6.8	13.8	103	103
78	Costa Rica	1,999	2,907	5.3	5.6	4.2	4.9	111	94
79	Ukraine[b]	6,300	4,700	..	..	..	..	..	..
80	Poland	13,997	18,834	..	2.8	..	2.8	95	95
81	Russian Federation[b]	43,900	33,100	..	..	..	..	..	..
82	Panama	553	2,188	–7.1 [c]	4.0	–3.3 [c]	–0.4	104	87
83	Czech Republic	12,929	13,487	..	..	..	..	..	..
84	Botswana	1,725	2,390	22.2	6.7	9.4	10.2	97	152
85	Turkey	15,343	29,174	4.1	9.1	5.6	11.0	82	109
86	*Iran, Islamic Rep.*	16,700	30,662	–10.5	4.2	12.5	1.2	176	96
	Upper-middle-income	**367,781** t	**391,116** t	**2.7** w	**4.2** w	**7.4** w	**3.0** w	**104** m	**102** m
87	Venezuela	13,239	10,979	–6.8	1.7	10.8	–3.6	166	93
88	Belarus[b]	737	777	..	..	..	..	..	..
89	Brazil	38,597	25,439	8.6	5.2	5.8	–0.8	101	97
90	South Africa	22,873	18,591	7.9	5.4	–1.8	–0.1	101	105
91	Mauritius	1,299	1,715	6.0	7.6	9.6	10.3	77	108
92	Estonia[b]	461	618	..	..	..	..	..	..
93	Malaysia	47,122	45,657	3.3	12.6	7.7	9.7	114	99
94	Chile	9,328	10,596	9.6	6.6	3.6	4.3	91	104
95	Hungary	8,886	12,597	3.9	2.3	2.0	0.8	103	..
96	Mexico	30,241	50,147	5.5	5.4	7.9	6.7	145	99
97	Trinidad and Tobago	1,612	1,448	–5.0	–2.1	–3.7	–8.0	138	92
98	Uruguay	1,645	2,300	5.2	2.6	5.7	1.2	91	114
99	Oman	*5,428*	4,114	–1.9	8.4	28.3	1.2	182	84
100	Gabon	*2,297*	835	0.1	1.7	11.9	–1.6	154	106
101	Slovenia	6,088	6,498	..	..	..	..	..	..
102	Puerto Rico	..	..	..	..	..	..	..	..
103	Argentina	13,118	16,784	8.9	3.2	3.1	–2.1	123	116
104	Greece	7,960	20,542	11.7	5.3	5.7	6.7	96	101
105	Korea, Rep.	82,236	83,800	22.7	12.3	13.2	11.4	94	100
106	Portugal	15,429	24,598	1.5	10.6	5.5	10.0	87	104
107	*Saudi Arabia*	40,858	28,198	4.4	–4.2	35.3	–5.5	175	98
108	*Turkmenistan[b]*	1,156	749	..	..	..	..	..	..
	Low- and middle-income	**804,692** t	**913,389** t						
	Sub-Saharan Africa	61,743 t	59,567 t	1.0 w	2.5 w	3.2 w	–2.2 w	110 m	95 m
	East Asia & Pacific	308,126 t	332,733 t	9.0 w	10.8 w	9.7 w	9.2 w	111 m	101 m
	South Asia	33,980 t	42,253 t	4.2 w	7.3 w	4.3 w	3.7 w	112 m	96 m
	Europe and Central Asia	160,818 t	195,995 t	..	..	..	..	..	..
	Middle East & N. Africa	105,058 t	118,999 t	–0.8 w	–1.0 w	16.6 w	–3.9 w	147 m	98 m
	Latin America & Caribbean	134,967 t	163,842 t	0.9 w	3.4 w	4.7 w	0.3 w	111 m	97 m
	Severely indebted	**101,188** t	**104,466** t	**2.0** w	**2.4** w	**6.4** w	**–2.3** w	**112** m	**98** m
	High-income economies	**2,896,774** t	**2,865,337** t	**6.0** w	**5.1** w	**5.2** w	**5.8** w	**94** m	**99** m
109	New Zealand	10,537	9,636	3.5	4.0	1.9	4.1	90	109
110	Ireland	28,611	21,386	9.2	9.0	6.9	4.9	96	95
111	Spain	62,872	78,626	12.6	7.4	7.0	10.5	82	114
112	† Israel	14,779	22,621	9.3	7.9	4.3	6.4	101	99
113	Australia	42,723	42,259	3.7	6.2	1.3	4.7	110	98
114	† Hong Kong	135,248	138,658	9.9	15.8	7.9	11.9	118	87
115	United Kingdom	180,579	206,321	4.3	4.0	3.3	5.2	104	106
116	Finland	23,446	18,032	4.5	2.2	2.5	2.2	88	91
117	† Kuwait	10,248	7,036	–8.3	–6.0	16.0	–4.4	165	86
118	Italy	168,460	146,789	6.9	4.3	3.8	5.0	84	104
119	† Singapore	74,012	85,234	..	12.7	..	9.7	108	94
120	Canada	145,178	131,675	4.5	5.6	5.1	5.5	99	97
121	Netherlands	139,075	126,557	5.2	4.7	3.9	4.6	101	101
122	† United Arab Emirates	20,500	19,520	6.3	6.0	28.2	1.9	181	98
123	Belgium[d]	112,512	125,058	5.6	4.5	6.2	4.3	93	100
124	France	206,259	202,271	6.8	4.5	6.9	4.8	89	103
125	Austria	40,174	48,578	7.3	6.7	7.2	6.0	92	93
126	Germany	380,154	348,631	5.6 [e]	4.2 [e]	4.9 [e]	5.8 [e]	84 [e]	100
127	Sweden	49,857	42,681	3.1	3.5	3.3	3.6	92	103
128	United States	464,773	603,438	7.0	5.1	5.8	6.0	101	101
129	Norway	31,853	23,956	6.5	7.2	3.5	3.3	141	97
130	Denmark	35,914	29,521	4.4	4.4	2.8	3.2	91	104
131	Japan	362,244	241,624	9.2	4.2	5.1	6.3	73	119
132	Switzerland	61,403	56,716	4.6	..	3.5	..	85	..
	World	**3,701,466** t	**3,778,726** t	..	..	..	..	..	..

a. Includes Eritrea. b. Excludes inter–republic trade. c. Excludes the Canal Zone. d. Includes Luxembourg. e. Data refer to the Federal Republic of Germany before unification.

Table 14. Structure of merchandise imports

		Percentage share of merchandise imports									
		Food		Fuels		Other primary commodities		Machinery & transport equip.		Other manufactures	
		1970	1993	1970	1993	1970	1993	1970	1993	1970	1993
Low-income economies											
Excluding China & India											
1	Mozambique	..	..	..	..	..	..	..	..	..	..
2	Tanzania	7	..	9	..	2	..	40	..	42	..
3	Ethiopia[a]	9	6	8	11	3	1	35	44	45	38
4	Sierra Leone	26	..	5	..	1	..	26	..	43	..
5	Viet Nam	..	..	..	..	..	..	..	..	..	..
6	Burundi	21	..	11	..	11	..	19	..	37	..
7	Uganda	7	..	2	..	3	..	34	..	55	..
8	Nepal	..	..	..	..	..	..	..	..	..	..
9	Malawi	18	..	6	..	2	..	30	..	44	..
10	Chad	21	..	16	..	3	..	23	..	38	..
11	Rwanda	19	..	6	..	9	..	18	..	49	..
12	Bangladesh	..	15	..	14	..	30	..	13	..	28
13	Madagascar	12	11	7	12	3	2	30	41	48	34
14	Guinea-Bissau	31	..	7	..	1	..	16	..	45	..
15	Kenya	6	8	10	33	4	5	34	25	46	29
16	Mali	29	..	9	..	6	..	21	..	36	..
17	Niger	14	..	4	..	4	..	27	..	51	..
18	Lao PDR	..	..	..	..	..	..	..	..	..	..
19	Burkina Faso	20	..	8	..	7	..	27	..	37	..
20	India	21	4	8	30	19	10	23	14	29	42
21	Nigeria	8	..	3	..	3	..	37	..	48	..
22	Albania	..	..	..	..	..	..	..	..	..	..
23	Nicaragua	10	23	6	15	3	1	28	26	54	34
24	Togo	23	23	4	10	3	3	22	28	47	36
25	Gambia, The	32	..	4	..	2	..	15	..	48	..
26	Zambia	11	..	10	..	2	..	39	..	38	..
27	Mongolia	..	..	..	..	..	..	..	..	..	..
28	Central African Republic	17	..	1	..	2	..	36	..	44	..
29	Benin	18	..	4	..	3	..	21	..	55	..
30	Ghana	21	..	6	..	4	..	26	..	44	..
31	Pakistan	21	14	7	17	7	6	31	35	35	27
32	Tajikistan[b]	..	1	..	0	..	96	..	0	..	2
33	China*	..	3	..	6	..	7	..	42	..	43
34	Guinea	..	..	..	..	..	..	..	..	..	..
35	Mauritania	23	..	8	..	2	..	38	..	30	..
36	Zimbabwe	..	18	..	12	..	4	..	36	..	31
37	Georgia[b]	..	17	..	42	..	15	..	0	..	26
38	Honduras	12	11	7	13	1	3	29	26	51	47
39	Sri Lanka	47	16	3	9	4	3	18	21	29	51
40	Côte d'Ivoire	16	..	5	..	2	..	33	..	44	..
41	Lesotho	..	..	..	..	..	..	..	..	..	..
42	Armenia[b]	..	0	..	0	..	2	..	0	..	98
43	Egypt, Arab Rep.	23	24	9	2	12	10	27	31	29	34
44	*Myanmar*	7	..	6	..	3	..	29	..	55	..
45	*Yemen, Rep.*	63	..	5	..	3	..	9	..	20	..
Middle-income economies											
Lower-middle-income											
46	Azerbaijan[b]	..	48	..	0	..	14	..	0	..	38
47	Indonesia	9	7	3	8	4	9	40	42	45	34
48	Senegal	29	29	5	11	4	3	25	23	38	34
49	Bolivia	20	9	1	5	2	4	37	48	40	34
50	Macedonia, FYR	..	..	..	..	..	..	..	..	..	..
51	Cameroon	12	16	5	3	1	2	32	27	49	51
52	Kyrgyz Republic[b]	..	38	..	0	..	15	..	0	..	47
53	Philippines	11	8	12	12	8	5	35	32	33	43
54	Congo	20	..	2	..	1	..	33	..	44	..
55	Uzbekistan[b]	..	42	..	0	..	38	..	0	..	20
56	Morocco	21	17	6	14	10	9	32	29	32	31
57	Moldova[b]	..	7	..	0	..	33	..	1	..	60
58	Guatemala	11	11	2	14	3	3	27	32	57	41
59	Papua New Guinea	20	..	3	..	1	..	38	..	38	..
60	Bulgaria	..	..	..	..	..	..	..	..	..	..
61	Romania	..	14	..	26	..	7	..	22	..	31
62	Jordan	31	20	6	13	4	3	17	27	42	37
63	Ecuador	8	5	6	2	2	4	35	49	49	41
64	Dominican Republic	14	..	7	..	6	..	34	..	40	..
65	El Salvador	14	15	3	14	4	5	23	26	56	41
66	Lithuania[b]	..	6	..	2	..	27	..	0	..	65
67	Colombia	8	8	1	4	8	5	47	39	37	44
68	Jamaica	18	14	6	19	3	3	33	23	40	41
69	Peru	20	20	2	8	5	3	35	36	38	34
70	Paraguay	19	11	15	12	1	1	32	40	33	35
71	Kazakhstan[b]	..	..	..	..	..	..	..	..	..	..
72	Tunisia	28	8	5	8	9	6	26	32	32	46
*	Data for Taiwan, China, are:	15	6	5	8	18	10	35	40	28	36

Note: For data comparability and coverage, see the technical notes. Figures in italics are for years other than those specified.

		Percentage share of merchandise imports								
		Food		Fuels		Other primary commodities		Machinery & transport equip.		Other manufactures	
		1970	1993	1970	1993	1970	1993	1970	1993	1970	1993
73	Algeria	13	*29*	2	*1*	6	*5*	37	*31*	42	*34*
74	Namibia	..	..	..	..	..	..	..	..	..	..
75	Slovak Republic	..	..	..	..	..	..	..	..	..	..
76	Latvia[b]	..	..	..	..	..	..	..	..	..	..
77	Thailand	5	5	9	8	7	7	36	45	43	36
78	Costa Rica	11	*8*	4	*9*	3	*3*	29	*26*	53	*55*
79	Ukraine[b]	..	..	..	..	..	..	..	..	..	..
80	Poland	..	*11*	..	*17*	..	*6*	..	*29*	..	*36*
81	Russian Federation[b]	..	..	..	..	..	..	..	..	..	..
82	Panama	10[c]	10	19[c]	13	2[c]	2	27[c]	31	43[c]	45
83	Czech Republic	..	..	..	..	..	..	..	..	..	..
84	Botswana	..	..	..	..	..	..	..	..	..	..
85	Turkey	8	6	8	14	8	10	41	38	36	33
86	*Iran, Islamic Rep.*	7	..	0	..	8	..	41	..	45	..
Upper-middle-income											
87	Venezuela	10	11	1	1	5	5	45	50	38	32
88	Belarus[b]	..	*24*	..	*10*	..	*9*	..	*28*	..	*29*
89	Brazil	11	10	12	16	8	7	35	33	34	33
90	South Africa	6	6	5	1	6	4	46	44	37	46
91	Mauritius	36	*13*	7	*9*	2	*3*	13	*25*	41	*50*
92	Estonia[b]	..	..	..	..	..	..	..	..	..	..
93	Malaysia	22	*7*	12	*4*	8	*4*	28	*54*	31	*30*
94	Chile	15	6	6	10	7	3	43	43	30	38
95	Hungary	11	6	9	13	19	5	31	37	31	39
96	Mexico	7	8	3	2	9	4	50	48	31	38
97	Trinidad and Tobago	11	15	53	16	1	3	13	33	22	32
98	Uruguay	13	8	15	9	12	4	31	40	29	39
99	Oman	2	19	5	3	1	2	17	44	75	32
100	Gabon	14	..	1	..	1	..	39	..	45	..
101	Slovenia	..	..	..	..	..	..	..	..	..	..
102	Puerto Rico	..	..	..	..	..	..	..	..	..	..
103	Argentina	6	5	5	2	16	4	31	49	42	39
104	Greece	11	*15*	7	*10*	10	*4*	48	*34*	25	*38*
105	Korea, Rep.	17	6	7	18	21	13	30	34	25	29
106	Portugal	14	*12*	9	*8*	13	*5*	30	*38*	34	*37*
107	*Saudi Arabia*	33	..	1	..	3	..	33	..	31	..
108	*Turkmenistan*[b]	..	*27*	..	*0*	..	*10*	..	*0*	..	*63*
Low- and middle-income											
Sub-Saharan Africa											
East Asia & Pacific											
South Asia											
Europe and Central Asia											
Middle East & N. Africa											
Latin America & Caribbean											
Severely indebted											
High-income economies											
109	New Zealand	7	8	7	6	10	4	34	38	43	44
110	Ireland	14	10	8	5	8	3	27	37	43	45
111	Spain	16	14	13	11	17	5	26	35	28	35
112	† Israel	14	7	5	7	8	4	30	33	42	49
113	Australia	6	5	6	6	7	3	41	43	42	43
114	† Hong Kong	20	6	3	2	9	3	17	33	52	56
115	United Kingdom	24	11	10	5	20	6	17	39	29	39
116	Finland	10	7	12	13	9	8	33	34	37	39
117	† Kuwait	20	*13*	1	*0*	2	*3*	36	*42*	42	*41*
118	Italy	19	13	14	9	21	9	20	29	26	39
119	† Singapore	16	6	14	11	12	3	23	49	35	31
120	Canada	9	6	6	4	6	4	49	50	31	35
121	Netherlands	15	15	11	9	10	5	26	30	39	41
122	† United Arab Emirates	16	..	3	..	3	..	26	..	52	..
123	Belgium[d]	13	*11*	9	*8*	19	*7*	26	*25*	33	*49*
124	France	15	11	12	9	15	5	25	34	33	41
125	Austria	10	5	8	5	12	6	31	37	39	47
126	Germany	19[e]	10	9[e]	8	18[e]	6	19[e]	33	36[e]	44
127	Sweden	11	8	11	9	10	5	30	36	39	42
128	United States	16	5	8	10	12	4	28	43	36	38
129	Norway	9	7	8	3	13	7	36	39	36	45
130	Denmark	11	*13*	11	*6*	9	*5*	28	*29*	42	*46*
131	Japan	17	18	21	21	37	13	11	17	14	32
132	Switzerland	13	7	5	4	9	5	27	29	46	55
World											

a. Includes Eritrea. b. Excludes inter-republic trade. c. Excludes the Canal Zone. d. Includes Luxembourg. e. Data refer to the Federal Republic of Germany before unification.

Table 15. Structure of merchandise exports

		Percentage share of merchandise exports									
		Fuels, minerals, metals		Other primary commodities		Machinery & transport equip.		Other manufactures		Textile fibers, textiles, and clothing[a]	
		1970	1993	1970	1993	1970	1993	1970	1993	1970	1993
	Low-income economies										
	Excluding China & India										
1	Mozambique	10	*14*	80	*66*	5	*3*	5	*18*	21	..
2	Tanzania	7	..	80	..	0	..	13	..	27	..
3	Ethiopia[b]	2	*1*	97	*95*	0	*0*	2	*4*	1	*3*
4	Sierra Leone	21	*45*	17	*28*	0	*0*	61	*27*	0	..
5	Viet Nam	..	..	..	..	..	..	..	..	..	..
6	Burundi	4	*0*	95	*70*	0	*3*	1	*27*	6	..
7	Uganda	9	*0*	91	*100*	0	*1*	0	*0*	20	..
8	Nepal	..	*0*	..	*16*	..	*0*	..	*84*	..	..
9	Malawi	1	*0*	96	*94*	0	*0*	3	*6*	8	..
10	Chad	0	..	95	..	1	..	4	..	69	..
11	Rwanda	35	..	64	..	0	..	1	..	0	..
12	Bangladesh	..	*0*	..	*18*	..	*0*	..	*81*	..	*78*
13	Madagascar	9	*8*	84	*73*	2	*2*	5	*18*	3	*13*
14	Guinea-Bissau	..	..	..	..	..	..	..	..	..	..
15	Kenya	13	..	75	..	0	..	12	..	6	..
16	Mali	1	..	89	..	0	..	10	..	29	..
17	Niger	0	..	96	..	1	..	2	..	2	..
18	Lao PDR	36	..	33	..	30	..	1	..	3	..
19	Burkina Faso	0	..	96	..	1	..	3	..	26	..
20	India	13	*7*	35	*18*	5	*7*	47	*68*	27	*30*
21	Nigeria	62	*94*	36	*4*	0	*0*	1	*2*	2	..
22	Albania	..	..	..	..	..	..	..	..	..	..
23	Nicaragua	3	*3*	81	*90*	0	*0*	16	*7*	23	*12*
24	Togo	25	*52*	69	*42*	2	*1*	4	*5*	3	*25*
25	Gambia, The	..	*0*	..	*63*	..	*0*	..	*37*	..	..
26	Zambia	99	..	1	..	0	..	0	..	..	..
27	Mongolia	..	..	..	..	..	..	..	..	..	..
28	Central African Republic	0	..	56	..	1	..	44	..	23	..
29	Benin	0	..	89	..	3	..	8	..	23	..
30	Ghana	13	*25*	86	*52*	0	*0*	1	*23*	..	..
31	Pakistan	2	*1*	41	*14*	0	*0*	57	*85*	75	*78*
32	Tajikistan[c]	..	*99*	..	*0*	..	*0*	..	*1*	..	..
33	China*	..	*6*	..	*13*	..	*16*	..	*65*	..	*31*
34	Guinea	..	..	..	..	..	..	..	..	..	..
35	Mauritania	88	*52*	11	*47*	0	*0*	1	*1*	..	..
36	Zimbabwe	..	*16*	..	*48*	..	*3*	..	*33*	..	*11*
37	Georgia[c]	..	*4*	..	*46*	..	*0*	..	*50*	..	..
38	Honduras	10	*3*	83	*83*	0	*0*	8	*13*	3	*3*
39	Sri Lanka	1	*1*	98	*27*	0	*2*	1	*71*	3	*52*
40	Côte d'Ivoire	2	*15*	92	*68*	1	*2*	5	*15*	3	..
41	Lesotho	..	..	..	..	..	..	..	..	..	..
42	Armenia[c]	..	*35*	..	*11*	..	*0*	..	*34*	..	..
43	Egypt, Arab Rep.	5	*55*	68	*12*	1	*1*	26	*32*	65	*20*
44	*Myanmar*	*7*	*7*	*92*	*82*	*0*	*2*	*2*	*9*	*1*	..
45	*Yemen, Rep.*	*10*	..	*90*	..	*0*	..	*0*	..	*0*	..
	Middle-income economies										
	Lower-middle-income										
46	Azerbaijan[c]	..	*19*	..	*1*	..	*0*	..	*80*	..	..
47	Indonesia	44	*32*	54	*15*	0	*5*	1	*48*	0	*17*
48	Senegal	12	*25*	69	*54*	4	*2*	15	*19*	7	*4*
49	Bolivia	93	*56*	4	*25*	0	*2*	3	*17*	1	*3*
50	Cameroon	10	*51*	82	*35*	3	*8*	6	*6*	9	*4*
51	Macedonia, FYR	..	..	..	..	..	..	..	..	..	..
52	Kyrgyz Republic[c]	..	*59*	..	*3*	..	*1*	..	*38*	..	..
53	Philippines	23	*7*	70	*17*	0	*19*	8	*58*	2	*9*
54	Congo	1	..	70	..	1	..	28	..	0	..
55	Uzbekistan[c]	..	*10*	..	*0*	..	*0*	..	*90*	..	..
56	Morocco	33	*14*	57	*29*	1	*6*	9	*51*	5	*25*
57	Moldova[c]	..	*12*	..	*45*	..	*1*	..	*42*	..	..
58	Guatemala	0	*2*	72	*68*	2	*2*	26	*28*	18	*6*
59	Papua New Guinea	*1*	*52*	*94*	*37*	*0*	*10*	*6*	*2*	..	*0*
60	Bulgaria	..	..	..	..	..	..	..	..	..	..
61	Romania	..	..	..	..	..	..	..	..	..	..
62	Jordan	24	*27*	60	*22*	3	*3*	13	*48*	3	*5*
63	Ecuador	1	*42*	97	*50*	0	*2*	2	*5*	1	*2*
64	Dominican Republic	8	*6*	88	*41*	0	*2*	5	*50*	0	..
65	El Salvador	2	*3*	70	*49*	3	*3*	26	*45*	22	*16*
66	Lithuania[c]	..	*3*	..	*36*	..	*1*	..	*60*	..	..
67	Colombia	11	*26*	81	*34*	1	*6*	7	*34*	7	*10*
68	Jamaica	31	*12*	23	*22*	0	*0*	46	*65*	2	*9*
69	Peru	49	*50*	49	*33*	0	*1*	1	*16*	6	*11*
70	Paraguay	0	*0*	91	*83*	0	*1*	9	*16*	7	*23*
71	Kazakhstan[c]	..	..	..	..	..	..	..	..	..	..
72	Tunisia	46	*13*	35	*12*	0	*10*	19	*66*	2	*43*
*	Data for Taiwan, China, are:	2	2	22	5	17	40	59	53	29	15

Note: For data comparability and coverage, see the technical notes. Figures in italics are for years other than those specified.

		Percentage share of merchandise exports									
		Fuels, minerals, metals		Other primary commodities		Machinery & transport equip.		Other manufactures		Textile fibers, textiles, and clothing[a]	
		1970	1993	1970	1993	1970	1993	1970	1993	1970	1993
73	Algeria	73	96	21	1	2	1	5	2	1	0
74	Namibia	..	..	..	..	..	..	..	..	..	..
75	Slovak Republic	..	..	..	..	..	..	..	..	..	..
76	Latvia[c]	..	..	..	..	..	..	..	..	..	..
77	Thailand	15	2	77	26	0	28	8	45	8	15
78	Costa Rica	1	1	80	66	3	4	17	29	4	5
79	Ukraine[c]	..	..	..	..	..	..	..	..	..	..
80	Poland	..	22	..	18	..	19	..	41	..	7
81	Russian Federation[c]	..	..	..	..	..	..	..	..	..	..
82	Panama	21 [d]	3	75 [d]	81	2 [d]	0	2 [d]	16	0 [d]	5
83	Czech Republic	..	..	..	..	..	..	..	..	..	..
84	Botswana	..	..	..	..	..	..	..	..	..	..
85	Turkey	8	4	83	25	0	8	9	64	35	40
86	*Iran, Islamic Rep.*	90	93	6	3	0	0	4	4	5	..
Upper-middle-income											
87	Venezuela	97	83	2	3	0	3	1	11	..	0
88	Belarus[c]	..	19	..	4	..	8	..	69	..	..
89	Brazil	11	12	75	28	4	21	11	39	9	4
90	South Africa	27	16	32	11	7	8	34	66	6	3
91	Mauritius	0	2	98	32	0	2	2	65	1	54
92	Estonia[c]	..	..	..	..	..	..	..	..	..	..
93	Malaysia	30	14	63	21	2	41	6	24	1	6
94	Chile	88	43	7	38	1	3	4	16	1	2
95	Hungary	7	8	26	24	32	24	35	44	9	12
96	Mexico	19	34	49	13	11	31	22	21	11	3
97	Trinidad and Tobago	78	58	9	8	1	3	12	32	1	1
98	Uruguay	1	0	79	57	1	8	20	35	34	28
99	Oman	100	90	0	2	0	6	0	3	..	1
100	Gabon	56	85	35	12	1	0	8	3	..	..
101	Slovenia	..	..	..	..	..	..	..	..	..	..
102	Puerto Rico	..	..	..	..	..	..	..	..	..	..
103	Argentina	1	11	85	57	4	11	10	21	8	3
104	Greece	15	11	51	36	2	5	33	49	14	28
105	Korea, Rep.	7	3	17	4	7	43	69	51	41	19
106	Portugal	5	5	31	12	8	21	56	62	26	30
107	*Saudi Arabia*	100	90	0	1	0	2	0	7	..	..
108	*Turkmenistan*[c]	..	40	..	5	..	0	..	55	..	..
Low- and middle-income											
Sub-Saharan Africa											
East Asia & Pacific											
South Asia											
Europe and Central Asia											
Middle East & N. Africa											
Latin America & Caribbean											
Severely indebted											
High-income economies											
109	New Zealand	1	7	88	66	2	6	10	22	19	7
110	Ireland	8	2	52	23	7	29	34	46	11	4
111	Spain	10	5	37	17	20	41	34	36	6	4
112	† Israel	4	2	26	7	5	31	66	60	14	6
113	Australia	28	36	53	29	6	8	13	28	17	9
114	† Hong Kong	2	2	3	5	12	26	84	67	44	..
115	United Kingdom	8	10	9	9	41	41	42	40	8	5
116	Finland	4	6	29	11	17	32	50	51	6	2
117	† Kuwait	94	..	1	..	1	..	4	..	0	..
118	Italy	7	3	10	7	37	37	46	52	14	12
119	† Singapore	25	14	45	6	11	55	20	25	6	4
120	Canada	26	17	22	17	32	40	19	26	1	1
121	Netherlands	14	11	29	25	20	24	37	40	8	4
122	† United Arab Emirates	..	..	..	..	..	..	..	..	..	..
123	Belgium[e]	13	7	11	12	21	27	55	54	12	8
124	France	6	5	19	17	33	38	42	40	9	5
125	Austria	6	4	14	7	24	38	56	52	12	8
126	Germany	6 [f]	4	5 [f]	6	47 [f]	48	43 [f]	42	6 [f]	5
127	Sweden	8	7	18	8	40	44	35	42	3	2
128	United States	9	4	21	14	42	49	28	33	3	3
129	Norway	25	59	20	10	23	13	32	18	3	1
130	Denmark	4	4	42	29	27	27	27	40	6	5
131	Japan	2	2	5	1	41	68	53	29	13	2
132	Switzerland	3	2	8	4	32	30	58	65	9	4
World											

a. Textile fibers are part of other primary commodities, textiles and clothing are part of other manufactures.   b. Includes Eritrea.   c. Excludes inter-republic trade.
d. Excludes the Canal Zone.   e. Includes Luxembourg.   f. Data refer to the Federal Republic of Germany before unification.

Table 16. OECD imports of manufactured goods

		Value of imports of manuf., by origin (million $)		Composition of 1993 imports of manufactures (%)				
		1970	1993	Textiles, clothing	Chemicals	Elect. machinery, electronics	Transport equipment	Other
	Low-income economies	1,257 t	97,400 t	38.5 w	3.8 w	9.0 w	1.1 w	47.7 w
	Excluding China & India	480 t	13,071 t	65.8 w	2.9 w	0.9 w	2.6 w	27.8 w
1	Mozambique	7	11	65.7	1.0	3.8	0.0	29.5
2	Tanzania	9	51	55.5	0.8	0.8	5.5	37.4
3	Ethiopia [a]	4	2	8.3	4.2	0.0	0.0	87.5
4	Sierra Leone	2	104	1.1	1.5	1.1	0.1	96.3
5	Viet Nam	1	..	..	..	..	..	..
6	Burundi	0	2	35.0	5.0	10.0	0.0	50.0
7	Uganda	1	3	10.3	0.0	48.3	3.4	37.9
8	Nepal	1	367	94.2	0.1	0.1	0.1	5.4
9	Malawi	1	14	93.0	0.0	0.7	0.0	6.3
10	Chad	0	3	0.0	..	3.6	..	96.4
11	Rwanda	0	1	0.0	0.0	23.1	0.0	76.9
12	Bangladesh	..	2,017	90.8	0.0	0.3	3.2	5.7
13	Madagascar	7	77	76.9	6.7	0.0	0.1	16.3
14	Guinea-Bissau	..	..	..	..	..	..	..
15	Kenya	16	133	32.7	5.9	7.6	1.9	51.8
16	Mali	2	45	2.0	0.7	56.6	0.4	40.3
17	Niger	0	158	0.4	97.5	0.2	0.1	1.9
18	Lao PDR	0	60	92.8	0.0	1.2	0.0	6.0
19	Burkina Faso	0	7	1.4	4.3	5.7	1.4	87.1
20	India	534	12,214	46.3	5.4	1.1	1.2	46.0
21	Nigeria	13	199	4.5	20.8	2.3	3.4	69.0
22	Albania	1	71	25.5	1.4	1.1	0.7	71.3
23	Nicaragua	6	32	39.1	3.2	0.3	1.6	55.8
24	Togo	0	12	17.5	2.5	7.5	0.8	71.7
25	Gambia, The	0	69	0.4	0.0	0.1	0.3	99.1
26	Zambia	4	31	47.3	0.6	0.6	1.0	50.5
27	Mongolia	0	37	68.8	27.2	0.0	0.0	4.1
28	Central African Republic	12	85	0.0	0.1	0.0	..	99.9
29	Benin	0	8	18.4	64.5	1.3	0.0	15.8
30	Ghana	8	183	0.7	0.9	1.1	0.6	96.7
31	Pakistan	207	3,588	86.8	0.3	0.2	0.1	12.5
32	Tajikistan [b]	..	2	10.0	10.0	5.0	0.0	75.0
33	China	243	72,115	32.2	3.6	11.8	0.8	51.6
34	Guinea	38	215	0.0	8.8	0.6	0.3	90.3
35	Mauritania	0	4	18.6	2.3	9.3	23.3	46.5
36	Zimbabwe	0	271	32.7	0.2	0.8	6.9	59.4
37	Georgia [b]	..	9	15.4	38.5	1.1	2.2	42.9
38	Honduras	3	611	88.0	0.6	0.0	0.1	11.3
39	Sri Lanka	9	2,057	73.7	1.0	1.6	0.1	23.6
40	Côte d'Ivoire	7	235	20.4	1.5	0.8	3.0	74.3
41	Lesotho [c]	..	..	..	..	..	..	..
42	Armenia [b]	..	15	7.1	3.2	0.0	0.0	89.6
43	Egypt, Arab Rep.	33	991	59.5	4.7	0.7	12.7	22.4
44	*Myanmar*	4	64	68.7	0.8	2.7	0.3	27.6
45	*Yemen, Rep.*	..	21	1.9	1.0	6.3	24.3	66.5
	Middle-income economies	..	230,097 t	22.7 w	6.2 w	19.2 w	7.1 w	44.8 w
	Lower-middle-income	..	86,935 t	33.1 w	7.0 w	10.7 w	3.2 w	46.0 w
46	Azerbaijan [b]	..	6	47.5	13.1	4.9	1.6	32.8
47	Indonesia	15	12,060	32.6	2.2	5.6	0.7	59.0
48	Senegal	4	19	21.6	3.8	7.6	1.1	65.9
49	Bolivia	1	88	14.5	6.9	0.3	0.5	77.8
50	Cameroon	4	38	18.5	3.4	2.6	2.6	72.8
51	Macedonia, FYR	..	..	..	..	..	..	..
52	Kyrgyz Republic [b]	..	4	30.2	34.9	4.7	2.3	27.9
53	Philippines	108	7,614	28.4	1.4	35.8	0.7	33.7
54	Congo	4	357	0.0	0.1	0.1	0.0	99.8
55	Uzbekistan [b]	..	13	20.5	71.2	0.0	0.0	8.3
56	Morocco	32	2,684	67.3	12.9	9.3	1.1	9.5
57	Moldova [b]	..	22	70.1	1.3	0.4	0.4	27.7
58	Guatemala	5	679	88.8	2.8	0.1	0.1	8.3
59	Papua New Guinea	4	21	7.2	1.0	1.0	8.7	82.1
60	Bulgaria	68	786	38.6	16.6	6.8	0.7	37.3
61	Romania	188	2,037	42.3	4.1	3.4	2.0	48.2
62	Jordan	1	85	27.6	26.3	5.4	20.2	20.5
63	Ecuador	3	117	19.8	3.1	5.1	15.3	56.6
64	Dominican Republic	10	2,547	59.5	0.6	7.8	0.0	32.1
65	El Salvador	2	370	76.5	3.1	12.6	0.0	7.7
66	Lithuania [b]	..	249	32.5	34.1	2.4	3.4	27.6
67	Colombia	52	1,253	34.6	5.4	0.4	0.3	59.3
68	Jamaica	117	962	48.2	45.9	0.4	0.1	5.5
69	Peru	12	430	54.8	7.5	0.7	0.3	36.7
70	Paraguay	5	87	5.4	12.6	11.0	0.1	70.9
71	Kazakhstan [b]	..	140	0.4	37.0	0.1	0.1	62.3
72	Tunisia	19	2,582	70.3	5.2	8.6	4.7	11.3

Note: For data comparability and coverage, see the technical notes. Figures in italics are for years other than those specified.

		Value of imports of manuf., by origin (million $)		Composition of 1993 imports of manufactures (%)				
		1970	1993	Textiles, clothing	Chemicals	Elect. machinery, electronics	Transport equipment	Other
73	Algeria	39	1,435	0.3	3.6	0.2	0.2	95.7
74	Namibia[c]	..	..	..	..	..	..	..
75	Slovak Republic	..	1,452	21.5	11.1	4.4	6.6	56.3
76	Latvia[b]	..	202	22.7	27.1	3.0	1.8	45.3
77	Thailand	32	16,882	18.5	1.8	19.0	1.0	59.6
78	Costa Rica	5	1,023	69.5	1.9	9.2	0.1	19.3
79	Ukraine[b]	..	803	14.0	32.3	2.2	1.8	49.7
80	Poland	287	7,066	25.0	8.4	6.9	13.3	46.4
81	Russian Federation[b]	..	5,600	3.9	27.5	1.4	5.0	62.2
82	Panama	18[d]	365	15.1	3.4	2.6	21.7	57.1
83	Czech Republic	..	5,800	15.0	9.2	7.8	9.1	59.0
84	Botswana[c]	..	..	..	..	..	..	..
85	Turkey	47	7,255	72.3	2.8	5.4	2.9	16.6
86	*Iran, Islamic Rep.*	133	723	84.9	1.0	1.8	0.6	11.7
Upper-middle-income		2,798 t	143,162 t	16.4 w	5.8 w	24.4 w	9.4 w	44.0 w
87	Venezuela	24	865	1.7	23.8	1.7	9.8	63.0
88	Belarus[b]	..	223	17.8	38.5	5.9	2.2	35.6
89	Brazil	197	10,126	7.5	10.5	4.7	8.3	68.9
90	South Africa[c]	325	3,620	8.2	10.5	2.8	4.4	74.2
91	Mauritius	1	868	86.4	0.2	0.6	0.1	12.6
92	Estonia[b]	..	237	42.2	11.9	5.4	2.0	38.5
93	Malaysia	39	20,571	10.7	2.2	47.1	1.3	38.7
94	Chile	15	774	7.3	27.1	0.7	1.2	63.6
95	Hungary	210	4,710	23.3	13.4	14.2	5.0	44.1
96	Mexico	508	35,317	5.6	3.3	32.3	21.4	37.5
97	Trinidad and Tobago	39	347	1.0	66.9	0.6	0.8	30.8
98	Uruguay	23	241	43.6	3.3	0.1	1.3	51.7
99	Oman	0	236	37.4	0.8	10.8	13.4	37.6
100	Gabon	8	48	0.0	51.9	1.1	0.6	46.4
101	Slovenia	..	3,721	21.3	3.6	12.7	12.4	50.0
102	Puerto Rico	..	..	..	..	..	..	..
103	Argentina	104	1,285	4.8	18.7	1.3	11.8	63.4
104	Greece	185	3,160	57.5	4.9	4.8	0.8	32.0
105	Korea, Rep.	524	39,473	19.8	4.0	24.8	6.2	45.2
106	Portugal	396	11,888	34.5	4.8	11.1	7.8	41.7
107	*Saudi Arabia*	16	2,060	0.5	40.5	9.0	9.4	40.6
108	*Turkmenistan[b]*	..	6	69.0	0.0	1.7	0.0	29.3
Low- and middle-income		..	327,497 t	27.4 w	5.5 w	16.2 w	5.3 w	45.6 w
Sub-Saharan Africa		515 t	7,879 t	17.5 w	8.5 w	2.1 w	3.8 w	68.2 w
East Asia & Pacific		1,086 t	171,044 t	25.7 w	3.1 w	20.3 w	2.1 w	48.8 w
South Asia		760 t	20,299 t	61.6 w	3.4 w	0.9 w	1.1 w	33.0 w
Europe and Central Asia		..	58,464 t	31.9 w	9.6 w	8.4 w	6.7 w	43.5 w
Middle East & N. Africa		304 t	11,535 t	44.2 w	14.3 w	6.3 w	4.9 w	30.3 w
Latin America & Caribbean		1,294 t	58,275 t	13.8 w	6.9 w	21.2 w	15.1 w	43.0 w
Severely indebted		889 t	24,890 t	22.9 w	11.7 w	5.3 w	8.4 w	51.7 w
High-income economies		120,190 t	120,190 t	5.5 w	13.1 w	11.8 w	19.0 w	50.6 w
109	New Zealand	121	2,191	9.5	22.2	6.4	4.2	57.7
110	Ireland	439	18,112	5.0	33.3	10.4	1.3	50.0
111	Spain	773	31,153	4.4	9.6	7.8	38.0	40.2
112	†Israel	308	9,234	9.6	13.4	11.0	2.2	63.8
113	Australia	471	6,261	4.3	28.4	5.0	11.2	51.1
114	†Hong Kong	1,861	25,524	40.1	0.6	13.8	0.4	44.9
115	United Kingdom	10,457	103,259	4.8	18.8	10.0	14.6	51.8
116	Finland	1,170	14,880	2.2	8.5	10.6	3.6	75.2
117	†Kuwait	6	215	24.3	0.7	12.4	19.3	43.3
118	Italy	7,726	96,742	15.5	8.9	7.8	10.2	57.6
119	†Singapore	112	26,022	3.6	4.3	23.0	1.7	67.4
120	Canada	8,088	88,067	1.7	7.6	6.8	41.4	42.5
121	Netherlands	5,678	60,312	6.7	26.2	8.5	8.2	50.3
122	†United Arab Emirates	1	990	50.0	2.8	4.2	6.3	36.7
123	Belgium[e]	7,660	68,771	7.9	21.7	5.5	23.0	42.0
124	France	9,240	123,610	5.3	17.0	9.0	24.9	43.9
125	Austria	1,637	28,206	8.2	8.8	11.2	7.9	63.9
126	Germany	23,342[f]	229,187	4.8	15.7	10.6	21.0	48.0
127	Sweden	4,143	32,918	1.4	12.4	11.3	17.5	57.4
128	United States	21,215	220,129	2.4	12.7	14.4	18.6	51.8
129	Norway	1,059	7,157	1.5	22.8	7.9	6.5	61.4
130	Denmark	1,413	16,317	6.7	16.6	10.5	3.2	63.0
131	Japan	8,851	195,574	1.0	4.1	19.5	28.9	46.5
132	Switzerland	3,568	48,238	4.5	24.2	9.3	2.7	59.3
World		..	1,832,379 t	9.4 w	11.8 w	12.6 w	16.5 w	49.7 w

Note: Data cover high-income OECD countries' imports only. For 1970, these are based on SITC, revision 1; for 1993, on revision 2.   a. Includes Eritrea.   b. Excludes inter-republic trade.   c. Data are for the South African Customs Union comprising South Africa, Namibia, Lesotho, Botswana, and Swaziland; trade among the component territories is excluded.   d. Excludes the Canal Zone.   e. Includes Luxembourg.   f. Data refer to the Federal Republic of Germany before unification.

Table 17. Balance of payments and reserves

		Current account balance (million $)				Net workers' remittances (million $)		Gross international reserves		
		After official transfers		Before official transfers				Million dollars		Months of import cov.
		1970	1993	1970	1993	1970	1993	1970	1993	1993
	Low-income economies							..	70,632 t	3.8 w
	Excluding China & India							9,722 t	28,609 t	4.2 w
1	Mozambique	..	–317	..	–820	..	60	..	..	2.2
2	Tanzania	–36	–408	–37	–935	..	..	65	203	2.1
3	Ethiopia[a]	–32	–183	–43	–433	..	248	72	500	2.8
4	Sierra Leone	–16	–89	–20	–128	..	..	39	33	0.9
5	Viet Nam	..	–869	..	–1,063	..	..	48	7	0.0
6	Burundi	2	–26	–2	–190	..	..	15	170	6.3
7	Uganda	20	–107	19	–369	–5	..	57	146	1.5
8	Nepal	–1	–195	–25	–263	..	..	94	*518*	*6.8*
9	Malawi	–35	–143	–46	–221	–4	..	29	62	0.7
10	Chad	2	–84	–33	–264	–6	–35	2	43	2.0
11	Rwanda	7	–112	–12	–360	–4	4	8	47	2.5
12	Bangladesh	–114	243	–234	–535	..	942	..	2,447	5.5
13	Madagascar	10	–167	–42	–326	–26	..	37	..	*1.2*
14	Guinea-Bissau	..	–25	..	–80	..	–2	..	14	1.7
15	Kenya	–49	153	–86	59	..	–3	220	437	0.4
16	Mali	–2	–103	–22	–374	–1	87	1	340	4.0
17	Niger	0	–29	–32	–165	–3	–34	19	196	6.1
18	Lao PDR	..	–13	..	–117	..	..	6	154	3.4
19	Burkina Faso	9	–117	–21	–493	16	71	36	387	4.4
20	India	–385	–315	–591	–685	80	3,050	1,023	14,675	3.6
21	Nigeria	–368	*2,268*	–412	*1,537*	..	22	223	1,640	*1.2*
22	Albania	..	–7	..	–304	..	278	7,075		..
23	Nicaragua	–40	–457	–43	–853	..	25	49	93	2.1
24	Togo	3	–98	–14	–129	–3	2	35	161	4.9
25	Gambia, The	0	7	0	–35	..	..	8	*94*	*4.5*
26	Zambia	108	–471	107	–471	–48	..	515	192	1.3
27	Mongolia	..	31	..	–40	..	..	..	66	0.6
28	Central African Republic	–12	–21	–24	–139	–4	..	1	116	3.7
29	Benin	–3	–52	–23	–212	..	87	16	248	3.8
30	Ghana	–68	–572	–76	–828	–9	8	43	517	2.5
31	Pakistan	–667	–3,327	–705	–3,688	86	1,562	195	1,995	1.4
32	Tajikistan	..	..	..	..	..	..	..	..	..
33	China*	–81	–11,609	–81	–11,898	..	93	..	27,348	3.8
34	Guinea	..	79	..	–67	..	–20	..	..	..
35	Mauritania	–5	–94	–13	–177	–6	23	3	49	1.2
36	Zimbabwe	–14	–116	–26	–295	..	..	59	628	1.8
37	Georgia	..	–191	..	–191	..	..	..	..	..
38	Honduras	–64	–393	–68	–496	..	..	20	106	1.6
39	Sri Lanka	–59	–381	–71	–541	3	632	43	1,686	2.9
40	Côte d'Ivoire	–38	–1,229	–73	–1,402	–56	–394	119	20	0.1
41	Lesotho	18	22	–1	–376	29	..	..	253	1.8
42	Armenia	..	–40	..	–184	..	..	..	..	..
43	Egypt, Arab Rep.	–148	1,566	–452	208	29	4,960	165	13,854	9.3
44	*Myanmar*	–63	..	–81	..	..	..	98	401	3.5
45	*Yemen, Rep.*	..	–1,344	..	–1,441	..	347	..	*337*	*1.3*
	Middle-income economies							..	..	..
	Lower-middle-income							..	..	..
46	Azerbaijan	..	*503*	..	*503*	..	..	..	..	..
47	Indonesia	–310	–2,016	–376	–2,298	..	346	160	12,474	3.3
48	Senegal	–16	–305	–66	–545	–16	40	22	15	0.1
49	Bolivia	4	–495	2	–693	..	..	46	572	3.7
50	Cameroon	–30	–638	–47	–794	–11	..	81	120	0.5
51	Macedonia, FYR	..	..	..	..	..	..	..	..	..
52	Kyrgyz Republic	..	*–101*	..	*–123*	..	..	..	..	..
53	Philippines	–48	–3,289	–138	–3,590	..	279	255	5,934	3.3
54	Congo	–45	–507	–53	–532	–3	–78	9	6	0.1
55	Uzbekistan	..	–405	..	–405	..	..	..	..	..
56	Morocco	–124	–525	–161	–679	27	1,945	142	3,930	4.8
57	Moldova	..	–149	..	–164	..	..	..	..	..
58	Guatemala	–8	–687	–8	–689	..	199	79	950	3.2
59	Papua New Guinea	–89	495	–239	323	..	69	..	166	1.3
60	Bulgaria	..	–523	..	–523	..	..	..	2,376	6.1
61	Romania	*–23*	–1,162	*–23*	–1,281	..	..	..	1,921	2.9
62	Jordan	–20	–472	–130	–472	..	1,040	258	1,946	2.7
63	Ecuador	–113	–360	–122	–490	..	..	76	1,542	3.2
64	Dominican Republic	–102	161	–103	–241	25	362	32	658	2.0
65	El Salvador	9	–77	7	–299	..	789	64	720	3.4
66	Lithuania	..	–69	..	–81	..	..	..	..	..
67	Colombia	–293	–2,220	–333	–2,220	6	455	207	7,670	8.6
68	Jamaica	–153	–182	–149	–247	29	..	139	*324*	*1.5*
69	Peru	202	–1,768	146	–2,217	..	220	339	3,918	6.3
70	Paraguay	–16	–492	–19	–492	..	..	18	645	2.7
71	Kazakhstan	..	*–1,479*	..	*–1,479*	..	..	..	..	..
72	Tunisia	–53	–912	–88	–1,023	20	590	60	938	1.4
*	Data for Taiwan, China, are:	1	6,714	2	6,741	..	..	627	88,869	11.0

Note: For data comparability and coverage, see the technical notes. Figures in italics are for years other than those specified.

		Current account balance (million $)				Net workers' remittances (million $)		Gross international reserves		
		After official transfers		Before official transfers				Million dollars		Months of import cov.
		1970	1993	1970	1993	1970	1993	1970	1993	1993
73	Algeria	−125	361	−163	361	178	993	352	3,656	3.2
74	Namibia	..	201	..	179	..	..	..	134	0.3
75	Slovak Republic	..	−435	..	−532	..	..	..	920	..
76	Latvia	..	..	..	..	..	..	..	..	..
77	Thailand	−250	−6,928	−296	−6,959	..	..	911	25,439	5.1
78	Costa Rica	−74	−470	−77	−537	..	..	16	1,038	3.8
79	Ukraine	..	−863	..	−970	..	..	..	..	..
80	Poland	..	−3,698	..	−5,927	..	..	..	4,277	2.2
81	Russian Federation	..	5,300	..	2,700	..	..	..	..	..
82	Panama	−64	70	−79	−136	..	..	16	597	0.8
83	Czech Republic	..	−228	..	369	..	..	..	4,551	..
84	Botswana	−30	..	−35	..	−9	..	..	4,153	0.0
85	Turkey	−44	−6,380	−57	−7,113	273	2,919	440	7,846	3.0
86	*Iran, Islamic Rep.*	−507	−3,765	−511	−3,765	..	..	217	..	..
	Upper–middle–income							**11,144 t**	**211,138 t**	**4.7 w**
87	Venezuela	−104	−2,223	−98	−2,216	−87	−746	1,047	13,693	7.8
88	Belarus	..	−404	..	−404	..	..	..	..	..
89	Brazil	−837	−637	−861	−608	..	..	1,190	31,747	7.6
90	South Africa	−1,215	1,805	−1,253	1,743	..	..	1,057	2,879	1.4
91	Mauritius	8	−92	5	−96	..	..	46	781	4.8
92	Estonia	..	−62	..	−60	..	..	..	..	..
93	Malaysia	8	−2,103	2	−2,100	..	..	667	28,183	4.5
94	Chile	−91	−2,093	−95	−2,418	..	..	392	10,369	8.4
95	Hungary	..	−4,262	..	−4,284	..	..	..	6,816	3.7
96	Mexico	−1,068	−23,393	−1,098	−23,393	..	..	756	25,299	2.7
97	Trinidad and Tobago	−109	*122*	−104	*123*	3	6	43	228	*1.1*
98	Uruguay	−45	−227	−55	−252	..	..	186	1,423	4.9
99	Oman	..	−1,069	..	−1,087	..	−1,329	13	1,021	4.8
100	Gabon	−3	−269	−15	−284	−8	−141	15	6	0.3
101	Slovenia	..	*932*	..	*885*	..	..	..	141	..
102	Puerto Rico	..	..	..	..	..	..	..	..	..
103	Argentina	−163	−7,452	−160	−7,363	..	..	682	15,499	5.9
104	Greece	−422	−747	−424	−4,832	333	2,360	318	9,135	3.0
105	Korea, Rep.	−623	384	−706	526	..	..	610	21,455	2.2
106	Portugal	−158	947	−158	−1,926	504	3,844	1,565	22,115	8.7
107	*Saudi Arabia*	71	−14,218	152	−13,278	−183	−15,717	670	9,224	1.4
108	*Turkmenistan*	..	*927*	..	*927*	..	..	..	..	..
	Low- and middle-income							..	..	..
	Sub–Saharan Africa							**3,085 t**	**15,164 t**	**2.4 w**
	East Asia & Pacific							..	**122,053 t**	**3.7 w**
	South Asia							**1,404 t**	**21,425 t**	**4.3 w**
	Europe and Central Asia							..	..	..
	Middle East & N. Africa							**4,477 t**	**49,511 t**	**4.3 w**
	Latin America & Caribbean							**5,527 t**	**118,421 t**	**5.6 w**
	Severely indebted							**3,691 t**	**68,277 t**	**5.7 w**
	High-income economies							**72,544 t**	**974,281 t**	**2.7 w**
109	New Zealand	−232	−932	−222	−885	16	256	258	3,337	2.7
110	Ireland	−198	3,848	−228	979	..	..	698	6,066	1.2
111	Spain	79	−6,258	79	−9,112	469	1,495	1,851	47,146	4.5
112	† Israel	−562	−1,373	−766	−5,268	..	..	452	6,386	2.2
113	Australia	−785	−10,369	−691	−9,955	..	..	1,709	14,189	2.4
114	† Hong Kong	225	..	225	..	..	..	..	..	..
115	United Kingdom	1,970	−16,391	2,376	−9,145	..	..	2,918	43,982	1.4
116	Finland	−240	−980	−233	−527	..	..	455	6,193	2.1
117	† Kuwait	853	6,344	853	6,474	..	−1,229	209	5,206	6.1
118	Italy	821	11,176	1,155	17,008	555	432	5,547	53,590	2.1
119	† Singapore	−572	2,039	−585	2,253	..	..	1,012	48,361	5.6
120	Canada	1,008	−23,869	960	−23,506	..	..	4,733	14,846	1.0
121	Netherlands	−485	9,775	−509	13,243	−51	−353	3,362	45,036	2.4
122	† United Arab Emirates	90	..	100	..	..	..	..	6,415	..
123	Belgium[b]	716	12,588	904	14,574	38	−365	..	..	..
124	France	−204	10,201	18	15,613	−641	−1,530	5,199	54,624	1.7
125	Austria	−79	−875	−77	−639	−7	44	1,806	21,878	2.8
126	Germany[c]	837	−25,563	1,839	*−1,222*	−1,366	*−4,375*	13,879	114,822	*2.6*
127	Sweden	−265	−1,835	−160	−244	..	90	775	21,421	3.4
128	United States	2,330	−103,925	4,680	−85,525	−650	−7,660	15,237	164,620	2.3
129	Norway	−242	2,453	−200	3,534	..	−234	813	20,085	3.1
130	Denmark	−544	4,711	−510	5,086	..	..	488	10,941	2.1
131	Japan	1,990	131,510	2,170	135,350	..	..	4,876	107,989	2.4
132	Switzerland	161	16,697	203	17,329	−313	−2,007	5,317	65,167	6.7
	World							..	..	..

a. Includes Eritrea.   b. Includes Luxembourg.   c. Data prior to July 1990 refer to the Federal Republic of Germany before unification.

Table 18. Official development assistance from OECD and OPEC members

OECD: Total net flows[a]		1970	1975	1980	1985	1989	1990	1991	1992	1993
						Millions of US dollars				
109	New Zealand	14	66	72	54	87	95	100	97	98
110	Ireland	0	8	30	39	49	57	72	70	81
113	Australia	212	552	667	749	1,020	955	1,050	1,015	953
115	United Kingdom	500	904	1,854	1,530	2,587	2,638	3,201	3,243	2,908
116	Finland	7	48	110	211	706	846	930	644	355
118	Italy	147	182	683	1,098	3,613	3,395	3,347	4,122	3,043
120	Canada	337	880	1,075	1,631	2,320	2,470	2,604	2,515	2,373
121	Netherlands	196	608	1,630	1,136	2,094	2,538	2,517	2,753	2,525
123	Belgium	120	378	595	440	703	889	831	870	808
124	France	971	2,093	4,162	3,995	5,802	7,163	7,386	8,270	7,915
125	Austria	11	79	178	248	282	394	548	556	544
126	Germany[b]	599	1,689	3,567	2,942	4,948	6,320	6,890	7,583	6,954
127	Sweden	117	566	962	840	1,799	2,007	2,116	2,460	1,769
128	United States	3,153	4,161	7,138	9,403	7,677	11,394	11,262	11,709	9,721
129	Norway	37	184	486	574	917	1,205	1,178	1,273	1,014
130	Denmark	59	205	481	440	937	1,171	1,200	1,392	1,340
131	Japan	458	1,148	3,353	3,797	8,965	9,069	10,952	11,151	11,259
132	Switzerland	30	104	253	302	558	750	863	1,139	793
	Total	**6,986**	**13,855**	**27,296**	**29,429**	**45,064**	**53,356**	**57,047**	**60,862**	**54,453**
						As percentage of donor GNP				
109	New Zealand	0.23	0.52	0.33	0.25	0.22	0.23	0.25	0.26	0.25
110	Ireland	0.00	0.09	0.16	0.24	0.17	0.16	0.19	0.16	0.20
113	Australia	0.59	0.65	0.48	0.48	0.38	0.34	0.38	0.37	0.35
115	United Kingdom	0.41	0.39	0.35	0.33	0.31	0.27	0.32	0.31	0.31
116	Finland	0.06	0.18	0.22	0.40	0.62	0.63	0.80	0.64	0.46
118	Italy	0.16	0.11	0.15	0.26	0.42	0.31	0.30	0.34	0.31
120	Canada	0.41	0.54	0.43	0.49	0.44	0.44	0.45	0.46	0.45
121	Netherlands	0.61	0.75	0.97	0.91	0.94	0.92	0.88	0.86	0.82
123	Belgium	0.46	0.59	0.50	0.55	0.46	0.46	0.41	0.39	0.39
124	France	0.66	0.62	0.63	0.78	0.61	0.60	0.62	0.63	0.63
125	Austria	0.07	0.21	0.23	0.38	0.22	0.25	0.34	0.30	0.30
126	Germany[b]	0.32	0.40	0.44	0.47	0.41	0.42	0.40	0.39	0.37
127	Sweden	0.38	0.82	0.78	0.86	0.96	0.91	0.90	1.03	0.98
128	United States	0.32	0.27	0.27	0.24	0.15	0.21	0.20	0.20	0.15
129	Norway	0.32	0.66	0.87	1.01	1.05	1.17	1.13	1.16	1.01
130	Denmark	0.38	0.58	0.74	0.80	0.93	0.94	0.96	1.02	1.03
131	Japan	0.23	0.23	0.32	0.29	0.31	0.31	0.32	0.30	0.26
132	Switzerland	0.15	0.19	0.24	0.31	0.30	0.32	0.36	0.45	0.33
						National currencies				
109	New Zealand (millions of dollars)	13	55	74	109	145	159	173	180	181
110	Ireland (millions of pounds)	0	4	15	37	35	34	45	41	55
113	Australia (millions of dollars)	189	402	591	966	1,287	1,222	1,348	1,380	1,401
115	United Kingdom (millions of pounds)	208	409	798	1,180	1,578	1,478	1,809	1,837	1,936
116	Finland (millions of markkaa)	29	177	414	1,308	3,025	3,228	3,749	2,873	2,026
118	Italy (billions of lire)	92	119	585	2,097	4,954	4,060	4,138	5,056	4,780
120	Canada (millions of dollars)	353	895	1,257	2,227	2,747	2,881	2,983	3,037	3,060
121	Netherlands (millions of guilders)	710	1,538	3,241	3,773	4,435	4,610	4,688	4,830	4,687
123	Belgium (millions of francs)	6,000	13,902	17,399	26,145	27,665	29,625	28,267	27,902	27,914
124	France (millions of francs)	5,393	8,971	17,589	35,894	36,973	38,901	41,517	43,673	44,774
125	Austria (millions of schillings)	286	1,376	2,303	5,132	3,726	4,468	6,374	6,095	6,32
126	Germany (millions of deutsche marks)[b]	2,192	4,155	6,484	8,661	9,290	10,186	11,390	11,812	11,490
127	Sweden (millions of kronor)	605	2,350	4,069	7,226	11,592	11,862	12,764	14,248	13,737
128	United States (millions of dollars)	3,153	4,161	7,138	9,403	7,677	11,394	11,262	11,709	9,721
129	Norway (millions of kroner)	264	962	2,400	4,946	6,327	7,527	7,609	7,787	7,203
130	Denmark (millions of kroner)	443	1,178	2,711	4,657	6,840	7,228	7,646	8,380	8,675
131	Japan (billions of yen)	165	341	760	749	1,234	1,307	1,472	1,411	1,248
132	Switzerland (millions of francs)	131	268	424	743	912	1,037	1,232	1,596	1,171
Summary						Billions of US dollars				
	ODA (current prices)	7.0	13.9	27.3	29.4	45.7	54.5	58.6	62.7	56.0
	ODA (1992 prices)	35.0	41.0	47.2	55.0	55.9	59.8	62.1	62.7	57.1
	GNP (current prices)	2,079.0	4,001.0	7,488.0	8,550.0	14,349.2	16,073.1	17,073.8	18,294.4	18,604.8
						Percent				
	ODA as a percentage of GNP	0.34	0.35	0.35	0.34	0.32	0.34	0.35	0.35	0.30
						Index (1992 = 100)				
	GDP deflator[c]	19.9	33.8	57.9	53.5	81.8	91.2	94.3	100.0	98.0

OECD: Net bilateral flows to low-income economies[a]		1980	1988	1989	1990	1991	1992	1993
					As percentage of donor GNP			
109	New Zealand	0.01	0.00	0.00	0.01	0.00	0.00	0.01
110	Ireland	..	0.00	0.05	0.06	0.07	0.07	0.08
113	Australia	0.05	0.04	0.06	0.06	0.05	0.06	0.06
115	United Kingdom	0.15	0.11	0.11	0.09	0.11	0.10	0.07
116	Finland	0.10	0.28	0.28	0.24	0.29	0.24	0.15
118	Italy	0.01	0.20	0.13	0.11	0.09	0.09	0.09
120	Canada	0.14	0.15	0.11	0.11	0.12	0.12	0.09
121	Netherlands	0.42	0.38	0.34	0.35	0.23	0.28	0.23
123	Belgium	0.26	0.17	0.12	0.15	0.10	0.12	0.11
124	France	0.11	0.17	0.19	0.20	0.18	0.19	0.19
125	Austria	0.03	0.04	0.07	0.11	0.13	0.04	0.04
126	Germany[b]	0.12	0.13	0.14	0.15	0.13	0.14	0.11
127	Sweden	0.41	0.36	0.41	0.34	0.36	0.34	0.37
128	United States	0.07	0.05	0.05	0.07	0.09	0.06	0.04
129	Norway	0.34	0.47	0.42	0.49	0.46	0.48	0.38
130	Denmark	0.33	0.37	0.39	0.35	0.36	0.33	0.36
131	Japan	0.09	0.11	0.11	0.09	0.12	0.09	0.09
132	Switzerland	0.09	0.12	0.12	0.12	0.16	0.13	0.12
	Total	**0.11**	**0.11**	**0.11**	**0.12**	**0.12**	**0.11**	**0.09**

OPEC: Total net flows[d]		1980	1988	1989	1990	1991	1992	1993
					Millions of US dollars			
21	Nigeria	35	14	70	13	..	..	..
	Qatar	277	4	−3	−2	1	1	1
73	Algeria	81	13	42	7	3	7	7
86	Iran, Islamic Rep.	−72	39	−94	2	..	..	..
87	Venezuela	135	55	52	15	..	..	..
	Iraq	864	−21	36	78	−3	−28	..
	Libya	376	129	174	37	15	40	27
107	Saudi Arabia[e]	5,943	2,223	1,441	4,556	1,873	962	811
117	† Kuwait	1,140	108	170	1,295	389	202	381
122	† United Arab Emirates	1,118	−17	65	888	558	169	236
	Total OPEC[d]	**9,897**	**2,547**	**1,953**	**6,889**	..	..	..
	Total OAPEC[f]	**9,799**	**2,439**	**1,925**	**6,859**	..	..	..
					As percentage of donor GNP			
21	Nigeria	..	0.04	0.25	0.04	..	..	..
	Qatar	4.16	0.06	−0.04	−0.03	0.01	0.01	0.02
73	Algeria	0.20	0.02	0.07	0.01	0.01	0.01	0.01
86	Iran, Islamic Rep.	..	..	−0.02	..	..	..	..
87	Venezuela	..	0.11	0.13	0.03	..	..	..
	Iraq	2.36	−0.04	0.05	0.11	0.00	−0.04	..
	Libya	1.16	0.62	0.80	0.14	0.05	0.15	0.12
107	Saudi Arabia[e]	4.15	2.73	1.64	3.42	1.60	0.80	0.70
117	† Kuwait	3.52	0.39	0.53	5.13	2.45	0.87	1.30
122	† United Arab Emirates	4.06	−0.07	0.23	2.64	1.64	0.48	0.66
	Total OPEC[d]	..	..	**0.19**	..	..	..	..
	Total OAPEC[f]	**3.26**	**0.85**	**0.56**	**1.80**	..	..	..

a. Organization for Economic Cooperation and Development high-income countries.   b. Data refer to the Federal Republic of Germany before unification.   c. See the technical notes.   d. Organization of Petroleum Exporting Countries.   e. Data are from national authorities.   f. Organization of Arab Petroleum Exporting Countries.

Table 19. Official development assistance: receipts

		Net disbursement of ODA from all sources								
		Millions of dollars							Per capita ($)	As percentage of GNP
		1987	1988	1989	1990	1991	1992	1993	1993	1993
	Low-income economies	16,909 t	18,904 t	20,344 t	23,274 t	23,404 t	29,897 t	31,394 t	9.2 w	2.5 w
	Excluding China & India	14,377 t	15,650 t	17,044 t	19,169 t	19,335 t	26,171 t	26,603 t	23.7 w	6.4 w
1	Mozambique	652	894	805	995	1,031	1,408	1,162	77.0	79.2
2	Tanzania	879	979	921	1,143	1,080	1,250	949	33.9	40.0
3	Ethiopia[a]	633	970	753	1,020	1,096	1,143	1,087	21.0	..
4	Sierra Leone	68	102	100	65	105	137	1,204	269.4	164.4
5	Viet Nam	111	148	129	194	248	579	319	4.5	2.5
6	Burundi	202	189	199	266	254	294	244	40.6	25.8
7	Uganda	280	363	447	552	539	670	616	34.2	19.0
8	Nepal	347	399	493	430	453	427	364	17.5	9.7
9	Malawi	280	366	412	481	504	570	503	47.8	25.5
10	Chad	198	264	244	308	265	241	229	38.1	19.1
11	Rwanda	245	252	232	294	352	353	361	47.7	24.1
12	Bangladesh	1,635	1,592	1,800	2,047	1,634	1,719	1,386	12.0	5.8
13	Madagascar	321	304	321	386	439	362	370	26.7	11.0
14	Guinea-Bissau	111	103	115	132	118	107	97	94.6	40.3
15	Kenya	572	808	966	1,053	873	893	894	35.3	16.1
16	Mali	366	427	454	468	458	424	360	35.5	13.5
17	Niger	353	371	296	391	377	371	347	40.5	15.6
18	Lao PDR	58	77	140	152	131	157	199	43.2	14.9
19	Burkina Faso	281	298	272	336	415	440	457	46.8	16.2
20	India	1,839	2,097	1,913	1,550	2,750	2,437	1,503	1.7	0.6
21	Nigeria	69	120	346	250	262	258	284	2.7	0.9
22	Albania	0	6	10	11	325	390	194	57.3	..
23	Nicaragua	141	220	244	334	841	658	323	78.5	17.9
24	Togo	126	199	183	241	202	212	101	25.9	8.1
25	Gambia, The	100	82	93	91	98	112	92	88.0	25.5
26	Zambia	426	475	389	482	880	1,031	870	97.3	23.6
27	Mongolia	3	3	6	13	70	123	113	48.6	10.3
28	Central African Republic	176	196	192	244	175	177	174	55.0	14.1
29	Benin	138	162	263	271	255	269	267	52.4	12.5
30	Ghana	373	474	552	502	723	616	633	38.5	10.4
31	Pakistan	879	1,408	1,129	1,149	1,223	1,072	1,065	8.7	2.1
32	Tajikistan	..	..	..	..	..	..	..	..	..
33	China	1,462	2,008	2,156	2,176	2,041	3,058	3,273	2.8	0.8
34	Guinea	213	262	346	296	370	441	414	65.6	13.0
35	Mauritania	185	187	244	229	220	183	331	153.2	34.9
36	Zimbabwe	293	272	264	340	393	715	460	42.8	8.1
37	Georgia	..	..	..	..	..	..	..	..	..
38	Honduras	258	325	253	456	303	349	324	60.7	9.7
39	Sri Lanka	502	598	547	674	815	483	551	30.8	5.3
40	Côte d'Ivoire	254	439	403	694	633	757	766	57.5	8.2
41	Lesotho	103	105	129	136	120	133	128	65.7	16.8
42	Armenia	..	..	..	..	..	..	..	..	..
43	Egypt, Arab Rep.	1,773	1,540	1,569	5,446	5,021	3,602	2,304	40.8	5.9
44	*Myanmar*	367	451	184	166	179	115	102	2.3	..
45	*Yemen, Rep.*	422	304	370	407	300	248	309	23.4	..
	Middle-income economies	..	..	..	..	..	..	..	..	..
	Lower-middle-income	..	..	..	..	..	..	..	..	..
46	Azerbaijan	..	..	..	..	..	..	..	..	..
47	Indonesia	1,245	1,632	1,840	1,747	1,874	2,095	2,026	10.8	1.4
48	Senegal	641	570	650	795	581	680	508	64.3	8.8
49	Bolivia	318	399	445	526	481	628	570	80.6	10.6
50	Cameroon	213	284	458	449	519	715	547	43.7	4.9
51	Macedonia, FYR	..	..	..	..	..	..	..	..	..
52	Kyrgyz Republic	..	..	..	..	..	..	..	..	..
53	Philippines	770	855	845	1,284	1,054	1,717	1,490	23.0	2.8
54	Congo	152	90	93	219	134	113	129	52.9	5.2
55	Uzbekistan	..	..	..	..	..	..	..	..	..
56	Morocco	448	482	464	1,055	1,233	962	751	29.0	2.8
57	Moldova	..	..	..	..	..	..	..	..	..
58	Guatemala	241	235	262	203	199	198	212	21.1	1.9
59	Papua New Guinea	322	380	339	416	397	442	303	73.7	6.0
60	Bulgaria	..	..	..	..	..	..	..	..	..
61	Romania	..	..	..	..	..	..	..	..	..
62	Jordan	577	417	276	888	921	355	245	59.7	4.4
63	Ecuador	228	172	161	163	238	244	240	21.9	1.7
64	Dominican Republic	130	118	143	101	67	64	2	0.2	0.0
65	El Salvador	426	420	446	352	294	409	405	73.4	5.3
66	Lithuania	..	..	..	..	..	..	..	..	..
67	Colombia	78	63	68	96	122	246	109	3.0	0.2
68	Jamaica	168	193	262	273	165	126	109	45.0	2.8
69	Peru	294	276	310	401	614	409	560	24.5	1.4
70	Paraguay	81	76	93	57	146	102	137	29.1	2.0
71	Kazakhstan	..	..	..	..	..	..	..	..	..
72	Tunisia	277	318	283	393	357	437	250	28.9	1.7

Note: For data comparability and coverage, see the technical notes. Figures in italics are for years other than those specified.

		Net disbursement of ODA from all sources								
		Millions of dollars							Per capita ($)	As percentage of GNP
		1987	1988	1989	1990	1991	1992	1993	1993	1993
73	Algeria	214	172	158	263	340	406	359	13.4	0.7
74	Namibia	17	22	59	123	184	143	154	105.6	6.2
75	Slovak Republic	..	..	..	..	..	..	..	..	..
76	Latvia	..	..	..	..	..	..	..	..	..
77	Thailand	504	563	739	802	722	776	614	10.6	0.5
78	Costa Rica	228	188	227	230	174	140	99	30.1	1.3
79	Ukraine	..	..	..	..	..	..	..	..	..
80	Poland	..	..	..	..	..	..	..	..	..
81	Russian Federation	..	..	..	..	..	..	..	..	..
82	Panama	40	22	19	98	102	162	79	31.3	1.2
83	Czech Republic	..	..	..	..	..	..	..	..	..
84	Botswana	156	151	160	149	136	115	127	90.4	3.3
85	Turkey	376	268	141	1,219	1,622	326	461	7.7	0.3
86	*Iran, Islamic Rep.*	71	82	96	105	194	107	141	2.2	..
Upper-middle-income		2,173 t	1,474 t	1,652 t	1,382 t	1,562 t	2,245 t	2,170 t	10.2 w	0.2 w
87	Venezuela	19	23	60	80	31	41	50	2.4	0.1
88	Belarus	..	..	..	..	..	..	..	..	..
89	Brazil	289	210	206	167	183	−235	238	1.5	0.0
90	South Africa	..	..	..	..	..	..	..	..	..
91	Mauritius	65	59	60	89	67	46	27	24.3	0.8
92	Estonia	..	..	..	..	..	..	..	..	..
93	Malaysia	363	104	140	469	289	209	100	5.2	0.2
94	Chile	21	45	62	108	126	136	184	13.3	0.4
95	Hungary	..	..	..	..	..	..	..	..	..
96	Mexico	156	174	99	160	278	316	402	4.5	0.1
97	Trinidad and Tobago	34	9	6	18	−2	9	3	2.0	0.1
98	Uruguay	18	41	39	54	51	73	121	38.5	0.9
99	Oman	16	1	18	66	15	54	1,071	538.8	9.2
100	Gabon	82	106	133	132	143	69	102	100.9	1.9
101	Slovenia	..	..	..	..	..	..	..	..	..
102	Puerto Rico	..	..	..	..	..	..	..	..	..
103	Argentina	100	153	212	184	299	292	283	8.4	0.1
104	Greece	35	35	30	37	39	47	44	4.2	0.1
105	Korea, Rep.	11	10	52	52	55	3	965	21.9	0.3
106	Portugal	..	..	..	..	..	..	..	..	..
107	*Saudi Arabia*	22	19	36	44	45	55	35	2.0	..
108	*Turkmenistan*	..	..	..	..	..	..	..	..	..
Low- and middle-income		..	..	..	..	..	..	..	..	..
Sub-Saharan Africa		9,511 t	10,574 t	11,924 t	13,473 t	13,973 t	16,784 t	16,441 t	35.7 w	11.5 w
East Asia & Pacific		4,722 t	4,722 t	5,749 t	6,736 t	7,095 t	8,068 t	7,700 t	6.1 w	0.8 w
South Asia		4,244 t	5,474 t	5,307 t	6,236 t	6,119 t	6,055 t	7,485 t	4.3 w	1.5 w
Europe and Central Asia		..	..	..	..	..	..	..	..	..
Middle East & N. Africa		4,710 t	4,474 t	4,704 t	..	..	9,831 t	9,560 t	22.9 w	3.2 w
Latin America & Caribbean		3,024 t	3,262 t	3,732 t	3,751 t	4,149 t	4,640 t	5,273 t	8.6 w	0.3 w
Severely indebted		3,324 t	3,473 t	3,788 t	3,118 t	3,310 t	5,543 t	6,189 t	13.4 w	0.4 w
High-income economies		..	..	..	..	..	..	..	..	..
109	New Zealand	..	..	..	..	..	..	..	..	..
110	Ireland	..	..	..	..	..	..	..	..	..
111	Spain	..	..	..	..	..	..	..	..	..
112	† Israel	1,251	1,241	1,192	1,372	1,749	2,066	1,266	242.5	1.8
113	Australia	..	..	..	..	..	..	..	..	..
114	† Hong Kong	19	22	40	38	36	−39	30	5.2	0.0
115	United Kingdom	..	..	..	..	..	..	..	..	..
116	Finland	..	..	..	..	..	..	..	..	..
117	† Kuwait	3	6	4	7	5	2	3	1.5	0.0
118	Italy	..	..	..	..	..	..	..	..	..
119	† Singapore	23	22	95	−3	8	20	24	8.5	0.0
120	Canada	..	..	..	..	..	..	..	..	..
121	Netherlands	..	..	..	..	..	..	..	..	..
122	† United Arab Emirates	115	−12	−6	5	−6	−8	−9	−4.8	0.0
123	Belgium	..	..	..	..	..	..	..	..	..
124	France	..	..	..	..	..	..	..	..	..
125	Austria	..	..	..	..	..	..	..	..	..
126	Germany	..	..	..	..	..	..	..	..	..
127	Sweden	..	..	..	..	..	..	..	..	..
128	United States	..	..	..	..	..	..	..	..	..
129	Norway	..	..	..	..	..	..	..	..	..
130	Denmark	..	..	..	..	..	..	..	..	..
131	Japan	..	..	..	..	..	..	..	..	..
132	Switzerland	..	..	..	..	..	..	..	..	..
World		..	..	..	..	..	..	..	..	..

a. Includes Eritrea.

Table 20. Total external debt

		Long-term debt (million $)		Use of IMF credit (million $)		Short-term debt (million $)		Total external debt (million $)		Total arrears on LDOD (million $)		Ratio of present value to nominal value of debt
		1980	1993	1980	1993	1980	1993	1980	1993	1980	1993	1993
Low-income economies												
Excluding China & India												
1	Mozambique	..	4,668	..	189	..	407	..	5,264	..	1,549	81
2	Tanzania	2,490	6,746	171	215	311	562	2,972	7,522	42	1,535	73
3	Ethiopia[a]	688	4,530	79	49	57	150	824	4,729	1	735	65
4	Sierra Leone	323	728	59	84	53	576	435	1,388	25	248	81
5	Viet Nam	40	21,554	0	100	0	2,570	40	24,224	0	7,610	86
6	Burundi	118	999	36	58	12	5	166	1,063	0	13	44
7	Uganda	549	2,617	89	334	64	105	702	3,056	103	283	58
8	Nepal	156	1,938	42	49	7	23	205	2,009	0	13	49
9	Malawi	625	1,724	80	86	116	12	821	1,821	4	8	45
10	Chad	204	705	14	28	11	25	229	757	35	36	49
11	Rwanda	150	836	14	12	26	62	190	910	0	50	47
12	Bangladesh	3,417	13,048	424	682	212	149	4,053	13,879	0	15	54
13	Madagascar	892	3,920	87	92	244	582	1,223	4,594	20	1,534	76
14	Guinea-Bissau	128	634	1	5	5	53	134	692	6	152	66
15	Kenya	2,499	5,721	254	363	640	909	3,394	6,994	6	690	76
16	Mali	669	2,506	39	71	24	73	732	2,650	76	345	58
17	Niger	687	1,535	16	52	159	118	863	1,704	2	223	67
18	Lao PDR	333	1,948	16	36	1	1	350	1,986	6	0	31
19	Burkina Faso	281	1,093	15	21	35	31	330	1,144	0	52	52
20	India	18,334	83,254	977	4,901	1,271	3,626	20,582	91,781	0	0	78
21	Nigeria	5,381	28,558	0	0	3,553	3,973	8,934	32,531	0	6,784	98
22	Albania	..	174	..	30	..	552	..	755	..	49	93
23	Nicaragua	1,671	8,773	49	23	472	1,648	2,192	10,445	44	4,335	91
24	Togo	899	1,128	33	69	120	95	1,052	1,292	49	85	62
25	Gambia, The	97	349	16	33	23	4	137	386	0	6	49
26	Zambia	2,227	4,679	447	777	586	1,332	3,261	6,788	39	2,073	81
27	Mongolia	..	344	..	32	..	15	..	391	..	36	72
28	Central African Republic	147	797	24	29	25	78	195	904	54	117	55
29	Benin	334	1,409	16	43	73	35	424	1,487	19	38	56
30	Ghana	1,162	3,378	105	738	131	474	1,398	4,590	9	155	62
31	Pakistan	8,515	20,429	674	1,122	737	4,500	9,926	26,050	0	0	79
32	Tajikistan	..	41	..	0	..	0	..	42	..	0	68
33	China	4,504	70,254	0	0	0	13,546	4,504	83,800	0	0	91
34	Guinea	1,004	2,675	35	60	78	128	1,117	2,864	129	412	65
35	Mauritania	717	1,960	62	63	65	180	843	2,203	54	379	71
36	Zimbabwe	696	3,287	0	282	90	600	786	4,168	0	2	84
37	Georgia	..	568	..	0	..	0	..	568	..	0	95
38	Honduras	1,167	3,568	33	118	272	179	1,472	3,865	3	173	81
39	Sri Lanka	1,231	6,026	391	516	220	241	1,841	6,783	0	0	64
40	Côte d'Ivoire	6,321	13,167	65	219	1,059	5,760	7,445	19,146	0	4,125	92
41	Lesotho	58	472	6	34	8	6	72	512	0	13	53
42	Armenia	..	..	..	..	..	..	..	..	..	..	..
43	Egypt, Arab Rep.	16,477	37,204	411	202	4,027	3,220	20,915	40,626	457	1,995	68
44	*Myanmar*	1,390	5,135	106	0	4	343	1,499	5,478	0	1,298	76
45	*Yemen, Rep.*	1,453	5,341	48	0	183	582	1,684	5,923	8	2,309	80
Middle-income economies												
Lower-middle-income												
46	Azerbaijan	..	36	..	0	..	0	..	36	..	0	96
47	Indonesia	18,169	68,865	0	0	2,775	20,674	20,944	89,539	0	1	91
48	Senegal	1,114	3,060	140	244	219	464	1,473	3,768	0	375	69
49	Bolivia	2,274	3,784	126	221	303	208	2,702	4,213	24	54	76
50	Cameroon	2,183	5,683	59	16	271	902	2,513	6,601	6	977	90
51	Macedonia, FYR	..	738	..	4	..	124	..	866	..	321	101
52	Kyrgyz Republic	..	248	..	60	..	0	..	308	..	0	90
53	Philippines	8,817	29,025	1,044	1,210	7,556	5,035	17,417	35,269	1	0	94
54	Congo	1,257	4,097	22	5	247	969	1,526	5,071	14	1,907	91
55	Uzbekistan	..	736	..	0	..	3	..	739	..	3	93
56	Morocco	8,475	20,660	457	285	778	486	9,710	21,430	6	434	89
57	Moldova	..	202	..	87	..	1	..	289	..	6	90
58	Guatemala	831	2,484	0	0	335	471	1,166	2,954	0	335	85
59	Papua New Guinea	624	2,860	31	44	64	264	719	3,168	0	0	86
60	Bulgaria	392	9,746	0	632	0	1,872	392	12,250	0	7,818	99
61	Romania	7,131	2,326	328	1,031	2,303	1,099	9,762	4,456	0	0	95
62	Jordan	1,490	6,825	0	81	486	66	1,975	6,972	30	301	89
63	Ecuador	4,422	10,176	0	71	1,575	3,863	5,997	14,110	1	5,199	96
64	Dominican Republic	1,473	3,813	49	186	480	634	2,002	4,633	20	929	91
65	El Salvador	659	1,905	32	0	220	107	911	2,012	0	9	79
66	Lithuania	..	164	..	121	..	7	..	291	..	0	87
67	Colombia	4,604	13,940	0	0	2,337	3,233	6,941	17,173	0	207	96
68	Jamaica	1,496	3,632	309	335	98	311	1,904	4,279	27	474	86
69	Peru	6,828	16,363	474	883	2,084	3,082	9,386	20,328	0	6,246	89
70	Paraguay	780	1,309	0	0	174	290	955	1,599	2	124	88
71	Kazakhstan	..	1,552	..	85	..	2	..	1,640	..	2	97
72	Tunisia	3,390	7,627	0	285	136	789	3,526	8,701	6	3	88

Note: For data comparability and coverage, see the technical notes. Figures in italics are for years other than those specified.

		Long-term debt (million $)		Use of IMF credit (million $)		Short-term debt (million $)		Total external debt (million $)		Total arrears on LDOD (million $)		Ratio of present value to nominal value of debt
		1980	1993	1980	1993	1980	1993	1980	1993	1980	1993	1993
73	Algeria	17,040	24,587	0	471	2,325	700	19,365	25,757	2	1	95
74	Namibia	..	..	..	..	..	..	..	..	..	..	..
75	Slovak Republic	..	2,059	..	557	..	715	..	3,330	..	0	94
76	Latvia	..	119	..	107	..	5	..	231	..	2	89
77	Thailand	5,646	26,079	348	0	2,303	19,740	8,297	45,819	0	0	98
78	Costa Rica	2,112	3,419	57	81	575	372	2,744	3,872	2	130	92
79	Ukraine	..	3,462	..	0	..	122	..	3,584	..	29	96
80	Poland	6,594	41,966	0	684	2,300	2,656	8,894	45,306	334	2,094	93
81	Russian Federation	..	72,769	..	2,469	..	7,851	..	83,089	..	7,729	98
82	Panama	2,271	3,709	23	113	681	2,980	2,975	6,802	1	3,607	97
83	Czech Republic	0	5,509	0	1,072	3,318	2,079	3,318	8,660	0	4	97
84	Botswana	143	666	0	0	4	8	147	674	0	15	76
85	Turkey	15,575	49,329	1,054	0	2,502	18,533	19,131	67,862	34	0	97
86	*Iran, Islamic Rep.*	4,500	11,666	0	0	0	8,884	4,500	20,550	1	40	109
Upper-middle-income												
87	Venezuela	13,795	30,103	0	2,680	15,550	4,682	29,345	37,465	51	1,023	97
88	Belarus	..	864	..	96	..	0	..	961	..	0	75
89	Brazil	57,466	105,283	0	304	13,546	27,162	71,012	132,749	469	15,370	98
90	South Africa	..	..	..	..	..	..	..	..	..	..	..
91	Mauritius	318	884	102	0	47	115	467	999	2	34	87
92	Estonia	..	97	..	58	..	0	..	155	..	0	91
93	Malaysia	5,256	16,384	0	0	1,355	6,951	6,611	23,335	0	0	97
94	Chile	9,399	16,031	123	476	2,560	4,130	12,081	20,637	0	0	95
95	Hungary	6,416	21,535	0	1,231	3,347	2,005	9,764	24,771	0	0	100
96	Mexico	41,215	85,960	0	4,787	16,163	27,281	57,378	118,028	0	0	99
97	Trinidad and Tobago	713	1,854	0	155	116	129	829	2,137	0	4	97
98	Uruguay	1,338	4,992	0	38	322	2,229	1,660	7,259	0	0	97
99	Oman	436	2,319	0	0	163	342	599	2,661	0	0	95
100	Gabon	1,272	2,889	15	45	228	883	1,514	3,818	0	1,105	96
101	Slovenia	..	1,794	..	12	..	117	..	1,923	..	125	97
102	Puerto Rico	..	..	..	..	..	..	..	..	..	..	..
103	Argentina	16,774	61,534	0	3,520	10,383	9,419	27,157	74,473	0	2,872	97
104	Greece	..	..	..	..	..	..	..	..	..	..	..
105	Korea, Rep.	18,236	35,003	683	0	10,561	12,200	29,480	47,203	0	0	97
106	Portugal	7,215	26,546	119	0	2,395	10,396	9,729	36,942	0	0	97
107	*Saudi Arabia*	..	..	..	..	..	..	..	..	..	..	..
108	*Turkmenistan*	..	9	..	0	..	0	..	9	..	0	56
Low- and middle-income												
Sub-Saharan Africa												
East Asia & Pacific												
South Asia												
Europe and Central Asia												
Middle East & N. Africa												
Latin America & Caribbean												
Severely indebted												
High-income economies												
109	New Zealand											
110	Ireland											
111	Spain											
112	† Israel											
113	Australia											
114	† Hong Kong											
115	United Kingdom											
116	Finland											
117	† Kuwait											
118	Italy											
119	† Singapore											
120	Canada											
121	Netherlands											
122	† United Arab Emirates											
123	Belgium											
124	France											
125	Austria											
126	Germany											
127	Sweden											
128	United States											
129	Norway											
130	Denmark											
131	Japan											
132	Switzerland											
World												

a. Includes Eritrea.

Table 21. Flow of public and private external capital

		Disbursements (million $)				Repayment of principal (million $)				Interest payments (million $)			
		Long-term public and publicly guaranteed		Private nonguaranteed		Long-term public and publicly guaranteed		Private nonguaranteed		Long-term public and publicly guaranteed		Private nonguaranteed	
		1980	1993	1980	1993	1980	1993	1980	1993	1980	1993	1980	1993
Low-income economies													
Excluding China & India													
1	Mozambique	..	156	..	4	..	23	..	3	..	41	..	0
2	Tanzania	403	234	31	0	53	78	16	0	59	66	7	0
3	Ethiopia[a]	110	379	0	0	17	35	0	0	17	28	0	0
4	Sierra Leone	86	64	0	0	32	3	0	0	8	2	0	0
5	Viet Nam	8	80	0	0	0	264	0	0	1	77	0	0
6	Burundi	39	78	0	0	4	19	0	0	2	12	0	0
7	Uganda	93	342	0	0	32	238	0	0	4	49	0	0
8	Nepal	50	187	0	0	2	39	0	0	2	27	0	0
9	Malawi	153	190	0	0	33	40	0	0	35	27	0	0
10	Chad	6	56	0	0	3	2	0	0	0	8	0	0
11	Rwanda	27	39	0	0	3	3	0	0	2	3	0	0
12	Bangladesh	657	618	0	0	63	274	0	0	47	153	0	0
13	Madagascar	350	120	0	0	30	28	0	0	26	23	0	0
14	Guinea-Bissau	69	19	0	0	3	1	0	0	1	2	0	0
15	Kenya	539	425	87	65	108	276	88	50	124	153	39	54
16	Mali	95	56	0	0	6	7	0	0	3	7	0	0
17	Niger	167	107	113	0	23	35	35	24	16	15	49	7
18	Lao PDR	55	78	0	0	1	24	0	0	1	5	0	0
19	Burkina Faso	65	145	0	0	11	17	0	0	6	16	0	0
20	India	2,166	6,849	285	1,120	664	3,822	91	253	473	3,956	30	139
21	Nigeria	1,187	514	565	0	65	499	177	10	440	1,269	91	2
22	Albania	..	63	..	0	..	0	..	0	..	0	..	0
23	Nicaragua	276	104	0	0	45	53	0	0	42	58	0	0
24	Togo	100	16	0	0	19	6	0	0	19	8	0	0
25	Gambia, The	51	26	0	0	0	19	0	0	0	6	0	0
26	Zambia	597	281	6	1	181	120	31	2	106	96	10	0
27	Mongolia	..	56	..	0	..	8	..	0	..	6	..	0
28	Central African Republic	25	54	0	0	1	2	0	0	0	4	0	0
29	Benin	62	78	0	0	6	18	0	0	3	14	0	0
30	Ghana	220	315	0	7	77	96	0	5	31	71	0	3
31	Pakistan	1,054	2,720	9	44	345	1,229	7	42	246	683	2	7
32	Tajikistan	..	14	..	0	..	0	..	0	..	0	..	0
33	China	2,539	19,250	0	230	613	6,683	0	0	318	2,614	0	0
34	Guinea	121	291	0	0	75	41	0	0	23	37	0	0
35	Mauritania	126	178	0	0	17	73	0	0	13	42	0	0
36	Zimbabwe	132	623	0	50	40	335	0	80	10	148	0	22
37	Georgia	..	141	..	0	..	5	..	0	..	8	..	0
38	Honduras	264	402	81	16	39	189	48	18	58	140	25	0
39	Sri Lanka	269	417	2	0	51	235	0	4	33	137	0	1
40	Côte d'Ivoire	1,413	458	325	190	517	227	205	189	353	214	237	157
41	Lesotho	13	62	0	0	3	20	0	0	2	12	0	0
42	Armenia	..	130	..	0	..	1	..	0	..	1	..	0
43	Egypt, Arab Rep.	2,803	1,437	126	40	368	931	46	140	378	1,126	23	34
44	*Myanmar*	268	79	0	0	66	25	0	0	45	90	0	0
45	*Yemen, Rep.*	566	136	0	0	25	78	0	0	10	21	0	0
Middle-income economies													
Lower-middle-income													
46	Azerbaijan	..	0	..	0	..	0	..	0	..	0	..	0
47	Indonesia	2,551	5,935	695	3,573	940	5,256	693	3,440	824	2,883	358	879
48	Senegal	327	147	0	1	152	48	4	2	67	20	0	2
49	Bolivia	441	307	16	0	126	301	19	27	164	112	9	8
50	Cameroon	562	390	50	65	82	149	32	72	104	129	15	15
51	Macedonia, FYR	..	1	..	0	..	5	..	0	..	3	..	0
52	Kyrgyz Republic	..	99	..	0	..	0	..	0	..	0	..	0
53	Philippines	1,382	3,288	472	668	221	2,582	320	121	375	1,661	204	98
54	Congo	522	459	0	0	34	75	0	0	37	20	0	0
55	Uzbekistan	..	512	..	0	..	27	..	0	..	7	..	0
56	Morocco	1,703	1,439	75	133	565	1,358	25	31	607	1,018	11	2
57	Moldova	..	95	..	0	..	1	..	0	..	0	..	0
58	Guatemala	138	84	32	62	15	138	62	20	30	86	30	7
59	Papua New Guinea	120	103	15	116	32	185	40	497	30	81	22	59
60	Bulgaria	364	3	0	0	25	42	0	0	20	197	0	0
61	Romania	2,797	932	0	104	824	128	0	20	332	75	0	12
62	Jordan	369	189	0	0	102	309	0	0	79	208	0	0
63	Ecuador	968	497	315	166	272	463	263	25	288	299	78	2
64	Dominican Republic	415	112	67	0	62	160	74	16	92	114	29	5
65	El Salvador	110	467	0	0	17	167	18	4	25	117	11	0
66	Lithuania	..	157	..	0	..	0	..	0	..	1	..	0
67	Colombia	1,016	1,547	55	150	250	1,890	13	193	279	871	31	63
68	Jamaica	328	199	25	6	91	208	10	6	114	169	7	2
69	Peru	1,248	1,492	60	59	959	960	60	47	547	751	124	16
70	Paraguay	158	87	48	12	44	191	36	6	35	79	9	1
71	Kazakhstan	..	290	..	0	..	0	..	0	..	8	..	0
72	Tunisia	558	1,088	53	30	216	807	43	35	212	412	16	7

Note: For data comparability and coverage, see the technical notes. Figures in italics are for years other than those specified.

		Disbursements (million $)				Repayment of principal (million $)				Interest payments (million $)			
		Long-term public and publicly guaranteed		Private nonguaranteed		Long-term public and publicly guaranteed		Private nonguaranteed		Long-term public and publicly guaranteed		Private nonguaranteed	
		1980	1993	1980	1993	1980	1993	1980	1993	1980	1993	1980	1993
73	Algeria	3,398	6,555	0	0	2,529	7,034	0	0	1,440	1,706	0	0
74	Namibia	..	..	..	..	..	..	..	..	..	..	..	..
75	Slovak Republic	..	701	..	0	..	424	..	0	..	127	..	0
76	Latvia	..	101	..	0	..	4	..	0	..	4	..	0
77	Thailand	1,315	1,832	1,288	4,607	172	1,445	610	4,858	269	721	204	1,100
78	Costa Rica	435	197	102	2	76	292	88	56	130	159	41	26
79	Ukraine	..	611	..	34	..	108	..	33	..	53	..	2
80	Poland	5,058	497	0	185	2,054	492	0	46	704	823	0	37
81	Russian Federation	..	4,936	..	0	..	1,558	..	0	..	642	..	0
82	Panama	404	25	0	0	215	136	0	0	252	82	0	0
83	Czech Republic	..	2,224	..	99	..	837	..	4	..	243	..	1
84	Botswana	28	104	0	0	6	55	0	0	8	33	0	0
85	Turkey	2,400	6,920	75	3,239	566	3,950	29	662	487	2,959	20	179
86	*Iran, Islamic Rep.*	264	1,577	0	300	527	390	0	0	431	172	0	53
Upper-middle-income													
87	Venezuela	2,870	1,877	1,891	260	1,737	779	1,235	736	1,218	1,521	257	239
88	Belarus	..	330	..	0	..	2	..	0	..	11	..	0
89	Brazil	8,335	3,265	3,192	8,930	3,861	3,006	2,970	3,206	4,200	1,973	2,132	1,047
90	South Africa	..	..	..	..	..	..	..	..	..	..	..	..
91	Mauritius	93	58	4	28	15	64	4	14	20	41	3	4
92	Estonia	..	64	..	0	..	10	..	3	..	4	..	1
93	Malaysia	1,015	2,465	441	110	127	2,500	218	440	250	831	88	173
94	Chile	857	293	2,694	1,889	891	881	571	592	483	693	435	280
95	Hungary	1,552	5,036	0	821	824	2,584	0	285	636	1,311	0	32
96	Mexico	9,131	7,874	2,450	7,910	4,010	5,653	750	7,075	3,880	4,708	700	827
97	Trinidad and Tobago	363	277	0	0	176	319	0	36	50	100	0	9
98	Uruguay	293	530	63	27	93	310	37	0	105	311	17	25
99	Oman	98	371	0	0	179	425	0	0	44	158	0	0
100	Gabon	171	92	0	0	279	29	0	0	119	32	0	0
101	Slovenia	..	137	..	187	..	104	..	153	..	83	..	46
102	Puerto Rico	..	..	..	..	..	..	..	..	..	..	..	..
103	Argentina	2,839	8,018	1,869	3,355	1,146	3,150	707	50	841	3,371	496	217
104	Greece	..	..	..	..	..	..	..	..	..	..	..	..
105	Korea, Rep.	3,429	4,354	551	3,898	1,490	4,620	64	1,650	1,293	1,594	343	521
106	Portugal	1,950	6,955	149	200	538	3,174	126	125	486	1,625	43	39
107	*Saudi Arabia*	..	..	..	..	..	..	..	..	..	..	..	..
108	*Turkmenistan*	..	9	..	0	..	0	..	0	..	0	..	0
Low- and middle-income													
Sub-Saharan Africa													
East Asia & Pacific													
South Asia													
Europe and Central Asia													
Middle East & N. Africa													
Latin America & Caribbean													
Severely indebted													
High-income economies													
109	New Zealand												
110	Ireland												
111	Spain												
112	† Israel												
113	Australia												
114	† Hong Kong												
115	United Kingdom												
116	Finland												
117	† Kuwait												
118	Italy												
119	† Singapore												
120	Canada												
121	Netherlands												
122	† United Arab Emirates												
123	Belgium												
124	France												
125	Austria												
126	Germany												
127	Sweden												
128	United States												
129	Norway												
130	Denmark												
131	Japan												
132	Switzerland												
World													

a. Includes Eritrea.

Table 22. Aggregate net resource flows and net transfers

		Total net flows long-term debt (million $)		Official grants (million $)		Net FDI in the reporting economy (million $)		Portfolio equity flows (million $)		Aggregate net resource flows (million $)		Aggregate net transfers (million $)	
		1980	1993	1980	1993	1980	1993	1980	1993	1980	1993	1980	1993
Low-income economies													
Excluding China & India													
1	Mozambique	..	134	76	700	0	30	..	0	..	864	76	823
2	Tanzania	365	156	485	749	0	20	0	0	850	924	785	823
3	Ethiopia[a]	93	343	125	700	0	6	0	0	218	1,049	201	1,021
4	Sierra Leone	54	62	24	100	−19	35	0	0	59	197	46	193
5	Viet Nam	8	−184	131	177	0	300[b]	0	65	139	82	138	6
6	Burundi	35	59	39	142	0	1	0	0	74	201	72	187
7	Uganda	61	104	62	300	0	3	0	0	123	407	119	345
8	Nepal	48	149	79	150	0	6	0	0	127	305	125	278
9	Malawi	120	150	49	217	10	0	0	0	178	366	135	339
10	Chad	3	54	22	100	0	6	0	0	25	160	25	153
11	Rwanda	25	37	68	236	16	3	0	0	109	276	98	269
12	Bangladesh	594	344	1,001	720	0	14	0	0	1,595	1,078	1,548	925
13	Madagascar	319	92	30	220	−1	30	0	0	348	342	321	318
14	Guinea-Bissau	66	18	37	53	0	0	0	0	103	71	102	69
15	Kenya	430	164	121	300	79	2	0	0	630	465	316	141
16	Mali	89	49	104	205	2	1	0	0	195	255	192	235
17	Niger	223	49	51	200	49	1	0	0	324	250	248	227
18	Lao PDR	54	54	16	75	0	48	0	0	70	177	69	172
19	Burkina Faso	55	128	88	200	0	0	0	0	142	328	128	313
20	India	1,696	3,894	649	560	79	273	0	1,840	2,423	6,567	1,920	2,472
21	Nigeria	1,510	5	3	100	−740	900	0	0	773	1,005	−1,357	−416
22	Albania	..	63	..	229	..	0	..	0	..	292	..	292
23	Nicaragua	231	52	48	200	0	39	0	0	279	290	217	223
24	Togo	82	9	15	75	42	0	0	0	139	84	119	68
25	Gambia, The	51	7	27	49	0	10	0	0	78	66	76	60
26	Zambia	391	160	71	500	62	55	0	0	524	715	324	573
27	Mongolia	..	48	..	45	..	8	..	0	..	101	..	96
28	Central African Republic	24	53	56	93	5	1	0	0	85	147	85	143
29	Benin	56	60	41	139	4	10	0	0	101	209	96	195
30	Ghana	143	221	23	222	16	25	0	0	181	468	135	385
31	Pakistan	711	1,493	482	250	63	347	0	185	1,256	2,275	1,002	1,523
32	Tajikistan	..	14	..	9	..	0	..	0	..	22	..	22
33	China	1,927	12,797	7	360	0	25,800	0	2,278	1,934	41,235	1,616	38,271
34	Guinea	47	250	25	180	34	25	0	0	106	455	43	392
35	Mauritania	109	106	61	145	27	1	0	0	198	252	162	206
36	Zimbabwe	93	258	127	200	2	28	0	0	221	486	133	256
37	Georgia	..	136	..	28	..	0	..	0	..	164	..	156
38	Honduras	258	211	20	81	6	65	0	0	283	357	123	127
39	Sri Lanka	221	178	161	141	43	195	0	0	425	513	377	342
40	Côte d'Ivoire	1,016	232	27	248	95	30	0	0	1,138	510	360	78
41	Lesotho	10	42	52	74	5	15	0	0	66	131	59	103
42	Armenia	..	129	..	25	..	0	..	0	..	154	..	153
43	Egypt, Arab Rep.	2,515	405	165	1,192	548	493	0	0	3,229	2,090	2,813	917
44	*Myanmar*	202	54	66	40	0	4	0	0	268	98	223	8
45	*Yemen, Rep.*	542	58	368	100	34	0	0	0	944	158	934	138
Middle-income economies													
Lower-middle-income													
46	Azerbaijan	..	0	..	14	..	0	..	0	..	14	..	14
47	Indonesia	1,613	812	109	280	180	2,004	0	1,836	1,902	4,932	−2,514	−1,407
48	Senegal	171	98	78	340	15	0	0	0	263	438	161	378
49	Bolivia	312	−21	48	195	47	150	0	0	407	324	214	178
50	Cameroon	498	234	29	200	130	−81	0	0	656	353	422	210
51	Macedonia, FYR	..	−5	..	0	..	0	..	0	..	−5	..	−7
52	Kyrgyz Republic	..	99	..	25	..	0	..	0	..	124	..	124
53	Philippines	1,313	1,253	59	249	−106	763	0	1,082	1,266	3,347	488	1,219
54	Congo	488	384	20	60	40	0	0	0	548	444	505	419
55	Uzbekistan	..	485	..	5	..	45	..	0	..	535	..	528
56	Morocco	1,188	182	75	179	89	522	0	0	1,353	884	685	−239
57	Moldova	..	94	..	22	..	14	..	0	..	130	..	130
58	Guatemala	93	−13	14	82	111	149	0	0	217	218	114	81
59	Papua New Guinea	64	−463	279	290	76	450	0	0	418	277	163	22
60	Bulgaria	339	−39	0	39	0	55	0	0	339	55	319	−141
61	Romania	1,973	888	0	84	0	94	0	0	1,973	1,066	1,641	975
62	Jordan	267	−120	1,127	155	34	−34	0	0	1,428	2	1,349	−206
63	Ecuador	748	174	7	51	70	115	0	0	825	340	349	−108
64	Dominican Republic	347	−64	14	45	93	183	0	0	454	163	267	−64
65	El Salvador	74	296	31	570	6	16	0	0	111	883	34	740
66	Lithuania	..	157	..	120	..	12	..	0	..	289	..	289
67	Colombia	808	−386	8	78	157	850	0	128	974	670	553	−1,463
68	Jamaica	251	−9	13	237	28	139	0	0	292	368	57	192
69	Peru	289	544	31	250	27	349	0	1,226	347	2,369	−580	1,541
70	Paraguay	127	−98	10	36	32	150	0	0	168	88	70	−17
71	Kazakhstan	..	290	..	10	..	150	..	0	..	450	..	443
72	Tunisia	352	276	26	135	235	239	0	0	612	650	232	−6

Note: For data comparability and coverage, see the technical notes. Figures in italics are for years other than those specified.

		Total net flows long-term debt (million $)		Official grants (million $)		Net FDI in the reporting economy (million $)		Portfolio equity flows (million $)		Aggregate net resource flows (million $)		Aggregate net transfers (million $)	
		1980	1993	1980	1993	1980	1993	1980	1993	1980	1993	1980	1993
73	Algeria	869	−479	77	82	349	15	0	0	1,295	−382	−831	−2,237
74	Namibia	..	..	..	..	..	..	..	..	..	..	..	..
75	Slovak Republic	..	277	..	24	..	0	..	0	..	301	..	174
76	Latvia	..	96	..	50	..	20	..	0	..	166	..	163
77	Thailand	1,822	137	75	200	190	2,400	0	3,117	2,087	5,854	1,576	3,613
78	Costa Rica	373	−149	0	22	53	280	0	0	425	153	234	−98
79	Ukraine	..	504	..	200	..	200	..	0	..	904	..	849
80	Poland	3,005	144	128	0	10	1,715	0	0	3,143	1,859	2,439	801
81	Russian Federation	..	3,378	..	2,800	..	700	..	0	..	6,878	..	6,236
82	Panama	189	−111	6	70	−47	−41	0	0	149	−82	−174	−196
83	Czech Republic	..	1,483	..	10	..	950	..	0	..	2,443	..	2,098
84	Botswana	21	49	51	53	112	55	0	0	184	157	68	−126
85	Turkey	1,880	5,546	185	400	18	636	0	178	2,083	6,761	1,545	3,203
86	*Iran, Islamic Rep.*	−263	1,487	1	57	0	−50	0	0	−262	1,494	−1,091	1,269
Upper-middle-income													
87	Venezuela	1,789	622	0	18	55	372	0	45	1,844	1,056	47	−1,279
88	Belarus	..	328	..	100	..	10	..	0	..	438	..	427
89	Brazil	4,696	5,983	14	60	1,911	802	0	5,500	6,621	12,345	−665	7,186
90	South Africa	..	..	..	..	..	..	..	..	..	..	..	..
91	Mauritius	79	8	13	20	1	8	0	17	93	53	69	-12
92	Estonia	..	51	..	120	..	160	..	0	..	331	..	327
93	Malaysia	1,111	−366	6	60	934	4,351	0	3,700	2,052	7,746	524	3,757
94	Chile	2,089	710	9	75	213	841	0	349	2,312	1,975	1,307	203
95	Hungary	728	2,989	0	71	0	2,349	0	13	728	5,422	92	4,013
96	Mexico	6,821	3,056	14	29	2,156	4,901	0	14,297	8,991	22,283	3,043	14,403
97	Trinidad and Tobago	187	−78	1	10	185	185	0	0	372	118	−157	−232
98	Uruguay	226	247	1	26	290	76	0	0	516	348	395	13
99	Oman	−81	−54	157	10	98	99	0	0	174	55	−156	−561
100	Gabon	−109	63	4	64	32	97	0	0	−73	224	−465	−8
101	Slovenia	..	67	..	0	..	112	..	0	..	179	..	51
102	Puerto Rico	..	..	..	..	..	..	..	..	..	..	..	..
103	Argentina	2,855	8,173	2	45	678	6,305	0	3,604	3,535	18,127	1,593	13,592
104	Greece	..	..	..	..	..	..	..	..	..	..	..	..
105	Korea, Rep.	2,426	1,982	8	7	6	516	0	6,029	2,440	8,534	740	6,166
106	Portugal	1,434	3,856	28	10	157	1,301	0	1,111	1,620	6,278	1,074	4,431
107	*Saudi Arabia*	..	..	..	..	..	..	..	..	..	..	..	..
108	*Turkmenistan*	..	9	..	1	..	0	..	0	..	10	..	10
Low- and middle-income													
Sub-Saharan Africa													
East Asia & Pacific													
South Asia													
Europe and Central Asia													
Middle East & N. Africa													
Latin America & Caribbean													
Severely indebted													
High-income economies													
109	New Zealand												
110	Ireland												
111	Spain												
112	† Israel												
113	Australia												
114	† Hong Kong												
115	United Kingdom												
116	Finland												
117	† Kuwait												
118	Italy												
119	† Singapore												
120	Canada												
121	Netherlands												
122	† United Arab Emirates												
123	Belgium												
124	France												
125	Austria												
126	Germany												
127	Sweden												
128	United States												
129	Norway												
130	Denmark												
131	Japan												
132	Switzerland												
World													

a. Includes Eritrea.   b. Revised recently.

Table 23. Total external debt ratios

| | | Net present value of external debt as % of | | | | Total debt services as % of exports[a] | | Interest payments as % of exports[a] | | Concessional debt as % of total external debt | | Multilateral debt as % of total external debt | |
| | | Exports[a] | | GNP | | | | | | | | | |
		1990	1993	1990	1993	1980	1993	1980	1993	1980	1993	1980	1993
	Low-income economies	**183.9 w**	**170.9 w**	**30.0 w**	**37.1 w**	**10.4 w**	**16.4 w**	**5.2 w**	**7.1 w**	**45.2 w**	**41.9 w**	**16.5 w**	**23.4 w**
	Excluding China & India	**269.1 w**	**270.4 w**	**63.9 w**	**75.6 w**	**12.4 w**	**18.2 w**	**6.6 w**	**7.9 w**	**40.8 w**	**47.6 w**	**14.5 w**	**24.3 w**
1	Mozambique	975.9	1,146.7	288.4	339.4	..	20.6	..	12.0	..	60.2	..	14.8
2	Tanzania	759.9	726.5	175.0	248.7	25.9	20.6	12.7	9.5	59.7	65.4	18.1	31.6
3	Ethiopia[b]	285.0	401.1	..	..	7.3	9.0	4.5	4.4	71.3	78.7	41.2	38.4
4	Sierra Leone	450.1	680.6	122.5	177.3	23.2	11.9	5.7	5.4	32.8	37.7	14.2	18.9
5	Viet Nam	..	568.5	..	161.8	..	13.6	..	3.7	26.4	80.9	22.1	0.4
6	Burundi	388.9	463.5	34.0	49.6	9.5	36.0	4.8	12.9	62.6	90.4	35.7	77.0
7	Uganda	650.0	844.5	37.2	55.7	17.3	143.6	3.7	25.6	36.3	68.8	11.6	56.9
8	Nepal	183.2	128.7	20.0	25.5	3.2	9.0	2.1	3.6	75.7	92.5	62.0	79.2
9	Malawi	180.1	246.9	46.7	42.6	27.7	22.3	16.7	8.4	33.8	85.2	26.7	78.8
10	Chad	83.9	215.6	19.7	31.7	8.3	7.2	0.7	5.0	50.9	77.1	32.6	72.2
11	Rwanda	208.8	362.6	13.6	28.8	4.2	5.0	2.8	2.8	74.4	91.5	47.8	74.9
12	Bangladesh	202.9	188.9	24.9	31.1	23.2	13.5	6.4	4.3	82.4	92.8	30.3	57.6
13	Madagascar	562.3	723.6	102.4	108.7	17.1	14.3	10.9	5.7	39.3	48.8	14.9	31.9
14	Guinea-Bissau	1,785.8	2,850.9	145.5	192.1	..	22.6	..	13.2	64.3	73.8	21.3	47.8
15	Kenya	234.6	228.7	64.8	103.0	21.0	28.0	11.1	11.3	20.8	43.7	18.6	38.0
16	Mali	224.3	266.8	51.6	58.8	5.1	4.5	2.3	1.8	84.7	92.3	23.7	41.9
17	Niger	279.8	379.3	44.6	52.1	21.7	31.0	12.9	8.4	18.0	55.3	16.5	44.0
18	Lao PDR	444.1	207.4	53.5	46.0	..	9.6	..	1.7	93.3	97.9	5.9	22.5
19	Burkina Faso	94.0	120.7	18.4	21.4	5.9	7.0	3.1	3.6	66.9	84.3	42.9	70.6
20	India	195.4	225.0	17.4	29.1	9.3	28.0	4.2	14.8	75.1	46.7	29.5	30.3
21	Nigeria	222.0	..	112.5	110.0	4.2	..	3.3	..	6.1	3.5	6.4	13.3
22	Albania	9.5	143.5	..	0.2	..	0.2	..	0.2	..	10.7	..	3.7
23	Nicaragua	2,429.5	2,397.4	741.6	695.4	22.3	29.1	13.4	15.9	21.8	32.9	19.2	11.1
24	Togo	126.4	251.5	46.7	66.2	9.0	8.5	5.8	4.0	24.2	65.4	11.3	48.3
25	Gambia, The	104.3	91.9	59.6	53.2	6.3	13.5	5.7	3.2	49.9	83.0	29.9	70.3
26	Zambia	430.7	518.5	195.0	160.8	25.3	32.8	8.7	14.8	25.4	42.0	12.2	25.9
27	Mongolia	4.1	71.6	1.0	26.6	..	4.4	..	2.3	..	50.3	..	18.3
28	Central African Republic	167.8	259.9	28.9	41.4	4.9	4.8	1.6	3.1	30.1	77.2	27.4	59.6
29	Benin	118.2	146.9	32.7	40.0	6.3	5.9	4.5	2.8	39.2	80.0	24.5	45.9
30	Ghana	217.6	234.4	35.2	47.6	13.1	22.8	4.4	9.0	58.3	61.1	19.9	52.0
31	Pakistan	173.1	205.1	34.3	39.1	17.9	24.7	7.6	10.6	73.0	51.4	15.4	38.0
32	Tajikistan	..	..	..	1.0	..	..	..	..	..	56.6	..	0.0
33	China	78.8	83.8	13.4	18.0	4.3	11.1	1.5	3.7	0.5	16.1	0.0	12.8
34	Guinea	193.0	211.2	62.3	60.9	19.8	9.5	6.0	4.5	59.4	78.1	11.6	39.2
35	Mauritania	311.4	342.3	158.3	177.9	17.3	27.4	7.9	10.2	60.9	73.0	14.8	34.1
36	Zimbabwe	131.5	172.6	41.4	64.6	3.8	31.1	1.5	10.5	2.3	29.3	0.4	31.4
37	Georgia	..	113.1	..	16.4	..	2.7	..	1.8	..	0.0	..	15.8
38	Honduras	272.4	272.2	104.7	101.2	21.4	31.5	12.4	13.1	23.4	42.6	31.2	50.5
39	Sri Lanka	121.2	104.1	42.3	41.9	12.0	10.1	5.7	3.7	56.2	78.2	11.7	34.8
40	Côte d'Ivoire	390.4	533.3	166.1	224.0	38.7	29.2	18.8	15.1	6.0	15.1	7.0	14.8
41	Lesotho	32.8	42.9	17.6	21.9	1.5	5.1	0.6	1.9	61.6	71.5	56.1	71.0
42	Armenia	..	62.3	..	5.6	..	0.9	..	0.7	..	3.7	..	44.0
43	Egypt, Arab Rep.	235.5	170.8	93.8	70.5	14.7	14.9	9.1	8.3	46.1	37.5	12.6	8.5
44	*Myanmar*	455.1	..	11.5	..	25.4	..	9.4	..	72.7	86.4	18.6	24.7
45	*Yemen, Rep.*	186.9	295.0	71.6	..	..	7.5	..	2.6	72.0	57.0	14.9	18.7
	Middle-income economies	..	**128.7 w**	..	**30.8 w**	..	**18.8 w**	..	**7.1 w**	..	**11.2 w**	..	**12.0 w**
	Lower-middle-income	..	**151.2 w**	..	**36.8 w**	..	**18.3 w**	..	**6.7 w**	..	**18.1 w**	..	**13.5 w**
46	Azerbaijan	..	..	..	0.7	..	..	..	..	..	0.0	..	0.0
47	Indonesia	192.6	194.6	56.9	58.5	13.9	31.8	6.5	11.0	36.4	27.9	8.8	19.9
48	Senegal	154.8	185.9	44.8	46.7	28.7	8.4	10.5	2.9	27.9	56.5	17.8	44.0
49	Bolivia	288.6	389.0	67.8	61.9	35.0	59.4	21.1	16.0	24.7	51.2	16.5	47.2
50	Cameroon	219.0	273.2	47.9	57.7	15.2	20.3	8.1	8.1	33.9	34.7	16.8	21.0
51	Macedonia, FYR	..	..	..	52.5	..	..	..	..	..	4.4	..	26.1
52	Kyrgyz Republic	..	..	..	7.2	..	..	..	..	..	9.9	..	18.0
53	Philippines	204.0	172.9	60.9	59.8	26.6	24.9	18.2	10.5	6.7	29.5	7.5	21.7
54	Congo	253.2	392.8	155.8	215.0	10.6	10.8	6.6	4.3	26.5	33.1	7.7	10.5
55	Uzbekistan	..	..	..	3.1	..	..	..	..	..	6.2	..	0.0
56	Morocco	241.1	231.5	80.4	72.8	32.7	31.7	17.0	13.0	37.6	27.2	7.4	26.2
57	Moldova	..	57.6	..	5.6	..	0.5	..	0.3	..	9.3	..	19.4
58	Guatemala	154.6	109.3	35.2	22.4	7.7	13.2	3.6	4.9	21.6	41.2	30.0	28.3
59	Papua New Guinea	145.8	95.6	73.4	60.0	13.8	30.2	6.6	5.8	12.2	22.9	21.2	26.7
60	Bulgaria	149.3	231.1	55.3	119.4	0.5	5.6	0.2	4.8	..	0.0	..	9.1
61	Romania	19.1	73.9	3.3	16.4	12.6	6.2	4.9	3.6	1.8	5.3	8.3	20.5
62	Jordan	240.3	156.5	204.6	117.1	8.4	14.4	4.3	5.4	41.6	45.0	8.0	13.0
63	Ecuador	356.2	378.2	118.3	98.8	33.9	25.7	15.9	11.3	5.0	9.7	5.4	16.6
64	Dominican Republic	163.6	153.5	53.7	45.1	25.3	12.1	12.0	5.3	20.5	42.2	10.2	19.2
65	El Salvador	123.1	81.1	28.4	21.0	7.5	14.9	4.7	6.2	25.9	47.7	28.3	52.4
66	Lithuania	..	11.9	..	5.5	..	0.2	..	0.2	..	11.5	..	34.3
67	Colombia	177.2	153.5	44.4	32.3	16.0	29.4	11.6	10.1	16.3	4.5	19.5	33.1
68	Jamaica	161.5	150.4	104.4	103.5	19.0	20.1	10.8	8.4	20.9	28.8	15.0	27.2
69	Peru	454.0	384.5	64.0	46.1	44.5	58.7	19.9	23.8	15.1	18.1	5.5	13.5
70	Paraguay	96.9	73.0	36.8	20.4	18.6	14.9	8.5	4.6	31.9	44.2	20.2	43.0
71	Kazakhstan	..	..	..	6.2	..	..	..	..	..	0.0	..	1.6
72	Tunisia	110.0	116.5	55.0	54.3	14.8	20.6	6.9	7.7	39.9	34.0	12.3	35.8

Note: For data comparability and coverage, see the technical notes. Figures in italics are for years other than those specified.

		Net present value of external debt as % of				Total debt services as % of exports[a]		Interest payments as % of exports[a]		Concessional debt as % of total external debt		Multilateral debt as % of total external debt	
		Exports[a]		GNP									
		1990	1993	1990	1993	1980	1993	1980	1993	1980	1993	1980	1993
73	Algeria	184.7	206.2	44.4	51.3	27.4	76.9	10.4	15.0	6.5	4.8	1.5	11.1
74	Namibia	..	..	..	..	..	..	..	..	..	..	..	..
75	Slovak Republic	..	41.6	0.0	28.5	..	8.1	..	2.5	..	0.6	..	10.9
76	Latvia	..	..	..	4.3	..	..	..	..	..	34.3	..	28.9
77	Thailand	81.3	91.7	30.1	36.5	18.9	18.7	9.5	5.8	10.9	13.0	12.0	6.6
78	Costa Rica	156.3	114.9	59.9	48.1	29.1	18.1	14.6	6.8	9.5	24.5	16.4	31.5
79	Ukraine	..	21.6	..	3.1	..	1.3	..	0.4	..	0.5	..	3.9
80	Poland	245.7	228.9	81.9	49.7	17.9	9.2	5.2	5.5	9.1	17.4	0.0	3.2
81	Russian Federation	..	162.1	..	25.4	..	4.6	..	1.5	..	4.5	..	1.5
82	Panama	117.9	86.5	136.9	101.6	6.3	3.1	3.3	1.2	9.0	6.6	11.0	9.2
83	Czech Republic	..	46.4	0.0	26.7	..	7.0	..	2.4	0.0	0.7	0.0	8.9
84	Botswana	19.0	..	14.3	13.6	2.1	..	1.2	..	42.3	42.5	57.5	71.8
85	Turkey	178.2	216.4	30.2	38.2	28.0	28.3	14.9	13.1	23.0	10.3	11.2	13.7
86	*Iran, Islamic Rep.*	44.6	106.0	7.5	..	6.8	6.7	3.1	4.7	7.4	0.2	13.8	1.1
	Upper-middle-income	96.8 w	110.3 w	24.9 w	26.3 w	32.1 w	19.4 w	17.4 w	7.4 w	3.4 w	3.0 w	4.7 w	10.2 w
87	Venezuela	137.8	210.8	62.7	62.6	27.2	22.8	13.8	12.5	0.4	0.9	0.7	7.7
88	Belarus	..	35.1	..	2.6	..	0.7	..	0.6	..	48.9	..	11.2
89	Brazil	304.9	296.0	23.7	26.3	63.1	24.4	33.7	9.2	2.5	1.9	4.4	7.1
90	South Africa	..	..	..	..	..	..	..	..	..	..	..	..
91	Mauritius	44.1	43.7	30.9	26.5	9.1	6.4	5.9	2.5	15.6	38.4	16.6	26.3
92	Estonia	..	12.2	..	2.6	..	1.6	..	0.5	..	23.5	..	29.3
93	Malaysia	43.6	42.6	36.7	37.0	6.3	7.9	4.0	2.4	10.1	12.3	11.3	7.0
94	Chile	172.9	159.7	64.1	44.7	43.1	23.4	19.0	9.4	6.2	1.5	2.9	21.0
95	Hungary	169.1	216.2	65.8	66.9	..	38.8	..	13.3	5.6	0.8	0.0	13.0
96	Mexico	175.4	175.6	40.0	32.8	48.1	31.5	26.6	10.5	0.9	1.2	5.6	13.6
97	Trinidad and Tobago	88.0	..	44.3	47.6	6.8	..	1.6	..	4.7	2.4	8.6	14.0
98	Uruguay	180.1	243.7	54.2	54.3	18.8	27.7	10.6	16.5	5.2	2.3	11.0	15.0
99	Oman	43.6	43.5	27.6	33.3	6.4	10.4	1.8	3.1	43.6	18.4	5.8	6.1
100	Gabon	131.9	148.8	74.7	77.7	17.7	6.0	6.3	3.3	8.3	10.6	2.7	10.5
101	Slovenia	..	..	..	15.7	..	..	..	..	..	1.1	..	24.1
102	Puerto Rico	..	..	..	..	..	..	..	..	..	..	..	..
103	Argentina	369.7	417.3	45.6	28.6	37.3	46.0	20.8	25.3	1.8	0.7	4.0	9.6
104	Greece	..	..	..	..	..	..	..	..	..	..	..	..
105	Korea, Rep.	41.2	46.2	12.7	13.9	19.7	9.2	12.7	2.9	9.7	10.0	8.0	6.8
106	Portugal	83.4	124.2	34.0	41.5	18.3	19.3	10.5	7.8	4.4	3.0	5.5	9.9
107	*Saudi Arabia*	..	..	..	..	..	..	..	..	..	..	..	..
108	*Turkmenistan*	..	..	..	..	..	..	..	..	..	..	..	..
	Low- and middle-income	..	136.2 w	..	32.1 w	..	18.3 w	..	7.1 w	..	20.1 w	..	15.3 w
	Sub-Saharan Africa	162.2 w	151.4 w	50.0 w	47.4 w	11.6 w	17.1 w	6.1 w	7.1 w	27.0 w	36.4 w	13.0 w	24.5 w
	East Asia & Pacific	84.0 w	91.0 w	23.1 w	28.5 w	13.4 w	14.4 w	7.6 w	4.8 w	16.6 w	25.0 w	8.6 w	13.1 w
	South Asia	185.0 w	206.2 w	20.3 w	31.1 w	11.9 w	24.4 w	5.1 w	12.1 w	74.4 w	54.3 w	25.1 w	35.4 w
	Europe and Central Asia	..	128.1 w	..	26.5 w	..	12.4 w	..	5.2 w	..	6.9 w	..	8.2 w
	Middle East & N. Africa	78.0 w	97.1 w	26.7 w	57.7 w	16.5 w	23.1 w	7.4 w	7.9 w	30.9 w	30.9 w	8.3 w	12.1 w
	Latin America & Caribbean	221.5 w	227.6 w	38.8 w	34.0 w	36.9 w	28.1 w	19.5 w	11.3 w	4.4 w	5.7 w	5.8 w	13.2 w
	Severely indebted	270.5 w	283.3 w	39.0 w	35.6 w	31.0 w	23.4 w	15.6 w	10.6 w	9.1 w	12.7 w	5.3 w	9.8 w
	High-income economies												
109	New Zealand												
110	Ireland												
111	Spain												
112	† Israel												
113	Australia												
114	† Hong Kong												
115	United Kingdom												
116	Finland												
117	† Kuwait												
118	Italy												
119	† Singapore												
120	Canada												
121	Netherlands												
122	† United Arab Emirates												
123	Belgium												
124	France												
125	Austria												
126	Germany												
127	Sweden												
128	United States												
129	Norway												
130	Denmark												
131	Japan												
132	Switzerland												
	World												

a. Refers to exports of goods and services.   b. Includes Eritrea.

Table 24. Terms of external public borrowing

		Commitments (million $)		Average interest rate (%)		Average maturity (years)		Average grace period (years)		Public loans with variable int. rates as % of public debt	
		1980	1993	1980	1993	1980	1993	1980	1993	1980	1993
	Low-income economies	29,273 t	40,705 t	6.2 w	4.5 w	23 w	20 w	6 w	6 w	16.5 w	17.1 w
	Excluding China & India	20,289 t	13,058 t	5.6 w	2.6 w	22 w	28 w	6 w	7 w	17.0 w	13.1 w
1	Mozambique	479	174	5.2	0.8	14	40	4	10	0.0	11.6
2	Tanzania	718	446	4.1	1.3	24	38	8	9	3.6	6.9
3	Ethiopia[a]	194	935	3.6	2.0	19	41	4	9	1.5	1.8
4	Sierra Leone	70	137	5.2	0.7	26	39	7	10	0.0	0.6
5	Viet Nam	1,460	522	3.5	1.9	18	32	1	8	1.2	3.0
6	Burundi	102	99	1.3	0.8	42	34	9	10	0.0	0.0
7	Uganda	209	357	4.6	1.7	25	28	6	8	1.3	3.7
8	Nepal	92	50	0.8	1.0	46	40	10	10	0.0	0.0
9	Malawi	130	146	6.0	1.3	24	38	6	9	23.2	1.7
10	Chad	0	79	0.0	0.8	0	42	0	13	0.2	0.0
11	Rwanda	48	48	1.5	0.6	39	35	9	10	0.0	0.0
12	Bangladesh	1,034	707	1.7	1.1	36	35	9	10	0.1	0.3
13	Madagascar	445	112	5.6	0.8	18	41	5	10	8.3	5.7
14	Guinea-Bissau	38	9	2.4	0.8	18	40	4	10	1.6	2.4
15	Kenya	518	92	3.5	0.8	31	39	8	9	27.6	13.2
16	Mali	145	63	2.2	0.9	23	41	5	10	0.0	0.1
17	Niger	341	94	7.4	2.3	18	28	5	7	56.4	12.2
18	Lao PDR	96	84	0.2	0.9	33	39	26	10	0.0	0.0
19	Burkina Faso	115	97	4.3	1.2	21	34	6	8	4.3	0.5
20	India	5,158	5,848	5.6	5.4	33	26	9	13	4.3	19.2
21	Nigeria	1,904	288	10.5	3.7	11	25	4	7	74.4	18.2
22	Albania	..	100	..	1.1	..	35	..	9	..	51.3
23	Nicaragua	434	255	4.0	5.4	25	25	7	6	47.6	27.1
24	Togo	97	0	4.0	0.0	24	0	7	0	12.0	3.3
25	Gambia, The	73	12	3.9	0.7	16	40	5	10	7.8	1.5
26	Zambia	645	235	6.7	1.3	19	41	4	10	12.6	9.7
27	Mongolia	..	174	..	1.1	..	34	..	10	..	8.9
28	Central African Republic	38	25	0.6	0.7	13	50	4	11	1.9	0.0
29	Benin	448	22	8.3	0.1	12	29	4	9	0.4	9.4
30	Ghana	170	269	1.4	0.7	44	40	10	10	0.9	1.9
31	Pakistan	1,115	3,297	4.4	3.5	30	21	7	6	1.5	20.8
32	Tajikistan	..	16	..	0.0	..	38	..	9	..	43.0
33	China	3,826	21,799	10.3	5.5	11	14	3	4	58.8	28.9
34	Guinea	269	76	4.6	2.9	19	31	6	8	0.3	3.5
35	Mauritania	211	197	3.6	1.8	20	30	7	9	2.4	8.4
36	Zimbabwe	171	322	7.1	2.9	15	28	6	8	0.4	25.8
37	Georgia	..	142	..	5.0	..	4	..	3	..	87.9
38	Honduras	495	582	6.8	3.1	24	24	7	5	34.2	20.9
39	Sri Lanka	752	583	3.9	2.2	31	32	8	9	6.9	4.9
40	Côte d'Ivoire	1,685	452	11.4	4.9	10	18	4	8	57.0	60.8
41	Lesotho	59	64	5.9	0.8	24	36	6	8	3.5	5.6
42	Armenia	..	163	..	4.5	..	11	..	4	..	64.4
43	Egypt, Arab Rep.	2,558	934	5.0	3.5	28	20	9	4	4.5	8.0
44	*Myanmar*	605	43	3.5	2.3	29	6	7	1	5.0	0.0
45	*Yemen, Rep.*	553	49	2.7	0.9	27	32	6	9	0.0	1.5
	Middle-income economies	..	92,953 t	..	6.3 w	..	13 w	..	5 w	..	50.6 w
	Lower-middle-income	..	48,213 t	..	6.0 w	..	14 w	..	5 w	..	48.7 w
46	Azerbaijan	..	..	..	..	..	..	..	..	..	..
47	Indonesia	4,277	7,415	8.1	5.2	19	19	6	5	30.7	43.6
48	Senegal	470	76	5.9	1.5	20	31	6	8	12.7	7.4
49	Bolivia	370	70	8.4	1.5	15	37	5	9	31.6	14.6
50	Cameroon	168	269	6.9	5.1	23	18	6	10	22.9	21.3
51	Macedonia, FYR	..	..	..	..	..	..	..	..	..	62.3
52	Kyrgyz Republic	..	222	..	4.5	..	22	..	7	..	86.2
53	Philippines	2,143	2,928	9.9	5.5	17	17	5	6	49.9	31.7
54	Congo	966	593	7.6	5.1	11	8	3	2	6.6	29.0
55	Uzbekistan	..	756	..	4.8	..	7	..	2	..	81.1
56	Morocco	1,686	2,063	8.0	7.0	15	18	5	6	31.0	53.8
57	Moldova	..	182	..	5.1	..	13	..	4	..	84.1
58	Guatemala	247	71	7.9	7.0	15	15	4	4	35.6	18.9
59	Papua New Guinea	184	113	11.2	5.6	18	24	5	6	43.5	58.1
60	Bulgaria	738	178	13.6	6.3	12	17	6	4	96.8	77.4
61	Romania	1,886	673	14.1	5.7	8	12	4	4	59.2	65.0
62	Jordan	768	218	7.3	6.4	16	18	4	5	13.4	28.0
63	Ecuador	1,148	312	10.7	5.7	14	14	4	4	62.5	60.9
64	Dominican Republic	519	86	8.9	4.1	12	25	4	6	47.2	46.8
65	El Salvador	225	522	4.2	6.0	28	21	8	4	27.4	17.7
66	Lithuania	..	159	..	5.1	..	13	..	6	..	43.8
67	Colombia	1,566	1,625	12.9	6.1	15	12	4	4	40.8	53.7
68	Jamaica	220	292	7.6	6.8	14	18	5	4	23.0	25.5
69	Peru	1,614	714	9.4	5.7	12	21	4	5	31.2	47.7
70	Paraguay	99	123	7.0	5.1	24	28	7	7	27.3	9.6
71	Kazakhstan	..	904	..	6.5	..	10	..	3	..	99.9
72	Tunisia	777	1,538	6.7	6.2	18	18	5	5	20.0	26.0

Note: For data comparability and coverage, see the technical notes. Figures in italics are for years other than those specified.

		Commitments (million $)		Average interest rate (%)		Average maturity (years)		Average grace period (years)		Public loans with variable int. rates as % of public debt	
		1980	1993	1980	1993	1980	1993	1980	1993	1980	1993
73	Algeria	3,538	5,813	8.1	5.7	12	9	4	4	25.0	51.0
74	Namibia	..	..	..	..	..	..	..	..	..	..
75	Slovak Republic	..	789	..	6.0	13	9	8	4	..	42.1
76	Latvia	..	119	..	3.6	..	7	..	7	..	89.5
77	Thailand	1,877	3,399	9.5	4.3	17	20	5	5	51.4	55.0
78	Costa Rica	621	269	11.2	6.0	13	12	5	3	57.0	28.8
79	Ukraine	..	720	..	6.6	..	8	..	3	..	98.5
80	Poland	1,715	1,182	9.3	7.3	11	16	4	4	37.8	69.0
81	Russian Federation	..	2,800	..	9.5	..	14	..	2	..	65.9
82	Panama	534	238	11.3	7.9	11	21	5	5	52.7	64.3
83	Czech Republic	8	1,794	8.2	6.9	12	9	4	3	0.0	48.0
84	Botswana	69	41	6.0	2.7	18	26	4	8	0.0	15.8
85	Turkey	2,925	7,580	8.3	6.0	16	10	5	6	26.5	36.1
86	*Iran, Islamic Rep.*	0	226	0.0	6.6	0	14	0	4	37.9	88.2
	Upper-middle-income	34,898 t	44,739 t	11.8 w	6.7 w	11 w	11 w	4 w	5 w	66.1 w	52.8 w
87	Venezuela	2,769	2,317	12.1	6.8	8	11	3	5	81.4	59.5
88	Belarus	..	361	..	6.8	..	13	..	5	..	52.1
89	Brazil	9,638	3,126	12.5	4.7	10	5	4	3	72.2	74.2
90	South Africa	..	..	..	..	..	..	..	..	..	..
91	Mauritius	121	67	10.4	4.5	14	17	4	5	47.0	36.5
92	Estonia	..	54	..	4.3	..	10	..	6	..	67.0
93	Malaysia	1,423	3,217	11.2	5.2	14	11	5	5	50.7	44.0
94	Chile	835	219	13.9	3.7	8	13	4	5	75.6	80.2
95	Hungary[b]	1,225	5,609	9.8	7.6	13	9	3	8	39.8	42.5
96	Mexico	7,632	9,986	11.3	6.6	10	8	4	5	75.9	46.9
97	Trinidad and Tobago	211	370	10.4	8.4	9	15	4	6	31.9	58.7
98	Uruguay	347	382	10.1	5.1	14	12	6	3	35.4	44.2
99	Oman	454	275	7.9	5.5	9	12	3	4	0.0	50.0
100	Gabon	196	394	11.2	7.8	11	20	3	6	39.3	14.7
101	Slovenia	..	379	..	7.3	..	8	..	2	..	76.0
102	Puerto Rico	..	..	..	..	..	..	..	..	..	..
103	Argentina	3,023	7,199	13.8	8.5	9	11	4	6	74.0	41.8
104	Greece	..	..	..	..	..	..	..	..	..	..
105	Korea, Rep.	4,928	4,432	11.3	5.7	15	10	4	5	36.4	43.2
106	Portugal	2,015	6,206	10.9	6.7	10	16	3	5	30.6	21.1
107	*Saudi Arabia*	..	..	..	..	..	..	..	..	..	..
108	*Turkmenistan*	..	10	..	3.0	..	37	..	9	..	0.0
	Low- and middle-income	..	133,657 t	..	5.8 w	..	15 w	..	5 w	..	40.3 w
	Sub-Saharan Africa	13,255 t	6,837 t	7.1 w	2.9 w	17 w	29 w	5 w	8 w	26.2 w	16.5 w
	East Asia & Pacific	20,932 t	44,317 t	9.3 w	5.3 w	16 w	16 w	5 w	5 w	39.8 w	35.5 w
	South Asia	8,181 t	10,514 t	4.7 w	4.3 w	33 w	25 w	8 w	10 w	3.2 w	16.5 w
	Europe and Central Asia	..	31,166 t	..	6.8 w	..	12 w	..	5 w	..	55.2 w
	Middle East & N. Africa	11,594 t	11,793 t	6.4 w	5.8 w	18 w	14 w	5 w	5 w	18.2 w	28.3 w
	Latin America & Caribbean	32,776 t	29,030 t	11.6 w	6.7 w	11 w	11 w	4 w	5 w	68.0 w	54.6 w
	Severely indebted	24,316 t	17,319 t	10.8 w	6.9 w	12 w	12 w	4 w	5 w	58.4 w	54.6 w
	High-income economies										
109	New Zealand										
110	Ireland										
111	Spain										
112	† Israel										
113	Australia										
114	† Hong Kong										
115	United Kingdom										
116	Finland										
117	† Kuwait										
118	Italy										
119	† Singapore										
120	Canada										
121	Netherlands										
122	† United Arab Emirates										
123	Belgium										
124	France										
125	Austria										
126	Germany										
127	Sweden										
128	United States										
129	Norway										
130	Denmark										
131	Japan										
132	Switzerland										
	World										

a. Includes Eritrea.   b. Includes debt in convertible currencies only.

Table 25. Population and labor force

		Population						Age 15-64 (millions)	Labor force			
		Total (millions)			Average annual growth (%)				Total (millions)	Average annual growth (%)		
		1993	2000	2025	1970–80	1980–93	1993–2000	1993	1993	1970–80	1980–93	1993–2000
	Low-income economies	3,092 t	3,518 t	4,987 t	2.1 w	2.0 w	1.8 w	1,738 t	1,434 t	2.3 w	2.1 w	1.6 w
	Excluding China & India	1,015 t	1,241 t	2,123 t	2.5 w	2.5 w	2.9 w	459 t	385 t	2.5 w	2.4 w	2.6 w
1	Mozambique	15	19	35	2.5	1.7	3.3	8	9	3.8	2.0	2.0
2	Tanzania	28	34	63	3.1	3.2	2.8	14	14	2.8	2.8	3.0
3	Ethiopia	52	64	127	2.3	2.7	3.0	24	23	2.0	1.9	2.2
4	Sierra Leone	4	..	..	2.0	2.5	..	2	2	1.0	1.2	..
5	Viet Nam	71	83	118	2.3	2.2	2.1	39	36	2.1	2.8	2.5
6	Burundi	6	7	13	1.6	2.9	2.8	3	3	1.3	2.2	2.5
7	Uganda	18	..	..	2.9	2.4	..	9	9	2.6	2.8	..
8	Nepal	21	25	41	2.6	2.6	2.5	11	8	1.8	2.3	2.2
9	Malawi	11	..	..	3.1	..	..	5	4	2.2	..	..
10	Chad	6	7	13	2.0	2.3	2.8	3	2	1.7	1.9	2.1
11	Rwanda	8	9	16	3.3	2.9	2.6	4	4	3.1	2.8	3.0
12	Bangladesh	115	..	..	2.8	2.1	..	60	37	2.0	2.9	..
13	Madagascar	14	17	34	2.8	3.3	3.1	7	5	2.2	2.1	2.3
14	Guinea-Bissau	1	1	2	4.1	2.0	2.1	1	0	3.8	1.3	1.6
15	Kenya	25	30	46	3.6	3.3	2.5	11	11	3.6	3.5	3.7
16	Mali	10	13	25	2.2	3.0	3.1	5	3	1.7	2.6	2.8
17	Niger	9	11	22	2.9	3.3	3.3	4	4	1.9	2.4	2.7
18	Lao PDR	5	6	10	1.7	2.8	2.8	2	2	1.3	2.0	2.1
19	Burkina Faso	10	12	22	2.3	2.6	2.6	5	4	1.7	2.0	2.3
20	India	898	1,022	1,392	2.2	2.0	1.8	506	341	1.7	1.9	1.7
21	Nigeria	105	129	238	2.7	2.9	2.9	50	46	3.1	2.7	2.9
22	Albania	3	4	5	2.2	1.8	1.0	2	2	3.0	2.6	2.2
23	Nicaragua	4	5	9	3.1	3.0	3.3	2	1	2.9	3.8	3.9
24	Togo	4	5	9	2.6	3.0	3.1	2	2	2.0	2.3	2.5
25	Gambia, The	1	1	2	3.2	3.7	3.1	1	0	1.9	1.4	1.6
26	Zambia	9	11	19	3.1	3.4	2.6	4	3	2.7	3.3	3.5
27	Mongolia	2	3	4	2.8	2.6	2.0	1	1	2.8	2.9	2.8
28	Central African Republic	3	4	6	2.2	2.4	2.4	2	1	1.2	1.5	1.9
29	Benin	5	6	12	2.5	3.0	3.0	3	2	2.0	2.2	2.6
30	Ghana	16	20	38	2.2	3.3	2.9	8	6	2.4	2.7	3.0
31	Pakistan	123	..	..	2.6	2.8	..	65	37	2.7	2.8	..
32	Tajikistan	6	7	12	3.0	2.9	2.7	3	..	..	..	..
33	China	1,178	1,255	1,471	1.8	1.4	0.9	773	707	2.4	2.0	1.0
34	Guinea	6	8	15	1.3	2.7	3.0	3	3	1.8	1.7	1.9
35	Mauritania	2	3	4	2.4	2.6	2.5	1	1	1.8	2.8	3.2
36	Zimbabwe	11	13	20	3.0	3.2	2.2	6	4	2.8	2.8	3.0
37	Georgia	5	6	6	0.7	0.6	0.2	4	..	..	..	..
38	Honduras	5	6	11	3.2	3.1	2.8	3	2	3.1	3.8	3.7
39	Sri Lanka	18	20	25	1.7	1.5	1.2	11	7	2.3	1.5	1.7
40	Côte d'Ivoire	13	17	37	4.0	3.7	3.3	6	5	2.5	2.6	2.5
41	Lesotho	2	2	4	2.3	2.9	2.6	1	1	2.0	2.0	2.2
42	Armenia	4	4	5	2.0	1.5	0.3	2	2	..	1.3	..
43	Egypt, Arab Rep.	56	..	..	2.2	2.0	..	32	16	2.1	2.6	..
44	*Myanmar*	45	52	76	2.2	2.1	2.1	24	19	2.2	1.9	1.7
45	*Yemen, Rep.*	13	..	..	2.6	3.6	..	6	3	1.6	2.6	..
	Middle-income economies	1,597 t	1,761 t	2,322 t	1.9 w	1.7 w	1.4 w	882 t	..	..	..	..
	Lower-middle-income	1,097 t	1,202 t	1,574 t	1.8 w	1.7 w	1.3 w	586 t	..	..	..	..
46	Azerbaijan	7	8	10	1.7	1.4	1.1	4	..	..	..	..
47	Indonesia	187	..	..	2.3	1.7	..	111	76	2.1	2.3	..
48	Senegal	8	9	17	2.9	2.7	2.6	4	3	3.2	1.9	2.1
49	Bolivia	7	8	13	2.4	2.1	2.4	4	2	2.1	2.7	2.6
50	Cameroon	13	15	29	2.7	2.8	2.8	7	5	1.5	2.0	2.3
51	Macedonia, FYR	2	2	3	1.4	1.1	1.1	1	..	..	..	..
52	Kyrgyz Republic	5	5	7	2.0	1.8	1.6	3	..	..	..	..
53	Philippines	65	75	105	2.5	2.3	2.0	35	24	2.4	2.5	2.4
54	Congo	2	3	6	2.8	2.9	2.8	1	1	2.1	2.0	2.4
55	Uzbekistan	22	25	38	2.9	2.4	2.1	11	..	..	..	..
56	Morocco	26	30	41	2.4	2.2	1.9	14	9	3.4	3.2	2.9
57	Moldova	4	5	5	1.1	0.7	0.3	3	..	..	..	..
58	Guatemala	10	12	22	2.8	2.9	2.8	5	3	2.1	3.0	3.3
59	Papua New Guinea	4	5	8	2.4	2.2	2.2	2	2	1.9	1.5	1.0
60	Bulgaria	9	9	8	0.4	0.0	–0.5	6	4	0.1	0.0	0.3
61	Romania	23	23	22	0.9	0.2	–0.1	15	12	0.0	0.7	0.7
62	Jordan	4	5	9	3.7	4.9	3.3	2	1	1.0	4.3	4.0
63	Ecuador	11	13	18	2.9	2.5	2.0	6	4	2.6	3.0	2.8
64	Dominican Republic	8	8	11	2.5	2.2	1.7	4	2	3.1	3.2	2.7
65	El Salvador	6	6	10	2.3	1.5	2.2	3	2	2.9	3.1	3.2
66	Lithuania	4	4	4	0.9	0.6	–0.1	3	2	1.5	0.1	0.6
67	Colombia	36	..	..	2.2	2.3	..	20	11	2.5	2.5	..
68	Jamaica	2	3	3	1.3	0.9	0.8	1	1	2.9	2.6	2.2
69	Peru	23	26	37	2.7	2.1	1.9	13	8	3.3	2.8	2.7
70	Paraguay	5	6	9	2.9	3.1	2.5	3	2	3.5	2.9	2.7
71	Kazakhstan	17	18	22	1.3	1.0	0.6	11	..	..	..	..
72	Tunisia	9	10	13	2.2	2.3	1.6	5	3	3.6	3.0	2.6

Note: For data comparability and coverage, see the technical notes. Figures in italics are for years other than those specified.

		Population						Age 15-64 (millions)	Labor force			
		Total (millions)			Average annual growth (%)				Total (millions)	Average annual growth		
		1993	2000	2025	1970–80	1980–93	1993–2000	1993	1993	1970–80	1980–93	1993–2000
73	Algeria	27	31	45	3.1	2.7	2.2	14	7	3.2	3.6	3.6
74	Namibia	1	2	3	2.6	2.7	2.6	1	1	1.8	2.4	2.8
75	Slovak Republic	5	5	6	0.9	0.5	0.4	3	2	..	..	..
76	Latvia	3	2	2	0.7	0.2	–0.8	2	..	1.7	..	..
77	Thailand	58	62	74	2.7	1.7	0.9	36	31	2.8	2.1	1.5
78	Costa Rica	3	..	..	2.8	..	..	2	1	3.8	..	..
79	Ukraine	52	51	49	0.5	0.2	–0.2	34	..	..	..	..
80	Poland	38	39	42	0.9	0.6	0.2	25	20	0.7	0.6	0.8
81	Russian Federation	149	147	146	0.6	0.5	–0.3	99	..	..	..	..
82	Panama	3	3	4	2.6	2.0	1.7	2	1	2.4	2.8	2.3
83	Czech Republic	10	10	11	0.5	0.0	0.1	7	5	0.3	–0.2	8.2
84	Botswana	1	2	3	3.5	3.4	2.9	1	0	3.0	3.3	3.4
85	Turkey	60	68	91	2.3	2.3	1.8	34	25	1.7	2.1	1.9
86	*Iran, Islamic Rep.*	64	..	..	3.2	..	..	30	17	3.1	..	..
	Upper-middle-income	**501 t**	**559 t**	**748 t**	**2.2 w**	**1.9 w**	**1.6 w**	**296 t**	**188 t**	**3.2 w**	**2.1 w**	**1.8 w**
87	Venezuela	21	24	35	3.4	2.5	2.1	12	7	4.8	3.2	2.8
88	Belarus	10	10	10	0.6	0.4	–0.2	7	5	..	–0.2	..
89	Brazil	156	175	230	2.4	2.0	1.6	90	59	3.4	2.2	2.1
90	South Africa	40	46	71	2.6	2.4	2.2	23	13	1.3	2.7	2.7
91	Mauritius	1	1	1	1.6	0.9	1.1	1	0	2.5	2.6	1.9
92	Estonia	2	1	1	0.8	0.4	–0.5	1	..	1.7	..	..
93	Malaysia	19	22	32	2.4	2.5	2.3	10	8	3.7	2.8	2.5
94	Chile	14	15	20	1.6	1.7	1.5	9	5	2.4	2.2	1.4
95	Hungary	10	10	9	0.4	–0.4	–0.4	7	5	–0.5	0.2	0.3
96	Mexico	90	102	137	2.8	2.3	1.8	50	33	4.3	3.1	2.7
97	Trinidad and Tobago	1	1	2	1.1	1.3	1.1	1	1	2.2	2.2	2.0
98	Uruguay	3	3	4	0.4	0.6	0.6	2	1	0.2	0.8	1.0
99	Oman	2	3	6	4.2	4.5	4.0	1	0	4.5	3.5	2.9
100	Gabon	1	2	3	4.7	1.7	5.9	1	1	0.8	0.7	1.1
101	Slovenia	2	2	2	0.9	0.4	0.1	1	..	..	..	..
102	Puerto Rico	4	4	5	1.7	0.9	0.8	2	1	2.4	2.0	0.4
103	Argentina	34	37	46	1.6	1.4	1.2	21	12	1.0	1.2	1.6
104	Greece	10	11	10	0.9	0.6	0.3	7	4	0.7	0.4	0.2
105	Korea, Rep.	44	47	54	1.8	1.1	0.9	31	20	2.6	2.3	1.8
106	Portugal	10	10	10	0.8	0.1	0.0	7	5	2.5	0.9	0.8
107	*Saudi Arabia*	17	21	43	5.1	4.4	3.1	10	5	5.5	3.8	3.3
108	*Turkmenistan*	4	5	7	2.7	2.4	2.1	2	..	..	..	..
	Low- and middle-income	**4,689 t**	**5,279 t**	**7,309 t**	**2.1 w**	**1.9 w**	**1.7 w**	**2,650 t**	**..**	**..**	**..**	**..**
	Sub-Saharan Africa	**559 t**	**683 t**	**683 t**	**2.7 w**	**2.9 w**	**2.9 w**	**290 t**	**228 t**	**2.4 w**	**2.5 w**	**2.7 w**
	East Asia & Pacific	**1,714 t**	**1,861 t**	**2,283 t**	**1.9 w**	**1.5 w**	**1.2 w**	**1,093 t**	**942 t**	**2.4 w**	**2.1 w**	**1.3 w**
	South Asia	**1,194 t**	**1,391 t**	**1,988 t**	**2.3 w**	**2.1 w**	**2.2 w**	**669 t**	**437 t**	**1.8 w**	**2.1 w**	**2.0 w**
	Europe and Central Asia	**495 t**	**507 t**	**553 t**	**1.0 w**	**0.8 w**	**0.4 w**	**316 t**	**..**	**..**	**..**	**..**
	Middle East & N. Africa	**262 t**	**313 t**	**507 t**	**2.9 w**	**3.0 w**	**2.5 w**	**148 t**	**71 t**	**3.0 w**	**3.2 w**	**3.3 w**
	Latin America & Caribbean	**465 t**	**523 t**	**709 t**	**2.4 w**	**2.0 w**	**1.6 w**	**274 t**	**169 t**	**3.1 w**	**2.5 w**	**2.3 w**
	Severely indebted	**386 t**	**433 t**	**604 t**	**2.1 w**	**1.9 w**	**1.7 w**	**233 t**	**146 t**	**2.3 w**	**2.0 w**	**2.1 w**
	High-income economies	**812 t**	**844 t**	**908 t**	**0.8 w**	**0.6 w**	**0.5 w**	**544 t**	**385 t**	**1.3 w**	**0.7 w**	**0.3 w**
109	New Zealand	3	4	4	1.0	0.9	1.1	2	2	1.7	1.7	0.8
110	Ireland	4	4	4	1.4	0.3	0.3	2	2	1.1	1.6	1.5
111	Spain	39	40	38	1.1	0.4	0.1	27	15	0.8	1.1	0.7
112	† Israel	5	6	8	2.7	2.3	2.1	3	2	2.8	2.2	1.9
113	Australia	18	19	25	1.5	1.5	1.3	11	8	2.3	1.6	1.2
114	† Hong Kong	6	6	6	2.5	1.1	0.4	4	3	4.3	1.9	–0.4
115	United Kingdom	58	59	61	0.1	0.2	0.3	38	28	0.5	0.3	0.1
116	Finland	5	5	5	0.4	0.4	0.4	3	3	0.8	0.6	0.2
117	† Kuwait	2	2	3	6.1	1.9	0.4	1	1	7.1	4.7	3.0
118	Italy	57	57	52	0.5	0.1	0.0	39	23	0.5	0.5	–0.1
119	† Singapore	3	3	3	1.5	1.1	0.9	2	1	4.3	1.3	0.5
120	Canada	29	31	38	1.4	1.2	1.1	19	14	3.1	1.1	0.8
121	Netherlands	15	16	16	0.8	0.6	0.6	10	6	1.5	1.0	0.2
122	† United Arab Emirates	2	2	3	15.2	4.4	2.2	1	1	17.2	3.5	1.7
123	Belgium	10	10	10	0.2	0.2	0.3	7	4	0.9	0.4	0.0
124	France	57	59	61	0.6	0.5	0.4	38	26	0.9	0.7	0.4
125	Austria	8	8	8	0.1	0.3	0.5	5	4	0.8	0.5	0.0
126	Germany	81	82	76	0.1	0.2	0.2	55	42	0.6	–0.8	–1.8
127	Sweden	9	9	10	0.3	0.3	0.5	6	4	1.1	0.4	0.2
128	United States	258	275	331	1.1	1.0	0.9	165	125	2.3	1.0	0.8
129	Norway	4	4	5	0.5	0.4	0.4	3	2	2.0	0.8	0.5
130	Denmark	5	5	5	0.4	0.1	0.1	4	3	1.3	0.5	0.0
131	Japan	124	126	122	1.1	0.5	0.2	86	63	0.7	0.8	0.2
132	Switzerland	7	7	8	0.2	0.6	0.9	5	3	0.3	0.3	–0.2
	World	**5,501 t**	**6,123 t**	**8,217 t**	**1.8 w**	**1.7 w**	**1.5 w**	**3,178 t**	**..**	**..**	**..**	**..**

Table 26. Demography and fertility

		Crude birth rate (per 1,000 population)		Crude death rate (per 1,000 population)		Total fertility rate			Percentage of births in 1993 to women aged		Married women of childbearing age using contraception[a] (%)
		1970	1993	1970	1993	1970	1993	2000	under 20	over 35	1988–93
	Low-income economies	39 w	28 w	14 w	10 w	5.9 w	3.6 w	3.3 w			
	Excluding China & India	45 w	40 w	19 w	13 w	6.5 w	5.5 w	4.9 w			
1	Mozambique	46	45	22	18	6.5	6.4	5.8	15	20	. .
2	Tanzania	50	43	19	14	6.8	5.8	5.2	17	14	10
3	Ethiopia	50	48	24	18	6.8	6.9	6.2	17	13	4
4	Sierra Leone	49	49	30	25	6.5	6.4	. .	22	13	. .
5	Viet Nam	38	30	15	8	5.9	3.8	3.3	3	16	53
6	Burundi	44	45	20	15	6.8	6.7	6.0	7	24	. .
7	Uganda	50	51	19	19	6.9	7.2	. .	22	14	5
8	Nepal	45	39	22	13	6.1	5.3	4.7	14	14	. .
9	Malawi	56	50	24	20	7.3	7.1	. .	18	17	13
10	Chad	45	43	26	18	6.0	5.8	5.3	22	13	. .
11	Rwanda	53	44	21	17	8.2	6.4	5.7	8	17	21
12	Bangladesh	48	35	21	11	7.0	4.3	. .	20	9	40
13	Madagascar	48	43	20	11	6.6	6.0	5.4	18	15	17
14	Guinea-Bissau	41	42	27	21	5.3	5.7	5.2	22	14	. .
15	Kenya	53	36	18	9	8.1	5.2	4.0	18	12	33
16	Mali	51	50	26	19	7.1	7.0	6.3	20	15	25
17	Niger	59	52	26	19	8.0	7.3	6.8	22	14	4
18	Lao PDR	44	44	23	15	6.1	6.6	5.6	6	24	. .
19	Burkina Faso	48	46	25	18	6.4	6.4	5.8	18	14	8
20	India	39	29	16	10	5.5	3.7	3.2	11	10	43
21	Nigeria	46	45	21	15	6.4	6.4	5.7	17	17	6
22	Albania	33	23	7	6	4.8	2.8	2.5	3	10	. .
23	Nicaragua	48	40	14	7	6.9	4.9	4.2	21	10	44
24	Togo	46	44	20	13	6.6	6.5	5.8	15	20	33
25	Gambia, The	49	43	28	19	6.5	5.5	5.0	19	14	. .
26	Zambia	49	44	19	15	6.8	5.9	5.2	18	13	15
27	Mongolia	42	27	14	7	5.8	3.5	3.1	7	13	. .
28	Central African Republic	43	41	22	17	5.7	5.6	5.1	20	17	. .
29	Benin	49	48	27	18	7.0	7.0	6.3	16	16	. .
30	Ghana	46	41	16	11	6.7	5.9	5.3	16	18	13
31	Pakistan	48	40	19	9	7.0	6.1	. .	7	21	14
32	Tajikistan	40	36	10	6	6.8	4.8	4.3	5	13	. .
33	China	33	19	8	8	5.8	2.0	1.9	4	4	83
34	Guinea	52	50	27	20	7.0	6.9	6.2	24	12	. .
35	Mauritania	45	40	22	14	6.5	5.3	4.8	18	15	. .
36	Zimbabwe	49	38	16	12	7.3	4.9	4.2	14	13	43
37	Georgia	19	16	10	9	2.6	2.1	2.1	12	7	. .
38	Honduras	48	36	14	6	7.2	4.8	4.0	18	13	47
39	Sri Lanka	30	20	8	6	4.3	2.4	2.2	8	14	. .
40	Côte d'Ivoire	51	49	20	15	7.4	7.3	6.6	23	13	. .
41	Lesotho	43	37	20	10	5.7	5.1	4.6	12	17	23
42	Armenia	23	20	6	6	3.2	2.6	2.3	12	5	. .
43	Egypt, Arab Rep.	40	29	17	8	5.9	3.8	. .	12	13	47
44	*Myanmar*	40	32	17	11	5.9	4.1	3.6	5	16	. .
45	*Yemen, Rep.*	49	49	23	15	7.6	7.5	. .	11	23	10
	Middle-income economies	31 w	23 w	12 w	8 w	4.5 w	3.0 w	2.7 w			
	Lower-middle-income	31 w	23 w	12 w	9 w	4.4 w	3.0 w	2.7 w			
46	Azerbaijan	29	22	7	6	4.6	2.5	2.2	4	7	. .
47	Indonesia	40	24	18	8	5.3	2.8	. .	14	12	50
48	Senegal	49	43	25	16	7.0	6.0	5.4	19	16	7
49	Bolivia	45	35	20	10	6.5	4.7	4.1	12	16	30
50	Cameroon	45	40	20	12	6.2	5.6	5.1	18	15	16
51	Macedonia, FYR	25	15	8	7	3.1	2.0	2.0	10	6	. .
52	Kyrgyz Republic	31	28	11	7	4.8	3.6	3.1	6	11	. .
53	Philippines	39	30	10	6	5.7	3.9	3.3	5	16	40
54	Congo	46	44	20	15	6.3	6.2	5.6	17	16	. .
55	Uzbekistan	36	31	10	6	6.1	3.8	3.3	6	9	. .
56	Morocco	47	28	16	8	7.0	3.6	2.8	7	18	42
57	Moldova	19	16	10	11	2.6	2.1	2.1	10	9	. .
58	Guatemala	45	38	14	8	6.5	5.3	4.6	17	13	. .
59	Papua New Guinea	42	33	18	11	6.1	5.0	4.4	4	27	. .
60	Bulgaria	16	10	9	13	2.2	1.5	1.5	21	3	. .
61	Romania	20	11	9	11	2.8	1.5	1.5	15	7	. .
62	Jordan	. .	37	. .	5	. .	5.1	4.3	7	14	40
63	Ecuador	41	28	11	6	6.2	3.4	2.9	15	14	58
64	Dominican Republic	41	26	11	6	6.1	3.0	2.7	18	9	56
65	El Salvador	44	33	12	7	6.3	3.9	3.4	24	9	53
66	Lithuania	17	13	9	11	2.3	1.8	1.9	8	7	. .
67	Colombia	36	24	9	6	5.3	2.6	. .	15	11	66
68	Jamaica	34	21	8	6	5.3	2.3	2.1	20	9	55
69	Peru	42	27	14	7	6.2	3.3	3.0	12	15	55
70	Paraguay	38	32	7	5	5.9	4.2	3.7	14	16	48
71	Kazakhstan	26	20	9	7	3.5	2.5	2.3	8	9	. .
72	Tunisia	39	25	14	6	6.4	3.1	2.6	5	13	50

Note: For data comparability, see the technical notes. Figures in italics are for years other than those specified.

		Crude birth rate (per 1,000 population)		Crude death rate (per 1,000 population)		Total fertility rate			Percentage of births in 1993 to women aged		Married women of childbearing age using contraception[a] (%)
		1970	1993	1970	1993	1970	1993	2000	under 20	over 35	1988–93
73	Algeria	49	29	16	6	7.4	3.8	3.1	6	15	..
74	Namibia	43	37	18	10	6.0	5.2	4.7	15	20	23
75	Slovak Republic	19	14	10	11	2.5	1.9	1.9	13	5	..
76	Latvia	14	11	11	13	1.9	1.6	1.6	10	8	..
77	Thailand	38	19	10	6	5.5	2.1	2.1	14	11	..
78	Costa Rica	34	26	6	4	4.9	3.1	..	17	11	..
79	Ukraine	15	11	9	13	2.0	1.6	1.6	13	6	..
80	Poland	17	13	8	11	2.3	1.9	1.9	8	9	..
81	Russian Federation	15	11	9	13	2.0	1.4	1.7	12	8	..
82	Panama	37	25	8	5	5.2	2.8	2.5	19	9	..
83	Czech Republic	16	13	13	13	2.1	1.8	1.8	14	4	69
84	Botswana	50	37	15	6	6.7	4.8	4.2	15	15	33
85	Turkey	36	27	12	7	5.3	3.3	2.8	8	10	63
86	*Iran, Islamic Rep.*	45	35	16	7	6.7	4.9	..	13	15	..
	Upper-middle-income	**33 w**	**24 w**	**10 w**	**7 w**	**4.7 w**	**3.0 w**	**2.7 w**			
87	Venezuela	37	27	7	5	5.3	3.2	2.8	19	11	..
88	Belarus	16	12	9	12	2.3	1.6	1.6	8	7	..
89	Brazil	35	24	10	7	4.9	2.8	2.5	16	12	..
90	South Africa	39	31	14	9	5.7	4.0	3.6	12	16	..
91	Mauritius	29	21	7	7	3.6	2.3	2.2	11	10	75
92	Estonia	15	11	11	13	2.1	1.6	1.6	11	8	..
93	Malaysia	36	28	9	5	5.5	3.5	3.0	5	14	56
94	Chile	29	22	10	6	4.0	2.5	2.4	11	9	..
95	Hungary	15	12	11	15	2.0	1.7	1.7	14	5	..
96	Mexico	43	27	10	5	6.5	3.1	2.6	15	10	..
97	Trinidad and Tobago	28	21	8	6	3.6	2.4	2.2	14	8	..
98	Uruguay	21	17	10	10	2.9	2.3	2.2	15	12	..
99	Oman	50	43	21	5	7.2	7.1	6.4	14	14	9
100	Gabon	31	38	21	15	4.2	5.4	5.5	18	17	..
101	Slovenia	17	11	10	11	2.2	1.4	1.4	11	6	..
102	Puerto Rico	25	18	7	7	3.2	2.2	2.1	17	7	..
103	Argentina	23	20	9	8	3.1	2.7	2.5	14	12	..
104	Greece	17	10	8	10	2.3	1.4	1.4	8	8	..
105	Korea, Rep.	30	16	10	6	4.3	1.7	1.8	2	2	77
106	Portugal	20	12	11	11	2.8	1.6	1.6	8	9	..
107	*Saudi Arabia*	48	35	18	5	7.3	6.3	5.7	17	25	..
108	*Turkmenistan*	37	31	11	7	6.3	3.9	3.4	3	13	
	Low- and middle-income	**36 w**	**27 w**	**13 w**	**9 w**	**5.4 w**	**3.4 w**	**3.1 w**			
	Sub-Saharan Africa	**48 w**	**44 w**	**21 w**	**15 w**	**6.6 w**	**6.2 w**	**5.6 w**			
	East Asia & Pacific	**35 w**	**21 w**	**10 w**	**8 w**	**5.7 w**	**2.3 w**	**2.2 w**			
	South Asia	**41 w**	**31 w**	**17 w**	**10 w**	**5.8 w**	**4.0 w**	**3.6 w**			
	Europe and Central Asia	**20 w**	**16 w**	**9 w**	**11 w**	**2.7 w**	**2.1 w**	**2.0 w**			
	Middle East & N. Africa	**45 w**	**33 w**	**16 w**	**7 w**	**6.7 w**	**4.7 w**	**4.1 w**			
	Latin America & Caribbean	**36 w**	**26 w**	**10 w**	**7 w**	**5.2 w**	**3.1 w**	**2.7 w**			
	Severely indebted	**33 w**	**26 w**	**11 w**	**8 w**	**4.7 w**	**3.3 w**	**3.0 w**			
	High-income economies	**17 w**	**13 w**	**10 w**	**9 w**	**2.3 w**	**1.7 w**	**1.8 w**			
109	New Zealand	22	17	9	8	3.0	2.2	2.1	8	9	..
110	Ireland	22	15	11	9	3.8	2.1	2.1	5	17	60
111	Spain	20	10	8	9	2.9	1.2	1.2	5	11	..
112	† Israel	27	21	7	7	3.8	2.8	2.5	4	15	..
113	Australia	20	15	9	7	2.7	1.9	1.9	5	10	..
114	† Hong Kong	21	11	5	6	3.3	1.2	1.2	2	13	..
115	United Kingdom	16	13	12	11	2.2	1.8	1.8	8	9	..
116	Finland	14	13	10	10	1.8	1.9	2.0	3	14	..
117	† Kuwait	47	24	6	2	7.1	3.1	2.8	8	13	..
118	Italy	17	10	10	10	2.4	1.3	1.3	3	11	..
119	† Singapore	23	16	5	6	3.0	1.7	1.7	2	13	..
120	Canada	17	15	7	8	2.2	1.9	2.0	6	9	..
121	Netherlands	17	13	8	9	2.3	1.6	1.6	2	12	76
122	† United Arab Emirates	35	23	11	3	6.5	4.2	3.7	12	18	..
123	Belgium	14	12	12	11	2.1	1.7	1.8	3	8	..
124	France	17	13	11	10	2.4	1.7	1.7	2	12	80
125	Austria	15	12	13	11	2.2	1.5	1.6	6	8	..
126	Germany	13	10	12	11	1.9	1.3	1.3	4	10	..
127	Sweden	14	14	10	11	2.0	2.1	2.1	3	11	74
128	United States	17	16	9	9	2.2	2.1	2.1	13	10	74
129	Norway	17	14	10	11	2.4	1.9	2.0	4	8	84
130	Denmark	15	12	10	12	2.1	1.7	1.7	3	8	..
131	Japan	19	10	7	8	2.0	1.5	1.5	1	8	56
132	Switzerland	16	13	9	9	2.0	1.6	1.7	1	12	..
	World	**32 w**	**25 w**	**12 w**	**9 w**	**4.8 w**	**3.2 w**	**2.9 w**			

a. Data include women whose husbands practice contraception; see the technical notes.

Table 27. Health and nutrition

		Population per				Low birthweight babies (%)	Infant mortality rate (per 1,000 live births)		Prevalence of malnutrition (under 5)	Under-5 mortality rate (per 1,000 live births)
		Physician		Nursing person						
		1970	1993	1970	1993	1991	1970	1993	1988–93	1993
	Low-income economies	**7,760 w**	..	**5,630 w**	..		**108 w**	**64 w**		**103 w**
	Excluding China & India	**20,640 w**	..	**12,780 w**	..		**135 w**	**89 w**		**144 w**
1	Mozambique	18,870	..	*4,280*	..	..	171	146	..	282
2	Tanzania	22,900	..	*3,400*	..	..	129	84	28	167
3	Ethiopia	85,690	..	..	..	..	159	117	47	204
4	Sierra Leone	17,830	..	2,700	..	13	197	164	..	284
5	Viet Nam	..	2,300	*4,310*	*400*	..	111	41	42	48
6	Burundi	58,570	*17,240*	6,910	*4,800*	..	138	101	..	178
7	Uganda	9,210	..	..	..	..	117	114	23	185
8	Nepal	52,050	*16,110*	*17,970*	*2,300*	26	157	96	50	128
9	Malawi	76,580	*50,360*	5,330	*1,980*	11	193	142	27	223
10	Chad	61,900	*29,410*	8,020	..	..	171	120	..	206
11	Rwanda	60,130	..	5,630	..	16	142	..	29	..
12	Bangladesh	8,450	*5,220*	65,810	*11,350*	34	140	106	67	122
13	Madagascar	10,310	..	*250*	..	10	181	93	39	164
14	Guinea-Bissau	17,500	..	2,860	..	12	185	138	..	235
15	Kenya	8,000	..	2,520	..	15	102	61	22	94
16	Mali	45,320	*21,180*	2,670	*2,050*	10	204	157	..	217
17	Niger	60,360	*35,140*	5,690	*660*	..	171	122	..	320
18	Lao PDR	15,160	*4,450*	1,380	*490*	30	146	95	41	141
19	Burkina Faso	95,690	..	..	..	12	178	129	..	175
20	India	4,950	..	*3,760*	..	..	137	80	63	122
21	Nigeria	20,530	..	*4,370*	..	17	114	83	43	191
22	Albania	1,070	..	230	..	..	66	29	..	41
23	Nicaragua	2,150	*1,490*	..	..	..	106	51	12	72
24	Togo	28,860	..	*1,590*	..	32	134	83	24	135
25	Gambia, The	24,420	..	..	..	10	185	130	..	..
26	Zambia	13,640	*11,430*	1,730	*610*	..	106	103	27	203
27	Mongolia	580	*360*	250	..	5	102	58	..	78
28	Central African Republic	44,020	..	2,480	..	18	139	101	..	177
29	Benin	28,960	..	2,610	..	10	146	85	..	144
30	Ghana	12,910	..	690	..	5	111	79	36	..
31	Pakistan	4,670	..	*7,020*	..	30	142	88	40	137
32	Tajikistan	630	430	190	140	..	77	47	..	83
33	China	*1,500*	*1,060*	2,500	1,490	6	69	30	25	54
34	Guinea	50,650	..	*3,730*	..	11	181	132	18	226
35	Mauritania	17,960	..	*3,750*	..	..	148	99	..	202
36	Zimbabwe	6,310	..	650	..	6	96	67	10	83
37	Georgia	280	180	110	*80*	..	35	19	..	28
38	Honduras	3,720	*2,330*	1,450	..	9	110	41	..	56
39	Sri Lanka	5,900	..	1,290	..	22	58	17	..	19
40	Côte d'Ivoire	15,540	..	1,930	..	..	135	91	..	120
41	Lesotho	30,400	..	3,860	..	..	134	77	..	156
42	Armenia	350	260	140	*100*	..	24	21	..	33
43	Egypt, Arab Rep.	2,030	*1,340*	2,480	*500*	12	158	64	10	86
44	*Myanmar*	8,820	*12,900*	3,050	*1,240*	13	128	82	32	111
45	*Yemen, Rep.*	34,790	..	..	..	..	192	117	30	137
	Middle-income economies	**5,820 w**	..	**1,730 w**	..		**74 w**	**39 w**		**57 w**
	Lower-middle-income	**7,470 w**	..	**1,600 w**	..		**75 w**	**40 w**		**63 w**
46	Azerbaijan	390	260	130	110	..	38	28	..	52
47	Indonesia	27,440	..	*4,910*	..	..	118	56	46	111
48	Senegal	15,810	..	*1,670*	..	10	135	67	20	120
49	Bolivia	1,970	..	2,990	..	9	153	73	11	114
50	Cameroon	29,390	*12,000*	2,610	*2,000*	13	126	61	14	113
51	Macedonia, FYR	..	430	..	..	..	82	26	..	..
52	Kyrgyz Republic	480	310	140	110	..	62	34	..	58
53	Philippines	9,270	..	*2,680*	..	..	71	42	34	59
54	Congo	9,940	..	810	..	..	101	84	..	109
55	Uzbekistan	490	280	150	90	..	66	40	..	66
56	Morocco	13,090	..	..	..	..	128	66	9	84
57	Moldova	490	250	130	90	..	38	25	..	36
58	Guatemala	3,660	..	..	..	..	100	46	..	73
59	Papua New Guinea	11,640	*12,750*	*1,710*	*1,160*	..	112	67	..	95
60	Bulgaria	540	..	240	..	6	28	18	..	19
61	Romania	840	*540*	430	..	..	45	23	..	29
62	Jordan	2,480	*770*	870	*500*	..	..	27	6	42
63	Ecuador	2,870	*960*	2,640	*600*	..	100	49	..	57
64	Dominican Republic	..	..	1,400	..	14	98	40	10	48
65	El Salvador	4,100	..	890	..	..	103	45	16	60
66	Lithuania	360	*230*	130	*90*	..	24	13	..	20
67	Colombia	2,260	..	..	..	17	77	36	10	44
68	Jamaica	2,630	..	530	..	11	43	14	7	17
69	Peru	1,920	*940*	..	..	..	116	63	11	92
70	Paraguay	2,300	*1,260*	2,210	..	5	57	37	4	46
71	Kazakhstan	460	250	120	90	..	52	29	..	49
72	Tunisia	5,930	*1,540*	940	*300*	4	127	42	8	52

Note: For data comparability and coverage, see the technical notes. Figures in italics are for years other than those specified.

		Population per				Low birthweight babies (%)	Infant mortality rate (per 1,000 live births)		Prevalence of malnutrition (under 5)	Under-5 mortality rate (per 1,000 live births)
		Physician		Nursing person						
		1970	1993	1970	1993	1991	1970	1993	1988–93	1993
73	Algeria	8,100	..	..	..	..	139	53	9	68
74	Namibia	..	4,320	..	..	14	118	59	..	79
75	Slovak Republic	..	290	..	110	..	25	12	..	18
76	Latvia	..	280	..	120	..	21	14	..	26
77	Thailand	8,290	4,420	1,170	910	10	73	36	13	45
78	Costa Rica	1,620	..	460	..	..	59	14	2	16
79	Ukraine	360	220	110	90	..	22	16	..	26
80	Poland	700	450	260	190	8	31	15	..	17
81	Russian Federation	340	220	110	90	..	29	21	..	31
82	Panama	1,630	..	1,540	..	..	47	24	7	28
83	Czech Republic	..	270	..	..	..	21	9	..	10
84	Botswana	15,540	..	1,920	..	..	95	42	..	56
85	Turkey	2,230	980	1,000	1,110	..	144	62	..	84
86	*Iran, Islamic Rep.*	3,270	..	1,780	..	12	131	35	..	54
	Upper-middle-income	**1,830 w**	**..**	**1,970 w**	**..**		**70 w**	**36 w**		**43 w**
87	Venezuela	1,130	640	450	330	..	53	23	6	24
88	Belarus	390	230	120	90	..	22	16	..	22
89	Brazil	2,030	..	4,140	..	15	95	57	7	63
90	South Africa	..	..	300	..	..	79	52	..	69
91	Mauritius	4,170	..	610	..	8	60	17	..	22
92	Estonia	300	260	110	130	..	22	16	..	23
93	Malaysia	4,310	2,410	1,270	470	8	45	13	..	17
94	Chile	2,160	2,150	460	330	7	77	16	..	17
95	Hungary	510	..	210	..	..	35	15	..	17
96	Mexico	1,480	..	1,620	..	5	72	35	14	43
97	Trinidad and Tobago	2,250	..	190	..	13	44	18	..	21
98	Uruguay	910	..	..	..	..	46	19	..	21
99	Oman	9,270	..	3,820	..	8	159	29	..	38
100	Gabon	5,250	..	570	..	10	138	92	25	154
101	Slovenia	..	..	..	..	..	24	8	..	..
102	Puerto Rico	..	..	..	..	..	28	11	..	..
103	Argentina	530	..	960	..	..	52	24	..	27
104	Greece	620	..	990	..	9	37	10	..	11
105	Korea, Rep.	2,220	950	1,190	450	..	46	11	..	12
106	Portugal	1,110	..	860	..	5	51	10	..	11
107	*Saudi Arabia*	7,460	710	2,080	460	..	119	28	..	38
108	*Turkmenistan*	460	280	140	90	..	81	56	..	89
	Low- and middle-income	**7,100 w**	**..**	**4,340 w**	**..**		**96 w**	**55 w**		**87 w**
	Sub-Saharan Africa	**31,810 w**	**24,180 w**	**3,210 w**	**1,840 w**		**132 w**	**93 w**		**172 w**
	East Asia & Pacific	**5,210 w**	**1,740 w**	**2,740 w**	**1,350 w**		**77 w**	**36 w**		**61 w**
	South Asia	**6,240 w**	**..**	**10,180 w**	**..**		**138 w**	**84 w**		**124 w**
	Europe and Central Asia	**630 w**	**370 w**	**270 w**	**250 w**		**44 w**	**25 w**		**37 w**
	Middle East & N. Africa	**6,370 w**	**1,260 w**	**2,010 w**	**400 w**		**136 w**	**52 w**		**70 w**
	Latin America & Caribbean	**2,020 w**	**..**	**2,640 w**	**..**		**82 w**	**43 w**		**52 w**
	Severely indebted	**3,350 w**	**2,000 w**	**2,560 w**	**450 w**		**84 w**	**49 w**		**63 w**
	High-income economies	**710 w**	**..**	**20 w**	**..**		**19 w**	**7 w**		**9 w**
109	New Zealand	870	..	150	..	6	17	9	..	12
110	Ireland	980	..	160	..	..	20	7	..	8
111	Spain	750	..	..	..	..	26	7	..	9
112	† Israel	410	..	..	..	7	24	9	..	12
113	Australia	840	..	..	..	..	17	7	..	8
114	† Hong Kong	1,510	..	570	..	..	19	7	..	8
115	United Kingdom	810	..	240	..	..	18	7	..	8
116	Finland	960	..	130	..	5	13	5	..	6
117	† Kuwait	1,050	..	260	..	..	48	17	..	21
118	Italy	550	..	..	..	..	29	8	..	9
119	† Singapore	1,520	..	280	..	7	21	6	..	7
120	Canada	680	..	140	..	6	18	7	..	8
121	Netherlands	800	..	300	..	..	13	7	..	8
122	† United Arab Emirates	1,120	1,100	..	580	..	68	18	..	21
123	Belgium	650	..	..	..	..	21	6	..	10
124	France	750	..	270	..	..	18	7	..	9
125	Austria	550	230	300	..	6	25	7	..	8
126	Germany	580ᵃ	..	..	..	..	22	6	..	7
127	Sweden	730	..	140	..	..	11	5	..	6
128	United States	630	..	160	..	7	20	9	..	10
129	Norway	720	..	160	..	..	13	8	..	9
130	Denmark	690	..	..	..	5	14	7	..	8
131	Japan	890	..	310	..	6	14	4	..	6
132	Switzerland	700	..	..	..	5	15	6	..	8
	World	**5,860 w**	**..**	**3,730 w**	**..**		**81 w**	**48 w**		**75 w**

a Data refer to the Federal Republic of Germany before unification.

Table 28. Education

		Percentage of age group enrolled in education														
		Primary				Secondary				Tertiary		Primary net enrollment (%)		Primary pupil/ teacher ratio	
		Total		Female		Total		Female							
		1970	1992	1970	1992	1970	1992	1970	1992	1980	1992	1975	1992	1970	1992
	Low-income economies	74 w	101 w	..	93 w	22 w	42 w	..	34 w	..	..	..	..	..	40 w
	Excluding China & India	50 w	74 w	37 w	66 w	12 w	26 w	8 w	21 w	3 w	5 w	..	57 w	42 w	41 w
1	Mozambique	47	60	..	51	5	8	..	5	0	0	..	42	..	53
2	Tanzania	34	68	27	67	3	5	2	4	0	..	..	50	47	36
3	Ethiopia	16	22	10	18	4	12	2	11	0	1	..	..	48	27
4	Sierra Leone	34	48	27	39	8	16	5	12	1	1	..	..	32	..
5	Viet Nam	..	108	..	103	..	33	..	..	2	2	..	..	..	..
6	Burundi	30	69	20	62	2	6	1	4	1	1	..	51	37	63
7	Uganda	38	71	30	63	4	13	2	..	1	1	..	..	..	..
8	Nepal	26	102	8	81	10	36	3	23	3	7	..	..	..	39
9	Malawi	..	66	..	60	..	4	..	3	1	..	..	48	43	68
10	Chad	35	65	17	41	2	7	0	3	..	..	..	..	65	64
11	Rwanda	68	71	60	70	2	8	1	7	0	..	..	67	60	58
12	Bangladesh	54	77	35	71	..	19	..	12	3	4	..	69	46	63
13	Madagascar	90	92	82	91	12	..	9	18	3	3	..	..	65	38
14	Guinea-Bissau	39	..	23	..	8	..	6	..	0	..	59	..	..	..
15	Kenya	58	95	48	93	9	29	5	25	1	2	88	..	34	31
16	Mali	22	25	15	19	5	7	2	5	0	1	..	19	40	47
17	Niger	14	29	10	21	1	6	1	4	0	..	..	25	39	38
18	Lao PDR	53	98	40	84	3	22	2	17	1	..	..	59	36	29
19	Burkina Faso	13	31	10	24	1	8	1	5	0	1	..	30	44	60
20	India	73	102	56	90	26	44	15	32	..	..	..	..	41	63
21	Nigeria	37	76	27	67	4	20	3	17	2	..	..	..	34	39
22	Albania	106	101	102	101	35	79	27	74	5	7	..	..	..	19
23	Nicaragua	80	102	81	104	18	44	17	46	14	10	65	80	37	37
24	Togo	71	111	44	87	7	23	3	12	2	..	..	76	58	59
25	Gambia, The	24	69	15	56	7	18	4	12	0	..	21	56	27	30
26	Zambia	90	97	80	92	13	31	8	26	2	2	..	..	47	..
27	Mongolia	113	89	..	100	87	77	..	..	..	14	..	..	30	..
28	Central African Republic	64	..	41	..	4	..	2	..	1	2	..	..	64	..
29	Benin	36	66	22	..	5	12	3	7	2	3	..	..	41	..
30	Ghana	64	74	54	67	14	38	8	29	2	2	..	..	30	29
31	Pakistan	40	46	22	31	13	21	5	13	4	..	..	..	41	41
32	Tajikistan	..	78	..	..	..	..	..	..	..	..	..	..	..	21
33	China	89	121	..	116	24	51	..	45	1	2	..	96	..	22
34	Guinea	33	42	21	27	13	10	5	5	5	..	..	..	..	49
35	Mauritania	14	55	8	48	2	14	0	10	..	3	..	..	24	51
36	Zimbabwe	74	119	66	118	7	48	6	42	1	6	..	..	..	38
37	Georgia	..	..	..	..	..	..	..	..	..	..	..	..	..	..
38	Honduras	87	105	87	107	14	19	13	34	8	9	..	93	35	38
39	Sri Lanka	99	107	94	105	47	74	48	77	3	6	..	..	..	29
40	Côte d'Ivoire	58	69	45	58	9	24	4	16	3	..	..	52	45	37
41	Lesotho	87	106	101	113	7	25	7	30	2	1	..	70	46	51
42	Armenia	..	..	..	..	..	..	..	..	..	..	..	..	..	..
43	Egypt, Arab Rep.	72	101	57	93	35	80	23	73	18	19	..	..	38	26
44	Myanmar	83	105	78	104	21	..	16	..	5	..	..	..	47	..
45	Yemen, Rep.	22	76	7	37	3	31	0	..	..	..	..	..	..	..
	Middle-income economies	..	104 w	..	..	..	..	..	..	..	..	..	..	..	..
	Lower-middle-income	..	103 w	..	..	..	..	..	..	..	..	..	..	..	..
46	Azerbaijan	..	97	..	..	..	83	..	..	..	..	..	..	..	..
47	Indonesia	80	115	73	113	16	38	11	..	4	10	72	97	..	23
48	Senegal	41	58	32	50	10	16	6	..	3	3	..	48	45	59
49	Bolivia	76	85	62	81	24	34	20	31	13	23	73	81	27	25
50	Cameroon	89	101	75	93	7	28	4	23	2	3	69	..	48	51
51	Macedonia, FYR	..	..	..	..	..	..	..	..	..	..	..	..	..	20
52	Kyrgyz Republic	..	..	..	..	..	..	..	..	..	..	..	..	..	..
53	Philippines	108	109	..	..	46	74	..	..	28	28	95	96	29	36
54	Congo	..	..	..	..	..	..	..	..	5	6	..	..	62	66
55	Uzbekistan	..	..	..	..	..	..	..	..	..	..	..	..	..	..
56	Morocco	52	69	36	57	13	28	7	29	6	10	47	59	34	28
57	Moldova	..	94	..	..	..	..	..	..	..	..	..	..	..	..
58	Guatemala	57	79	51	73	8	28	8	..	8	..	53	..	36	34
59	Papua New Guinea	52	73	39	66	8	12	4	10	2	..	..	..	30	31
60	Bulgaria	101	90	100	88	79	71	..	73	16	30	96	80	22	14
61	Romania	112	88	113	87	44	80	38	80	11	..	..	78	21	21
62	Jordan	..	105	..	105	..	..	..	..	27	19	..	99	..	22
63	Ecuador	97	..	95	..	22	..	23	..	37	20	78	..	37	..
64	Dominican Republic	100	..	100	..	21	..	..	..	..	..	..	..	55	..
65	El Salvador	85	78	83	79	22	25	21	27	4	16	..	70	37	44
66	Lithuania	..	92	..	91	..	..	..	..	..	..	..	..	..	..
67	Colombia	108	117	110	117	25	55	24	60	10	15	..	83	38	28
68	Jamaica	119	106	119	108	46	62	45	66	7	9	90	100	..	38
69	Peru	107	119	99	..	31	30	27	..	19	39	..	..	35	..
70	Paraguay	109	110	103	109	17	30	17	31	9	8	83	98	32	23
71	Kazakhstan	..	..	..	..	..	..	..	..	..	..	..	..	..	..
72	Tunisia	100	117	79	112	23	43	13	42	5	11	..	99	47	26

Note: For data comparability and coverage, see the technical notes. Figures in italics are for years other than those specified.

		Percentage of age group enrolled in education													
		Primary				Secondary				Tertiary		Primary net enrollment (%)		Primary pupil/ teacher ratio	
		Total		Female		Total		Female							
		1970	1992	1970	1992	1970	1992	1970	1992	1980	1992	1975	1992	1970	1992
73	Algeria	76	99	58	92	11	60	6	53	6	12	77	90	. .	27
74	Namibia	. .	124	. .	127	. .	41	. .	47	. .	3	. .	81	. .	32
75	Slovak Republic	. .	100	. .	. .	. .	96	. .	. .	. .	28	. .	. .	. .	22
76	Latvia	. .	. .	. .	. .	. .	. .	. .	. .	. .	23	. .	82	. .	. .
77	Thailand	83	97	79	88	17	33	15	32	13	19	. .	. .	35	17
78	Costa Rica	110	105	109	104	28	43	29	45	23	28	92	90	30	32
79	Ukraine	. .	. .	. .	. .	. .	. .	. .	. .	. .	. .	. .	. .	. .	. .
80	Poland	101	98	99	97	62	83	65	86	18	23	96	96	23	17
81	Russian Federation	. .	98	. .	. .	. .	. .	. .	. .	. .	. .	. .	. .	. .	. .
82	Panama	99	106	97	105	38	60	40	. .	22	24	87	92	27	23
83	Czech Republic	. .	95	. .	96	. .	88	. .	. .	. .	. .	. .	. .	. .	18
84	Botswana	65	116	67	118	7	54	6	57	1	5	58	96	36	29
85	Turkey	110	112	94	107	27	60	15	50	6	15	. .	100	38	29
86	*Iran, Islamic Rep.*	72	109	52	104	27	57	18	49	4	12	. .	98	32	32
Upper-middle-income		**94 w**	**104 w**	**93 w**	**104 w**	**33 w**	**54 w**	**30 w**	**63 w**	**14 w**	**19 w**	**81 w**	**91 w**	**35 w**	**24 w**
87	Venezuela	94	99	94	100	33	34	34	40	21	30	81	91	35	23
88	Belarus	. .	87	. .	. .	. .	91	. .	. .	. .	. .	. .	. .	. .	. .
89	Brazil	82	106	82	. .	26	39	26	. .	12	12	71	86	28	23
90	South Africa	99	. .	99	. .	18	. .	17	. .	. .	14	. .	. .	. .	. .
91	Mauritius	94	106	93	108	30	54	25	56	1	2	82	89	32	21
92	Estonia	. .	85	. .	85	. .	. .	. .	. .	. .	23	. .	81	. .	25
93	Malaysia	87	93	84	94	34	58	28	59	4	7	. .	. .	. .	20
94	Chile	107	96	107	95	39	72	42	75	13	23	94	83	50	25
95	Hungary	97	89	97	89	63	81	55	81	13	15	. .	86	18	12
96	Mexico	104	113	101	111	22	55	17	55	14	14	. .	100	46	30
97	Trinidad and Tobago	106	95	107	95	42	81	44	82	5	7	87	89	34	26
98	Uruguay	112	108	109	107	59	84	64	. .	18	32	. .	93	24	21
99	Oman	3	100	1	96	. .	57	. .	53	0	6	32	85	18	27
100	Gabon	85	. .	81	. .	8	. .	5	. .	. .	3	. .	. .	46	44
101	Slovenia	. .	. .	. .	. .	. .	. .	. .	. .	. .	. .	. .	. .	. .	18
102	Puerto Rico	117	. .	. .	. .	71	. .	. .	. .	48	. .	. .	. .	26	. .
103	Argentina	105	107	106	114	44	. .	47	. .	22	43	96	. .	19	. .
104	Greece	107	. .	106	. .	63	. .	55	. .	17	25	97	. .	31	19
105	Korea, Rep.	103	105	103	106	42	90	32	91	16	42	99	100	57	33
106	Portugal	98	120	96	118	57	68	51	74	11	23	91	100	34	14
107	*Saudi Arabia*	45	78	29	75	12	46	5	41	7	14	42	64	24	14
108	*Turkmenistan*	. .	94	. .	. .	. .	. .	. .	. .	. .	. .	. .	. .	. .	. .
Low- and middle-income		**. .**	**102 w**	**. .**	**. .**	**. .**	**. .**	**. .**	**. .**	**. .**	**. .**	**. .**	**. .**	**. .**	**. .**
Sub-Saharan Africa		**50 w**	**67 w**	**41 w**	**60 w**	**7 w**	**18 w**	**5 w**	**16 w**	**1 w**	**4 w**	**67 w**	**47 w**	**42 w**	**40 w**
East Asia & Pacific		**88 w**	**117 w**	**. .**	**113 w**	**24 w**	**52 w**	**. .**	**46 w**	**4 w**	**5 w**	**. .**	**96 w**	**. .**	**23 w**
South Asia		**67 w**	**94 w**	**50 w**	**82 w**	**24 w**	**39 w**	**14 w**	**29 w**	**. .**	**. .**	**. .**	**. .**	**42 w**	**59 w**
Europe and Central Asia		**. .**	**99 w**	**. .**	**. .**	**. .**	**. .**	**. .**	**. .**	**. .**	**. .**	**. .**	**. .**	**. .**	**. .**
Middle East & N. Africa		**68 w**	**97 w**	**50 w**	**89 w**	**24 w**	**56 w**	**15 w**	**51 w**	**10 w**	**15 w**	**65 w**	**86 w**	**34 w**	**26 w**
Latin America & Caribbean		**95 w**	**106 w**	**94 w**	**105 w**	**28 w**	**45 w**	**26 w**	**54 w**	**15 w**	**18 w**	**77 w**	**89 w**	**34 w**	**26 w**
Severely indebted		**89 w**	**101 w**	**84 w**	**92 w**	**34 w**	**46 w**	**31 w**	**56 w**	**14 w**	**19 w**	**78 w**	**85 w**	**28 w**	**24 w**
High-income economies		**. .**	**103 w**	**. .**	**103 w**	**. .**	**. .**	**. .**	**. .**	**36 w**	**51 w**	**88 w**	**97 w**	**24 w**	**. .**
109	New Zealand	110	104	109	103	77	84	76	85	29	50	100	100	21	16
110	Ireland	106	103	106	103	74	101	77	105	20	38	91	90	. .	25
111	Spain	123	107	125	107	56	. .	48	. .	24	40	100	100	34	21
112	† Israel	96	94	95	94	57	85	60	89	29	34	. .	. .	. .	16
113	Australia	115	107	115	107	82	82	80	83	25	40	98	98	. .	17
114	† Hong Kong	117	108	115	. .	36	. .	31	. .	11	20	92	. .	33	. .
115	United Kingdom	104	104	104	105	73	86	73	88	20	28	97	97	. .	. .
116	Finland	82	100	79	99	102	121	106	133	32	57	. .	. .	22	. .
117	† Kuwait	89	61	76	60	63	51	57	51	11	14	68	45	16	16
118	Italy	110	95	109	97	61	76	55	76	28	34	97	. .	22	12
119	† Singapore	105	107	101	. .	46	. .	45	. .	8	. .	100	. .	30	. .
120	Canada	101	107	100	106	65	104	65	104	42	99	. .	100	23	17
121	Netherlands	102	98	102	99	75	97	69	96	30	39	92	95	30	. .
122	† United Arab Emirates	93	118	71	117	22	69	9	73	2	10	. .	100	. .	17
123	Belgium	103	99	104	100	81	102	80	103	26	38	. .	95	20	10
124	France	117	106	117	105	74	101	77	104	26	46	98	100	26	12
125	Austria	104	103	103	104	72	104	73	100	23	37	89	91	21	11
126	Germany	. .	107	. .	107	. .	. .	. .	. .	27	36	. .	89	. .	16
127	Sweden	94	101	95	101	86	91	85	93	31	34	100	100	20	10
128	United States	. .	104	. .	103	. .	. .	. .	. .	56	76	72	98	23	. .
129	Norway	89	99	94	99	83	103	83	104	26	49	100	99	20	6
130	Denmark	96	95	97	95	78	108	75	110	29	38	. .	95	9	11
131	Japan	99	102	99	102	86	. .	86	. .	31	32	99	100	26	20
132	Switzerland	. .	105	. .	105	. .	91	. .	88	18	31	. .	96	. .	. .
World		**. .**	**102 w**	**. .**	**. .**	**. .**	**. .**	**. .**	**. .**	**. .**	**. .**	**. .**	**. .**	**. .**	**. .**

Table 29. Gender comparisons

		Health			Maternal mortality per 100,000 live births, 1988–93	Education								Employment	
		Life expectancy at birth (years)				Percentage of cohort persisting to grade 4				Females per 100 males				Female share of labor force (%)	
		Female		Male		Female		Male		Primary		Secondary[a]			
		1970	1993	1970	1993		1970	1988	1970	1988	1970	1992	1970	1992	1970	1993
	Low-income economies	**54 w**	**63 w**	**53 w**	**61 w**		..	..	..	..	..	**80 w**	..	**67 w**	**36 w**	**36 w**
	Excluding China & India	**47 w**	**57 w**	**45 w**	**54 w**		**65 w**	**63 w**	**71 w**	**64 w**	**57 w**	**76 w**	**40 w**	**64 w**	**32 w**	**31 w**
1	Mozambique	44	48	40	45	..	..	54	..	60	..	75	..	65	50	47
2	Tanzania	47	53	44	50	..	86	90	90	89	65	96	38	77	51	47
3	Ethiopia	42	50	39	46	..	58	56	55	56	46	69	32	87	40	37
4	Sierra Leone	36	41	33	38	..	62	..	58	..	67	..	40	56	36	32
5	Viet Nam	52	68	47	63	105	..	..	..	..	..	..	..	..	48	47
6	Burundi	45	52	42	49	..	55	79	51	79	49	82	17	62	50	47
7	Uganda	48	46	45	43	550[b]	..	..	..	..	..	..	31	..	43	40
8	Nepal	42	54	43	55	..	..	..	..	..	..	62	16	..	35	33
9	Malawi	41	46	40	45	380	55	68	60	73	..	89	36	54	45	40
10	Chad	40	50	37	46	..	59	65	63	74	..	46	9	19	23	21
11	Rwanda	46	49	43	46	300	67	76	66	73	79	98	44	61	50	47
12	Bangladesh	43	56	45	56	600	..	46	..	44	47	81	..	49	5	8
13	Madagascar	47	59	44	56	350	69	72	70	68	86	95	70	98	42	39
14	Guinea-Bissau	38	46	35	42	..	..	..	..	..	..	..	62	..	43	40
15	Kenya	52	60	48	57	..	98	78	97	76	71	95	42	75	42	39
16	Mali	40	48	36	45	..	53	..	64	..	55	59	29	50	17	16
17	Niger	40	49	37	45	..	73	..	72	..	53	60	35	49	49	46
18	Lao PDR	42	53	39	50	660	..	..	..	..	59	77	36	62	46	44
19	Burkina Faso	42	49	39	46	..	71	90	74	86	57	63	33	51	48	46
20	India	49	61	50	61	420	44	..	49	..	60	74	39	58	30	25
21	Nigeria	45	52	41	49	800	..	76	..	74	59	79	49	..	37	34
22	Albania	69	75	66	69	..	..	..	..	..	..	93	92	124	40	41
23	Nicaragua	55	69	52	65	..	58	60	39	63	101	102	89	114	20	26
24	Togo	46	57	43	54	..	84	82	89	87	45	65	26	34	39	36
25	Gambia, The	38	47	35	44	..	97	..	95	..	44	71	33	..	43	40
26	Zambia	48	49	45	47	..	..	..	..	..	80	..	49	..	28	30
27	Mongolia	54	65	52	63	140	..	..	..	..	..	..	..	..	45	46
28	Central African Republic	45	52	40	47	..	65	81	69	85	49	..	20	..	49	45
29	Benin	41	50	38	46	..	75	..	76	..	45	..	44	39	48	47
30	Ghana	51	58	48	55	1,000	75	..	82	..	75	84	35	64	42	39
31	Pakistan	49	63	50	61	270[c]	50	45	62	55	36	52	25	41	9	13
32	Tajikistan	65	73	60	68	39	..	..	..	..	..	94	..	..	..	..
33	China	63	71	61	68	115[d]	..	78	..	98	..	87	..	76	42	43
34	Guinea	37	45	36	44	559[e]	..	78	..	81	..	46	26	32	42	39
35	Mauritania	44	54	41	50	800	..	77	..	81	..	80	13	51	22	23
36	Zimbabwe	52	54	49	52	80	82	77	88	77	82	98	63	79	38	34
37	Georgia	72	77	64	69	55	..	..	..	..	..	..	..	..	..	..
38	Honduras	55	71	51	66	221	..	..	..	..	99	101	79	113	14	20
39	Sri Lanka	66	74	64	70	..	..	99	..	99	89	93	101	105	25	27
40	Côte d'Ivoire	46	52	43	49	..	82	82	93	85	57	71	27	48	38	34
41	Lesotho	52	64	47	59	220	87	85	70	75	150	118	111	146	48	43
42	Armenia	75	76	69	70	35	..	..	..	..	..	..	..	..	..	..
43	Egypt, Arab Rep.	52	65	50	63	..	86	..	93	..	61	81	48	81	7	11
44	*Myanmar*	50	60	47	57	..	..	..	..	..	89	..	65	96	39	36
45	*Yemen, Rep.*	41	51	41	50	..	..	..	..	..	..	..	..	..	8	14
	Middle-income economies	**63 w**	**71 w**	**58 w**	**65 w**		..	..	..	..	..	..	..	**102 w**	..	..
	Lower-middle-income	**63 w**	**70 w**	**58 w**	**64 w**		..	..	..	..	..	..	..	**100 w**	..	..
46	Azerbaijan	72	75[h]	64	67	29	..	..	..	..	..	94	..	96	..	..
47	Indonesia	49	65	47	61	450	67	83	89	99	..	94	59	81	30	31
48	Senegal	40	51	38	49	933[f]	..	90	..	94	63	74	39	53	41	39
49	Bolivia	48	61	44	58	600	49	..	57	..	69	90	64	..	21	26
50	Cameroon	46	58	43	55	430	78	..	79	..	74	85	36	71	37	33
51	Macedonia, FYR	68	75	65	69	..	..	..	..	..	..	93	..	160	..	..
52	Kyrgyz Republic	67	73	58	65	43	..	..	..	..	..	..	..	..	..	..
53	Philippines	59	69	56	65	76	..	85	..	84	..	..	..	..	33	31
54	Congo	49	53	43	49	..	86	87	89	88	..	87	43	72	40	39
55	Uzbekistan	67	72	60	66	43	..	..	..	..	..	..	..	..	..	..
56	Morocco	53	66	50	62	..	82	81	81	83	51	68	40	70	14	21
57	Moldova	68	72	61	64	34	..	..	..	..	..	..	..	..	..	..
58	Guatemala	54	68	51	63	..	33	..	67	..	79	84	65	..	13	17
59	Papua New Guinea	47	57	47	56	700	82	70	90	72	57	80	37	66	29	35
60	Bulgaria	74	75	69	68	..	92	92	100	89	94	92	..	211	44	47
61	Romania	71	73	66	67	..	..	..	..	..	97	95	151	108	44	47
62	Jordan	..	72	..	68	..	..	97	..	99	..	96	..	117	6	11
63	Ecuador	60	72	57	67	170	69	..	69	..	94	..	76	..	16	19
64	Dominican Republic	61	72	57	68	..	..	..	..	..	99	..	..	..	11	16
65	El Salvador	60	69	56	64	..	56	..	56	..	90	98	77	92	20	25
66	Lithuania	75	76	67	65	29	..	..	..	..	..	..	..	107	50	..
67	Colombia	63	73	59	67	110	56	74	53	72	101	98	73	105	21	22
68	Jamaica	70	76	66	72	..	..	100	..	98	..	99	103	..	42	46
69	Peru	56	68	52	64	..	..	..	..	..	85	..	74	..	20	24
70	Paraguay	67	72	63	68	180	70	78	71	79	89	93	91	104	21	21
71	Kazakhstan	69	74	59	65	53	..	..	..	..	..	..	..	..	..	..
72	Tunisia	55	69	54	67	127	..	93	..	95	..	87	38	82	12	25

Note: For data comparability and coverage, see the technical notes. Figures in italics are for years other than those specified.

		Health					Education								Employment	
		Life expectancy at birth (years)				Maternal mortality per 100,000 live births, 1988–93	Percentage of cohort persisting to grade 4				Females per 100 males				Female share of labor force (%)	
		Female		Male			Female		Male		Primary		Secondary[a]			
		1970	1993	1970	1993		1970	1988	1970	1988	1970	1992	1970	1992	1970	1993
73	Algeria	54	69	52	66	..	90	95	95	96	..	83	40	81	6	10
74	Namibia	49	61	47	58	..	..	..	..	..	..	102	..	124	24	24
75	Slovak Republic	73	75	67	67	..	..	..	..	..	..	95	..	104		46
76	Latvia	74	75	66	63	..	..	..	..	..	..	..	..	..	51	..
77	Thailand	61	72	56	66	..	75	..	75	..	88	95	69	97	47	44
78	Costa Rica	69	79	65	74	..	84	90	82	91	96	95	111	104	18	22
79	Ukraine	74	74	66	64	33	..	..	..	..	..	..	127	109	..	..
80	Poland	74	76	67	67	..	99	..	97	..	93	94	251	259	45	46
81	Russian Federation	74	74	63	62	..	..	..	..	..	..	..	..	112	..	..
82	Panama	67	75	64	71	..	84	86	81	84	92	92	99	103	25	28
83	Czech Republic	73	75	67	68	..	..	..	..	..	..	99	..	134	..	45
84	Botswana	54	67	50	63	..	94	94	99	90	113	105	88	116	44	34
85	Turkey	59	69	55	65	146[c]	77	98	82	98	73	89	37	64	38	34
86	*Iran, Islamic Rep.*	54	68	55	67	..	77	93	79	94	55	89	49	78	13	19
	Upper-middle-income	**64 w**	**72 w**	**59 w**	**66 w**	..		**..**	**71 w**	..	..	**95 w**	..	**106 w**	**25 w**	**30 w**
87	Venezuela	68	75	63	69	200	84	*84*	60	*87*	99	99	102	137	21	28
88	Belarus	75	75	66	65	25	..	..	..	..	..	..	..	104	..	..
89	Brazil	61	69	57	64	..	56	..	54	..	..	..	99	..	22	28
90	South Africa	56	66	50	60	..	..	..	..	..	..	98	95	114	33	36
91	Mauritius	65	74	60	67	..	98	99	98	99	94	98	66	103	20	27
92	Estonia	74	75	66	64	41	..	..	..	..	..	96	..	..	51	..
93	Malaysia	63	73	60	69	34[g]	..	99	..	98	..	95	69	105	31	35
94	Chile	66	78	59	71	40	80	..	82	..	98	96	130	115	22	29
95	Hungary	72	74	67	65	..	91	99	99	98	93	96	202	*194*	40	45
96	Mexico	64	74	60	68	..	..	74	..	95	..	94	..	93	18	27
97	Trinidad and Tobago	68	74	63	70	..	76	97	73	96	97	*97*	113	*100*	30	30
98	Uruguay	72	76	66	69	36	..	*98*	..	*98*	..	95	129	..	26	32
99	Oman	49	72	46	68	..	..	*97*	..	*100*	16	90	0	89	6	9
100	Gabon	46	56	43	52	..	78	*80*	78	*82*	91	*98*	43	..	40	37
101	Slovenia	73	78	66	68	..	..	..	..	..	..	95	..	108		
102	Puerto Rico	75	79	69	72	21	..	..	..	..	..	..	..	..	27	..
103	Argentina	70	76	64	69	140	..	..	..	..	97	..	156	..	25	28
104	Greece	74	80	70	75	..	97	99	97	98	91	*94*	98	*104*	26	27
105	Korea, Rep.	63	75	58	68	30	95	100	94	100	92	94	65	88	32	34
106	Portugal	71	78	64	71	..	94	..	93	..	95	*92*	98	*153*	25	37
107	*Saudi Arabia*	54	72	51	69	..	93	..	92	..	46	88	16	79	5	8
108	*Turkmenistan*	64	69	57	62	55	..	..	..	..	..	..	..	..	..	..
	Low- and middle-income	**57 w**	**66 w**	**55 w**	**63 w**	..	**..**	**..**	**..**	**..**	**..**	**..**	**..**	**78 w**	**..**	**..**
	Sub-Saharan Africa	**46 w**	**53 w**	**42 w**	**50 w**	..	..	**73 w**	..	**73 w**	**61 w**	**81 w**	**44 w**	**72 w**	**40 w**	**37 w**
	East Asia & Pacific	**60 w**	**70 w**	**58 w**	**66 w**	..	..	**80 w**	..	**97 w**	..	**89 w**	..	**78 w**	**41 w**	**42 w**
	South Asia	**48 w**	**60 w**	**50 w**	**60 w**	..	**45 w**	..	**50 w**	..	**56 w**	**73 w**	**37 w**	**56 w**	**26 w**	**22 w**
	Europe and Central Asia	**71 w**	**74 w**	**64 w**	**65 w**	..	**..**	**..**	**..**	**..**	**..**	**..**	**..**	**124 w**	**..**	**..**
	Middle East & N. Africa	**54 w**	**67 w**	**52 w**	**65 w**	..	**85 w**	**91 w**	**88 w**	**93 w**	..	**83 w**	..	**79 w**	**10 w**	**16 w**
	Latin America & Caribbean	**63 w**	**72 w**	**58 w**	**66 w**	..	**60 w**	..	**58 w**	..	**94 w**	**95 w**	**101 w**	**104 w**	**22 w**	**27 w**
	Severely indebted	**62 w**	**69 w**	**58 w**	**64 w**	..	**71 w**	**83 w**	**71 w**	**86 w**	**81 w**	**87 w**	**113 w**	**138 w**	**28 w**	**30 w**
	High-income economies	**75 w**	**80 w**	**68 w**	**74 w**	..	**95 w**	**99 w**	**95 w**	**98 w**	**96 w**	**95 w**	**97 w**	**98 w**	**36 w**	**38 w**
109	New Zealand	75	79	69	73	..	..	99	..	98	94	94	94	97	29	..
110	Ireland	74	78	69	73	..	..	99	..	98	..	95	124	100	26	30
111	Spain	75	81	70	75	..	89	100	88	99	99	*93*	84	*102*	19	25
112	† Israel	73	79	70	75	..	*96*	97	*96*	98	..	95	131	118	30	34
113	Australia	75	81	68	75	..	76	*100*	74	*98*	..	95	91	98	31	38
114	† Hong Kong	75	82	68	76	..	96	..	95	..	90	..	74	..	35	..
115	United Kingdom	75	79	69	74	..	..	..	..	..	..	..	94	*96*	36	39
116	Finland	74	80	66	72	..	..	98	..	98	..	95	112	114	44	47
117	† Kuwait	68	77	64	73	..	96	..	98	..	79	*96*	74	97	8	16
118	Italy	75	81	69	74	..	..	..	..	..	94	95	86	98	29	32
119	† Singapore	71	78	67	73	10	*98*	*100*	99	*100*	88	94	103	..	26	31
120	Canada	76	81	69	74	..	96	98	95	95	95	94	95	95	32	40
121	Netherlands	77	81	71	75	..	99	..	96	..	96	..	91	110	26	31
122	† United Arab Emirates	63	76	59	73	..	*97*	98	*93*	97	..	93	23	105	4	7
123	Belgium	75	80	68	73	..	81	..	79	..	94	94	87	..	30	34
124	France	76	81	68	73	..	*91*	..	*98*	..	95	94	107	106	36	40
125	Austria	74	79	67	73	..	95	99	92	97	95	95	95	95	39	40
126	Germany	74	79	68	73	..	97[h]	99[h]	96[h]	97[h]	96[h]	96[h]	93[h]	100[h]	40	40
127	Sweden	77	81	72	76	..	98	..	97	..	96	95	92	110	36	45
128	United States	75	79	67	73	..	..	..	..	..	..	94	98	*94*	37	41
129	Norway	77	80	71	74	..	*99*	..	*98*	..	105	95	97	106	29	41
130	Denmark	76	78	71	73	..	99	100	96	100	97	96	102	106	36	45
131	Japan	75	83	70	76	..	100	100	100	100	96	95	101	*99*	39	38
132	Switzerland	76	81	70	75	..	*94*	..	*93*	..	..	97	93	101	33	36
	World	**61 w**	**68 w**	**58 w**	**64 w**	..	**..**	**..**	**..**	**..**	**..**	**..**	**..**	**81 w**	**..**	**..**

a. See the technical notes.   b. Midpoint of national range.   c. Based on indirect estimation using survey data.   d. Based on study covering 30 provinces.   e. Based on community study in urban center of Conakry.   f. Government estimate.   g. Based on civil registration.   h. Data refer to the Federal Republic of Germany before unification.

Table 30. Income distribution and PPP estimates of GNP

			Percentage share of income or consumption						PPP estimates of GNP per capita (United States = 100)		Current intl. dollars
		Year	Lowest 20 percent	Second quintile	Third quintile	Fourth quintile	Highest 20 percent	Highest 10 percent	1987	1993	1993
Low-income economies											
Excluding China & India											
1	Mozambique		..	..	..	..	..	..	2.6[a]	2.2[a]	550[a]
2	Tanzania	1991[b,c]	2.4	5.7	10.4	18.7	62.7	46.5	2.4[d]	2.3[d]	580[d]
3	Ethiopia	1981–82[b,e]	8.6	12.7	16.4	21.1	41.3	27.5	..	..	..
4	Sierra Leone		..	..	..	..	..	..	3.5[d]	3.0[d]	750[d]
5	Viet Nam	1992[b,c]	7.8	11.4	15.4	21.4	44.0	29.0	..	..	..
6	Burundi		..	..	..	..	..	..	3.4[a]	3.0[a]	740[a]
7	Uganda	1989–90[b,c]	8.5	12.1	16.0	21.5	41.9	27.2	3.2[a]	3.6[a]	900[a]
8	Nepal	1984–85[f,g]	9.1	12.9	16.7	21.8	39.5	25.0	4.0[a]	4.1[a]	1,020[a]
9	Malawi		..	..	..	..	..	..	3.1[d]	2.8[d]	690[d]
10	Chad		..	..	..	..	..	..	2.8[a]	2.9[a]	720[a]
11	Rwanda	1983–85[b,c]	9.7	13.1	16.7	21.6	38.9	24.6	3.8[d]	3.0[d]	740[d]
12	Bangladesh	1988–89[b,c]	9.5	13.4	17.0	21.6	38.6	24.6	4.9[d]	5.2[d]	1,290[d]
13	Madagascar		..	..	..	..	..	..	3.2[d]	2.7[d]	670[d]
14	Guinea-Bissau	1991[b,c]	2.1	6.5	12.0	20.6	58.9	42.4	3.1[a]	3.4[a]	840[a]
15	Kenya	1992[b,c]	3.4	6.7	10.7	17.3	61.8	47.9	5.8[d]	5.2[d]	1,290[d]
16	Mali		..	..	..	..	..	..	2.3[d]	2.1[d]	520[d]
17	Niger		..	..	..	..	..	..	3.9[a]	3.2[a]	780[a]
18	Lao PDR		..	..	..	..	..	..	..	..	..
19	Burkina Faso		..	..	..	..	..	..	3.4[a]	3.1[a]	770[a]
20	India	1989–90[b,c]	8.8	12.5	16.2	21.3	41.3	27.1	4.5[d]	4.9[d]	1,220[d]
21	Nigeria	1992[b,c]	5.1	10.1	14.8	21.0	49.0	34.2	5.0[d]	5.7[d]	1,400[d]
22	Albania		..	..	..	..	..	..	..	..	..
23	Nicaragua	1993[b,c]	4.2	8.0	12.6	19.9	55.3	39.8	12.4[a]	7.7[a]	1,900[a]
24	Togo		..	..	..	..	..	..	5.9[a]	4.0[a]	1,000[a]
25	Gambia, The		..	..	..	..	..	..	4.7[a]	4.7[a]	1,170[a]
26	Zambia	1991[b,c]	5.6	9.6	14.2	21.0	49.7	34.2	4.6[d]	4.2[d]	1,040[d]
27	Mongolia		..	..	..	..	..	..	21.8[a]	8.2[a]	2,020[a]
28	Central African Republic		..	..	..	..	..	..	5.1[a]	4.1[a]	1,010[a]
29	Benin		..	..	..	..	..	..	7.1[d]	6.5[d]	1,620[d]
30	Ghana	1988–89[b,c]	7.0	11.3	15.8	21.8	44.1	29.0	7.8[a]	8.0[a]	1,970[a]
31	Pakistan	1991[b,c]	8.4	12.9	16.9	22.2	39.7	25.2	8.5[d]	8.8[d]	2,170[d]
32	Tajikistan		..	..	..	..	..	..	12.3[h]	5.6[h]	1,380[h]
33	China	1990[f,g]	6.4	11.0	16.4	24.4	41.8	24.6	6.3[h]	9.4[h]	2,330[h]
34	Guinea		..	..	..	..	..	..	..	..	..
35	Mauritania	1987–88[b,c]	3.5	10.7	16.2	23.3	46.3	30.2	6.5[d]	6.0[a]	1,490[a]
36	Zimbabwe	1990–91[b,c]	4.0	6.3	10.0	17.4	62.3	46.9	8.7[d]	8.1[d]	2,000[d]
37	Georgia		..	..	..	..	..	..	28.5[h]	7.1[h]	1,750[h]
38	Honduras	1989[f,g]	2.7	6.0	10.2	17.6	63.5	47.9	8.2[i]	7.7[i]	1,910[i]
39	Sri Lanka	1990[b,c]	8.9	13.1	16.9	21.7	39.3	25.2	10.7[d]	12.1[d]	2,990[d]
40	Côte d'Ivoire	1988[b,c]	6.8	11.2	15.8	22.2	44.1	28.5	8.6[d]	5.7[d]	1,400[d]
41	Lesotho	1986–87[b,c]	2.9	6.4	11.3	19.5	60.0	43.6	6.5[a]	6.5[a]	1,620[a]
42	Armenia		..	..	..	..	..	..	26.4[h]	8.2[h]	2,040[h]
43	Egypt, Arab Rep.		..	..	..	..	..	..	14.7[d]	15.3[d]	3,780[d]
44	*Myanmar*		..	..	..	..	..	..	..	..	..
45	*Yemen, Rep.*		..	..	..	..	..	..	..	..	..
Middle-income economies											
Lower-middle-income											
46	Azerbaijan		..	..	..	..	..	..	22.1[h]	8.9[h]	2,190[h]
47	Indonesia	1990[b,c]	8.7	12.1	15.9	21.1	42.3	27.9	10.1[i]	12.7[i]	3,150[i]
48	Senegal	1991–92[b,c]	3.5	7.0	11.6	19.3	58.6	42.8	7.5[d]	6.7[d]	1,650[d]
49	Bolivia	1990–91[b,c]	5.6	9.7	14.5	22.0	48.2	31.7	9.2[i]	9.8[i]	2,420[i]
50	Cameroon		..	..	..	..	..	..	15.3[d]	8.5[d]	2,100[d]
51	Macedonia, FYR		..	..	..	..	..	..	..	..	..
52	Kyrgyz Republic	1992[b,c]	2.5	7.1	12.5	20.9	57.0	40.3	13.7[h]	9.4[h]	2,320[h]
53	Philippines	1988[b,c]	6.5	10.1	14.4	21.2	47.8	32.1	10.6[d]	10.8[d]	2,670[d]
54	Congo		..	..	..	..	..	..	11.7[d]	9.9[d]	2,440[d]
55	Uzbekistan		..	..	..	..	..	..	12.6[h]	10.1[h]	2,510[h]
56	Morocco	1990–91[b,c]	6.6	10.5	15.0	21.7	46.3	30.5	13.4[d]	12.5[d]	3,090[d]
57	Moldova		..	..	..	..	..	..	23.4[h]	11.6[h]	2,870[h]
58	Guatemala	1989[f,g]	2.1	5.8	10.5	18.6	63.0	46.6	13.5[i]	13.5[i]	3,350[i]
59	Papua New Guinea		..	..	..	..	..	..	8.8[a]	9.5[a]	2,350[a]
60	Bulgaria	1992[f,g]	8.4	13.0	17.0	22.3	39.3	24.7	28.5[d]	16.6[a]	4,100[a]
61	Romania		..	..	..	..	..	..	18.4[j]	11.3[j]	2,800[j]
62	Jordan	1991[b,c]	6.5	10.3	14.6	20.9	47.7	32.6	21.4[a]	16.6[a]	4,100[a]
63	Ecuador		..	..	..	..	..	..	16.1[i]	17.1[i]	4,240[i]
64	Dominican Republic	1989[f,g]	4.2	7.9	12.5	19.7	55.6	39.6	14.0[i]	14.7[i]	3,630[i]
65	El Salvador		..	..	..	..	..	..	9.1[i]	9.5[i]	2,350[i]
66	Lithuania		..	..	..	..	..	..	27.9[h]	12.6[h]	3,110[h]
67	Colombia	1991[f,g]	3.6	7.6	12.6	20.4	55.8	39.5	21.0[i]	22.2[i]	5,490[i]
68	Jamaica	1990[b,c]	6.0	9.9	14.5	21.3	48.4	32.6	10.6[j]	12.1[j]	3,000[j]
69	Peru	1985–86[b,c]	4.9	9.2	13.7	21.0	51.4	35.4	18.7[i]	13.0[i]	3,220[i]
70	Paraguay		..	..	..	..	..	..	13.4[i]	13.7[i]	3,390[i]
71	Kazakhstan		..	..	..	..	..	..	24.6[h]	15.0[h]	3,710[h]
72	Tunisia	1990[b,c]	5.9	10.4	15.3	22.1	46.3	30.7	18.7[d]	19.3[d]	4,780[d]

Note: Data on income distribution should be treated with caution; for data comparability and coverage, see the technical notes. Figures in italics are for years other than those specified.

		Year	Lowest 20 percent	Second quintile	Third quintile	Fourth quintile	Highest 20 percent	Highest 10 percent	PPP estimates of GNP per capita (United States = 100) 1987	1993	Current intl. dollars 1993
					Percentage share of income or consumption						
73	Algeria	1988[b,c]	6.9	11.0	14.9	20.7	46.5	31.7	27.0[a]	21.7[a]	5,380[a]
74	Namibia		..	..	..	..	..	..	14.9[a]	15.3[a]	3,790[a]
75	Slovak Republic		..	..	..	..	..	..	35.0[k]	25.4[k]	6,290[k]
76	Latvia		..	..	..	..	..	..	35.7[h]	20.3[h]	5,010[h]
77	Thailand	1988[b,g]	6.1	9.4	13.5	20.3	50.7	35.3	16.7[d]	25.3[d]	6,260[d]
78	Costa Rica	1989[f,g]	4.0	9.1	14.3	21.9	50.8	34.1	20.3[i]	22.3[i]	5,520[i]
79	Ukraine		..	..	..	..	..	..	26.6[h]	18.0[h]	4,450[h]
80	Poland	1989[f,g]	9.2	13.8	17.9	23.0	36.1	21.6	23.0[d]	20.2[d]	5,000[d]
81	Russian Federation	1992[b,c]	4.2	9.8	15.3	22.8	48.0	31.5	35.8[h]	20.4[h]	5,050[h]
82	Panama	1989[f,g]	2.0	6.3	11.6	20.3	59.8	42.1	25.7[i]	23.6[i]	5,840[i]
83	Czech Republic		..	..	..	..	..	..	39.2[k]	30.5[k]	7,550[k]
84	Botswana	1985–86[l,e]	3.6	6.9	11.4	19.2	58.9	42.9	15.5[d]	20.9[d]	5,160[d]
85	Turkey		..	..	..	..	..	..	15.9[m]	15.8[m]	3,920[m]
86	Iran, Islamic Rep.		..	..	..	..	..	..	22.0[d]	21.7[d]	5,380[d]
Upper-middle-income											
87	Venezuela	1989[f,g]	4.8	9.5	14.4	21.9	49.5	33.2	34.1[i]	32.9[i]	8,130[i]
88	Belarus		..	..	..	..	..	..	30.1[h]	25.2[h]	6,240[h]
89	Brazil	1989[f,g]	2.1	4.9	8.9	16.8	67.5	51.3	24.8[i]	21.7[i]	5,370[i]
90	South Africa	1993[b,c]	3.3	5.8	9.8	17.7	63.3	47.3	..	..	..
91	Mauritius		..	..	..	..	..	..	40.0[d]	50.2[d]	12,420[d]
92	Estonia		..	..	..	..	..	..	45.0[h]	..	..
93	Malaysia	1989[f,g]	4.6	8.3	13.0	20.4	53.7	37.9	23.8[i]	32.1[j]	7,930[j]
94	Chile	1992[f,g]	3.3	6.9	11.2	18.3	60.4	45.8	25.3[i]	34.0[i]	8,400[i]
95	Hungary	1989[f,g]	10.9	14.8	18.0	22.0	34.4	20.8	28.5[d]	24.5[d]	6,050[d]
96	Mexico	1984[f,g]	4.1	7.8	12.3	19.9	55.9	39.5	28.2[j]	27.5[j]	6,810[j]
97	Trinidad and Tobago		..	..	..	..	..	..	39.5[a]	32.7[a]	8,080[a]
98	Uruguay		..	..	..	..	..	..	24.3[i]	25.8[i]	6,380[i]
99	Oman		..	..	..	..	..	..	35.7[a]	36.5[a]	9,020[a]
100	Gabon		..	..	..	..	..	..	..	..	..
101	Slovenia		..	..	..	..	..	..	..	..	..
102	Puerto Rico		..	..	..	..	..	..	42.1[a]	43.1[a]	10,670[a]
103	Argentina		..	..	..	..	..	..	32.6[i]	33.3[i]	8,250[i]
104	Greece		..	..	..	..	..	..	35.8[m]	36.4[m]	9,000[m]
105	Korea, Rep.	1988[n,o]	7.4	12.3	16.3	21.8	42.2	27.6	27.7[d]	38.9[d]	9,630[d]
106	Portugal		..	..	..	..	..	..	37.6[m]	43.3[m]	10,710[m]
107	*Saudi Arabia*		..	..	..	..	..	..	43.6[a]	..	..
108	*Turkmenistan*		..	..	..	..	..	..	17.2[h]	..	..
Low- and middle-income											
Sub-Saharan Africa											
East Asia & Pacific											
South Asia											
Europe and Central Asia											
Middle East & N. Africa											
Latin America & Caribbean											
Severely indebted											
High-income economies											
109	New Zealand	1981–82[n,o]	5.1	10.8	16.2	23.2	44.7	28.7	67.6[m]	64.8[m]	16,040[m]
110	Ireland		..	..	..	..	..	..	43.2[m]	54.5[m]	13,490[m]
111	Spain	1988[n,o]	8.3	13.7	18.1	23.4	36.6	21.8	51.2[m]	54.6[m]	13,510[m]
112	† Israel	1979[n,o]	6.0	12.1	17.8	24.5	39.6	23.5	57.3[i]	60.4[i]	14,940[i]
113	Australia	1985[n,o]	4.4	11.1	17.5	24.8	42.2	25.8	73.3[m]	72.4[m]	17,910[m]
114	† Hong Kong	1980[n,o]	5.4	10.8	15.2	21.6	47.0	31.3	73.2[d]	87.1[d]	21,560[d]
115	United Kingdom	1988[n,o]	4.6	10.0	16.8	24.3	44.3	27.8	70.6[m]	69.6[m]	17,210[m]
116	Finland	1981[n,o]	6.3	12.1	18.4	25.5	37.6	21.7	72.8[m]	62.8[m]	15,530[m]
117	† Kuwait		..	..	..	..	..	..	85.1[a]	87.4[a]	21,630[a]
118	Italy	1986[n,o]	6.8	12.0	16.7	23.5	41.0	25.3	70.6[m]	72.1[m]	17,830[m]
119	† Singapore	1982–83[n,o]	5.1	9.9	14.6	21.4	48.9	33.5	54.8[a]	78.9[a]	19,510[a]
120	Canada	1987[n,o]	5.7	11.8	17.7	24.6	40.2	24.1	87.6[m]	81.8[m]	20,230[m]
121	Netherlands	1988[n,o]	8.2	13.1	18.1	23.7	36.9	21.9	67.0[m]	70.0[m]	17,330[m]
122	† United Arab Emirates		..	..	..	..	..	..	84.6[a]	84.6[a]	20,940[a]
123	Belgium	1978–79[n,o]	7.9	13.7	18.6	23.8	36.0	21.5	74.1[m]	79.4[m]	19,640[m]
124	France	1989[n,o]	5.6	11.8	17.2	23.5	41.9	26.1	76.2[m]	76.8[m]	19,000[m]
125	Austria		..	..	..	..	..	..	73.1[m]	78.5[m]	19,430[m]
126	Germany[p]	1988[n,o]	7.0	11.8	17.1	23.9	40.3	24.4	66.0[m]	68.1[m]	16,850[m]
127	Sweden	1981[n,o]	8.0	13.2	17.4	24.5	36.9	20.8	77.8[m]	69.5[m]	17,200[m]
128	United States	1985[n,o]	4.7	11.0	17.4	25.0	41.9	25.0	100.0[m]	100.0[m]	24,740[m]
129	Norway	1979[n,o]	6.2	12.8	18.9	25.3	36.7	21.2	80.5[m]	80.0[m]	19,780[m]
130	Denmark	1981[n,o]	5.4	12.0	18.4	25.6	38.6	22.3	79.1[m]	79.1[m]	19,560[m]
131	Japan	1979[n,o]	8.7	13.2	17.5	23.1	37.5	22.4	74.6[m]	84.3[m]	20,850[m]
132	Switzerland	1982[n,o]	5.2	11.7	16.4	22.1	44.6	29.8	100.7[m]	95.6[m]	23,660[m]
World											

a. Based on regression estimates.   b. Refers to expenditure shares by fractiles of persons.   c. Ranked by per capita expenditure.   d. Extrapolated from 1985 ICP estimates. e. Ranked by household expenditure.   f. Refer to income shares by fractiles of persons.   g. Ranked by per capita income.   h. These values are subject to more than the usual margin of error (see technical notes).   i. Extrapolated from 1980 ICP estimates.   j. Extrapolated from 1975 ICP estimates.   k. Extrapolated from 1990 ICP estimates. l. Refer to expenditure shares by fractiles of households.   m. Extrapolated from 1993 ICP estimates.   n. Refer to income shares by fractiles of households.   o. Ranked by household income.   p. Distribution data refer to the Federal Republic of Germany.

Table 31. Urbanization

		Urban population				Population in capital city as % of		Population in urban agglomerations of 1 million or more in 1993, as % of			
		As % of total population		Average annual growth rate (%)				Urban		Total	
		1970	1993	1970–80	1980–93	Urban 1990	Total 1990	1970	1993	1970	1993
	Low-income economies	**18 w**	**28 w**	**3.6 w**	**3.9 w**	**12 w**	**3 w**	**41 w**	**38 w**	**8 w**	**11 w**
	Excluding China & India	**19 w**	**27 w**	**4.2 w**	**4.2 w**	**30 w**	**7 w**	**39 w**	**40 w**	**7 w**	**12 w**
1	Mozambique	6	31	10.8	8.4	42	11	69	41	4	13
2	Tanzania	7	23	11.0	6.5	31	6	43	25	3	6
3	Ethiopia	9	13	4.3	4.3	32	4	29	30	3	4
4	Sierra Leone	18	35	5.0	5.1	52	17	0	0	0	0
5	Viet Nam	18	20	2.8	2.7	24	5	35	32	6	6
6	Burundi	2	7	7.4	6.7	71	4	0	0	0	0
7	Uganda	8	12	3.9	4.8	37	4	0	0	0	0
8	Nepal	4	13	7.7	7.7	17	2	0	0	0	0
9	Malawi	6	13	7.3	6.7	28	3	0	0	0	0
10	Chad	12	21	6.6	3.2	64	13	0	0	0	0
11	Rwanda	3	6	7.1	4.7	76	4	0	0	0	0
12	Bangladesh	8	17	6.8	5.3	39	6	47	51	4	9
13	Madagascar	14	26	5.4	5.9	23	5	0	0	0	0
14	Guinea-Bissau	15	21	5.2	3.8	37	7	0	0	0	0
15	Kenya	10	26	8.1	7.0	27	6	45	28	5	7
16	Mali	14	26	4.8	5.5	30	7	0	0	0	0
17	Niger	9	16	6.8	5.3	50	8	0	0	0	0
18	Lao PDR	10	20	5.0	6.0	52	10	0	0	0	0
19	Burkina Faso	6	23	6.3	10.4	26	5	0	0	0	0
20	India	20	26	3.7	3.0	4	1	32	37	6	10
21	Nigeria	20	38	5.7	5.5	23	8	26	27	5	10
22	Albania	32	37	2.8	2.5	21	7	0	0	0	0
23	Nicaragua	47	62	4.3	4.1	46	28	0	43	0	27
24	Togo	13	30	8.2	5.1	51	15	0	0	0	0
25	Gambia, The	15	24	5.2	6.0	96	22	0	0	0	0
26	Zambia	30	42	5.9	3.8	29	12	0	31	0	13
27	Mongolia	45	60	4.2	3.6	37	22	0	0	0	0
28	Central African Republic	30	39	3.7	3.1	66	25	0	0	0	0
29	Benin	16	30	7.0	4.5	16	5	0	0	0	0
30	Ghana	29	35	2.9	4.2	22	7	29	27	8	10
31	Pakistan	25	34	3.8	4.2	1	0	49	53	12	18
32	Tajikistan	37	32	2.2	2.4	..	..	0	0	0	0
33	China	17	29	3.0	4.3	4	1	48	37	8	11
34	Guinea	14	28	4.6	5.6	87	23	47	76	7	21
35	Mauritania	14	51	9.9	6.9	81	38	0	0	0	0
36	Zimbabwe	17	31	5.8	5.6	30	9	0	0	0	0
37	Georgia	48	58	1.5	1.4	..	..	0	42	0	24
38	Honduras	29	43	5.1	4.6	39	16	0	0	0	0
39	Sri Lanka	22	22	1.6	1.6	17	4	0	0	0	0
40	Côte d'Ivoire	27	42	6.4	5.2	45	18	37	45	10	19
41	Lesotho	9	22	6.7	6.6	18	3	0	0	0	0
42	Armenia	59	68	3.0	1.8	..	..	0	50	0	34
43	Egypt, Arab Rep.	42	44	2.5	2.1	39	17	53	55	22	24
44	*Myanmar*	23	26	2.7	2.6	32	8	23	32	5	8
45	*Yemen, Rep.*	13	32	6.8	7.1	11	3	0	0	0	0
	Middle-income economies	**46 w**	**60 w**	**3.3 w**	**2.8 w**	..	..	**42 w**	**37 w**	**17 w**	**22 w**
	Lower-middle-income	**42 w**	**54 w**	**3.0 w**	**2.8 w**	..	..	**39 w**	**34 w**	**13 w**	**18 w**
46	Azerbaijan	50	55	2.3	1.7	..	..	0	44	0	25
47	Indonesia	17	33	4.9	4.8	17	5	45	38	5	13
48	Senegal	33	41	3.6	3.8	51	20	43	56	14	23
49	Bolivia	41	59	3.5	4.1	33	19	29	28	12	16
50	Cameroon	20	43	7.1	5.3	17	7	22	40	5	17
51	Macedonia, FYR	47	59	2.6	1.9	..	..	0	0	0	0
52	Kyrgyz Republic	37	39	2.2	1.9	..	..	0	0	0	0
53	Philippines	33	52	3.8	4.8	29	14	29	29	9	15
54	Congo	33	57	5.0	5.4	53	28	0	66	0	38
55	Uzbekistan	37	41	3.9	2.5	..	..	32	25	12	10
56	Morocco	35	47	4.1	3.4	10	4	38	37	13	17
57	Moldova	32	50	3.3	2.5	..	..	0	0	0	0
58	Guatemala	36	41	3.3	3.5	23	9	0	0	0	0
59	Papua New Guinea	10	16	5.2	3.6	35	5	0	0	0	0
60	Bulgaria	52	70	2.1	1.0	20	13	20	22	10	15
61	Romania	42	55	2.5	1.0	18	10	20	17	8	9
62	Jordan	51	70	5.4	6.1	46	31	0	31	0	22
63	Ecuador	40	57	4.6	4.0	22	12	50	45	20	26
64	Dominican Republic	40	63	4.8	3.9	51	31	47	71	19	44
65	El Salvador	39	45	2.8	2.1	26	11	0	0	0	0
66	Lithuania	50	71	3.0	1.7	..	..	0	0	0	0
67	Colombia	57	72	3.3	3.2	21	15	40	38	23	27
68	Jamaica	42	53	2.5	1.9	53	27	0	0	0	0
69	Peru	57	71	3.9	2.9	41	29	39	43	22	31
70	Paraguay	37	51	4.0	4.7	46	22	0	0	0	0
71	Kazakhstan	50	59	2.0	1.7	..	..	0	12	0	7
72	Tunisia	45	56	3.6	3.0	37	20	33	39	14	22

Note: For data comparability and coverage, see the technical notes. Figures in italics are for years other than those specified.

		Urban population				Population in capital city as % of		Population in urban agglomerations of 1 million or more in 1993, as % of			
		As % of total population		Average annual growth rate (%)		Urban	Total	Urban		Total	
		1970	1993	1970–80	1980–93	1990	1990	1970	1993	1970	1993
73	Algeria	40	54	4.0	4.4	24	12	24	24	10	13
74	Namibia	19	35	4.7	6.0	34	11	0	0	0	0
75	Slovak Republic	41	58	3.2	1.4	..	..	0	0	0	0
76	Latvia	62	72	1.6	0.7	..	..	0	0	0	0
77	Thailand	13	19	5.1	2.7	69	13	65	56	9	11
78	Costa Rica	40	49	3.6	3.7	71	33	0	0	0	0
79	Ukraine	55	69	1.8	1.1	..	..	0	27	0	19
80	Poland	52	64	2.0	1.3	9	6	32	35	17	22
81	Russian Federation	63	75	1.7	1.1	..	..	0	27	16	20
82	Panama	48	53	3.0	2.5	38	20	0	0	0	0
83	Czech Republic	52	65	2.5	0.2	..	..	25	18	11	12
84	Botswana	8	26	9.4	7.6	44	10	0	0	0	0
85	Turkey	38	66	3.6	5.4	8	5	37	35	14	23
86	*Iran, Islamic Rep.*	42	58	4.9	5.0	20	11	43	34	18	20
	Upper-middle-income	**55 w**	**71 w**	**3.7 w**	**2.7 w**	**22 w**	**16 w**	**47 w**	**44 w**	**26 w**	**32 w**
87	Venezuela	72	92	4.8	3.3	23	21	28	33	20	30
88	Belarus	44	69	3.2	2.0	..	..	0	24	0	17
89	Brazil	56	71	4.1	2.5	2	2	49	46	27	32
90	South Africa	48	50	2.7	2.7	13	6	40	42	19	21
91	Mauritius	42	41	1.7	0.6	37	15	0	0	0	0
92	Estonia	65	73	1.5	0.7	..	..	0	0	0	0
93	Malaysia	34	52	4.6	4.2	19	10	12	12	4	6
94	Chile	75	84	2.4	1.9	43	36	40	42	30	35
95	Hungary	49	64	1.9	0.5	33	20	39	31	19	20
96	Mexico	59	74	4.0	3.1	33	24	43	40	25	30
97	Trinidad and Tobago	63	71	1.1	2.2	12	8	0	0	0	0
98	Uruguay	82	90	0.7	1.0	44	39	51	46	42	42
99	Oman	5	12	8.0	8.3	35	4	0	0	0	0
100	Gabon	26	48	8.0	4.0	68	31	0	0	0	0
101	Slovenia	37	62	3.5	2.4	..	..	0	0	0	0
102	Puerto Rico	58	73	3.0	1.6	55	39	44	42	26	30
103	Argentina	78	87	2.2	1.8	41	36	53	47	42	42
104	Greece	53	64	1.9	1.4	54	34	55	68	29	44
105	Korea, Rep.	41	78	5.1	3.6	35	26	75	64	30	50
106	Portugal	26	35	2.0	1.3	48	16	45	52	12	18
107	*Saudi Arabia*	49	79	8.3	5.7	16	12	27	27	13	21
108	*Turkmenistan*	48	45	2.5	2.0	..	..	0	0	0	0
	Low- and middle-income	**28 w**	**38 w**	**3.4 w**	**3.3 w**	**..**	**..**	**41 w**	**38 w**	**11 w**	**15 w**
	Sub-Saharan Africa	**19 w**	**30 w**	**4.8 w**	**4.8 w**	**33 w**	**9 w**	**34 w**	**34 w**	**7 w**	**11 w**
	East Asia & Pacific	**19 w**	**31 w**	**3.4 w**	**4.2 w**	**12 w**	**4 w**	**46 w**	**37 w**	**9 w**	**12 w**
	South Asia	**19 w**	**26 w**	**3.8 w**	**3.3 w**	**8 w**	**2 w**	**35 w**	**40 w**	**7 w**	**10 w**
	Europe and Central Asia	**51 w**	**65 w**	**2.1 w**	**1.7 w**	**..**	**..**	**34 w**	**29 w**	**15 w**	**19 w**
	Middle East & N. Africa	**41 w**	**55 w**	**4.3 w**	**4.1 w**	**26 w**	**13 w**	**42 w**	**40 w**	**18 w**	**22 w**
	Latin America & Caribbean	**57 w**	**71 w**	**3.6 w**	**2.7 w**	**24 w**	**16 w**	**45 w**	**43 w**	**26 w**	**31 w**
	Severely indebted	**53 w**	**67 w**	**3.5 w**	**2.6 w**	**18 w**	**11 w**	**43 w**	**42 w**	**24 w**	**28 w**
	High-income economies	**74 w**	**78 w**	**1.1 w**	**0.8 w**	**11 w**	**9 w**	**43 w**	**46 w**	**32 w**	**36 w**
109	New Zealand	81	86	1.3	1.1	12	10	0	0	0	0
110	Ireland	52	57	2.1	0.6	46	26	0	0	0	0
111	Spain	66	76	2.0	0.7	18	13	27	31	18	23
112	† Israel	84	90	3.2	2.4	12	11	41	40	35	36
113	Australia	85	85	1.6	1.4	2	1	68	68	58	58
114	† Hong Kong	88	95	2.9	1.3	100	95	100	100	90	95
115	United Kingdom	89	89	0.2	0.3	14	13	31	26	27	23
116	Finland	50	62	2.1	0.8	33	20	22	31	11	19
117	† Kuwait	78	97	7.6	2.4	53	50	97	64	75	62
118	Italy	64	67	0.8	0.1	8	5	43	35	27	24
119	† Singapore	100	100	1.5	1.1	100	100	100	100	100	100
120	Canada	76	77	1.4	1.3	4	3	39	50	29	38
121	Netherlands	86	89	1.1	0.6	8	7	19	16	16	14
122	† United Arab Emirates	57	83	17.4	5.6	..	..	0	0	0	0
123	Belgium	94	97	0.3	0.3	10	10	12	12	11	11
124	France	71	73	0.9	0.4	21	15	30	31	21	22
125	Austria	52	55	0.7	0.4	49	27	51	47	26	26
126	Germany	80	86	0.4	0.5	1	1	50	51	40	44
127	Sweden	81	83	0.6	0.3	23	19	17	21	14	18
128	United States	74	76	1.1	1.2	2	1	51	55	38	42
129	Norway	65	73	1.3	0.6	22	16	0	0	0	0
130	Denmark	80	85	0.9	0.2	32	27	35	30	28	26
131	Japan	71	77	1.8	0.6	19	15	43	49	30	38
132	Switzerland	55	60	0.7	1.3	7	4	0	0	0	0
	World	**37 w**	**44 w**	**2.6 w**	**2.6 w**	**..**	**..**	**42 w**	**39 w**	**15 w**	**18 w**

Table 32. Infrastructure

		Electric power		Telecommunications		Paved roads		Water		Railways	
		Production (kwh per person) 1992	System losses (% of total output) 1992	Telephone mainlines (per 1,000 persons) 1992	Faults (per 100 mainlines per year) 1992	Road density (km per million persons) 1992	Roads in good cond. (% of paved roads) 1988	Population with access to safe water (% of total) 1991	Losses (% of total water provision) 1986	Rail traffic units (per thousand $ GDP) 1992	Diesels in use (% of diesel inventory) 1992
Low-income economies											
Excluding China & India											
1	Mozambique	24	24	3	10	*343*	12	22	..	..	..
2	Tanzania	66	12	3	..	*142*	25	52	..	..	50
3	Ethiopia[a]	25	3	3	74	*77*	48	18	46	..	*60*
4	Sierra Leone	..	..	3	17	295	62	43	..	..	..
5	Viet Nam	139	24	2	..	..	..	*50*	..	..	*60*
6	Burundi	..	..	2	81	177	58	38	46	..	..
7	Uganda	..	..	2	58	*118*	10	*15*	..	20	67
8	Nepal	45	24	3	168	*139*	40	37	45	..	..
9	Malawi	..	..	3	..	*278*	56	*53*	..	26	70
10	Chad	..	..	1	152	56	..	..	..	..	..
11	Rwanda	..	..	2	38	*162*	41	64	..	..	..
12	Bangladesh	79	32	2	..	*59*	15	78	47	37	*74*
13	Madagascar	..	..	3	78	433	56	..	..	..	..
14	Guinea-Bissau	..	..	6	4	..	..	25	..	..	..
15	Kenya	130	16	8	..	*324*	32	..	18	*105*	*52*
16	Mali	..	..	1	..	*308*	63	49	..	*104*	48
17	Niger	..	..	1	79	*400*	60	59	..	..	..
18	Lao PDR	..	..	2	12	516	..	28	..	..	..
19	Burkina Faso	..	..	2	..	158	24	67	..	..	..
20	India	373	23	8	218	*893*	20	*75*	..	488	90
21	Nigeria	137	39	3	327	*376*	67	*42*	..	*17*	18
22	Albania	1,002	13	13	28	*414*	..	100	..	..	78
23	Nicaragua	..	..	14	..	414	..	53	20	..	..
23	Togo	..	..	4	22	470	40	71	..	..	..
25	Gambia, The	..	..	14	120	*772*	..	*77*	..	..	..
26	Zambia	900	11	9	33	795	40	59	..	169	*44*
27	Mongolia	..	..	30	43	..	..	66	..	..	58
28	Central African Republic	..	..	2	..	135	30	12	..	..	..
29	Benin	44	1	3	150	241	26	*50*	..	..	..
30	Ghana	386	2	3	159	474	28	56	47	*28*	..
31	Pakistan	435	17	10	120	826	18	*50*	40	137	*78*
32	Tajikistan	3,001	7	48	218	..	..	b	..	..	..
33	China	647	7	10	..	..	..	71	..	847	*82*
34	Guinea	..	..	2	..	229	27	33	..	..	..
35	Mauritania	..	..	3	165	*804*	58	66	..	..	..
36	Zimbabwe	790	7	12	215	1,406	27	*36*	..	523	83
37	Georgia	2,120	23	105	43	..	..	c	..	..	..
38	Honduras	..	..	21	40	*443*	50	..	..	..	..
39	Sri Lanka	200	17	8	..	*536*	10	60	..	*65*	..
40	Côte d'Ivoire	144	4	7	80	357	75	83	16	32	44
41	Lesotho	..	..	6	..	452	53	46	..	..	..
42	Armenia	1,850	22	157	..	*2,024*	..	c	..	..	..
43	Egypt, Arab Rep.	849	*12*	39	..	633	39	41	..	465	75
44	*Myanmar*	61	35	2	..	*210*	..	33	..	..	75
45	*Yemen, Rep.*	156	11	11	22	372	39	..	45	..	..
Middle-income economies											
Lower-middle-income											
46	Azerbaijan	2,699	13	89	..	..	..	d	..	..	..
47	Indonesia	233	17	8	49	*160*	30	42	29	27	*75*
48	Senegal	99	9	*8*	*36*	542	28	*51*	..	75	68
49	Bolivia	349	14	*33*	28	258	21	46	..	81	*62*
50	Cameroon	223	4	5	74	299	38	*34*	..	96	72
51	Macedonia, FYR	2,812	8	*148*	*13*	2,310	..	..	..	..	..
52	Kyrgyz Republic	2,636	10	75	30	..	..	d	..	..	..
53	Philippines	419	13	10	10	*242*	31	81	53	..	..
54	Congo	181	0	7	54	509	50	..	..	140	31
55	Uzbekistan	2,390	10	67	..	..	..	d	..	..	..
56	Morocco	383	3	25	84	*179*	20	..	5	125	81
57	Moldova	2,562	11	117	45	2,832	..	c	..	..	..
58	Guatemala	290	15	22	58	320	7	60	..	..	..
59	Papua New Guinea	..	..	9	..	*196*	34	33	..	..	..
60	Bulgaria	4,000	14	275	48	3,986	..	100	..	297	78
61	Romania	2,386	10	113	116	*3,431*	30	100	28	..	*52*
62	Jordan	1,120	13	71	89	1,767	..	99	41	*74*	76
63	Ecuador	675	24	48	197	*476*	53	58	47	..	..
64	Dominican Republic	..	..	66	133	*364*	52	62	..	..	..
65	El Salvador	..	..	31	..	323	..	41	..	..	..
66	Lithuania	5,050	9	222	46	9,529	..	c	..	..	64
67	Colombia	1,032	18	85	83	383	42	..	38	5	35
68	Jamaica	897	20	70	84	1,881	10	72	31	..	..
69	Peru	587	11	27	47	347	24	58	..	*16*	..
70	Paraguay	6,693	0	28	..	..	..	33	..	..	..
71	Kazakhstan	4,826	9	88	..	6,747	..	d	..	..	*54*
72	Tunisia	731	6	45	113	2,080	55	67	30	119	57

Note: For data comparability and coverage, see the Key and the technical notes. Figures in italics are for years other than those specified.

		Electric power		Telecommunications		Paved roads		Water		Railways	
		Production (kwh per person) 1992	System losses (% of total output) 1992	Telephone mainlines (per 1,000 persons) 1992	Faults (per 100 mainlines per year) 1992	Road density (km per million persons) 1992	Roads in good cond. (% of paved roads) 1988	Population with access to safe water (% of total) 1991	Losses (% of total water provision) 1986	Rail traffic units (per thousand $ GDP) 1992	Diesels in use (% of diesel inventory) 1992
73	Algeria	701	15	37	82	2,403	40	..	..	76	88
74	Namibia	..	..	40	78	*2,722*	..	..	..	..	..
75	Slovak Republic	4,251	8	*167*	*23*	..	..	77	..	..	..
76	Latvia	1,460	26	247	26	4,437	..	e	..	..	93
77	Thailand	1,000	10	*31*	*32*	841	50	*72*	48	*75*	*72*
78	Costa Rica	..	..	102	..	1,756	22	94	..	..	*46*
79	Ukraine	4,900	9	145	49	3,085	..	c	..	..	60
80	Poland	3,473	11	103	..	6,132	69	100	..	610	67
81	Russian Federation	6,820	8	154	..	..	..	c	..	..	..
82	Panama	1,167	24	97	10	*1,332*	36	83	..	..	..
83	Czech Republic	5,740	7	176	..	..	..	..	..	..	..
84	Botswana	..	..	27	55	*1,977*	94	..	25	..	..
85	Turkey	1,154	13	160	27	5,514	..	91	44	65	76
86	*Iran, Islamic Rep.*	1,101	12	50	..	..	..	89	..	61	*39*
	Upper-middle-income										
87	Venezuela	3,404	15	91	5	*10,269*	40	89	..	..	..
88	Belarus	3,692	11	169	..	4,707	..	c	..	..	92
89	Brazil	1,570	15	71	43	929	30	96	30	*61*	62
90	South Africa	4,329	7	89	..	*1,394*	..	d	..	804	*82*
91	Mauritius	..	..	72	67	*1,549*	95	100	..	..	..
92	Estonia	7,599	9	215	45	5,180	..	c	..	..	77
93	Malaysia	1,612	9	112	78	..	..	78	29	*30*	*76*
94	Chile	1,646	11	94	82	*808*	42	86	..	*42*	*57*
95	Hungary	3,080	10	125	60	7,756	..	100	..	369	78
96	Mexico	1,381	14	80	..	1,019	85	78	..	73	75
97	Trinidad and Tobago	3,122	13	142	6	*1,724*	72	96	..	..	..
98	Uruguay	2,842	14	*168*	*16*	*2,106*	26	..	..	13	62
99	Oman	2,729	1	*74*	*24*	2,992	66	57	..	..	..
100	Gabon	928	11	23	74	511	30	72	22	90	..
101	Slovenia	6,238	5	247	..	5,525	..	..	..	..	81
102	Puerto Rico	..	..	317	71	..	..	..	..	..	..
103	Argentina	1,670	15	*123*	*13*	1,856	35	64	..	*120*	68
104	Greece	3,624	7	*487*	*80*	10,341	..	100	..	*37*	47
105	Korea, Rep.	2,996	5	357	13	1,090	70	78	..	*146*	88
106	Portugal	3,055	11	306	52	*6,130*	50	100	..	· *97*	86
107	*Saudi Arabia*	4,417	9	93	24	3,601	..	95	..	..	90
108	*Turkmenistan*	3,422	11	65	53	..	..	d	..	..	..
	Low- and middle-income										
	Sub-Saharan Africa										
	East Asia & Pacific										
	South Asia										
	Europe and Central Asia										
	Middle East & N. Africa										
	Latin America & Caribbean										
	Severely indebted										
	High-income economies										
109	New Zealand	9,086	8	449	..	15,725	..	97	..	64	*90*
110	Ireland	4,545	9	314	38	24,468	..	100	..	54	60
111	Spain	4,022	9	353	6	8,540	..	100	..	67	87
112	† Israel	4,870	3	353	21	2,658	..	100	..	26	*82*
113	Australia	9,221	7	471	..	*16,221*	e	100	..	*75*	*81*
114	† Hong Kong	6,051	11	485	22	268	e	100	..	..	..
115	United Kingdom	5,660	8	473	16	6,224	e	100	..	64	*74*
116	Finland	11,409	5	544	11	9,429	..	100	..	180	*99*
117	† Kuwait	8,924	9	245	30	..	..	100	..	..	..
118	Italy	3,963	7	410	17	*5,283*	e	100	..	96	79
119	† Singapore	6,353	5	415	11	*993*	..	100	8	..	..
120	Canada	18,309	7	592	..	11,451	..	100	..	325	*91*
121	Netherlands	5,089	4	487	4	6,078	e	100	..	90	85
122	† United Arab Emirates	9,917	6	321	..	2,706	..	100	..	..	..
123	Belgium	7,215	5	425	8	*12,909*	e	100	..	120	83
124	France	8,089	6	525	8	13,008	e	100	..	140	93
125	Austria	6,554	6	440	35	13,954	e	100	..	213	83
126	Germany^f	6,693	2	*457*	*14*	..	..	100	..	107	88
127	Sweden	16,913	6	682	10	11,747	..	100	..	201	*88*
128	United States	12,900	8	565	..	14,453	e	..	..	344	*90*
129	Norway	27,501	8	529	16	14,698	..	100	..	..	..
130	Denmark	5,983	7	581	..	13,741	e	100	..	89	..
131	Japan	7,211	4	464	2	6,426	e	..	..	147	88
132	Switzerland	8,471	6	606	21	10,299	e	100	..	..	..
	World										

a. Includes Eritrea.   b. Estimates range from 25 to 49 percent.   c. Estimates range from 75 to 94 percent.   d. Estimates range from 50 to 74 percent.   e. 85 percent or more of roads are in good condition; see the technical notes.   f. Data refer to the Federal Republic of Germany before unification.

Table 33. Natural resources

		Total area (thousand sq. km.)		Forest area		Nationally protected areas, 1993			Freshwater resources: annual withdrawal, 1970–92[b]				
				Annual deforest., 1981–90[a]						As % of total water resources	Per capita (cu m)		
		1980	1990	Thousand sq. km.	(% of total area)	Thousand sq. km.	Number	As % of total area	Total (cu km)		Total	Domestic	Industrial and agricultural

Low–income economies
Excluding China & India

		1980	1990										
1	Mozambique	187	173	1.4	0.7	0.0	1	0.0	0.8	1.3	55	13	42
2	Tanzania	379	336	4.4	1.2	138.9	30	14.7	0.5	0.6	35	7	28
3	Ethiopia[c]	146	142	0.4	0.3	60.2	23	4.9	2.2	2.0	49	5	43
4	Sierra Leone	20	19	0.1	0.6	0.8	2	1.1	0.4	0.2	96	7	89
5	Viet Nam	97	83	1.4	1.5	13.3	59	4.0	28.9	7.7	416	54	362
6	Burundi	2	2	0.0	0.6	0.9	3	3.2	0.1	2.8	20	7	13
7	Uganda	70	63	0.6	1.0	19.1	31	8.1	0.2	0.3	20	7	14
8	Nepal	56	50	0.5	1.0	11.1	12	7.9	2.7	1.6	148	6	142
9	Malawi	40	35	0.5	1.4	10.6	9	8.9	0.2	1.8	20	7	13
10	Chad	123	114	0.9	0.7	114.9	9	9.0	0.2	0.5	34	6	29
11	Rwanda	2	2	0.0	0.3	3.3	2	12.4	0.1	2.4	23	6	18
12	Bangladesh	11	8	0.4	3.9	1.0	8	0.7	22.5	1.0[d]	212	6	206
13	Madagascar	171	158	1.3	0.8	11.2	37	1.9	16.3	40.8	1,642	16	1,625
14	Guinea-Bissau	22	20	0.2	0.8	..	..	..	0.0	0.0	11	3	8
15	Kenya	13	12	0.1	0.6	35.0	36	6.0	1.1	7.4	51	14	37
16	Mali	132	121	1.1	0.8	40.1	11	3.2	1.4	2.2	162	3	159
17	Niger	25	24	0.1	0.4	84.2	5	6.6	0.3	0.7[d]	41	9	33
18	Lao PDR	145	132	1.3	0.9	24.4	17	10.3	1.0	0.4	259	21	239
19	Burkina Faso	47	44	0.3	0.7	26.6	12	9.7	..	..	..	..	..
20	India	551	517[e]	3.4	0.6	143.5	374	4.4	380.0	18.2[d]	612	18	594
21	Nigeria	168	156	1.2	0.7	29.7	19	3.2	3.6	1.2[d]	37	11	25
22	Albania	14	14	0.0	0.0	0.3	11	1.2	0.2	0.9[d]	94	6	88
23	Nicaragua	73	60	1.2	1.9	9.0	59	6.9	0.9	0.5	367	92	275
24	Togo	16	14	0.2	1.5	6.5	11	11.4	0.1	0.8	28	17	11
25	Gambia, The	1	1	0.0	0.8	0.2	5	2.0	0.0	0.1[d]	29	2	27
26	Zambia	359	323	3.6	1.1	63.6	21	8.5	0.4	0.4	86	54	32
27	Mongolia	152	139	1.3	0.9	61.7	15	3.9	0.6	2.2	273	30	243
28	Central African Republic	319	306	1.3	0.4	61.1	13	9.8	0.1	0.0	25	5	20
29	Benin	56	49	0.7	1.3	7.8	2	6.9	0.1	0.4	26	7	19
30	Ghana	109	96	1.4	1.3	11.0	9	4.6	0.3	0.6	35	12	23
31	Pakistan	26	19	0.8	3.4	37.2	55	4.7	153.4	32.8[d]	2,053	21	2,032
32	Tajikistan	..	..	..	..	0.9	3	0.6	12.6	13.2[d]	2,376	119	2,257
33	China	1,334	1,247	8.8	0.7	580.7	463	6.1	460.0	16.4	462	28	434
34	Guinea	76	67	0.9	1.2	1.6	3	0.7	0.7	0.3	140	14	126
35	Mauritania	6	6	0.0	0.0	17.5	4	1.7	0.7	9.9[d]	495	59	436
36	Zimbabwe	95	89	0.6	0.7	30.7	25	7.9	1.2	5.3	136	19	117
37	Georgia	..	..	..	..	1.9	15	2.7	4.0	6.5[d]	733	154	579
38	Honduras	57	46	1.1	2.1	8.6	44	7.7	1.5	2.1[d]	279	11	268
39	Sri Lanka	20	17	0.3	1.4	8.0	56	12.1	6.3	14.6	503	10	493
40	Côte d'Ivoire	121	109	1.2	1.0	19.9	12	6.2	0.7	1.0	66	15	52
41	Lesotho	..	..	..	..	0.1	1	0.2	0.1	1.3	31	7	24
42	Armenia	..	..	..	..	2.1	4	7.2	3.8	45.9[d]	1,140	148	992
43	Egypt, Arab Rep.	..	..	..	..	7.9	12	0.8	56.4	97.1[d]	1,028	72	956
44	*Myanmar*	329	289	4.0	1.3	1.7	2	0.3	..	..	..	..	..
45	*Yemen, Rep.*	41	41	..	..	..	..	..	3.4	136.0	324	16	308

Middle-income economies
Lower-middle-income

46	Azerbaijan	..	..	..	..	1.9	12	2.2	15.8	56.5[d]	2,215	89	2,126
47	Indonesia	1,217	1,095	12.1	1.0	185.7	175	9.7	16.6	0.7	95	12	83
48	Senegal	81	75	0.5	0.7	21.8	10	11.1	1.4	3.9[d]	202	10	192
49	Bolivia	557	493	6.3	1.2	92.3	25	8.4	1.2	0.4	186	19	167
50	Cameroon	216	204	1.2	0.6	20.5	14	4.3	0.4	0.2	38	17	20
51	Macedonia, FYR	9	9	0.0	0.1	2.2	16	8.4	..	..	..	..	..
52	Kyrgyz Republic	..	..	..	..	2.8	5	1.4	11.7	24.0	2,663	80	2,583
53	Philippines	110	78	3.2	3.3	6.1	27	2.0	29.5	9.1	686	123	562
54	Congo	202	199	0.3	0.2	11.8	10	3.4	0.0	0.0[d]	20	12	7
55	Uzbekistan	..	..	..	..	2.4	10	0.5	82.2	76.4[d]	4,007	160	3,847
56	Morocco	78	90	−1.2	−1.5	3.6	10	0.8	10.9	36.2	412	23	390
57	Moldova	..	..	..	..	0.1	2	0.2	3.7	29.1[d]	848	59	788
58	Guatemala	50	42	0.8	1.7	8.3	17	7.6	0.7	0.6	139	13	127
59	Papua New Guinea	371	360	1.1	0.3	0.8	5	0.2	0.1	0.0	28	8	20
60	Bulgaria	36	37	−0.1	−0.2	3.7	46	3.3	13.9	6.8[d]	1,545	43	1,502
61	Romania	63	63	0.0	0.0	10.8	39	4.6	19.7	9.4[d]	853	68	785
62	Jordan[f]	1	1	0.0	−1.1	2.9	10	3.3	0.5	31.6[d]	173	50	123
63	Ecuador	143	120	2.4	1.8	111.1	15	39.2	5.6	1.8	567	40	528
64	Dominican Republic	14	11	0.4	2.8	10.5	17	21.5	3.0	14.9	442	22	420
65	El Salvador	2	1	0.0	2.2[e]	0.1	2	0.2	1.0	5.3	245	17	228
66	Lithuania	..	..	..	..	6.3	76	9.7	4.4	19.0[d]	1,179	83	1,097
67	Colombia	577	541	3.7	0.7	93.6	79	8.2	5.3	0.5	174	71	103
68	Jamaica	5	2	0.3	7.2	0.0	1	0.1	0.3	3.9	159	11	148
69	Peru	706	679	2.7	0.4	41.8	22	3.2	6.1	15.3	301	57	244
70	Paraguay	169	129	4.0	2.7	14.8	19	3.6	0.4	0.1[d]	110	16	93
71	Kazakhstan	..	..	..	..	8.9	9	0.3	37.9	30.2[d]	2,264	91	2,173
72	Tunisia	5	7	−0.1	−1.9	0.4	7	0.3	2.3	52.9[d]	317	41	276

Note: For data comparability and coverage, see the technical notes. Figures in italics are for years other than those specified.

		Forest area				Nationally protected areas, 1993			Freshwater resources: annual withdrawal, 1970–92[b]				
		Total area (thousand sq. km.)		Annual deforest., 1981–90[a]						As % of total water resources	Per capita (cu m)		
		1980	1990	Thousand sq. km.	(% of total area)	Thousand sq. km.	Number	As % of total area	Total (cu km)		Total	Domestic	Industrial and agricultural
73	Algeria	44	41	0.3	0.8	119.2	19	5.0	3.0	15.7[d]	160	35	125
74	Namibia	130	126	0.4	0.3	102.2	12	12.4	0.1	1.5	104	6	98
75	Slovak Republic	19	18	0.0	0.1	10.2	40	20.7	..	..	..	..	..
76	Latvia	..	..	..	..	7.7	45	12.0	0.7	2.2[d]	261	109	151
77	Thailand	179	127	5.2	3.3	70.2	111	13.7	31.9	17.8[d]	606	24	582
78	Costa Rica	19	14	0.5	2.9	6.4	29	12.5	1.4	1.4	780	31	749
79	Ukraine	90	92	−0.2	−0.3	5.2	20	0.9	34.7	40.0[d]	669	107	562
80	Poland	86	87	−0.1	−0.1	30.6	111	9.8	14.5	25.8[d]	383	51	332
81	Russian Federation	..	..	..	..	655.4	199	3.8	117.0	2.7[d]	787	134	653
82	Panama	38	31	0.6	1.9	13.3	15	17.6	1.3	0.9	744	89	654
83	Czech Republic	26	26	0.0	0.0	10.7	34	13.5	..	..	..	..	..
84	Botswana	150	143	0.8	0.5	106.6	9	18.3	0.1	0.5[d]	100	5	95
85	Turkey	202	202	0.0	0.0	8.2	44	1.1	23.8	12.3[d]	433	104	329
86	*Iran, Islamic Rep.*	180	180	0.0	0.0	83.0	68	5.0	45.4	38.6	1,362	54	1,307
Upper-middle income													
87	Venezuela	517	457	6.0	1.2	263.2	100	28.9	4.1	0.3[d]	387	166	220
88	Belarus	60	63	−0.3	−0.4	2.4	10	1.2	3.0	5.4[d]	292	94	199
89	Brazil	5,978	5,611	36.7[e]	0.6	321.9	273	3.8	36.5	0.5[d]	245	54	191
90	South Africa	42	45	−0.4	−0.8	69.3	237	5.7	14.7	29.3	386	46	340
91	Mauritius	1	1	0.0	0.2	0.0	3	2.0	0.4	16.4	410	66	344
92	Estonia	..	..	..	..	4.4	39	9.8	3.3	21.2[d]	2,085	104	1,980
93	Malaysia	215	176	4.0	2.0	14.8	54	4.5	9.4	2.1	768	177	592
94	Chile	87	88	−0.1	−0.1	137.3	66	18.1	16.8	3.6	1,623	97	1,526
95	Hungary	16	17	−0.1	−0.5	5.7	53	6.2	6.4	5.5[d]	596	54	543
96	Mexico	554	486[e]	6.8[e]	1.3	97.3	65	5.0	54.2	15.2	921	55	865
97	Trinidad and Tobago	2	2	0.0	−2.2	0.2	6	3.1	0.2	2.9	148	40	108
98	Uruguay	6	7	0.0	−0.7	0.3	8	0.2	0.7	0.5[d]	241	14	227
99	Oman	41	41	0.0	0.0	37.4	29	17.6	0.5	23.9	623	19	604
100	Gabon	194	182	1.2	0.6	10.5	6	3.9	0.1	0.0	57	41	16
101	Slovenia	10	10	0.0	0.0	1.1	10	5.3	..	..	..	..	..
102	Puerto Rico	3	3	0.0	0.0	..	..	..	..	..	..	..	..
103	Argentina	601	592	0.9	0.1	43.7	86	1.6	27.6	2.8[d]	1,042	94	948
104	Greece	60	60	0.0	0.0	2.2	24	1.7	7.0	11.8[d]	721	58	663
105	Korea, Rep.	66	65	0.1	0.1	6.9	28	7.0	27.6	41.7	625	116	509
106	Portugal	30	31	−0.1	−0.5	5.8	25	6.3	10.5	16.0[d]	1,075	161	914
107	*Saudi Arabia*	12	12	0.0	0.0	62.0	10	2.9	3.6	163.8	497	224	273
108	*Turkmenistan*	..	..	..	..	11.1	8	2.3	22.8	32.6[d]	6,216	62	6,154
Low- and middle-income													
Sub-Saharan Africa													
East Asia & Pacific													
South Asia													
Europe and Central Asia													
Middle East & N. Africa													
Latin America & Caribbean													
Severely indebted													
High-income economies													
109	New Zealand	..	75	..	..	61.5	206	22.7	1.9	0.5	585	269	316
110	Ireland	4	4	0.0	−1.2	0.5	12	0.7	0.8	1.6	235	38	198
111	Spain	256	256	0.0	0.0	42.5	215	8.4	45.8	41.2[d]	1,188	143	1,045
112	†Israel	1	1	0.0	−0.3	3.1	15	14.6	1.8	86.0[d]	410	66	344
113	Australia	1,456	1,456	0.0	0.0	935.5	892	12.1	17.8	5.2	1,306	849	457
114	†Hong Kong	0	0	0.0	−0.5	..	..	..	..	..	..	..	..
115	United Kingdom	21	24	−0.2	−1.1	51.3	191	20.9	14.5	12.1	253	51	203
116	Finland	233	234	−0.1	0.0	27.3	82	8.1	3.0	2.7[d]	604	72	532
117	†Kuwait	0	0	0.0	0.0	0.3	2	1.5	0.5	..	525	336	189
118	Italy	..	86	..	..	22.7	172	7.6	56.2	30.1[d]	996	139	856
119	†Singapore	0	0	0.0	0.9	0.0	1	4.5	0.2	31.7	84	38	46
120	Canada	..	4,533	..	..	825.5	640	8.3	43.9	1.5	1,688	304	1,384
121	Netherlands	3	3	0.0	−0.3	3.9	79	10.4	14.5	16.1[d]	994	50	944
122	†United Arab Emirates	0	0	0.0	0.0	..	..	..	0.9	299.0	884	97	787
123	Belgium	6	6	0.0	−0.3	0.8	3	2.5	9.0	72.2[d]	917	101	816
124	France	134	135	−0.1	−0.1	56.0	110	10.2	43.7	23.6[d]	778	125	654
125	Austria	37	39	−0.1	−0.4	20.1	170	23.9	2.1	2.3[d]	276	52	224
126	Germany	103	107	−0.5	−0.4	92.0	504	25.8	53.7	31.4[d]	687	73	614
127	Sweden	279	280	−0.1	0.0	29.9	214	6.6	3.0	1.7[d]	352	127	225
128	United States	2,992	2,960	3.2	0.1	1,042.4	1,494	10.6	467.0	18.8	1.868	244	1,624
129	Norway	..	96	..	..	55.4	114	17.1	2.0	0.5[d]	491	98	393
130	Denmark	5	5	0.0	0.0	13.9	113	32.2	1.2	9.0[d]	228	68	160
131	Japan	238	238	0.0	0.0	27.6	80	7.3	89.3	16.3	732	125	607
132	Switzerland	11	12	−0.1	−0.6	7.3	109	17.7	1.1	2.2[d]	168	39	129
World													

a. Negative values represent an increase in forest area. b. Water withdrawal data refer to any year from 1970 to 1992. c. Data includes Eritrea. d. Total water resources include river flows from other countries in addition to internal renewable resources. e. See the technical notes for alternative estimates. f. Except for water withdrawal estimates, data for Jordan cover the East Bank only.

Table 1a. Basic indicators for other economies

		Population (thousands) mid-1993	Area (thousands of sq. km)	GNP per capita[a]		Avg. annual rate of inflation (%)		Life expect. at birth (years) 1993	Adult illiteracy (percent)	
				Dollars 1993	Avg. ann. growth (%), 1980–93	1970–80	1980–93		Female 1990	Total 1990
1	Guyana	816	215.00	350	−3.0	9.6	34.5	66	5	4
2	São Tomé and Principe	122	1.00	350	−3.6	4.0	24	..	..	..
3	Equatorial Guinea	379	28.00	420	1.2	..	−0.6	48	63	50
4	Comoros	471	2.20	560	−0.4	..	5.2	55	..	..
5	*Afghanistan*	17,691	652.10	b	..	..	..	44	86	71
6	*Bhutan*	..	47.00	b	..	..	8.1	..	75	62
7	*Bosnia and Herzegovina*	3,776	51.10	b	..	..	..	72	..	..
8	*Cambodia*	9,683	181.00	b	..	..	..	52	78	65
9	*Eritrea*	..	125.00	b	..	..	..	..	..	..
10	*Haiti*	6,893	27.70	b	..	9.3	9.5	57	53	47
11	*Liberia*	2,845	97.70	b	..	9.2	..	56	71	61
12	*Somalia*	8,954	637.70	b	..	15.2	49.7	47	86	76
13	*Sudan*	26,641	2,505.80	b	..	14.5	42.8	53	88	73
14	*Zaire*	41,231	2,344.90	b	..	31.4	..	52	39	28
15	Kiribati	76	0.70	710	0.5	10.6	5.4	..	..	10
16	Solomon Islands	354	28.90	740	2.6	8.4	12.1	71	..	..
17	Djibouti	557	23.20	780	..	..	3.6	49	..	..
18	Maldives	238	0.30	820	7.2	..	10	63	..	..
19	Cape Verde	370	4.00	920	3.0	9.4	8.7	65	..	..
20	Western Samoa	167	2.80	950	..	..	11.2	..	..	30
21	Suriname	414	163.30	1,180	−2.0	11.8	11.8	71	5	5
22	Swaziland	880	17.40	1,190	2.3	12.3	13.3	58	..	..
23	Tonga	98	0.70	1,530	0.6	..	10.2	..	..	..
24	Vanuatu	161	12.20	1,230	0.5	..	5.3	66	..	30
25	St. Vincent and the Grenadines	110	0.40	2,120	5.0	13.8	4.6	..	..	..
26	Fiji	762	18.30	2,130	0.5	12.8	5.6	72	..	..
27	Grenada	92	0.30	2,380	3.8	..	4.6	..	..	..
28	Belize	204	23.00	2,450	2.9	8.6	3.4	74	..	..
29	Dominica	71	0.70	2,720	4.6	16.8	5.5	..	..	..
30	*Angola*	10,276	1,246.70	c	..	..	..	47	72	58
31	*Croatia*	4,511	56.50	c	..	..	..	72	..	..
32	*Cuba*	10,862	110.90	c	..	..	..	76	7	6
33	*Iraq*	19,465	438.30	c	..	17.9	..	66	51	40
34	*Korea, Dem. Rep.*	23,036	120.50	c	..	..	..	71	..	..
35	*Lebanon*	3,855	10.40	c	..	..	..	69	27	20
36	*Marshall Islands*	51	0.20	c	..	..	..	..	..	9
37	*Micronesia, Fed. Sts.*	105	0.70	c	..	..	..	..	..	..
38	*Northern Mariana Islands*	45	0.48	c	..	..	..	..	..	..
39	*Syrian Arab Rep.*	13,696	185.20	c	..	11.8	15.5	68	49	36
40	*West Bank and Gaza*	..	6.10	c	..	..	..	..	..	..
41	*Yugoslavia, Fed. Rep.*	10,566	102.17	c	..	..	..	72	12	7
42	St. Lucia	142	0.60	3,380	4.4	..	3.5	..	..	..
43	St. Kitts and Nevis	42	0.40	4,410	5.4	..	6.3	..	..	..
44	Barbados	260	0.40	6,230	0.5	13.5	4.3	76	..	..
45	Seychelles	72	0.45	6,280	3.4	16.7	3.2	..	..	..
46	Antigua and Barbuda	65	0.40	6,540	5.2	..	5.9	..	..	..
47	Malta	361	0.30	7,970	3.2	4.2	2.3	76	..	..
48	Bahrain	533	0.70	8,030	−2.9	..	−0.3	72	31	23
49	*American Samoa*	51	0.20	d	..	..	..	..	..	..
50	*Aruba*	69	0.20	d	..	..	..	..	..	..
51	*French Guiana*	134	90.00	d	..	..	..	..	..	..
52	*Gibraltar*	28	0.01	d	..	..	..	..	..	..
53	*Guadeloupe*	413	1.70	d	..	..	..	75	..	..
54	*Guam*	143	0.50	d	..	..	..	76	..	..
55	*Isle of Man*	72	0.57	d	..	..	..	..	..	..
56	*Libya*	5,044	1,759.50	d	..	18.4	0.2	64	50	36
57	*Macao*	381	0.02	d	..	..	8.5	..	..	..
58	*Martinique*	371	1.10	d	..	..	..	76	..	..
59	*Mayotte*	101	0.37	d	..	..	..	..	..	..
60	*Netherlands Antilles*	195	0.80	d	..	..	..	73	..	..
61	*New Caledonia*	176	18.60	d	..	..	..	72	..	..
62	*Reunion*	633	2.50	d	..	..	..	74	..	..
63	Cyprus	726	9.20	10,380	4.9	..	5.2	77	..	..
64	Bahamas, The	268	13.90	11,420	1.4	6.4	4.2	73	..	..
65	Qatar	524	11.00	15,030	−7.2	..	..	72	..	..
66	Iceland	263	103.00	24,950	1.2	35.0	25.4	78	..	..
67	Luxembourg	396	3.00	37,320	2.8	6.9	5	76	..	..
68	*Andorra*	61	0.40	e	..	..	..	..	..	..
69	*Bermuda*	62	0.05	e	..	8.4	9.1	..	..	..
70	*Brunei*	274	5.80	e	..	12.6	−5.1	74	..	..
71	*Cayman Islands*	29	0.30	e	..	..	..	..	..	..
72	*Channel Islands*	146	0.19	e	..	..	..	..	..	..
73	*Faeroe Islands*	47	0.40	e	..	..	..	..	..	..
74	*French Polynesia*	211	4.00	e	..	..	..	70	..	..
75	*Greenland*	57	341.70	e	..	..	..	..	..	..
76	*San Marino*	24	0.10	e	..	..	..	..	..	..
77	*Virgin Islands (U.S.)*	104	0.30	e	..	6.9	3.9	..	..	..

a. See the technical note for Table 1.   b. Estimated to be low-income ($695 or less).   c. Estimated to be lower-middle income ($696 to $2,785).   d. Estimated to be upper-middle-income ($2,786 to $8,625).   e. Estimated to be high-income ($8,626 or more).

Technical notes

THE MAIN CRITERION FOR COUNTRY CLAS-sification is gross national product (GNP) per capita. For this reason, the 132 economies included in the main tables are listed in ascending GNP per capita order. A separate table (Table 1a) shows basic indicators for 77 economies that have sparse data or have populations of fewer than 1 million. For changes in this edition, see the Introduction.

Data reliability

Considerable effort has been made to standardize the data, but full comparability cannot be ensured, and care must be taken in interpreting the indicators. Many factors affect availability and reliability; statistical systems in many developing economies are still weak; statistical methods, coverage, practices, and definitions differ widely among countries; and cross-country and cross-time comparisons involve complex technical problems that cannot be unequivocally resolved. For these reasons, although the data are drawn from the sources thought to be most authoritative, they should be construed only as indicating trends and characterizing major differences among economies rather than offering precise quantitative measures of those differences. In particular, data issues have yet to be resolved for the fifteen economies of the former Soviet Union. Coverage is sparse, and the data are subject to more than the normal range of uncertainty.

Most social data from national sources are drawn from regular administrative files, although some come from special surveys or periodic census inquiries. Issues related to the reliability of demographic indicators are reviewed in United Nations, *World Population Trends and Policies*. Readers are urged to take these limitations into account in interpreting the indicators, particularly when making comparisons across economies.

Base years

To provide long-term trend analysis, facilitate international comparisons, and include the effects of changes in intersectoral relative prices, constant price data for most economies are partially rebased to three base years and linked together. The year 1970 is the base year for data from 1960 to 1975, 1980 for 1976 to 1982, and 1987 for 1983 and beyond. These three periods are "chain-linked" to obtain 1987 prices throughout all three periods.

Chain-linking is accomplished for each of the three subperiods by rescaling; this moves the year in which current and constant price versions of the same time series have the same value, without altering the trend of either. Components of gross domestic product (GDP) are individually rescaled and summed to provide GDP and its subaggregates. In this process a rescaling deviation may occur between the constant price GDP by industrial origin and the constant price GDP by expenditure. Such rescaling deviations are absorbed under the heading *private consumption, etc.* on the assumption that GDP by industrial origin is a more reliable estimate than GDP by expenditure.

Because private consumption is calculated as a residual, the national accounting identities are maintained. Rebasing does involve incorporating in private consumption whatever statistical discrepancies arise for expenditure. The value added in the services sector also includes a statistical discrepancy, as reported by the original source.

Summary measures

The summary measures are calculated by simple addition when a variable is expressed in reasonably comparable units of account. Economic indicators that do not seem naturally additive are usually combined by a price-weighting scheme. The summary measures for social indicators are weighted by population except for infant mortality, which is weighted by the number of births.

The World Development Indicators provide data for, usually, two reference points rather than annual time series. For summary measures that cover many years, the calculation is based on the same country composition over time and across topics. The Indicators permit group measures to be compiled only if the country data available for a given year account for at least two-thirds of the full group, as defined by the 1987 benchmarks. As long as that criterion is met, noncurrent reporters (and those not providing ample history) are, for years with missing data, assumed to behave like the sample of the group that does provide estimates. Readers should keep in mind that the purpose is to maintain an appropriate relationship across topics, despite myriad problems with country data, and that nothing meaningful can be deduced about behavior at the country level by working back from group indicators. In addition, the weighting process may result in discrepancies between summed subgroup figures and overall totals. This is explained more fully in the introduction to the *World Tables*.

Sources and methods

Data on external debt are compiled directly by the World Bank on the basis of reports from its developing member countries through the Debtor Reporting System. Other data are drawn mainly from the United Nations (U.N.) and its specialized agencies, the International Monetary Fund (IMF), and country reports to the World Bank. Bank staff estimates are also used to improve currentness or consistency. For most countries, national accounts estimates are obtained from member governments through World Bank economic missions. In some instances these are adjusted by Bank staff to ensure conformity with international definitions and concepts, consistency, and currentness.

Growth rates

For ease of reference, only ratios and rates of growth are usually shown; absolute values are generally available from other World Bank publications, notably the 1995 edition of the *World Tables*. Most growth rates are calculated for two periods, 1970–80 and 1980–93, and are computed, unless otherwise noted, by using the least-squares regression method. Because this method takes into account all observations in a period, the resulting growth rates reflect general trends that are not unduly influenced by exceptional values, particularly at the end points. To exclude the effects of inflation, constant price economic indicators are used in calculating growth rates. Details of this methodology are given at the beginning of the technical notes. Data in italics are for years or periods other than those specified—up to two years earlier for economic indicators and up to three years on either side for social indicators, since the latter tend to be collected less regularly and change less dramatically over short periods of time.

All growth rates shown are calculated from constant price series and, unless otherwise noted, have been computed using the least-squares method. The least-squares growth rate, r, is estimated by fitting a least-squares linear regression trend line to the logarithmic annual values of the variable in the relevant period. More specifically, the regression equation takes the form $\log X_t = a + bt + e_t$, where this is equivalent to the logarithmic transformation of the compound growth rate equation, $X_t = X_0 (1 + r)^t$. In these equations, X is the variable, t is time, and $a = \log X_0$ and $b = \log (1 + r)$ are the parameters to be estimated; e is the error term. If b^* is the least-squares estimate of b, then the average annual percentage growth rate, r, is obtained as [antilog (b^*)] –1 and is multiplied by 100 to express it as a percentage.

Table 1. Basic indicators

For basic indicators for economies with sparse data or with populations of fewer than 1 million, see Table 1a.

Population estimates for mid-1993 are from a variety of sources, mainly from the U.N. Population Division, but also from national statistical offices, and World Bank country departments. Note that refugees not permanently settled in the country of asylum are generally considered to be part of the population of their country of origin.

The data on *area* are from the Food and Agriculture Organization (FAO). Area is the total surface area, measured in square kilometers, comprising land area and inland waters.

GNP per capita figures in U.S. dollars are calculated according to the *World Bank Atlas* method, which is described below.

GNP per capita does not, by itself, constitute or measure welfare or success in development. It does not distinguish between the aims and ultimate uses of a given product, nor does it say whether it merely offsets some natural or other obstacle, or harms or contributes to welfare. For example, GNP is higher in colder countries, where people spend money on heating and warm clothes, than in balmy climates, where people are comfortable wearing light clothes in the open air.

More generally, GNP does not deal adequately with environmental issues, particularly natural resource use. The World Bank has joined with others to see how national accounts might provide insights into these issues. "Satellite" accounts that delve into practical and conceptual difficulties (such as assigning a meaningful economic value to resources that markets do not yet perceive as "scarce" and allocating costs that are essentially global within a framework that is inherently national) have been included in the 1993 revision of the *U.N. System of National Accounts* (SNA). This will provide a framework for national accountants to consider environmental factors in estimating alternative measures of income.

GNP measures the total domestic and foreign value added claimed by residents. It comprises GDP (defined in the note for Table 2) plus net factor income from abroad, which is the income residents receive from abroad for factor services (labor and capital) less similar payments made to nonresidents who contributed to the domestic economy.

In estimating GNP per capita, the Bank recognizes that perfect cross-country comparability of GNP per capita estimates cannot be achieved. Beyond the classic, strictly intractable index number problem, two obstacles stand in the way of adequate comparability. One concerns the GNP and population estimates themselves. There are differences in national accounting and demographic reporting systems and in the coverage and reliability of underlying statistical information among various countries. The other obstacle relates to the use of official exchange rates for converting GNP data, expressed in different national currencies, to a common denomination—conventionally the U.S. dollar—to compare them across countries.

Recognizing that these shortcomings affect the comparability of the GNP per capita estimates, the World Bank has introduced several improvements in the estimation procedures. Through its regular review of member countries' national accounts, the Bank systematically evaluates the GNP estimates, focusing on the coverage and concepts employed, and, where appropriate, making adjustments to improve comparability. As part of the review, Bank staff estimates of GNP (and sometimes of population) may be developed for the most recent period. For example, the dollar estimate for China's per capita income is a preliminary figure based on on-going World Bank study on China's GDP. It was calculated to facilitate inter-country comparisons. Official statistics are used as the basis for all other economic analysis contained in this document.

The World Bank also systematically assesses the appropriateness of official exchange rates as conversion factors. An alternative conversion factor is used (and reported in the *World Tables*) when the official exchange rate is judged to diverge by an exceptionally large margin from the rate effectively applied to foreign transactions. This applies to only a small number of countries. For all other countries the Bank calculates GNP per capita using the *World Bank Atlas* method.

The *Atlas* conversion factor for any year is the average of a country's exchange rate for that year and its exchange rates for the two preceding years, after adjusting them for differences in rates of inflation between the country and the G-5 countries (France, Germany, Japan, the United Kingdom, and the United States.) The inflation rate for G-5 countries is represented by changes in the SDR deflators. This three–year average smooths fluctuations in prices and exchange rates for each country. The resulting GNP in U.S. dollars is divided by the midyear population for the latest of the three years to derive GNP per capita.

Some sixty low- and middle-income economies suffered declining real GNP per capita in constant prices during the late 1980s and early 1990s. In addition, significant currency and terms of trade fluctuations have affected relative income levels. For this reason the levels and ranking of GNP per capita estimates, calculated by the *Atlas* method, have sometimes changed in ways not necessarily related to the relative domestic growth performance of the economies.

The following formulas describe the procedures for computing the conversion factor for year t:

$$(e^*_{t-2,t}) = \frac{1}{3}[e_{t-2}\left(\frac{P_t}{P_{t-2}} / \frac{P_t^s}{P_{t-2}^s}\right) + e_{t-1}\left(\frac{P_t}{P_{t-1}} / \frac{P_t^s}{P_{t-1}^s}\right) + e_t]$$

and for calculating per capita GNP in U.S. dollars for year t:

$$(Y_t^\$) = (Y_t / N_t) \div e^*_{t-2,t}$$

where

    Y_t = current GNP (local currency) for year t
    P_t = GNP deflator for year t
    e_t = average annual exchange rate (local currency to the U.S. dollar) for year t
    N_t = midyear population for year t
    P_t^s = SDR deflator for year t

Because of problems associated with the availability of comparable data and the determination of conversion factors, information on GNP per capita is not shown for some economies.

The use of official exchange rates to convert national currency figures to U.S. dollars does not reflect the relative domestic purchasing powers of currencies. The U. N. International Comparison Programme (ICP) has developed measures of real GDP on an internationally comparable scale, using purchasing power parities (PPPs) instead of exchange rates as conversion factors. Table 30 shows the most recent PPP-based GNP per capita estimates. The ICP estimates are expressed in GNP rather than in GDP terms to make them consistent with the estimates in Table 1. Information on the ICP has been published in four studies and in a number of other reports. The most recent study is for 1993, part of which has already been published by the Organization for Economic Cooperation and Development (OECD).

The United Nations and its regional economic commissions, as well as other international agencies, such as the European Union (EU), the OECD, and the World Bank, are working to improve the methodology and to extend annual purchasing power comparisons to all countries. However, exchange rates remain the only generally available means of converting GNP from national currencies to U.S. dollars.

Average annual rate of inflation is measured by the growth rate of the GDP implicit deflator for each of the periods shown. The GDP deflator is first calculated by dividing, for each year of the period, the value of GDP at current values by the value of GDP at constant values, both in national currency. The least-squares method is then used to calculate the growth rate of the GDP deflator for the period. This measure of inflation, like any other, has limitations. For some purposes, however, it is used as an indicator of inflation because it is the most broadly based measure, showing annual price movements for all goods and services produced in an economy.

Life expectancy at birth indicates the number of years a newborn infant would live if prevailing patterns of mortality at the time of its birth were to stay the same throughout its life. The data are from the U.N. Population Division's *World Population Prospects: The 1994 Edition*. These rates are linear interpolations between the projected 1990–94 and 1995–99 rates.

Adult illiteracy is defined here as the proportion of the population over the age of fifteen who cannot, with understanding, read and write a short, simple statement on their everyday life. This is only one of three widely accepted definitions, and its application is subject to qualifiers in a number of countries. The data are from the illiteracy estimates and projections prepared in 1989 by the U.N. Educational, Scientific, and Cultural Organization (UNESCO).

The summary measures for GNP per capita, life expectancy, and adult illiteracy in this table are weighted by population. Those for average annual rates of inflation are weighted by the 1987 share of country GDP valued in current U.S. dollars.

Tables 2 and 3. Growth and structure of production

Most of the definitions used are those of the *U.N. System of National Accounts* (SNA), Series F, No. 2, Revision 3. Revision 4 of the SNA was completed only in 1993, and it is likely that many countries will still be using the recommendations of Revision 3 for the next few years. Estimates are obtained from national sources, sometimes reaching the World Bank through other international agencies but more often collected during World Bank staff missions.

World Bank staff review the quality of national accounts data and in some instances, through mission work or technical assistance, help adjust national series. Because of the sometimes limited capabilities of statistical offices and basic data problems, strict international comparability cannot be achieved, especially in economic activities that are difficult to measure, such as parallel market transactions, the informal sector, or subsistence agriculture.

GDP measures the total output of goods and services for final use produced by residents and nonresidents, regardless of the allocation to domestic and foreign claims. It is calculated without making deductions for depreciation of "fabricated" assets or depletion and degradation of natural resources. Although the SNA envisages estimates of GDP by industrial origin to be at producer prices, many countries still report such details at factor cost. International comparability of the estimates is affected by differing country practices in valuation systems for reporting value added by production sectors. As a partial solution, GDP estimates are shown at purchaser values if the components are on this basis, and such instances are footnoted. However, for a few countries in Tables 2 and 3, GDP at purchaser values has been replaced by GDP at factor cost.

The figures for GDP are U.S. dollar values converted from domestic currencies using single-year official exchange rates. For a few countries where the official exchange rate does not reflect the rate effectively applied to actual foreign exchange transactions, an alternative conversion factor is used (and reported in the *World Tables*). Note that this table does not use the three-year averaging technique applied to GNP per capita in Table 1.

Agriculture covers forestry, hunting, and fishing as well as agriculture. In developing countries with high levels of subsistence farming, much agricultural production is either not exchanged or not exchanged for money. This increases the difficulty of measuring the contribution of agriculture to GDP and reduces the reliability and comparability of such numbers.

Industry comprises value added in mining; *manufacturing* (also reported as a separate subgroup); construction;

and electricity, water, and gas. Value added in all other branches of economic activity, including imputed bank service charges, import duties, and any statistical discrepancies noted by national compilers, are categorized as *services, etc.*

Partially rebased, chain-linked 1987 series in domestic currencies, as explained at the beginning of the technical notes, are used to compute the growth rates in Table 2. The sectoral shares of GDP in Table 3 are based on current price series.

In calculating the summary measures for each indicator in Table 2, partially rebased constant 1987 U.S. dollar values for each economy are calculated for each year of the periods covered; the values are aggregated across countries for each year; and the least-squares procedure is used to compute the growth rates. The average sectoral percentage shares in Table 3 are computed from group aggregates of sectoral GDP in current U.S. dollars.

Table 4. Agriculture and food

The basic data for *value added in agriculture* are from the World Bank's national accounts series at current prices in national currencies. Value added in current prices in national currencies is converted to U.S. dollars by applying the single-year conversion procedure, as described in the technical note for Tables 2 and 3.

The figures for the remainder of this table are from the FAO. *Cereal imports* are measured in grain equivalents and defined as comprising all cereals in the *Standard International Trade Classification* (SITC), Revision 2, Groups 041-046. *Food aid in cereals* covers wheat and flour, bulgur, rice, coarse grains, and the cereal component of blended foods. The figures are not directly comparable because of reporting and timing differences. Cereal imports are generally based on calendar-year data reported by recipient countries, and food aid in cereals is based on data for crop years reported by donors and international organizations, including the International Wheat Council and the World Food Programme. Furthermore, food aid information from donors may not correspond to actual receipts by beneficiaries during a given period because of delays in transportation and recording or because aid is sometimes not reported to the FAO or other relevant international organizations. Food aid imports may also not show up in customs records. The time reference for food aid is the crop year, July to June.

Fertilizer consumption measures the plant nutrients used in relation to arable land. Fertilizer products cover nitrogenous, potash, and phosphate fertilizers (which include ground rock phosphate). Arable land is defined as land under permanent crops and under temporary crops (double-cropped areas are counted once), temporary meadows for mowing or for pasture, as well as land under market or kitchen gardens, and land temporarily fallow or lying idle.

The time reference for fertilizer consumption is the crop year, July to June.

Average growth rate of *food production per capita* has been computed from the index of food production per capita. The index relates to the average annual growth rate of food produced per capita in 1979–93 in relation to the average produced annually in 1979–81 (1979–81=100). The estimates are derived by dividing the quantity of food production by the total population. For the index, food is defined as comprising nuts, pulses, fruits, cereals, vegetables, sugar cane, sugar beet, starchy roots, edible oils, livestock, and livestock products. Quantities of food production are measured net of annual feed, seeds for use in agriculture, and food lost in processing and distribution.

Fish products are measured by the level of daily protein supply derived from the consumption of fish in relation to total daily protein supply from all food. This estimate indirectly highlights the relative importance or weight of fish in total agriculture, especially since fish is not included in the index of food production.

The summary measures for fertilizer consumption are weighted by total arable land area; the summary measures for food production are weighted by population.

Table 5. Commercial energy

The data on *energy production and consumption* are primarily from International Energy Agency (IEA) and U.N. sources. They refer to commercial forms of primary energy—petroleum (crude oil, natural gas liquids, and oil from nonconventional sources), natural gas, solid fuels (coal, lignite, and other derived fuels), and primary electricity (nuclear, hydroelectric, geothermal, and other)—all converted into oil equivalents. For converting nuclear electricity into oil equivalents, a notional thermal efficiency of 33 percent is assumed; hydroelectric power is represented at 100 percent efficiency.

Energy consumption refers to domestic primary energy supply before transformation to other end-use fuels (such as electricity, refined petroleum product) and is calculated as indigenous production plus imports and stock changes, minus exports and international marine bunkers. Energy consumption also includes products for nonenergy uses, mainly derived from petroleum. The use of firewood, dried animal excrement, and other traditional fuels, although substantial in some developing countries, is not taken into account because reliable and comprehensive data are not available.

Energy use is expressed as kilogram oil equivalent per capita. The output indicator is the U.S. dollar estimate of GDP produced per kilogram of oil equivalent.

Energy imports refer to the dollar value of energy imports—Section 3 in the SITC, Revision 1—and are expressed as a percentage of earnings from merchandise exports. Because data on energy imports do not permit a distinction between petroleum imports for fuel and those for use in the petrochemicals industry, these percentages may overestimate dependence on imported energy.

The summary measures of energy production and consumption are computed by aggregating the respective volumes for each of the years covered by the periods and applying the least-squares growth rate procedure. For energy consumption per capita, population weights are used to compute summary measures for the specified years.

The summary measures of energy imports as a percentage of merchandise exports are computed from group aggregates for energy imports and merchandise exports in current dollars.

Table 6. Structure of manufacturing

The basic data for *value added in manufacturing* are from the World Bank's national accounts series at current prices in national currencies. Value added in current prices in national currencies is converted to U.S. dollars by applying the single-year conversion procedure, as described in the technical note for Tables 2 and 3.

The data for *distribution of manufacturing value added* among industries are provided by the United Nations Industrial Development Organization (UNIDO), and distribution calculations are from national currencies in current prices.

The classification of manufacturing industries is in accordance with the U.N. *International Standard Industrial Classification of All Economic Activities* (ISIC), Revision 2. *Food, beverages, and tobacco* comprise ISIC Division 31; *textiles and clothing*, Division 32; *machinery and transport equipment*, Major Groups 382–84; and *chemicals*, Major Groups 351 and 352. *Other* comprises wood and related products (Division 33), paper and related products (Division 34), petroleum and related products (Major Groups 353–56), basic metals and mineral products (Divisions 36 and 37), fabricated metal products and professional goods (Major Groups 381 and 385), and other industries (Major Group 390). When data for textiles, machinery, or chemicals are shown as not available, they are also included in *other*.

Summary measures given for value added in manufacturing are totals calculated by the aggregation method noted at the beginning of the technical notes.

Table 7. Manufacturing earnings and output

Four indicators are shown: two relate to real earnings per employee, one to labor's share in total value added generated, and one to labor productivity in the manufacturing sector. The indicators are based on data from UNIDO; the deflators are from other sources, as explained below.

Earnings per employee are in constant prices and are derived by deflating nominal earnings per employee by the country's consumer price index (CPI). The CPI is from the IMF's *International Financial Statistics.*

Total earnings as a percentage of value added are derived by dividing total earnings of employees by value added in current prices to show labor's share in income generated in the manufacturing sector. *Gross output per employee* is in constant prices and is presented as an index of overall labor productivity in manufacturing, with 1980 as the base year. To derive this indicator, UNIDO data on gross output per employee in current prices are adjusted using implicit deflators for value added in manufacturing or in industry, taken from the World Bank's national accounts data files.

To improve cross-country comparability, UNIDO has, where possible, standardized the coverage of establishments to those with five or more employees.

The concepts and definitions are in accordance with the *International Recommendations for Industrial Statistics,* published by the United Nations. Earnings (wages and salaries) cover all remuneration to employees paid by the employer during the year. The payments include (a) all regular and overtime cash payments and bonuses and cost of living allowances; (b) wages and salaries paid during vacation and sick leave; (c) taxes and social insurance contributions and the like, payable by the employees and deducted by the employer; and (d) payments in kind.

The term "employees" in this table combines two categories defined by the United Nations: regular employees and persons engaged. Together these groups comprise regular employees, working proprietors, active business partners, and unpaid family workers; they exclude homeworkers. The data refer to the average number of employees working during the year.

"Value added" is defined as the current value of gross output less the current cost of (a) materials, fuels, and other supplies consumed; (b) contract and commission work done by others; (c) repair and maintenance work done by others; and (d) goods shipped in the same condition as received.

The value of gross output is estimated on the basis of either production or shipments. On the production basis it consists of (a) the value of all products of the establishment; (b) the value of industrial services rendered to others; (c) the value of goods shipped in the same condition as received; (d) the value of electricity sold; and (e) the net change in the value of work-in-progress between the beginning and the end of the reference period. In the case of estimates compiled on a shipment basis, the net change between the beginning and the end of the reference period in the value of stocks of finished goods is also included.

Tables 8 and 9. Growth of consumption and investment; structure of demand

GDP is defined in the note for Tables 2 and 3, but here it is in purchaser values for all countries.

General government consumption includes all current expenditure for purchases of goods and services by all levels of government. Capital expenditure on national defense and security is regarded as consumption expenditure.

Private consumption, etc. is the market value of all goods and services, including durable products (such as cars, washing machines, and home computers) purchased or received as income in kind by households and nonprofit institutions. It excludes purchases of dwellings but includes imputed rent for owner-occupied dwellings. In practice, it includes any statistical discrepancy in the use of resources. At constant prices, it also includes the rescaling deviation from partial rebasing, which is explained at the beginning of the technical notes.

Gross domestic investment consists of outlays on additions to the fixed assets of the economy plus net changes in the level of inventories.

Gross domestic savings are calculated by deducting total consumption from GDP.

*Exports of goods and nonfactor service*s represent the value of all goods and nonfactor services provided to the rest of the world; they include merchandise, freight, insurance, travel, and other nonfactor services. The value of factor services, such as investment income, interest, and labor income, is excluded. Current transfers are also excluded.

The *resource balance* is the difference between exports of goods and nonfactor services and imports of goods and nonfactor services.

Partially rebased 1987 series in constant domestic currency units are used to compute growth rates in the Table 8. Distribution of GDP in Table 9 is calculated from national accounts series in current domestic currency units.

The summary measures are calculated by the method explained in the note for Tables 2 and 3.

Table 10. Central government expenditure

The data on central government finance in Tables 10 and 11 are from the IMF, *Government Finance Statistics Yearbook* (1994), and IMF data files. The accounts of each country are reported using the system of common definitions and classifications found in the IMF's *Manual on Government Finance Statistics* (1986).

For complete and authoritative explanations of concepts, definitions, and data sources, see these IMF sources. The commentary that follows is intended mainly to place these data in the context of the broad range of indicators reported in this edition.

The shares of *total expenditure* and current revenue by category are calculated from series in national currencies. Because of differences in coverage of available data, the individual components of central government expenditure and current revenue shown in these tables may not be strictly comparable across all economies.

Moreover, inadequate statistical coverage of state, provincial, and local governments dictates the use of central government data; this may seriously understate or distort the statistical portrayal of the allocation of resources for various purposes, especially in countries where lower levels of government have considerable autonomy and are responsible for many economic and social services. In addition, "central government" can mean either of two accounting concepts: consolidated or budgetary. For most countries, central government finance data have been consolidated into one overall account, but for others only the budgetary central government accounts are available. Since budgetary accounts do not always include all central government units, the overall picture of central government activities is usually incomplete. Countries reporting budgetary data are footnoted.

Consequently, the data presented, especially those for education and health, are not comparable across countries. In many economies, private health and education services are substantial; in others, public services represent the major component of total expenditure but may be financed by lower levels of government. Caution should therefore be exercised in using the data for cross-country comparisons. Central government expenditure comprises the expenditure by all government offices, departments, establishments, and other bodies that are agencies or instruments of the central authority of a country. It includes both current and capital (development) expenditure.

Defense comprises all expenditure, whether by defense or other departments, on the maintenance of military forces, including the purchase of military supplies and equipment, construction, recruiting, and training. Also in this category are closely related items such as military aid programs. Defense does not include expenditure on public order and safety, which are classified separately.

Education comprises expenditure on the provision, management, inspection, and support of preprimary, primary, and secondary schools; of universities and colleges; and of vocational, technical, and other training institutions. Also included is expenditure on the general administration and regulation of the education system; on research into its objectives, organization, administration, and methods; and on such subsidiary services as transport, school meals, and school medical and dental services.

Health covers public expenditure on hospitals, maternity and dental centers, and clinics with a major medical component; on national health and medical insurance schemes; and on family planning and preventive care.

Housing, amenities, social security, and welfare cover expenditure on housing (excluding interest subsidies, which are usually classified with *other*) such as income-related schemes; on provision and support of housing and slum-clearance activities; on community development; and on

sanitation services. These categories also cover compensation for loss of income to the sick and temporarily disabled; payments to the elderly, the permanently disabled, and the unemployed; family, maternity, and child allowances; and the cost of welfare services, such as care of the aged, the disabled, and children. Many expenditures relevant to environmental defense, such as pollution abatement, water supply, sanitary affairs, and refuse collection, are included indistinguishably in this category.

Economic services comprise expenditure associated with the regulation, support, and more efficient operation of business; economic development; redress of regional imbalances; and creation of employment opportunities. Research, trade promotion, geological surveys, and inspection and regulation of particular industry groups are among the activities included.

Other covers general public services, interest payments, and items not included elsewhere; for a few economies it also includes amounts that could not be allocated to other components (or adjustments from accrual to cash accounts).

Total expenditure is more narrowly defined than the measure of general government consumption given in Tables 8 and 9 because it excludes consumption expenditure by state and local governments. At the same time, central government expenditure is more broadly defined because it includes government's gross domestic investment and transfer payments.

Overall surplus/deficit is defined as current and capital revenue and official grants received, less total expenditure and lending minus repayments.

Table 11. Central government current revenue

Information on data sources and comparability and the definition of central government is given in the first four paragraphs of the note for Table 10. Current revenue by source is expressed as a percentage of *total current revenue,* which is the sum of tax revenue and nontax revenue and is calculated from national currencies.

Tax revenue comprises compulsory, unrequited, nonrepayable receipts for public purposes. It includes interest collected on tax arrears and penalties collected on nonpayment or late payment of taxes and is shown net of refunds and other corrective transactions. *Taxes on income, profit, and capital gains* are taxes levied on the actual or presumptive net income of individuals, on the profits of enterprises, and on capital gains, whether realized on land sales, securities, or other assets. Intragovernmental payments are eliminated in consolidation. *Social security* contributions include employers' and employees' social security contributions as well as those of self-employed and unemployed persons. *Domestic taxes on goods and services* include general sales and turnover or value added taxes, selective excises on goods, selective taxes on services, taxes on the use of goods or property, and profits of fiscal monopolies. *Taxes on international trade and transactions* include import duties, export duties, profits of export or import monopolies, exchange profits, and exchange taxes. *Other taxes* include employers' payroll or labor taxes, taxes on property, and taxes not allocable to other categories. They may include negative values that are adjustments, for instance, for taxes collected on behalf of state and local governments and not allocable to individual tax categories.

Nontax revenue comprises receipts that are not a compulsory nonrepayable payment for public purposes, such as fines, administrative fees, or entrepreneurial income from government ownership of property. Proceeds of grants and borrowing, funds arising from the repayment of previous lending by governments, incurrence of liabilities, and proceeds from the sale of capital assets are not included.

Table 12. Money and interest rates

The data on *broadly defined money* are based on the IMF's *International Financial Statistics* (IFS). Broadly defined money comprises most liabilities of a country's monetary institutions to residents other than the central government. For most countries, broadly defined money is the sum of money (IFS line 34) and quasi-money (IFS line 35). Money comprises the economy's means of payment: currency outside banks and demand deposits. Quasi-money comprises time and savings deposits and similar bank accounts that the issuer can exchange for money with little if any delay or penalty. Where nonmonetary financial institutions are important issuers of quasi-monetary liabilities, these are often included in the measure of broadly defined money.

The growth rates for broadly defined money are calculated from year-end figures, while the average of the year-end figures for the specified year and the previous year is used for the ratio of broadly defined money to GDP.

The *nominal interest rates of banks*, also from IFS, represent the rates paid by commercial or similar banks to holders of their quasi-monetary liabilities (deposit rate) and charged by the banks on loans to prime customers (lending rate). The data are, however, of limited international comparability partly because coverage and definitions vary.

Since interest rates (and growth rates for broadly defined money) are expressed in nominal terms, much of the variation among countries stems from differences in inflation. For easy reference, the Table 1 indicator of recent inflation is repeated in this table.

Table 13. Growth of merchandise trade

The main data source for current trade values is the U.N. Conference on Trade and Development (UNCTAD) trade

database supplemented by the data from the IMF's *International Financial Statistics* (IFS), the U.N.'s Commodity Trade (COMTRADE) database, and World Bank estimates.

Merchandise *exports* and *imports*, with some exceptions, cover international movements of goods across customs borders; trade in services is not included. Exports are valued f.o.b. (free on board) and imports c.i.f. (cost, insurance, and freight) unless otherwise specified in the foregoing sources. These values are in current U. S. dollars.

The growth rates of merchandise exports and imports are based on constant price data, which are obtained from export or import value data as deflated by the corresponding price indicies. The World Bank uses the price indexes produced by UNCTAD for low- and middle-income economies, and those presented in the IMF's IFS for high-income economies. These growth rates can differ from those derived from national sources because national price indexes may use different base years and weighting procedures from those used by UNCTAD.

The *terms of trade*, or the net barter terms of trade, measure the relative movement of export prices against that of import prices. Calculated as the ratio of a country's index of average export prices to its average import price index, this indicator shows changes over a base year in the level of export prices as a percentage of import prices. The terms of trade index numbers are shown for 1985 and 1993, where 1987 = 100. The price indexes are from the source cited above for the growth rates of exports and imports.

The summary measures for the growth rates are calculated by aggregating the 1987 constant U.S. dollar price series for each year and then applying the least-squares growth rate procedure for the periods shown.

Tables 14 and 15. Structure of merchandise imports and exports

The shares in these tables are derived from trade values in current dollars reported in the UNCTAD trade data system, supplemented by data from the U.N. COMTRADE system.

Merchandise *exports* and *imports* are defined in the technical note for Table 13.

The categorization of exports and imports follows the *Standard International Trade Classification* (SITC), Series M, No. 34, Revision 1. For some countries, data for certain commodity categories are unavailable and the full breakdown cannot be shown.

In Table 14, *food* commodities are those in SITC Sections 0, 1, and 4 and Division 22 (food and live animals, beverages and tobacco, animal and vegetable oils and fats, oilseeds, oil nuts and oil kernels). *Fuels* are the commodities in SITC Section 3 (mineral fuels, and lubricants and related materials). *Other primary commodities* comprise SITC Section 2 (inedible crude materials, except fuels), less Division 22 (oilseeds, oilnuts, and oil kernels) and Division 68 (nonferrous metals). *Machinery and transport equipment* are the commodities in SITC Section 7. *Other manufactures*, calculated residually from the total value of manufactured imports, represent SITC Sections 5 through 9, less Section 7 and Division 68.

In Table 15, *fuels, minerals, and metals* are the commodities in SITC Section 3 (mineral fuels, and lubricants and related materials), Divisions 27 and 28 (crude fertilizers and crude minerals, excluding coal, petroleum and precious stones, and metalliferous ores and metal scrap), and Division 68 (nonferrous metals). *Other primary commodities* comprise SITC Sections 0, 1, 2, and 4 (food and live animals, beverages and tobacco, inedible crude materials, except fuels, and animal and vegetable oils and fats), less Divisions 27 and 28. *Machinery and transport equipment* are the commodities in SITC Section 7. *Other manufactures* represent SITC Sections 5 through 9, less Section 7 and Division 68. *Textile fibers, textiles, and clothing*, representing SITC Divisions 26, 65 and 84 (textiles, textile fibers, yarn, fabrics, made-up articles, and related products and clothing), are a subgroup of *other primary commodities* and of *other manufactures*; it is a memo item.

Table 16. OECD imports of manufactured goods

The data are from the United Nations and were reported by high-income OECD economies—the OECD members excluding Greece, Mexico, Portugal, and Turkey.

The table reports the *value of imports of manufactures* of high-income OECD countries by the economy of origin and the composition of such imports by major manufactured product groups. These data are based on the U.N. COMTRADE database—Revision 1 SITC for 1970 and Revision 2 SITC for 1993.

Manufactured imports of the predominant markets from individual economies are the best available proxy of the magnitude and composition of the manufactured exports of developing economies to all destinations taken together.

Manufactured goods are the commodities in the SITC, Revision 1, Sections 5 through 9 (chemical and related products, basic manufactures, manufactured articles, machinery and transport equipment, and other manufactured articles and goods not elsewhere classified), excluding Division 68 (nonferrous metals). This definition is somewhat broader than the one used to define exporters of manufactures.

The major manufactured product groups reported are defined as follows: *textiles and clothing* (SITC Sections 65 and 84), *chemicals* (SITC Section 5), *electrical machinery*

and electronics (SITC Section 72), *transport equipment* (SITC Section 73), and *other*, defined as the residual. SITC Revision 1 data are used for the year 1970, whereas the equivalent data in Revision 2 are used for the year 1993.

Table 17. Balance of payments and reserves

The statistics for this table are mostly as reported by the IMF but do include estimates by World Bank staff and, in rare instances, the Bank's own coverage or classification adjustments to enhance international comparability. Values in this table are in U.S. dollars converted at current exchange rates.

The *current account balance after official transfers* is the difference between (a) exports of goods and services (factor and nonfactor), as well as inflows of unrequited transfers (private and official) and (b) imports of goods and services, as well as all unrequited transfers to the rest of the world.

The *current account balance before official transfers* is the current account balance that treats net official unrequited transfers as akin to official capital movements. The difference between the two balance of payments measures is essentially foreign aid in the form of grants, technical assistance, and food aid, which, for most developing countries, tends to make current account deficits smaller than the financing requirement.

Net workers' remittances cover payments and receipts of income by migrants who are employed or expect to be employed for more than a year in their new economy, where they are considered residents. These remittances are classified as private unrequited transfers and are included in the balance of payments current account balance, whereas those derived from shorter-term stays are included in services as labor income. The distinction accords with internationally agreed guidelines, but many developing countries classify workers' remittances as a factor income receipt (hence, a component of GNP). The World Bank adheres to international guidelines in defining GNP and therefore may differ from national practices.

Gross international reserves comprise holdings of monetary gold, special drawing rights (SDRs), the reserve position of members in the IMF, and holdings of foreign exchange under the control of monetary authorities. The data on holdings of international reserves are from IMF data files. The gold component of these reserves is valued throughout at year-end (December 31) London prices: that is, $37.37 an ounce in 1970 and $390.6 an ounce in 1993. Because of differences in the definition of international reserves, in the valuation of gold, and in reserve management practices, the levels of reserve holdings published in national sources do not have strictly comparable significance. The reserve levels for 1970 and 1993 refer to the end of the year indicated and are in current U.S. dollars at prevailing exchange rates. Reserve holdings at the end of 1993, *months of import coverage*, are also expressed in terms of the number of months of imports of goods and services they could pay for.

The summary measures are computed from group aggregates for gross international reserves and total imports of goods and services in current dollars.

Table 18. Official development assistance from OECD and OPEC members

Official development assistance (ODA) consists of net disbursements of loans and grants made on concessional financial terms by official agencies of the members of the Development Assistance Committee (DAC) of the Organization for Economic Cooperation and Development (OECD) and members of the Organization of Petroleum Exporting Countries (OPEC) to promote economic development and welfare. Although this definition is meant to exclude purely military assistance, the borderline is sometimes blurred; the definition used by the country of origin usually prevails. ODA also includes the value of technical cooperation and assistance. All data shown are supplied by the OECD, and all U.S. dollar values are converted at official exchange rates.

Total net flows are net disbursements to developing countries and multilateral institutions. The disbursements to multilateral institutions are now reported for all DAC members on the basis of the date of issue of notes; some DAC members previously reported on the basis of the date of encashment.

The nominal values shown in the summary for ODA from high-income OECD countries were converted at 1992 prices using the dollar GDP deflator. This deflator is based on price increases in OECD countries (excluding Greece, Mexico, Portugal, and Turkey) measured in dollars. It takes into account the parity changes between the dollar and national currencies. For example, when the dollar depreciates, price changes measured in national currencies have to be adjusted upward by the amount of the depreciation to obtain price changes in dollars.

The table, in addition to showing totals for OPEC, shows totals for the Organization of Arab Petroleum Exporting Countries (OAPEC). The donor members of OAPEC are Algeria, Iraq, Kuwait, Libya, Qatar, Saudi Arabia, and United Arab Emirates. ODA data for OPEC and OAPEC are also obtained from the OECD.

Table 19. Official development assistance: receipts

Net disbursements of ODA from all sources consist of loans and grants made on concessional financial terms by all bilateral official agencies and multilateral sources to promote economic development and welfare. They include the value of technical cooperation and assistance. The disbursements

shown in this table are not strictly comparable with those shown in Table 18 since the receipts are from all sources; disbursements in Table 18 refer only to those made by high-income members of the OECD and members of OPEC. Net disbursements equal gross disbursements less payments to the originators of aid for amortization of past aid receipts. Net disbursements of ODA are shown per capita and as a percentage of GNP.

The summary measures of per capita ODA are computed from group aggregates for population and for ODA. Summary measures for ODA as a percentage of GNP are computed from group totals for ODA and for GNP in current U.S. dollars.

Table 20. Total external debt

The data on debt in this and successive tables are from the World Bank Debtor Reporting System, supplemented by World Bank estimates. The system is concerned solely with developing economies and does not collect data on external debt for other groups of borrowers or from economies that are not members of the World Bank. The dollar figures on debt shown in Tables 20 through 24 are in U.S. dollars converted at official exchange rates.

The data on debt include private nonguaranteed debt reported by thirty developing countries and complete or partial estimates for an additional twenty that do not report but for which this type of debt is known to be significant.

Long-term debt has three components: public, publicly guaranteed and private non-guaranteed loans. Public loans are external obligations of public debtors, including the national government, its agencies, and autonomous public bodies. Publicly guaranteed loans are external obligations of private debtors that are guaranteed for repayment by a public entity. These two categories are aggregated in the tables. Private nonguaranteed loans are external obligations of private debtors that are not guaranteed for repayment by a public entity.

Use of IMF credit denotes repurchase obligations to the IMF for all uses of IMF resources, excluding those resulting from drawings in the reserve tranche. It is shown for the end of the year specified. It comprises purchases outstanding under the credit tranches, including enlarged access resources, and all special facilities (the buffer stock, compensatory financing, extended fund, and oil facilities), trust fund loans, and operations under the enhanced structural adjustment facilities. Use of IMF credit outstanding at year-end (a stock) is converted to U.S. dollars at the dollar-SDR exchange rate in effect at year-end.

Short-term debt is debt with an original maturity of one year or less. It includes interest arrears on LDOD due but not paid, on a cumulative basis. Available data permit no distinctions between public and private nonguaranteed short-term debt.

Total external debt is defined here as the sum of public, publicly guaranteed, and private nonguaranteed long-term debt, use of IMF credit, and short-term debt.

Total arrears on long-term debt outstanding and disbursed (LDOD) denotes principal and interest due but not paid.

Ratio of present value to nominal value is the discounted value of the future debt service payments divided by the face value of debt.

Table 21. Flow of public and private external capital

Data on disbursements, repayment of principal (amortization), and payment of interest are for public, publicly guaranteed, and private nonguaranteed long-term loans.

Disbursements are drawings on long-term loan commitments during the year specified.

Repayment of principal is the actual amount of principal (amortization) paid in foreign currency, goods, or services in the year specified.

Interest payments are actual amounts of interest paid in foreign currency, goods, or services in the year specified.

Table 22. Aggregate net resource flows and net transfers

Total net flows on long-term debt are disbursements less the repayment of principal on public, publicly guaranteed, and private nonguaranteed long-term debt. *Official grants* are transfers made by an official agency in cash or in kind in respect of which no legal debt is incurred by the recipient. Data on official grants exclude grants for technical assistance.

Net foreign direct investment (FDI) in the reporting economy is defined as investment that is made to acquire a lasting interest (usually 10 percent of the voting stock) in an enterprise operating in a country other than that of the investor (defined according to residency), the investor's purpose being an effective voice in the management of the enterprise.

Portfolio equity flows is the sum of the country funds (note that the sum of regional or income-group flows does not add up to the total due to the global funds), depository receipts (American or global), and direct purchases of shares by foreign investors.

Aggregate net resource flows are the sum of net flows on long-term debt (excluding use of IMF credit), plus official grants (excluding technical assistance) net foreign direct investment and portfolio equity flows. *Aggregate net transfers* are equal to aggregate net resource flows minus interest payments on long-term loans and remittance of all profits.

Table 23. Total external debt ratios

Net present value of total external debt as a percentage of exports of goods and services is the discounted value of future debt service to exports of goods and services.

The present value can be higher or lower than the nominal value of debt. The determining factor for the present value being above or below par are the interest rates of loans and the discount rate used in the present value calculation. A loan with an interest rate higher than the discount rate yields a present value that is larger than the nominal value of debt: the opposite holds for loans with an interest rate lower than the discount rate. Throughout this table, goods and services include workers' remittances. For estimating *net present value of total external debt as a percentage of GNP*, the debt figures are converted into U.S. dollars from currencies of repayment at end-of-year official exchange rates. GNP is converted from national currencies to U.S. dollars by applying the conversion procedure described in the technical note for Tables 2 and 3.

Total debt service as a percentage of exports of goods and services is the sum of principal repayments and interest payments on total external debt (as defined in the note for Table 20). It is one of several conventional measures used to assess a country's ability to service debt.

Interest payments as a percentage of exports of goods and services are actual payments made on total external debt.

Concessional debt as a percentage of total external debt conveys information about the borrower's receipt of aid from official lenders at concessional terms as defined by the DAC, that is, loans with an original grant element of 25 percent or more.

Multilateral debt as a percentage of total external debt conveys information about the borrower's receipt of aid from the World Bank, regional development banks, and other multilateral and intergovernmental agencies. Excluded are loans from funds administered by an international organization on behalf of a single donor government.

The summary measures are weighted by exports of goods and services in current dollars and by GNP in current dollars, respectively.

Table 24. Terms of external public borrowing

Commitments refer to the public and publicly guaranteed loans for which contracts were signed in the year specified. They are reported in currencies of repayment and converted into U.S. dollars at average annual official exchange rates.

Figures for *interest rates, maturities*, and *grace periods* are averages weighted by the amounts of the loans. Interest is the major charge levied on a loan and is usually computed on the amount of principal drawn and outstanding. The maturity of a loan is the interval between the agreement date, when a loan agreement is signed or bonds are issued, and the date of final repayment of principal. The grace period is the interval between the agreement date and the date of the first repayment of principal.

Public loans with variable interest rates, as a percentage of public debt refer to interest rates that float with movements in a key market rate; for example, the London interbank offered rate (LIBOR) or the U.S. prime rate. This column shows the borrower's exposure to changes in international interest rates.

The summary measures in this table are weighted by the amounts of the loans.

Table 25. Population and labor force

For changes in source and content of demographic data, see the introduction.

Population estimates for mid-1993 are from a variety of sources, including the UN Population Division, national statistical offices, and World Bank country departments. Note that refugees not permanently settled in the country of asylum are generally considered to be part of the population of their country of origin.

The projections of population for 2000 and 2025, are from the UN Population Division.

Total labor force estimates are from the International Labor Organization and cover the "economically active" population; a restrictive concept that includes the armed forces and the unemployed but excludes homemakers and other unpaid caregivers. Labor force numbers in several developing countries reflect a significant underestimation of female participation rates.

Population and labor force growth rates are exponential period averages calculated from midyear populations and total labor force estimates.

Table 26. Demography and fertility

For changes in source and content of demographic data, see the introduction.

The *crude birth rate* and *crude death rate* indicate, respectively, the number of live births and deaths occurring per thousand population in a year. The data are from the U.N. Population Division. The rates for 1970 and 1993 are linear interpolation between the 1965–69 and 1970–74 and projected 1990–94 and 1995–99 rates respectively.

The *total fertility rate* represents the number of children that would be born to a woman if she were to live to the end of her childbearing years and bear children at each age in accordance with prevailing age-specific fertility rates. The data sources and methodology are the same as in the crude birth rate. The rate for the year 2000 is the linear interpolation between the projected 1995–99 and 2000–04 rates.

Births to women under age 20 and *over age 35* are shown as a percentage of all births. These births are often high-risk because of the greater risk of complications during pregnancy and childbirth. Children born to very young or to older women are also more vulnerable. The data are from the U.N. Population Division.

Married women of childbearing age using contraception are women who are practicing, or whose husbands are practicing, any form of contraception. Contraceptive usage is generally measured for married women age 15 to 49. A few countries use measures relating to other age groups, especially 15 to 44.

Data are mainly derived from demographic and health surveys, contraceptive prevalence surveys, and World Bank country data. For a few countries for which no survey data are available and for several African countries, program statistics are used. Program statistics may understate contraceptive prevalence because they do not measure use of methods such as rhythm, withdrawal, or abstinence, or use of contraceptives not obtained through the official family planning program. The data refer to rates prevailing in a variety of years, generally not more than three years before and one year after the year specified in the table.

All summary measures are country data weighted by population.

Table 27. Health and nutrition

For changes in source and content of demographic data, see the introduction.

The estimates of *population per physician* and *per nursing person* are derived from World Health Organization (WHO) data and are supplemented by data obtained directly by the World Bank from national sources. The data refer to a variety of years, generally no more than two years before the year specified. Nursing persons include auxiliary nurses, as well as paraprofessional personnel such as traditional birth attendants. The inclusion of auxiliary and paraprofessional personnel provides more realistic estimates of available nursing care. Because definitions of doctors and nursing personnel vary—and because the data shown are for a variety of years—the data for these two indicators are not strictly comparable across countries.

Low birthweight babies are children born weighing less than 2,500 grams. Low birthweight is frequently associated with maternal malnutrition. It tends to raise the risk of infant mortality and to lead to poor growth in infancy and childhood, thus increasing the incidence of other forms of retarded development. The figures are derived from both WHO and U.N. Children's Fund (UNICEF) sources and are based on national data. The data are not strictly comparable across countries because they are compiled from a combination of surveys and administrative records that may not have representative national coverage.

The *infant mortality rate* is the number of infants who die before reaching one year of age, per thousand live births in a given year. The data and methodology are the same as in the crude birth rate.

Prevalence of malnutrition measures the percentage of children under 5 with a deficiency or an excess of nutrients that interfere with their health and genetic potential for growth. Methods of assessment vary, but the most commonly used are the following: less than 80 percent of the standard weight for age; less than minus 2 standard deviation from the 50th percentile of the weight-for-age reference population; and the Gomez scale of malnutrition. Note that for a few countries the figures are for children 3 or 4 years of age and younger.

The *under-5 mortality* rate shows the probability of a newborn baby dying before reaching age 5. It is subject to current age-specific mortality rates. The data for this edition are from UNICEF's *State of the World's Children 1995*, except for countries for which the U.N. Population Division estimates of infant mortality rate are higher. For such countries, models are used to adjust the under-5 mortality rate. Because most of the under-5 mortality rates do not come from the same source as the infant mortality rate and life expectancy at birth, mortality rates are not always consistent.

The summary measures in this table are country data weighted by population, except for infant mortality rate, which in this edition is weighted by births.

Table 28. Education

The data in this table refer to a variety of years, generally not more than two years distant from those specified. Figures for females, however, sometimes refer to a year earlier than that for overall totals. The data are mostly from UNESCO.

Primary school enrollment data are estimates of the ratio of children of all ages enrolled in primary school to the country's population of school-age children. Although many countries consider primary school age to be 6 to 11 years, others do not. For some countries with universal primary education, the gross enrollment ratios may exceed 100 percent because some pupils are younger or older than the country's standard primary school age.

The data on *secondary* school enrollment are calculated in the same manner, and again the definition of secondary school age differs among countries. It is most commonly considered to be 12 to 17 years. Late entry of more mature students as well as repetition and the phenomenon of "bunching" in final grades can influence these ratios.

The *tertiary* enrollment ratio is calculated by dividing the number of pupils enrolled in all post-secondary schools and universities by the population in the 20–24 age group. Pupils attending vocational schools, adult education programs, two-year community colleges, and distant education centers (primarily correspondence courses) are included. The distribution of pupils across these different types of institutions varies among countries. The youth population—that is, 20 to 24 years— has been adopted by UNESCO as the denominator, since it represents an average tertiary level cohort even though people above and below this age group may be registered in tertiary institutions.

Primary net enrollment is the percentage of school-age children who are enrolled in school. Unlike gross enrollment, the net ratios correspond to the country's primary-school age group. This indicator gives a much clearer idea of how many children in the age group are actually enrolled in school without the numbers being inflated by over- or under-age children.

The *primary pupil–teacher ratio* is the number of pupils enrolled in school in a country divided by the number of teachers in the education system.

The summary measures in this table are country enrollment rates weighted by each country's share in the aggregate population.

Table 29. Gender comparisons

For changes in source and content of demographic data, see the introduction.

This table provides selected basic indicators disaggregated to show differences between the sexes that illustrate the condition of women in society. The measures reflect the demographic status of women and their access to health and education services. Statistical anomalies become even more apparent when social indicators are analyzed by gender because reporting systems are often weak in areas related specifically to women. Indicators drawn from censuses and surveys, such as those on population, tend to be about as reliable for women as for men; but indicators based largely on administrative records, such as maternal mortality, are less reliable. More resources are now being devoted to developing better information on these topics, but the reliability of data, even in the series shown, still varies significantly.

The maternal mortality statistics draw attention, in particular, to discrimination affecting women, and to the conditions associated with childbearing. Childbearing still carries the highest risk of death for women of reproductive age in developing countries. The indicator reflects, but does not measure, both the availability of health services for women and the general welfare and nutritional status of mothers.

Life expectancy at birth is defined in the note to Table 1. The data source and methodology are as in the crude birth rate (Table 26).

Maternal mortality refers to the number of female deaths that occur during childbirth per 100,000 live births. Because deaths during childbirth are defined more widely in some countries to include complications of pregnancy or the period after childbirth, or of abortion, and because many pregnant women die from lack of suitable health care, maternal mortality is difficult to measure consistently and reliably across countries. The data are drawn from diverse national sources and collected by the World Health Organization (WHO), although many national administrative systems are weak and do not record vital events in a systematic way. The data are derived mostly from official community reports and hospital records, and some reflect only deaths in hospitals and other medical institutions. Sometimes smaller private and rural hospitals are excluded, and sometimes even relatively primitive local facilities are included. The coverage is therefore not always comprehensive, and the figures should be treated with extreme caution.

Clearly, many maternal deaths go unrecorded, particularly in countries with remote rural populations. This accounts for some of the very low numbers shown in the table, especially for several African countries. Moreover, it is not clear whether an increase in the number of mothers in hospital reflects more extensive medical care for women or more complications in pregnancy and childbirth because of poor nutrition, for instance. (Table 27 shows data on low birth weight.)

These time series attempt to bring together readily available information not always presented in international publications. WHO warns that there are inevitably gaps in the series, and it has invited countries to provide more comprehensive figures.

The *education* indicators, based on UNESCO sources, show the extent to which females have equal access to schooling.

Percentage of cohort persisting to grade 4 is the percentage of children starting primary school in 1970 and 1988, respectively, who continued to the fourth grade by 1973 and 1991. Figures in italics represent earlier or later cohorts. The data are based on enrollment records. The slightly higher persistence ratios for females in some African countries may indicate male participation in activities such as animal herding.

All things being equal, and opportunities being the same, the ratios for *females per 100 males* should be close to 100. However, inequalities may cause the ratios to move in different directions. For example, the number of females per 100 males will rise at secondary school level if male attendance declines more rapidly in the final grades because of males' greater job opportunities, conscription into the army, or migration in search of work. In addition, since the numbers in these columns refer mainly to general secondary education, they do not capture those (mostly males) enrolled in technical and vocational schools or in full-time apprenticeships, as in Eastern Europe.

Females as a percentage of total labor force, based on ILO data, shows the extent to which women are "gainfully employed" in the formal sector. These numbers exclude homemakers and other unpaid caregivers and in several developing countries reflect a significant underestimate of female participation rates.

All summary measures are country data weighted by each country's share in the aggregate population or population subgroup.

Table 30. Income distribution and PPP estimates of GNP

The first set of columns reports distribution of income or expenditure accruing to percentile groups of population

ranked by per capita income, expenditure, or, as in the case of the high-income countries, by total household income. The last three columns contain estimates of per capita GNP based on purchasing power parities (PPPs) rather than exchange rates (see the definition of PPP below).

Columns 2 through 7 give the shares of population or household quintiles and the top decile in total income or consumption expenditure for 51 low- and middle-income countries and 20 high-income countries. The data sets for these countries refer to different years between 1978 and 1993 and are drawn mostly from nationally representative household surveys.

The data sets for the low- and middle-income countries have been compiled from two main sources: government statistical agencies (often using published reports) and the World Bank (mostly data originating from the Living Standards Measurement Study and the Social Dimensions of Adjustment Project for Sub-Saharan Africa). Where the original unit record data from the household survey were available, these have been used to calculate directly the income (or expenditure) shares of different quantiles; otherwise, the latter have been estimated from the best available grouped data. For further details on both the data and the estimation methodology for low- and middle-income countries, see Chen, Datt, and Ravallion, "Is Poverty Increasing in the Developing World?" Policy Research Working Papers WPS 1146, World Bank, 1993. The data for Australia, Canada, Israel, Italy, Norway, Sweden, Switzerland, and the United States are from the Luxembourg Income Study database (1990); those for France, Germany, Netherlands, Spain and the United Kingdom from the Statistical Office of the European Union. The data for Belgium, Denmark, Finland, Japan, and New Zealand come from the U.N. *National Accounts Statistics: Compendium of Income Distribution Statistics, 1985*. Data for other high-income countries come from national sources.

There are significant comparability problems across countries in the income distribution data presented here. The underlying household surveys are not fully comparable across countries, even though these problems are diminishing over time as survey methodologies are both improving and becoming more standardized, particularly under the initiatives of the United Nations (under the Household Survey Capability Program) and the World Bank (under the Living Standards Measurement Study and the Social Dimensions of Adjustment Project for Sub–Saharan Africa). In particular, the following three sources of noncomparability ought to be noted. First, the surveys differ in the use of income or consumption expenditure as the living standard indicator. For 34 of the 51 low- and middle-income countries, the data refer to consumption expenditure. Typically, income is more unequally distributed than consumption. Second, the surveys differ in the use of the household or the individual as their unit of observation. Further, household units differ in the number of household members and the extent of income sharing among members. Individuals differ in age and need for consumption. Where household is used as the observation unit, the quintiles refer to the percentage of households, rather than the percentage of persons. Third, the surveys differ according to whether the units of observation are ranked by household or per capita income (or consumption). The footnotes to the table identify these differences for each country. Although the income distribution estimates shown are considered to be the best available, they still reflect all the problems mentioned above.

The international comparability of high-income country data is particularly limited, since the observation unit is a household unadjusted for size, and households are ranked according to total household income rather than income per household member. These data are presented pending the publication of improved data from the *Luxembourg Income Study*, where household members are ranked by the average disposable income per adult-equivalent person. The estimates in the table, therefore, should be treated with considerable caution.

The 1987 indexed figures on PPP-based GNP per capita (US=100) are presented in column 8. PPP is the commonly used term to refer to the parities computed for a fixed basket of products, even though theoretically these are more appropriately labeled Purchasing Power of Currencies. The data include (a) results of the International Comparison Programme (ICP) for 1993 for OECD countries, extrapolated backward to 1987; (b) results for 1985 for non-OECD countries, extrapolated to 1987; (c) the latest available results for either 1980 or 1975, extrapolated to 1987 for countries that participated in the earlier phases only; (d) a World Bank estimate for China and the economies of the former Soviet Union; and (e) ICP estimates obtained by regression for the remaining countries. Economies whose 1987 estimates are based on regressions are footnoted. The values are expressed in "international dollars" to distinguish them from those based on exchange rates.

The blend of extrapolated and regression-based 1987 figures underlying column 8 is extrapolated to 1993, using Bank estimates of real per capita GNP growth rates and scaled up by inflation rates measured by SDR deflators. These estimates are expressed as an index (US=100) in column 9. For countries that have participated in the ICP as well as for China and the economies of the FSU, the latest available PPP-based values are extrapolated to 1993. The blend of extrapolated and regression based 1993 estimates are presented in column 10. Economies whose 1987 figures are extrapolated from another year or imputed by regression are footnoted accordingly. The adjustments do not take account of changes in the terms of trade.

At the individual country level, ICP recasts traditional national accounts through special price collections and disaggregation of GDP by expenditure components. ICP details are prepared by national statistical offices, and the results are coordinated by the U.N. Statistical Division (UNSTAT) with support from other international agencies, particularly the Statistical Office of the European Communities (Eurostat) and the OECD. The World Bank, the Economic Commission for Europe, and the Economic and Social Commission for Asia and the Pacific (ESCAP) also contribute to this exercise. For Nepal, which participated in the 1985 exercise, total GDP data were not available, and comparisons were made for consumption only. Luxembourg and Swaziland are the only two economies with populations under 1 million that have participated in the ICP; their 1987 results, as percentages of the U.S. values, are 121.0 and 15.0, respectively. The current round of ICP surveys, for 1993, is expected to cover more than 80 countries, including China and the FSU economies.

The "international dollar" (I$), used as the common currency, is the unit of account that equalizes price levels in all participating countries. It has the same purchasing power over total GNP as the U.S. dollar in a given year, but purchasing power over subaggregates is determined by average international prices at that level rather than by U.S. relative prices. These dollar values, which are different from the dollar values of GNP or GDP shown in Tables 1 and 3 (see the technical notes for these tables), are obtained by special conversion factors designed to equalize the purchasing powers of currencies in the respective countries. This conversion factor, the purchasing power parities (PPP), is defined as the number of units of a country's currency required to buy the same amounts of goods and services in the domestic market as one dollar would buy in the United States. The computation involves deriving implicit quantities from national accounts expenditure data and specially collected price data, and then revaluing the implicit quantities in each country at uniform prices. The average price index thus equalizes dollar prices in every country so that cross-country comparisons of GNP based on them reflect differences in quantities of goods and services free of price-level differentials. This procedure is designed to bring cross-country comparisons in line with cross-time real value comparisons that are based on constant price series.

The ICP figures presented here are the results of a two-step exercise. Countries within a region or group such as the OECD are first compared using their own group average prices. Next, since group average prices may differ from each other—making the countries in different groups not comparable—the group prices are adjusted to make them comparable at the world level. The adjustments, done by UNSTAT and Eurostat, are based on price differentials observed in a network of "link" countries representing each group. However, the linking is done in a manner that retains in the world comparison the relative levels of GDP observed in the group comparisons, called "fixity."

The two-step process was adopted because the relative GDP levels and rankings of two countries may change when more countries are brought into the comparison. It was felt that this should not be allowed to happen within geographic regions; that is, that the relationship of, say, Ghana and Senegal should not be affected by the prices prevailing in the United States. Thus overall GDP per capita levels are calculated at "regional" prices and then linked together. The linking is done by revaluing GDPs of all the countries at average "world" prices and reallocating the new regional totals on the basis of each country's share in the original comparison.

Such a method does not permit the comparison of more detailed quantities (such as food consumption). Hence these subaggregates and more detailed expenditure categories are calculated using world prices. These quantities are indeed comparable internationally, but they do not add up to the indicated GDPs because they are calculated at a different set of prices.

Some countries belong to several regional groups. A few of the group have priority; others are equal. Thus fixity is maintained between members of the European Union, even within the OECD and world comparisons. For Austria and Finland, however, the bilateral relationship that prevails within the OECD comparison is also the one used within the global comparison. But a significantly different relationship (based on Central European prices) prevails in the com-parison within that group, and this is the relationship presented in the separate publication of the European comparison.

To derive ICP-based 1987 figures for countries that are yet to participate in any ICP survey, an estimating equation is first obtained by fitting the following regression to 1987 data:

$$\ln{(r)} = 0.605 \ln{(\text{ATLAS})} + 0.239 \ln{(\text{ENROL})} + 0.717;$$
$$\qquad (0.276) \qquad\qquad (0.052) \qquad\qquad (0.160)$$

$$\text{RMSE} = 0.223; \text{Adj.R-Sq.} = 0.96; N=81$$

where all variables and estimated values are expressed as US=100 and where

r = ICP estimates of per capita GDP converted to U.S. dollars by PPP, the array of r consisting of extrapolations of the most recent actual ICP values available for countries that ever participated in ICP

ATLAS = per capita GNP estimated by the *Atlas* method

ENROL = secondary school enrollment ratio

RMSE = root mean squared error.

ATLAS and ENROL are used as rough proxies of intercountry wage differentials for unskilled and skilled human capital, respectively. Following Isenman 1980, the rationale adopted here is that ICP and conventional estimates of GDP differ mainly because wage differences persist among nations due to constraints on the international mobility of labor. A technical paper (Ahmad 1992) providing fuller explanation is available on request. For further details on ICP procedures, readers may consult the ICP Phase IV report, *World Comparisons of Purchasing Power and Real Product for 1980* (New York: United Nations, 1986). Readers interested in detailed ICP survey data for 1975, 80, 85, and 90 may refer to *Purchasing Power of Currencies: Comparing National Incomes Using ICP Data* (World Bank 1993).

Table 31. Urbanization

Data on urban population and agglomeration in large cities are from the U.N.'s *World Urbanization Prospects*. The growth rates of urban population are calculated from population estimates (see Table 1); the estimates of urban population shares are calculated from both of the above.

Because the estimates in this table are based on different national definitions of what is urban, cross-country comparisons should be made with caution.

The summary measures for urban population as a percentage of total population are calculated from country percentages weighted by each country's share in the aggregate population. The other summary measures in this table are weighted in the same fashion, using urban population.

Table 32. Infrastructure

This table provides selected basic indicators of the coverage and performance of infrastructure sectors.

Indicators of coverage are based on the infrastructure data most widely available across countries which measure the extent, type, and sometimes condition of physical facilities in each infrastructure sector. Such data are divided by national population totals to derive indicators of coverage or availability (as in telephone mainlines per thousand persons or road kilometers per million persons). More direct measures of coverage are based on household surveys of actual access, reported as percentage of households with electricity or access to safe water.

Performance quality can be assessed from the perspectives of both the infrastructure providers and of the users. Indicators from the providers' perspective measure operating efficiency (such as power system losses, unaccounted for water, and locomotive availability), capacity utilization, or financial efficiency (such as cost recovery). Indicators from the users' perspectives measure the effectiveness of the service ultimately delivered. Service quality indicators (such as faults per 100 main lines per year) are the most difficult data to obtain on a comparable and recurrent basis for a large sample of countries. Some indicators represent both system efficiency and service quality such as the share of paved roads in good condition.

Although the data reported here are drawn from the most authoritative sources available, comparability may be limited by variation in data collection, statistical methods, and definitions.

Coverage of *electric power* is measured by *production (kilowatt-hour per person)*. This refers to gross production, which includes the consumption by station auxiliaries and losses in the transformers that are considered integral parts of the station. Excluded is electricity produced from pumped storage. The data is from *U.N. Energy Statistics Yearbook*. System losses, which are obtained from the "Power Data Sheets" compiled by the Industry and Energy Department of the World Bank and IEA Energy Statistics, combine technical and nontechnical losses. Technical losses, due to the physical characteristics of the power system, consist mainly of resistance losses in transmission and distribution. Nontechnical losses consist mainly of illegal connection to electricity and other sources of theft. System losses are expressed as percentage of total output (net generation).

Telecommunications coverage is the number of telephone exchange *mainlines per thousand persons*. A telephone mainline connects the subscriber's equipment to the switched network and has a dedicated port in the telephone exchange. This term is synonymous with "main station," also commonly used in telecommunication documents. *Faults (per 100 main lines per year)* refer to the number of reported faults per 100 main telephone lines for the year indicated. Some operators include malfunctioning customer premises equipment as faults while others include only technical faults. Data on main lines and faults per 100 main lines are from the International Telecommunication Union database.

The indicators used to represent *paved road* coverage in this sector are *road density* (kilometers per million population). As the measure of performance, *roads in good condition* is defined as roads substantially free of defects and requiring only routine maintenance. Data for paved roads are from C. Queiroz and S. Gautam, "Road Infrastructure and Economic Development," (Working Paper 921, World Bank, 1992) and are available for 1988 only.

The measure of coverage for *water* is the *percentage of the population with access to safe water* either by standpipe or house connection, and is drawn primarily from the World Health Organization's, *The International Drinking Water Supply and Sanitation Decade* series, for various years. Data for losses are from H. Garn, "Patterns in the Data Reported on Completed Water Supply Projects," World Bank, 1987 and are for metropolitan area systems. Where 1986 was not available, the closest available year was taken. *Losses* include physical losses (pipe breaks and overflows) and commercial losses (meter under-registration; illegal use including fraud-

ulent or unregistered connections; and legal, but usually not metered, uses like fire fighting).

The coverage indicator for *railways* is the number of rail traffic units per thousand U.S. dollars of GDP. *Rail traffic units* are the sum of passenger-kilometers and ton-kilometers, and were obtained from the database maintained by the Transport Division of the Transportation, Water and Urban Development Department, World Bank. *Diesels in use* is one of the better measures of technical and managerial performance because locomotives are the most expensive rolling stock the railways own. Data are from the same World Bank database. GDP figures are from R. Summers and A. Heston, *The Penn World Tables (Mark 5.6)*, forthcoming.

Table 33. Natural resources

This table represents a step toward including environmental data in the assessment of development and the planning of economic strategies. It provides a partial picture of the status of forests, the extent of areas protected for conservation or other environmentally related purposes, and the availability and use of fresh water. The data reported here are drawn from the most authoritative sources available, which are cited in World Resources Institute, *World Resources 1994–95*. Perhaps even more than other data in this Report, however, these data should be used with caution. Although they accurately characterize major differences in resources and uses among countries, true comparability is limited because of variation in data collection, statistical methods, definitions, and government resources.

No conceptual framework that integrates natural resource and traditional economic data has yet been agreed on. Nor are the measures shown in this table intended to be final indicators of natural resource wealth, environmental health, or resource depletion. They have been chosen because they are available for most countries, are testable, and reflect some general conditions of the environment.

Forest area refers to natural stands of woody vegetation in which trees predominate. These estimates are derived from country statistics assembled by the Food and Agriculture Organization (FAO) and the United Nations Economic Commission for Europe (UNECE). New assessments were published in 1993 for tropical countries (FAO) and temperate zones (UNECE/FAO). The FAO and the UNECE/FAO use different definitions in their assessments. FAO defines natural forest in tropical countries as either a closed forest where trees cover a high proportion of the ground and there is no continuous grass cover or an open forest, defined as mixed forest/grasslands with at least 10 percent tree cover and a continuous grass layer on the forest floor. A tropical forest encompasses all stands except plantations and includes stands that have been degraded to some degree by agriculture, fire, logging, or acid precipitation.

UNECE/FAO defines a forest as land where tree crowns cover more than 20 percent of the area. Also included are open forest formations; forest roads and firebreaks; small, temporarily cleared areas; young stands expected to achieve at least 20 percent crown cover on maturity; and windbreaks and shelterbelts. Plantation area is included under temperate country estimates of natural forest area. Some countries in this table also include other wooded land, defined as open woodland and scrub, shrub, and brushland.

Deforestation refers to the permanent conversion of forest land to other uses, including shifting cultivation, permanent agriculture, ranching, settlements, or infrastructure development. Deforested areas do not include areas logged but intended for regeneration or areas degraded by fuelwood gathering, acid precipitation, or forest fires. The extent and percentage of total area shown refer to the average annual deforestation of natural forest area.

Some countries also conduct independent assessments using satellite data or extensive ground data. A 1991 country-wide assessment using Landsat imagery estimated India's forest cover at 639,000 square kilometers. An inventory based on 1990 LANDSAT^{TM} imagery estimated Mexico's forest cover at 496,000 square kilometers, with a deforestation rate of 4.06 square kilometers per year between 1980 and 1990. In Brazil two recent satellite-imagery-based assessments of deforestation in the Brazilian Amazon have resulted in different deforestation rate estimates for this region. A study by the U.S. National Space and Aeronautics Administration (NASA) and the University of New Hampshire estimated forest loss at 15,000 square kilometers per year during 1978–88. Brazil's National Institute for Space Research (INPE) and National Institute for Research in the Amazon (INPA) estimated deforestation at 20,300 square kilometers per year for the same period. Deforestation in secondary forest areas and dry scrub areas were not included in either study. The FAO data presented in this table include forestation in all Brazil, including secondary forest areas and other forested areas. Note also that according to the FAO Brazil has an estimated 70,000 square kilometers of plantation land, defined as forest stands established artificially by afforestation and reforestation for industrial and nonindustrial usage. India has an estimated 189,000 square kilometers of plantation land and Indonesia an estimated 87,500 square kilometers.

Nationally protected areas are areas of at least 1,000 hectares that fall into one of five management categories: scientific reserves and strict nature reserves; national parks of national or international significance (not materially affected by human activity); natural monuments and natural landscapes with some unique aspects; managed nature reserves and wildlife sanctuaries; and protected landscapes and seascapes (which may include cultural landscapes). This table does not include sites protected under local or provincial law or areas where consumptive uses of wildlife are allowed. These data are subject to variations in defini-

tion and in reporting to the organizations, such as the World Conservation Monitoring Centre, that compile and disseminate them. Total surface area is used to calculate the percentage of total area protected.

Freshwater resources: annual withdrawal data are subject to variation in collection and estimation methods but accurately show the magnitude of water use in both total and per capita terms. These data, however, also hide what can be significant variation in total renewable water resources from one year to another. They also fail to distinguish the seasonal and geographic variations in water availability within a country. Because freshwater resources are based on long-term averages, their estimation explicitly excludes decade-long cycles of wet and dry. The Département Hydrogéologie in Orléans, France, compiles water resource and withdrawal data from published documents, including national, United Nations, and professional literature. The Institute of Geography at the National Academy of Sciences in Moscow also compiles global water data on the basis of published work and, where necessary, estimates water resources and consumption from models that use other data, such as area under irrigation, livestock populations, and precipitation. These and other sources have been combined by the World Resources Institute to generate data for this table. Withdrawal data are for single years and vary from country to country between 1970 and 1992. Data for small countries and countries in arid and semiarid zones are less reliable than those for larger countries and countries with higher rainfall.

Total water resources includes both internal renewable resources and, where noted, river flows from other countries. Estimates are from 1992. Annual internal renewable water resources refer to the average annual flow of rivers and aquifers generated from rainfall within the country. The total withdrawn and the percentage withdrawn of the total renewable resource are both reported in this table. Withdrawals include those from nonrenewable aquifers and desalting plants but do not include losses from evaporation. Withdrawals can exceed 100 percent of renewable supplies when extractions from nonrenewable aquifers or desalting plants are considerable or if there is significant water reuse. Total per capita water withdrawal is calculated by dividing a country's total withdrawal by its population in the year for which withdrawal estimates are available. For most countries, sectoral per capita withdrawal data are calculated using sectoral withdrawal percentages estimated for 1987. Domestic use includes drinking water, municipal use or supply, and use for public services, commercial establishments, and homes. Direct withdrawals for industrial use, including withdrawals for cooling thermoelectric plants, are combined in the final column of this table with withdrawals for agriculture (irrigation and livestock production). Numbers may not sum to the total per capita figure because of rounding.

Data sources

Production and domestic absorption	U.N. Department of International Economic and Social Affairs. Various years. *Statistical Yearbook*. New York.
	———. Various years. *Energy Statistics Yearbook*. Statistical Papers, series J. New York.
	U.N. International Comparison Program Phases IV (1980), V (1985), and Phase VI (1990) reports, and data from ECE, ESCAP, Eurostat, OECD, and U.N.
	FAO, IMF, UNIDO, and World Bank data; national sources.
Fiscal and monetary accounts	International Monetary Fund. *Government Finance Statistics Yearbook*. Vol. 11. Washington, D.C.
	———. Various years. *International Financial Statistics*. Washington, D.C.
	IMF data, and World Bank data.
Core international transactions	International Monetary Fund. Various years. *International Financial Statistics*. Washington, D.C.
	U.N. Conference on Trade and Development. Various years. *Handbook of International Trade and Development Statistics*. Geneva.
	U.N. Department of International Economic and Social Affairs. Various years. *Monthly Bulletin of Statistics*. New York.
	———. Various years. *Yearbook of International Trade Statistics*. New York.
	FAO, IMF, U.N., and World Bank data.
External finance	Organization for Economic Cooperation and Development. Various years. *Development Co-operation*. Paris.
	———. 1988. *Geographical Distribution of Financial Flows to Developing Countries*. Paris.
	IMF, OECD, and World Bank data; World Bank Debtor Reporting System.
Human resources and environmentally sustainable development	Bos, Eduard, My T. Vu, Ernest Massiah, and Rodolfo A. Bulatao. *World Population Projections, 1994–95 Edition* (1994). Baltimore, Md.: Johns Hopkins University Press.
	Garn, Harvey. April 1987. *Patterns in the Data Reported on Completed Water Supply Projects*. Washington, D.C.: World Bank.
	Heiderian, J. and Wu, Gary. 1993. *Statistics of Developing Countries (1987–91)*. Washington, D.C.: Industry and Energy Department, World Bank.
	Institute for Resource Development/Westinghouse. 1987. Child Survival: Risks and the Road to Health. Columbia, Md.
	International Energy Agency. 1993. *IEA Statistics: Energy prices and taxes*. Paris: OECD.
	International Road Transport Union. 1990. World Transport Data.
	International Telecommunication Union. *1994 World Telecommunications Development Report*. Geneva.
	Kurian, G.T. 1991. *The New Book of World Rankings*. New York: Facts on File.
	Queiroz, Cesar and Surhid Gautam. June 1992. "Road Infrastructure and Economic Development." World Bank Working Paper No. 921. Washington, D.C.: World Bank.
	Ross, John and others. 1993. *Family Planning and Population: A Compendium of International Statistics*. New York: The Population Council.
	Sivard, Ruth. 1985. *Women—A World Survey*. Washington, D.C.: World Priorities.
	U.N. Department of Economic and Social Information and Policy Analysis. (formerly U.N. Department of International Economic and Social Affairs). Various years. *Demographic Yearbook*. New York.
	———. Various years. *World Energy Supplies*. Statistical Papers, series J. New York.
	———. Various years. *Statistical Yearbook*. New York.
	———. 1989. *Levels and Trends of Contraceptive Use as Assessed in 1988*. New York.
	———. 1988. *Mortality of Children under Age 5: Projections 1950–2025*. New York.
	———. 1986. *World Comparisons of Purchasing Power and Real Product for 1980*. New York.
	———. *World Population Prospects: The 1994 Edition (forthcoming)*. New York.
	———. *World Urbanization Prospects, 1994 Revision (forthcoming)*. New York.
	U.N. Educational Scientific and Cultural Organization. Various years. *Statistical Yearbook*. Paris.
	———. 1990. *Compendium of Statistics on Illiteracy*. Paris.
	UNICEF. 1995. *The State of the World's Children 1995*. Oxford: Oxford University Press.
	World Bank. 1993. *Purchasing Power of Currencies: Comparing National Incomes Using ICP Data*. Washington, D.C.
	World Health Organization. Various years. *World Health Statistics Annual*. Geneva.
	———. 1986. *Maternal Mortality Rates: A Tabulation of Available Information*, 2nd edition. Geneva.
	———. 1991. *Maternal Mortality: A Global Factbook*. Geneva.
	———. Various years. *World Health Statistics Report*. Geneva.
	———. Various years. *The International Drinking Water Supply and Sanitation Decade*. Geneva.
	World Resources Institute. 1994. *World Resources 1994–95*. New York.
	FAO, ILO, U.N., and World Bank data; national sources.

Table 1 Classification of economies by income and region, 1995

Income group	Subgroup	Sub-Saharan Africa		Asia		Europe and Central Asia		Middle East and North Africa		
		East and Southern Africa	West Africa	East Asia and Pacific	South Asia	Eastern Europe and Central Asia	Rest of Europe	Middle East	North Africa	Americas
Low-Income		Burundi Comoros Eritrea Ethiopia Kenya Lesotho Madagascar Malawi Mozambique Rwanda Somalia Sudan Tanzania Uganda Zaire Zambia Zimbabwe	Benin Burkina Faso Central African Republic Chad Côte d'Ivoire Equatorial Guinea Gambia, The Ghana Guinea Guinea-Bissau Liberia Mali Mauritania Niger Nigeria São Tomé and Principe Sierra Leone Togo	Cambodia China Lao PDR Mongolia Myanmar Viet Nam	Afghanistan Bangladesh Bhutan India Nepal Pakistan Sri Lanka	Albania Armenia Bosnia and Herzegovina Georgia Tajikistan		Yemen, Rep.	Egypt, Arab Rep.	Guyana Haiti Honduras Nicaragua
Middle-income	Lower	Angola Botswana Djibouti Namibia Swaziland	Cameroon Cape Verde Congo Senegal	Fiji Indonesia Kiribati Korea, Dem. Rep. Marshall Islands Micronesia Fed. Sts. N. Mariana Is. Papua New Guinea Philippines Solomon Islands Thailand Tonga Vanuatu Western Samoa	Maldives	Azerbaijan Bulgaria Croatia Czech Republic Kazakhstan Kyrgyz Republic Latvia Lithuania Macedonia FYR[a] Moldova Poland Romania Russian Federation Slovak Republic Turkmenistan Ukraine Uzbekistan Yugoslavia, Fed. Rep.	Turkey	Iran, Islamic Rep. Iraq Jordan Lebanon Syrian Arab Rep. West Bank and Gaza	Algeria Morocco Tunisia	Belize Bolivia Colombia Costa Rica Cuba Dominica Dominican Republic Ecuador El Salvador Grenada Guatemala Jamaica Panama Paraguay Peru St. Vincent and the Grenadines Suriname
	Upper	Mauritius Mayotte Reunion Seychelles South Africa	Gabon	American Samoa Guam Korea, Rep. Macao Malaysia New Caledonia		Belarus Estonia Hungary Slovenia	Gibraltar Greece Isle of Man Malta Portugal	Bahrain Oman Saudi Arabia	Libya	Antigua and Barbuda Argentina Aruba Barbados Brazil Chile French Guiana Guadeloupe Martinique Mexico Netherlands Antilles Puerto Rico St. Kitts and Nevis St. Lucia Trinidad and Tobago Uruguay Venezuela
Subtotal:	170	27	23	26	8	27	6	10	5	38

Table 1

Income group	Subgroup	Sub-Saharan Africa East and Southern Africa	West Africa	Asia East Asia and Pacific	South Asia	Europe and Central Asia Eastern Europe and Central Asia	Rest of Europe	Middle East and North Africa Middle East	North Africa	Americas
High-income	OECD Countries			Australia Japan New Zealand			Austria Belgium Denmark Finland France Germany Iceland Ireland Italy Luxembourg Netherlands Norway Spain Sweden Switzerland United Kingdom			Canada United States
	NonOECD Countries			Brunei French Polynesia Hong Kong Singapore OAE[b]			Andorra Channel Islands Cyprus Faeroe Islands Greenland San Marino	Israel Kuwait Qatar United Arab Emirates		Bahamas, The Bermuda Cayman Islands Virgin Islands (US)
Total:	210	27	23	34	8	27	28	14	5	44

a. Former Yugoslav Republic of Macedonia.
b. Other Asian economies—Taiwan, China.

For operational and analytical purposes the World Bank's main criterion for classifying economies is gross national product (GNP) per capita. Every economy is classified as low-income, middle-income (subdivided into lower-middle and upper-middle), or high-income. Other analytical groups, based on geographic regions, exports, and levels of external debt, are also used.

Low-income and middle-income economies are sometimes referred to as developing economies. The use of the term is convenient; it is not intended to imply that all economies in the group are experiencing similar development or that other economies have reached a preferred or final stage of development. Classification by income does not necessarily reflect development status.

Definitions of groups

These tables classify all World Bank member economies, and all other economies with populations of more than 30,000.

Income group: Economies are divided according to 1993 GNP per capita, calculated using the *World Bank Atlas* method. The groups are: low-income, $695 or less; lower-middle-income, $696–$2,785; upper-middle-income, $2,786–$8,625; and high-income, $8,626 or more.

The estimates for the republics of the former Soviet Union are preliminary and their classification will be kept under review.

Table 2 Classification of economies by major export category and indebtedness, 1995

| | Low- and middle-income | | | | | | | High-income | |
| | Low-income | | | Middle-income | | | | | |
Group	Severely indebted	Moderately indebted	Less indebted	Severely indebted	Moderately indebted	Less indebted	Not classified by indebtedness	OECD	nonOECD
Exporters of manufactures			Armenia China Georgia	Bulgaria Poland	Hungary Russian Federation	Belarus Estonia Korea, Rep. Korea, Dem. Rep. Kyrgyz Republic Latvia Lebanon Lithuania Macao Moldova Romania Ukraine Uzbekistan		Canada Finland Germany Ireland Italy Japan Sweden Switzerland	Hong Kong Israel Singapore OAE[a]
Exporters of nonfuel primary products	Afghanistan Burundi Côte d'Ivoire Equatorial Guinea Ethiopia Ghana Guinea Guinea-Bissau Guyana Honduras Liberia Madagascar Mali Mauritania Myanmar Nicaragua Niger Rwanda São Tomé and Principe Somalia Sudan Tanzania Uganda Viet Nam Zaire Zambia	Albania Chad Malawi Togo Zimbabwe	Mongolia	Argentina Bolivia Cuba Peru	Chile Papua New Guinea	Botswana Guatemala Namibia Paraguay Solomon Islands St. Vincent and the Grenadines Suriname Swaziland	American Samoa French Guiana Guadeloupe Reunion	Iceland New Zealand	Faeroe Islands Greenland
Exporters of fuels (mainly oil)	Nigeria			Angola Congo Iraq	Algeria Gabon Venezuela	Bahrain Iran, Islamic Rep. Libya Oman Saudi Arabia Trinidad and Tobago Turkmenistan			Brunei Qatar United Arab Emirates
Exporters of services	Yemen, Rep.	Benin Egypt, Arab Rep. Gambia, The Nepal	Bhutan Burkina Faso Cambodia Haiti Lesotho	Jamaica Jordan Panama	Antigua and Barbuda Dominican Republic Greece Western Samoa	Barbados Belize Cape Verde Djibouti El Salvador Fiji Grenada Kiribati Maldives Malta Seychelles St. Kitts and Nevis St. Lucia Tonga Vanuatu	Aruba Cayman Islands Martinique	United Kingdom	Bahamas, The Bermuda Cyprus French Polynesia Kuwait

Table 2

| | Low- and middle-income | | | | | | | High-income | |
| | Low-income | | | Middle-income | | | | | |
Group	Severely indebted	Moderately indebted	Less indebted	Severely indebted	Moderately indebted	Less indebted	Not classified by indebtedness	OECD	nonOECD
Diversified exporters[b]	Central African Rep. Kenya Lao PDR Mozambique Sierra Leone	Bangladesh Comoros India Pakistan	Sri Lanka Tajikistan	Brazil Cameroon Ecuador Morocco Syrian Arab Rep. Uruguay	Colombia Costa Rica Indonesia Mexico Philippines Senegal Tunisia Turkey	Azerbaijan Dominica Kazakhstan Malaysia Mauritius Netherlands Antilles Portugal South Africa Thailand Yugoslavia, Fed. Rep.		Australia Austria Belgium Denmark France Luxembourg Netherlands Norway Spain United States	
Not classified by export category				Gibraltar	Croatia Czech Republic Macedonia FYR[c] New Caledonia Slovak Republic Slovenia		Bosnia and Herzegovina Eritrea Guam Isle of Man Marshall Islands Mayotte Micronesia Fed. Sts. Northern Mariana Islands Puerto Rico West Bank and Gaza		Andorra Channel Islands San Marino Virgin Islands (US)
Number of economies 210	33	13	11	18	20	59	17	21	18

a.   Other Asian economies—Taiwan, China.
b.   Economies in which no single export category accounts for more than 50 percent of total exports.
c.   Former Yugoslav Republic of Macedonia.

Definitions of groups

These tables classify all World Bank member economies, plus all other economies with populations of more than 30,000.

Major export category: Major exports are those that account for 50 percent or more of total exports of goods and services from one category, in the period 1988–92. The categories are: nonfuel primary (SITC 0,1,2, 4, plus 68), fuels (SITC 3), manufactures (SITC 5 to 9, less 68), and services (factor and nonfactor service receipts plus workers' remittances). If no single category accounts for 50 percent or more of total exports, the economy is classified as *diversified.*

Indebtedness: Standard World Bank definitions of severe and moderate indebtedness, averaged over three years (1991–93) are used to classify economies in this table. *Severely indebted* means either of the two key ratios is above critical levels: present value of debt service

to GNP (80 percent) and present value of debt service to exports (220 percent). *Moderately indebted* means either of the two key ratios exceeds 60 percent of, but does not reach, the critical levels. For economies that do not report detailed debt statistics to the World Bank Debtor Reporting System, present-value calculation is not possible. Instead the following methodology is used to classify the non-DRS economies. *Severely indebted* means three of four key ratios (averaged over 1991–93) are above critical levels: debt to GNP (50 percent); debt to exports (275 percent), debt service to exports (30 percent); and interest to exports (20 percent). *Moderately indebted* means three of four key ratios exceed 60 percent of, but do not reach, the critical levels. All other classified low- and middle-income economies are listed as *less-indebted.*